Language Production, Cognition, and the Lexicon

TEXT, SPEECH AND LANGUAGE TECHNOLOGY

VOLUME 48

Series editor

Nancy Ide, *Vassar College, New York, USA*

Editorial Board

Emily M. Bender, *University of Washington, Washington, USA*
Mona Diab, *Columbia University, New York, USA*
Pascale Fung, *The Hong Kong University of Science and Technology, Kowloon, Hong Kong SAR*
Roberto Navigli, *Sapienza University of Rome, Rome, Italy*
Virach Sornlertlamvanich, *NECTEC, Bangkok, Thailand*
Fei Xia, *University of Washington, Washington, USA*

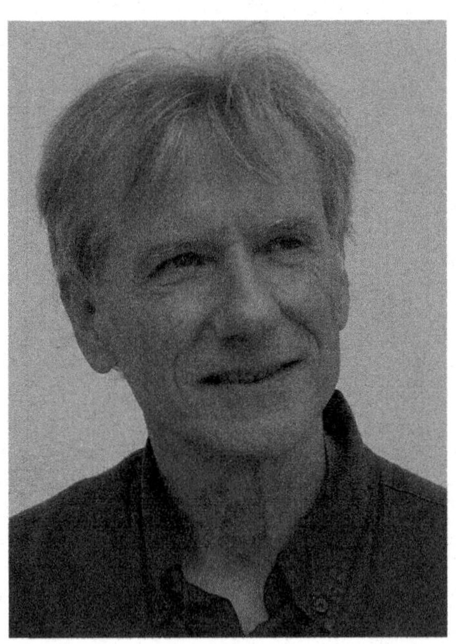

More information about this series at http://www.springer.com/series/6636

Núria Gala · Reinhard Rapp
Gemma Bel-Enguix
Editors

Language Production, Cognition, and the Lexicon

Springer

Editors
Núria Gala
Gemma Bel-Enguix
CNRS-LIF, UMR 7279
Aix-Marseille University
Marseille
France

Reinhard Rapp
CNRS-LIF, UMR 7279
Aix-Marseille University, University of Mainz
Marseille
France

ISSN 1386-291X Text, Speech and Language Technology
ISBN 978-3-319-35847-5 ISBN 978-3-319-08043-7 (eBook)
DOI 10.1007/978-3-319-08043-7

Springer Cham Heidelberg New York Dordrecht London

© Springer International Publishing Switzerland 2015
Softcover reprint of the hardcover 1st edition 2015
This work is subject to copyright. All rights are reserved by the Publisher, whether the whole or part of the material is concerned, specifically the rights of translation, reprinting, reuse of illustrations, recitation, broadcasting, reproduction on microfilms or in any other physical way, and transmission or information storage and retrieval, electronic adaptation, computer software, or by similar or dissimilar methodology now known or hereafter developed. Exempted from this legal reservation are brief excerpts in connection with reviews or scholarly analysis or material supplied specifically for the purpose of being entered and executed on a computer system, for exclusive use by the purchaser of the work. Duplication of this publication or parts thereof is permitted only under the provisions of the Copyright Law of the Publisher's location, in its current version, and permission for use must always be obtained from Springer. Permissions for use may be obtained through RightsLink at the Copyright Clearance Center. Violations are liable to prosecution under the respective Copyright Law.
The use of general descriptive names, registered names, trademarks, service marks, etc. in this publication does not imply, even in the absence of a specific statement, that such names are exempt from the relevant protective laws and regulations and therefore free for general use.
While the advice and information in this book are believed to be true and accurate at the date of publication, neither the authors nor the editors nor the publisher can accept any legal responsibility for any errors or omissions that may be made. The publisher makes no warranty, express or implied, with respect to the material contained herein.

Printed on acid-free paper

Springer is part of Springer Science+Business Media (www.springer.com)

Preface

It was early in 2013 that we learnt that Michael Zock was retiring after more than 30 years of research. Retired? Michael? For those who have had the chance to know Michael, to work with him or just to share a little bit of his time (during a conference, a dinner, a coffee break, etc.) these two words together make no sense. Michael is a passionate and an experienced researcher, a trusted colleague with a stellar career, an untiring worker, a globetrotter fascinated by different cultures, and an easygoing man disseminating humanistic values wherever he goes.

It is thus a great pleasure and honor to present him this festschrift, *Language Production, Cognition, and the Lexicon*, on the occasion of his retirement. We, the editors, have tried to bring together well-known researchers whose contributions reflect Michael's interests at the crossroads of psycholinguistics, cognitive science, natural language processing, and computer science. We hope and believe that he will like the volume, which contains 30 chapters written by 49 authors from 16 countries on four continents, and that the book will lead to fruitful scientific interaction and exchange.

The volume is organized into six different parts, preceded by a personal and introductory chapter presenting Michael's career (by Mark T. Maybury). They include scientific papers grouped into specific domains at the intersection of theoretical and applied research, language engineering, and advanced text technology.

- Part I begins with a paper on sentiment analysis and opinion mining (by Ed Hovy) from the perspective of *Natural Language Processing* and providing a long-term Cognitive View on Opinion. This part also overviews the field of Cognitive Natural Language Processing (by Bernadette Sharp), as well as Artificial Intelligence and Cognitive Modelling (by Sergei Nirenburg).
- Part II addresses the *Lexicon and Lexical Analysis*. Alain Polguère makes a theoretical contribution arguing against dogmatic contextualism in lexical studies; Marie-Claude L'Homme investigates predicative lexical units in terminology; Mathieu Lafourcade and Alain Joubert present an application of lexical access, namely the tip-of-the-tongue problem; Olivier Ferret studies the type of relations that can be found in distributional thesauri; Chu-Ren Huang

and Ya-Min Chou elaborate on conceptual access to a multilingual lexicon based on shared orthography (the ideographic aspect of the Chinese writing system and its borrowed version in the Japanese writing system); Yves Lepage addresses the issue of proportional analogy applied to natural language processing. Pushpak Bhattacharyya's paper addresses the issue of multilingual projection whereby an annotated resource of one language can be used for the processing of another language, with a case study in word sense disambiguation in a multilingual framework (Indian languages WordNets).

- Part III is about *Semantics* by and large. Gregory Grefenstette discusses the notion of personal semantics, an idea which one of the reviewers thinks "provides much food for thought"; Didier Schwab, Jérôme Goulian, Gilles Sérasset, and Andon Tchechmedjiev cast a new light on evaluating semantic relatedness by considering the task of word sense disambiguation; Yorick Wilks sheds light on metaphor detection and interpretation in large-scale corpora in different languages (cross-linguistically and cross-culturally); Rodolfo Delmonte proposes a linguistic and computational perspective on the crucial notions of recursion and ambiguity.
- Part IV is devoted to *Language and Speech Generation*. Kumiko Tanaka-Ishii verifies the statistical structure underlying text through the analysis of the role of vowels and consonants. Rebecca Smaha and Christiane Fellbaum raise concerns about the analysis of artificial languages compared to natural ones. Rolf Schwitter investigates how defaults and exceptions can be incorporated into an existing controlled natural language; Line Jakubiec-Jamet disusses issues on natural language generation by presenting a resource integrating a linguistically motivated ontology; Kristiina Jokinen describes an interactive open-domain spoken dialog system generating speech using Wikipedia as knowledge source. Nicolas Daoust and Guy Lapalme propose a system that allows its user to generate French text to be easily integrated into web pages (dynamic output depending on the content of the page).
- Part V concerns *Reading and Writing Technologies*. Sanja Štajner, Ruslan Mitkov, and Gloria Corpas Pastor explore existing readability formulae applied to assess the level of simplification offered by a text simplification system; Juyeon Kang and Patrick Saint-Dizier present some general ideas related to an interactive system, which assists technical writers with requirements when producing documents; Cerstin Mahlow describes ongoing research on analyzing complex writing errors for improving writing technology.
- Part VI is focused on *Language Resources and Language Engineering*. Joseph Mariani and Gil Francopoulo propose a general survey of language resources available in Europe; Eric Wehrli and Luka Nerima report on a multilingual parser which can be used for any natural language application which requires lexical, morphological or syntactic information; Dan Tufis and Verginica Barbu Mititelu present an ontology for Romanian; Dan Cristea and collaborators describe collective work aimed to build a corpus including annotations of semantic relations; Dominique Estival contributes with an Australian corpus for

human communication science collaboration; Asanee Kawtrakul describes a framework for handling knowledge extraction and integration across websites.

Thanks to these contributions, we have been able to edit a book which is not only a Festschrift, but also serves as an excellent reference for the current state of the research in the areas Michael has worked on. Many have referred to his work, so we think that this has been a good way to honor a great researcher and colleague.

In closing, we would like to acknowledge the support from the Laboratoire d'Informatique Fondamentale (LIF) and from the projects AutoWordNet and DynNetLAc which took place within the seventh European Community Framework Programme. We would also like to sincerely acknowledge the excellent and very pleasant cooperation with Springer, in particular with Federica Corradi dell Aqua, but also with Alice Blanck, series editor Nancy Ide, and the production team. We likewise wish to thank the reviewers whose feedback was indispensable to select and improve the contributions. Particular thanks also go to Ed Hovy, Christian Boitet, and Debela Tesfaye for their advice and support. Last but not least, we would like to thank our authors for their enthusiasm, encouragement, and for their high quality contributions.

Marseille, Spring 2014

Núria Gala
Reinhard Rapp
Gemma Bel-Enguix

Contents

Michael Zock: A Life of Interdisciplinary Research and International Engagement

Mark T. Maybury

Abstract Language scientist, translator, German radio journalist, free-lance photographic reporter, and scientific ambassador are just some of the titles held by the multitalented Michael Zock. This opening chapter chronicles the professional milestones of this boundary spanning, cross cultural, psycholinguistic pioneer, while exposing his politeness, modesty and warmth. Following a brief introduction of Michael's origins, this chapter accounts, in part through the words of his colleagues, Michael's life-long interest in computational modelling and simulation of the natural cognitive process of language production and his quest to create practical systems for language learning. The chapter summarizes his contributions to the literature, his scientific leadership, and transdisciplinary engagements across Europe, America and Asia. Cultured, creative, and communicative, Michael's cross domain insights spanning theory and practice and his passion for language and cognition continue to inspire students and colleagues alike.

Keywords History · Scientific contributions · Language production · Language learning · Psycholinguistics · Scientific leadership · Translation · Transdisciplinary · Students · Books

---

M.T. Maybury (✉)
The MITRE Corporation, Bedford, MA 01730, USA
e-mail: maybury@mitre.org

© Springer International Publishing Switzerland 2015
N. Gala et al. (eds.), *Language Production, Cognition, and the Lexicon*,
Text, Speech and Language Technology 48, DOI 10.1007/978-3-319-08043-7_1

1 In the Beginning

Born 22 September 1948 in Rosenheim, Germany, Michael Zock entered the world just after the blockade of Berlin by Russia. On the day of his birth, the British Foreign Secretary stressed that western powers were not committed to going to war over the situation as they believed there would be a political solution in the short term. Perhaps prophetically, international engagement would become a hallmark of Michael's life. It was in the very city of Berlin that Michael graduated with his baccalaureate on the 13th of January 1970. After studying languages (French, English, Spanish, and Russian) at the University of Paris-VIII from 1971–1973, he was awarded a degree to become a trainer of language teachers from the École Normale Supérieure de Saint-Cloud, an elite French high school for male students near Paris. Michael received a Masters of Linguistics in 1974 and then in 1980 a Doctorate of Experimental Psychology with a specialization in Psycholinguistics from Paris-VIII. He completed his habilitation in Cognitive Science in April 1997.

2 Dissertation Research

After completing his doctorate in Experimental Psychology, Michael was appointed by the CNRS to work at LIMSI, an AI-lab close to Paris (Orsay). He stayed for 20 years before moving in 2006 to southern France (Marseille) to join TALEP, the NLP group of the LIF (Aix-Marseille Université).

The depth and completeness of Michael's work was evident early on. In the French report by Jury President and world reknown computational linguist Joseph Mariani, Michael's thesis work is called "clair et bien construit" (clear and well-constructed), "brillamment présenté", including nothing less than a 3,000 title bibliography that would be "un outil très précieux", a most precious utility for the scientific community. His dissertation jury particularly noted the interdisciplinary character of Michael's research, spanning linguistics, computing, and psycho-linguistics.

3 Work Life

The time line of Michael's life illustrated in Fig. 1 reveals that Michael's passion for language and cognition was an early and constant focus of his career, starting from early education. An initial professional example was from 1971–1972 when he served

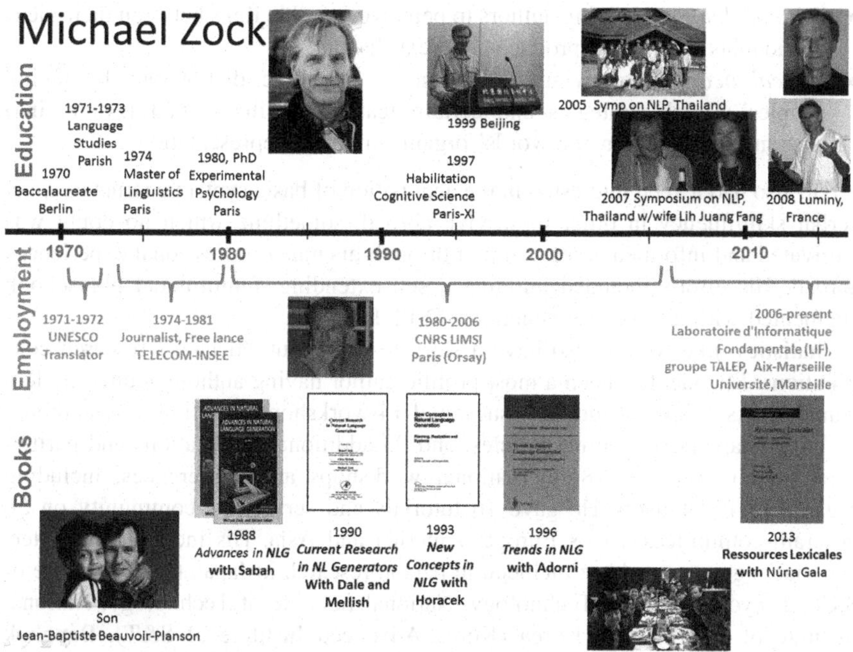

Fig. 1 Michael Zock time line

as a translator for UNESCO. Quadralingual in German, English, French, and Spanish, Michael also has knowledge of Russian and Japanese and (later of) Chinese. With a global perspective, Michael served naturally as a French scientific ambassador. The breadth and practicality of his interests were also apparent early on as he served as a German radio journalist and a free-lance photographic reporter before he commenced his research career (meeting and taking pictures of VIPs including Roman Polanski and Jacques Chirac). His international engagement was a persistent theme, starting with his reporting career in the late seventies in international affairs and then in the late eighties at LIMSI participating in diverse European Community projects.

Michael's principal domain of expertise is linguistics, psycholinguistics and automated generation of language. His research interests include language learning and cognitive simulation. Starting from user needs and empirical findings, he built tools to help people acquire speaking or writing skills and also advanced the simulation of the cognitive process of language production (words, phrases, texts).

A life-long investigator of human language production and machine generation of language, Michael was persistent in his pursuit of employing machines to augment cognition through the development of language aids for humans. Michael's research foci included the areas of:

- *Message planning*: creation of a conceptual interface, (i.e. linguistically motivated ontology augmented with a graph generator) to help people compose their thoughts;

- *Outline planning*: helping authors to perceive possible links between their ideas or thoughts in order to produce coherent discourse;
- *Lexical access*: improving navigation in electronic dictionaries by taking peoples' search strategies and certain features of the mental lexicon into account, in particular, the words' organization and representation.

He also had a keen interested in the acquisition of basic syntactic structures, i.e. verbal skill/fluency in order to survive abroad, something which no doubt was motivated and informed at least in part through his many professional experiences abroad. His efforts included building a self-extending, multilingual phrasebook augmented with an exercise generator (Drill Tutor).

Statistics, like words, also have a story to tell about Michael's research contributions. Michael has been a most prolific author having authored/edited no less than 5 books, 3 special journal issues, and 14 workshop collections. He authored 21 book chapters, 13 journal articles, and 93 additional publications and participated in no less than 78 international workshops and conferences, including organizing 19 of them. He gave 16 tutorials and served his community on 56 program committees across Europe, America and Asia. His indefatigable international engagements have included in person research in Japan (Nara Institute of S&T, Tokyo Institute of Technology, National Institute of Technology, National Institute of Informatics), Korea (Korea Advanced Institute of S&T), Bangkok (University of Kasetsart), Canada (University of Montreal), Bulgaria (Academy of Sciences), Canada (McGill University), Togo (UNESCO Mission) and Ethiopia (Addis Ababa University School of Information Science). In Paris, he has given 13 technical courses and received 20 invitations to speak at conferences.

Michael's collaborative research and publication is evident in the many text books he co-edited with colleagues from around the world. This is illustrated in Table 1 which also exemplifies his sustained contribution to the field of natural language generation.

4 Michael's Work Through His Colleagues Eyes

A particularly insightful picture of Prof. Zock's contributions comes into view from the eyes of his peers. For example University of Exeter Professor of French and Renaissance Studies Keith Cameron notes Zock's considerable influence both on French and international linguistic research directions. Professor Guy Lapalme from the University of Montreal describes Michael as an internationally known natural language generation expert with an original blended vision of computing and psycholinguistics. Noting his broad career spanning a master of linguistics, journalism, psycholinguistics doctorate, and French and international research, this enabled transdisciplinary and cross domain insights spanning theory and practice, providing an authoritative view of language production. Professor Lapalme notes Michael's establishment in 1987 of the European Language Generation Workshop, his service as a thesis examiner (Canada, Spain), invited speaker at international conferences (e.g., US, Bulgaria,

Table 1 Michael Zock's book co-editorship

Co-editors	Title	Publishers	Year
Núria Gala and Michael Zock	Ressources lexicales: Contenu, construction, utilisation, évaluation Lingvisticæ Investigationes Supplementa)	John Benjamin Publishing Company	2013
Giovanni Adorni and Michael Zock	Trends in natural language generation—An artificial intelligence perspective: fourth European workshop (EWNLG)	Springer Verlag, New York	1996
Helmut Horacek and Michael Zock	New concepts in natural language generation: planning, realization, systems	Pinter Publishers, London	1995
Robert Dale, Chris Mellish and Michael Zock	Current research in natural language generation	Academic Press, Harcourt Brace and Jovanovich, New York	1990
Michael Zock	Advances in natural language generation: an interdisciplinary perspective: volume 2	Pinter, London, Ablex, Norwood, N.J	1988
Michael Zock, and Gerard Sabah	Advances in natural language generation: an interdisciplinary perspective: volume 1	Pinter, London, Ablex, Norwood, N.J	1988

Romania, Mexico, Japan, Australia), committee member of international conferences such as COLING and ECAI, and evaluator of NSF projects.

University of Paris Professor Laurence Danlos notes Michael's impressive publication record and research community contributions, and reports that Michael is not interested solely in creating a machine that will faithfully produce a coherent text from the input but rather an accurate computational model and simulation of the natural cognitive process of language production as well as a practical system for language learning.

University of Montreal Professor Alain Polguère, knowing Michael for more than 15 years, notes how Michael came to work on a range of American and Canadian contracts on text generation in the context of the R&D company, Odyssey Research Associates, making foundational contributions to both text generation and lexical knowledge. In 1991, they helped organize the First Natural Language Pacific Rim Symposium in Singapore. Michael's originality and clairvoyance provided him a grand capacity for analysis and synthesis which he applied to the systematic study not only of his own research but of the entire research community. Also noted was his system SWIM and his lexical multilingual lexical research in Papillon. Professor Polguère also notes Michael's important influence on his colleague Igor Mel'čuk possessive Sense-Text linguistic theory and his contributions to the lexical database DiCo, adopted in Papillon. Reflecting on his scientific role, Professor Polguère called Michael the prototype researcher of the highest caliber, with exceptional domain knowledge and productivity, an impressive ability to collaborate with others and enhance their scientific capacity.

Christiane Fellbaum, Senior Research Scientist at Princeton, describes Michael as "an extraordinarily active, original, and productive member of the international scientific community". She notes his global involvement in France, Europe, Eastern Europe, and Asia. She cites his multidisciplinary (psychology and computer science) perspective noting his expertise in lexical access and tip-of-the-tongue phenomena and his (then) recent contributions on multilingual wordnets.

In his collaboration with Michael during the multilingual lexical Papillon project, Professor Christian Boitet from the Groupe d'Études pour la Traduction Automatique (GETA) recognized all that he had heard about Michael in the past: competent, original, creative, relevant, high quality, high impact, and communication excellence. His research was well thought very ambitious, yet practical (e.g., his use of the semantic graph language UNL to facilitate lexical knowledge management). Christian was impressed by Michael's ability to rapidly discover, create practical solutions, publish and engage and influence external research community. For example, he introduced psycholinguistically naturalistic extensions to the Sense-Text models of Mel'čuk.

Dr. Dominique Estival, Head of the Natural Language Processing group at Syrinx Speech Systems in North Sydney Australia, in 2001 writes of Michael's long and fruitful research career. Describing Michael as enthusiastic and persevering, Dr. Estival used one of Michael's overview publications when teaching a course on natural language processing at University of Melbourne. Moreover, Dominique notes Michaels' devotion to students and researchers across the world—from Eastern Europe to Bulgaria or Romania. His research is of long term interest to industrial researchers at IBM, Apple-Europe, and Thomson-CSF.

Professor Dan Tufis, Director of the Research Institute for Artificial Intelligence of the Romanian Academy and Full Member of the Romanian Academy, recalls Michael as a "fascinating person, a broad-view scientist and man of culture, a gifted lecturer" and a "major influencer" of his career. Dan recounts in 1988 when Michael was a VIP invited lecturer at an international conference in Prague that in spite of suffering "assaults from participants" he exhibited "modesty and politeness". Dan was impressed by not only his clarity of ideas, but also his generosity, including gifting in early 1990 a MAC-Plus and an Apple printer where in Romania, personal computers didn't appeared until 1987 and only then in public institutions. He recounts this "real friend" who "fought for it more than once" to obtain a 1-year NATO scholarship at LIMSI for Dan. On the occasion of the Festschrift, Dan expresses "Thanks Mika! Be happy, surrounded by lots of friends, followers and peers who love you both as a scholar and a gentleman."

Gerard Sabah, Director of Research at the Centre National de la Recherche Scientifique/Laboratoire d'Informatique pour la Mécanique et les Sciences de l'Ingénieur (CNRS/LIMSI) notes his recognition at a global level, exemplified by his 2001 Generation Workshop in Toulouse or his invitation by Kathy McKeown to give a course at the University of Columbia in New York City, his invitation by James Pustejovsky to spend three months at Brandeis University, or his invitation to the Tokyo Institute of Technology. Gerard notes his expertise in text generation, lexicography, and dictionaries, his multidisciplinary approach and foundation on valid cognitive theories yet with practical application, and highlights the strong connection with the Human Machine Communication department at LIMSI and its groups on Architecture and Models for Interaction and Language Information and Representation.

Professor Jean-Pierre Desclés at the University of Paris-Sorbonne notes how Michael Zock contributed greatly to the clarification of the challenging research area focused on the relationship of language and thought. Professor Desclés describes the important application domains addressed by Michael's psycholinguistically motivated research in text generation including computer-based education assistants. His impressive international reputation has enabled him to bring his theoretical and practical insights to Romania, Bulgaria, and Mexico as well as facilitated the development of many junior researchers in France and beyond.

Joseph Mariani, Director of Research at CNRS and at that time Director of the ICT Department at the French Ministry for Research, recognized the quality of Michael's work and its impact on the international community, describing him as a "recognized pioneer" in text generation and dictionaries. Dr. Mariani notes his major role in organizing international workshops, conferences (e.g., COLING, ACL) as well as citations of his contributions in reviews in the leading journals *Artificial Intelligence* and *Computational Linguistics*. In addition to a multiplicity of publications, Joseph notes this most interesting trilingual scientist has acted as a global scientist … called upon to serve as a reviewer in Washington at NSF and in Brussels by the European Commission, as well as being invited to research in Tokyo or give a tutorial in Beijing (COLING) or conference paper in Cuba or a psychology review in Mexico. These strengths are echoed by Michel Denis from the Human Cognition Group at CNRS/LIMSI.

Professor Pieter Seuren at the Max Planck Institute for Psycholinguistics in Nijmegen notes Michael's contributions are not only to deeper understanding of "the human ability to produce coherent speech" but also "important contributions to psycholinguistics and the theory of language in general". He characterizes his approach as "ambitious" and "developing theories that are computer-testable" resulting in his ability to "establish an impressive reputation". In a companion area of automated dictionary making, Dr. Zock's "expertise is recognized by formal lexicographers all over the world." "He is appreciated not only for the intellectual content of his contributions but also for the quality of his teaching." Notably, Pieter characterizes Michael as "a person of total integrity and great personal warmth, without any of the arrogance that too often grows in leading academic figures, of whom he is clearly one."

5 Technical Leadership and Recognition

Michael exhibited leadership throughout his career, notably not only in his unofficial role as an international scientific ambassador but also through sustained contributions and organization of scientific events. In addition to edited collections cited above, Dr. Zock helped organize at least 6 Workshops on Natural Language Processing and Cognitive Science (NLPCS 2013, 2012, 2011, 2010, 2009, 2008, 2007), four—European Workshops on Natural Language Generation (EWNLG 1995, 1993, 1991, 1989), four CogALex workshops (2012, 2010, 2008 and a forerunner 2004) in conjunction with COLING, Tools for Authoring Aids—(2008), and LREC, Marrakech) and the 7th International Conference on Cognitive Science (ICCS 2010). A sampling of some of his recent contributions illustrates his sense of humor and wit (e.g., "If all roads lead to Rome, they are not created equal. The problem of lexical access" (IA + TAL), "Wheels for the mind" (LREC'10), and "The mental lexicon, blueprint of the dictionaries of tomorrow?" (ESSLI '09)). I had the great fortunate of co-organizing two workshops with Michael (Jokinen et al. 1996, 1997) and his leadership was natural but laser focused. Tireless worker, he is still organizing scientific workshops: one in COLING 2014 (Cognitive Aspects of the Lexicon, CogALex) and another one within the French NLP conference TALN 2014 (Réseaux Lexicaux et Traitement des Langues Naturelles, Lexical Networks and NLP).

Not surprisingly, Michael's work has been recognized across the world. For example, in Mexico (1995) he was recognized with the *Unam School of Psychology 20th Anniversary Award*, for his work on SWIM. In Santiago de Cuba in 2001 he received the best paper in the Computational Linguistics section of the 7th Symposium of Social Communication. He has received four grants from the Japanese government (1995, 2003, 2004, 2009) and his research was twice supported by Apple Computer Europe.

6 Next Generation

Michael's passion for international technical leadership and progress, however, was complemented by his concern for the next generation of research talent. A persistent aspect of Michael's professional career has been his constant mentoring of the future science leaders. One example of this has been his service on doctoral thesis committees. Table 2 illustrates how graduate students from Australia, Italy, Spain, and Canada have benefited from Michael's sage technical counsel.

And as yet another manifestation of his practicality and efficiency, Table 3 is a blended example of Michael's thesis oversight together with simultaneous collaboration with other researchers. His generous and collaborative approach has helped shape the landscape and futures of computing and linguistics researchers. He is currently supervising the PhD thesis of Valérie Clerc (2011–2015): Génération automatique d'exercices de formation en ligne pour l'apprentissage du japonais—niveau intermédiaire (automatic generation of on-line training exercices to learn Japanese—intermediate level).

Table 2 Michael Zock's doctoral committee service

Student	University	Topic	Year
Lars Yencken	Computer Science and Software Engineering, University of Melbourne, Australia	Orthographic support for Japanese vocabulary acquisition	2009
Alberto G. Bramati	Catholic University of Milan, Italy	Linguistics	2008
Anastasis Daradoumis	Polytechnic University of Catalonia, Barcelona Spain	Intelligent tutoring systems and human-computer interaction	1997
Nicole Tourigny	Université de Montréal, Canada	Computer science	1994

Table 3 Michael Zock's thesis direction

Student	Discipline	Co director	University
Nikolai Vazov	Linguistics Thesis	Jean-Pierre Desclés	Sorbonne
Laroui	Computing	Gérard Sabah	Paris Sud
Nicolas Nicolov	Computing	Chris Mellish	Edinburgh-Sofia

7 Conclusion

Multilingual translator, global researcher, and language generator, Michael's legacy is indicated by many scientific artifacts deposited along his journey, from novel concepts and interdisciplinary approaches to intriguing inventions and communications. However, his true contribution is to a better connected interdisciplinary science and, most important, the lasting influence he has left in the hearts and minds of those he collaborated with taught, and mentored.

References

Adorni, G., & Zock, M. (Eds). (1996). *Trends in Natural Language Generation—An Artificial Intelligence Perspective: Fourth European Workshop (EWNLG)*. New York: Springer.

Centre National de la Recherche Scientifique (2014). Retrieved July 1, 2014 from http://www.cnrs.fr.

Dale, R., Chris Mellish, C., & Michael Zock, M. (1990). *Current research in natural language generation*. New York: Academic Press, Harcourt Brace and Jovanovich.

Gala, N., & Zock, M. (Eds.). (2013). *Ressources Lexicales: Contenu, construction, utilisation, évaluation (Lingvisticæ Investigationes Supplementa)*. Amsterdam: John Benjamin Publishing Company.

Horacek, H., & Zock, M. (1993). *New concepts in natural language generation: planning, realization, systems*. London: Pinter Publishers.

Jokinen, K., Maybury, M., Zock, M., & Zukerman, I. (1997). Gaps and bridges: New directions in planning and natural language generation. *AI Magazine, 18*(1), 133–136.

Jokinen, K., Maybury, M., Zock, M., & Zukermann, I. (1996). Introduction to the workshop gaps and bridges: new directions in planning and natural language generation. *12th European Conference on Artificial Intelligence (ECAI)* (pp. 1–4). Budapest. Retrieved form http://www.aaai.org/ojs/index.php/aimagazine/article/view/1283/1184.

Kawtrakul, A., & Zock, M. (Eds.). (2006). Electrical Engineering/Electronics, Computer, Communications and Information TechnologyAssociation (ECTI) [Special issue]. *Transaction on Computer and Information Technology*, 2(2), 73. ISSN 2286–9131.

Zock, M. (2014). Home page. Retrieved July 1, 2014 from http://pageperso.lif.univ-mrs.fr/~michael.zock/.

Zock, M. (1988). *Advances in natural language generation: an interdisciplinary perspective:* (Vol. 2). London, Ablex, Norwood, NJ: Pinter.

Zock, M., & Sabah, G. (1988). *Advances in Natural Language Generation: an Interdisciplinary Perspective:* (Vol. 1). London, Ablex, Norwood, N.J: Pinter.

Zock, M. (1998). Computer assisted language learning in the francophone world. *CALL, Exeter, 11*(5), 138.

Part I
Cognitive Natural Language Processing

What are Sentiment, Affect, and Emotion? Applying the Methodology of Michael Zock to Sentiment Analysis

Eduard H. Hovy

Abstract In Natural Language Processing or Computational Linguistics (NLP or CL), researchers assume almost universally that speakers hold some affective value or sentiment with regard to (some aspects of) a topic such as a film or camera, that this sentiment has a fixed value (typically, something like *good* or *bad*), and that the sentiment is expressed in text through a word or small combination of words. However, one finds in the NLP literature essentially no discussion about what 'sentiment' or 'opinion' really is, how it is expressed in actual language usage, how the expressing words are organized and found in the lexicon, and how in fact one can empirically verify cognitive claims, if any, implied in or assumed by an NLP implementation. Even the Wikipedia definition, which is a little more careful than most of the NLP literature, uses words like "polarity", "affective state", and "emotional effect" without definition. In this situation we can usefully try to duplicate Michael's mindset and approach. What do people actually do? How does what they do illustrate the complexities of the problem and disclose unusual and interesting aspects that computer scientists are simply blind to? In this paper I first provide interesting examples of real-world usage, then explore some definitions of sentiment, affect, opinion, and emotion, and conclude with a few suggestions for how computational studies might address the problem in a more informed way. I hope in the paper to follow the spirit of Michael's research, in recognizing that there is much more to language usage than simply making some computer system mimic some annotated corpus, and that one can learn valuable lessons for NLP by looking at what people do when they make language.

Keywords Sentiment analysis · Opinion mining · Computational sentiment determination · Cognitive view on opinion

---

Dedicated to Michael Zock.

E.H. Hovy (✉)
Carnegie Mellon University, Pittsburgh, PA, USA
e-mail: hovy@cmu.edu

© Springer International Publishing Switzerland 2015

N. Gala et al. (eds.), *Language Production, Cognition, and the Lexicon*,
Text, Speech and Language Technology 48, DOI 10.1007/978-3-319-08043-7_2

1 Introduction

Throughout his career, Michael has been interested in one of the core issues of psycholinguistics: how we access and use the lexicon. Time and again he has pointed out the mismatch between computational and psycholinguistic approaches to the lexicon: in Computational Linguistics research the focus is always the content and use of lexical items, while finding the word(s) we need is never a problem; however real human language behavior shows clearly that lexical access is complicated and error-prone, and is just as interesting a problem as lexical content.

In this paper I address a similar mismatch between computational studies and real-world uses, on a different topic. Over the past decade, computational linguistics has developed a new area commonly called *sentiment analysis* or *opinion mining*. As Wikipedia defines it.

> **Sentiment analysis** or **opinion mining** refers to the application of natural language processing, computational linguistics, and text analytics to identify and extract subjective information in source materials. Generally speaking, sentiment analysis aims to determine the attitude of a speaker or a writer with respect to some topic or the overall contextual polarity of a document. The attitude may be his or her judgment or evaluation (see appraisal theory), affective state (that is to say, the emotional state of the author when writing), or the intended emotional communication (that is to say, the emotional effect the author wishes to have on the reader).

In Natural Language Processing or Computational Linguistics (NLP or CL), researchers assume almost universally that speakers hold some affective value or sentiment with regard to (some aspects of) a topic such as a film or camera, that this sentiment has a fixed value (typically, something like *good* or *bad*), and that the sentiment is expressed in text through a word or small combination of words. However, one finds in the NLP literature essentially no discussion about what 'sentiment' or 'opinion' really is, how it is expressed in actual language usage, how the expressing words are organized and found in the lexicon, and how in fact one can empirically verify cognitive claims, if any, implied in or assumed by an NLP implementation. Even the Wikipedia definition, which is a little more careful than most of the NLP literature, uses words like "polarity", "affective state", and "emotional effect" without definition.

In this situation we can usefully try to duplicate Michael's mindset and approach. What do people actually do? How does what they do illustrate the complexities of the problem and disclose unusual and interesting aspects that computer scientists are simply blind to?

In this paper I first provide interesting examples of real-world usage, then explore some definitions of sentiment, affect, opinion, and emotion, and conclude with a few suggestions for how computational studies might address the problem in a more informed way. I hope in the paper to follow the spirit of Michael's research, in recognizing that there is much more to language usage than simply making some computer system mimic some annotated corpus, and that one can learn valuable lessons for NLP by looking at what people do when they make language.

2 Current Tasks and Approaches

There has been a rapidly growing desire for automated sentiment/opinion detection systems. Companies are eager to read popular critiques of their products and learn the effects of their advertising campaigns; politicians are eager to assess their image among the electorate, and normal people overwhelmed by the variety of text on the web about almost any topic, with too many different voices and too little trustworthiness, are eager for some automated assistance.

But the lack of standardization—the absence even of clear definitions of the major topics under discussion—hampers any serious work. For example, restaurant reviews in Yelp, book reviews in Amazon, and similar crowdsourcing sites all include some sort of star rating system, the more stars meaning the more positive. But even a cursory glance shows that different raters apply very different standards, and that almost no review discusses just a single aspect, making a single star rating system a crude average of little specific value.

Reflecting this fact, the linguistic expression of opinion is often quite complex. For example, the opinion expressed in the following excerpt from the web

> I have been working as a stylist at great clips for about 7 months now, and I like it and I hate it at the same time I only have to work a 6 h shift and I get tips from customers but I hate it cuz I don't really like being close to strangers and I hate getting hair all over my shoes…

is nuanced in a way that makes a simple star rating for the job impossible.

In response, many NLP researchers have taken the approach of trying to identify 'aspects' or 'facets' of the topic and then discovering the author's opinion for each of them; for example, positive on hours and tips but negative on proximity to strangers and messy shoes. This resembles the periodical *Consumer Reports*, whose well-known faceted rating system of nicely composed tables rate facets of hundreds of products. But while this approach may work well for products, real life is often much harder to compartmentalize into facets. Unlike the price, weight, and lens quality of a camera, 'getting hair over my shoes' is not a common and easily quantifiable aspect of life.

The problem goes beyond nuancing and facets. People's attitudes change, and change again. For example, also from the web

> the movement…. er…. sometimes I like it and sometimes I hate it. It would've been sooooo much better if they had used head tracking rather than rotating the shoulders

Even assuming one can identify which facet is being discussed, the author holds about it two radically opposite opinions. What star rating system can express this?

Finally, there is the assumption that when one has identified the author's opinion then one has done one's job. But just assigning a sentiment value is not always enough. In

Why I won't buy this game even though I like it.

the author is probably saying something of prime importance to the makers of the game, far more serious than just some reasons for satisfaction of a happy customer.

3 Current Computational Sentiment Determination

There is a great deal of recent research on automated sentiment detection. Politicians, advertisers, product manufacturers, and service providers are all driven by the exciting promise of being able to determine easily and quickly the general public's response to them and/or their ideas or products. Computational systems and services like Media Tenor (http://us.mediatenor.com/en/) provide beautifully crafted results that show in dramatic color the level of popularity of, for example, the US President George W. Bush in 2005, shown in Fig. 1.

Despite its apparent sophistication, automated sentiment determination is almost universally very simple. The very simplest systems match words in the immediate context of the target item's name against lists of positive-affect and negative-affect words, and compute some sort of possibly weighted average. That is, the sentences

I hate George Bush
I have trouble with Bush's policies

are given the label *bad* for Bush because of the presence of "hate" and "trouble"; often also a strength score is provided when "hate" is scored as 'more-negative' than "trouble". The fact that one person's 'having trouble with' may be worse than another's 'hate' is simply ignored.

Recent research papers extend this simple scheme in one of three ways: (1) more elaborate signals of affect not just longer lists of words, but also other features such as part of speech tags, negation as expressed by words like "not", "don't", "never…", etc. (Pang et al. 2002; Turney 2002); (2) additional facets or components of the problem including facets of the topic, the holder of the affect, etc. (Kim and Hovy 2006; Snyder and Barzilay 2007); and (3) more elaborate methods to compose individual signals, in order to handle mixed-affect sentences such as

Although I hate Bush's policies on immigrants, I really love his fiscal policy

Modern techniques propagate affect up the sentence parse tree and perform various kinds of affect combination at nodes where values meet. The most sophisticated sentence sentiment computation engine at the time of writing is that

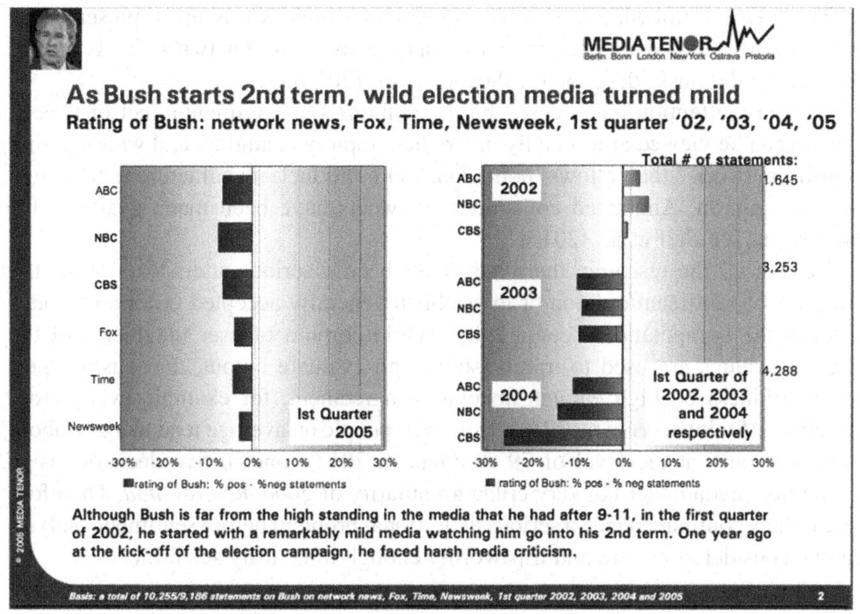

Fig. 1 Media Tenor's analysis of public popularity of then US President George W. Bush in 2005

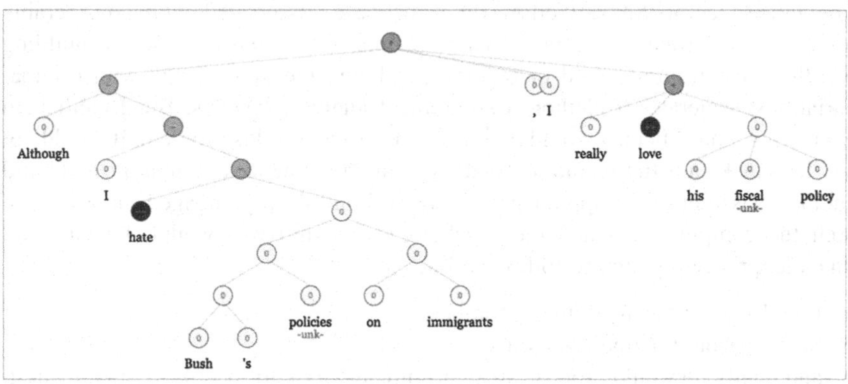

Fig. 2 Analysis of "Although I hate Bush's policies on immigration, I really love his fiscal policy"

of Richard Socher, whose online demo system at http://nlp.stanford.edu:8080/sentiment/rntnDemo.html produces for the above sentence the analysis in Fig. 2. Here brown nodes (in the left half of the sentence) reflect negative and blue nodes (right half) positive sentiment, and the intensity of the node's color expresses the strength of affect.

This system embodies a complex model in which words are represented as vectors of values and are combined using a recursive neural network that is trained for exactly this task, described in Socher et al. (2013).

Recently, attention has focused on determining the sentiment/affect of tweets. Tweets can be viewed as a socially diversified, rapidly changing, and wide-ranging 'sensor network' that allows politicians and product manufacturers to gauge popular opinion. Annotated collections of tweets have been made available for evaluation; see Saif et al. (2013).

Despite all the research, there has never been a serious attempt to define the concepts of sentiment/opinion or to establish generally accepted criteria for judgment in the computational community. While corpora of user judgments of the affective values are used to train systems and evaluate output, they justify their trustworthiness on high enough annotation agreement, for example even across languages (Steinberger et al. 2011). However, people on average tend to agree about sentiment only at the level of 79 % (Ogneva 2012): one in five decisions is in contention, even under the very crude granularity of *good–neutral–bad*. Therefore researchers continue to face a serious definitional problem before sentiment analysis can be considered mature and trustworthy enough to be truly scientific.

4 What Would Michael Do?

The intense computational effort (in some cases associated with considerable private sector funding) attracts many people. The relative ease of building wordlists and training word or feature matching algorithms (even with original variations) generates a plethora of sentiment analysis systems. But I can't help wondering what Michael would do if he were to address this problem. It would not be "let's make a better feature list and break up the sentence a little more and build another classifier". His approach —thoughtful and deeply engaged, interested in both the computational and the psychological/cognitive— would, I venture to imagine, proceed along the following lines:

- first, he would analyze the phenomena,
- then he would define his terms,
- and finally he would propose an algorithm, and look for people to implement it.

In other words, one has to address the following open questions if one wants to know what one is talking about:

1. Definitions: What are *Sentiment*? *Opinion*? *Affect*?
2. Theory: What is the structure of these concepts?
3. Practice: Is sentiment recognition all just a matter of identifying the appropriate keyword(s) (perhaps in combinations)? What do people do when they assign (generate) and understand (interpret) sentiment?
4. Evaluation: How do people assign values? Do they agree?

5 Types and Definitions of Opinions

One can identify at least two kinds of Sentiment expressed in text:

- **Opinions**, such as *like/dislike/mixed/don't-know… believe/disbelieve/unsure… want/don't-want/sometimes-want…* . This is something the subject decides.
- **Feelings/emotions**, such as *happy/sad/angry… calm/energetic/patient/relaxed* … . This is something the subject feels.

What exactly these notions are is not simple to define. The concepts are connected; they cause and/or reinforce one another. Researchers in Emotion/Affect, mostly in Psychology, have written dozens of books on the topic (see *Affective Computing* in Wikipedia). We do not address Emotion in this chapter.

Turning to opinions, the Merriam-Webster dictionary defines an *opinion* as "a view, judgment, or appraisal formed in the mind about a particular matter", or "a belief stronger than an impression and less strong than positive knowledge". This indicates that there are at least two kinds of opinion:

Judgment opinions: *good, bad, desirable, disgusting…*: "The food is horrible"
Belief opinions: *true, false, possible, likely…*: "The world is flat"

Analysis of examples indicates that they both have the same internal structure, which can be defined at minimum as a quadruple: (Topic, Holder, Claim, Valence):

- **Topic** = theme/topic of consideration
- **Holder** = person or organization holding or making the opinion
- **Claim** = statement about the topic
- **Valence** (judgment opinions):
  - *Positive* or *Negative* or *Mixed* or
  - *Neutral*: "I don't care one way or the other about him" or
  - *Unstated*: "they had strong political feelings"
- **Valence** (belief opinions):
  - *Believed* or *Disbelieved* or *Unsure* or
  - *Neutral*: "I don't care one way or the other about him" or
  - *Unstated*: "perhaps he believed it, I don't know"

Armed with this knowledge, one can define opinions and its types as follows:

Definition An *opinion* is a decision made by someone (the Holder) about a topic (the Topic). This decision assigns the Topic to one of a small number of classes (the Valences) that affect the role that the topic will play in the Holder's future goals and planning decisions (discussed below).

Definition *Judgment opinions* express whether or not the Holder will follow goals to try to own/control/obtain the Topic.

Definition *Belief opinions* express whether or not the Holder will assume the Topic is true/certain/etc. in later communication and reasoning.

One can include additional components to extend the structure:

- **Strength** of opinion
  - This is very difficult to normalize across Holders
- **Facet(s) of topic**
  - It may be useful to differentiate subfacets of the Topic; not "the camera" but "the weight of the camera". This is simply a narrower Topic.
- **Conditions** on opinion
  - Adding conditions is possible, at the cost of complexity: "I like it only when X"/"If X then I like it".
- **Reasoning/warrant** for opinion
  - "The reason I like it is X". As argued below, this is important, even though it opens up the question of reasoning and argument structure.

6 Identification of Opinion

The question now arises, how are opinions of both kinds expressed in text? It is clear from the examples above that the current computational practice of using simple word lists is not adequate. Opinion are expressed by units of various sizes:

- **Word level**: individual words are opinion clues
  - Yes: "hate", "disgusting", "anger"
  - No opinion: "run", "announce", "tall"
- **Sentence level**: compositions of words
  - Yes: "Actions with negative consequences include the US attack on Iraq."
  - No opinion: "To receive a copy of our catalogue, send mail."
- **Text level** (implicature): opinions are obtained via rhetorical relations
  - "Not only did he eat the meat, he spoiled all the rest of the food as well"
  - "Sure he ate the meat. But he still didn't clean the kitchen!"

Computational linguistics research has devoted a lot of effort to creating lists of words and phrases to be used for opinion recognition, including, at the lexical level, wordlists, better word/feature combination functions, etc. (Yu and Hatzivassiloglou 2003; Riloff and Wiebe 2003; Kim and Hovy 2005; Agarwal and

Mittal 2013; and other recent work); at the structural level, sentence and discourse structure analysis (Socher et al. 2013; Wang et al. 2012a, b) and document-level sentiment (Pang et al. 2002; Turney 2002; Wiebe et al. 2005). Additional supporting information includes knowledge about user–user relationships in online social networks like Twitter (Balahur and Tanev 2012; Tan et al. 2011), or general ideology (Wang et al. 2012a, b; Gryc and Moilanen 2010; Kim and Hovy 2006).

7 A Longer-Term Cognitive View on Opinion

As is so nicely described in the opening chapters of this book, Michael's primary research interest would focus on the cognitive aspects of the problem. It would be axiomatic to him that it is simply not interesting to assign labels in a simplistic word- or feature-matching manner (even though, for some corpora, this approach may work quite well). I can imagine him saying: let's look at *why* people say what they say. That is, sentiment reflects the deeper psychological state of the holder, enabling people to give reasons why they like or dislike something. Where does this lead one?

On analysis, one readily discovers two principal types of reason:

- Goals and plans regarding future actions
- Emotional attachments and preferences/attitudes toward objects and people

First, considering the goals and plans of the speaker: when the topic is something of utility to the holder, one can match up its characteristics to the holder's plans and goals. Characteristics that align with a goal or a plan pursued by the holder would receive a positive rating, and vice versa. For example, a sturdy and perhaps heavy camera would match up well with the goals and plans of a mountaineer (and hence be *positive*), but absolutely not with the goals and plans of a teenage girl going to the beach (and hence for her be *negative*). Simple keyword matching can never explain *why* someone makes his or her opinion judgment. But if you understand this first category of sentiment properly, you can explain why. (Ask anyone who does not study NLP why some sentiment decision is made, and they will readily and easily provide their view of the reasoning.)

Second, considering emotional attachments and preferences: when the topic is not of primarily utilitarian value, it does not relate to plans, but generally only to the holder's highest-level goal(s) to be interested/amused/happy. In this case, one can try to identify the general conceptual types of entity and event that he or she prefers or disprefers: Western or crime stories, Action or SciFi movies, conservative or informal clothes, classical or jazz or rock music. When people say "I prefer cotton over polyester even though it needs ironing because it is cooler", that reflects their goal to be comfortable at the cost of their goal of being groomed. But not everything relates back to a goal or plan. People will generally have a hard time saying "I prefer jazz over rock because…". For the second category of sentiment, *de gustibus non est disputandem*. In this case, referring to the prototypes of the preferred/dispreferred actions and entities usually provides sufficient justification.

Following this line of thought, one can extend the structural definition of opinion as follows:

Opinion type 1:

- Topic: camera
- Claim: strength is good
- Holder: buyer
- Valence: +
- Reason:
  - Personal profile: mountaineer
  - Goals: climb mountains, protect camera
  - Plans: take photos while climbing

Opinion type 2:

- Topic: music
- Claim: jazz is good
- Holder: listener
- Valence: +
- Reason:
  - Features: free-form, complex harmonies and rhythms, etc.

To address the problem of reason determination computationally, one can perform automated goal and plan harvesting, using match patterns such as "*a * camera because* *" to link topic features relative to the relevant plans, as shown in Fig. 3.

While the causes for type 2 opinions will range widely over emotions, and hence probably not be tractable computationally, the causes for type 1 might be easily categorized into a small ontology of physical features relating to actions, including notions of movement, cognition, social acts, construction, money, and a few others.

In conclusion, the challenge for Opinion (Sentiment) Analysis is not just sentiment classification, but deeper explanation generation. (In fact, precisely this is what the companies and politicians really want!) discovering how to do so is an interesting and longer-term research challenge that will provide a rich dividend to the researcher. But it is not easy, and not likely to be popular with people interested in a lot of quick-win publications.

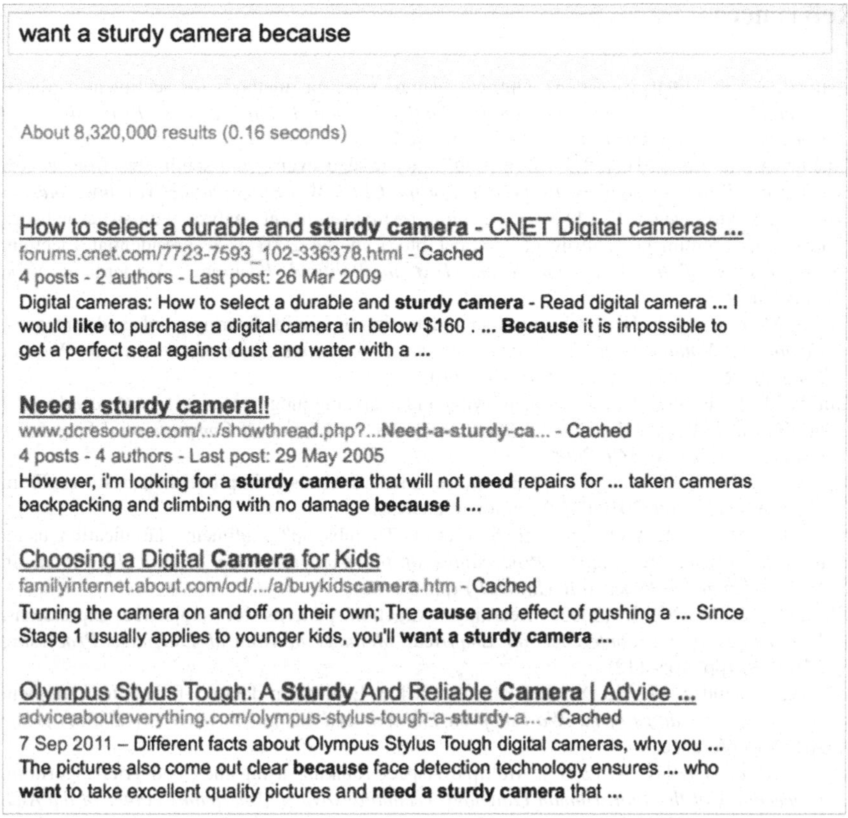

want a sturdy camera because

About 8,320,000 results (0.16 seconds)

How to select a durable and **sturdy camera** - CNET Digital cameras ...
forums.cnet.com/7723-7593_102-336378.html - Cached
4 posts - 2 authors - Last post: 26 Mar 2009
Digital cameras: How to select a durable and **sturdy camera** - Read digital camera ... I would **like** to purchase a digital camera in below $160 . ... **Because** it is impossible to get a perfect seal against dust and water with a ...

Need a sturdy camera!!
www.dcresource.com/.../showthread.php?...**Need-a-sturdy-ca**... - Cached
4 posts - 4 authors - Last post: 29 May 2005
However, i'm looking for a **sturdy camera** that will not **need** repairs for ... taken cameras backpacking and climbing with no damage **because** I ...

Choosing a Digital **Camera** for Kids
familyinternet.about.com/od/.../a/buykids**camera**.htm - Cached
Turning the camera on and off on their own; The **cause** and effect of pushing a ... Since Stage 1 usually applies to younger kids, you'll **want a sturdy camera** ...

Olympus Stylus Tough: A **Sturdy** And Reliable **Camera** | Advice ...
adviceabouteverything.com/olympus-stylus-tough-a-**sturdy**-a... - Cached
7 Sep 2011 – Different facts about Olympus Stylus Tough digital cameras, why you ... The pictures also come out clear **because** face detection technology ensures ... who **want** to take excellent quality pictures and **need a sturdy camera** that ...

Fig. 3 Harvesting goal and plan information, and associated features, from the web

8 Conclusion

Over his long career, Michael has shown a remarkable talent to connect with people. The existence of this book demonstrates the respect and affection we hold for him. I think our regard has both emotional and intellectual grounds; we empathize with his humanity, personal humility, and genuine concern for people, but we equally much respect and value his tenacity, intellectual humility toward problems, and seriousness in addressing the questions that have occupied most of his research life. Michael's unwillingness just to follow an easy computational approach and accept as an answer "because it works", but instead to keep asking "but how, and why, do people do it?", despite having papers rejected and contributions ignored—this is the spirit that moves us who contribute to this book. These qualities have influenced me, and I believe, most of us.

I am grateful for having known Michael, and I hope that I have the privilege for a long time to come. Happy birthday!

References

Agarwal, A., & Mittal, N. (2013). Optimal feature selection methods for sentiment analysis. *Proceedings of the 14th International Conference on Intelligent Text Processing and Computational Linguistics (CICLing)* (Vol. 7817, pp. 13–24).

Balahur, A., & Tanev, H. (2012). Detecting entity-related events and sentiments from tweets using multilingual resources. *Proceedings of the CLEF Workshop Online Working Notes.*

Gryc, W., & Moilanenm, K. (2010). Leveraging textual sentiment analysis with social network modelling: sentiment analysis of political blogs in the 2008 U.S. Presidential Election. *Proceedings of the workshop 'From Text to Political Positions'* Amsterdam: Vrije Universiteit.

Kim, S.-M., & Hovy, E. H. (2005). Automatic detection of opinion bearing words and sentences. *Companion Volume to the Proceedings of the International Joint Conference on Natural Language Processing (IJCNLP)* (pp. 61–66).

Kim, S.-M., & Hovy, E. H. (2006). Identifying and analyzing judgment opinions. *Proceedings of the Human Language Technology/North American Association of Computational Linguistics conference (HLT-NAACL 2006).*

Ogneva, M. (2012). How companies can use sentiment analysis to improve their business. From http://mashable.com/2010/04/19/sentiment-analysis/.

Pang, B., Lee, L., & Vaithyanathan, S. (2002). Thumbs up? sentiment classification using machine learning techniques. *Proceedings of the Conference on Empirical Methods in Natural Language Processing (EMNLP)* (pp. 79–86).

Riloff, E., & Wiebe, J. (2003). Learning extraction patterns for subjective expressions. *Proceedings of the conference on Empirical Methods in Natural Language Processing (EMNLP)* (pp. 105–112).

Saif, H., Fernandez, M., He, Y., & Alani, H. (2013). Evaluation datasets for twitter sentiment analysis. *Proceedings of the Workshop on Emotion and Sentiment Analysis (ESSEM)* at the AI*IA Conference.

Snyder, B., & Barzilay, R. (2007). Multiple Aspect Ranking using the good grief algorithm. *Proceedings of the Joint Human Language Technology/North American Chapter of the ACL Conference (HLT-NAACL)* (pp. 300–307).

Socher, R., Perelygin, A., Wu, J., Chuang, J., Manning, C., Ng, A., et al. (2013). Recursive deep models for semantic compositionality over a sentiment treebank. *Proceedings of the Conference on Empirical Methods in Natural Language Processing (EMNLP 2013).*

Steinberger, J., Lenkova, P., & Kabadjov, M., Steinberger, R., & van der Goot, E. (2011). Multilingual entity-centered sentiment analysis evaluated by parallel corpora. *Proceedings of the Conference on Recent Advancements in Natural Language Processing (RANLP).*

Tan, C., Lee, L., Tang, J., Jiang, L., Zhou, M., & Li, P. (2011). User-level sentiment analysis incorporating social networks. *Proceedings of the KDD conference.*

Turney P. (2002). Thumbs up or thumbs down? semantic orientation applied to unsupervised classification of reviews. *Proceedings of the Association for Computational Linguistics* (pp.417–424). arXiv:cs.LG/0212032.

Wang, F., Wu, Y., & Qiu, L. (2012a). Exploiting discourse relations for sentiment analysis. *Proceedings of COLING conference posters* (pp. 1311–1320).

Wang, J., Yu, C. T., Yu, P. S., Liu, B., & Meng, W. (2012b). Diversionary comments under political blog posts. *Proceedings of the 21st ACM international conference on Information and knowledge management (CIKM).*

Wiebe, J., Wilson, T., & Cardie, C. (2005). Annotating expressions of opinions and emotions in language. *Language Resources and Evaluation, 39*(2–3), 165–210.

Yu, H., & Hatzivassiloglou, V. (2003). Towards answering opinion questions: Separating facts from opinions and identifying the polarity of opinion sentences. *Proceedings of the conference on Empirical Methods in Natural Language Processing (EMNLP)* (pp. 129–136).

Towards a Cognitive Natural Language Processing Perspective

Bernadette Sharp

Abstract The advances in artificial intelligence and the post-Google interests in information retrieval, in the recent decades, have made large-scale processing of human language data possible and produced impressive results in many language processing tasks. However, the wealth and the multilingualism of digital corpora have generated additional challenges for language processing and language technology. To overcome some of the challenges an adequate theory of this complex human language processing system is needed to integrate scientific knowledge from the fields of cognitive science and cognitive neuroscience, in particular. Over the last few years, emerging applications of NLP have taken a cognitive science perspective recognising that the modelling of the language processing is simply too complex to be addressed within a single discipline. This paper provides a synopsis of the latest emerging trends, methodologies, and applications in NLP with a cognitive science perspective, contributed by the researchers, practitioners, and doctoral students to the international workshops in Natural Language processing and Cognitive Science (NLPCS).

Keywords Natural language understanding · Natural language processing · Cognitive language perspective · NLPCS · NLP history · NLP challenges · Connectionist language processing · Symbolic language processing · Cognitive modelling

1 Introduction

The field of Natural Language Processing (NLP) has developed rapidly in recent years and is actively pursued by commercial and industrial organisations. The primary goal of NLP is to develop methods and systems which will allow

B. Sharp (✉)
Staffordshire University, Stafford, UK
e-mail: b.sharp@staffs.ac.uk

© Springer International Publishing Switzerland 2015

N. Gala et al. (eds.), *Language Production, Cognition, and the Lexicon*,
Text, Speech and Language Technology 48, DOI 10.1007/978-3-319-08043-7_3

computers to analyse, understand and interact with users in a normal human language. NLP is still an evolving discipline though it began in the 1950s. In her paper Sparck Jones (2001) identified four distinctive phases in the history of NLP. The first phase, which covered the period up to late 1960s, focused on machine translation primarily by researcher from the Soviet Union, the USA, Europe and Japan. Most of the research focused first on syntactic processing such as the work by Plath (1967) though few considered the challenges of semantic processing, namely the group led by Ceccato (1967) who also made use of the world knowledge to extend linguistic semantics. The emphasis on semantics and world knowledge and the use of artificial intelligence methods became more prominent in the second phase which covered the period to late 1970s. NLP researchers (e.g. Winograd 1976; Rustin 1973; Shank 1986; Woods 1986) became involved in developing knowledge based driven systems designed to interpret and respond to language input. The third phase is described as a grammatico-logical phase as the researchers moved towards logical knowledge representation and reasoning between the late 1970s and 1980s. Computational grammar theory linked with logics and knowledge representation helped the development of discourse processing projects (e.g. Brady and Berswick 1983; Gross et al. 1986; Briscoe et al. 1987) and of resources such as grammars and lexical tools (e.g. the Alvey Natural language Tools). This phase also included the adoption of connectionist approaches to NLP offering an alternative approach to the symbolic processing approach. The availability of large machine readable data and advances in computer power in the 1990s stimulated the development of the lexicalist approach to grammar and the revival of statistical processing in the fourth phase. Concepts such language engineering and language technology emerged; with the rapid growth of the internet, the emergence of the information society and knowledge economy, a number of governmental initiatives (e.g. DARPA, MUC, HLT, EU RTD Framework programmes, …) have funded the development of rich linguistic resources, namely written and spoken corpora, lexical databases, parsers and grammars, terminologies as well as software document management tools. These initiatives, which marked the fifth phase, have helped the NLP community not only to address important issues such as reliability, robustness, and portability, but also brought together researchers from a wide variety of traditional fields (e.g. computational linguistics, cognitive linguistics, natural language processing, information science) and stimulated the emergence of new areas (e.g. semantic web, web ontologies, text mining, machine learning, etc.) working on large digitised multilingual corpora.

The history of NLP has been marked by a gradual shift from lexical semantics to compositional semantics to narrative based NLP technology (Cambria and White 2014) and from symbolic processing to connectionist models of language processing. Though the relative merits of connectionist and symbolic models of language are continuously debated these two models should be viewed as complementary contributing to different aspects of language processing (Steedman 1999).

2 Towards a Cognitive Science Approach to Natural Language Processing

The advances in artificial intelligence and the post-Google interests in information retrieval, in the recent decades, have made large-scale processing of human language data possible and produced impressive results in many language processing tasks, such as speech recognition, morphological analysis, parsing, and semantic interpretation. However, the wealth and the multilingualism of digital corpora have generated additional challenges for language processing and language technology. To overcome some of the challenges an adequate theory of this complex human language processing system is needed to integrate scientific knowledge from several fields: linguistics, information science, epistemology, computer science, and, in particular, the fields of cognitive science and cognitive neuroscience, both of which investigate language function in the human brain and can contribute significantly to language comprehension and language processing.

Over the last few years, emerging applications of NLP have taken a cognitive science perspective recognising that the modelling of the language processing is simply too complex to be addressed within a single discipline. To deal with a natural or artificial system (people or computers) or a combination of both (interactive NLP) systems must rely on many types of very different knowledge sources. Hence, strategies varied considerably depending on the person (novice, expert), on the available knowledge (internal and external) and on the nature of the information processor: human machines or both (human-machine communication).

To foster interactions among researchers and practitioners in NLP taking a cognitive science perspective a series of international workshops have been launched to encourage cross-fertilisation, potentially leading to the creation of true semiotic extensions, i.e. the development of brain inspired (or brain compatible) cognitive systems. These workshops have welcomed papers from many perspectives, including computational linguistics, psycholinguistics, cognitive psychology, language learning, artificial intelligence, and, in particular, cognitive science. In 2004, the first workshop of Natural Language Understanding and Cognitive Science (NLUCS) was launched in conjunction with the 4th international conference on Enterprise Information Systems in Porto and in 2007; the name of the workshop changed to Natural Language Processing and Cognitive Science (NLPCS) to include advances in information processing and human language technologies. These workshops were held in Porto in 2004, Miami in 2005, Paphos in 2006, Funchal in 2007, Barcelona in 2008, Milan in 2009, Funchal in 2010, Copenhagen in 2011, Wroclaw in 2012, Marseille in 2013, and the next workshop is to be held in Venice. A comprehensive account of the 170 papers presented at these workshops is beyond the scope of this paper as they cover a wide range of topics ranging from lexical, syntactical and semantic based approaches to text analysis, text mining, natural language interface, machine translation, information processing, decision modelling and sentiment analysis. Consequently, the following sections will focus on the dominant and representative themes of NLUCS/NLPCS which demonstrate their connection to cognitive approaches of language processing.

3 Cognitive Modelling of Language Understanding

Narayanan (2005) explained that one is driven to computational theories and models that link neural structure to linguistic behaviour in our aim to understand how humans acquire and exploit language. He suggested that a formally grounded computational cognitive linguistics can provide the basic mechanisms for understanding human language processing. He introduced his Neural Theory of Language (NTL) which is a synthesis of cognitive linguistics and biologically plausible computational modelling. Ball (2004) argued that our linguistic abilities derive from our basic cognitive abilities and knowledge of language is mostly learned. He discussed the Double R Grammar which is the cognitive linguist theory which underlies Double R Model. Double R Grammar is focused on the representation and integration of two dimensions of meaning: referential meaning and relational meaning, which are constructed directly from input texts. There is no separate syntactic analysis which feeds into a semantic interpretation, so the processing of language is driven by the input text using a bottom-up and lexically driven approach. Double R Model is implemented using the ACT-R which is a theory of human cognition implemented as a computational system. This model is capable of processing a wide range of grammatical constructions namely intransitive, transitive and ditransitive verbs, verbs with clausal complements, and various types of predicates (nominal, adjectives and prepositions). In a later paper, the ACT-R cognitive architecture is used to develop an incremental and plausible model of human language processing (Ball 2010). Whereas a serial pseudo-deterministic processor is built to integrate linguistic representations relying on a non-monotonic mechanism of context accommodation and to capture the incremental nature of the model, a parallel probabilistic mechanism is used to capture its interactive nature. Context accommodation makes use of the full context to carry out any modest adjustment required to the evolving representation. It can also construe the current input to allow its integration into the representation.

Yokota (2005) proposed an approach to language understanding based on a mental image model to support users accessing necessary information from the multimedia information over the web. The proposed Mental Image Directed Semantic Theory (MIDST) is based on predicate logic consisting of axioms and postulates related to human perceptive processes of space and time. MIDST associates word meanings with mental images, not only limited to visual but also 'omnisensual' aspects. For example, a moving black triangular object is perceived in terms of its location, colour and shape by an observer. Yokota has applied MIDST successfully to perform cross-media references between Japanese, Chinese, Albanian, and English texts. Feng and Hovy (2005) explored the evolutionary language understanding approach to build a natural language understanding system in their attempt at addressing the problem that most dialogue systems suffer from lack of well annotated data. Their approach is applied using an initial training data and is based on the concepts of finite state machine, naïve Bayes classifier, and shallow semantic frame.

Modelling cognitive frames for situations was the focus of Murray and Jain (2011) who claimed that Markov Logic Networks can represent situations better than either logic or probabilistic graphical models. They argued that we represent concepts such as situations with cognitive frames, a prototype-based psychological model of the world. Situational frames are inferred from the props, actions, roles, and the setting of situations. Their approach was able to represent generalities through logic and exceptions through probabilities. Representing radial concepts, contradictory beliefs or metaphorical reasoning are to be investigated further.

An interdisciplinary approach to implicit knowledge of spatial cognition in common sense geography was presented by Goerz et al. (2013). Their aim is to examine space as a cognitive, linguistic, and operative category by reconstructing the mental models of ancient people. Their proposed methodology combined annotating and parsing techniques with semantic role labelling and constraint based construction with word sense disambiguation and co-reference resolution, and cognitive linguistic description and mark-up. They argued that the survey of ancient texts can provide insights into whether basic epistemological expressions of spatial orientation can be candidates for universals.

4 Information Processing and Knowledge Extraction

As a large number of NLPCS papers fell into this category, this section will select typical applications to describe the range of approaches presented at the workshops. The first area of significant interest which emerged in 1958 with the work of Luhn (1958) is information extraction and summarisation. In opposition to the traditional linguistic approaches the researchers' aim is to extract meaning from a text using a more pragmatic and heuristic approach to text understanding. Summarisation, which is perceived as a cognitive task by Endres-Niggemeyer and Wasorra (2004) consists of "building a mental representation of the information of a body of mostly external information, reducing it to the most relevant items, and uttering or generation the content of the reduced representation—the summary" (Endres-Niggemeyer and Wasorra 2004, p. 86). They discussed their Summ-It-BMT (Summarize It in Bone Marrow Transplantation) system which was based on the strategies employed by six human summarisers. The first implementation of Summ-It-BMT was carried out by a system of cognitive agents undertaking a series of tasks reproducing the human processing model. The shortcomings of Summ-It-BMT included the problem of anaphora resolution and the performance of the cognitive agents. Textual entailment was an approach pursued by Lloret et al. (2008) aimed at showing the positive influence of textual entitlement on summarisation. Their system generated extracts from documents related to newswire stories.

Closely associated with summarisation is the work on knowledge extraction. In recent years, one of the most important directions of improvement of NLP and of knowledge extraction tasks is by exploiting semantics. In the past, systems were based mostly on statistical and machine learning methods for the analysis of large amount of textual data; today, the availability of rich and complete semantic descriptions has provided a valuable source of semantics. For instance, the paper by Tesfaye and Zock (2012) proposed a novel approach to perform semantic analysis to extract Part-Whole relations by clustering noun co-occurrences with identical tail nouns. Their approach depended on the classification features which were based on the N-gram value of concepts and the distribution of words. Clematide and Klenne (2013) proposed a method based on annotation and maximum entropy to classify the semantic contributions of prepositional phrases across different languages such as German, French, and English.

Information search is another related activity discussed by Lopez-Orozco et al. (2012). In their paper they described a cognitive computation model which was based on the way decisions were made to determine if a given paragraph was more interesting than others. They argued that such a decision model must be based on a model of semantic memory capable of imitating human judgements of semantic associations. Their model was an attempt at predicting the sequence of words likely to be fixated before a paragraph was abandoned given a search goal. Latent semantic analysis was used to compute the semantic similarities between the search goal and the fixated set of words.

5 Machine Translation

NLPCS 2011 was dedicated to machine translation, one of the oldest applications of NLP. The themes of translation memory system and technology were covered by Christensen and his colleagues. Christensen and Schjoldager (2011) argued that the use of translation memory technology and other translation software is bound to influence translators' cognitive processes. A pilot study was carried out to investigate the impact of translation memory technology on a small cohort of 22 students. The findings revealed that the greatest impact occurred during the drafting phase of the translation process; the comprehension phase became less thorough, the transfer phase was largely neglected, and the production phase consisted of more revisions than the actual production.

Teixeira (2011) explained that, until recently, machine translation and translation memories were perceived as different approaches. However, today there are being integrated due to quality improvements and availability of statistical based machine translation systems. This integration has affected the productivity for all parties involved in the translation process. For instance, source files were pre-translated using a combination of customised machine translation and translation memory systems before reaching the translators, and translators became reviewers or post-editors. To study the provenance information about translation suggestions, in the integrated translation environment, Teixeira devised an experiment to test whether the translation speed was higher when provenance information was available, and whether the quality level was of no significance when provenance information was available. Although the results were inconclusive the study concluded that provenance information was relevant for translators working with translations proposed from machine translation and translation memory systems.

The translators' productivity in the post-editing phase was further explored by Carl et al. (2011) who carried out experiments comparing manual translation with automatically translated texts which were post-edited. Translog tool was used to perform the post-editing, to monitor and collect keystrokes, and to record gaze movements during translation. The quality of the translations was evaluated by professional translators. The small scale study has shown that translation speeds were on average faster with post-editing together with a modest increase in the quality of translation. They concluded that post editing machine translation has indeed a positive effect on productivity. Carl (2011) discussed further the patterns of shallow text production in translation. Two experimental settings were described, one related to a copying task and another to a translation task. Translog was also used to track keystrokes and gaze movements. They concluded that translators tended to proceed preferably in a shallow mode which resembled text copying rather than full text understanding. Alves et al. (2011) examined the ongoing meaning construction in translation, namely grammatical metaphor, using a systemic functional linguistics perspective. By analysing recorded logs of keystrokes and eye tracking they have developed a methodology to gain insights into the cognitive processes of human translators.

6 Ontological Issues for NLP

Ontologies are now being acknowledged as important components of language processing and information processing. They are widely used in dialogue management, information extraction, text analysis, named entity recognition, etc. In his paper, Ontotherapy or How to Stop Worrying about What There is, Wilks (2007) focused on the definition of ontologies and their distinction from thesauri, lexicons, semantic nets and taxonomies, in general, and Wordnet, in particular. He concluded that "ontological and lexical resources do not differ in content, only in principle, and the fact that Wordnet is of mixed type does not disqualify it from practical use" (Wilks 2007, p. 20). Roche (2007) claimed that the conceptual modelling built from text produced rarely an ontology since it was corpus dependent and suffered from reusability and soundness. To support his claim he carried out an ontology reverse engineering from text and demonstrated that such ontology did not match the ontology defined by expert using a formal language.

He concluded that ontology design remains an epistemological issue and epistemological oriented languages.

A two-level semantic approach based on the principles of ontological engineering was proposed by Bateman (2009) in order to address the complexity of representing spatial relationships and spatial activities. An ontology-like organisation was constructed; this was motivated by grammatical and lexical evidence using natural usage of spatial expressions. This ontology mediated between linguistic form and contextualised interpretation. He concluded that it was beneficial to separate the linguistics semantics of space from the non-linguistics, situation-specific interpretation of space.

Access to ontology has also supported significantly the research into dialogue management, knowledge sharing, and metaphor processing. Delmonte (2006) proposed an approach in which the domain ontology was learnt from the linguistic analysis of texts representing the domain itself. GETARUN system was used to generate a semantic representation of a text in XML format, a top level ontology and a discourse model. The approach was tested using 450 factoid questions from TREC with some success. Glueckstad (2011) argued that terminological ontology could be a potential application for simulating the cognitive theories or models to explain real-world inter-cultural communication scenarios. The study produced terminological ontologies capturing the educational system of two countries, Denmark and Japan; feature matching based on Tversky's contrast model was applied showing modest results. Russell (2008) argued that an abstract ontology can play a significant role in the interpretation of creative cross-modal metaphor. Her cross-modal metaphor-relevant ontology was "based not on any objective reality but on a certain unconventional view of reality through language, which is itself conceptualized from reality" (Russell 2008, p. 54). An ontology based metaphor analysis program was developed (MAP) to interpret dead and novel metaphors. The paper suggested that such ontology was well capable of interpreting conventional and unconventional metaphor that is similarity-creating. The problem of metaphor is one of the many challenges faced by the applications of NLP. The implications of this problem for ontologies, lexical resources, discourse processing and text mining was explored by Barnden (2004). He argued that metaphors can also be a useful guide to the structure of dialogue and to summarisation as some metaphor types can signal topic changes and/or summarise a topic.

7 Conclusions

As Neustein (2012) explained the history of NLP has been marked by cyclical developments as evidenced by the fluctuations and the diversity of approaches to modelling human language. Language processing is a complex task, both for human and machines. What makes language processing difficult? Blache explained (2013) that this is due to the fact that our knowledge concerning the non-linearity of human language processing in still incomplete. The complexity of this phenomenon is still partially explained by psycholinguists and cognitive linguists.

The first decade of NLPCS has seen an increasing interest in pursuing a cognitive science perspective to modelling and processing language making use of statistical, machine learning, and artificial intelligence methods, contributing to the six phase of natural language processing. A variety of approaches and applications have been presented with authors from various disciplines. The tutorial, entitled Natural Language Processing from a Cognitive NeuroScience Perspective, which was presented at NLPCS 2013 by M. Besson and F. Xavier Alario from Universite Aix Marseille, has motivated the delegates and the organisation to integrate developments in cognitive neuroscience into future workshops.

Acknowledgements The authors would like to take this opportunity to thank Michael Zock for his commitments and support in co-chairing the last seven workshops and to wish him a very happy retirement.

References

Alves, F., Pagano, A. & da Silva, I. (2011). Modeling (un)packing of meaning in translation: Insights from effortful text production. *Proceedings of the 8th International Workshop on Natural Language Processing and Cognitive Science* (pp. 153–164).

Ball, J. (2004). A computational psycholinguistic model of natural language understanding. *Proceedings of the 1st International Workshop on Natural Language Processing and Cognitive Science* (pp. 3–14).

Ball, J. (2010). Context accommodation in human language processing. *Proceedings of the 7th International Workshop on Natural Language Processing and Cognitive Science* (pp. 27–36).

Barnden, J. A. (2004). Challenges in natural language processing: The case of metaphor. *Proceedings of the 1st International Workshop on Natural Language Processing and Cognitive Science* (pp. 1–2).

Bateman, J. A. (2009). Language and space: A two-level semantic approach based on principles of ontological engineering. *Proceedings of the 6th International Workshop on Natural Language Processing and Cognitive Science* (pp. 3–10).

Blache, P. (2013). What makes language processing difficult or easy. *Proceedings of the 10th International Workshop on Natural Language Processing and Cognitive Science* (p. 5).

Brady, M., & Berswick, R. C. (1983). *Computational models of discourse*. Cambridge: MIT Press.

Briscoe, E., Grover, C., Boguraev, B. & Carroll, J. (1987). A formalism and environment for the development of a large grammar of English. *Proceedings of the 10th International Joint Conference on Artificial Intelligence*, Milan, Italy (pp. 703–708).

Cambria, E., & White, B. (2014). Jumping NLP curves: A review of natural language processing research. *IEEE Computational Intelligence Magazine, 9*(2), 48–57.

Carl, M. (2011). Patterns of shallow text production in translation. *Proceedings of the 8th International Workshop on Natural Language Processing and Cognitive Science* (pp. 143–152).

Carl, M., Dragsted, B., Elming, J., Hardt, D. & Jakobsen, A. L. (2011). The process of post-editing: A pilot study. *Proceedings of the 8th International Workshop on Natural Language Processing and Cognitive Science* (pp. 131–142).

Ceccato, S. (1967). Correlational analysis and mechanical translation. In A. D. Booth (Ed.), *Machine translation* (pp. 77–135). Amsterdam: North-Holland.

Christensen, T. & Schjoldager, A. (2011). The Impact of translation-MEMORY (TM) technology on cognitive processes: Student-translators' retrospective comments in an online questionnaire. *Proceedings of the 8th International Workshop on Natural Language Processing and Cognitive Science* (pp. 119–130).

Clematide, S. & Klenne, M. (2013). Disambiguation of the semantics of German prepositions: A case study. *Proceedings of the 10th International Workshop on Natural Language Processing and Cognitive Science* (pp. 137–150).

Delmonte, R. (2006). Building domain ontologies from text analysis: N application for question answering. *Proceedings of the 3rd International Workshop on Natural Language Processing and Cognitive Science* (pp. 3–16).

Endres-Niggemeyer, B. & Wasorra, E. (2004). Making cognitive summarisation agents work in a real-world domain. *Proceedings of the 1st International Workshop on Natural Language Processing and Cognitive Science* (pp. 86–96).

Feng, D. & Hovy, E. (2005). MRE: A study on evolutionary language understanding. *Proceedings of the 2nd International Workshop on Natural Language Processing and Cognitive Science* (pp. 45–54).

Glueckstad, F. K. (2011). Application of classical psychological theory to terminological ontology. *Proceedings of the 8th International Workshop on Natural Language Processing and Cognitive Science* (pp. 227–238).

Goerz, G., Llyushechkina, E. & Martin, T. (2013). Towards a cognitive-linguistic reconstruction of mental maps from ancient texts. The example of dionysios periegetes. *Proceedings of the 10th International Workshop on Natural Language Processing and Cognitive Science* (pp. 20–34).

Grosz, B. J., Sparck Jones, K., & Webber, B. L. (Eds.). (1986). *Readings in natural language processing*. Los Altos: Morgan Kaufmann.

LLoret, E. Fernandez, O. Munoz, R. & Palomar, M. (2008). A text summarisation approach under the influence of textual entailment. *Proceedings of the 5th International Workshop on Natural Language Processing and Cognitive Science* (pp. 22–31).

Lopez-Orozco, F., Guerin-Dugue, A. & Lemaire, B. (2012). Continue or stop reading? Modeling decisions in information search. *Proceedings of the 9th International Workshop on Natural Language Processing and Cognitive Science* (pp. 96–105).

Luhn, H. P. (1958). The automatic creation of literature abstracts. *IBM Journal of Research and Development, 2*(2), 159–165.

Murray, W. & Jain, D. (2011). Modelling cognitive frames for situations with Markov logic networks. *Proceedings of the 8th International Workshop on Natural Language Processing and Cognitive Science* (pp. 167–178).

Narayanan, S. (2005). Computational cognitive semantics. *Proceedings of the 2nd International Workshop on Natural Language Processing and Cognitive Science* IS3-IS10.

Neustein, A. (2012). Think before you talk: The role of cognitive science in natural language processing. *Proceedings of the 9th International Workshop on Natural Language Processing and Cognitive Science* (pp. 3–11).

Plath, W. (1967). Multiple path analysis and automatic translation. In A. D. Booth (Ed.), *Machine translation* (pp. 267–315). Amsterdam: North-Holland.

Roche, C. (2007). Saying is not modelling. *Proceedings of the 4th International Workshop on Natural Language Processing and Cognitive Science* (pp. 47–56).

Russell, S. W. (2008). The role of an abstract ontology in the computational interpretation of creative cross-modal metaphor. *Proceedings of the 5th International Workshop on Natural Language Processing and Cognitive Science* (pp. 52–63).

Rustin, R. (Ed.). (1973). *Natural language processing*. New York: Algorithmics Press.

Schank, R. C. (1986). Language and memory. In B. J. Grosz, K. Sparck Jones & B. L. Webber (Eds.), *Readings in natural language processing* (pp. 171–191). Los Altos: Morgan Kaufmann.

Sparck Jones, K. (2001). *Natural language processing: a historical review*. Retrieved February 2, 2013, from http://www.cl.cam.ac.uk/archive/ksj21/histdw4.pdf

Steedman, M. (1999). Connectionist sentence processing in perspective. *Cognitive Science, 23*, 615–634.

Teixeira, C. (2011). Knowledge of provenance and its effects on translation performance. *Proceedings of the 8th International Workshop on Natural Language Processing and Cognitive Science* (pp. 107–118).

Tesfaye, D. & Zock, M. (2012). Automatic extraction of part-whole relations. *Proceedings of the 9th International Workshop on Natural Language Processing and Cognitive Science* (pp. 130–142).

Yokota, M. (2005). An approach to natural language understanding based on a mental image model. *Proceedings of the 2nd International Workshop on Natural Language Processing and Cognitive Science* (pp. 22–21).

Winograd, T. A. (1976). Towards a procedural understanding of semantics.

Wilks, Y. (2007). Ontotherapy, or how to stop worrying about what there is. *Proceedings of the 4th International Workshop on Natural Language Processing and Cognitive Science* (pp. 3–26).

Woods, W. A. (1986). Semantics and quantification in natural language question answering. In B. J. Grosz, A. K. Joshi & S. Weinstein (Eds.), Towards a computational theory of discourse interpretation (Unpublished manuscript).

Cognitive Systems as Explanatory Artificial Intelligence

Sergei Nirenburg

Abstract This paper argues for a revival of a mentalist approach to modeling human intelligence. The fields of artificial intelligence and natural language processing have over the past two decades been dominated by empirical approaches based on analogical reasoning, distributional semantics, machine learning and what is today called Big Data. This has led to a variety of gradual technological advances. True advances, however, are predicated on developing and testing explanatory theories of human behavior. This latter activity must include accounts of "directly unobservable" phenomena, such as human beliefs, emotions, intentions, plans and biases. This task is addressed by the field of cognitive systems. It is extraordinarily complex but unavoidable if the goal is success in modeling complex—and not entirely rational—human behavior.

Keywords Artificial intelligence · Cognitive science · Cognitive systems · Knowledge representation · Knowledge acquisition · Intelligent agents

1 Dedication to Michael Zock

Over the course of his illustrious career to date Michael Zock has made significant contributions to a number of fields, including natural language generation, the lexicon and cognitive modeling. I singled out the three areas above solely for the reason that I have studied them myself and therefore am in a good position to appreciate the quality of and impact of Michael's work, which are stellar. The two of us also share an interest in assessing the state of our discipline and analyzing metalevel processes in our research community, such as trajectories of research paradigms. Even though most of our attention is devoted to computational linguistics, by virtue of our

S. Nirenburg (✉)
Department of Cognitive Science, Rensselaer Polytechnic Institute, Troy
NY 12170, USA
e-mail: nirens@rpi.edu

© Springer International Publishing Switzerland 2015
N. Gala et al. (eds.), *Language Production, Cognition, and the Lexicon*,
Text, Speech and Language Technology 48, DOI 10.1007/978-3-319-08043-7_4

background and personal "quirks," we tend to consider the state of affairs in adjacent disciplines, most notably cognitive science and artificial intelligence. In his 2010 COLING debate with Ed Hovy, Michael defended the need for computational linguists to include the points of view and findings from other disciplines in computational-linguistic research. In the essay that follows I attempt to extend Michael's thesis by arguing that, similarly to computational linguistics, artificial intelligence has gravitated over the past several decades toward research methodology that deemphasizes theoretical work in favor of practical studies oriented at developing tools for exploiting newly available resources, such as "big data."

In the essay, I argue that from a long-term perspective, ultimate success in the science and technology of "intelligent machinery" depends on the construction of explanatory theories of human cognitive abilities. While the argument below is framed in terms of cognitive systems and artificial intelligence, it is equally applicable to computational linguistics. I dedicate this essay to Michael and hope that it provides fodder for continuing discussion and debate.

2 Cognitive Systems and Artificial Intelligence

It has become fashionable to describe artificial intelligence (AI) research as work on solving classes of problems that have not yet become routine. This weak, all-inclusive definition accepts a broad variety of types and directions of work. Remarkably, it does not in any way relate to the metaphor of intelligence that is a part of the field's name—a metaphor that was chosen precisely because the original idea was to replicate human intelligent behavior using computer programs. Today the replication of human-like intelligence is concentrated in the field of cognitive systems, a subfield of AI that is broadly concerned with computer implementations of explanatory theories of human perception, reasoning and action. Over the years, a number of differences have developed between the concerns and methods of cognitive systems and general AI. This essay presents a brief and partial overview of these differences.

What separates cognitive systems research from other approaches to developing automated means to solve problems and exhibit skills that have traditionally been considered uniquely human capabilities? Cognitive systems research is characterized by its focus on simulating human intelligence in silico. It further differs from what we might call "mainstream" modern artificial intelligence because cognitive systems research insists on grounding its system-building efforts on *explanatory theories* as the basis for simulating human intelligence. By contrast, most big data-driven, largely statistics-oriented approaches to building AI application systems tend to deemphasize theories of human functioning as formulated by philosophers or cognitive psychologists. Thus, to give just one example, latent semantic analysis, LSA (Landauer et al. 1998) claims, among other things, the ability to capture the semantics of natural language texts while being essentially a method of computing co-occurrences of semantically uninterpreted text strings in a corpus. As a result, LSA will yield different meanings of "love" if unleashed over a *Wall Street Journal* corpus rather than, say, the Gutenberg Project database. This is quite a counterintuitive state of affairs. When one adds to this the fact that the metalanguage of meaning specification in LSA is essentially a list of string co-occurrence counts, one can see why formulating explanatory theories is largely outside the focus of work on LSA applications.

While cognitive systems are oriented at modeling human abilities and performance, "mainstream" AI is at least equally interested in building systems that are claimed to be capable of *exceeding* levels of human performance on specific tasks: to give a recent example, an automatic system for distinguishing between grades of breast cancer cells has proven in one study to provide a more accurate prognosis than human pathologists (as reported in Economist 2011). The desire to exceed human capabilities is squarely in the tradition of ever ongoing and accelerating technological progress of humanity—building machines that are faster, cheaper and less error-prone than unaided human labor. Two well-publicized recent instances of such mainstream AI systems have been developed at IBM. The Deep Blue (Campbell et al. 2002) chess player is a star example of a successful modern AI program. It does not model human chess players but beat the world chess champion. While, as far as one can conclude from published materials (e.g., Ferrucci et al. 2010), the Watson question-asking system that played the game show *Jeopardy!* does not in principle preclude the use of explanatory theories of human performance, it is motivated primarily by the success of the intended application, not the quality of the underlying theory. Watson is certainly not as successful in its field (human-computer dialog) as Deep Blue is in chess, though one must not forget that its task is much more daunting.

Before discussing the merits of working on explanatory theories, let us briefly review a few trends and desiderata in avowedly engineering-oriented system development efforts in AI. Viewed as application-oriented efforts, both mainstream AI and Cognitive systems can be characterized by a few general parameters, such as:

- **Presence or absence of a theoretical model**, which, if present, might, or might not, be psychologically motivated;
- **Extent of coverage of real-world phenomena**, for example, in the domain of human language processing, extent of coverage can be assessed by whether—and at what grain size of description—an application addresses such complex topics as propositional and lexical meaning, reference and ellipsis, modality, non-literal language—as well as many more specialized phenomena contributing to the treatment of the above;
- **Extent of coverage of agent capabilities**, including perception (vision, language, etc.), human characteristics (beliefs, preferences, traits, attitudes, decision-making abilities) as well as mental and emotional states;
- **Level of automation**, from entirely manual to fully automatic;
- **Output quality**, from far below to far above human performance on corresponding tasks;
- **cost** of development, operation and maintenance.

Faced with choosing the type of work to pursue in a system-building project, AI researchers must take into account a variety of trade-offs between the desired values of the above parameters, for example, the three trade-offs illustrated in Fig. 1. It is common knowledge that systems with modest expectations of the quality of their outputs are drastically less expensive to build than those whose output quality is expected to be very high. A variant of the Pareto principle (also known as the 80-20 rule) seems to be applicable: if X is the amount of resources it takes to attain 80 % of quality objectives in a system, then it will take at least 4X to reach all of the quality objectives.

A not quite surprising consequence is the negative short-term impact of incorporating treatments of more and deeper phenomena in a system on its output quality. This is due, in part, to these new treatments being theoretically immature and descriptively insufficient. The complexity of engineering systems with ever growing sets of components is another important factor, especially if we take into account their ever-growing need for large-scale and content-rich knowledge resources. Developing explanatory theories of a wide range of relevant phenomena and then operationalizing such theories by developing algorithms and supporting knowledge is a difficult task fraught with uncertainties. In view of this, it is natural to opt for less labor-intensive—and, therefore, less expensive—alternative solutions. It is in this context that we must interpret the famous quip by the late Fred Jelinek (at that time, the manager of the speech recognition project at IBM): "Every time I fire a linguist, the quality of the system's output improves." It may indeed have improved but not beyond the—admittedly, approximate—80 % quality mark. Speech recognition systems have not yet attained the level of quality that would be comparable with human capabilities.

One conclusion from this experience is that while knowledge-lean methods that do not stress explanatory description of phenomena may serve well in the short term to build moderate-quality applications, they soon hit a ceiling of quality. Knowledge-rich, theoretically motivated approaches seeking explanations for natural phenomena still hold the promise of supporting such a breakthrough. They have never been proven false. They just fell out of fashion on account of their cost and the natural human desire for instant gratification in every endeavor.

The third trade-off applies to applications where output quality is paramount. At the present time, most AI applications of this kind cannot avoid involving humans not only as users but, critically, as contributors to the overall system output. The demarcation line between the contributions of people and those of the machines is, of course, expected to shift over time. One can argue that progress will come through building computational models based on explanatory theories of human behavior.

Of course, to be useful, AI application systems do not necessarily have to attain human levels of performance—witness the suboptimal quality but nontrivial utility of statistical translation systems or the SIRI personal assistant for the iPhone. Indeed, an application may be justifiably considered useful if it reduces the cost of carrying out a task, which can be achieved without full automation. Consequently, human-aided AI applications become a natural short-term solution. The differences between fully automatic and human-aided systems were first discussed in the

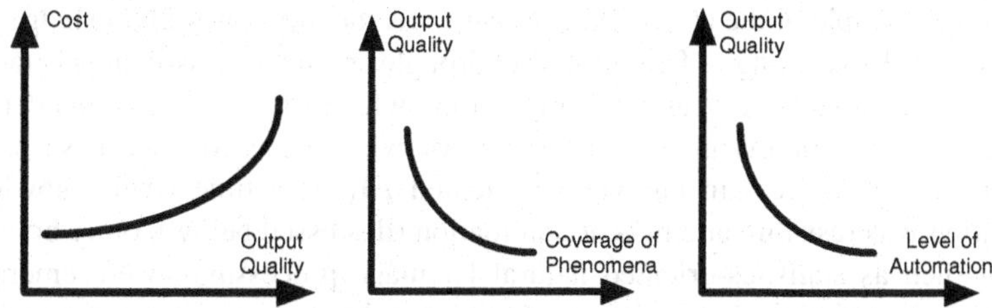

Fig. 1 Some of the trade-offs in AI application system development. At a given moment in time, AI developers must weigh hard constraints against the promise of success in an application. Thus, constraints on development costs limit expectations of output quality of a fully automatic application with broad coverage of phenomena

framework of machine translation over 60 years ago, and human-aided machine translation has been shown to be quite useful.

In the discussion above we assumed that the measure of a system's success is based on an "objective" comparison between system performance and human performance on some task. For example, Watson's responses to *Jeopardy!* answers can be compared with human responses; similarly, the output of a machine translation system can be compared to human translations (though, for the latter task, current automatic comparison metrics fall short, for example, by failing to account for the rich opportunities for paraphrase in natural language).

Another measure of success in AI systems is user acceptance, which was discussed at least as far back as Turing. In commerce and everyday life this has, of course, always been a motive force. Claiming high user acceptance of a moderate-quality and/or narrow-coverage computing application, such as a robot or a conversational companion, can be used as justification for declaring continued research in cognitive systems superfluous to requirements. Indeed, even an incomplete or low-quality technology can be viewed as successful—a realization that encourages developers because traditional prerequisites for success of an application system can be declared null and void. Even more importantly, the hope of imminent success influences society's science and technology policy and often results in additional support channeled into applications adjudged as promising, regardless of the quality of underlying technology or the potential of that technology to lead to further advances. While this may be a prudent policy in general, when it comes to applications emulating human capacity of communicating, reasoning and acting, it is nearsighted, considering the overwhelming complexity of these tasks.[1] Still, this complexity is not universally acknowledged, and optimistic hopes often prevail.

[1] Unfortunately, this complexity was not sufficiently understood even by many of the early AI researchers who on numerous occasions overplayed their hands by claiming imminent success of advanced applications—from machine translation to expert systems—that never materialized. Note, however, that this does not mean that the scientific paradigm in which they worked is invalid.

A good example of the above phenomenon was the turn toward knowledge-lean AI of about 20 years ago. This turn was brought about by less-than-spectacular progress in the quality, cost and coverage of knowledge acquisition, as availability of large amounts of machine-interpretable knowledge has long been seen as a prerequisite for success in knowledge-oriented AI. At a time when knowledge acquisition was resisting attempts at automation (discussed below), other branches of AI—such as statistics-oriented natural language processing—were emerging, and were adopted with alacrity as a source of new hope, promising to forestall the boredom and pessimism imposed by the so-called knowledge bottleneck.

User acceptance as a major criterion of success played an important role in the new approaches to AI (see, e.g., Christian 2011 for a non-technical discussion of AI systems and their acceptance by a judge in the 2009 Loebner competition). One cannot discount the success—particularly with children and the elderly—of not-very-intelligent little furry robots capable of saying a few words and producing cuddly sounds. That Joseph Weizenbaum, the pioneering author of Eliza (Weizenbaum 1966), spent a significant amount of time after releasing the system arguing that it is not really intelligent is similarly significant. Instead of dismissing these and similar devices as worthy of P.T. Barnum, one should rather try to analyze the reasons for their wide acceptance. There may be many such reasons, but the one most relevant to our discussion seems to be pervasive cognitive biases, such as the halo effect (e.g., Nisbett and Wilson 1977) or the "what you see is all there is" (WYSIATI) effect (e.g., Kahneman 2011, pp. 85–88). These biases capture people's tendencies to judge other people (or, by extension, computer programs) on the basis of a subset of relevant features, thus assuming that high scores on some features (e.g., the looks of Hollywood actors) imply high scores on other features (e.g., their wisdom or political acumen). Thus, if a robot is capable of, say, smiling and being cuddly, it is considered adequate for communication tasks that require a deeper understanding of the world and significantly more involved models of self and others. In any case, no matter how one explains acceptance phenomena, they license AI program developers to create simpler programs than those that would be expected to be subjected to more strict evaluations. Still, while lenient user acceptance metrics might be sufficient in certain areas involving "affective computing," defined as building systems that simulate empathy, in many more applications the content of the results—decisions taken, information retrieved, processed and output, etc.—should have priority. Which brings us back to explanatory theories underlying cognitive systems.

In an ideal world, developers of cognitive systems might prefer to step entirely away from the real-world pressures that favor near-term, user-accepted systems and, instead, study cognitive theories without building applications at all. However, this is not possible or, arguably, even desirable since all theories must be subject to experimental validation and falsification—even on a modest scale—so as not to be dismissed as pure abstractions.

Since comprehensive, theoretically grounded applications cannot be configured at once, I believe that many differences among alternative approaches to cognitive systems can be traced to the selection of a particular subset of phenomena and operations about which to theorize and for which to build experimental systems.

3 Cognitive Systems and Cognitive Psychology

It is no surprise that explanatory theories underlying cognitive systems are typically related to theories originally formulated in psychology. Just like in the case of cognitive systems and AI, there are important differences between the methodologies of cognitive systems and cognitive psychology. Let us consider two such differences. First, "pure" psychologists typically test their theories through human experimentation while builders of cognitive systems aim to simulate human behavior but have to implement underlying psychological theories using "hardware" and "software" instead of observing and interpreting the results of the operation of the "wetware" of the human brain. A second distinction relates to the presence vs. absence of native human capabilities. Computer systems do not have the native capabilities of humans, and therefore a variety of prerequisites for modeling human functioning have to be overtly developed instead of being assumed to exist. For example, human decision-making reflects the effects of the phenomenon called *priming*, which Kahneman (2011, pp. 52–54) describes as essentially "automatic" activation into working memory of concepts related to an idea in the focus of a human agent's attention. Priming supports the basic operations associated with all cognitive systems—perception, reasoning and action. It relates to subconscious, automatic, skill-oriented, System 1 (in Kahneman's 2011 terminology) thinking, as contrasted with conscious, deliberate, center-of-attention, reasoning-oriented (System 2, for Kahneman) thinking. Priming is used to guide disambiguation in perception, to help control reasoning, and to assist in choosing actions.

Psychologists, especially experimental psychologists, do not have to be concerned with modeling priming mechanism in silico—priming is assumed to exist, and the main research issue was to detect and analyze the content that is primed in an existing memory. Developers of cognitive systems face a different task. When cognitive system developers want to be informed by any information that psychological experiments provide about different cases of priming, they must first encode the concepts and their priming relations in a knowledge base and then suggest a method for activating elements of this knowledge base due to priming effects.

While the distinction between subconscious (System 1) and conscious (System 2) thinking has been addressed in cognitive systems work, the theoretical and methodological underpinnings of its modeling require further investigation. For example, the Icarus cognitive architecture (e.g., Langley and Choi 2006) maintains a distinction between executing skills and conceptual reasoning and operationalizes it by implementing the former as a top-down processing in a hierarchy of skills and the latter as a bottom-up processing in the hierarchy of concepts. Further studies must address the questions of what knowledge is shared between the two hierarchies; similarities between conclusions derived during inference making and skill execution; and how to conform to the psychological reality that skills are more "automatic" than deliberate reasoning.

4 The Theoretical Primacy of Knowledge

Knowledge is a core component of all cognitive systems, though its depth, coverage, and integration with models of cognitive functioning (e.g., how it is leveraged by decision-making functions) differ substantially across existing approaches. Continuing with our example of priming, a core prerequisite for implementing this psychological bias in a cognitive system is the existence of a comprehensive knowledge of concepts, concept instances and other entities—such as word forms or images of scenes—capable of being remembered. It can be argued that *the content and organization of knowledge in a simulated cognitive agent constitutes the core of an explanatory theory underlying this cognitive system*. Under such a view, the nature of the operations on the knowledge is constrained and determined by computability and efficiency considerations related to applications and are extraneous to a cognitive theory. In fact, most if not all the processing methods and specific algorithms used in engineering cognitive systems are not special to this field and are used in AI in general and in other areas of computer engineering. The distinction between theory and applications has been noted in related fields too. For example, Manning (2004) suggests that the role of linguistic theory in facilitating natural language processing applications consists in suggesting adequate inventories of descriptive features (parameters) whose values can be determined using theory-free (in this case, statistics-based) methods; those feature values are then used in a variety of decision functions relevant to the application at hand.

In sum, the knowledge in cognitive systems acquires theoretical weight because the features (conceptual parameters) used to formulate models of a cognitive agent's knowledge and memory of a cognitive agent are theoretically and descriptively motivated. Defining and using such features is not an easy task; first, because the meaning of many concepts is difficult to pinpoint precisely; and, second, because of difficulties in establishing interdependencies among such concepts.

The work of theoretically motivating inventories of features for intelligent agents has been recently pursued, for example, by Wilks (2010) in the context of developing conversational companions. The inventory of features Wilks finds desirable in a "Victorian" artificial companion include, among others, politeness, discretion, modesty, wit, cheerfulness, trustworthiness. Wilks' feature list can be expanded, for example, by adding character traits—e.g., shyness or obstinacy or earnestness—so that the user would have a choice of companion personality. Also, Wilks understandably omits any overt mention of features that are present in people but cannot be simply assumed in companions—basic capabilities of perception, reasoning and (to a lesser degree) action, including the important capabilities of learning by being told and collaborating on tasks.

An important thing to notice about the items on the Wilks list is that before they can be used in computational modeling they must be first given an interpretation. This is because most of these items are essentially metaphorical or at least refer to metaphorical concepts (this is a different, less general, interpretation of metaphoricity than the one meant, e.g., by Bryson 2010). Feature descriptions bring to mind Minsky's (2006) "suitcase words", which have vague meaning but refer to important though not universally clearly defined (or definable) concepts, such as consciousness, emotion, perception, awareness, intelligence, attention or, for that matter, happiness. Minsky points out that it might be counterproductive to try to make the corresponding notions more precise: "we need to use those suitcase words in our everyday lives to keep from being distracted by thinking about how our thinking works" (2006, p. 128). This approach licenses our everyday use of metaphorical quasi-definitions—as when we say that somebody is boiling with indignation or has the eye of an eagle when it comes to impropriety. Note that Wilks specifically states that his list of features was compiled "in no scientific manner": it is intended for people and is expected to be broadly understood without precise definitions.[2] The implication is, one must presume, that for building actual systems one will have to make the definitions of the objects of modeling more precise.

As an example of how difficult it is to define features in cognitive modeling, consider Traum et al. (2005) SASO-ST system, which models certain capabilities of "virtual humans". Among the features of these virtual humans is *trust*, which is operationally modeled using the features of *familiarity*, *solidarity* and *credibility*. In SASO-ST, *solidarity* is calculated on the basis of the percentage of the user's assertions or demands that are congruent with the agent's goals (which raises the question of how one calculates congruence). *Credibility* is interpreted as a count of how many times the user makes assertions consistent with the agent's beliefs. *Familiarity* is understood as a measure of obeying the norms of *politeness* (another suitcase category; alas, the authors do not dwell on how the norms are defined or interpreted). While this kind of modeling of psychological categories is quite possibly the most interesting conceptual part of the system, it is equally clear that trust-related computations in the system differ from the everyday interpretations of the "suitcase words" used to label the features in the model. *Credibility* and *solidarity* are suitcase categories: using them to describe the actual properties computed relies on human interpretation outside the operation of the system. The choice and the interpretation of the features and functions for determining their

[2] Minsky believes that "a clear definition can make things worse, until we are sure that our ideas are right" (op.cit., p. 95).

values may be entirely sufficient for the purposes of the SASO-ST system. But more descriptive and theoretical work is needed to formulate an explanatory and computationally implementable model of human social cognition.

The role of metaphor in the scientific enterprise is quite important and should not be disparaged. Still, when defining basic concepts for a theory, it is, at the very least, necessary to provide a precise interpretation of each instance of metaphorical usage. It is quite tempting in developing cognitive systems to rely on an imprecise interpretation of metaphors—after all, this strategy often works in human communication. Indeed, people are very good at judging the importance of each instance of ambiguity (of which metaphor is an important subclass) and can often avoid the risk of incorrect interpretation by deciding to leave certain parts of input uninterpreted or underinterpreted. This can be theoretically justified because many instances of ambiguity in perceptory input are benign, in the sense that their resolution is not necessary to maintain adequate functioning of a human or artificial cognitive agent. The problem for developers of cognitive systems is to replicate or simulate the human ability to judge whether an ambiguity is benign and whether the cost of a potential error in overall interpretation due to the incomplete interpretation of a component of input is acceptable from the point of view of the overall efficiency of the cognitive system. Note that considerations of system efficiency are theoretically grounded (and not motivated just in terms of utility of an application or relative ease of system development) only when they are called upon to account for observable differences in behavior, such as the differences between the fast and slow thinking of Kahneman's (2011) title.

A theoretically viable approach to modeling cognitive systems will view all perception-, reasoning- and action-oriented processing as decision making over a system's knowledge resources. As such, there will be considerable similarity in an agent's approach to making decisions related to subtasks as different as disambiguating the word senses of language input and carrying out goal-oriented selection of the agent's next action. Both types of decisions will be computed by functions using theoretically motivated properties of concepts in the agent's memory. Moreover, the arguments for these decision functions can be drawn from diverse components of the model of the agent's mind—ontology, fact repository, situation model, model of other agents' minds, repositories of personality and physical states of the agent, etc. This capability facilitates breaking the barriers of modular pipeline architectures of many models of complex cognitive processes, such as, for example, natural language processing. The idea about multifaceted influences on specific decision making needs is not new; it can be said that blackboard architectures (e.g., Erman et al. 1980 or Hayes-Roth 1985) were introduced to make such enriched decision making possible. Maybe it is time to revisit this approach and see whether it can now be made sufficiently efficient to be practical.

The actual computation of a given instance of a decision function can in turn be modeled as a decision function, since each decision involves context-specific determinations of the values of parameters as well as the contribution of each parameter to the final decision. This computation can clearly be multi-step and is often described using the "intentional stance" terminology of goal-directed processing. That is, an externally motivated goal of having made a decision causes the instantiation of a number of subgoals, including that of knowing the values of the relevant features (the determination of which, by the way, can involve calculations of the cost of finding the information, the system's confidence in the found value, etc.). Sometimes, however, decisions cannot be modeled using a subgoal hierarchy: e.g., decisions about word sense disambiguation depend on the choice of other word senses in the input, making necessary specialized knowledge about process control preferences.

5 Ideal-World and Real-World Methodologies

Theoretical work on cognitive systems is far from complete. It must remain the core focus of activity in the field if cognitive systems should continue *qua* cognitive systems and not merge with general AI applications. Whenever possible, cognitive system developers should concentrate on formulating and implementing explanatory theories of cognitive agency as a whole, along with its various functional components. Realistically, though, at any time during this research enterprise some theories will be missing or in some ways inadequate—being either too strong or too weak, providing insufficient coverage or even being not explanatory at all. What methodological choices are open for developers of comprehensive cognitive systems?

From a purely theoretical point of view it is appropriate to persist in pursuing maximum explanatory power and coverage by developing larger inventories of better knowledge-based heuristics even in the face of all too real efficiency and cost constraints that may make the approach practically infeasible at the moment. Indeed, knowledge-based systems have not been proven wrong, despite the multiple pronouncements of AI developers who switched to knowledge-lean methods;[3] rather, they have not yet been truly tested, as the costs of theory development, acquisition of knowledge about the world and about intelligent agents and system development have so far proved too steep. The members of the research community did not help the cause by promising imminent utility of applications of knowledge-based systems that never fully materialized. Still, real progress in simulating human performance cannot be achieved by relying exclusively on analogy-based textual pattern matching, even when supported by the currently fashionable crowd sourcing, whose main theoretical insight is the vague and empirically questionable statement that people do exactly the same thing in similar situations.

---

[3] This opinion may be a manifestation of the exposure effect cognitive bias described by Kahneman (2011): "A reliable way to make people believe in falsehoods is frequent repetition, because familiarity is not easily distinguished from truth" (ibid: 62).

While real-world pressures must be fully appreciated, they are not an excuse for the failure to test, validate and falsify theories; the challenge is to develop methodologies for building, evaluating and interpreting the evaluations of systems that are sophisticated enough for the domain of cognitive modeling. For example, to facilitate system building and evaluation in the presence of theoretical lacunae, cognitive systems can be (and usually are) viewed as hybrid systems—combinations of semi-independent processing components, some of which are based on well-developed theories and others of which are viewed as temporary placeholders awaiting the development of better microtheories of specific phenomena or operations. These placeholder components may not be motivated by explanatory theories, and/or they may cover only a subset of phenomena in the purview of the microtheory in question. One corollary of agreeing that not all components of a cognitive system must rely on explanatory theories is agreeing to evaluate only those of their components that do rely on explanatory theories. As such, blame assignment is clear and system development can continue in two directions: by improving the already theoretically motivated aspects, and/or by replacing placeholder modules by increasingly theoretically motivated ones.

6 Methodological Decisions Must Be Overt

Considering the overall complexity of the task of developing cognitive systems, it seems appropriate to adopt a lenient methodological stance and welcome any and all approaches as long as they clearly recognize the theoretical and methodological status of their work vis-à-vis the overall goal of building cognitive systems. Thus, system developers must make conscious decisions and publish reasoned statements about such issues as:

(a) which components of their work are motivated by theory and which components are included simply to ensure that an application system is complete;
(b) the breadth of the domain covered by a system;
(c) the breadth and depth of descriptions of world- and language-related phenomena addressed by a system;
(d) the expected quality of results of a system;
(e) if choosing to work on a hybrid system, the nature, scope and sufficiency of selected system evaluation methods;
(f) any and all simplifying assumptions and decisions made in designing a system.

The last point is especially important. Any discussion of issues relating to it must include a description of the benefits and expected limitations of each assumption or decision—for example, one should explain why it might be desirable to use a uniform processing engine for all the different kinds of processing that a cognitive system is called upon to perform, or to use a uniformly encoded world model and agent memory for both understanding-oriented and action-oriented decision making by a cognitive agent. Such methodological clarity will both help system development and promote "truth in advertisement" about the capabilities of any intelligent system.

Acknowledgements Many thanks to Marge McShane for productive criticism, apt suggestions and editorial help and to Pat Langley for critiquing an earlier draft of this paper.

References

Bryson, J. (2010). Robots should be slaves. In Y. Wilks (Ed.), *Close engagements with artificial companions*. Amsterdam: John Benjamins.

Campbell, M., Hoane, A. J., & Hsu, F. H. (2002). Deep blue. *Artificial Intelligence, 134*, 57–83.

Christian, B. (2011). Mind vs. machine, *The Atlantic*.

Economist. (2011). Indolent or aggressive: A computerized pathologist that can outperform its human counterparts could transform the field of cancer diagnosis. *The Economist*, December 3, 2011.

Erman, L. D., Hayes-Roth, F., Lesser, V. R., & Reddy, D. R. (1980). The Hearsay-II speech-understanding system: Integrating knowledge to resolve uncertainty. *ACM Computing Surveys, 12*(2), 213.

Ferrucci, D., Brown, E., Jennifer, C. -C., Fan, J., Gondek, D., & Kalyanpur, A. A. et al. (2010). Building Watson: An overview of the DeepQA Project. *AI Magazine*.

Hayes-Roth, B. (1985). A blackboard architecture for control. *Artificial Intelligence, 26*(3), 251–321.

Kahneman, D. (2011). *Thinking: Fast and slow*. New York: Farrar, Straus and Giroux

Landauer, T. K., Foltz, P. W., & Laham, D. (1998). Introduction to latent semantic analysis. *Discourse Processes, 25*, 259–284.

Langley, P., & Choi, D. (2006). A unified cognitive architecture for physical agents. *Proceedings of the Twenty-First National Conference on Artificial Intelligence*. Boston: AAAI Press.

Manning, C. (2004). Beyond the Thunderdome. *Proceedings of CONLL-04*.

Minsky, M. (2006). *The emotion machine: Commonsense thinking, artificial intelligence, and the future of the human mind*. Simon and Schuster.

Nisbett, R. E., & Wilson, T. D. (1977). The halo effect: Evidence for unconscious alteration of judgments. *Journal of Personality and Social Psychology, 35*(4), 250–256.

Traum, D. R., Swartout, W., Marsella, S., & Gratch, J. (2005). Virtual humans for non-team interaction training. *Proceedings of the AAMAS Workshop on Creating Bonds with Embodied Conversational Agents*.

Weizenbaum, J. (1966). ELIZA - a computer program for the study of natural language communication between man and machine. *Communications of the ACM, 9*(1), 36–45.

Wilks, Y. (2010). On being a Victorian companion. In Y. Wilks (Ed.), *Close engagements with artificial companions*. Amsterdam: John Benjamins.

Part II
Lexicon and Lexical Analysis

Lexical Contextualism: The Abélard Syndrome

Alain Polguère

Abstract The term *contextualism* is used in linguistics to refer to approaches that are based on the following credo: linguistic entities cannot be considered outside contexts of use as it is only in context that they do make sense. Contextualism has always existed (at least, since antiquity) and it does not correspond to a uniform approach to language studies. It is however striking that much resonance is given in lexical studies to what could be called *lexical contextualism*, a radical conception by which words do not have meaning of their own, and by which only contexts "give meanings" to words. This position has many non-trivial implications on lexicographic methodologies, language teaching strategies, and even on the very acceptance of core notions such as polysemy. The goal of this paper is twofold. First, it characterizes lexical contextualism: the axioms it is based on and its implications on lexical studies. Second, it tries to provide explanations for why lexical contextualism can appeal to many in their attempt to account for how words convey meanings.

Keywords Context · Lexical contextualism · Lexical semantics · Monosemy · Polysemy · Sense denial · Speaker perspective · Addressee perspective · Lexicology · Philosophy of language

1 Introduction

Before being a matter of proof and discovery, science is a matter of belief. Without beliefs, without knowledge that one does not reconsider in the course of reasoning on an object of study, there is no scientific activity. In linguistics, as in any

A. Polguère (✉)
Université de Lorraine and ATILF CNRS, 44 avenue de la Libération, BP 30687
54063 Nancy Cedex, France
e-mail: alain.polguere@univ-lorraine.fr

© Springer International Publishing Switzerland 2015
N. Gala et al. (eds.), *Language Production, Cognition, and the Lexicon*,
Text, Speech and Language Technology 48, DOI 10.1007/978-3-319-08043-7_5

descriptive science, beliefs play a crucial role as no progress can be made if some facts are not taken for granted, if there are no "truths" and if everything has to be perpetually reconsidered and put to a test. The author of the present text is not ashamed to assert that he believes in the primarily descriptive nature of linguistics as a science, in the notion of part of speech, in syntactic dependencies and, unlike some (Kilgarriff 1997), in word senses. The moment one doubts axiomatic facts, the research activity is stopped, the fundamental descriptive component of linguistic study is paralyzed and one can do nothing but turn philosophical. There is only one thing that should make scientists reconsider their beliefs: it is if they cannot achieve what they try to achieve with the notional toolkit they are using. Under such circumstances, they have to pause and reflect, and are faced with two options. They can try to diagnose what goes wrong with their approach, see if something can be fixed, see if a better alternative already exists or if a theoretical revolution is required. The alternative approach, more radical and, strangely enough, quite popular is **pure and simple denial of the object of study: if I cannot explain X, it means that X does not exist.**

This paper tries to be a remedy against this easy way out in lexical studies and, more specifically, against the denial of word senses. Our present target is the doctrine of lexical contextualism, that is so widespread in language studies whether in its explicit or rampant form.

The term *contextualism* is used in the philosophy of language to refer to approaches that are based on the following credo: the content of linguistic utterances results from contextual (pragmatic) parameters and it is only in context that utterances do make sense (Cappelen and Lepore 2005; Recanati 2004; Searle 1980; Stanley 2004). Contextualism in the philosophy of language has been extensively discussed—see (Montminy 2010) for a recent criticism of the approach—and we are in no position to add a single piece of relevant comment to what has already been said on this topic. Rather, our focus is on a peculiar manifestation of the radical contextualist doctrine in the field of lexical studies (i.e. lexicology, lexicography, vocabulary teaching, etc.): what can be termed *lexical contextualism*, a conception by which words do not possess meaning of their own, and by which only contexts give meanings to words. Lexical contextualism has always existed (at least, since antiquity) and it does not pertain to a specific approach to language studies. It is however striking that it appeals to many and that it has non-trivial implications on lexicographic methodologies, language teaching strategies, and even on the very acceptance of core notions such as polysemy.

This paper is only a modest essay on lexical contextualism and it does not pretend to "reveal" or build new pieces of knowledge. We will be satistisfed if the fact of expressing our opinion on lexical contextualism and synthesizing observations we have been able to make while studying lexical knowledge can help put linguistic context in its right place in lexical studies. The principle we want to argue for is probably an uninteresting piece of self evidence for those already convinced and an absurd backward conception for the others, but truths often look this way. This principle can be phrased as follows, in three logically related statements:

1. Linguistic context of linguistic units in utterances is determined primarily by lexical rules and grammatical rules that make up the bulk of the Speaker's linguistic knowledge.
2. The meaning and individual combinatorial properties of a lexical unit L are, in that respect, the fundamental inherent rules associated to L that condition the various contexts in which the speaker will use L in speech.
3. Under no circumstances should lexical meaning be considered as determined by context as this would boil down to confusing meaning (Speaker's knowledge) with the process of meaning recognition/identification (Addressee's mental process).

The aim of our essay is two-fold. First, it presents both theoretical and practical arguments against lexical contextualism. Second, it tries to provide explanations for why lexical contextualism can appeal to many in their attempt to account for how words convey meanings.

Well, to be honest, this paper has another purpose: it is meant to be a token of friendship to our colleague and old friend Michael Zock. *Old* is used here as a collocate of *friend*, synonym of *long-time*,[1] and it should definitely not be understood in its literal meaning. Talking about meaning ... let's get down to business.

2 Contextualism in Lexical Studies

By *lexical studies*, we mean all disciplines for which the study, understanding and treatment of words play a central role. It includes lexicology and lexicography, but also terminology, vocabulary teaching, etc. This section tries, first, to clarify the nature and impact of contextualism in lexical studies (Sect. 2.1) and, second, to put forward arguments against a radical contextualist perspective on the study of words, that we will refer to as *lexical contextualism* (Sect. 2.2). The inadequacy of lexical contextualism can only be pointed at, and not demonstrated. However, laying down arguments against lexical contextualism is a non-trivial exercise as the approach negates the existence of inherent lexical meaning, whereas the focus should be on their study and description. In so doing, lexical contextualism undermines the very foundations of linguistics. To quote Anna Wierzbicka on this matter (Wierzbicka 1992 p. 146):

> My basic premise is that language is a tool for conveying meaning. Though a truism, this proposition is what imparts direction, purpose, and a sense of identity to linguistics as a science.

[1] A **Magn**^{temp} of *friend*, in terms of Meaning-Text lexical functions (Mel'čuk 1996).

2.1 To Have or Not to Have a Meaning

Being a philosophical ignoramus, we would not dare comment on what exactly contextualism is, in its broad sense. We have to humbly admit that we perceive definitions such as the one below—proposed by Jason Stanley (Stanley 2004 p. 119)—as being totally opaque:

> Contextualism in epistemology is the doctrine that the proposition expressed by a knowledge attribution relative to a context is determined in part by the standards of justification salient in that context.

It is however clearer to us, though not absolutely clear, what contextualism is in linguistics. To rephrase in very simple terms the definition given earlier in Sect. 1, linguistic contextualism is the credo according to which what is expressed by a linguistic utterance is radically determined by the context in which this utterance occurs. As mentioned in the introduction, there are many variants of linguistic contextualism, and this variability can be explained by at least three facts.

Firstly, *context* (in which an utterance occurs) is a vague term. It can be the linguistic context, i.e. the *co-text*, it can be the pragmatic context, or it can be both. Unfortunately, authors do not always make absolutely clear what type of context they are considering. In this paper, only co-text will be considered as relevant. And by *co-text*, we mean exclusively the linguistic material itself. Non-linguistic knowledge that can be associated with the co-text of an utterance is but pragmatic context.

Secondly, one should make a clear distinction between the notion of informational content and that of linguistic meaning. While the content of an utterance is the information it carries in speech, its linguistic meaning is the information it carries as an assemblage of linguistic signs. We feel almost ashamed to write such a statement, that seems a piece of self-evidence a century after Ferdinand de Saussure's conceptualization of the distinction between *langue* and *parole* (Saussure 1916). But what is an evidence for linguists, lexicographers and grammarians involved in actual descriptive work is often overlooked by those who are in the business of discussing, rather than describing, languages.

Finally, linguistic contextualism is a gradable notion, ranging from "mild" (Recanati 2004) to "radical" (Searle 1980) variants. From a radical perspective, nothing can be said about the meaning of lexical units, phrases, etc., as it is only once they appear in given linguistic and pragmatic contexts that they do carry a given informational content.

There is no point discussing mild linguistic contextualism. It goes without saying that context plays a definite role in determining the semiotic value of utterances, the same way it participates in any Peircian semiosis (Queiroz and Merrell 2006). The following quotation from Martin Montminy (Montminy 2010 p. 320) seems to summarize perfectly well this rather non-controversial approach to contextualism:

> What is asserted is closely related to the sentence uttered: figuring out what is asserted is a matter of "fleshing out" the meaning of the sentence so as to obtain the proposition that the speaker primarily means by her utterance. We could characterize what is asserted as a slightly enriched version of what is explicitly expressed by the utterance. Thus, what is asserted could have been made explicit simply by inserting some lexical material at the relevant place in the sentence uttered.

Additionally, we should not argue against the fact that words do not "mean" by themselves. They "have a meaning," i.e. an inherent property that conditions their denotational effect in semiosis but, considered by itself, a word is just like an unlit lightbulb. This is why authors often call on the term [*a*] *potential* when characterizing the nature of word meanings. See, from a contextualist perspective, François Recanati's *semantic potential* (Recanati 2004 p. 152):

> There is something which words do contribute, and which is sufficient to account for the difference it makes when we substitute a word for another one. That thing is not a 'meaning' in the traditional sense: it is what I called the 'semantic potential' of words. 'Red' and 'rectangle' have very different semantic potentials. The semantic potential of a word is the collection of past uses on the basis of which similarities can be established between the source situations (that is, the situations such uses concerned) and the target situation (the situation of current concern). So there is, indeed, interaction between the 'context' and what words themselves contribute. Context does not do everything, even on the most extreme form of Contextualism.

In the same vein, but in a more descriptive perspective, Kerstin Norén and Per Linell (Norén and Linell 2007) adopt the notion of *meaning potential*.

Anna Wierzbicka, from a lexicologist perspective, acknowledges the notion of meaning as a non-autonomous property seen as *descriptive potential*, while insisting on the fact that word meanings are constant values **that can be identified and described if the proper tools are used** (Wierzbicka 1992 p. 147):

> (…) a word is not a container with hidden contents which can be extracted or a black hole whose contents can be suddenly illuminated. Different words "mean" different things in the sense that they can make different contributions to communication. These contributions can be compared if we have some standard of measure for "measuring" (describing) different words' communicative potential (that is, their "meaning").

In what follows, word meanings as non-autonomous properties and contexts as necessary parameters in linguistic semiosis are taken for granted. Only radical contextualism is subject to discussion as it boils down to negating the existence of linguistic meaning. As specified above, within radical contextualism, it is specifically lexical contextualism that will be our focus of attention. Lexical contextualism can be more of less equated with what François Recanati terms *meaning eliminativism* and claims "is implicit in the writings of some of the early contextualists (Austin, Wittgenstein, and others)" (Recanati 2004 p. 141).

2.2 Lexical Contextualism "at Work"

The most direct consequence of lexical contextualism is the negation of the lexico-semantic module of natural languages. As no inherent information can be associated to words, lexical meanings (among others) cannot be considered as part of the language. And the corollary of this is that any enterprise that aims at identifying and describing lexical meanings is by nature futile.

It is interesting to notice that radical contextualists are quicker at working on the omnipotence of context in regards to lexical meanings than they are in regards to, say, grammar rules. But if lexical meaning can be negated, why not also consider that grammar rules do not exist *per se* and that structural organization of utterances exists only in context? Afterall, no one has ever "seen" a syntactic or morphological structure. If meanings do not exist, we can as well consider that grammar also, and the whole of language do not exist. If languages do not exist, what are we doing here?

Languages—lexical units, their individual properties, grammar rules, etc.—are learnt. Learning means acquiring information. In the specific case of languages, we acquire rules from our interaction with the social environment. Language is not reflex. Language is knowledge. And the primary role of linguistics is to account for that knowledge. Therefore, radical contextualism, and particularly lexical contextualism, has simply no place in linguistics. It can be discussed from a philosophical point of view, like any productive or counter-productive idea. But it can only act as an intellectual poison once poured in the field of linguistics because, as has just been said, it simply negates the object of study of this science.

Science is not only meant to satisfy our curiosity. Curiosity is an important factor in the dynamics of science, which allows some to state that science is self-justified as a means to satisfy an inherent "knowledge hunger" in human beings. However, giving science a free-ride is a dangerous and self-destructive attitude. Ultimately, the outcome of scientific activity is not the publishing of texts, the organization of conferences and the thickening of CVs, it is the successful exploitation of scientific results for external purposes, i.e. activities that are either non-scientific or belong to other scientific domains. In the specific case of linguistics, these activities can be language teaching, translation, computer processing of texts, diagnosis and treatment of language-related pathologies, etc.

And what do we need to obtain from the study of words? The following are obvious answers:

- models of the lexicons (dictionaries, lexical databases) that can be used by language teachers and learners, translators, etc., as references on word-related language rules (meanings or "descriptive potentials" being central);
- formal models that can be used by computer programs to perform linguistic tasks;
- greater insight on how lexical knowledge evolves;
- greater insight on the global structuring of lexical information from linguistic, neurological, psychological, etc., perspectives.

Now: which approach, considering word meanings (i) identifiable properties or (ii) evanescent and fully context-bound phenomena, will get us closer to meeting the above-mentioned societal needs? The answer seems obvious. Additionally, we wonder if the advocates of lexical contextualism realize that, because of their belief that words do not have meaning, they are not entitled to ask or answer such natural questions as "What does *irony* <*grin, poneytail, direct object* ...> mean?" One can wonder what kind of parents, teachers or friends they would be if they were to truly stick to their principles in daily life. For this reason, we tend to not believe those who say that they do not believe in word senses (Kilgarriff 1997).

All this being said, one cannot ignore the influence of lexical contextualism in linguistics, and because we are daily faced with it, it is worth trying to answer a very simple question, the only question that is worth asking, in our opinion: why does sense denial exist?

3 Why Does Sense Denial Exist?

We see at least two interrelated facts that explain the overwhelming presence of lexical contextualism in lexical studies: a quasi-metaphysical or philosophical attitude towards words—examined in Sect. 3.1 below—and a methodological linguistic tradition—Sect. 3.2. As will be shown in Sect. 3.3, both are related.

3.1 Prata (Scolaresque) Rident

In an article entitled *Prata rident* (Rosier-Catach 1997), Irène Rosier-Catach analyses Latin texts written by three medieval scholars—Pierre Abélard, Thierry de Chartres and Guillaume de Conches—and elaborates on their conceptualization of metaphorical "semantic transfer" (*translatio* or *transumptio*, in Latin).

The Latin expression that serves as title for (Rosier-Catach 1997) can be translated as follows, though we will have to discuss this translation later in Sect. 3.1.2[2]:

(1)

Lat. *Prata rident*
meadows$_{\text{NOM}}$ laugh
'The meadows bloom'

[2] In the literal translation, the subscript "$_{\text{NOM}}$" stands for the nominative case.

First, we will explain why the above example is such an emblematic illustration of metaphorical semantic transfer (Sect. 3.1.1); a detailed structural linguistic analysis of (1) and of other closely related expressions will follow (Sect. 3.1.2). Finally, we will focus on Abélard's perspective on this type of metaphor—as accounted for in (Rosier-Catach 1997)—in order to extrapolate on some possible "philosophical" roots of contemporary lexical contextualism (Sect. 3.1.3).

3.1.1 *Prata Rident*: An Emblematic Example

The expression *prata rident* has been much cited by theologians and rhetoricians. Its recurrent mention in scholarly texts as an object of study can probably be explained by the fact that it clearly belongs to the poetical literary genre and has a strong presence in poems and hymns that find their roots in Christian tradition; for instance, in the *Carmina Burana* (Carmina Burana ca. 1230)—see *Carmina amatoria* 'love songs' N° 114 (2a) and N° 139 (2b)[3]:

(2)

a. ***Prata*** *iam* ***rident*** *omnia,*
est dulce flores carpere
b. *flore* ***rident*** *vario*
prata *iam serena;*

The English counterparts—with either *meadows* or *pastures* as grammatical subject of *laugh*—can also easily be found in the same literary genre; for instance in (Winkworth 1863 p. 90), the 19th century English translation of a German hymn written in the 17th century by Henriette Maria Luise von Hayn:

(3) *Guided by his gentle staff*
Where the sunny ***pastures laugh***,[4]
I go in and out and feed,
Lacking nothing that I need;
When I thirst, my feet he brings
To the fresh and living springs.

or in a famous poem by William Blake called *Laughing Song* (Blake 1789):

(4) *When the* ***meadows laugh*** *with lively green*
And the grasshopper laughs in the merry scene.

---

[3] Considered profane songs, the *Carmina Burana* were written by itinerant clerics (called *golliards*) and are in reality deeply rooted in Christian culture and rhetorics.

[4] There is no German "pastures laugh" metaphor in the original hymn (entitled *Weil ich Jesu Schäflein bin*); the German corresponding verse only says *Unaussprechlich süße Weide* 'inexpressibly sweet meadow'.

When Mary and Susan and Emily
With their sweet round mouths sing Ha, Ha, He.

We will show, in Sect. 3.1.3, that Abélard's analysis of the metaphor involved in *prata rident* and presented in (Rosier-Catach 1997) is directly relevant to the question of lexical contextualism. But before we do so, let us offer our own linguistic analysis of what is at stake in the structural design of this expression.

3.1.2 Preliminary Linguistic Analysis: Two Distinct Collocational Patterns

It is essential to first distinguish two Latin constructions **C1** and **C2**, together with their English equivalents[5]:

C1	Lat.	$N1_{NOM}$ *ridet* $N2_{ABL}$ → used in (2b)
	Eng.	N_1 *laughs with* N_2 → used in (4)
C2	Lat.	$N1_{NOM}$ *ridet* → used in (1) and (2a)
	Eng.	N_1 *laughs* → used in (3)

Though lexically and syntactically more complex, **C1** has to be considered first because it somehow "explains" **C2**. In order to contrast the two constructions, we will consider (5) below as a typical example for **C1** and (1) above as a typical example for **C2**:

(5)

Lat. *Prata rident floribus.*
meadows $_{NOM}$ laugh flowers $_{ABL}$
'The meadows bloom with flowers'

Both constructions **C1** and **C2** are **collocations** (Hausmann 1979; Mel'čuk 1995), i.e. semi-idiomatic constructions that are made up of two distinct elements:

(i) a **base**, that is chosen by the Speaker as a proper lexicalization for the meaning intended;
(ii) a **collocate**, that is chosen by the Speaker "under the instruction of the base" in order to express a specific meaning next to the base.

One can see that this notion of collocation is mildly contextualist: it implies that the individual meaning (= the definition) of the collocate does not have to

[5] The subscript " $_{ABL}$" stands for the ablative case. Because of the properties of Latin grammar, linear order is not relevant here and construction **C1** could be expressed as "$N2_{ABL}$ *ridet* $N1_{NOM}$" to better reflect the linearization of lexical elements in (2b). The linearization used above was chosen because it shows better the parallel between the Latin and English versions of **C1** and **C2**.

correspond exactly to the meaning it expresses once combined with the base. This contextualist flavor of the notion of collocation is however non-pragmatic in nature: a collocation is indeed to be conceived of as a lexical rule of the language, that is part of the lexical restricted combinatorics of the lexical unit functioning as base.

Using the notion of collocation, we can identify a major functional distinction between the two constructions we have identified.

FUNCTIONAL ANALYSIS of **C1** In (5), our prototypical example for construction **C1**, *rident* functions primarily as collocate of its complement *floribus*. It is used by the Speaker to express the fact that flowers are present in the meadows, and that this looks nice. In terms of Meaning-Text formal modelling of collocations, *rident* expresses here the standard lexical function **BonInvolv** (Mel'čuk 1996; Polguère 2007). However, because the meaning 'meadows' and not 'flowers' is expressed in (5) in thematic position (as syntactic subject of the verb), a syntactic conversion applies in the collocation, which thus corresponds to a slightly more complex lexical function: **Conv$_{21}$BonInvolv**.

In other words, a dictionary for medieval Latin should specify in the entry for the noun FLŌS 'flower' that it can be used as oblique complement of the collocative verb RĪDĔO, with **any** noun denoting a place as subject of this verb, in order to express the fact that the place in question is nicely covered with flowers. The same applies to dictionaries of contemporary English: if complete, they should indicate in their article for FLOWER that the verb BLOOM can take this noun as complement in order to express roughly the same collocational meaning:

(6) *The meadow/garden/balcony/... blooms with flowers.*

Again, the very fact that any noun denoting a place can be the subject of *blooms* in (6), whereas only *flowers* (or names of flowers) can be used in the *with*-phrase complement, shows that it is the complement noun N_2, and not the subject N_1, that functionally controls construction **C1**—i.e., that is the base of the collocation.

FUNCTIONAL ANALYSIS of **C2** Sentence (1) is as much a collocation as (5). However, as there is no N_2 to talk about, it is obvious that the subject noun *prata* functions here as base. Now, it is not clear what exactly the collocate verb *rident* expresses in this collocation. Does (1) mean 'The meadows bloom'—the translation we offered earlier, when introducing the example—or simply something like 'The meadows are resplendent' (because their grass is very green, or because they are covered with flowers, etc.)? This question is legitimate and, unfortunately, only "native" speakers of medieval Latin could have answered it. In the absence of an informant, at least two facts can allow us to postulate a vaguer meaning for the collocate. First, this use of *rident* without complement is clearly derived from the full construction **C1**; in the process of losing a complement, the verb gains some lexical flesh but it does not necessarily incorporate 'flower' in its meaning. Going back in time, we know of at least one Roman text where the verb is used, in a collocation of the **C1** type, with a vague meaning of 'be resplendent'—Horace, Ode XI, Book 4:

(7)

Lat. *ridet argento domus*
laugh silver $_{ABL}$ house $_{NOM}$
'The house is resplendent with silver'

If in ancient Latin the verb RĪDĔO could be used as collocate of ARGENTUM in construction **C1** to express 'be resplendent (with)', why could it not retain this vague meaning in medieval Latin when functioning as collocate of PRĀTUM in a **C2** construction? Afterall, and this is our second argument, one finds in French a trace of this vague meaning in a collocative sense of the adjective RIANT lit. 'laughing':

(8)

Fr. *riante prairie*
laughing meadow
'resplendent meadow'

This collocation can well be used to refer to a meadow that is very green and radiant in the sun, but where flowers are not particularly noticeable. In conclusion, in (1), we simply cannot be sure of the exact meaning expressed by the verb, but we can be pretty sure the verb is indeed a collocate of its subject. Therefore, collocations of the **C2** type are to be lexicographically accounted for in the dictionary entry for N_1, where the verb RĪDĔO is mentioned as potential candidate for expressing the collocational meaning 'to look nice'. This is the same meaning expressed by the verb in construction **C1**, and it corresponds to the standard lexical function **PredBon** 'to be good'.

As we are clearly dealing with a specific, lexicalized sense of the vocable RĪDĔO, it is preferable to use a lexicographic numbering in order to clearly identify this lexical unit. We adopt the numbering of the *Gaffiot* Latin-French dictionary (Gaffiot 1934 p. 1364), where this unit is identified as RĪDĔO **I.2[fig.]**. Figure 1 below sumarizes the lexical function links that connect the three Latin lexical units PRĀTUM, FLŌS and RĪDĔO **I.2[fig.]**, according to our linguistic analysis.

This figure shows that being able to use collocational constructions **C1** and **C2** is all about learning very specific lexical rules. These rules are making up part of our knowledge of a language and by no means should the use of that knowledge be forgotten when explaining how words make sense in given utterances. They make sense because the Speaker uses them to make sense, by diligently applying linguistic rules or, eventually, by creatively transgressing them.

It is not contexts that give meaning to words, it is the Speaker who uses linguistic rules to build sentences, and contexts are only symptoms: perceivable consequences of rule applications or transgressions.

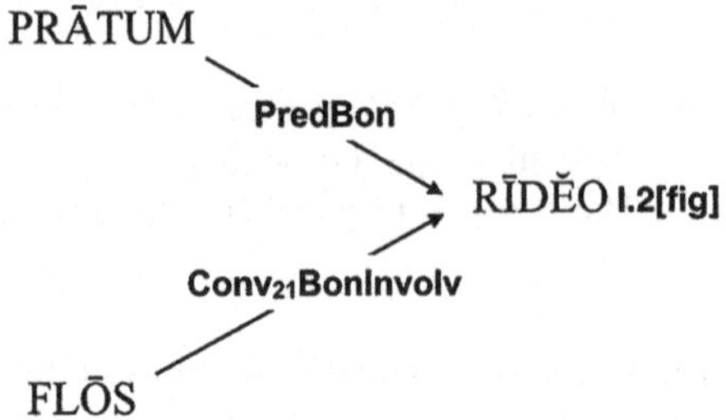

Fig. 1 Lexical function relations involved in collocations *Prata rident floribus* (construction **C1** → *floribus* is the base) ~ *Prata rident* (construction **C2** → *prata* is the base)

Now that the system of lexical rules involved in **C1** and **C2** has been elicited, let us turn our attention to Pierre Abélard's analysis of *Prata rident*, as presented in (Rosier-Catach 1997).

3.1.3 Abélard's Monosemic Credo

Pierre Abélard—in his writings on logic—uses expressions such as *Prata rident* in order to elaborate on a strong postulate about words: each word has one and only one intrinsic meaning. This monosemic credo clearly follows from a biblical principle: each word has been **institutionalized** by Man, through the power granted to him by God, in order to name a given thing.[6]

> And out of the ground the LORD God formed every beast of the field, and every fowl of the air; and brought *them* unto Adam to see what he would call them: and whatsoever Adam called every living creature, that *was* the name thereof.
> Genesis 2:19, (King James Bible 1611).

It follows from Abélard's perspective that, if a word does happen to be used in order to designate something of a different nature than what it has been institutionalized for, then:

1. this is a form of transgression—i.e., it is not something very good;
2. this can only happen by virtue of the context in which the word appears.

According to Abélard, if a word conveys in a sentence another content than its intrinsic meaning (because of a Speaker's rhetorical figure, error, etc.), this "improper" content is given to the word by the context in which it appears. Thus, in (1), the context "*Prata*___" gives to *rident* the meaning 'to flower', that cannot

[6] The religious origin of Abélard's "monosemicism" is probably to be traced in other parts of the Bible as well. For instance, in the New Testament, more precisely the first verse of John's Gospel: "In the beginning was the Word, and the Word was with God, and the Word was God." If there can be only one God, and if the Word was God, it seems natural for a catholic to consider the word as deeply univocal.

belong to the verb RĪDĔO on the premise that it has one and only one meaning 'to laugh' (Rosier-Catach 1997 p. 158).

Abélard fails to notice that a much vaguer meaning than 'to flower' could be associated to the verb—as we did in our analysis, Sect. 3.1.2—, in order to account for other similar usages. He also does not identify the fundamental functional differences between constructions **C1** and **C2**, focussed as he is on the "deviant" use of the verb. His credo about the fundamental semantic univocity of words forbids him completely from seeing that some subtle lexical rules are activated when *ridere* is used as collocate (Fig. 1) and that context has very little to do in terms of explaining where meaning comes from.

Abélard's attitude towards word meaning is a prototypical illustration of philosophical, non-linguistic approaches to the study of language. Instead of being driven by systematic logical observation of linguistic facts, it is designed to abide by general axioms about God, Man and the relation between them.

3.2 The Upside-Down Approach to Linguistic Meaning

Clearly, Abélard is a die-hard lexical contextualist. But his monosemic credo is somehow logical and fully justified from a philosophical point of view. It is less understandable though that the same credo about the unicity of meaning finds its way into contemporary linguistics. For instance, while the Generative Lexicon put forward by James Pustejovsky (Pustejovsky 1995) aims primarily at dealing with polysemy, it presupposes that each polysemic word happens to possess one core, orignal meaning, from which all other senses can be derived through inference rules by virtue of the word being used in given contexts; cf. (Pustejovsky 1998 p. 293):

> Whereas sense enumeration approaches to meaning construct a Linnaeus-like museum of word senses, with genus and species neatly classified and separated into distinct cases, in Generative Lexicon Theory the methodology has been to construct differential structures that have functional behaviors. More specifically, (a) the semantics of lexical items are underspecified expressions, (b) every element in a phrase may function "actively" in the composition of the phrase, and (c) the notion of word sense only emerges at the level of the sentence, namely, its "sense in context."

The motivation behind Abélard's postulate is clear, but what motivates this urge for unicity among modern scholars, whose frame of analysis is supposed to be unrelated to any theological doctrine?

One has to grant the Generative Lexicon a practical motivation: natural language processing—in particular, automatic text analysis—has to cope with any sense a word could carry while, at the same time, no lexical ressource will ever be rich and detailed enough to provide computer programs with a complete enumeration of these senses and solve the **ambiguity problem**. And here, we put our finger on another fact that should help us understand the omnipresence of lexical contextualism:

When studying language, people have the unconscious reflex of putting themselves in the Addressee's shoes instead of systematically adopting the Speaker perspective.

Take a sentence, any sentence; *Prata rident*, for instance. The very presence before us of *Prata rident* presupposes at least three essential participating elements, besides the sentence itself:

1. the Language—*Prata rident* is a Latin sentence, not an English or Russian one, and this means that it follows the rules of a complex system, that we call *Latin*;
2. the Speaker—if *Prata rident* exists in speech, someone has uttered or written it;
3. the Addressee—if *Prata rident* is bound to function in semiosis, it means that there is or will be at least one person performing the act of comprehending it (and the Speaker knows this).

Linguists or philosophers who are reflecting on this sentence can identify themselves to two of these participating elements: the Speaker or the Addressee. This leaves us with three logically possible methodologies for examining language: one can take the Speaker perspective, the Addressee perspective or a combo Speaker-Addressee perspective.

The last perspective, the combo one, can hardly be adopted as it is virtually impossible to focus on the description of a sentence by taking simultaneously the place of the Speaker and the Addressee. As stated above, it is the Addressee perspective that is almost always adopted in language studies. Because most people are unaware of this, it is worth listing a few facts that directly reflect the omnipresence of the Addressee perspective in language studies:

- the fact that *Linguistics 101* courses or, more generally, introductions to the study of language, are generally structured from phonetics to semantics, through morphology and syntax, instead of proceeding exactly the other way round (from meanings to be expressed to modes of expression of these meanings);
- the fact of focussing on ambiguity—a **problem** the Addressee has to solve—instead of focussing on synonymy/paraphrase—a **set of choices** made available to the Speaker by natural languages;
- the fact that the terms *analysis*, *interpretation*, *parsing* are omnipresent in linguistic texts, whereas *synthesis*, *production*, *generation* are much rarer;
- the fact that the semantic module of languages is often presented as being an *interpretation* module, for instance in so-called formal semantics (Montague 1970; Montague 1973);

- the fact of referring to a *syntax-semantics interface* instead of a *semantics-syntax interface*.[7]

We could continue this enumeration almost endlessly. As a rule, language studies are wall-to-wall Addressee-oriented. Let us mention two black sheeps, two theoretical approaches in modern linguistics that are designed specifically in order to model languages from content to form, and not the other way round:

- Michael Halliday's Systemic Functional Linguistics (Halliday 2004);
- Igor Mel'čuk's Meaning-Text linguistics (Mel'čuk 1973, 1997; Milićević 2006).

In Meaning-Text linguistics, in particular, the Meaning-to-Text orientation is explicitly presented as a methodological prerequisite for effective linguistic study. As stated by Mel'čuk (Mel'čuk 2012 p. 122):

> From the viewpoint of linguistic communication, the two directions are equally important as well: both the Speaker and the Addressee are vital for an act of communication. As a consequence, one might think that choosing the orientation of linguistic description in an MTM [= Meaning-Text Model] is of not too great an importance. Thus, in the majority of linguistic theories I know of the description of a language is carried out in the direction "Texts ⇒ Meanings," i.e., in the direction of analysis. However, I think that the orientation of linguistic description is of utmost importance, and the opposite direction—"Meanings ⇒ Texts," i.e., synthesis—seems by far more useful and promising.

It is this Speaker-oriented approach that we have adopted in our analysis of *Prata rident* and other related sentences (Sect. 3.1.2), because only this can make us "see" fully the linguistic rules that allow for these sentences to be assembled and, therefore, to exist. However, in our experience, the systematic examination of linguistic objects from the Speaker viewpoint is one of the main reasons why it seems so difficult for many to follow Meaning-Text arguments and demonstrations.

While the Speaker perspective is explicitly stated in Meaning-Text linguistics as a necessary condition for good linguistic study, the Addressee perspective is generally chosen by default, in an unconscious way, by people who are more often than not simply unaware (a) that two alternative approaches logically exist and (b) that they are *de facto* adopting one of them.

Reasons for considering that the Speaker perspective is the right one in linguistics need to be discussed at length, and a detailed argumentation can be found in (Mel'čuk 2012 p. 122–148). We will limit ourselves to two observations, that may not be definite arguments but that are based, at least, on rather objective facts about language and linguistic processes.

Firstly, there is inherent sequentiality in the communication process:

1. the Speaker makes up and expresses a linguistic content;
2. then the utterance exists as a fact;
3. finally the Addressee interprets this utterance.

---

[7] At the time of writing, the `syntax-semantics+interface` query returned 81,000 hits on Google, against a meager 2,840 hits for `semantics-syntax + interface`.

Though the interpretation process may occur almost simultaneously, a chunk of utterance is interpreted inasmuch as it has been uttered in spoken language. In written language, the sequentiality is more obvious, even though the Addressee may anticipate what he/she is about to read: the actual interpretation takes place (as confirmation of anticipation) only when actual reading is performed. Therefore, the synthesis process is primary in time.

Secondly, language is knowledge, i.e. information in mind. This knowledge is knowledge of signs and sign combination rules that are used both by the Speaker in the production process and by the Addressee in the interpretation process. But the difference between active and passive mastering of language shows, at the level of performance, that the interpretation process relies heavily on extra-linguistic knowledge as well, to the extent that we may be able to interpret sentences in a language that we do not master, whereas we could never assemble sentences in order to express given contents without a good mastering of the language. Therefore, adopting the Speaker perspective helps us to focus on linguistic knowledge because speaking is a much more language-based activity than interpreting.

Of course, everyone is entitled to reject these arguments; but at least researchers should, first, acknowledge the fact that they do make a choice by adopting an opposite Addressee perspective and, second, explain why their approach is better.

Adopting the Speaker perspective truly makes things easier for linguists, language teachers, etc. In contrast, we are convinced that the analytical approach has catastrophic effects: it is an **upside-down approach**, leading to **inside-out models**, to spending much time and energy on trying to solve problems that either are not the right ones or do not exist in language use. Methodology should be as central in linguistics as it is in any other science, and the fact of adopting the Speaker perspective does make a difference in language studies. As stated very clearly by Mel'čuk (Mel'čuk 2012 p. 147):

> The intuition of a linguist, which is so important in linguistic research, functions much better in the direction of synthesis. It seems easier for introspection to figure out the ways in which a given meaning can be expressed than to deal with formally possible (even if absurd) interpretations of a given text.

In a nutshell, the right question to ask ourselves when faced with a linguistic expression should be:

"How did the Speaker do it?"

So why is the Addressee perspective so systematically adopted? On the one hand, it can be the result of an academic conditioning.[8] Most linguists, students, language teachers are just acting the way they have been trained to act, because of

[8] This is at least our own personal experience. As a Ph.D. student, we had to go through a rather long process of deconditioning, which made us aware of the fact that the upside-down view of language was instilled in us by the sheer fact that it is overwhelmingly present in language studies. Yes, our deconditioning took place via a reverse process of reconditioning. At least, we went through it consciously, and it felt good because it simply helped "doing things" with language and linguistics.

a conditioning that results from reading over and over again statements such as the following upside-down definition of language offered by the philosopher David Lewis (Lewis 1975 p. 3):

> What is a language? Something which assigns meanings to certain strings of types of sounds or of marks. It could therefore be a function, a set of ordered pairs of strings and meanings.

Another possible explanation is that this Addressee-identification reflex finds some of its roots deep in cultural conditioning and in the structures of language itself. For instance, one can easily find in English, French, etc., words that relate to the fact of speaking too much (*to babble*, *to blather*, *to gossip*, *babbler*, *chatter*, *chatterbox*, *gabbler*, *magpie*, *pratter*, *garrulous*, *gassy*, *gossipy*, *long-winded*, *verbose*, *wordy*…), but it is much harder to find in our lexicons words denoting excessive listening. Language itself imposes on us a vision of linguistic interaction where speaking has more chance to be the wrong thing to do than listening. God speaks and Man listens, as it goes. Whether we are believers or atheists, we cannot escape the fact that in occidental cultures our right place seems to be the place of the listener.[9] This explanation may seem far-fetched, and maybe it is, but we find it quite appealing as a working hypothesis for someone who may want to study the question of general linguistic methodologies from an epistemological viewpoint. Indeed, it nicely connects our two explanations for the omnipresence of lexical contextualism: the word monosemy dogma (Sect. 3.1) and the upside-down Addressee perspective.

For this reason, let us call this lexical contextualism of mixed origins, that manifests itself in linguistics and in the philosophy of language, the *Abélard syndrome*.

3.3 Connecting the Dots

Not only the Abélard syndrome acts as blinders in languages studies, but it seems to breed pure and simple sense denial, especially when scholars start to voice out murderous ideas about polysemy; cf. Geoffrey Nunberg concluding his analysis of the notion of word meaning as regards to polysemy (Nunberg 1979 p. 177):

> In the end, my point is simply this. Linguists have postulated that words have 'meanings-in-the-language' because it seemed necessary to do so, in order to explain how novel utterances are understood. It turns out, however, that this hypothesis is too strong, and that it would force us to make assumptions about our language over and above what simple understanding would require. We do not have to know what a word names to be able to say what it is being used to refer to.

[9] We do not intend to imply that this is a distinctive characteristic of occidental cultures. Confucianism, for instance, clearly puts very strong emphasis on listening as a virtue: "Listen widely to remove your doubts and be careful when speaking about the rest and your mistakes will be few" (Confucius 2:18). What we mean is that such is not necessarily the case in all cultures and that adopting the Speaker perspective may indeed seem like a more natural thing to do in some.

And a few lines below:

> All that linguistic semantics should be asked to provide is an account of how languages come to be used and understood, and we can do that, it turns out, without having to say that speakers know what words mean.

These ideas are also promoted by trigger-happy philosophers when they turn upon polysemy, word meaning and any attempt at offering descriptive models of word senses; cf. Jerry Fodor on Ray Jackendoff's semantic theory (Fodor 1998 p. 50):

> I claim that Jackendoff's account of polysemy offers no good reason to think that there are definitions. As often happens in lexical semantics, the problem that postulating definitions is supposed to solve is really only begged; it's, as it were, kicked upstairs into the metalanguage.

And because Fodor loves his own metaphors, he does not hesitate to do some recycling when attacking this time, with Ernest Lepore, the Generative Lexicon approach to polysemy (Fodor and Lepore 1998 pp. 279–280):[10]

> This is just the polysemy problem all over again; all that's happened is that it has been kicked upstairs from the semantics to the ontology: whereas we used to worry about how to count senses, we are now invited to worry about how to count processes. Six of one, half a dozen of the other.

Ideologues of linguistics and the philosophy of language such as Nunberg or Fodor are successful because they sow on fertile soil: the Abélard syndrome prevails and sense denial rhetoric probably echoes a need for comfort experienced by people who find themselves unable to apprehend language as a true object of study. It seems easier to say that there is no meaning and therefore to dispense with the burden of performing actual descriptive work.

4 In Form of Conclusion

It is time to conclude this reflection on lexical contextualism with an important remark: at no time do we pretend that linguistic context has no role to play in shaping the semiotic content carried by linguistic expressions **as speech tokens**. For instance, we have no problem with John Firth's famous aphorism (Firth 1957 p. 190):

> [The use of the word 'meaning' is subject to the general rule that] each word when used in a new context is a new word.

---

[10] See Pustejovsky (1998) for a detailed answer by James Pustejovsky to Fodor and Lepore criticisms.

But this sentence has to be put in its context, whereas meaning negationists citing Firth almost systematically fail to recall (maybe because they have not read the text from which the quote comes) that Firth's concern in his essay *Modes of Meanings* is primarily about tokens and not types, about *parole* in the Saussurian sense and not *langue*. Essentially, people forget that this paper deals with what Firth calls *phonological modes of meaning* and *collocational modes of meaning* in literary texts, mainly poetry, and epistolary literature. It is focussing on creativity and individual realization. To quote another of Firth's aphorisms, p. 193:

> [To begin with, we must apprehend language events in their contexts as shaped by the creative acts of speaking persons.] Whenever a man speaks, he speaks in some sense as a poet.

Even if we disregard the creative aspect of language use, we have no doubt that words do not make sense in isolation. Within language as knowledge—in the mental lexicon (Aitchison 2012; Wierzbicka 2009; Zock and Schwab 2011)—, words are not isolated: their inherent semiotic value is a factor of their position in the global **lexical system** (Polguère 2009; Polguère 2014).[11] Experienced lexicographers, translators or language teachers never consider a word in isolation. They will never consider, for instance, just the form *wave*; they will mentally picture *wave* in various contexts that act as signatures for corresponding senses:

(9)

a. *sea, high, strong wave*
b. *wave of protests, strikes*
c. *Wave your hand*
etc.

As speakers who construct and utter sentences, they will focus on actual lexical signs, not forms. In their mind, they will necessarily associate each word with a network of paradigmatic and syntagmatic connections that conditions a specific sense.

Thinking about it: if it were to be understood in reference to lexical networks as contexts, lexical contextualism could even be said to be the right approach to lexical semantics.

Acknowledgements Many thanks to Helen Lim for her feedback on the draft version of this paper, and for accepting to indulge in philosophical chats with us.

[11] For instance, Fig. 1, Sect. 3.1.2, is a hypothesized micro-sample of the global lexical system of Latin.

References

Aitchison, J. (2012). *Words in the mind: An introduction to the mental lexicon* (4th ed.). Oxford: Wiley.

Blake, W. (1789). *Songs of innocence*. Retrieved from http://www.blakearchive.org/exist/blake/archive/work.xq?workid=s-inn&java=no.

Cappelen, H., & Lepore, E. (2005). *Insensitive semantics: A defense of semantic minimalism and speech act pluralism*. Oxford: Wiley.

Carmina Burana. (ca. 1230). *Codex latinus Monacensis*. Codex clm 4660 and 4660a. Munich: Bavarian State Library.

Confucius. *Analects of Confucius*. Retrieved from http://www.acmuller.net/con-dao/analects.html.

Firth, J. R. (1957). Modes of meaning. In *Papers in linguistics 1934–1951* (pp. 190–215). London: Oxford University Press [First published in *Essays and Studies* (The English Association), 1951].

Fodor, J. A. (1998). *Concepts. Where cognitive science went wrong*. Oxford: Oxford Cognitive Science Series, Oxford University Press.

Fodor, J. A., & Lepore, E. (1998). The emptiness of the lexicon: Reflections on James Pustejovsky's *The Generative Lexicon*. *Linguistic Inquiry, 29*(2), 269–288.

Gaffiot, F. (1934). *Dictionnaire latin-français*. Paris: Hachette.

Halliday, M. A. K., & Christian M. I. M. M. (2004). *An introduction to functional grammar* (3rd edn). London: Hodder Arnold [First edition by Michael Halliday in 1985].

Hausmann, F. J. (1979). Un dictionnaire des collocations est-il possible? *Travaux de littérature et de linguistique de l'Unviersité de Strasbourg, XVII*(1), 187–195.

Kilgarriff, A. (1997). I don't believe in word senses. *Computers and the Humanities, 31*, 91–113.

King James Bible. (1611). *King James Bible "authorized version"*. Cambridge edition. Retrieved from http://www.kingjamesbibleonline.org/.

Lewis, D. (1975). Languages and language. In K. Gunderson (Ed.), *Language, mind and knowledge* (pp. 3–35). Minneapolis: University of Minnesota Press.

Mel'čuk, I. (1973). Towards a linguistic "Meaning ⟺ Text" model. In F. Kiefer (Ed.), *Trends in soviet theoretical linguistics* (pp. 33–57). Dordrecht: Reidel.

Mel'čuk, I. (1995). Phrasemes in language and phraseology in linguistics. In M. Everaert, E.-J. van der Linden, A. Schenk & R. Schreuder (Eds.), *Idioms: Structural and psychological perspectives* (pp. 167–232). Hillsdale, NJ.–Hove, UK: Laurence Erlbaum Associates.

Mel'čuk, I. (1996) Lexical functions: A tool for the description of lexical relations in the lexicon. In L. Wanner (Eds.), *Lexical functions in lexicography and natural language processing* (pp. 37–102). Amsterdam/Philadelphia: Language Companion Series 31, John Benjamins.

Mel'čuk, I. (1997). *Vers une Linguistique Sens-Texte. Leçon inaugurale*. Paris: Collège de France.

Mel'čuk, I. (2012). *Semantics: From meaning to text*. Amsterdam/Philadelphia: Studies in Language Companion Series 129, John Benjamins.

Milićević, J. (2006). A short guide to the meaning-text linguistic theory. *Journal of Koralex, 9*, 187–233.

Montague, R. (1970). Universal grammar. *Theoria, 36*(3), 373–398.

Montague, R. (1973). The proper treatment of quantification in ordinary english. In J. Hintikka, J. Moravcsik, & P. Suppes (Eds.), *Approaches to natural language* (pp. 221–242). Dordrecht: Reidel.

Montminy, M. (2010). Two contextualist fallacies. *Synthese, 173*(3), 317–333.

Norén, K., & Linell, P. (2007). Meaning potentials and the interaction between lexis and contexts: An empirical substantiation. *Pragmatics, 17*(3), 387–416.

Nunberg, G. (1979). The non-uniqueness of semantic solutions: Polysemy. *Linguistics and Philosophy, 3*(2), 143–184.

Polguère, A. (2007). Lexical function standardness. In L. Wanner (Eds.), *Selected lexical and grammatical issues in the meaning-text theory. In honour of Igor Mel'čuk* (pp.43–95). Amsterdam/Philadelphia: Language Companion Series 84, Benjamins.

Polguère, A. (2009). Lexical systems: Graph models of natural language lexicons. *Language Resources and Evaluation, 43*(1), 41–55.

Polguère, A. (2014). To appear. Principes de modélisation systémique des réseaux lexicaux. *Actes de la 21e Conférence sur le Traitement Automatique du Langage Naturel (TALN 2014)*, Marseille.

Pustejovsky, J. (1995). *The generative lexicon*. Cambridge, Massachusetts and London, England: MIT Press.

Pustejovsky, J. (1998). Generativity and explanation in semantics: A reply to Fodor and Lepore. *Linguistic Inquiry, 29*(2), 289–311.

Queiroz, J., & Merrell, F. (2006). Semiosis and pragmatism: Toward a dynamic concept of meaning. *Sign Systems Studies, 34*(1), 37–65.

Recanati, F. (2004). *Literal meaning*. Cambridge: Cambridge University Press.

Rosier-Catach, I. (1997). Prata rident. In A. Libera, A. Elamrani-Jamal & A. Galonnier (Eds.), *Langages et philosophie : Hommage à Jean Jolivet* (pp. 155–176). Paris: Études de philosophie médiévale 74, J. Vrin.

Saussure, F. (1916). In C. Bally, A. Sechehaye & with the collaboration of A. Riedlinger (Eds.), *Cours de linguistique générale*. Lausanne-Paris: Payot.

Searle, J. (1980). The background of meaning. In J. Searle, F. Kiefer, & M. Bierwisch (Eds.), *Speech act theory and pragmatics* (pp. 221–232). Dordrecht: Reidel.

Stanley, J. (2004). On the linguist basis for contextualism. *Philosophical Studies, 119*, 119–146.

Wierzbicka, A. (1992). Back to definitions: Cognition, semantics, and lexicography. *Lexicographica, 8*, 146–174.

Wierzbicka, A. (2009). The theory of the mental lexicon. In S. Kempgen, P. Kosta, T. Berger & K. Gutschmidt (Eds.), *Die slavischen Sprachen/The Slavic Languages An international handbook of their structure, their history and their investigation* (pp. 848–863). Berlin and New York: Mouton de Gruyter.

Winkworth, C. (1863). *Lyra Germanica: Second series: The christian life*. London: Longman, Green, Longman, and Roberts.

Zock, M., & Schwab, D. (2011). Storage does not guarantee access: The problem of organizing and accessing words in a speaker's lexicon. *Journal of Cognitive Science, 12*, 233–259.

Predicative Lexical Units in Terminology

Marie-Claude L'Homme

Abstract Predicative lexical units have been largely ignored in terminology for a number of reasons: one of them is the focus on entities viewed as the nodes of knowledge representations; another is the lack of linguistic perspective on the data to be represented. Things are changing though and an increasing number of researchers in the field of terminology and other areas interested in processing specialized corpora recognize that predicative units (verbs, adjectives and many nouns) play a key role in the expression and organization of specialized knowledge. However, the models traditionally used in terminology to describe terms are not equipped to capture the properties of predicative units adequately. In this contribution, I review a selection of works in the area and discuss how they aim at unveiling the contribution of predicative terms to the expression of specialized knowledge. I also show how two specific lexical semantics frameworks (Explanatory Combinatorial Lexicology, ECL (Mel'čuk et al. 1984–1999, 1995) and Frame Semantics (Fillmore 1977, 1982, 1985)) can be applied to the description of predicative terms and help us represent their linguistic properties. I will refer to data taken from the specialized fields of cycling, environment and computing.

Keywords Predicative lexical unit · Terminology · Verb · Argument structure · Contextual annotation · Specialized lexical resource · Lexical relation · Environment · Cycling · Computing

1 Introduction

Terminologists have long recognized that "structure" is an inherent aspect of terminological description. Usually, the focus has been placed on the structure of knowledge in a given specialized area and many terminologists assume that terms

M.-C. L'Homme (✉)
Observatoire de linguistique Sens-Texte, Université de Montréal, C.P. 6128,
Succ. Centre-ville, Montréal, QC, Canada
e-mail: mc.lhomme@umontreal.ca

© Springer International Publishing Switzerland 2015
N. Gala et al. (eds.), *Language Production, Cognition, and the Lexicon*,
Text, Speech and Language Technology 48, DOI 10.1007/978-3-319-08043-7_6

are closely connected to the way this knowledge is organized. However, if this knowledge structure is defined before analyzing the terms themselves or is considered as the reference to which everything else must be linked, terminologists might miss important linguistic expressions that contribute to the expression of knowledge. My assumption is that part of this structure can only be discovered after a fine-grained analysis of terms, including predicative terms, is carried out. This will be dealt with in more detail in Sects. 2 and 3.

An increasing number of researchers in terminology now recognize that predicative units (verbs, adjectives and many nouns) play an important role in the conveyance of specialized knowledge and have suggested models and methods to take them into account. From the point of view of other areas such as Lexical Semantics or Natural Language Processing (NLP) where different projects focus on predicative units (e.g. FrameNet 2014; PropBank 2014; VerbNet 2014), it might appear surprising that these units have been under-investigated in terminology. I will try to explain why it took so long for terminologists to start taking them into consideration in Sect. 2.

In Sect. 3, I review a selection of works that focus on predicative terms (especially verbs since other predicative units have been less studied in terminology). In Sects. 4 and 5, I describe work carried out at the Observatoire de linguistique Sens-Texte (OLST) that aims at capturing the specific nature of specialized predicative units based on Explanatory Combinatorial Lexicology, ECL (Mel'čuk et al. 1984–1999, 1995) and Frame Semantics (Fillmore 1977, 1982, 1985) and more specifically its application in FrameNet (Fillmore et al. 2003; FrameNet 2014; Ruppenhofer et al. 2010). I will also show that predicative units can reveal different kinds of structures that complement those usually considered in terminology. I will refer to data taken from the fields of cycling, environment and computing. (The field of cycling was chosen specifically for Michael Zock and the first steps have been taken to compile a dictionary on this specific topic.)

2 The "Knowledge" Paradigm

Figure 1 shows what a knowledge structure (in this case, an ontology) can look like in a specific field: i.e. the bicycle (Theory Simple-Bikes 2013 http://www.ksl.stanford.edu/htw/dme/thermal-kb-tour/simple-bikes.html).

In this example, items of knowledge (*concepts* or *classes*) that represent the parts of the bicycle are organized in a hierarchy.[1] The ontology concentrates on

[1] Much more can be said about this type of knowledge structure and the way it is defined: attributes can be associated with each class; in some cases, definitions of classes are provided. Experts must define and agree on criteria according to which items can be organized in specific fields (for instance, in the bicycle example, other organization principles could have been chosen). Hence a consensus must necessarily be reached for such representations to be usable (Guarino 2009).

parts and it can be argued that important concepts are missing, such as types of bicycles. But we would be dealing with entities in both cases, as do many ontologies or other types of knowledge representations. I will argue below that other equally important concepts are still missing and that the field of cycling is not only a collection of entities. The example chosen is simple, but still representative of the kind of reasoning applied when building knowledge structures.

This kind of work is certainly interesting from the point of view of organizing knowledge in specialized fields since it can later be used as a reference for making conceptual distinctions. However, it only considers a portion of what is necessary to convey that knowledge. In the bicycle example, one can discover the relationship between a "wheel" and a "bicycle", but cannot learn how to express the installation of a wheel on a bicycle or what the specific functions of a wheel or a bicycle are. In addition, the linguistic items used in the field are considered after concepts are defined and are often viewed as labels that are superimposed on knowledge structures. In the bicycle example, the labelling of concepts is secondary and some labels do not even correspond to real terms (e.g. *Wheel-Assy*).[2] The purpose is to represent concepts (linguistic expressions are listed somewhere else when necessary).

Hence, these methodologies (that I will refer to as *knowledge-driven methodologies*) raise a number of questions with regard to the way knowledge is expressed in texts[3]:

- Often, only nouns are considered. This is a consequence of the focus on entities. Even in cases where activity concepts need to be taken into account (linguistically expressed by nouns or verbs), nouns are still preferred. One can easily think of activities associated with the bicycle ("cycling", "riding", "shifting speeds", etc.) or even properties, but incorporating them in a structure such as that shown in Fig. 1 is not straightforward.
- Even when other types of concepts (processes, events and properties) appear in knowledge structures, the specific nature of the units that express them, namely the fact that they require arguments (e.g., X *rides* Y, Y *cycles*, X *shifts* Y), is not taken into account.

Terminologists resort to less formal methods when defining the contents of specialized dictionaries. However, they are still guided by a reasoning similar to the one described above. In a small dictionary on cycling (À vos vélos 2013), one can find terms linked to the following topics: types of bicycles (*city bicycle*, *electric bicycle*), bicycle parts (*back wheel*, *cable*), accessories (*dynamo*, *fender*), tools, as well as repair and maintenance equipment (*file*, *patch*), and infrastructure

[2] The linguistic label may be chosen among a list of possible labels used be experts (in some ontologies, a unique identifier is used to represent an item of knowledge unambiguously).

[3] Other linguistic consequences are listed in L'Homme (2014a).

Fig. 1 A simple ontology of the bicycle

30 classes defined:

- Bike-Component
  - Bicycle
  - Transmission
  - Brake-System
    - Coaster-Brake
    - Hand-Brakes
  - Frame
    - Battaglin-Sl
    - Battaglin-Slx
  - Stem
    - Itm-400
    - Superitalia-Pro
    - Control-Tech
  - Handlebars
  - Seat
  - Wheel-Assy
    - Front-Wheel
    - Rear-Wheel
  - Multi-Spd-Transmission
  - Saddle
  - Seat-Post
  - Chain
  - Pedals
  - Crankset
  - Bottom-Bracket
  - Freewheel
  - Front-Derailer
  - Rear-Derailer
  - Wheel
  - Tire

(*bike route*, *paved shoulder*). All entries are devoted to noun terms. A small portion of these nouns denote activities (e.g., *two-way cycling*), but they are treated exactly as the other ones that refer to entities.

3 Predicative Units in Terminology

Let us know consider matters from a different perspective. Appendix 1 shows the first results of term extraction (by TermoStat, Drouin 2003) applied to a corpus of texts on cycling of approx. 150,000 words. Among the 50 most specific items identified by the term extractor, 8 are verbs (one verb appears in third position) and 2 are adjectives. Some might argue that some of these units do not correspond to valid terms in the field of cycling. Although this can be said for some units (and for some nouns, for that matter), it would be difficult to discard *cycle*, *ride* or *brake* (especially if their nominal counterparts are already defined as terms). In addition, 4 nouns refer to activities and can thus be defined as predicative units (e.g., *adjustment*, *cycling*, *ride*, *race*). Eight others refer to entities, while still being truly predicative (e.g., *intersection, rider*).[4] If a knowledge-based analysis such as that described in the previous section is applied, more than half the items that could be identified as relevant terms in the field of cycling would either be neglected or described in a way that does not fully capture their semantic properties.

I argue that predicative units are not only necessary to communicate knowledge: they are also an important part of the structure of this knowledge. However, the structures such as the ontology discussed in Sect. 2 (and other similar ones) are not well suited to represent them. Other methods need to be (and have been) devised. We mention some of them in the following sections.

3.1 When Does a Predicative Unit Become a Term?

A view strongly held a few decades ago was that terms belonging to parts of speech other than nouns had to correspond to a noun to become relevant for terminology.[5]

> Concepts represented in terminological dictionaries are predominantly expressed in the form of nouns; concepts which are linguistically expressed as adjectives and verbs in technical languages are frequently found only in the corresponding noun form and some theorists deny the existence of adjective and verb concepts (Sager 1990, p. 58).

This allows us to validate the verbs *brake* and *cycle* as terms since they are related to noun forms. Linguistically though it is difficult to argue that all nouns precede the other parts of speech: the nouns *ride* and *rider* are defined on the basis of the meaning of the verb *ride*. This also applies to *cycling* and *race*: the meaning of *cycling* is explained according to that of the verb *cycle*; the meaning of the noun *race* is based on that of the verb *race*.

Intuitively, it is also difficult to deny the important role played by some predicative units, even those that are not related to noun terms. Corpus data confirms this as discussed above. We mentioned the problem raised by some verbs in the list of candidate terms produced after processing a corpus on cycling. Similar examples can be found in many other fields of knowledge: *configure*, *develop, write* (computing); *code*, *replicate*, *synthetize* (genetics); *pollute*, *recycle*, *warm* (environment). Some adjectives also convey a meaning that it would be difficult not to consider as specialized: *dynamic*, *static*, *virtual* (computing); *clean*, *green, sustainable* (environment).

This was pointed out by a number of scholars (who discussed the importance of verbs in terminology; other parts of speech have not attracted as much attention):

---

[4] Other items in the list could be considered as predicative units (*frame* of x, *lever* of x, etc.), but we did not consider them in this quick count.

[5] This view was also shared by Rey (1979). Traces can still be found in more recent work (e.g., Lorente 2007) for whom a verb can become a "quasi-term" when it is morphologically related to a noun term.

Condamines (1993), in the field of banking, L'Homme (1998) in the field of computing, Lerat (2002), in the field of law, Lorente (2007) in various fields of knowledge (see L'Homme 2012a), for a more detailed account). Three types of verbs can be found in specialized texts: 1. Specialized verbs (that are specific to a given field); 2. Verbs that acquire a new meaning in the field [6]; 3. General language verbs (that can be further divided into support verbs (Lerat 2002) and discursive verbs (Lorente 2007)). Verbs in groups 1 and 2 would potentially correspond to terms.

However, the strategy normally employed by terminologists to decide whether a unit can qualify as a term (by defining its position in a knowledge structure specific to a domain) cannot be applied to parts of speech such as verbs or adjectives. Apart from L'Homme (1998) and Lorente (2007), few authors provide criteria to guide the selection of terms that do not refer to entities. Here are two of the criteria defined in L'Homme (1998) (they were defined for verbs but also apply to other predicative units):

1. Given a corpus containing texts on a subject, if the linguistic realizations of actants (i.e. arguments) of a verb are defined as terms, the verb is likely to be a term itself. For example, *ride* (*X rides Y*) is likely to be a term in the field of cycling since, realizations for X will be terms such as *cyclist* or *rider* (or a specific name referring to one) and instantiations for Y will be terms such *bike*, *bicycle* (and specific types of bicycles or brands).
2. If a verb is morphologically and semantically related to lexical units that have already been defined as terms, it is a term itself. For example, if the noun *brake* is defined as a term, then the verb *brake* is one.

3.2 Representing Predicative Units

Predicative units are not only defined as terms using criteria that differ from those that apply to other types of terms, they must also be described in order to fully capture their meaning. Authors have devised different methods to achieve this, but they appear to agree on the fact that their argument structure should be represented, ideally in a way that explains the meaning of the predicative unit when used in a specialized field. Again, verbs have attracted the most attention, but what is said in this section also applies to other predicative units.

For example, assuming that *ride* has two arguments (x, y), they can be represented using *classes of objects* ("classes d'objets", Lerat 2002), semantic classes defined specifically for a given subject field (Tellier 2007; Wandji et al. 2013),

[6] In some cases, new meanings viewed from the perspective of a special subject field do not necessarily correspond to a meaning that a lexicographer or a linguist would consider as truly different from meanings already recorded for that unit. This phenomenon has been labeled by Cruse (2011) as *micro-sense* or *subsense*.

Table 1 Argument structures of predicative terms with typical terms

Subject field	Predicative unit	Argument structure
Cycling	Ride	cyclist ~ bicycle
	Rider	~of bicycle
Computing	Download_1	user ~ file, application from computer, network to computer
	$\text{Download}_{1.1}$	~of file, application from computer, network to computer
	Downloadable	~file, application
	Upload	user ~ file, application from computer to computer, network
Environment	Impact_1	change ~ on environment
	Impact_2	~of change on environment
	Effect	~of change, gas on environment

frame elements labels (Pimentel 2013), semantic roles (L'Homme 2012b).[7] In the examples given in Table 1, typical terms (i.e., terms that are considered to be representative of what can be expected in a given argument position) are used.[8] Other examples are given for terms in the subject fields of computing and the environment.

4 Describing Predicative Units in Specialized Lexicons

Assuming like I did that predicative units should be considered as valid terms and that their argument structures should be considered as important parts of their descriptions, some principles based on lexical semantics can guide us when adding these units to lexicons. In what follows, I show how this can be carried out using two different lexical frameworks, namely Explanatory Combinatorial Lexicology, ECL (Mel'čuk et al. 1984–1999, 1995) and Frame Semantics (Fillmore 1977, 1982, 1985; Fillmore et al. 2003). In addition to a few aforementioned examples in

[7] The definition of argument structures (i.e. the number of arguments; the determination of arguments vs. adjuncts; the nature of arguments) can differ substantially according to the theoretical perspective taken. Often in terminology, arguments are defined at an abstract and semantic level (i.e. those participants that are necessary to understand the meaning of the predicative unit). This differs from perspectives based on syntactic evidence. Of course, as will be shown in this paper, there is a relation between semantics and syntax. However, at the semantic level, arguments may be considered obligatory and be realized in specific cases in syntax (this is the case for nominalization of verbs, for instance).

[8] In this kind of approach, authors implicitly assume that predicative units can be defined regardless of their possible uses in other fields or situations. For instance, the arguments defined for *ride* are valid from the point of view of *cycling* but not for *ride* in general. The same applies to *impact* (verb and noun) and *effect*.

the field of cycling, I will refer to two specialized lexical resources: one is dedicated to the fields of computing and the Internet (*DiCoInfo. Dictionnaire fondamental de l'informatique et de l'Internet* Homme 2014c) and the other to the environment (*DiCoEnviro. Dictionnaire fondamental de l'environnement* Homme 2014b). (A short description of these resources is given in Sect. 4.1.)

4.1 A Short Presentation of Two Specialized Lexical Resources

DiCoInfo and DiCoEnviro are freely available online resources that contain terms in English, French and Spanish (the coverage, however, differs from one language to the other). The resources describe terms that belong to different parts of speech such as nouns (*configuration, data, environment, biodiversity*), verbs (*to configure, to download, to pollute, to warm*), adjectives (*configurable, environmental, sustainable, virtual*) and adverbs (e.g., *dynamically, environmentally*), part of which are predicative units.

The theoretical and methodological principles used to compile these resources are based chiefly on ECL. (However, as will be seen below, other principles were borrowed from Frame Semantics.) They adhere to ECL principles in the following ways:

1. Each article is devoted to a specific lexical unit (and not to a lexical item); for instance, *address* appears in three different articles in the DiCoInfo: "the unique identifier of a user in a network", "the unique identifier of a computer or a site in a network", "a location on a storage device";
2. Meanings are distinguished by analyzing the series of interactions (similarities and oppositions) of a unit with other units of the field;[9]
3. The argument structure (called *actantial structure*) is stated and given a central role in the description of the meaning of lexical units (although, here it differs from ECL, in the sense that semantic roles are used to label arguments; ECL uses variables, such as X, Y, Z);
4. Much emphasis is placed on the listing of lexical relationships (e.g., in the entry for *pollute*, the nouns *pollution, polluter, pollutant*, the adjective *polluting*, and the verbs *contaminate, depollute* are listed along with an explanation of their relationships with *pollute*).[10]

[9] In both resources, only specialized meanings are considered. Hence, even if the corpus does contain occurrences of general meanings, only those related to computing or the Internet are included in the word list of the DicoInfo and those meanings linked to the environment appear in the DiCoEnviro.

[10] This is beyond the scope of the article, but all lexical relationships are described using the formal system of lexical functions (a system devised within ECL) that provides a formal basis to specify the structure and meaning of relationships (paradigmatic as well as syntagmatic) (More information about the application of ECL principles to the specialized resources can be found in L'Homme 2012b).

4.2 A Unified Treatment of Specialized Predicative Units

In our resources, entries provide information on the argument structure of terms and supply contexts (some of which are annotated as will be seen below). The argument structure states the obligatory participants, and labels them in terms of general semantic roles (**Agent**, **Patient**, **Instrument**[11]) and typical terms (the term that is the most representative of those that instantiate a given semantic role in corpora).

These systems (and especially semantic roles) enable us to capture the relationships between semantically related predicative units.[12] Table 2 gives a few examples of relationships that can be captured using this system.

4.3 Linking Syntax to Semantics

An abstract argument structure can also be linked to instantiations of a predicative unit and of its arguments in corpora. This can be done using an annotation method such as that devised in the FrameNet Projet (Ruppenhoffer et al. 2010).

Our resources include a module that shows how predicative terms combine with their arguments. Up to 20 sentences are extracted from specialized corpora (environment or computing) and relevant parts of these sentences are tagged using XML. The following properties are indicated:

- The predicative unit under analysis is identified (it then appears in capital letters in the annotated sentences);
- The participants are tagged and analyzed (the analysis takes into account the following):
  - Obligatory or non-obligatory participants (called *actants* (i.e. arguments) and *circumstants*))[13] are distinguished;
  - The semantic roles of actants and circumstants are specified (participants labeled with a specific role are displayed in a different color in the annotated sentences);
  - Their syntactic function is labeled;
  - The syntactic group to which they belong is identified.

[11] The role **Instrument** as an argument has been questioned by a number of authors. However, in specialized subject fields, it often becomes an obligatory participant. In addition, it often appears in regular alternations (e.g. *the user prints a document with a laser printer; the printer prints the file*).

[12] In fact, the system is also extended to quasi-predicative units, but we do not deal with this in this contribution.

[13] This is the terminology used in ECL and in our resources. Frame Semantics refers to core frame elements and non-core frame elements. Although the examples do not show this, circumstants (i.e. non-obligatory participants) are also annotated.

Table 2 Argument structures of semantically related predicative terms

Relationships between different parts of speech	Degrade: **Agent** or **Cause** ~ **Patient**	*Water quality generally would be degraded by higher water temperatures*
	Degradation: ~ of **Patient** by **Agent** or **Cause**	*… floods increasing sediment loads and causing degradation of water quality …*
	Degraded: ~ **Patient**	*… as different areas of degraded land spread and merge together to form desert-like conditions*
	Ride: **Agent** ~ **Patient**	*Even if you have ridden a bicycle for years …*
	Rider: **Agent** is a ~ of **Patient**	*Ride one at a time when you ride with other bicycle riders*
Relationships between derivatives that belong to the same part of speech	Install: **Agent** ~ **Patient** on **Destination**	*If a user decides to install a firewall program on a laptop …*
	Reinstall: **Agent** ~ **Patient** on **Destination**	*you can reinstall most of your software*
	Preinstall: **Agent** ~ **Patient** on **Destination**	*… software that is preinstalled on a new computer by an original equipment manufacturer …*
Relationships between certain types of antonyms	Install: **Agent** ~ **Patient** on **Destination**	*If a user decides to install a firewall program on a laptop …*
	Uninstall: **Agent** ~ **Patient** from **Source**	*This is the applet you should use to uninstall programs that you no longer want*
Semantic distinctions	Write$_1$: **Agent** ~ **Patient** to **Destination**	*… you write small files to a disc …*
	Write$_2$: **Agent** ~ **Patient** in **Material**	*… you can use Perl to write shell scripts …*
Alternations	start$_{1a}$: **Patient** ~	*If successful, the program will start in that mode each time*
	start$_{1b}$: **Agent** ~ **Patient**	*These icons allow you to click and start the programs you use most*

The results of these annotations appear in the form of annotated sentences and a summary of the properties of participants. I reproduced in Tables 3 and 4 samples of these annotations for the verb *install* in computing and the noun *impact* in the environment. Role labels are presented between brackets (however, the online version displays them in different colors).

Table 3 Annotations for *install*

Install: **Agent** ~ **Patient** on **Destination**		
*When **you**[Agent] INSTALL a **game**[Patient], it generally also copies a huge array of samples on to your hard disk*		
***You**[Agent] can even run Linux directly from a CD, without having to INSTALL **anything**[Patient] **on your PC**[Destination]*		
***The operating system**[Patient] IS INSTALLED **on your hard disk**[Destination]*		
Agent	Subject (NP)	you (2)
	Indirect Link (NP)	
Patient	Object (NP) (2)	anything
	Subject (NP)	game
		operating system
Destination	Complement (PP-on) (2)	hard disk
		PC

Table 4 Annotations for *impact*

Impact: ~ of **Cause** or **Agent** on **Patient**		
*It so happens that the IMPACT **of climate change**[Cause] **on world heritage sites**[Patient] will be the subject of a meeting taking place at UNESCO just two months from now, on 16 and 17 March*		
*Theories concerning the **climatic**[Patient] IMPACT **of such emissions**[Cause] vary*		
*In general, these scientific workshops focused on the drivers of global change and the IMPACT **of those changes**[Cause] **on ecosystems**[Patient], …*		
Cause	Complement (PP-of) (3)	change (2)
		emission
Patient	Complement (PP-on) (2)	climatic
	Modifier (AP)	ecosystem
		site

4.4 Cohesive Descriptions Based on the Argument Structure

If we assume that arguments are an essential part of the meaning of a predicative unit (as do ECL (Mel'cuk et al. 1995) and Frame Semantics (Fillmore et al. 2003), and other frameworks), they should appear in many other parts of the semantic description of these units. ECL provides many useful tools to link relevant parts of a lexical entry (definition, lexical relationships) to the argument structure.

We adapted these tools to our resources as shown in the entry *attach* that we reproduced below. Arguments are labeled with semantic roles (**Agent**, **Patient**, **Destination**) that are further specified with typical terms (*user*, *file*, *email*). Reference to these typical terms is made in the definition, lexical relationships (in this case, the **Patient** is involved in the meaning of the related term *attached*) and in the annotations. Again, role labels are reproduced between brackets.

Attach, vt.

Agent{user} ~ **Patient{file}** to **Destination{email}**
Definition: A **user**$_{[Agent]}$ links a **file**$_{[Patient]}$ to an **email**$_{[Destination]}$ in order to send this **file**$_{[Patient]}$ along with the **email**$_{[Destination]}$.

Lexical relationships:

A **file**$_{[Patient]}$ that has been a. *attached*

Annotations

***You**$_{[Agent]}$ can also ATTACH **files**$_{[Patient]}$ **to email messages**$_{[Destination]}$* ...
Non-ASCII files, known as binary files**$_{[Patient]}$, may BE ATTACHED **to e-mail
***messages**$_{[Destination]}$*
***You**$_{[Agent]}$ can ATTACH **more than one file**$_{[Patient]}$ **to a single email message**$_{[Destination]}$.*

5 Taking Things a Step Forward: Capturing Different Kinds of Structures

Coming back to the importance of "structures" in specialized fields of knowledge mentioned in the introduction, I will now show how the descriptions listed in Sect. 4 can help us discover different types of structures within a specific field. This work has not been carried out systematically on our resources yet, but the examples I present below are, in my opinion, quite convincing. Of course, the resulting structures differ substantially from the ones sought by a knowledge-based approach (such as that presented in Sect. 2) since they are based on the lexicon rather than on knowledge.

This first structure that can be unveiled is based on the lexical relationships identified between terms and described as was mentioned above with lexical functions. Figure 2 shows how such a structure can be discovered and presented

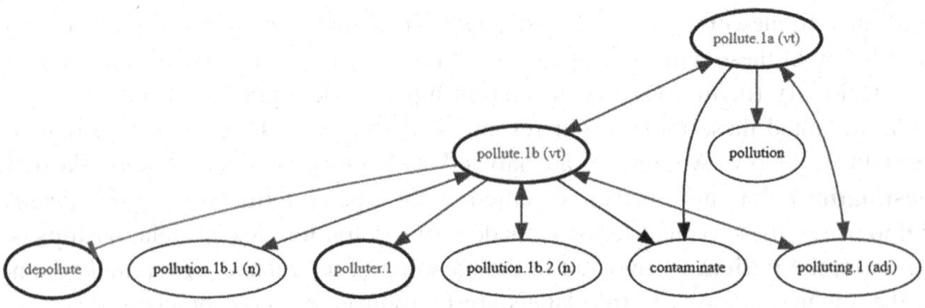

Fig. 2 Lexical relationships between *pollute* and other terms in the field of the environment

graphically based on the information given in the entries.[14] The arc between *pollute*$_{1b}$ and *depollute* indicates an antonymy relationship. The arcs between *pollute*$_{1a}$ and *contaminate* and between *pollute*$_{1b}$ and *contaminate* represent similarity relationships (in this case near synonymy). Finally, all the other arcs show relationships between morphologically related terms (further specified with lexical functions: e.g. the relationship between *pollute* and *pollution* is encoded as an S_0 that means "a noun that has the same meaning"; the relationship between *pollute* and *polluter* is encoded with S_1 that can be explained as "noun for the typical Agent").

A different kind of structure can be discovered based on an analysis of the arguments of predicative terms, the lexical relationships in which they appear, and their annotations. I will call this structure a *frame*, based on Frame semantics. A frame represents a conceptual scenario associated with a given situation in which participants are involved. In the Frame Semantics framework, lexical units can evoke a frame from different perspectives. In addition, participants are defined as core frame elements (obligatory) and non-core frame elements (non-obligatory).

We carried out an analysis using English and French verbs and predicative nouns already recorded in the DiCoEnviro in order to discover such frames. This analysis is based partly on the one devised in the FrameNet project.[15] The analysis was performed manually and took into account four sets of data (L'Homme et al. 2014):

1. A comparison with data available in the English FrameNet: This could only be done with the English terms in DiCoEnviro. The comparison was carried out in order to find whether the lexical units recorded in the DiCoEnviro could be related to lexical items recorded in FrameNet or not. If a lexical item could be identified in FrameNet, then we needed to establish whether the environment term evoked the same frame. For example, the verb *affect* appears both in DiCoInfo and FrameNet. However, in FrameNet it appears in two different frames (Objective_influence and Feigning). The lexical unit recorded in DiCoEnviro evokes the Objective_influence frame.
2. A comparison of the arguments structures of verbs and predicative nouns in the DiCoEnviro: This was done in order to identify predicative terms that shared similarities with regard to their argument structures (same semantic roles). We hypothesized that similar argument structures could lead to the identification of lexical units evoking a frame.
3. A comparison of the circumstants found in the annotations of verbs and predicative nouns: Again, this data was used to try to locate similarities between lexical units.

[14] The graph is generated with a tool developed by Robichaud (2012). In the original graph, arcs are colored.

[15] Our methodology differs from that applied in FrameNet in the sense that frames are discovered afterwards based on the descriptions already available in our databases. In the FrameNet project, frames are defined and then validated on corpus data (Fillmore et al. 2003).

Objective_influence

Note: A Frame based on *Objective_influence* in FrameNet	
Definition: An **Agent** or a **Cause** has an influence (that is often negative) on a **Patient**. The Patient can undergo changes due to this influence.	
Participants (1): 1. **Agent | Cause** 2. **Patient** **Participants (2)**: Degree, Descriptor, Duration, Expanse, Location, Manner, Method, Time,Value	
Lexical Units:	
English: • affect 1 • effect 1 • impact 1 • impact 2 • influence 1 • influence 2	French: • affecter 1 • effet 1 • impact 1 • influence 1 • influencer 1 • influer 1

Fig. 3 A frame with lexical units evoking it in the field of the environment

4. A comparison of the lexical functions associated with these verbs and predicative nouns: Since a lexical function provides an abstract and general description of meanings, this information was used to locate lexical units with close meanings.

Although the analysis was carried out on a preliminary set of data (about 100 terms in English, 150 in French), our results indicate that frames can be a useful way to capture a specific kind of structure in specialized domains. Up to know, we identified more than 40 frames, some of which are based on those recorded in FrameNet, others are adaptations of existing frames; others, finally, are new frames that could be specific to the field of the environment. Figure 3 is an illustration of what the Objective_influence frame (based on the one given in FrameNet) could be in the field of the environment and lists the predicative terms that evoke it.

6 Concluding Remarks

In this contribution, I emphasized the importance of the notion of "structure" in terminology and the role it plays in knowledge understanding. Capturing and representing concepts is an ontology or other types of knowledge repositories is or should be an important part of terminology work. Unfortunately, most efforts carried out up to now have focused on representations that allow us to take into account entity concepts and, indirectly, terms that refer to these entities. However, in order to convey knowledge in text, other types of units are necessary as evidenced by the small term extraction on a corpus of cycling.

I argued and tried to show that predicative units are an essential part in the conveyance of knowledge and that they must appear in terminological descriptions. I also underlined the fact that, even though they are important, they cannot be properly described using the tools devised for terms that refer to entities. Their argument structure must be stated in such a way as to capture their specialized nature (for instance, by specifying the type of unit that would instantiate an argument).

Finally, I showed that predicative terms can also participate in two different kinds of structures. The first one is based on the relationships terms share with other terms. This can be achieved if the links between terms have been properly identified and distinguished from one another. The second one is based on the notion of "frame"; terms can be said to evoke frames and a first subset of data seems to confirm this. There might be cognitive implications in the ideas reported in this chapter, but I will let experts such as Michael Zock dwell on them.

One question, however, remains unanswered. Would it be possible to connect knowledge structures (at least ones that also represent terms) to descriptions of predicative units such as those that we proposed in this contribution? Intuitively, we can certainly think of some kind of connection. As shown in Fig. 4, the argument structure stated for *ride* in which *bicycle* appears could be linked to a

Fig. 4 Argument structure for *ride* and types of bicycles

Ride: cyclist ~ bicycle

According to function
- road bicycle
- touring bicycle
- hybrid bicycle
- ....

According to sport
- road racing bicycle
  - time trial bicycle
  - triathlon bicycle
- cyclo-cross bicycle
- mountain bike
- ...

According to frame design
- ...

According to material
- ...

According to rider position
- upright bicycle
- recumbent bicycle
- ...

knowledge representation in which types of "bicycles" are listed (the classes for bicycle are based on those given in Wikipedia 2014). From this, we could infer that we can ride hybrid bicycles, upright bicycles, touring bicycles, etc.

This indicates that there might be a connection between lexical representations and conceptual ones, at least a partial one. However, this would need to be tested on a more substantial amount of data.

7 Appendix: Term Extraction by TermoStat

Lemma	Frequency	Score (specificity)	Inflected forms	Part of Speech
bicycle	1360	225.93	bicycle, bicycles	Noun
bike	773	168.37	bike, bikes	Noun
ride	719	143.62	ride, rides, ridden, riding	Verb
brake	550	134.74	brake, brakes	Noun
cycling	466	130.99	cycling	Noun
rider	340	104.73	rider, riders	Noun
wheel	521	102.6	wheel, wheels	Noun
lever	284	100.02	lever, levers	Noun
cyclist	274	98.04	cyclist, cyclists	Noun
pedal	235	96.1	pedal, pedals	Noun
bicyclist	215	91.64	bicyclist, bicyclists	Noun
gear	279	91.29	gear, gears	Noun
tire	211	90.76	tire, tires	Noun
traffic	435	88.94	traffic	Noun
cycle	194	85.82	cycle, cycles, cycling	Verb
rear	213	79.82	rear	Adjective
lane	270	78.85	lane, lanes	Noun
saddle	178	78.54	saddle, saddles	Noun
ride	219	76.46	ride, rides	Noun
road	499	71.64	road, roads	Noun
dealer	218	69.92	dealer, dealers	Noun
intersection	141	69.4	intersection, intersections	Noun
derailleur	115	67.37	derailleur, derailleurs	Noun
handlebar	119	66.79	handlebar, handlebars	Noun
rim	125	65.22	rim, rims	Noun

(continued)

(continued)

Lemma	Frequency	Score (specificity)	Inflected forms	Part of Speech
bicycle	105	64.03	bicycle, bicycles, bicycling	Verb
fork	116	63.99	fork, forks	Noun
norco	97	61.82	norco	Noun
frame	173	58.1	frame, frames	Noun
brake	95	57.18	brake, brakes, braking	Verb
adjust	197	56.53	adjust, adjusted, adjusting	Verb
bolt	107	55.11	bolt, bolts	Noun
reflector	78	54.63	reflector, reflectors	Noun
helmet	128	54.08	helmet, helmets	Noun
pedal	80	53.66	pedal, pedals, pedaled, pedaling	Verb
pedestrian	94	52.79	pedestrian, pedestrians	Noun
jersey	98	52.45	jersey, jerseys	Noun
motorist	113	51.52	motorist, motorists	Noun
race	283	49.32	race, races	Noun
adjustment	137	48.81	adjustment, adjustments	Noun
nut	101	47.81	nut, nuts	Noun
front	176	47.78	front	Adjective
page	60	47.24	page	Verb
hub	73	46.84	hub, hubs	Noun
clamp	56	46.79	clamp	Noun
axle	65	46.48	axle, axles	Noun
sprocket	55	46.36	sprocket, sprockets	Noun
clamp	71	46.3	clamp, clamps, clamped, clamping	Verb
organiser	95	46.03	organiser, organisers	Noun
tube	126	45.99	tube, tubes	Noun

References

À vos vélos. (2013). Retrieved December 9, 2013, from http://www.oqlf.gouv.qc.ca/ressources/bibliotheque/dictionnaires/terminologie_velo/fiches/indexFRA.html).

Condamines, A. (1993). Un exemple d'utilisation de connaissances de sémantique lexicale : Acquisition semi-automatique d'un vocabulaire de spécialité. *Cahiers de lexicologie, 62*, 25–65.

Cruse, A. (2011). *Meaning in language: A introduction to semantics and pragmatics.* Oxford: Oxford University Press.

Drouin, P. (2003). Term extraction using non-technical corpora as a point of leverage. *Terminology, 9*(1), 99–115.

Fillmore, C. J. (1977). Scenes-and-frames Semantics, linguistic structures processing. In A. Zampolli (Ed.), *Fundamental studies in computer science* (Vol. 59, pp. 55–88). Amsterdam: North Holland Publishing.

Fillmore, C. J. (1982). Frame semantics. In The Linguistic Society of Korea (Ed.). *Linguistics in the morning calm* (pp. 111–137). Seoul: Hanshin.

Fillmore, C. J. (1985). Frames and the semantics of understanding. *Quaderni di Semantica, 6*(2), 222–254.

Fillmore, C. J., Petruck, M. R. L., Ruppenhofer, J., & Wright, A. (2003). FrameNet in action: The case of attaching. *International Journal of Lexicography, 16*(3), 297–332.

FrameNet. (2014). *FrameNet.* Retrieved January 24, 2014, from (https://framenet.icsi.berkeley.edu/fndrupal/).

Guarino, N., Oberle, D., & Staab, S. (2009). What is an ontology? In S. Staab & R. Studer (Eds.), *Handbook on ontologies* (pp. 11–17). Berlin: Springer.

L'Homme, M. C. (1998). Le statut du verbe en langue de spécialité et sa description lexicographique. *Cahiers de lexicologie, 73*(2), 61–84.

L'Homme, M. C. (2012a). Le verbe terminologique : un portrait de travaux récents. In F. Neveu et al. (Eds.), *Actes du 3e Congrès mondial de linguistique française.* Lyon, France: EDP Sciences.

L'Homme, M. C. (2012b). Adding syntactico-semantic information to specialized dictionaries: An application of the FrameNet methodology. In R. Gouws et al. (Eds.), *Lexicographica* (Vol. 28, pp. 233–252). Berlin: De Gruyter.

L'Homme, M. C. (2014a). Terminologies and taxonomies. In J. Taylor (Ed.), *The handbook of the word.* Oxford: Oxford University Press.

L'Homme, M. C. (dir.) (2014b). *DiCoEnviro. Dictionnaire fondamental de l'environnement.* Retrieved January 6, 2014 from (http://olst.ling.umontreal.ca/cgi-bin/dicoenviro/search-enviro.cgi).

L'Homme, M. C. (dir.) (2014c). *DiCoInfo. Dictionnaire fondamental de l'informatique et de l'Internet.* Retrieved January 6, 2014, from (http://olst.ling.umontreal.ca/cgi-bin/dicoinfo/search.cgi).

L'Homme, M. C., Robichaud, B., & Subirats, C. (2014). Discovering frames in specialized domains. In *Language Resources and Evaluation, LREC 2014.* Iceland: Reykjavik. Retrived July 2, 2014, from www.rec.cont.org/proceeding/rec2014/index.html

Lerat, P. (2002). Qu'est-ce que le verbe spécialisé ? Le cas du droit. *Cahiers de Lexicologie, 80*, 201–211.

Lorente, M. (2007). Les unitats lèxiques verbals dels textos especialitzats. Redefinició d'una proposta de classificació. In M. Lorente et al. (Ed.) *Estudis de lingüístics i de lingüística aplicada en honor de M. Teresa Cabré Catellví. Volum II: De deixebles*, (pp. 365–380). Barcelona: Institut Universitari de Lingüística Aplicada de la Universitat Pompeu Fabra, Sèrie Monografies 11–12.

Mel'čuk, I. et al. (1984–1999). *Dictionnaire explicatif et combinatoire du français contemporain. Recherches lexico-sémantiques I-IV*, Montréal: Presses de l'Université de Montréal.

Mel'čuk, I., Clas, A., & Polguère, A. (1995). *Introduction à la lexicologie explicative et combinatoire.* Louvain-la-Neuve: Duculot/Aupelf-UREF.

Pimentel, J. (2013). Methodological bases for assigning terminological equivalents. A contribution. *Terminology, 19*(2), 237–257.

PropBank (2014). *PropBank.* Retrieved April 11, 2014, from (http://verbs.colorado.edu/propbank/).

Rey, A. (1979). *La terminologie: noms et notions.* Paris: Presses universitaires de France.

Robichaud, B. (2012). Logic based methods for terminological assessment. In *Language Resources and Evaluation (LREC 2012)*. Turkey: Istanbul. Retrived July 2, 2014 from www.rec.cmf.org/proceedings/rec2014/index.html

Ruppenhofer, J., Ellsworth, M., Petruck, M. R. L., Johnson, C., & Scheffczyk J. (2010). *FrameNet II: Extended theory and practice*. Retrieved November 12, 2013, from http://framenet.icsi.berkeley.edu/.

Sager, J. C. (1990). *A practical course in terminology*. Amsterdam/Philadelphia: John Benjamins.

Tellier, C. (2007). *Verbes spécialisés en corpus médical: une méthode de description pour la rédaction d'articles terminographiques*, Travail dirigé présenté au Département de linguistique et de traduction, Université de Montréal. *Theory simple bikes*. Retrieved December 11, 2013, from http://www.ksl.stanford.edu/htw/dme/thermal-kb-tour/simple-bikes.html.

Theory Simple Bikes. http://www.ksl.stanford.edu/htw/dme/thermal-kb-tour/simple-bikes.html. Accessed 11 December 2013.

VerbNet. (2014). *VerbNet*. Retrieved April 11, 2014, from (http://verbs.colorado.edu/~mpalmer/projects/verbnet/downloads.html).

Wandji, O., L'Homme, M.-C., & Grabar, N. (2013). Discovering semantic frames for a contrastive study of verbs in medical corpora. In *Actes de la 9e Conférence Internationale Terminology and Artificial Intelligence (TIA'13)*, Paris, France.

Wikipedia. (2014). *List of bicycle types*. Retrieved July 2, 2014, from (http://en.wikipedia.org/wiki/List_of_bicycle_types).

TOTAKI: A Help for Lexical Access on the TOT Problem

Mathieu Lafourcade and Alain Joubert

Abstract The JDM lexical network has been built thanks to on-line games the main of which, JeuxDeMots (JDM), was launched in 2007. It is currently a large lexical network, in constant evolution, containing more than 310,000 terms connected by more than 6.5 million relations. The riddle game Totaki (Tip Of the Tongue with Automated Knowledge Inferences), the initial version of which was elaborated with Michael Zock, was launched in a first version in 2010. The initial aim of this project is to cross validate the JDM lexical network. Totaki uses this lexical network to make proposals from user given clues, and in case of failure players can supply new information, hence enriching the network. Endogenous processes of inference, by deduction, induction, abduction, also allow to find new information not directly available in the network and hence lead to a densification of the network. The assumption about the validation is that if Totaki is able to guess proper terms from user clues, then the lexical network contains appropriate relations between words. Currently, Totaki achieves a 75 % success rate, to be compared to less than 50 % if the guessing is done by human users. One serious application of Totaki is to be viewed as a tool for lexical access and a possible remedy for the tip of the tongue problem. The Wikipedia encyclopaedia, built in a collaborative way, represents a very important volume of knowledge (about 1.5 million articles in its French version). The idea developed in this chapter consists in benefiting from Wikipedia to enrich the JDM network and evaluate the impact on Totaki performance. Instead of relying only on the JDM network, Totaki also makes use of information extracted from Wikipedia. The overall process is then both endogenous and exogenous. In a first part, we shall remind the reader the basic principles of a lexical network, then the aims and the underlying principles of the Totaki game. We shall see on examples Totaki may be used as a game to evaluate and enrich the JDM network, but also it may be considered as a tool for

M. Lafourcade (✉) · A. Joubert
LIRMM, Université de Montpellier, Montpellier, France
e-mail: lafourcade@lirmm.fr

A. Joubert
e-mail: joubert@lirmm.fr

© Springer International Publishing Switzerland 2015
N. Gala et al. (eds.), *Language Production, Cognition, and the Lexicon*,
Text, Speech and Language Technology 48, DOI 10.1007/978-3-319-08043-7_7

the Tip Of the Tongue problem; partial syntactic or morphologic information may be added to semantic information to help the user. In a second part, we shall show the results of the evaluation of the JDM network, results we obtained playing Totaki. We shall clarify the process allowing the introduction in the Totaki game of data extracted from Wikipedia as a complement in the information from the JDM network, and we shall briefly present the results provided by the first experiments.

Keywords JeuxDeMots · Lexical network · Lexical network evaluation and enrichment · Totaki · Riddle game · TOT problem · Clue terms · Wikipedia

1 Introduction

The JDM lexico-semantic network has been built thanks to on-line games (Games With A Purpose or GWAPs) the main of which, JeuxDeMots (JDM), was launched in 2007 (Lafourcade 2007). It is a large lexical network, in constant evolution, containing currently more than 310,000 terms connected by more than 6.5 million relations. The riddle game Totaki (Tip Of the Tongue with Automated Knowledge Inferences), the initial version of which was elaborated with Michael Zock, was launched in its first version in 2010 (Lafourcade et al. 2011). The initial purpose of this project was to cross validate the JDM lexical network. In particular, we wanted to answer the question: "*Is the lexical network complete enough with terms and relations (between terms) it contains*?". With "*enough*", we mean data into the network are sufficient in number and quality to allow in a satisfying way the realization of classical tasks in NLP, such as textual semantic analysis with lexical disambiguation. It is obvious that, in an exhaustive way, such a network can never be complete, only because of the permanent evolution of the language and the linguistic data.[1] Totaki uses the data of the network to allow the system to develop its proposals from clues supplied by the players, but in case of failure of the system the players can supply new information, thus enriching the network. Recently, endogenous processes, working by deduction, induction and abduction (Zarrouk et al. 2013), also allowed a densification of the network: approximately 1 million new relations were so inferred.

In a first part, we shall remind the reader the basic principles of a lexical network and these of Totaki game. We shall show that Totaki, initially designed to estimate the JDM network, can be an interesting solution to the Tip Of the Tongue (TOT) problem, but also allows an enrichment of this network, in particular of the long tail of its relations. The second part of this chapter will be dedicated to the

[1] In particular, new terms (e.g.: *obamania* or *to vapote*) or new meanings of already existing terms (e.g.: *tablet*) regularly arise.

results of the evaluation of the JDM network, obtained thanks to Totaki. Then, we shall clarify a new process (still unpublished) allowing the introduction in the Totaki game of data extracted from Wikipedia as a complement of the information from the JDM network. This process will be illustrated by an example, before presenting the first results of this experiment.

2 Lexical Networks and Totaki

2.1 Structure of a Lexical Network

The structure of a lexical network, like the one we are building, is composed of nodes and links between nodes, as it was initially introduced in the end of 1960s by (Collins and Quillian 1969) and more recently clarified by (Polguère 2006). A node (a vertex) of the network refers to a term (or a multiple word expression or any textual segment), usually in its canonical form (lemma). The links between nodes are typed and are interpreted as a possible relation holding between the two terms. Some of these relations correspond to lexical functions, some of which have been made explicit by (Mel'čuk et al. 1995), others are semantically motivated like hypernym, hyponym, agent, patient…

More formally, a lexical network is a graph structure composed of nodes (vertices) and links.

- A node is a 3-tuple: <label, type, weight>
- A link is a 4-tuple <start-node, type, end-node, weight>

The label is simply the string holding the term. The type is an encoding referring to the information holding by the node. For instance a node can be a term or a Part of Speech (POS) like :Noun, :Verb. The link type refers to the relation considered, for instance: is_a, synonym, part_of. A node weight refers to the number of times a term has been used by players. Similarly, the weight of a relation refers to the strength of the relation. Figure 1 shows a very small example of the kind of lexical network we are dealing with.

2.2 Presentation of the JDM Network

The interest in and the feasibility of on-line games for acquisition of high quality lexical resources have clearly been established by (Lafourcade and Joubert 2013, published by Gala and Zock). The JDM network, which is in constant evolution, has been built by means of several games:

- JeuxDeMots: it is the very first game of the project, launched in July 2007, and its purpose is the constitution of the JDM network, from an already existing base of 150,000 terms. In a JDM game, two players, anonymously and in an

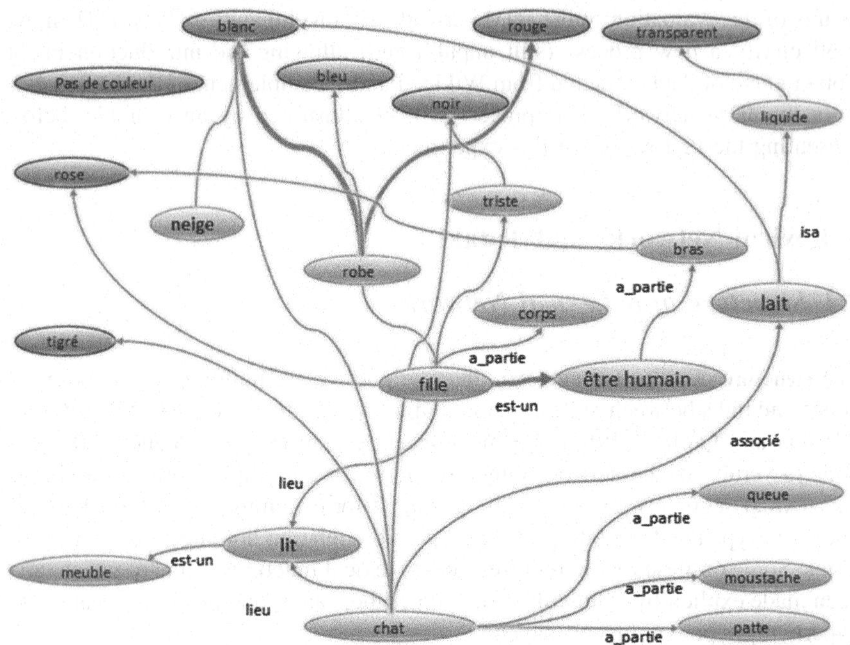

Fig. 1 An example (partial) of a lexical network. For sake of clarity, the relation weights are not represented here. Only nodes corresponding to terms are displayed

asynchronous way, propose typed associations for a term randomly picked up in the base. JDM allowed to acquire approximately 2 million relations,[2] as well as to increase the base to more than 310,000 terms.

- PtiClic: this game was launched in 2008. Contrary to JDM, it is a "closed" game in which the player has to associate terms which are displayed on the screen. These terms come from the JDM network, but also from a voluminous corpus analyzed with LSA.
- Games with choice such as AskIt or LikeIt: these games were most recently launched, from 2010. They suggest the user he answers "true" or "false", "like" or "unlike", on simple statements about lexical data. They are very fast games, the user generally can give his answer within a few seconds. These games allow to obtain polarities about the terms of the network.
- Another game, called Tierxical, ask the player to sort (and bet) three proposals among a set of nine proposals which are associated to a term and a directive.

[2] Here, it is about relations acquired thanks to JDM game. The main part of the other relations present in the network was acquired by deduction, induction, abduction processes (about 1 million relations) or using data from Wikipedia (about 3.5 million relations).

Diko is a tool allowing to display of the information contained in the network. For a target term, the screen presents in a clear way relations it is concerned with. In the example reproduced in Figs. 2 and 3, the target term corresponds to a well known researcher (unfortunately not very well lexicalized in the network).

Diko, besides being a visualisation tool for the JDM network, also allows contributions from interested and experimented players. Indeed, some relations turn out to be poorly playable: they are relations either too specific (e.g.: *magn* indicating an intensification of the target term[3]), or scarcely lexicalized, that is for which there are only very few possible answers (e.g.: *instrument* > *action*[4]). A significant number of players, mainly among those who spent a lot of hours playing JDM, wished to become contributors to inform specific terms or more difficult relations, and thus weakly lexicalized (e.g.: the *parasitology* domain was mainly lexicalized this way): it allows the players, so become contributors, to take part on domains which interest them more particularly or on which they have specific knowledge. Currently, approximately 1 million contributed relations are awaiting validation. These validations are manually realized by expert validators: when several contributors proposed the same relation, this one is posted first and foremost for the expert validator; at the moment, there is no automatic validation. A process of automatic validation is currently been studied; it leans on the notion of minimal vote: when a number of contributors will have proposed the same relation, with a very strong proportion of corresponding votes, then this relation could be automatically validated, with a type indicating that it results from contributions and with a relatively low weight.

2.3 Validation of the JDM Network

The basic principles of the design of Totaki, developed in association with Michael Zock, were presented by (Lafourcade et al. 2011). The initial aim was to obtain a qualitative evaluation of the JDM network, also thanks to an on-line game. The motivation to obtain this evaluation from a game relies on the idea that the number of participants would be much more important with a game than with a classical approach based on the simple voluntary service. With the aim of such an evaluation, the question of the comprehensiveness of our network settles in a more practical way: "*for a given term, are the typed and weighted relations it possesses with the other terms of the network sufficient to determine it in a unique way*?". If the answer is positive, any term can be found by means of a reduced number of typed terms (which are clues).

The principle of the Totaki game consists in making guess a word to the system by proposing it clues. Following each clue given by the player, the system proposes a possible answer term. The clues can be typed (e.g.: *is_a* for hyperonymy or

[3] e.g.: *magn (fever)* = *high fever.*

[4] e.g.: *scissors* → *cut.*

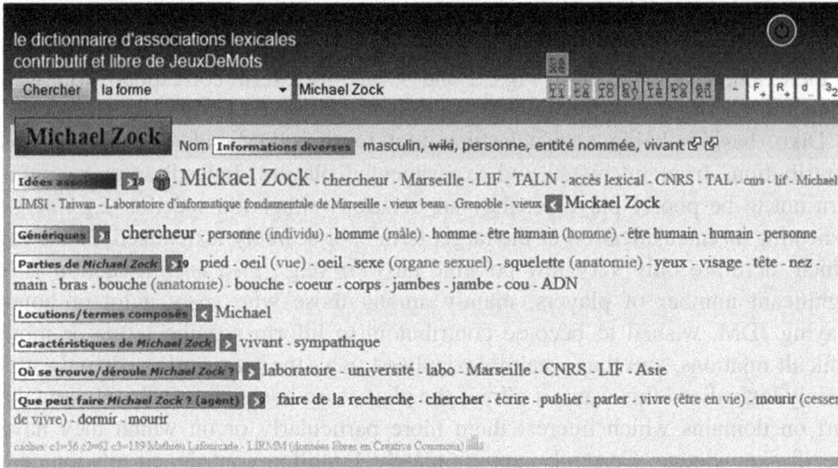

Fig. 2 Diko screen for the term *Michael Zock*

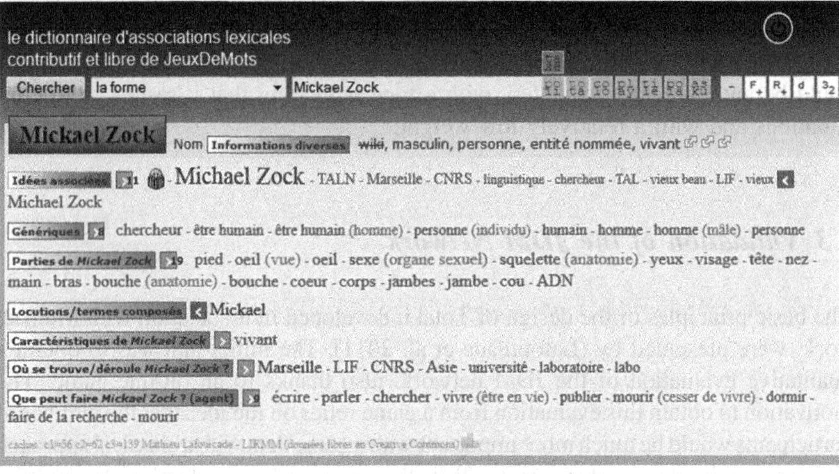

Fig. 3 Diko screen for the term *Mickael Zock*. The reader may notice that players have some difficulties spelling correctly *Michael Zock*'s first name, because when his first name is spelt with a *k* (what is not the correct spelling) the term is strongly lexicalized, almost as well as when its first name is correctly written (with a *h*)

syn for the synonymy), otherwise we consider them as simply associated to the word to be found. The type of a clue corresponds to one of the types of relations existing in the network (e.g.: *is_a animal*). The answers proposed by the system result from typed and weighted relations stored in the JDM network: Totaki proposes the term which is the most strongly connected to the clues given by the player and not already previously given neither by the player nor by Totaki itself in the same game. The process Totaki relies on was exposed in (Joubert and Lafourcade 2012). After each clue supplied by the user, the system computes the intersection of all the terms associated to the previously given clues with all the terms associated to this last clue. If no term may be proposed by the system (in case of an empty intersection), then the system computes the union of these sets: naturally, in it fall-back position, the precision is strikingly less good.

If, after several clues, Totaki does not find the term which tried to make it guess the player, Totaki admits defeat. The player supplies the target term he thought, so realizing an enrichment of the network: the relations *clue* → *target term* are added in the JDM network, typed "Totaki" in order to make the distinction with the relations resulting from other games, but also the target term is added if this one was until then unknown by the network.

In its initial version, Totaki was based only on semantic data contained in the JDM network, that is on the relations between terms, their types and their weights. A more recent version introduces the exploitation of morphological and phonetic notions, by allowing the user to specify:

- the length of the target term (e.g. *:long* = *4* in order to select only terms of 4 characters long)
- elements of spelling, even phonetics (e.g. *:reg_tion* for terms containing 1 character followed by the characters *tion*, or *:reg%tion* for terms of any number of characters followed by characters *tion*).

Figures 4, 5 and 6 show an example of a game partially played using these last possibilities. Figure 7 shows other examples of clues allowing to obtain the same target term.

Another semantic learning system, Never-Ending Language Learning (NELL), developed by Tom Mitchell's team (Carlson et al. 2010), regularly parse web pages looking for semantic relationships between information it already knows and what it finds through its search process; thus, it makes new connections in a manner that is intended to mimic the way humans learn new information. NELL, such as IBM's Watson (Ferrucci et al. 2010), aims at to be able to develop means of answering questions posed by users in natural language with no human intervention in the process.

2.4 Help for the TOT Problem

Totaki can also be used as a help for the TOT problem, as clearly analyzed by Michael Zock in (Lafourcade et al. 2011). Indeed, in the case of a real TOT problem, the user does not find spontaneously a term which nevertheless he knows very well.[5] He knows many elements about this term, but he does not manage to

[5] The TOT problem has been studied by a lot of authors. One of the most recent analysis (Zock and Schwab 2013) also supplies very promising elements of answer.

Vos indices	Mes réponses
TALN	grammaire
:reg Mi%	Mickael Zock

Fig. 4 Example of the beginning of a game: part of the screen showing the clues supplied by the user, as well as the answers Totaki made; the user looks for a term connected to the clue *NLP* (Totaki proposed the term *grammar*) and beginning with the characters *Mi*: guess which researcher was proposed by Totaki!

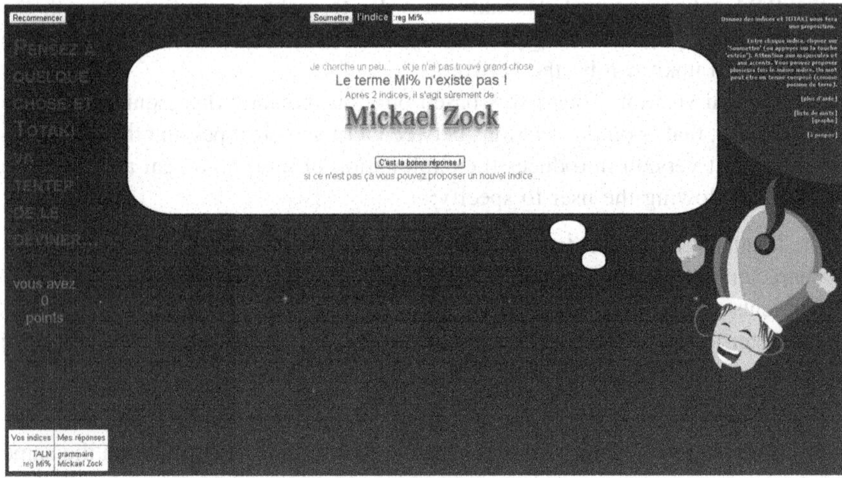

Fig. 5 Example of the beginning of a game in which the user asked terms connected with *NLP* and beginning with the characters *Mi*. Look at Totaki answer!

Fig. 6 Screen obtained after the user validates Totaki proposal

Vos indices	Mes réponses
TALN	grammaire
Marseille	Mickael Zock

Vos indices	Mes réponses
LIF	Mickael Zock

Vos indices	Mes réponses
Marseille	bouillabaisse
Taiwan	lieu
Grenoble	Michael Zock

Vos indices	Mes réponses
sympathique	gentil
faire de la recherche	Michael Zock

Fig. 7 Several examples of set of clues allowing Totaki to find *Michael Zock* (not always correctly spelt!). The last example (with *nice* and *doing research* as clues) is, in our mind, the most characteristic one to find Michael

have access on it. The user generally knows semantic information about this term (its context, as well as its lexical field), morphological information (its lexical category: name, verb, adjective…, his genre: male, feminine), phonological information (intonative outline, approximate number of syllables). He is then going to supply a series of targeted clues, possibly semantically typed. One of the real examples of the TOT problem is reproduced in Fig. 8: the user was not finding the term *saltcellar*, he supplied as first clue the term *salt*, the proposal made by Totaki was *sugar*, because *sugar* was the most strongly connected term with *salt*, then the user supplied the clue *bowl*, the proposal of Totaki was then *salt cellar*, which was the term the user looked for.

A second example of Totaki used as tool for a TOT problem is reproduced in Fig. 9. The user not finding any more the term *washbasin* supplied the clues *latin* (remembering that there is a joke in Latin with the target term), then the clues *white*, *hard* and *bathroom*.

The first version of Totaki allowed the exploitation of the only semantic information at the disposal of a user looking for a term. Even if the latter possessed morphological or phonological information, these could not be taken into account. As seen previously, the current version of Totaki allows a partial exploitation of this information.

2.5 Enrichment of the JDM Network Thanks to Totaki

When a player discovers Totaki, most of his games are played to verify the scale of the knowledge of the network, beginning generally with common terms with frontal indications (e.g.: *feline*, *mouse* to make guess *cat*). Very quickly, the players try to test the limits of the system and are going to propose thus either games on common terms but with side clues (e.g.: *booted*, *angora* for *cat*), or games on infrequent terms generally with frontal clues (e.g.: *cat*, *tale* for *Puss in Boots*). In both cases, the players try "to trap" the system: there is learning of new

Vos indices	Mes réponses
sel	mer
récipient	salière

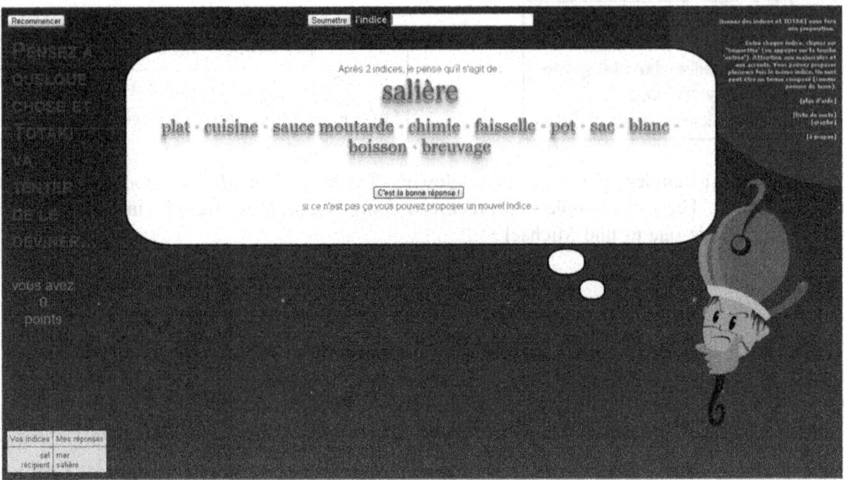

Fig. 8 Extract from the screen, then the complete screen of an example of real case where Totaki allowed a user to find the term that he had on the tip of the tongue, namely *saltcellar* from the clues *salt* and *bowl*. It is to notice that when we did this example again the first proposal of Totaki was not the term *sugar*, but the term *sea*, what clearly shows the evolution of our network: between the real game of the user and the reproduction which we made for this paper (a few weeks), the term the most strongly connected with *salt* was not any more *sugar*, but *sea*

Vos indices	Mes réponses
latin	langue
blanc	noir
dur	plastique
salle de bain	lavabo

Fig. 9 Extract from the screen of another example of help for a TOT problem in which Totaki found the target term

relations (in the first case), but also of new terms often connected to the current events (in the second case). For example, the set of the names of Pokemons (*Pikachu*, *Dracaufeu*…) was mainly constituted thanks to Totaki. So, Totaki allows enrichment on terms directly chosen by the users.

However, these new relations or these new terms introduced into the JDM network thanks to Totaki are initially supplied only by a single player. It would be possible that, faithfully or not, the player introduces erroneous information. It is the reason why the relations introduced by Totaki into the network are differently typed ("Aki" type) and weighted with a low value (equal to 10, while the weight of a relation introduced by a single couple of players into JDM values 50).

2.6 Enrichment of the Long Tail

Due to the concept of the JDM game, most of the relations in the network are "direct" or "frontal" (e.g.: *dog* → *animal*, of "associated idea" type and the weight of which is currently more than 820); they are the ones which were the most spontaneously given by the users. However, certain relations are "indirect" or "lateral" (e.g.: *dog* → *sit down, don't move, slaver, bring back*… also of "associated idea" type and all of them with a current weight less or equal to 60). These last relations constitute the *long tail*. For most of the terms present in the network, the major part of the relations, in number, is in the long tail. Currently, the distribution of the relations for a given term follows a power law (more exactly, a Zipf law): so, the cumulated weight of the 80–85 % weaker relations is similar to the weight of the 15–20 % stronger relations. In a classic Totaki game, the user can supply the clues he wishes; during a Totaki game in taboo mode, we are going to make guess to the system a target term, forbidding the user to supply as clues ten terms the most strongly connected with this target term in the network, that is forbidding the strongest "frontal" indications. For the example *dog*, the ten forbidden terms in taboo mode are: *cat*, *animal*, *Snowy*, *Idefix*, *to bark*, *poodle*, *niche*, *wolf*, *bone* and *she-dog*. The user is thus obliged to supply clues less strongly connected with the target term and thus belonging to the long tail. The principle reminds the one of the Taboo board game. This process, presented by (Lafourcade and Joubert 2012) inevitably increases the recall.

3 Evaluation of the JDM Network…

3.1 …Thanks to Totaki

The initial idea of the design of Totaki is that the success rate to find a target term from clues is covariant to the rate of comprehensiveness of the JDM network: the more our network will be complete, the more the success rate of Totaki will be important. Totaki so allows us to have an empirical evaluation of the network JDM.

The evaluation, just like the learning, is made only according to what the players informed. As already mentioned, Totaki can be envisaged as a game or a tool for the TOT problem. A priori, our software does not know how to make the distinction between both uses. Indeed, after a single game and if AKI finds the solution, we cannot know a priori if the user knew or if he looked for the target term. On the other hand, if in a relatively short lapse of time (within a few minutes) the same term is played several times, we can make the hypothesis that it is about a use of game (at least from the second game) where the user tries to make find the target term by Totaki, generally proposing more and more side different clues. In both cases, game or TOT tool, the target terms are mainly terms of average or low frequency. Indeed, play to find a frequent word does not present a big interest, and generally we do not look for a common term thanks to a TOT tool. Figure 10 shows the evolution in time of the ratio between the number of games Totaki won (games the user indicated that the software found the target term) and the number of played games. The result we obtained seems to stabilize towards a value of the order of 75 %. It should be noted that this value is probably only an underestimate of the comprehensiveness of the JDM network (on the played vocabulary), because, as we have already indicated it, a large number players look for the limits of Totaki.

3.2 …and Wikipédia

3.2.1 Principle

The Wikipedia encyclopedia, constructed in a collaborative way, represents a very important volume of knowledge (about 1.5 million articles in its French version). The idea we develop in this section consists in benefiting from Wikipedia to enrich the JDM network. Instead of leaning only on the data of the JDM network, Totaki will also use information extracted from Wikipedia. Thus, it is here about an endogenous and exogenous process.

During a game of Totaki, every clue the player supplies serves as entry to Wikipedia. The software selects, on the Wikipedia page of this entry, the different links, except the links of numerical type.[6] In the JDM network, all the relations *clue* → *link* are then added, with the "Wiki" type and a low valuable weight 10, unless these relations already existed (whatever is their type). If the term corresponding to this link does not exist in the JDM network, it is added to it, in particular to be able to add the correspondent "Wiki" relation *clue* → *link*. Naturally, for the target term of this game of Totaki, the similar relations (between this target term and the corresponding links on the Wikipedia page) are also added to the JDM network. When the player confirms the proposal from Totaki, if Totaki had found this proposal thanks to "Wiki" relations, these relations are then added as "AKI" relations, also with a weight of 10.

In order to not slowing down the Totaki games, it was decided to make a scan on all the terms of the JDM network and thus to create all the "Wiki" relations

[6] Years (e.g.: *1984*) are not taken into account; on the other hand, dates (e.g.: *September 11th*) are.

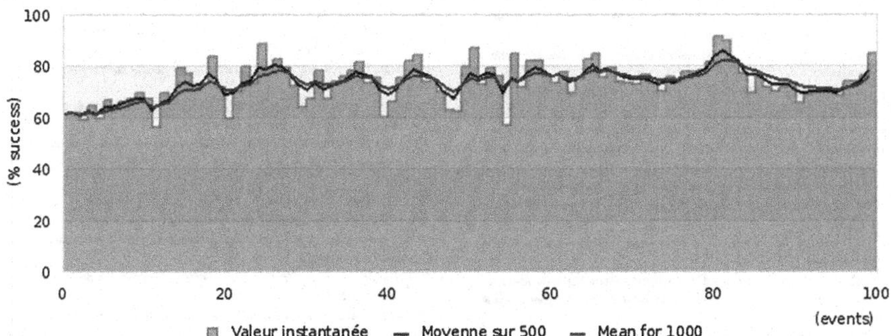

Fig. 10 Evolution in time of the success rate of Totaki. We notice a light progress of the averages since 60 % to values which can exceed 85 %, but generally in the order of 70 to 80 %: the network is thus complete in approximately 75 %! It would seem that the light reduction in the success rate in last thousands of played games results from the fact that a largest number of players learnt new terms to Totaki. Histogram (immediate value) is drawn with a chunk size of 1 % of the number of played games; we also give mean values for 500 and for 1,000

clue → *link*. So, when a player proposes a clue, the system will not need to scan the corresponding Wikipedia page.

Wikipedia contains much more information than the JDM network; Figs. 11 and 12 clearly show this difference on an example: while the Wikipedia page relative to *Gérard Philippe* draws up a relatively exhaustive list of its movies, the corresponding Diko screen only gives a few of them. On the other hand, a number of Wikipedia links, relative to general terms, corresponds to noise (that is the reason why we chose a low value weight of 10 for "Wiki" relations). Figure 13, extracted from the Wikipedia page of *Gérard Philippe*, contains links which are absolutely not characteristic for him, such as the terms *war* or *baccalaureate*.

3.2.2 Evolutionary Aspect

The JDM network, just like the encyclopaedia Wikipedia, is in a Never Ending Learning context. In order to take into account the evolutionary character of Wikipedia, the "Wiki" relations are created with a deadline date (currently arbitrarily chosen 1 month). When a "Wiki" relation is called, it is really used only if its deadline date is not overtaken.

With the aim of minimizing the "Wiki" importance of the relations *target_term* → *link*, in particular compared with the "AKI" relations, their weight is decreased of 1 for each Totaki game concerning this target term. When the weight of a "Wiki" relation reaches the 0 value, this relation is deleted from the JDM network. The next time this relation will be found thanks to Wikipedia, it will be created with a weight equal to 10. This process allows to take into account the evolutionary character of the Wikipedia articles.

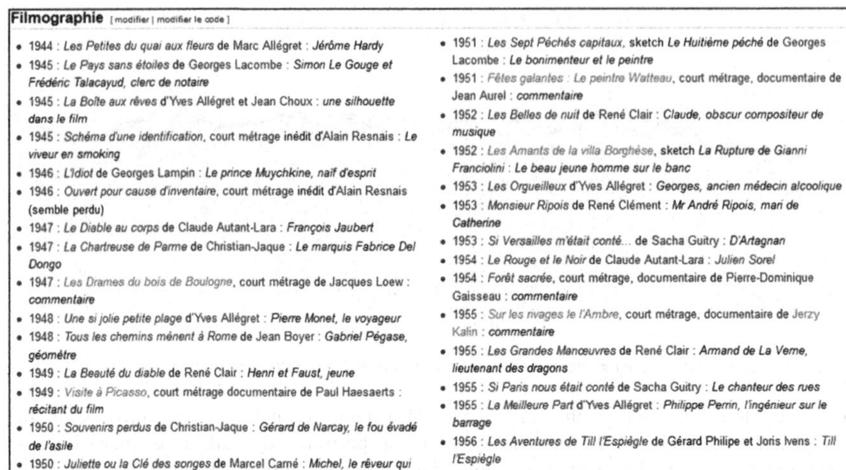

Filmographie [modifier | modifier le code]

- 1944 : *Les Petites du quai aux fleurs* de Marc Allégret : *Jérôme Hardy*
- 1945 : *Le Pays sans étoiles* de Georges Lacombe : *Simon Le Gouge et Frédéric Talacayud, clerc de notaire*
- 1945 : *La Boîte aux rêves* d'Yves Allégret et Jean Choux : *une silhouette dans le film*
- 1945 : *Schéma d'une identification*, court métrage inédit d'Alain Resnais : *Le viveur en smoking*
- 1946 : *L'Idiot* de Georges Lampin : *Le prince Muychkine, naïf d'esprit*
- 1946 : *Ouvert pour cause d'inventaire*, court métrage inédit d'Alain Resnais (semble perdu)
- 1947 : *Le Diable au corps* de Claude Autant-Lara : *François Jaubert*
- 1947 : *La Chartreuse de Parme* de Christian-Jaque : *Le marquis Fabrice Del Dongo*
- 1947 : *Les Drames du bois de Boulogne*, court métrage de Jacques Loew : *commentaire*
- 1948 : *Une si jolie petite plage* d'Yves Allégret : *Pierre Monet, le voyageur*
- 1948 : *Tous les chemins mènent à Rome* de Jean Boyer : *Gabriel Pégase, géomètre*
- 1949 : *La Beauté du diable* de René Clair : *Henri et Faust, jeune*
- 1949 : *Visite à Picasso*, court métrage documentaire de Paul Haesaerts : *récitant du film*
- 1950 : *Souvenirs perdus* de Christian-Jaque : *Gérard de Narcay, le fou évadé de l'asile*
- 1950 : *Juliette ou la Clé des songes* de Marcel Carné : *Michel, le rêveur qui*
- 1951 : *Les Sept Péchés capitaux*, sketch *Le Huitième péché* de Georges Lacombe : *Le bonimenteur et le peintre*
- 1951 : *Fêtes galantes : Le peintre Watteau*, court métrage, documentaire de Jean Aurel : *commentaire*
- 1952 : *Les Belles de nuit* de René Clair : *Claude, obscur compositeur de musique*
- 1952 : *Les Amants de la villa Borghèse*, sketch *La Rupture de Gianni Franciolini* : *Le beau jeune homme sur le banc*
- 1953 : *Les Orgueilleux* d'Yves Allégret : *Georges, ancien médecin alcoolique*
- 1953 : *Monsieur Ripois* de René Clément : *Mr André Ripois, mari de Catherine*
- 1953 : *Si Versailles m'était conté...* de Sacha Guitry : *D'Artagnan*
- 1954 : *Le Rouge et le Noir* de Claude Autant-Lara : *Julien Sorel*
- 1954 : *Forêt sacrée*, court métrage, documentaire de Pierre-Dominique Gaisseau : *commentaire*
- 1955 : *Sur les rivages de l'Ambre*, court métrage, documentaire de Jerzy Kalin : *commentaire*
- 1955 : *Les Grandes Manœuvres* de René Clair : *Armand de La Verne, lieutenant des dragons*
- 1955 : *Si Paris nous était conté* de Sacha Guitry : *Le chanteur des rues*
- 1955 : *La Meilleure Part* d'Yves Allégret : *Philippe Perrin, l'ingénieur sur le barrage*
- 1956 : *Les Aventures de Till l'Espiègle* de Gérard Philipe et Joris Ivens : *Till l'Espiègle*

Fig. 11 Part of the Wikipedia page relative to *Gérard Philippe*, showing a part of his filmography: the links are the colored terms (*red* when the Wikipedia page does not still exist)

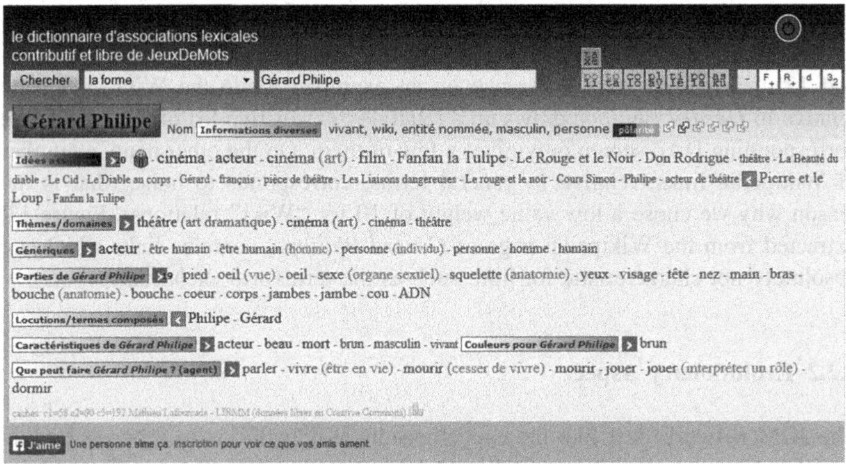

Fig. 12 Diko screen about *Gérard Philippe*: only a few of his movies are listed

In the Sect. 3.2.1, we mentioned that a scan on all the terms of the JDM network, with scan of the correspondent Wikipedia pages, had been realized. To take into account the evolutionary character of the JDM network and of Wikipedia, such a process must be regularly made (currently every 30 days, according to the deadline period of the “Wiki” relations).

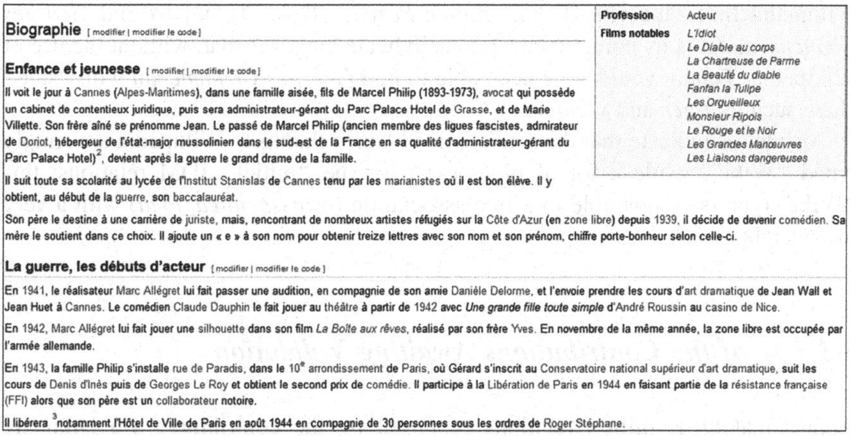

Biographie [modifier | modifier le code]

Profession	Acteur
Films notables	*L'Idiot* *Le Diable au corps* *La Chartreuse de Parme* *La Beauté du diable* *Fanfan la Tulipe* *Les Orgueilleux* *Monsieur Ripois* *Le Rouge et le Noir* *Les Grandes Manœuvres* *Les Liaisons dangereuses*

Enfance et jeunesse [modifier | modifier le code]

Il voit le jour à Cannes (Alpes-Maritimes), dans une famille aisée, fils de Marcel Philip (1893-1973), avocat qui possède un cabinet de contentieux juridique, puis sera administrateur-gérant du Parc Palace Hotel de Grasse, et de Marie Villette. Son frère aîné se prénomme Jean. Le passé de Marcel Philip (ancien membre des ligues fascistes, admirateur de Doriot, hébergeur de l'état-major mussolinien dans le sud-est de la France en sa qualité d'administrateur-gérant du Parc Palace Hotel)[2], devient après la guerre le grand drame de la famille.

Il suit toute sa scolarité au lycée de l'Institut Stanislas de Cannes tenu par les marianistes où il est bon élève. Il y obtient, au début de la guerre, son baccalauréat.

Son père le destine à une carrière de juriste, mais, rencontrant de nombreux artistes réfugiés sur la Côte d'Azur (en zone libre) depuis 1939, il décide de devenir comédien. Sa mère le soutient dans ce choix. Il ajoute un « e » à son nom pour obtenir treize lettres avec son nom et son prénom, chiffre porte-bonheur selon celle-ci.

La guerre, les débuts d'acteur [modifier | modifier le code]

En 1941, le réalisateur Marc Allégret lui fait passer une audition, en compagnie de son amie Danièle Delorme, et l'envoie prendre les cours d'art dramatique de Jean Wall et Jean Huet à Cannes. Le comédien Claude Dauphin le fait jouer au théâtre à partir de 1942 avec *Une grande fille toute simple* d'André Roussin au casino de Nice.

En 1942, Marc Allégret lui fait jouer une silhouette dans son film *La Boîte aux rêves*, réalisé par son frère Yves. En novembre de la même année, la zone libre est occupée par l'armée allemande.

En 1943, la famille Philip s'installe rue de Paradis, dans le 10ᵉ arrondissement de Paris, où Gérard s'inscrit au Conservatoire national supérieur d'art dramatique, suit les cours de Denis d'Inès puis de Georges Le Roy et obtient le second prix de comédie. Il participe à la Libération de Paris en 1944 en faisant partie de la résistance française (FFI) alors que son père est un collaborateur notoire.

Il libérera [3]notamment l'Hôtel de Ville de Paris en août 1944 en compagnie de 30 personnes sous les ordres de Roger Stéphane.

Fig. 13 Part of the Wikipedia page relative to *Gérard Philippe*, showing a part of his bibliography; links such as *war* or *baccalaureate* are absolutely not characteristic for *Gérard Philippe*

3.2.3 Interest for Totaki Game

For the terms poorly lexicalized in the JDM network but suitably informed in Wikipedia, (for example named entities), this process allows to supply them with relations. These relations have a low weight: if the clues the user supplies are correctly lexicalized, these relations will not be used by Totaki; on the other hand, if the clues are weakly (even not) lexicalized, then these relations allow Totaki to make proposals, while the first experiments showed that it would have been able not to be able to make them. For the strongly lexicalized terms, there are relatively few modifications: most of the relations *term* → *link* already existed in the network.

This process, just like the use of Totaki in taboo mode (Sect. 2.6), should allow to enrich the long tail, and thus increases the recall.

3.2.4 First Results

In the current state of our experiments, the JDM network contains about 3,500,000 "Wiki" relations making the total over 6,500,000 relations. Let us remind these relations have a low valuable weight (10 or less), while a relation introduced via JDM by a single couple of players has a higher weight (equal to 50). This translates the ascendancy we want to give to these "initial" JDM relations with regard to those obtained thanks to Wikipedia. The use of Wikipedia so allows to improve the capacities of the JDM network. So, for example, thanks to the

Wikipedia links, the clue *Mouilleron-en-Pareds* allows Totaki to find *Georges Clemenceau* (it is its home town). Let us indicate however that, without the use of Wikipedia, Totaki would have been able to find *Georges Clemenceau* with "side" clues such as *tiger* and *victory*.

Also let us indicate that these relations obtained thanks to Wikipedia are simply typed "Wiki", while a lot of types exist for the "initial" JDM relations: this "Wiki" type is comparable to a free association (or *associated_idea*) with a very low weight.

3.3 Use of the Contributions Awaiting Validation

Approximately 1 million relations proposed by the contributors via Diko are currently awaiting validation. Thus, they are not present, even temporarily, in the JDM network. Why to ignore such a mass of information which by experiment we found very relevant in almost all of the cases? The basic idea thus consists in using these relations, by allocating them a low weight, much lower than that of the relations of the JDM network. As a consequence, the relations of the JDM network have priority compared with these pseudo-relations, in the same way as the "Wiki" relations. These pseudo-relations, informed as we previously saw on often very specific and little lexicalized terms, can allow Totaki to provide answers, in particular in cases it could not be able to supply them.

4 Conclusion and Perspectives

Totaki on-line game was initially designed in association with Michael Zock with the aim of estimating the validity of the JDM network. From the beginning of this design, a duality appeared: Totaki can be considered as a game (just like JDM), but also as a tool for the TOT problem. In this second approach, Michael Zock's contribution was determining.

Thanks to the help of players looking ceaselessly for its limits, Totaki allows to enrich in a consequent way the JDM network, mainly by allowing the acquisition of "side" relations, as well as that of new terms.

The use by Totaki of links from Wikipedia pages in the search for proposals, from the clues supplied by the players, as well as the use of the contributions of certain players (proposed, but not yet validated relations) allowed an important densification of the JDM network, mainly for terms which the games of the JDM project had relatively weakly lexicalized.

5 Annexes

Other examples of Totaki games

Vos indices	Mes réponses
nourriture :good	manger viande

Vos indices	Mes réponses
nourriture :bad	manger junk food

Vos indices	Mes réponses
sentiment :bad	amour haine

Vos indices	Mes réponses
:isa animal :good peluche	tigre chat ours

Vos indices	Mes réponses
:isa animal :long = 13	tigre poisson rouge

Vos indices	Mes réponses
:isa animal WWF	tigre panda

References

Carlson, A., Betteridge, J., Kisiel, B., Settles, B., Hruschka, E. R., & Mitchell, T. M. (2010). Toward an architecture for never-ending language learning. *In Proceedings of the Conference on Artificial Intelligence (AAAI)*, (p. 8).

Collins, A., & Quillian, M. R. (1969). Retrieval time from semantic memory. *Journal of Verbal Learning and Verbal Behaviour, 8*(2), 240–248.

Ferrucci, D., Brown, E., Chu-Carroll, J., Fan, J., Gondek, D., Kalyanpur, A., et al. (2010). Building watson: An overview of the DeepQA project. *AI Magazine, 31*(3), 59–79.

Joubert, A., & Lafourcade, M. (2012). A new dynamic approach for lexical networks evaluation. *In Proceedings of the 8th edition of Language Resources and Evaluation Conference (LREC 2012)*, (p. 5). Istanbul: ELRA.

Lafourcade, M. (2007). Making people play for lexical acquisition. *In Proceedings of the 7th Symposium on Natural Language Processing (SNLP 2007)*, (p. 8). December 13–15, 2007, Pattaya, Thaïland.

Lafourcade, M., Joubert, A., Schwab, D., et Zock, M. (2011). Évaluation et consolidation d'un réseau lexical grâce à un assistant ludique pour le "mot sur le bout de la langue". *In Proceedings of TALN'11*, (pp. 295–306). Montpellier, France, 27 juin-1er juillet 2011.

Lafourcade, M., & Joubert, A. (2013). Bénéfices et limites de l'acquisition lexicale dans l'expérience JeuxDeMots. In N. Gala & M. Zock (Eds.), *Ressources lexicales* (pp. 187–216).

Mel'čuk, I. A., Clas, A., & Polguère, A. (1995). *Introduction à la lexicologie explicative et combinatoire*. Louvain-la-Neuve: Duculot AUPELF-UREF.

Polguère, A. (2006). Structural properties of lexical systems: monolingual and multilingual perspectives. *In Workshop on Multilingual Language Resources and Interoperability (COLING/ACL 2006)*, (pp. 50–59). Sydney.

Zarrouk, M., Lafourcade, M., & Joubert, A. (2013). Inductive and deductive inferences in a crowdsourced lexical-semantic network. *In proceedings of the 9th International Conference on Recent Advances in Natural Language Processing (RANLP 2013)*, (p. 6). September 7–13, 2013, Hissar, Bulgaria.

Zock, M., & Schwab, D. (2013). L'index, une ressource vitale pour guider les auteurs à trouver le mot bloqué sur le bout de la langue. In N. Gala & M. Zock (Eds.) *Ressources lexicales* (pp. 313–354).

Typing Relations in Distributional Thesauri

Olivier Ferret

Abstract Dictionaries are important tools for language producers but they are rarely organized for an easy access to words from concepts. Such access can be facilitated by the presence of relations between words in dictionaries for implementing associative lookup. Lexical associations can be quite easily extracted from a corpus as first or second order co-occurrence relations. However, these associations face two related problems: they are noisy and the type of relations on which they are based is implicit. In this article, we propose to address to some extent the second problem by studying the type of relations that can be found in distributional thesauri. This study is more precisely performed by relying on a reference lexical network, WordNet in our case, in which the type of the relations is known. This reference network is first used for identifying directly the relations of the thesauri that are present in this network but also for characterizing, through the detection of patterns of composition of known relations, new kinds of relations that do not appear explicitly in it.

Keywords Distributional thesaurus · Lexical relation · Lexical network · Co-occurrence · Topical relation · Topic segmentation · Composition of relations · WordNet · Semantic similarity · Semantic relatedness

1 Introduction

Everyone is now familiar with Information Retrieval through the use of Web search engines and more particularly with its more widespread form, consisting in searching documents from a restricted set of words. The implicit objective of users in this kind of task is to find the minimal set of words, called a query, that is likely to

O. Ferret (✉)
CEA LIST, Vision and Content Engineering Laboratory, 91191 Gif-Sur-Yvette, France
e-mail: olivier.ferret@cea.fr

© Springer International Publishing Switzerland 2015
N. Gala et al. (eds.), *Language Production, Cognition, and the Lexicon*,
Text, Speech and Language Technology 48, DOI 10.1007/978-3-319-08043-7_8

retrieve documents that correspond to their information need. But what about the problem of finding the words of a query? The problem of turning an information need into a query has of course been considered in the field of Information Retrieval, but in a limited way as a significant part of its content is outside of the scope of this domain. Indeed, it is related to the psycholinguistic problem of expressing concepts into words, a problem that was addressed centrally by the work of Michael Zock since many years through different viewpoints, from Natural Language Generation (NLG) (Zock 1996) to the study of the *tip-of-the-tongue* state (Zock 2002) and the learning of foreign languages (Zock and Quint 2004).

Through the diversity of these viewpoints, the work of Michael Zock is characterized by a common set of principles that can be summarized as follows: the process of turning concepts into words is not a straightforward process only consisting in a choice between several solutions, as it was considered for many years in the field of NLG, but rather a complex process that implies many interactions between conceptual and linguistic levels. This complex process heavily relies on the notion of *lexicon* and consequently, *lexical access* is a central problem that is generally hidden but can be observed in situations of failure such as in the tip-of-the-tongue state. This lexical access is more precisely viewed as a navigational process in which words are accessed in an associative mode through the lexical relations present in the lexicon.

This model stands for the mental lexicon but one of the specificities of the work of Michael Zock is the application of this theoretical framework for building tools dedicated to the help of speakers or writers in the expression of what they have in mind. In this context, the lexicon keeps a central role but has to take the concrete form of a lexical network in which a language producer can navigate for finding the right word for expressing an idea. Such a lexical network must fit at least three main requirements:

- it has to be large and densely connected, i.e. containing a large number of relations between a large number of words, as it should be possible to access a word from one or several other words expressing its meaning by going through a very limited number of relations;
- it has to contain a high number of different relation types, which ensures that a word can be accessed through different paths, according to the mental context of the language producer. It is also an indirect way to limit the length of paths, as it contributes to increasing the density of the network;
- the type of relations in such a network must be explicit, which means that the relation between each pair of words has to be labeled, as the navigation in the network is performed by a human.

Unfortunately, these three requirements are difficult to take into account simultaneously for building a concrete lexical network. More particularly, the first two requirements are difficult to fulfill together with the third one. On one side, building automatically a large network of lexical associations by recording the co-occurrences between words in the documents of a corpus is quite straightforward and such a network will certainly contain a large variety of relations. However, identifying in this network the associations that actually correspond to semantic relations and determining the type of these relations is a far more difficult task that is still a research issue. On the other side, building such a lexical network manually is a way to control precisely the type of relations it comprises but represents such a heavy task that it is difficult to perform at a large scale. Even a large manually-built resource such as WordNet contains only a restricted set of types of relations and is globally rather sparse.

In this article, we adopt the perspective of the automatic construction of a lexical network. However, our objective is to control and identify as much as we can the type of its relations. We present more precisely two approaches that contribute to this goal. The first one, that we will mention briefly in the next section, was developed in a joint work with Michael Zock (Ferret and Zock 2006) and is based on the idea that a certain type of relations, based in our case on first-order co-occurrences, is closely linked to a certain process and that this link can be exploited for selecting relations accordingly. The second one, which focuses in our case on relations resulting from second-order co-occurrences, relies on the relations present in a reference resource and their composition to characterize the relations of a specific type of lexical network, more precisely distributional thesauri.

2 A Process-Based Approach for Identifying Lexical Relations

Manually-built lexical resources such as WordNet mainly contains paradigmatic relations, such as synonymy, hypernymy, hyponymy or meronymy, but generally lack association relations such as the ones referred by Halliday and Hasan (1976) as non-systematic semantic relations, by Morris and Hirst (2004) as "non-classical relations" or by Zock and Bilac (2004) as TIORA (Typically Involved Object, Relation or Actor) relations. These relations are also the core of the "tennis problem'' mentioned by Roger Schaffin, cited in Fellbaum (1998), and correspond to some of the lexical functions of the Meaning-test theory Mel'čuk and Polguère (1987). Associations like *surgeon–hospital*, *law–policeman* or *pilot–airport* are typical examples of such relations, which can also be viewed, at least for a significant part of them, as topical relations, that is to say, relations between concepts co-occurring in the same topic or the same situation.

From this definition, one straightforward way to capture automatically such relations is to collect co-occurrences between words in segments of texts that are topically homogeneous. The method does not label the resulting associations with a type but the exploitation of a topical segmentation of texts is supposed to restrict the extracted associations to topical relations. The direct application of this principle leads to extract a too large number of associations that do not actually correspond to topical relations. To alleviate the problem, we proposed a bootstrapping method

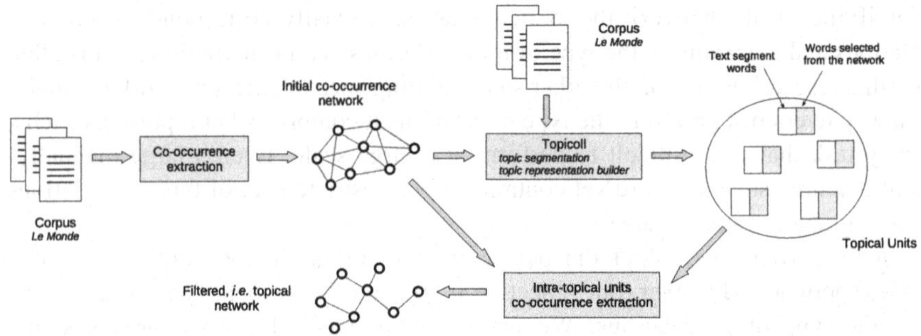

Fig. 1 Overall process for extracting topical relations from texts

that links more closely the topical segmentation of texts to the extraction of topic relations (Ferret and Zock 2006).

The starting point of this method, globally presented in Fig. 1, is the building of a large co-occurrence network from a corpus[1] (see Ferret (2006) for the details) with the objective to capture as many topical relations as possible. Hence, a rather large window of 20 content words is used for collecting co-occurrences inside the space of each document of the corpus. The resulting network is exploited by a text segmenter, called TOPICOLL (Ferret 2002), that produces both a linear segmentation of texts, as text segmenters after Hearst (1994), and a representation of the topic of each text segment, called a Topical Unit. This representation is made of both the words of the segment and the word of the co-occurrence network that are the more representative of the topic of the segment. Both types of words are selected by TOPICOLL from a sliding window used for computing the cohesion of a text at a given position. Similarly to Hearst (1994), such computation is the core part of the segmentation method as topic shifts are detected from the breaks in text cohesion. For the building of Topical Units, some of the words of the network are selected from their co-occurrence connections with the words of the window and as a feedback, some of the words of the windows are selected according to their links with the selected words of the network.

In comparison with text segments, Topical Units should only contain words that belong to the same topic. As a consequence, their co-occurrences in the space of a Topical Unit are supposed to correspond to topical relations. Hence, a new network, called topical network, is built by recording the co-occurrences between the words inside each Topical Unit. In practice, we restrict this process to the co-occurrences already present in the initial network, as our goal is first to identify the associations in the initial network that are likely to be topical relations.

The resulting network is 46 % smaller than the initial one but an evaluation performed with TOPICOLL shows that this filtered network, used by TOPICOLL for topic segmentation, leads to the same performance than the initial network while a

[1] The experiments were performed on 24 months of the French *Le Monde* newspaper.

network filtered according to the frequency of co-occurrences, with the same level of cut, causes a significant decrease of results. As a consequence, we can assume that the proposed method mostly filters associations that do not correspond to topical relations. For instance, for the word *acteur* (*actor*) it discards co-occurrents such as *cynique* (*cynical*) or *allocataire* (*beneficiary*), which are found strongly associated to *acteur* (*actor*) but not topically linked to it, while it keeps co-occurrents such as *gros-plan* (*close-up*) or *scénique* (*theatrical*), which are topically coherent with *acteur* (*actor*) but more weakly associated to it than the discarded co-occurrents.

As illustrated by these results, such approach can be interesting for discarding lexical associations that do not fit a category of relations defined in a holistic way, such as topical relations here, but is not precise enough for characterizing a particular type of relations. Hence, we propose in what follows another approach that leverages a reference resource made of relations whose type is already known for characterizing new relation types. First, we will present the target of this work, distributional thesauri, and more particularly the way they are classically built and evaluated. Then, we will make some proposals for characterizing the type of the relations they contain by relying on WordNet.

3 Distributional Thesauri

Distributional semantic resources, and more precisely distributional thesauri, are used in a comprehensive set of tasks, ranging from relation extraction (Min et al. 2012) to machine translation (Marton 2013). A widespread way to build such thesaurus from a corpus is to follow the implementation of the distributional hypothesis (Firth 1957) first proposed by Hindle (1990): each word is characterized by the set of contexts from a corpus in which it appears and the semantic similarity of two words is computed from the contexts they share. This similarity is then used for selecting the list of the closest semantic neighbors of a word. This approach was extended by Grefenstette (1994) and Lin (1998) and explored in detail in Curran and Moens (2002, Weeds (2003) or Heylen et al. (2008).

In the perspective of a resource used for supporting word access, a distributional thesaurus can also be viewed as a lexical network in which it is possible to go from one word to another through a link of semantic similarity based on second-order co-occurrences. However, the term *semantic similarity* is very general and ambiguous. In addition, it is not unanimously defined in the literature: one part considers paradigmatic relations, such as hypernymy or synonymy; the other part considers association relations such as those mentioned in Sect. 2. The distinction between these two approaches refers to the distinction between the notions of *semantic similarity* and *semantic relatedness* as it was made in Budanitsky and Hirst (2006) or in Zesch and Gurevych (2010) for instance. However, the limit between these two notions is sometimes hard to see in existing work as terms *semantic similarity* and *semantic relatedness* are often used interchangeably. Moreover, *semantic similarity* can be considered as included into *semantic relatedness* and the two problems are often tackled by using the same methods. In what follows, we will first try to differentiate *semantic similarity* and *semantic relatedness* globally through the use of two different reference resources and then, we will examine more closely what types of relations are present in a resource that accounts for *semantic relatedness*.

3.1 Building of a Distributional Thesaurus

The first step of the work we present here is evidently the building of a distribution thesaurus. In our case, this building was done from the AQUAINT-2 corpus, a corpus of about 380 million words comprising news articles in English. We chose to limit deliberately the preprocessing of texts to part-of-speech tagging and lemmatization. This seems to be a reasonable compromise, concerning the balance between the number of languages for which such tools exist and the quality of the resulting thesaurus, between the approach of Freitag et al. (2005), in which no normalization of words is carried out, and the more widespread use of syntactic parsers in work such as Curran and Moens (2002). More precisely, we used *TreeTagger* (Schmid 1994) for performing the linguistic preprocessing of the AQUAINT-2 corpus.

For the extraction of distributional data and the definition of a similarity measure from them, we selected the following parameters by relying on the extended TOEFL test of Freitag et al. (2005), similarly to Ferret (2010):

- distributional contexts based on graphical co-occurrents: co-occurrents collected in a fixed-size window centered on each occurrence of the target word. These co-occurrents were restricted to content words, i.e. nouns, verbs and adjectives;
- size of the window = 3 (one word on the left and right sides of the target word), i.e. very short range co-occurrents;
- soft filtering of contexts: removal of co-occurrents with only one occurrence;
- weighting function of co-occurrents in contexts = *Pointwise Mutual Information* (PMI) between the target word and the co-occurrent;
- similarity measure between contexts, for evaluating the semantic similarity of two words = *Cosine* measure.

The building of the thesaurus based on the similarity measure described above was performed as in Lin (1998) or Curran and Moens (2002) by extracting the closest semantic neighbors of each of its entries. More precisely, the selected measure was computed between each entry and its possible neighbors. These neighbors were then ranked in the decreasing order of the values of this measure and the first N ($N = 100$) neighbors were kept as the semantic neighbors of the entry. Both entries and possible neighbors were made of the AQUAINT-2 nouns whose frequency was higher than 10. Table 1 gives as examples the first neighbors

Table 1 First neighbors of some entries of our distributional thesaurus

Abnormality	defect [0.30], disorder [0.23], deformity [0.22], mutation [0.21], prolapse [0.21], anomaly [0.21] …
Agreement	accord [0.44], deal [0.41], pact [0.38], treaty [0.36], negotiation [0.35], proposal [0.32], arrangement [0.30] …
Cabdriver	waterworks [0.23], toolmaker [0.22], weaponeer [0.17], valkyry [0.17], wang [0.17], amusement-park [0.17] …
Machination	hollowness [0.15], share-price [0.12], clockmaker [0.12], huguenot [0.12], wrangling [0.12], alternation [0.12] …

of some entries of the resulting thesaurus with their similarity (in the range [0–1]) to their entry.

3.2 Evaluation of a Distributional Thesaurus

The examples of Table 1 clearly show that while *defect* or *disorder* for the entry *abnormality* or *accord* or *deal* for the entry *agreement* actually correspond to interesting semantic neighbors accounting for semantic similarity, *waterworks* for the entry *cabdriver* or *hollowness* for the entry *machination* do not appear as good semantic neighbors, even from the semantic relatedness viewpoint. From a general point of view, the evaluation of a distributional thesaurus can be achieved by means of an intrinsic or an extrinsic method. As our global objective is to have a deeper analysis of the kind of relations that are present in such thesaurus, we have chosen to adopt an intrinsic type of evaluation, as (Morlane-Hondère and Fabre 2012) for French, by comparing the semantic neighbors of our thesaurus with two complementary reference resources: WordNet 3.0 synonyms (Fellbaum 1998) [W], which characterize a semantic similarity based on paradigmatic relations, and the Moby thesaurus (Ward 1996) [M], which gathers a larger set of types of relations and is more representative of *semantic relatedness*.[2]

Table 2 shows the results of this evaluation. Its fourth column, which gives the average number of synonyms and similar words in our references for the AQUAINT-2 nouns, illustrates the difference of these two resources in terms of richness. A fusion of the two resources was also considered [WM]. As our main objective is to evaluate the extracted semantic neighbors and not the ability of our measure to rebuild the reference resources, these resources were filtered to discard entries and synonyms that are not part of the AQUAINT-2 vocabulary (see the difference between the number of words in the first column and the number of evaluated words of the third column). In distributional approaches, the frequency of words related to the size of the corpus is an important factor. Hence, we give our

[2] Although the Moby thesaurus contains not only synonyms, we will sometimes use the term *synonym* for referring to all the words associated to one of its entries.

Table 2 Evaluation of semantic neighbor extraction

Frequency	Ref.	#eval. words	#syn. / word	Recall	R-prec.	MAP	P@1	P@5	P@10	P@100
All 14,670	W	10,473	2.9	24.6	8.2	9.8	11.7	5.1	3.4	0.7
	M	9,216	50.0	9.5	6.7	3.2	24.1	16.4	13.0	4.8
	WM	12,243	38.7	9.8	7.7	5.6	22.5	14.1	10.8	3.8
High 4,378	W	3,690	3.7	28.3	11.1	12.5	17.2	7.7	5.1	1.0
	M	3,732	69.4	11.4	10.2	4.9	41.3	28.0	21.9	7.9
	WM	4,164	63.2	11.5	11.0	6.5	41.3	26.8	20.8	7.3
Middle 5,175	W	3,732	2.6	28.6	10.4	12.5	13.6	5.8	3.7	0.7
	M	3,306	41.3	9.3	6.5	3.1	18.7	13.1	10.4	3.8
	WM	4,392	32.0	9.8	9.3	7.4	20.9	12.3	9.3	3.2
Low 5,117	W	3,051	2.3	11.9	2.1	3.3	2.6	1.2	0.9	0.3
	M	2,178	30.1	2.8	1.2	0.5	2.5	1.5	1.5	0.9
	WM	3,687	18.9	3.5	2.1	2.4	3.3	1.7	1.5	0.7

results globally but also for three ranges of frequencies that split our vocabulary into roughly equal parts: *high* frequency nouns (frequency > 1,000), *middle* frequency nouns (100 < frequency ≤ 1,000) and *low* frequency nouns (10 < frequency ≤ 100). These results take the form of several measures and start at the fifth column by the proportion of the synonyms and similar words of our references that are found among the first 100 extracted neighbors of each noun. As these neighbors are ranked according to their similarity value with their target word, the evaluation measures can be taken from the Information Retrieval field by replacing documents with synonyms and queries with target words (see the four last columns of Table 2). The R-precision (R-prec.) is the precision after the first R neighbors were retrieved, R being the number of reference synonyms; the Mean Average Precision (MAP) is the average of the precision value after a reference synonym is found; precision at different cut-offs is given for the 1, 5, 10 and 100 first neighbors. All these values are given as percentages.

The results of Table 2 lead to three main observations. First, they have globally a low level. This weakness concerns both the recall of synonyms and their rank among semantic neighbors. Second, the level of results depends heavily on the frequency range of target words: the best results are obtained for high frequency words while evaluation measures decrease significantly for low frequency words. Finally, the characteristics of the reference resources have a significant impact on results. WordNet provides a restricted number of synonyms for each noun while the Moby thesaurus contains for each entry a large number of synonyms and similar words. As a consequence, the precision values at different cut-offs are significantly higher when Moby is used as a reference when compared to WordNet.

These three observations have to be kept in mind when these results are compared to other works. Curran and Moens (2002) is certainly the most comparable work to ours. It tested a large number of similarity measures based on syntactic co-occurrences by using them for extracting semantic neighbors. The evaluation of this extraction was done against the fusion of three thesauri: the Macquarie, Roget's and Moby thesauri. It focused on 70 nouns randomly chosen from WordNet such that they were representative of WordNet's nouns in terms of frequency, number of senses, specificity (depth in the hierarchy of WordNet) and domain. Among all tested measures, its best results were 76 % as precision at rank 1, 52 % at rank 5 and 45 % at rank 10 for 70 nouns while our best precision (high frequency words and [M] as reference) is 41.3 % at rank 1, 28.0 % at rank 5 and 21.9 % at rank 10 for 3,732 nouns. One possible explanation of this difference is the use of syntactic co-occurrences in Curran and Moens (2002) whereas our work exploits only window-based co-occurrences. However, we observed that the use of syntactic co-occurrences in our framework (see line A2ST-SYNT of Table 4 for global results with [WM] as reference) does not actually explain the difference with the results obtained by Curran and Moens (2002). The best precision, once again for high frequency words and [M] as reference (results not given in Table 4)—44.0 % at rank 1, 31.6 % at rank 5 and 25.2 % at rank 10 for 3,727 nouns—illustrates the fact that even if these values are significantly higher than the results of Table 2, it is also clear that this improvement is not very high in comparison with the values of Curran and Moens (2002).

The difference between our results and those of Curran and Moens (2002) is more completely explained by two other factors. The first one is the difference of richness of the two gold standards. In our case, the Moby thesaurus provides 50 synonyms on average while 331 synonyms are available for each of the 70 nouns considered in Curran and Moens (2002). The impact of the difference of richness we have noted above between WordNet and the Moby thesaurus—2.9 synonyms for each entry compared to 50 with a precision at rank 5 raising globally from 5.1 to 16.4—is a good illustration of that phenomenon. The second factor is the frequency range of words in the test sets. The test set of Curran and Moens (2002) was supposed to be balanced according to different parameters, including frequency. In fact, among the 69 words of this test set that are included in the AQUAINT-2 vocabulary, 65 words are part of our high frequency nouns while none are part of the low frequency nouns. Moreover, the *70w* line of Table 3 shows that the results for this test set are far better than for the whole set of our high frequency nouns. This observation is also valid for the larger test set used in Curran (2003) as 244 of its 296 evaluated entries are part of our high frequency nouns, only 3 are part of our low frequency nouns and the values of the evaluation measures for the line *300w* of Table 3 are far higher than the corresponding values for the whole set of our high frequency nouns.

Table 4 gives a larger perspective on the results by comparing, with [WM] as reference, our thesaurus (*A2ST*) to several thesauri built with other methods.

Table 3 Evaluation of extracted semantic neighbors for test sets of Curran (2003)

Test set	Ref.	#eval. words	#syn./ word	Recall	R-prec.	MAP	P@1	P@5	P@10	P@100
70w # 69	W	59	5.2	23.6	9.3	9.6	20.3	8.1	5.6	1.2
	M	64	103.2	11.2	11.4	5.1	54.7	43.1	33.3	11.6
	WM	65	103.1	11.2	12.0	5.8	55.4	43.4	33.5	11.6
300w # 296	W	247	4.7	27.2	12.3	12.7	19.8	8.4	5.8	1.3
	M	253	97.6	11.1	11.5	5.6	53.0	37.0	29.0	10.8
	WM	269	93.0	11.2	12.2	6.7	52.0	36.0	28.2	10.4

Table 4 Comparison of several approaches for building distributional thesauri

Method	#eval. words	#syn./ word	Recall	R-prec.	MAP	P@1	P@5	P@10	P@100
A2ST	12,243	38.7	9.8	7.7	5.6	22.5	14.1	10.8	3.8
A2ST-SYNT	11,887	39.4	13.2	10.7	7.9	29.4	18.9	14.6	5.2
Lin (1998)	9,823	44.5	12.7	11.6	8.1	36.1	23.7	18.2	5.6
Huang et al. (2012)	10,537	42.6	3.8	1.9	0.8	7.1	5.0	4.0	1.6
Mikolov et al. (2013)	12,326	38.6	6.2	5.5	4.2	16.3	9.5	7.0	2.4
ESA	7,756	44.3	7.0	6.9	5.1	13.2	9.1	7.3	3.1

(Lin 1998) is the thesaurus made available by Lin[3] and clearly outperforms all the thesauri of Table 4. The first reason of this superiority is the use of syntactic co-occurrences, which are known to give better results than window-based approaches (Curran and Moens 2002; Heylen et al. 2008). This is confirmed in our case by the superiority of A2ST-SYNT, a thesaurus based on the co-occurrences collected from the application of the Minipar parser (Lin 1994) to the AQUAINT-2 corpus,[4] over A2ST. The second reason of the superiority of the Lin thesaurus is its bias towards high and middle frequency words, which has clearly a positive impact as shown by the analysis of ours results: while the number of evaluated entries against WM for low frequency words is equal to 3,687 for AS2T, it is equal to 1,510 for the Lin thesaurus. This bias can be further perceived when considering the fact that the average number of synonyms and related words for each evaluated

[3] http://webdocs.cs.ualberta.ca/lindek/Downloads/sim.tgz.

[4] As for A2ST, the weighting function of co-occurrents was PMI, only the co-occurrents with one occurrence were filtered and the *Cosine* measure was applied for comparing distributional contexts.

entry is the highest among all thesauri of Table 4. Finally, it should be noted that the corpus of Lin was much larger than the AQUAINT-2 corpus, which is also a favorable factor.

At the other extremum, the worst results are obtained by the (Huang et al. 2012) thesaurus. As (Mikolov et al. 2013), (Huang et al. 2012) is a recent approach based on neural networks and produces word embeddings that can be used as distributional contexts for evaluating the semantic similarity of words. In the case of Huang et al. (2012), we relied on embeddings computed from Wikipedia[5] by the authors while for (Mikolov et al. 2013), we computed the embeddings from the AQUAINT-2 corpus with the best parameters of Mikolov et al. (2013). In both cases, the thesaurus was built by following the same process and the same similarity measure between contexts as for AS2ST and A2ST-SYNT. The weak performance of the (Huang et al. 2012) thesaurus may be partly explained by the fact that Wikipedia is quite different from the AQUAINT-2 corpus and perhaps not very well adapted to this task. But even if the (Mikolov et al. 2013) thesaurus outperforms significantly the (Huang et al. 2012) thesaurus, its performance is significantly worse than A2ST, which suggests that such models are probably not very suitable for building distributional thesauri, at least until now.

Finally, we also report on the results of a thesaurus built by relying on the Explicit Semantic Analysis (ESA), another popular approach for evaluating semantic similarity between words (Gabrilovich and Markovitch 2007). In this case, the thesaurus was constructed from ESA data coming from (Popescu and Grefenstette 2011)[6] for a smaller set of mainly high and middle frequency words. While ESA gets very good results on benchmarks such as WordSim 353, its performance in thesaurus building is not so high and quite close to the (Mikolov et al. 2013) thesaurus. A more complete overview should have included the use of Latent Semantic Analysis (Landauer and Dumais 1997) or Non-negative Matrix Factorization for building thesauri but Van de Cruys (2010) has already showed that these approaches do not lead to better results than A2ST, or A2ST-SYNT when syntactic analysis is exploited.

4 A Resource-Based Approach for Identifying Lexical Relations

4.1 Background

The kind of evaluation we have presented in the previous section is a first step for identifying the type of relations in distributional thesauri. However, if using the synonyms of WordNet as a reference provides direct knowledge of the presence of

---

5 http://nlp.stanford.edu/~socherr/ACL2012_wordVectorsTextFile.zip.

6 We thank more particularly Adrian Popescu for having given access to these data.

one type of relations, other relations such as those encoded in a resource such as the Moby thesaurus are not defined and seem in practice rather heterogeneous and sometimes even quite obscure, as for instance the relation between *accuracy* and *subtlety* or between *alarm* and *rocket*. As a consequence, going further in the analysis of the content of distributional thesauri requires considering explicitly a larger set of relations. A first step in this direction was taken by Heylen et al. (2008), who focused on a larger set of elementary relations, including synonymy, hypernymy and hyponymy, in addition to the composed relation of cohyponymy. However, such relations are far from covering all the relations in a resource such as the Moby Thesaurus, even by adding other "classical" elementary relations such as meronymy, holonymy or antonymy.

The most direct way to characterize these uncovered relations is to assume that they can be described as the composition of elementary relations, such as for cohyponymy. The idea of leveraging the compositionality of semantic relations is not new and was already developed in the context of textual inferences, first by Harabagiu and Moldovan (1998), who applied it to WordNet, and recently in a more formalized form by Blanco and Moldovan (2011). However, the objective of these works is not to account for the semantic similarity of words but to find relations between clauses or sentences. Hirst and St-Onge (1998) adopt a global perspective more focused on textual cohesion than on textual coherence but more importantly, define a set of patterns of composition of WordNet semantic relations that can be applied for building paths between words that are "indicative of some reasonable proximity". More precisely, they distinguish three kinds of elementary links:

- upward links (U), that correspond to generalization relations. They include hypernymy and meronymy;
- downward links (D), that correspond to specialization relations. They include hyponymy and holonymy;
- horizontal links (H), that keep the same meaning. They include synonymy and antonymy.

For building a semantic path between two words by combining these three kinds of links, Hirst and St-Onge (1998) defines three rules:

- an upward link cannot be preceded by another link, except an upward link. This means that a generalization can not be done after a specialization or even the passage through a word with a similar meaning, as this generalization may concern a dimension of the specialization that is not present in the source word;
- "at most one change of direction is allowed" as such change represents a significant semantic step.
- the second rule has one exception: a horizontal link is permitted between an upward and a downward link.

The application of these rules leads to the eight patterns of Fig. 2. In a pattern, each vector represents a sequence of elementary relations of the same type (U, D

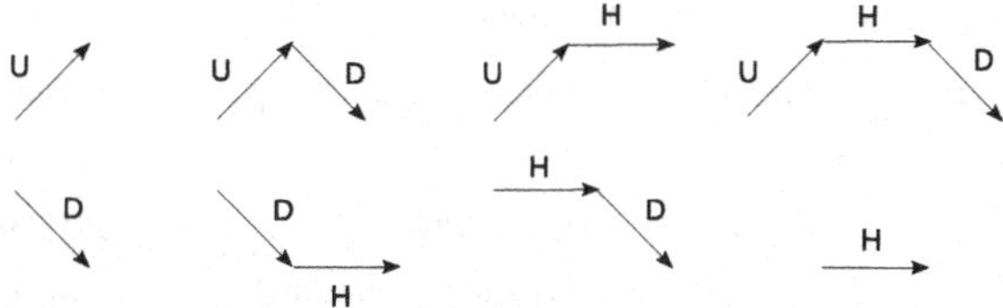

Fig. 2 Patterns of semantic relations from (Hirst and St-Onge 1998)

or H), with the global constraint that a path of relations is made at least of two elementary relations and at most of five relations.

The composition of different types of relations was also considered in work focusing on semantic similarity or relatedness measures in ontologies, such as (Mazuel and Sabouret 2008). However, Mazuel and Sabouret (2008) adopted the principles of Hirst and St-Onge (1998) for defining valid semantic paths between words and their proposal was mainly focused on a specific weighting of theses paths for the computation of a global similarity value.

4.2 Methodology

Despite the interest of the semantic paths defined in Hirst and St-Onge (1998) and used in Mazuel and Sabouret (2008), the main objective of these two works is different from ours: they want to define valid semantic paths between words to determine whether these words are semantically close while we are interested in characterizing the semantic relation underlying a pair of words found as semantically close, either by a human or an algorithm. More precisely, we do not want to be prescriptive but rather to observe what compositions of elementary semantic relations the given associations correspond to. The implementation of this approach is quite straightforward: given a reference resource containing known elementary semantic relations, WordNet in our case, a graph is built in such a way that each word of this resource is turned into a vertex and each semantic relation between two words is turned into an edge between the corresponding vertices. This edge is labeled by the identifier of the relation between the two words. The resulting graph is directed and unweighted as no type of relations is given preference over another. As a consequence, finding the combination of relations underlying the association of two words consists in searching the path that minimizes the number of relations between the two words, which is done by a breadth-first search in the graph.

The reference resource we have used for our experiments was the nominal subset of WordNet 3.0. We used NLTK (http://www.nltk.org) for the extraction of WordNet data and the igraph library (http://igraph.sourceforge.net) for representing the graph of relations and searching shortest paths in it. The resulting graph was made of 119,034 vertices, i.e. nouns (single terms and compounds), and 996,848 edges, i.e. semantic relations. All types of semantic relations between

Table 5 Semantic relations in WordNet for nouns

Macro-relation type	Macro id	WordNet relation type	Frequency	(%)
Equivalence	E	Synonymy	210,064	(21.0)
Generalization	G	Hypernymy	257,038	(25.8)
		Hypernymy (instance)	34,340	(3.4)
Specialization	G^{-1}	Hyponymy	257,038	(25.8)
		Hyponymy (instance)	34,340	(3.4)
Compound	C	Holonymy (part)	38,004	(3.8)
		Holonymy (substance)	2,789	(0.3)
		Holonymy (member)	60,229	(6.0)
Component	C^{-1}	Meronymy (part)	38,004	(3.8)
		Meronymy (substance)	2,789	(0.3)
		Meronymy (member)	60,229	(6.0)
Opposite	O	Antonymy	1,984	(0.2)

nouns in WordNet were considered, that is to say, the twelve types given by Table 5 together with their frequency in our graph. From the viewpoint of their extraction from WordNet (see Algorithm 1), the only difference to note is between relations whose arguments are directly words, more precisely synonymy and antonymy, and relations whose arguments are synsets, all the others, for which the extracted relations results from the Cartesian product of the synsets.

Algorithm 1 Extraction of all semantic relations between nouns in WordNet[7]

```
for all synset in noun_synsets do
    syns_lemmas ← synset.lemmas()
    ▷ dump synonyms
    print all pairs of syns_lemmas
    ▷ dump antonyms
    for all lemma in syns_lemmas do
        for all anto in lemma.antonyms() do
            print relations lemma → anto and anto → lemma
    ▷ dump all relations between synsets
    enumerateRelationsBetweenSynsets(syns_lemmas, synset.hyponyms())
    enumerateRelationsBetweenSynsets(syns_lemmas, synset.hypernym())
    idem with {part,substance,member}_meronyms(),
        {part,substance,member}_holonyms(),
        instance_hyponyms() and instance_hypernym

procedure ENUMERATERELATIONSBETWEENSYNSETS(source_lemmas,target_synsets)
    for all trgt_synset in target_synsets do
        for all srce_lem in source_lemmas do
            for all trgt_lem in trgt_synset.lemmas() do
                print relation srce_lem → trgt_lem and
                    inverse relation trgt_lem → srce_lem
```

As (Hirst and St-Onge 1998), we have grouped these relations types into larger sets, more precisely six macro-relations, organized in four groups:

- equivalence [E] (21.0 % of relations): two words have the same meaning, such as *car* and *automobile*;
- generalization/specialization [G/G^{-1}] (58.4 %): the source word refers to a generalization or a specialization of the concept referred by the target word. Specialization [G^{-1}] is considered as the inverse of Generalization [G];
- compound/component [C/C^{-1}] (20.2 %): one word refers to the component of a compound referred by the second word of the relation. Component [C^{-1}] is considered as the inverse of Compound [C];
- opposite [O] (0.2 %): two words with opposite meanings.

In comparison with (Hirst and St-Onge 1998), our macro-relations are less abstract as they do not focus only on the notion of level of generality, which makes the observation of a larger set of more precise patterns possible. From the viewpoint of frequency, the generalization/specialization relations are clearly dominant (nearly 60 % of relations) while the equivalence and compound/component relations have roughly the same number of occurrences. The opposite relations are marginal. This distribution of relations is naturally expected to have an impact on the observed patterns of relations, as we will first see for the Moby Thesaurus.

4.3 Application to the Moby Thesaurus

Following the methodology described in the previous section, we have used our graph of WordNet relations for finding what paths of those relations can be found between the 9,269 entries of the Moby Thesaurus and their semantic neighbors, which represents a set of 461,645 pairs of words. Only 3,129 of these pairs (0.7 %) were discarded, partly because at least one of their words was not part of WordNet. A total of 3,872 path types[7] were produced but the 75 most frequent path types represent 80 % of all types and the 190 most frequent represent 90 % of them. 1,319 (34.07 %) path types occurs only once.

Figure 3 gives the distribution of path lengths both at the level of occurrences and types. More precisely, it shows that while for occurrences, paths of length 3 and 4 are the most frequent, for types, paths of length 5 and 6 are dominant, which can be partly explained in this last case by a simple combinatorial effect as the number of types of paths tends to grow exponentially with their length.

Table 6 offers a more precise view of the most frequent types of paths found in the Moby Thesaurus. These path types are numbered according to the decreasing order of their frequency, given at the fourth column together with the percentage of

[7] A path type is made of a sequence of elementary relations while a path occurrence also includes the specific words that are linked.

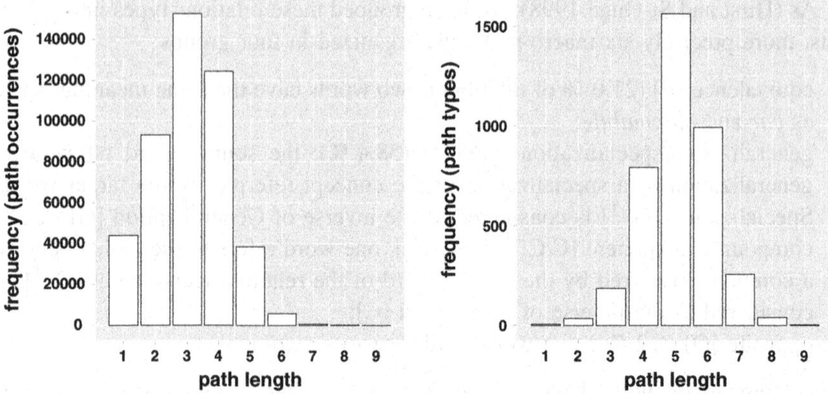

Fig. 3 Distribution of path lengths, both at the level of occurrences (*left*) and types (*right*)

all paths (in brackets). A ✔ in the second column indicates whether the path type corresponds to one of the patterns of Hirst and St-Onge (1998). Finally, path types are defined as sequences of elementary relations represented by their macro identifier of Table 5, with two specific notations: first, the sequence of n successive identical relations R is written as $R\{n\}$; second, two subsequences corresponding to well-known lexical relations are replaced by a specific identifier: h for the subsequence GG^{-1}, which corresponds to the cohyponymy relation and m for the subsequence CC^{-1}, which corresponds to the comeronymy relation.

The first thing to notice from Table 6 is the great diversity of path types and the limited number of occurrences of each type: the most frequent type covers only 9 % of all paths. Despite their diversity, these path types are far from exploiting the full range of available elementary relations equally: they are mainly made of generalization (G), specialization (G^{-1}) and equivalence (E) relations. Compound/ component relations occur in only the 54th and 58th types and the opposite relation in the 143th type. This is hardly surprising for the opposite relation, which is not very frequent in WordNet, but compound/component relations are almost as frequent in WordNet as the equivalence relation while they are present in only 3 path types among the first 80 % of them and in 32 types for the first 90 %.

Table 6 also illustrated the interest of the notion of compound relation as the first four path types are made of several elementary relations. The first one is somehow special in this respect as it corresponds to a known relation—cohyponymy—but the three others are not considered as "classical" lexical relations. The second can be interpreted as a specialization of a cohyponym, such as in the associations (*abolition*, *annulment*) or (*cataclysm*, *debacle*), the third one as a cohyponym of a generalization, such as in the associations (*abyss*, *rift*) or (*algorithm*, *routine*), and the fourth one as a kind of cohyponymy one level higher, such as in the associations (*maelstrom*, *turmoil*) or (*liturgy*, *vesper*).

This kind of analysis is also a way to detect associations that are questionable in a resource such as Moby. For instance, the association (*ablation*, *waste*) is not very

Table 6 First 60 most frequent semantic paths for the associations of the Moby Thesaurus

1	✔	h	41,508	(9.0)	21	✔	$G^{-1}\{3\}$	4,254	(0.9)	41		$G^{-1}Gh$	1,940	(0.4)
2	✔	hG^{-1}	29,853	(6.5)	22		GhE	4,078	(0.9)	42		$G^{-1}G\{2\}$	1,894	(0.4)
3	✔	Gh	26,969	(5.8)	23	✔	$G^{-1}E$	3,965	(0.9)	43	✔	$G^{-1}\{2\}E$	1,824	(0.4)
4	✔	GhG^{-1}	17,476	(3.8)	24		EG	3,798	(0.8)	44		GEh	1,736	(0.4)
5		E	15,708	(3.4)	25		EhG^{-1}	3,720	(0.8)	45	✔	$GE\{2\}$	1,618	(0.4)
6		G^{-1}	13,930	(3.0)	26	✔	$G\{3\}$	3,675	(0.8)	46	✔	$E\{2\}G^{-1}$	1,540	(0.3)
7		G	13,078	(2.8)	27		GhG	3,606	(0.8)	47		$EG\{2\}$	1,534	(0.3)
8		hh	11,993	(2.6)	28	✔	GEG^{-1}	3,309	(0.7)	48		$EG^{-1}G$	1,483	(0.3)
9		hG	10,156	(2.2)	29		$G^{-1}hG^{-1}$	3,186	(0.7)	49		GEG	1,412	(0.3)
10		hE	9,657	(2.1)	30		$hG^{-1}E$	3,159	(0.7)	50		$G^{-1}\{2\}h$	1,383	(0.3)
11	✔	$G^{-1}\{2\}$	9,240	(2.0)	31	✔	$GhG^{-1}\{2\}$	3,098	(0.7)	51		$G^{-1}EG^{-1}$	1,378	(0.3)
12		$G^{-1}h$	8,883	(1.9)	32	✔	$EG^{-1}\{2\}$	2,910	(0.6)	52		$hG\{2\}$	1,365	(0.3)
13	✔	$hG^{-1}\{2\}$	8,489	(1.8)	33	✔	$G\{2\}hG^{-1}$	2,813	(0.6)	53		hGE	1,364	(0.3)
14		Eh	8,459	(1.8)	34	✔	$G\{2\}E$	2,696	(0.6)	54	✔	hC^{-1}	1,359	(0.3)
15	✔	$G\{2\}$	8,267	(1.8)	35		$hG^{-1}G$	2,632	(0.6)	55		$G^{-1}GE$	1,311	(0.3)
16	✔	$G\{2\}h$	6,929	(1.5)	36		Ghh	2,338	(0.5)	56		$EG^{-1}h$	1,286	(0.3)
17	✔	EG^{-1}	5,356	(1.2)	37		EGh	2,298	(0.5)	57		$EG^{-1}E$	1,264	(0.3)
18	✔	GE	5,223	(1.1)	38		$G^{-1}\{2\}G$	2,251	(0.5)	58	✔	Ch	1,231	(0.3)
19		$G^{-1}G$	5,095	(1.1)	39		hhG^{-1}	2,216	(0.5)	59		EhE	1,204	(0.3)
20	✔	$E\{2\}$	4,979	(1.1)	40		hEG^{-1}	2,044	(0.4)	60	✔	$GEG^{-1}\{2\}$	1,128	(0.2)

intuitive but is "justified" by the path type *Gh* with the following path: *ablation* –(G)– *operation* –(G)– *activity* –(G^{-1})– *waste*. In this case, the generalization up to a general term such as *activity* explains that *ablation* and *waste* can be linked. This does not invalidate a path type such as *Gh* but suggests that the level of the WordNet hierarchy associated to a term could be taken into account, similarly to Wu and Palmer (1994) for their measure, to detect associations whose validity or interest are probably low.

Finally, it is interesting to note that even among the most frequent path types, a significant part of them, even if we let aside one-relation paths, are not considered as valid according to the criteria of Hirst and St-Onge (1998). The generalization of a cohyponym (*hG*) is for instance a very frequent compound relation, giving associations such as (*newsletter*, *journalism*) or (*opinion*, *appraisal*), but is not permitted by Hirst and St-Onge (1998). Conversely, the association (*ablation*, *waste*) is not filtered by these criteria, despite its questionable validity. In practice, the rules defined by Hirst and St-Onge (1998) are probably too strict given variabilities in the intuition-based construction of the hierarchy of WordNet and moreover, they are not adapted to the level of terms in this hierarchy.

4.4 Application to a Distributional Thesaurus

In the previous section, we have reported on the analysis of the associations that are present in one reference resource used for evaluating distributional thesauri. We now report on the analysis of our A2ST distributional thesaurus according to the same criteria. 10,473 entries of this thesaurus were considered with the subset of their neighbors that are part of WordNet, which represents 1,120,530 associations. A total of 15,683 path types were found for these associations, with the 342 most frequent types representing 80 % of all types and the 939 most frequent, 90 % of them. 6,374 path types (40.6 %) have only one occurrence. Finally, at the level of occurrences, paths of lengths 4 and 5 are the two most frequent while at the level of types, paths of lengths 5 and 6 are dominant.

A clear difference with the Moby Thesaurus appears when considering these global statistics only: path types for A2ST are far more numerous than for Moby, with a larger proportion of them being hapaxes, their distribution is more flat and they have a higher length. All these tendencies characterize the fact that semantic paths in WordNet are more representative of relations in Moby than in A2ST and as a consequence, that the relations in A2ST are not as good as the relations in Moby from a semantic viewpoint.

Table 7 offers a closer look at the differences between A2ST and Moby by comparing their first 20 most frequent path types. The most noticeable point is the absence of one-relation paths in the case of A2ST whereas three of them are present among the first seven paths for Moby. Moreover, the first path for A2ST is more complex, which also means more uncertain, than for Moby and a path such as *hh*, which is discarded according to Hirst and St-Onge (1998), is more frequent

Table 7 Comparison of the 20 most frequent semantic paths for the A2ST and the Moby thesauri

A2ST					Moby				
1	✔	GhG^{-1}	50,706	(4.5)	1	✔	h	41,508	(9.0)
2	✔	Gh	38,852	(3.5)	2	✔	hG^{-1}	29,853	(6.5)
3	✔	hG^{-1}	38,838	(3.5)	3	✔	Gh	26,969	(5.8)
4		hh	36,940	(3.3)	4	✔	GhG^{-1}	17,476	(3.8)
5	✔	h	35,937	(3.2)	5		E	15,708	(3.4)
6	✔	$hG^{-1}\{2\}$	23,523	(2.1)	6		G^{-1}	13,930	(3.0)
7	✔	$GhG^{-1}\{2\}$	22,613	(2.0)	7		G	13,078	(2.8)
8	✔	G{2}h	22,331	(2.0)	8		hh	11,993	(2.6)
9	✔	$G\{2\}hG^{-1}$	20,269	(1.8)	9		hG	10,156	(2.2)
10		Ghh	19,349	(1.7)	10		hE	9,657	(2.1)
11		hhG^{-1}	17,789	(1.6)	11	✔	$G^{-1}\{2\}$	9,240	(2.0)
12		hG	16,323	(1.5)	12		$G^{-1}h$	8,883	(1.9)
13		$G^{-1}h$	12,377	(1.1)	13	✔	$hG^{-1}\{2\}$	8,489	(1.8)
14		GhG	10,810	(1.0)	14		Eh	8,459	(1.8)
15		EhG^{-1}	9,870	(0.9)	15	✔	G{2}	8,267	(1.8)
16		Eh	9,259	(0.8)	16	✔	G{2}h	6,929	(1.5)
17		$hG^{-1}h$	8,778	(0.8)	17	✔	EG^{-1}	5,356	(1.2)
18		GhE	8,315	(0.7)	18	✔	GE	5,223	(1.1)
19		hE	8,261	(0.7)	19		$G^{-1}G$	5,095	(1.1)
20		$hG^{-1}G$	8,202	(0.7)	20	✔	E{2}	4,979	(1.1)

than the cohyponymy relation *h*, the most frequent relation in Moby. This tendency is more general as the average length of these 20 path types is significantly higher for A2ST (3.85) than for Moby (2.55).

5 Conclusion

As pointed out in a large part of the work by Michael Zock, the notion of dictionary is central for lexical access tasks. Moreover, this dictionary must be associated with an index structure made of a large set of various relations between words. When the lexical access is performed by a writer or a speaker who wants to express an idea, these relations have to be labeled by their type. If building large networks of lexical associations from corpora is not a difficult problem, labeling such lexical associations is still an open issue. In this chapter, we have presented two different ways to tackle this problem. The first one, resulting from a joint work with Michael Zock (Ferret and Zock 2006), is an indirect method that relies on a process associated with a specific type of relations, in our case topical relations, for selecting this type of relations. The second work explores the use of the semantic relations of a reference resource, more precisely WordNet, for characterizing the relations underlying the semantic neighbors in distributional thesauri. This characterization is performed by creating compound relations from the sequences of relations built for linking thesaurus' entries with their neighbors. We have first applied this method to analyze the relations of the Moby Thesaurus, one of the resources we use for evaluating distributional thesauri, and then, to analyze directly the relations in such thesaurus.

Our use of WordNet for creating compound relations is a preliminary work that can be extended in many ways. Until now, we have built compound relations without looking at their semantic validity. The most straightforward extension in this direction would be to rely on compound relations built from a resource such as Moby for defining more generally which compound relations are valid. However, as we have seen that some Moby's relations are questionable, a more complex solution has to be found, probably by taking into account the position of the terms to link in the WordNet hierarchy. Another limit of the current work is that we have considered only relations between nouns. As WordNet is not very rich in terms of relations between words belonging to different morphosyntactic categories, we will have to use resources such as FrameNet for enlarging the set of types of relations we can characterize.

References

Blanco, E., & Moldovan, D. (2011). Unsupervised learning of semantic relation composition. In *49th Annual Meeting of the Association for Computational Linguistics: Human Language Technologies (ACL-HLT 2011)* (pp. 1456–1465). Portland, Oregon.

Budanitsky, A., & Hirst, G. (2006). Evaluating WordNet-based measures of lexical semantic relatedness. *Computational Linguistics, 32*(1), 13–47.

Curran, J. R. (2003). *From distributional to semantic similarity*. Ph.D. thesis, University of Edinburgh.

Curran, J. R., & Moens, M. (2002). Improvements in automatic thesaurus extraction. In *Workshop of the ACL Special Interest Group on the Lexicon (SIGLEX)* (pp. 59–66). Philadelphia, USA.

Fellbaum, C. (Ed.). (1998). *WordNet: An electronic lexical database*. Cambridge: The MIT Press.

Ferret, O. (2002). Using collocations for topic segmentation and link detection. In *19th International Conference on Computational Linguistics (COLING 2002)* (pp. 260–266). Taipei, Taiwan.

Ferret, O. (2006). Building a network of topical relations from a corpus. In *5th International Conference on Language Resources and Evaluation (LREC 2006)* (pp. 575–580). Genova, Italy.

Ferret, O. (2010). Testing semantic similarity measures for extracting synonyms from a corpus. In *Seventh conference on international language resources and evaluation (LREC'10)*. Valletta, Malta.

Ferret, O., & Zock, M. (2006). Enhancing electronic dictionaries with an index based on associations. In *21st International Conference on Computational Linguistics and 44th Annual Meeting of the Association for Computational Linguistics (COLING-ACL 2006)* (pp. 281–288). Sydney, Australia.

Firth, J. R. (1957). A synopsis of linguistic theory 1930–1955. In *Studies in linguistic analysis* (pp. 1–32). Oxford: Blackwell.

Freitag, D., Blume, M., Byrnes, J., Chow, E., Kapadia, S., & Rohwer, R., et al. (2005). New experiments in distributional representations of synonymy. In *Ninth Conference on Computational Natural Language Learning (CoNLL)* (pp. 25–32). Ann Arbor, MI, USA.

Gabrilovich, E., & Markovitch, S. (2007). Computing semantic relatedness using wikipedia-based explicit semantic analysis. In *20th International Joint Conference on Artificial Intelligence (IJCAI 2007)* (pp. 6–12).

Grefenstette, G. (1994). *Explorations in automatic thesaurus discovery.* Boston: Kluwer Academic Publishers.

Halliday, M. A. K., & Hasan, R. (1976). *Cohesion in English.* London: Longman.

Harabagiu, S., & Moldovan, D. (1998). Knowledge processing on extended WordNet. In C. Fellbaum (Ed.), *WordNet: An electronic lexical database* (pp. 379–405). Cambridge: MIT Press.

Hearst, M. A. (1994). Multi-paragraph segmentation of expository text. In *32th Annual Meeting of the Association for Computational Linguistics (ACL'94)* (pp. 9–16). Las Cruces, New Mexico, USA.

Heylen, K., Peirsmany, Y., Geeraerts, D., & Speelman, D. (2008). Modelling word similarity: An evaluation of automatic synonymy extraction algorithms. In *Sixth Conference on International Language Resources and Evaluation (LREC 2008).* Marrakech, Morocco.

Hindle, D. (1990). Noun classification from predicate-argument structures. In *28th Annual Meeting of the Association for Computational Linguistics (ACL 1990)* (pp. 268–275). Pittsburgh, Pennsylvania, USA.

Hirst, G., & St-Onge, D. (1998). Lexical chains as representations of context for the detection and correction of malapropisms. In C. Fellbaum (Ed.), *WordNet: an electronic lexical database* (pp. 305–332). Cambridge: MIT Press.

Huang, E. H., Socher, R., Manning, C. D., & Ng, A. Y. (2012). Improving word representations via global context and multiple word prototypes. In *50th Annual Meeting of the Association for Computational Linguistics (ACL'12)* (pp. 873–882).

Landauer, T. K., & Dumais, S. T. (1997). A solution to Plato's problem: The latent semantic analysis theory of acquisition, induction, and representation of knowledge. *Psychological Review, 104*(2), 211–240.

Lin, D. (1994). PRINCIPAR: An efficient, broad-coverage, principle-based parser. In *COLING'94* (pp 42–48). Kyoto, Japan.

Lin, D. (1998). Automatic retrieval and clustering of similar words. In *17th International Conference on Computational Linguistics and 36th Annual Meeting of the Association for Computational Linguistics (ACL-COLING'98)* (pp. 768–774). Montréal, Canada.

Marton, Y. (2013). Distributional phrasal paraphrase generation for statistical machine translation. *ACM Transactions on Intelligent Systems and Technology, 4*(3), 1–32.

Mazuel, L., & Sabouret, N. (2008). Semantic relatedness measure using object properties in an ontology. In *7th International Conference on The Semantic Web (ISWC'08)* (pp. 681–694). Springer, Karlsruhe, Germany.

Mel'čuk, I. A., & Polguère, A. (1987). A formal lexicon in the meaning-text theory or (how to do lexica with words). *Computational Linguistics, 13*(3–4), 261–275.

Mikolov, T., Yih, W. -T., & Zweig, G. (2013). Linguistic regularities in continuous space word representations. In *2013 Conference of the North American Chapter of the Association for Computational Linguistics: Human Language Technologies (NAACL HLT 2013)* (pp. 746–751). Atlanta, Georgia.

Min, B., Shi, S., Grishman, R., & Lin, C. Y. (2012). Ensemble semantics for large-scale unsupervised relation extraction. In *2012 Joint Conference on Empirical Methods in Natural Language Processing and Computational Natural Language Learning (EMNLP-CoNLL 2012)* (pp. 1027–1037). Jeju Island, Korea.

Morlane-Hondère, F., & Fabre, C. (2012). Le test de substituabilité à l'épreuve des corpus : utiliser l'analyse distributionnelle automatique pour l'étude des relations lexicales. In *Congrès Mondial de Linguistique Française (CMLF 2012)* (pp. 1001–1015). EDP Sciences, Lyon, France.

Morris, J., & Hirst, G. (2004). Non-classical lexical semantic relations. In *Workshop on Computational Lexical Semantics of Human Language Technology Conference of the North American Chapter of the Association for Computational Linguistics* (pp, 46–51). Boston, MA.

Popescu, A., & Grefenstette, G. (2011). Social media driven image retrieval. In *1st ACM International Conference on Multimedia Retrieval (ICMR'11), ACM* (pp. 1–8). Trento, Italy.

Schmid, H. (1994). Probabilistic part-of-speech tagging using decision trees. In *International Conference on New Methods in Language Processing.*

Van de Cruys, T. (2010). Mining for meaning. *The extraction of Lexico-semantic knowledge from text.* Ph.D. thesis. The Netherlands: University of Groningen.

Ward, G. (1996). Moby thesaurus. Moby Project.

Weeds, J. (2003). *Measures and applications of lexical distributional similarity.* Ph.D. thesis, Department of Informatics, University of Sussex.

Wu, Z., & Palmer, M. (1994). Verbs semantics and lexical selection. In *32nd Annual Meeting of the Association for Computational Linguistics (ACL'94)* (pp. 133–138). Las Cruces, New Mexico, USA.

Zesch, T., & Gurevych, I. (2010). Wisdom of crowds versus wisdom of linguists: Measuring the semantic relatedness of words. *Natural Language Engineering, 16*(1), 25–59.

Zock, M. (1996). The power of words in message planning. In *16th International Conference on Computational Linguistics (COLING 1996)* (pp. 990–995). Copenhagen, Denmark.

Zock, M. (2002). Sorry, what was your name again, or how to overcome the tip-of-the tongue problem with the help of a computer? In *SEMANET'02: Workshop on Building and Using Semantic Networks* (pp. 1–6), Taipei, Taiwan.

Zock, M., & Bilac, S. (2004). Word lookup on the basis of associations: From an idea to a roadmap. In *COLING 2004 Workshop: Enhancing and Using Electronic Dictionaries* (pp. 29–35). Geneva, Switzerland.

Zock, M., & Quint, J. (2004). Why have them work for peanuts, when it is so easy to provide reward? Motivations for converting a dictionary into a drill tutor. In *5th Workshop on Multilingual Lexical Databases*. Grenoble, France.

Multilingual Conceptual Access to Lexicon Based on Shared Orthography: An Ontology-Driven Study of Chinese and Japanese

Chu-Ren Huang and Ya-Min Chou

Abstract In this paper we propose a model for ontology-driven conceptual access to multilingual lexicon taking advantage of the cognitive-conceptual structure of radical system embedded in shared orthography of Chinese and Japanese. Our proposal rely crucially on two facts. First, both Chinese and Japanese use Chinese characters (hanzi/kanji) in their orthography. Second, the Chinese character orthography is anchored on a system of radical parts which encodes basic concepts. Each character as an orthographic unit contains radicals which indicate the broad semantic class of the meaning of that unit. Our study utilizes the homomorphism between the Chinese hanzi and Japanese kanji systems, but goes beyond the character-to-character mapping of kanji-hanzi conversion, to identify bilingual word correspondences. We use bilingual dictionaries, including WordNets, to verify semantic relation between the cross-lingual pairs. These bilingual pairs are then mapped to ontology of characters structured according to the organization of the basic concepts of radicals. The conceptual structure of the radical ontology is proposed as the model for simultaneous conceptual access to both languages. A study based on words containing characters composed of the "口 (mouth)" radical is given to illustrate the proposal and the actual model. It is suggested that the proposed model has the conceptual robustness to be applied to other languages based on the fact that it works now for two typologically very different languages and that the model contains Generative Lexicon (GL)-like coercive links to account for a wide range of possible cross-lingual semantic relations.

C.-R. Huang (✉)
The Hong Kong Polytechnic University, Hong Kong, China
e-mail: churen.huang@polyu.edu.hk

Y.-M. Chou
National Taipei University, Taipei, Taiwan
e-mail: milesymchou@gmail.com

© Springer International Publishing Switzerland 2015

N. Gala et al. (eds.), *Language Production, Cognition, and the Lexicon*,
Text, Speech and Language Technology 48, DOI 10.1007/978-3-319-08043-7_9

Keywords Ontology · Chinese hanzi · Japanese kanji · orthography · Generative Lexicon · SUMO · Cross-lingual cognitive access

1 Motivation

Computational conceptual access to multilingual lexicon can be achieved through the use of ontology or WordNet as interlingual links. Some languages do conventionally encode semantic classification information, such as the linguistic system of classifiers (e.g. Huang and Ahrens 2003; Shirai et al. 2008) or the orthographic system of characters (e.g. Chou and Huang 2006, 2010; Chu et al. 2012). We attempt to make use of conventionally encoded linguistic knowledge for conceptual access to lexical information.

On the other hand, even though ontology seems to be a natural choice for conceptual framework to access multilingual lexical information, there is no large-scale implementation nor is there any direct evidence for psychological reality of the frameworks of ontology. Hence, we hope that using a conventionalized semantic classification system will mitigate some of the problems and provide the constructed ontology some motivation since they are the shared and implicit conceptual systems.

2 Background

2.1 *Hanzi and Kanji: Shared Orthography of Two Typologically Different Languages*

Chinese and Japanese are two typologically different languages sharing the same orthography since they both use Chinese characters in written text. What makes this sharing of orthography unique among languages in the world is that Chinese characters (*kanji* in Japanese and *hanzi* in Chinese) explicitly encode information of semantic classification bases on a system of radicals to represent basic concepts shared by a family of characters (Xyu CE 121; Hsieh and Lin 1997; Chou and Huang 2006, 2010). This partially explains the process of Japanese adopting Chinese orthography even though the two languages are not related. The adaptation is supposed to be based on meaning and not on cognates sharing some linguistic forms. However, this meaning-based view of kanji/hanzi orthography faces a great challenge given the fact that Japanese and Chinese form-meaning pair do not have strict one-to-one mapping. There are meanings instantiated with different forms, as well as same forms representing different meanings. The character 湯 is one of most famous *faux amis*. It stands for 'hot soup' in Chinese and 'hot spring' in Japanese. In sum, these are two languages where their forms are supposed to be organized according to meanings, but show inconsistencies. It is this fact that these two languages adopt the same cognitive-conceptual based organization of the radical system yet each, through natural evolution, added variations to the kind of associations link to the same semantic primitive (and sometimes the same character), which limited the success rate of the earlier studies based on direct character-to-character kanji-kanzi mapping (Tan and Nagao 1995; Goh et al. 2005, among others). This is also the reason why the radical system as ontology approach proposed by Chou and Huang (2006) and followed by others (Huang et al. 2008; Chou and Huang 2010; Chu et al. 2012, etc.) is not only very successful but has the potential to shed light on how potentially different cognitive strategies are employed to access lexical concepts in these two languages.

It is important to note that WordNet and the Chinese character orthography are not as different as they appear. WordNet assumes that there are some generalizations in how concepts are clustered and lexically organized in languages and proposes an explicit lexical level representation framework which can be applied to all languages in the world. Chinese character orthography intuited that there are some conceptual bases for how meaning are lexical realized and organized, hence devised a sub-lexical level representation to represent semantic clusters. Based on this observation, the study of cross-lingual homo-forms between Japanese and Chinese in the context of WordNet offers a window for different approaches to lexical conceptualization. Since Japanese and Chinese use the same character set with the same semantic primitives (i.e. radicals), we can compare their conceptual system with the same atoms when there are variations in meanings of the same word-forms. When this is overlaid over WordNet, we get to compare the ontology of the two representation systems.

2.2 Hantology and the Ontologization of the Semantic Classification of the Radicals

Our design of Hantology (Chou and Huang 2006, 2010) differs from other word-based ontology. A typical word-based ontology is WordNet which describes the different relations among synonyms (Miller 1995; Fellbaum 1998). All of the relations among synonyms are based on the senses of words. Therefore, WordNet only needs to take senses into consideration. Hantology is more complicated than WordNet because it describes orthographic forms, pronunciations, senses, variants, lexicalization. This approach can systematically illustrate the development of the Chinese writing system.

Hantology also provides mapping with Sinica Bilingual Ontological WordNet (Sinica BOW, Huang et al. 2010). Sinica BOW is a Chinese-English Ontology and have mapping with WordNet and Suggested Upper Merged Ontology (SUMO, Niles and Pease 2001). In this resource, character-based and word-based ontologies are integrated to provide resources from character to word for Chinese language processing (Fig. 1).

Fig. 1 The mapping among Hantology, Sinica BOW and WordNet

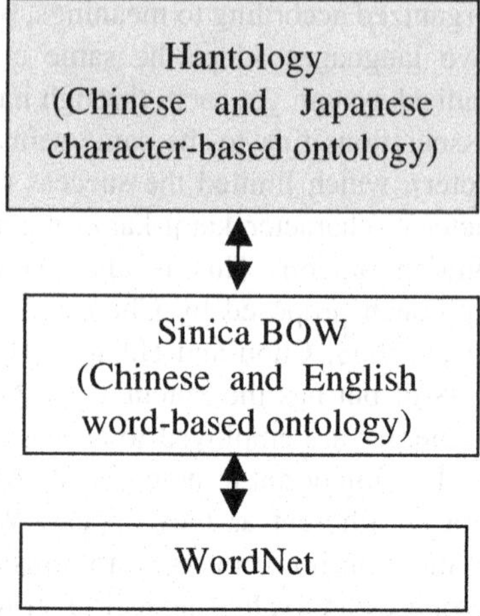

The structure of Hantology is divided into three parts: orthography, pronunciation, and lexicalization. The orthographic part of Hantology describes the structure of characters, the principles of formatting characters, the evolution of script, glyph expression, the relation of variant and the spread of Chinese characters.

(1) The structure of characters describes the components of each hanzi/kanji, including semantic and phonetic symbols.
(2) The principles of formatting Chinese characters encode the classification of the relation used to compose the character from its components: The pictographic characters were formed by reformatting the pictures of concrete objects. The ideographic (zhi3shi4, refer-event) characters are formed by abstract representation of a concept. The compound ideographic characters are formed by combining two or more semantic symbols. The semantic-phonetic (xing2-sheng1) characters, representing over 90 % of Chinese character in Kaiti script, are formed by combining a semantic symbol and a phonetic symbol (Li 1997).
(3) The evolution of script illustrates the different scripts of Chinese characters. The script is a kind of writing style. Because Chinese characters have been used for thousands years, the scripts have changed. The orthographic forms do not change with different scripts. Hantology provides Bronze, Lesser Seal, Kaishu scripts to illustrate evolution of Chinese scripts used from 3,000 years ago.
(4) Variants are the characters with different orthographic forms with identical pronunciation and meaning. For example, Chinese characters 台 and 臺 are variants. Variants relations are an important feature in Hantology, similar to WordNet synset relations.

The Japanese language continues to evolve and change after the adoption of Chinese characters. Hence the kanji system includes both historical changes and cross-lingual variations (Nakada and Hayashi 2000; Sugimoto 1998; Chou 2012). The kanji system has its own variants which are not necessarily the same set of variants in the hanzi system. Most of Chinese characters adopted by simplified kanji are the variants already used in Chinese. For example, '国' is a simplified kanji of traditional kanji '國'. In addition, Chinese character '国' is also the variant of Chinese character '國'. So, '國' and '国' both are variants in Chinese and Japanese. But, some simplified kanji are not variants used in Chinese. For example, new kanji '欠' is the variant of old kanji '缺' in Japan (Morohashi 1960; Hiroyuki et al. 2003). However, '欠' is not the variant of '缺' in Chinese.

The second reason of the kanji orthographic form to be changed is that Japan not only adopted Chinese characters but also have created hundreds of kanji known as Kokuji (国字). Most Kokuji characters have only Japanese pronunciations. Some of Kokuji have been adopted in Chinese. For example, Kokuji '癌' is also borrowed by Chinese. The meaning of '癌' is the same both in Japanese and Chinese.

3 Preliminaries: Orthography Based Mapping of Chinese and Japanese Words

3.1 EDR Japanese-English Dictionary

The Japanese-English dictionary of *EDR Electronic Dictionary* is a machine-tractable dictionary that contains the lexical knowledge of Japanese and English (Yokoi 1995).[1] It contains list of 165,695 Japanese words (jwd) and each of their related information. In this experiment, the English synset, definition and the Part-of-Speech category (POS) of each jwd are used to determine the semantic relations.

We assume that the concept, synonyms, near-synonyms, and paraphrases are the synset of each jwd. In the case when there is no English definition for the word, we assume that there are no equivalent English terms. Hence concept definition of the jwd is directly adopted.

3.2 SinicaBow

In the previous experiment, the CWN, which contains a list of 8,624 Chinese word (cwd) entries, was used as the cwd data, however since the number of cwds was too small, many jwds were not mapped, even when there is actually a corresponding Chinese and Japanese word pairs exists. This time we adopt SinicaBow, which contains 99,642 entries, hoping to find more valid corresponding Chinese and Japanese word pairs. In SinicaBow, each entry is a definition and it contains one or more cwds corresponds to the definition. In this experiment, the English synset, definition and the POS of each cwd are used to determine the semantic relations.

[1] http://www2.nict.go.jp/r/r312/EDR/index.html.

3.3 List of Kanji Variants

List of 125 pairs of manually matched Chinese and Japanese characters with variant glyph forms provided by Kyoto University. Some Japanese kanji and Chinese hanzi have identical property but have different font and Unicode. This resource contains list of Japanese kanji and Chinese hanzi pairs that the kanji properties are exactly the same but the forms and the Unicode are different.

During the mapping procedure, whenever a Japanese kanji and a Chinese hanzi being compared are in the variant list and are the variants of each other, they are considered to be the identical hanzi.

3.4 Procedure

3.4.1 Kanji Mapping

Each jwd is mapped to the corresponding cwd according to their kanji similarity. Such mapping pairs are divided into the following three groups:

(1) *Identical Kanji Sequence Pairs,* where the numbers of kanji in the jwd and cwd are identical and the nth characters in the two words are also identical. E.g. 頭, 歌手

(2) *Different Kanji Order Pairs,* where the numbers of kanji in the jwd and cwd are identical, and the kanji appear in the two words are identical, but the order is different.

E.g. Japanese	Chinese
制限	限制
律法	法律

(3) *Partially Identical Pairs,* where at least half kanji in the shorter word matches with the part of the longer word. In the case when the shorter word has 4 or less kanji, 2 of the kanji have to be in the longer word. In the case when the shorter word is only 1 kanji, the pair is not considered. jwd matches with a kanji in the cwd.

E.g., Japanese	Chinese
浅黄色	棕黄色
	蛋黄色的
	黄色的
宇宙飛行体	飛行
	飛行的
	etc...

In the case no corresponding pair relation (one of the three groups explained above) is found for a jwd or a cwd, each word is classified to one of the following group

Table 1 Chinese and Japanese Hanzi similarity distribution

	Number of words	Number of Chinese and Japanese word pairs
(1) Identical hanzi sequence pairs	2,815 jwds	20,199
(2) Different hanzi order pairs	204 jwds	473
(3) Partly identical pairs	264,917 jwds	8,438,099
(4) Independent japanese	57,518 jwds	–
(5) Independent chinese	851 cwds	–

(4) unmapped jwd is classified to an independent Japanese
(5) unmapped cwd is classified to an independent Chinese

Chinese and Japanese word pairs in such mapping groups are classified in the following manner:

(1) A jwd and a cwd are compared. If the words are identical, then they are an identical kanji sequence pair.
(2) If the pair is found to be not an identical kanji sequence pair, check if the pair has identical kanji in different order (equal length). If so, then they are a different kanji order pair.
(3) If the pair is found to be not a different kanji order pair, then check the partial identity of the pair. Meanwhile, if they are partially identical (according to the characteristics of partially identical pairs described above), the pair is classified to a partially identical pair.

After the mapping process, if the jwd is not mapped to any of the cwd, the jwd is classified to (4) independent Japanese group. If a cwd is not mapped by any of the jwd, it is classified to (5) independent Chinese group.

The number of Japanese kanji- Chinese hanzi pairs' similarity distribution is shown in Table 1.

3.4.2 Finding Synonymous Relation (Word Relation)

After the kanji mapping, each of (1) identical kanji sequence pairs, (2) different kanji order pairs and (3) partially identical pairs is divided into three subgroups;

(1-1, 2-1, 3-1) Synonym pairs with identical POS: words in a pair are synonym with identical POS.

E.g. (1-1) 歌手: singer (noun)
(2-1) 藍紫色 (Japanese) and 紫藍色 (Chinese):blue-violet color (noun)
(3-1) 赤砂糖 (Japanese) and 紅砂糖 (Chinese):brown sugar (noun)

(1-2, 2-2, 3-2) Synonym pairs with unmatched POS: words in a pair are synonym with different POS or POS of at least one of the words in the pair is missing.

E.g. (1-2) 包:(Japanese) action of wrapping (noun) (Chinese) to wrap (verb)
(2-2) 嗽咳 (Japanese): a cough (noun) 咳嗽 (Chinese): cough (verb)

(1-3, 2-3, 3-3) Relation Unidentified: the relation is not determinable by automatic processing with the given information at this point.

E.g.	Japanese	Chinese
(1-3)	湯: hot spring (noun)	湯: soup (noun)
(2-3)	生花:	花生: flower arrangement
	(noun) peanut (noun)	
(3-3)	青葡萄: blue grapes (noun)	葡萄牙: Portugal (noun)

In order to find the semantic relation of Chinese and Japanese word pairs by machine analysis, the jwd and the cwd in a pair are compared according to the following information:

Jwd: English synset (jsyn), definition (jdef) and POS
Cwd: English synset (csyn), definition (cdef) and POS

The process of checking the synonymy of each pair is done in the following manner:

If any of the following conditions meets, we assume that the pair is a synonym pair:

at least any one of the synonym from each of jsyn and csyn are identical
at least one of the word definition contains a synonym of the other word

If any synonym pair was found, check if the POS are identical. If the POS are identical, the pair is classified to a synonym pair with identical POS. Otherwise the pair is classified to a synonym pair with non-identical POS. If the pair is not a synonym pair then they are classified to a relation-unidentified pair. After the process, each of the subgroups is manually examined to check the actual semantic relations of each word pair.

4 Results

4.1 Word Family as Domain Ontology Headed by a Basic Concept

Chinese radical (*yi4fu2*, ideographs; semantic symbols) system offers a unique opportunity for systematic and comprehensive comparison between formal and linguistic ontologies. Chou and Huang (2010) suggests that the family of Chinese characters sharing the same radical can be linked to a basic concept by Qualia relations. Based on Pustejovsky (1995) Qualia Structure and the original analysis of "ShuoWenJieXi" (Xyu CE 121), each radical group can be as domain ontology headed by one basic concept.

Chou and Huang assume that 540 radicals in "ShuoWenJieXi" can each represent a basic concept and that all derivative characters are conceptually dependent on that basic concept. Also, they hypothesize that a radical can be classified into six main types: formal, constitutive, telic, participating, descriptive (state, manner) and agentive. Modes of conceptual extension capture the generative nature of lexical creativity while preserving the conceptual clustering of characters sharing the same radical. Huang et al. (2013) show that all derived characters are conceptually dependent on the basic concept and forms an ontology. In their preliminary studies, word family could be headed by a basic concept and also could be represented ontologies in OWL format (Chou and Huang 2013).

4.2 Data Analysis: Japanese and Chinese Words with Identical Orthography

4.2.1 Kanji Mapping

We present our study over Japanese and Chinese lexical semantic relation based on the kanji sequences and their semantic relations. We compared Japanese-English dictionary of Electric Dictionary Research (EDR) with the SinicaBow in order to examine the nature of cross-lingual lexical semantic relations (Tables 2, 3, 4 and 5).

The following tables are summarized tables showing the Japanese-Chinese form-meaning relation distribution examined in our preliminary study (Tables 6, 7 and 8).

Since each entry in SinicaBow corresponds to a definition and each jwd has at least a definition or a concept definition, no pairs with insufficient information to check the semantic relation was found. The data shows that as the word forms of the two languages are closer, the more synonyms are found. In order to confirm this observation and to see the actual semantic relation of each pairs, we will continue with more detailed analysis. In addition, in order to pursue the further details of the Japanese-Chinese words relation, we will also analyze the semantic relations (not only synonymous relation) of the relation-unidentified pairs.

4.2.2 "口(Mouth)"Analysis Procedure

Chinese and Japanese share orthography not only at characters level but also at radical level. We have analyzed the characters level in Sect. 4.2.1. In this section, we will express shared orthography on the radical level, which allows us to map characters sharing same conceptual primitive but possibly different glyph forms. Because there are more than 540 radicals in Chinese hanzi, and the analysis cannot be automatically, we chose the most typical radical "口 (mouth)" as an example. In characters level, there are many identical or partly identical Chinese-Japanese word pairs using the radical "口 (mouth)", we select the identical kanji Sequence

Table 2 Chinese and Japanese kanji

	Identical	Different order	Part- identical
Synonym (identical POS)	13,610 pairs	567 pairs	37,466 pairs
Synonym (unmatched POS)	2,265 pairs	214 pairs	22,734 pairs
Relation unidentified	21,154 pairs	2,336 pairs	1,116,141 pairs
Total	37,029 pairs	3,117 pairs	1,176,341 pairs
	16,950 jwds	1,497 jwds	39,821 jwds

Table 3 Identical kanji sequence pairs (37,029 pairs) synonymous relation distribution

	Number of 1-to-1 form-meaning pairs by machine analysis	% in (1)
(1-1) Synonym (identical POS)	13,610	36.8
(1-2) Synonym (unmatched POS)	2,265	6.1
(1-3) Relation unidentified	21,154	57.1

Table 4 Identical kanji but different order pairs (3,117 pairs) synonymous relation distribution

	Number of 1-to-1 form-meaning pairs by machine analysis	% in (2)
(2-1) Synonym (identical POS)	567	18.2
(2-2) Synonym (unmatched POS)	214	6.9
(2-3) Relation unidentified	2,336	74.9

Table 5 Partially identical pairs (1,176,341 pairs) synonymous relation distribution

	Number of 1-to-1 form-meaning pairs by machine prcessing	% in (3)
(3-1) Synonym (identical POS)	37,466	3.2
(3-2) Synonym (unmatched POS)	22,734	1.9
(3-3) Relation unidentified	1,116,141	94.9

Table 6 Identical kanji sequence pairs (37,029 pairs) lexical semantic relation

	Pairs found to be synonym	% in (1)	Relation unidentified	% in (1)
Machine analysis	15,875	42.9	21,154	57.1

Table 7 Identical kanji but different order pairs (3,117 pairs) lexical semantic relation

	Pairs found to be synonym	% in (2)	Relation unidentified	% in (2)
Machine analysis	781	25.1	2,336	74.9

Table 8 Partially identical pairs (1,176,341 pairs) lexical semantic relation

	Pairs found to be synonym	% in (3)	Relation unidentified	% in (3)
Machine analysis	60,200	5.1	1,116,141	94.9

Pairs (POS) as our main resources. In addition, if any character of the words owns the radical "口 (mouth)", then it would be included here for analysing the detailed semantic relation between jwd and cwd.

We would like to define the semantic relations of Chinese and Japanese word pairs in more details. We examined the actual semantic relation of Chinese and Japanese word pairs by classifying into 8 semantic relations and marked the relation into [ ] remark.

1. [SYN](Synonym)
2. [NSN](Near-Synonym)
3. [HYP](Hypernym)
4. [HPO](Hyponym)
5. [HOL](Holonym)
6. [MER](Meronym)
7. [/](No Corresponding Semantic Relation)
8. [??](unable to decide)

The pattern is as follows.

[(JWD > jsyn > 詞類 > jdef >)-[Semantic Relation]-(CWD) > csyn > 詞類 > cdef]]

Sample:

[(J)-[HYP]-(C)]@

(J is the hypernym of C)

The examples are shown here. In each pair, we define the semantic relation between the jwd and the cwd. The mapping process would be as follows.

E.g

1. [(唖 > JWD0028646 > N > a condition of being incapable of speaking using the voice >)-[SYN]-(啞 > 10137481 N > N > paralysis of the vocal cords resulting in an inability to speak > alalia,)]@
2. [(嘴 > JWD0378514 > N > of a bird, a bill > bill)-[SYN]-(嘴 > 01278388 N > N > horny projecting jaws of a bird > nib,neb,bill,beak,)]@
3. [(咽喉 > JWD0161758 > N > part of an animal called a throat >)-[SYN]-(咽喉 > 04296952 N > N > the passage to the stomach and lungs; in the front part of the neck below the chin and above the collarbone > pharynx,throat,)]@
4. [(啄木鳥 > JWD0398785 > N > a bird that is related to the picidae, called woodpecker > woodpecker)-[SYN]-(啄木鳥 > 01355454 N > N > bird with strong claws and a stiff tail adapted for climbing and a hard chisel-like bill for boring into wood for insects > woodpecker,)]@
5. [(人工呼吸器 > JWD0401642 > N > a medical instrument with which a patient can breathe artificially > respirator)-[SYN]-(人工呼吸器 > 03233384 N > N > a device for administering long-term artificial respiration > inhalator, respirator,)]@

According to our observation, we notice that most of the Japanese kanji can get their synonyms or near-synonyms in Chinese hanzi and the percentage for this relation is about 63 % in characters with the radical "口(mouth)" selected from

Table 9 Semantic relation distribution in characters with the radical "口 Mouth"

Semantic relations between Chinese and Japanese word	Distribution in characters with the radical 口 (mouth)	% in characters with the radical 口(mouth) 486 total pairs
[SYN]	190	39
[NSN]	129	27
[HYP]	16	4
[HPO]	7	2
[HOL]	11	3
[MER]	12	3
[/]	118	25
[??]	1	1

Identical Synonym POS data. Please refer to Table 1. The distributions of Semantic Relations comparing jwd to cwd in characters with the radical "口 (mouth)" chosen from Identical Syno POS are as follows (Table 9).

4.3 Conceptual Access: A Preliminary Model

In this part, we try to apply dimension of conceptual extension of "口(mouth)" radical into the data we have chosen from the Identical Synonym POS data comparing with Japanese kanji and Chinese hanzi. (Please refer to the Appendix A[2]). A study based on words containing characters composed of the "口(mouth)" radical is given for illustration in this preliminary study. It shows that the conceptual robustness can also be applied to other languages, such as Japanese kanji.

5 Conclusions

In this paper, we examine and analyze the form of kanji/hanzi characters and the semantic relations between Japanese and Chinese. Our study utilizes the homomorphism of radical encoded conceptual structure between the Chinese hanzi and Japanese kanji systems to identify bilingual word correspondences. We use bilingual dictionaries, including WordNet and Sinica BOW, to verify semantic relation between the cross-lingual pairs. These bilingual pairs are then mapped to an ontology constructed based on relations to the relation between the meaning of each character and the basic concept of their radical parts. The conceptual structure of the radical ontology is proposed as the model for simultaneous conceptual access to both languages. The results have two implications. First, a ontology-driven,

[2] The categories of the concepts represented by radicals are extended based on Qualia structure. Each category in Table 10 and appendix was manually analyzed and assigned.

Table 10 Jwd correspondence to "口 (mouth) conceptual extension" Graph (口 (mouth), basic concept: the body part which used mainly in language and food)

Categories in "口(mouth) conceptual extension"	Examples in "口 (mouth) conceptual extension"	Japanese kanji and Chinese hanzi example
Formal -Sense-vision and size	嘩	
Formal-sense-hearing	叫	
Constitutive	吻、嚨、喉	吻、口吻、嘴、咽喉、喉頭、喉頭炎、喉頭鏡
Descriptive-active	吐、叫	嘔吐
Descriptive-state	含	含量、含意、含糊、嗜好
Participating-action	咳、啞、呼、吸	啞、咳嗽、吸血鬼、呼吸、吸盤
Participating-others	哼、噓	
Participating-instrument	右	左右、右側、右手,周到
Metaphor	启	入口、門口、出入口、出口
TELIC-subordinate concept 1 and subordinate concept 2		
Subordinate concept 1(speaking)		
Formal-property	唐	
Formal-sense-hearing	呷	
Constitutive	名、吾	匿名、名詞、名言、名人、物質名詞
Descriptive-active	吃、哽	吃、吃水線
Participator	吠、喔	狗吠、唯我論、唯心論
Participating-action-way	呻、吟	唱歌
Participating-others	君、命	君、命令、革命、生命、命運
Subordinate concept 2 (eating)		
Formal-sense-taste	味、啜	味、趣味
Descriptive-active	噎	
Participating-action	啜	
Participating-state	饞	
Participator	啄	啄木鳥、啄木鳥目

orthographic system based mapping goes beyond glyph-based approaches to kanji/hanzi conversion and offers a conceptual/cognitive base for this NLP task. Second, our success, especially our ability to identify Chinese-Japanese word mapping even when word-forms and meaning association variations, suggests that a concept-based lexical mapping between two or more languages with or without related orthography, as proposed by Huang et al. (2007) and Soria et al. (2009) is feasible. We hope that this line of ontology-driven study can lead to better understanding of cognitive access to the lexicon from multicultural and multilingual perspectives.

Acknowledgments Earlier version of this paper was presented at CogALex 2008 and we would like to thank Michael Zock and other participants for their helpful comments. We would also like to thank anonymous reviewers of this volume for their constructive suggestions. Work done on this paper was partially supported by grant GRF-543512 from Hong Kong RGC.

6 Appendix A: The Dimension of "口(Mouth) Conceptual Extension"

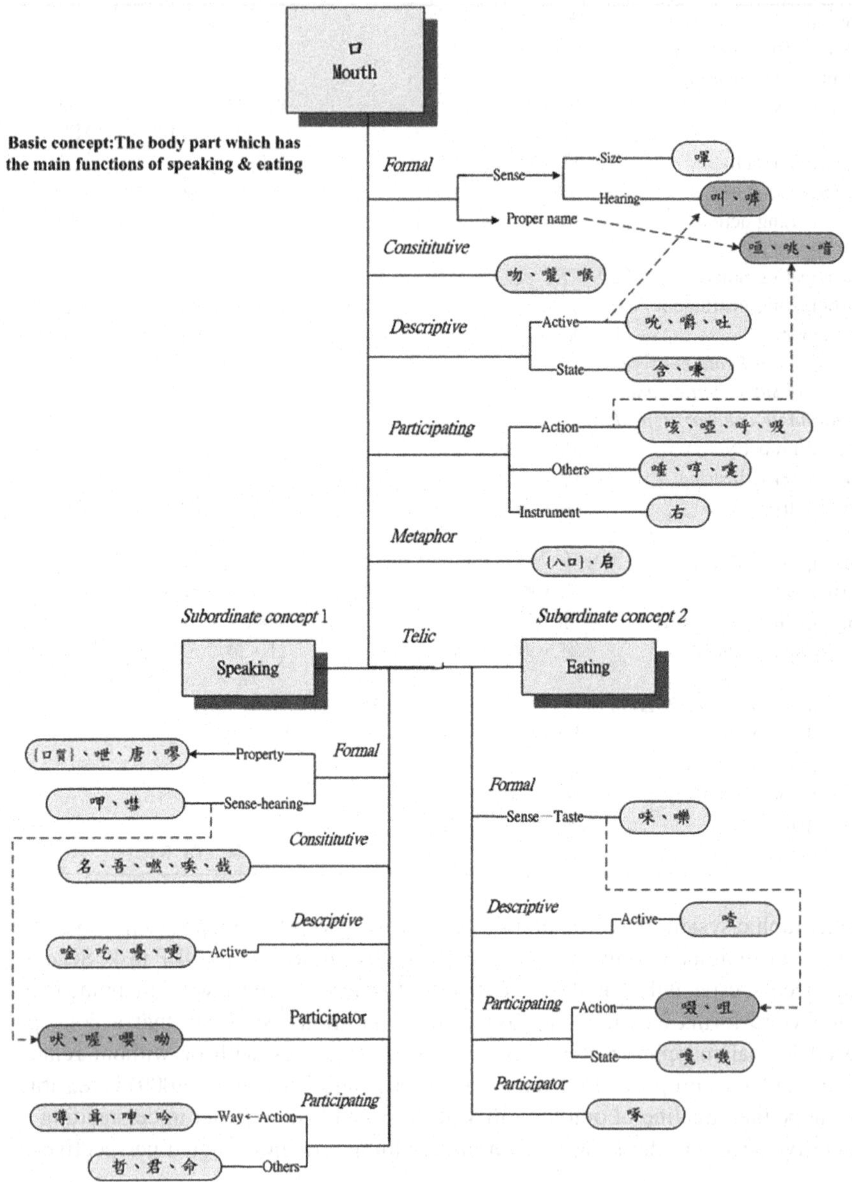

References

Chou, Y. M., & Huang, C. R. (2007). Hantology: A linguistic resource for chinese language processing and studying. *Proceedings of the 5th LREC* (pp. 587–590).

Chou, Y. M., & Huang, C. R. (2010). Hantology: conceptual system discovery based on orthographic convention. In C. R. Huang (Ed.), *ontology and the lexicon: A natural language processing perspective* (pp. 122–143). Cambridge: Cambridge University Press.

Chou, Y. M. (2012). The application of chinese-japanese characters and words knowledgebase: DaoZhaiSuiBi and Sheng WenZuanKao as examples. *Journal of Chinese Literature of National Taipei University, 12*, 41–56.

Chou, Y. M., & Huang, C. R. (2013). The formal representation for chinese characters. In C. R. Huang, Y. M. Sophia, & Y. Lee (Eds.), *Special issues on ontology and chinese language processing. contemporary linguistics* (pp.142–161) (in Chinese).

Chu, C., Nakazawa, T., & Kurohashi S. (2012). Chinese character mapping table of japanese, traditional chinese, and simplified chinese. *Proceedings of the 8th LREC* (pp. 2149–2152).

Fellbaum, C. (1998). *WordNet: An electronic lexical database*. Cambridge: MIT Press.

Goh, C.-L., Asahara, M., & Matusmoto, Y. (2005). Building a Japanese-Chinese dictionary using Kanji/Hanzi conversion. natural language processing-IJCNLP 2005. In Lecture notes in computer science (Vol. 3651, pp. 670–681). Heidelberg: Springer.

Hiroyuki, S., Shoichi, Y., & Eric, Long. (2003). *Linguistic ecology of kanji variants in contemporary Japan*. Tokyo: Sanseido Co., Ltd. (in Japanese).

Hsieh, C. C., & Lin, S. (1997). A survey of full-text data bases and related techniques for chinese ancient documents in Academia Sinica. *International Journal of Computational Linguistics and Chinese Language Processing*, 2(1), 105-130 (in Chinese).

Huang, C. R., & Ahrens, K. (2003). Individuals, kind and events: Classifier coercion of nouns. *Language Sciences, 25*(4), 353–373.

Huang, C. R., Prévot, L., Su, I. L., & Hong, J. F. (2007). Towards a conceptual core for multicultural processing: A multilingual ontology based on the Swadesh list. In T. Ishida, S. R. Fussell, P. T. J. M. Vossen, (Eds.), *Intercultural collaboration I. Lecture notes in computer science, state-of-the-art survey* (pp. 17–30). Springer-Verlag.

Huang, C. R., Chiyo, H., Kuo, T. Y., Su, I. L., & Hsieh, S. K. (2008). WordNet-anchored comparison of Chinese-Japanese kanji word. *Proceedings of the 4th Global WordNet Conference.* Szeged, Hungary.

Huang, C. R., Chang, R. Y., & Li, S. (2010). Sinica BOW: Integration of bilingual wordnet and SUMO. In H. Chu-Ren, N. Calzolari, A. Gangemi, A. Lenci, A. Oltramari, L. Prevot (Eds.), *Ontology and the Lexicon (*pp. 201–211). Cambridge: Cambridge University Press.

Huang, C. R., Yang, Y. J., & Chen, S. Y. (2013). Radicals as ontologies: Concept derivation and knowledge representation of Four-Hoofed mammals as semantic symbols. In Guangshun Cao, Hilary Chappell, Redouane Djamouri, & Thekla Wiebusch (Eds.), *Breaking down the barriers: interdisciplinary studies in Chinese linguistics and beyond. A Festschrift for Professor Alain Peyraube* (pp. 1117–1133). Taipei: Institute of Linguistics. Academia Sinica.

Li, X. D. (1997). *Hanzi de Qi Yuan Yu Yan Bian Lun Cong(the origin and evolution of han characters).* Taipei: Lian-Keng. (in Chinese).

Miller, G. A. (1995). WordNet: A lexical database for english. *Communications of the ACM, 38* (11), 39–41.

Morohashi, T. (1960). *Dai Kan-Wa Jiten(the great han-japanese dictionary).* Tokyo: Taishukan Publishing Co., Ltd. (in Japanese).

Nakada, N., & Hayashi, C. (2000). *Nihon no Kanji(Japanese Kanji).* Toyko: Chuo Koron new company.

Niles, I., & Pease, A. (2001).Towards a standard upper ontology. *Proceedings of the 2nd International Conference on Formal Ontology in Information Systems*, Ogunquit, Maine, October 17–19.

Pustejovsky, J. (1995). *The generative lexicon.* MA: The MIT Press.

Shirai, K., Tokunaga, T., Huang, C.-R., Hsieh, S.-K., Kuo, T.-Y., Sornlertlamvanich, V., & Charoenporn, T. (2008). Constructing taxonomy of numerative classifiers for Asian languages. *Proceedings of the Third International Joint Conference on Natural Language Processing (IJCNLP2008)*, Hyderabad, India.

Soria, C., Monachini, M., Bertagna, F., Calzolari, N., Huang, C. R., Hsieh, S. K., Marchetti, A., & Tesconi, M. (2009). Exploring interoperability of language resources: The case of cross-lingual semi-automatic enrichment of wordnets. In S. Gilles et al. (Eds.), *Special issue on interoperability of multilingual language processing. Language Resources and Evaluation* (Vol. 43, No. 1, pp. 87–96).

Sugimoto, T. (1998). *Nihon Mojishi no Kenkyu (Research on the History of Japanese Kangi).* Tokyo: Yasakashobo. (in Japanese).

Tan, C. L., & Nagao, M. (1995). Automatic alignment of japanese-chinese bilingual texts. *IEICE Transactions of Information Systems, E78-D*(1), 68–76.

Xyu, S. (121/2004). *ShuoWenJieZi (The explanation of words and the parsing of chinese characters).* This edition. Beijing: ZhongHua. (in Chinese).

Yokoi, T. (1995). The EDR electronic dictionary. *Communications of the ACM, 38*(11), 42–44.

Proportional Analogy in Written Language Data

Yves Lepage

Abstract The purpose of this paper is to summarize some of the results obtained over many years of research in proportional analogy applied to natural language processing. We recall some mathematical formalizations obtained based on general axioms drawn from a study of the history of the notion from Euclid to modern linguistics. The obtained formalization relies on two articulative notions: conformity and ratio, and on two constitutive notions: similarity and contiguity. These notions are applied on a series of objects that range from sets to strings of symbols through multi-sets and vectors, so as to obtain a mathematical formalization on each of these types of objects. Thanks to these formalizations, some results are presented that were obtained in structuring language data by the characters (bitmaps), words or short sentences in several languages like Chinese or English. An important point in using such formalizations that rely on form only, concerns the truth of the analogies retrieved or produced, i.e., whether they are valid on both the levels of form and meaning. Results of evaluation on this aspect are recalled. It is also mentioned how the formalization on string of symbols can be applied to two main tasks that would correspond to 'langage' and 'parole' in Saussurian terms: structuring language data and generating language data. The results presented have been obtained from reasonably large amounts of language data, like several thousands of Chinese characters or hundred thousand sentences in English or other languages.

Keywords Analogy · Proportional analogy · Language data

Y. Lepage (✉)
Graduate School of Information, Production and Systems, Waseda University, Hibikino 2–7, Wakamatsu-Ku, Kitakyushu-Shi, Fukuoka-Ken 808-0135, Japan
e-mail: yves.lepage@waseda.jp

© Springer International Publishing Switzerland 2015

N. Gala et al. (eds.), *Language Production, Cognition, and the Lexicon*,
Text, Speech and Language Technology 48, DOI 10.1007/978-3-319-08043-7_10

1 Introduction

The purpose of this paper is to summarize some of the results obtained over many years of research in proportional analogy applied to natural language processing.

Firstly, based on a study of the history of the notion from Euclid up to modern linguistics, briefly reported in the sequel of this section, we rapidly recall the formalization that we arrived at. Two constitutive notions, those of *similarity* and *contiguity* and two basic articulative notions, those of *ratio* and *conformity* are the foundations of this formalization, presented in Sect. 2. We then recall the general basic properties that can be exploited on different objects that underly, by relaxation, strings of symbols: sets and multi-sets. We also present recent works on clustering by analogy vectors representing binary images, more precisely, bitmaps of Chinese characters.

Secondly, in Sect. 3, we recall the results obtained in the inspection of the number of true analogies, i.e., analogies of form that are analogies in meaning among various units of texts, namely, words, *N*-grams, chunks and sentences. The striking result is the number of 95 %, the number of true analogies among analogies of form gathered using our proposed formalization, that was obtained in different experiments.

Thirdly, in Sect. 4, we summarize some experiments performed structuring sets of short sentences by proportional analogy,

Finally, in Sect. 5, we briefly report some experiments in filling holes in a corpus of short sentences, generating paraphrases for the same corpus, or trying to build a quasi-parallel corpus of short Chinese-Japanese sentences from unrelated sentences extracted from the Web. We rapidly touch on the subject of machine translation and related issues but leave any elaboration out of the scope of this paper.

1.1 Informal Definition

Proportional analogy[1] is defined in various ways by different authors (Gentner 1983; Itkonen 2005; Lepage 2001; Richard and Prade 2014; Yvon et al. 2004) but all agree on the following common basis:

[1] We use this term to denote the notion. By doing this, we follow the German tradition (*proportionale Analogiebildung* (Osthoff 1979, p. 132) *proportionale Analogiebildung* (Paul 1920, p. 132) *Proportionalanalogie*, (Becker 1990, p. 14) The other term, *analogical proportion,* is usually understood as the result, i.e., the lists of forms or paradigms, (Welcomme 2010, p. 91), i.e., analogical clusters for us (see Fig. 2 or Table 1). But this last term is also used for the notion itself by some authors [e.g., Richard and Prade (2014)].

Four objects, A, B, C and D, form a proportional analogy if the first object is to the second object in the same way as the third object is to the fourth object. A proportional analogy is noted $A : B :: C : D$.

1.2 Articulative Notions: Conformity and Ratio

In all generality, if the relation between two objects (noted by the colon :) is called a *ratio* and the relation between the two pairs of objects (noted by the two colons ::) is called a *conformity*, then a proportional analogy is a conformity of ratios between two pairs of objects, usually of the same type. Conformity and ratio are the two *articulative notions* in proportional analogies.

1.3 True Analogies

Proportional analogies can be seen between words on the level of form or on the level of meaning or on both at the same time (Hoffman 1995) studies non standard cases). Table 1 gives examples of proportional analogies that hold on these two levels at the same time or only on one of these two levels.

Proportional analogies on the levels of form and meaning at the same time are called *true analogies*. Between chunks or short sentences, their number has been shown to be quite important (Lepage 2004; Lepage et al. 2007, 2009). Forms which depart from declension or conjugation paradigms (groups of proportions in Paul (1920) were called anomalies in classical grammar (Varro 1954). On the semantic level, lexical analogies, i.e., analogies between the meanings of four given words, (water : riverbed :: traffic : road) it has been shown that vector space models can help in capturing them (Turney 2006, 2008; Turney and Littman 2005). The role of proportional analogy as an organizational principle to enlarge knowledge-bases by incremental addition of lexical analogies has also been explored in Veale and Li (2014).

1.4 Positive or Negative Judgements About Proportional Analogy

A review of the history of proportional analogy, especially from the grammatical and linguistic point of view (Lepage 2003, Part I; Lavie 2003, Chap. 2), at different times, shows that proportional analogy has taken positive or negative connotations (see Table 2). In the Antiquity, analogy was just another name for regularity in derivational or flexional morphology. Varro (1954) illustrates this by:

Table 1 Examples of proportional analogies between words

Proportional analogy	Levels on which the analogy holds:		True analogy
	Form	Meaning	
to walk : walked :: to work : worked	Yes	Yes	Yes
wings : fins :: a wing : a fin	Yes	Yes	Yes
to walk : walked :: to be : was	No	Yes	No
wings : fins :: bird : fish	No	Yes	No
to walk : walked :: to me : meed	Yes	No	No
wings : fins :: winged : fined	Yes	No	No

Table 2 Analogy and its opposite notions in the history of grammar and linguistics and the judgements made on them ($\oplus$: positive, $\ominus$: negative, $\otimes$: neutral)

Analogy	Place of analogy	Opposite place
Greek and Latin antiquity	Analogy, regularity $\oplus$	Anomaly, irregularity $\ominus$
Comparative linguists	Analogical reconstruction, perturbation $\ominus$	Sound change, natural law $\oplus$
Neogrammairians (Brugmann, Osthoff, Paul)	Synchrony, reorganization through analogy, order $\oplus$	Diachrony, sound changes, desorder $\ominus$
Structuralists (Saussure)		
Kazan's school (Kuryłowicz) (Mańczak)	Diachronic effect, secondary forms, low frequencies $\otimes$	Synchronic effect, primary forms, high frequencies $\otimes$
Generativists (Chomsky)	Acquisition, induction, over-generation $\ominus$	Innateness, parameter setting, adequacy $\oplus$

Roma : *Romanus* :: *Padua* : $x \Rightarrow x =$ *Paduanus* and Quintilianus explains the form *pepigi* by the proportional analogy: *cado* : *cecidi* :: *pago* : $x \Rightarrow x =$ *pepigi*. In the middle of the nineteenth century, with sound change becoming the main object of research for a nascent comparative linguistics, analogical change, i.e., the creation of new forms in conformity with regular models, as in *actorem* : *actor* :: *honorem* : $x \Rightarrow x =$ *honor*, has been perceived as an infelicitous phenomenon that hides the regular application of sound changes. Analogical changes often replace forms that would otherwise reflect sound changes, a fact this is referred to as Sturtevant's paradox (Anttila 1989):

> Sound change is regular and causes irregularity. Analog[ical change] is irregular and causes regularity.

In this view, analogy is a hindrance in the quest for the laws of sound changes. It took the Neogrammarian revolution with its manifesto by Osthoff and Brugmann (Lehmann 1967) to recognize that the two main factors of evolution are sound changes and analogy. Paul is the first modern linguist to dedicate a good part of his studies to analogy (see the entire Chap. 5 in Paul (1920)). Similarly, the students of Saussure dedicate an entire part (Part III) of the Course in General Linguistics (de Saussure 1995) to analogy. Saussure contributed a lot to the move from a negative attitude to a positive attitude (Stankiewicz 1986):

> [it is] more sound changes that disturb regular relations between grammatical forms and [···] analogical uniformisations counter the blind action of sound changes.

1.5 Constitutive Notions: Similarity and Contiguity

Considered from the point of view of cognition or linguistics, analogy can be found to take the central place between several fundamental concepts as illustrated in Table 3. Whatever the point of view and their denominations, the two extreme concepts can be understood as instantiating the two *constitutive notions* of similarity and contiguity. In mere comparison, the two notions are kept apart while in proportional analogy, they work on both directions, as illustrated in Fig. 1.

2 Formalization of Proportional Analogy Between Strings of Symbols

In this section, we give the basic set of properties that characterize proportional analogies between any kind of objects. By using this set of basic properties and by giving a specific meaning to some of the notions involved when dealing with

Table 3 Analogy as playing a central role between some extreme notions

	First extreme notion	Place of analogy	Other extreme notion
Sense of being	Univocity	–	Equivocity
Word associations	Synonymy	Paronymy	Homonymy
Word usage	Metaphor	–	Metonymy
Linguistic axes	Paradigmatic	–	Syntagmatic
Mind operations	Selection	–	Combination
Intellect operations	Perception	–	Knowledge
Set operations	Intersection	–	Inclusion
Constitutive notions	Similarity	–	Contiguity

Mere comparison	← similarity →	
	bird	fish
↑	wings	fins
contiguity	lungs	gills
↓	feathers	scales
	to fly	to swim

Proportional analogy	← similarity → & contiguity	
↑	aslama	muslim
contiguity & similarity	arsala	mursil
↓		

Fig. 1 Similarity and contiguity are kept separated in mere comparison (on the *left*), while they are merged in proportional analogy between objects of the same type (on the *right*)

specific objects, it is possible to derive a mathematical definition of proportional analogies between some specific data structures. We illustrate this below on sets, multi-sets and strings of symbols.

2.1 A Set of Basic Properties

A first fact easily understandable is that, when taking any two objects, because their ratio is tautologically equal to itself, this ratio should necessarily be conform to itself.

(o) reflexivity of *conformity* $A : B :: A : B$

A second important property identified by the Greeks, Aristotle for instance, is that, for an analogy $A : B :: C : D$, there always exists the possibility of exchanging objects B and C. This property is called the *exchange of the means* in the scholastic tradition.

(v) exchange of the means If $A : B :: C : D$ then: $A : C :: B : D$

The combination of the previous two properties implies that, for any two objects, $A : A :: B : B$. It is a good question to ask whether $A : A :: B_1 : B_2$ may hold with $B_1 \neq B_2$. As for ourselves, we refuse such a possibility and call this hypothesis the *determinism hypothesis.* We shall come back to this point when dealing with strings of symbols in Sect. 2.4.

As a third property, *symmetry of conformity* or *inversion of conformity,* i.e., the possibility of exchanging the terms on both sides of the :: sign, seems to always hold. In combination with the exchange of the means, inversion of conformity leads to the fact that, for a given proportional analogy, the eight different expressions are possible [see Theorem 2.1 in Lepage (2004)]. This system with only two basic properties is the simplest one (see Table 4), but adding inversion of ratios as a third property leads to a redundant system, but it has the advantage of making central the notion of inversion.

By introducing the term *inversion*, it becomes apparent that this notion can be applied to each of the important terms in the definition of a proportional analogy: a *conformity* of *ratios* between *objects* of the same type. Conformity and ratio are the articulative notions in proportional analogy. Inversion of objects concerns contiguity as taking the inverse, or the opposite, or the contrary of an object. It is the most elementary form of contiguity as any object is contiguous to its negation or inverse. So as to cover both constitutive notions, it remains to add a property for similarity. We express it through the notion of distribution of features. With all of the above, one gets the following set of basic properties for proportional analogies between objects of the same type.

Table 4 Equivalent forms of a given analogy. Proofs of equivalence in two systems, one with only two basic properties, and one with three basic properties

Equivalent forms	Proofs with two basic properties	Proofs with three basic properties	Name of equivalent form
$A : B :: C : D$	–	–	–
$A : C :: B : D$	Exch. means	Exch. means	Exchange of the means
$B : A :: D : C$	Exch. means + sym. :: + exch. means	Inv. :	Inverse of ratios
$B : D :: A : C$	Exch. means + sym. ::	Inv. : + exch. means	–
$C : A :: D : B$	Sym. :: + exch. means	Inv. :: + exch. means	–
$C : D :: A : B$	Sym. ::	Inv. ::	Inverse of conformity
$D : B :: C : A$	Sym. :: + exch. means + sym. ::	Inv. : + inv. :: + exch. means	Exchange of the extremes
$D : C :: B : A$	Exch. means + sym. :: + exch. means + sym. ::	Inv. : + inv. ::	Inverse reading

Table 5 A set of fundamental axioms for proportional analogy between objects of the same type

No.	Axioms	if $A : B :: C : D$ then:
(i)	Inversion of *conformity*	$C : D :: A : B$
(ii)	Inversion of *ratios*	$B : A :: D : C$
(iii)	Inversion of *objects* ($\Leftarrow$ contiguity)	$A^{-1} : B^{-1} :: C^{-1} : D^{-1}$
(iv)	Distribution in *objects* ($\Leftarrow$ similarity)	Any feature in A must be present in either B or C or both
(v)	Exchange of the means	$A : C :: B : D$

As an important remark, it should be noticed that the previous properties do not imply nor assume transitivity for conformity (the sign ::). This means that conformity is not an equivalence relation in the general case. This remark is linked with the determinism hypothesis and we shall come back to this in Sect. 2.4 (Table 5).

2.2 The Case of Sets and Multi-sets

For sets, the solution of an analogical equation $A : B :: C : x$ can be directly deduced from the sets of basic properties by giving a meaning to the basic property (iv), which corresponds to the constitutive notion of similarity. By taking features to mean the members of the sets considered, one translates (iv) into: $A \subset B \cup C$. The use of the eight equivalent forms of analogy and complementation for the inverse of the sets, leads to the result that the previous analogical equation has a solution if and only if $A \subset B \cup C$ and $A \supset B \cap C$. In this case, the solution is unique and is given by Eq. 1. This result can be visualized as shown below, where A, B and C are visualized as circles. The necessary and sufficient condition for an analogy to hold, on the inclusion of A in $B \cup C$ and on the inclusion of $B \cap C$ in A, is captured by the very particular configuration shown here. The solution x of the equation $A : B :: C : x$ is the area in gray.

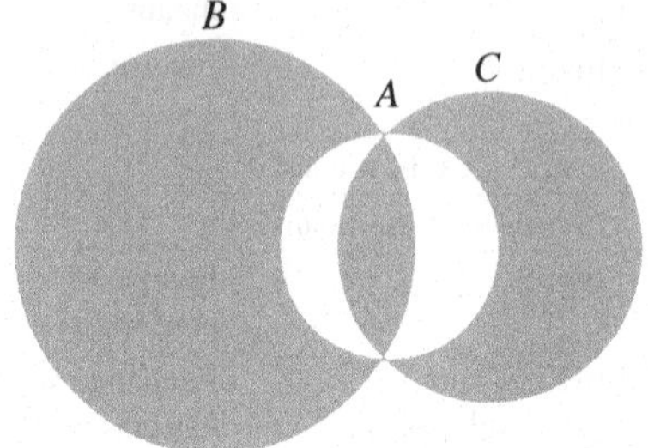

$$x = ((B \cup C) \backslash A)) \cup (B \cap C) \tag{1}$$

With this, it can be easily checked that the basic property (iii), which states that the analogy holds on the inverse of the objects, is met by taking the inverse of an object to mean the complement of the set relatively to any set that contains the union of the four sets. Also, a particular case of analogy between sets is worth mentioning: for any two sets A and B, $A \cap B : A :: B : A \cup B$.

The structure of multi-sets is closer than sets to the structure of strings of symbols in that it adds the notion of repetition of the members. But it still lacks the notion of order of the members which exists in strings of symbols. We define a multi-set A as a mapping from a domain $\mathscr{D}(A)$ to $\mathbb{N}$. Again, the translation of the basic property (iv) into: $A(a) \leq B(a) + C(a)$ and the use of the eight equivalent forms of analogy leads to the following result. The analogical equation $A : B :: C : x$ on the multi-sets A, B, and C has a solution if and only if:

$$\forall a \in (\mathscr{D}(A) \cup \mathscr{D}(B) \cup \mathscr{D}(C)), \quad A(a) \leq B(a) + C(a) \tag{2}$$

In this case, there exists a unique solution D with domain:

$$\mathscr{D}(D) = \{a \in (\mathscr{D}(A) \cup \mathscr{D}(B) \cup \mathscr{D}(C))/A(a) < B(a) + C(a)\} \tag{3}$$

and images:

$$\forall a \in \mathscr{D}(D), \quad D(a) = B(a) + C(a) - A(a) \tag{4}$$

Similarly to sets, by defining a multi-set which contains all the members appearing in some given multi-sets repeated a number of times which is greater than the max over all the given multi-sets, it is possible to write the basic property (iii) on inverses of objects. In addition, and similarly to sets, by positing for any two multi-sets A and B:

$$\begin{aligned}(A \wedge B)(a) &= \max(A(a), B(a)),\\ (A \vee B)(a) &= \min(A(a), B(a))\end{aligned} \tag{5}$$

the particular analogy $A \wedge B : A :: B : A \vee B$ always holds. It is just a generalization of the previous particular analogy on sets mentioned above.

Finally, for a set or a multi-set A, one can define its cardinality, noted $|A|$, as the number of members it contains (counting repetitions for multi-sets). It is possible to prove that in both cases, when $A : B :: C : D$, then $|A| + |D| = |B| + |C|$. This can be spelled as follows: for an analogy between sets or between multi-sets, the sum of the cardinalities of the extremes is equal to the sum of the cardinalities of the means.

2.3 The Case of Vectors: Application to Binary Images and Bitmaps of Chinese Characters

Vectors with non-negative integer values can be seen as just a slight generalization of multi-sets where the universe of members is known in advance, i.e., they are the dimensions of the vectorial space. Vector difference as a ratio, and equality between vectors as conformity, consistently define analogies that meet the intuitive notions about proportional analogies. An analogy between vectors can be illustrated by the following example.

$$\begin{pmatrix}1\\0\\0\\1\\0\end{pmatrix} - \begin{pmatrix}0\\0\\0\\0\\0\end{pmatrix} = \begin{pmatrix}3\\2\\2\\1\\2\end{pmatrix} - \begin{pmatrix}2\\2\\2\\0\\2\end{pmatrix} \tag{6}$$

It is worth mentioning that, although conformity is not transitive in the general case, in the particular case of vectors, it is transitive. In natural language processing, the use of vector space models has a long history. We used such a model, not on texts but on the problem of re-discovering the structure of Chinese characters. To simplify, the problem is to structure Chinese characters by keys without using any a priori knowledge, on the contrary to other approaches (Veale and Chen 2006). The only knowledge allowed in this approach is the given of the bitmap of each character. The problem then tantamounts to extract features from the bitmaps

倔:掘
恨:振
怕:拍
惜:措
快:抉
怜:拎
惦:掂
俸:捧

诘:结
调:绸
谝:编
谁:维

捂:梧
抗:杭
拮:桔

偏:惆
谝:调
编:绸

诅:祖
诈:祚

铂:珀
锂:理

湟:徨
注:往

技:扛
肢:胚

Fig. 2 A sample of 8 analogical clusters output by our method on 5,000 characters from the font FireflyR16 using 51 pixel positions selected at random as features. Each of these clusters shows commutations of the *left* part of characters (usually a phonetic key) with the *right* part (usually a semantic radical). The *rightmost* cluster is not acceptable for the human eye. Similarly, the first, the second and the last lines in the *leftmost* cluster should have been left out

and to enumerate all analogies between vectors of features like the one above so that, showing the bitmaps the vectors stand for, visualizes analogies between characters, like the one below:

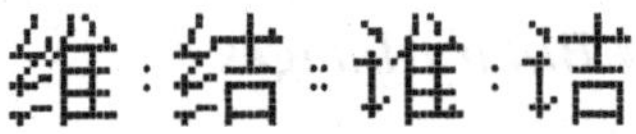

维 : 结 :: 谁 : 诘

In Lepage (2014), we showed that the original problem, which complexity is $O(n^4)$, can be reduced to a problem quadratic in the number of characters thanks to the transitivity of conformity in this special case. Additional practical gains in time can be obtained. We used various features ranging from the number of black pixels on the lines or rows to decomposition by quad trees. In general it takes about half an hour on a modern computer to output clusters of Chinese characters like the ones shown in Fig. 2 from a set of several thousands of bitmaps. The number of analogies that are not valid for the human eye, i.e., the number of analogies that are not *true analogies,* is negligible (see cluster (8) as an example in Fig. 2). In other words, the precision is excellent. Some valid analogies are not captured by our proposal (like). Their number, i.e., the recall of the method, is difficult to estimate, especially by sampling, due to the sparseness of true analogies relatively to the set of all possibilities.

2.4 The Case of Strings of Symbols

Strings of symbols are a specialization of the structure of multi-sets in the sense that an order on the members is added to each string.

Before going further, we examine the relation between the determinism hypothesis and transitivity for conformity (already mentioned at the beginning and end of Sect. 2.1). It should first be said that there exist analogical equations on strings of symbols that admit several solutions. For instance, $a : aa :: b : x$, has several possible solutions: *ba*, or *ab*, or even *bb*. Hence, in all generality, there exist proportional analogies between strings of symbols $A : B :: C : x$ with at least two different solutions D_1 and D_2 ($D_1 \neq D_2$). Now, for such an analogical equation, if conformity would be transitive, then:

$$\begin{cases} A : B :: C : D_1 \\ A : B :: C : D_2 \end{cases} \Rightarrow \begin{cases} C : D_1 :: A : B \,(\text{inv. ::}) \\ A : B :: C : D_2 \end{cases}$$
$$\Rightarrow C : D_1 :: C : D_2 \,(\text{transitivity of ::})$$
$$\Rightarrow C : C :: D_1 : D_2 \,(\text{exch. means})$$

As D_1 and D_2 were supposed to be different, this shows that transitivity of conformity and the determinism hypothesis are in conflict. Our first result on proportional analogy between strings of symbols will be directly linked with this.

Let us first mention that four kinds of proportional analogies can be distinguished between strings of symbols. They are named and illustrated below.

Repetition: *guru* : *guru–guru* :: *pelajar* : *pelajar–pelajar* (Malay)
Reduplication: *cado* : *cecidi* :: *pago* : *pepigi* (Latin)
Commutation: *aslama* : *muslim* :: *arsala* : *mursil* (Arabic)
Mirror: *abcd* : *dcba* :: *xyz* : *zyx*

Mirror is not a kind of analogy attested in language data. Although reduplication and repetition are well attested phenomena in language data (Gil 2002; Tkaczyk 2004), our work concerns only analogies of commutation. We illustrated it above with an example from Arabic morphology to stress the fact that the interesting property to reproduce is parallel infixing, not only mere substitution of prefixes or suffixes.

From the observation of a large amount of linguistic and formal examples [see Lepage (2003) pages 140–143 and 158–160] it is possible to propose a sufficient condition for the analogical equation $A : B :: C : x$ to have *no* solution: if some symbol in A appears neither in B nor in C, there exists no solution to the equation. By contraposition, a necessary condition for the analogy $A : B :: C : D$ to hold is that all symbols in A appear in B, in C, or in both (in the same order). If we denote by *sim* the similarity between strings, i.e., the length of the longest common subsequence, this means that A is covered by the subsequences it has in common with B and C. Thus: $A : B :: C : D \Rightarrow sim(A,B) + sim(A,C) \geq |A|$. By using the eight equivalent forms of proportional analogy, and by assuming that the differences of the type $sim(A,B) + sim(A,C) - |A|$ are all equal for A, B, C and D,[2] the following system of equalities is obtained:

[2] This assumption comes from the observation of language data and formal data. It is not derived from any theoretical consideration and should thus be added to the set of basic properties for strings of symbols as such.

$$\begin{cases} |A| + |B| - 2 \times sim(A,B) = |C| + |D| - 2 \times sim(C,D) \\ |A| + |C| - 2 \times sim(A,C) = |B| + |D| - 2 \times sim(B,D) \end{cases} \tag{7}$$

Because it is known that for any two strings of symbols, $dist(A,B) = |A| + |B| - 2 \times sim(A,B)$ where *dist* is the canonical edit distance that involves insertion and deletion only as edit operations, the previous system is equivalent to:

$$\begin{cases} dist(A,B) = dist(C,D) \\ dist(A,C) = dist(B,D) \end{cases} \tag{8}$$

This result implies the determinism hypothesis. For any proportional analogy of the form $A : A \ :: B_1 : B_2$, $dist(A,A) = 0 = dist(B_1,B_2)$ implies that $B_1 = B_2$. It means that conformity is not transitive in this setting.[3]

In addition to this result on distances, if we note $|A|_a$ the number of occurrences of symbol a in string A,

$$|A|_a + |D|_a = |B|_a + |C|_a \tag{11}$$

is clearly met by all data. This merely meets the fact that strings of symbols are a specialization of multi-sets.[4] It is trivial to show that both separately, the result on distances or the result on counting of symbols, imply: for an analogy between strings of symbols, $A : B \ :: \ C : D$, the sum of the lengths of the extremes is equal to the sum of the lengths of the means $|A| + |D| = |B| + |C|$.

The results above can be partially visualized by a parallelogram, exemplified by the geometrical figure given in Fig. 3.

---

[3] The alternative proposal for the definition of proportional analogies between strings of symbols found in Stroppa (2005; Stroppa and Yvon 2004; Yvon et al. 2004) does not share the same property. That proposal allows the particular proportional analogy $a : a :: ab : ba$ which is barred by our definition, and more generally all the proportional analogies of the type: $p_1.u.s_1 : p_1.u.s_1 :: p_2.u.v.s_2 : p_2.v.u.s_2$ which do not hold in general in our definition (notice the inversion of u and v in the right part of the proportion analogy although the first two members of the analogy are equal). According to that proposal, $A : B :: C : D$ iff $A \bullet D \cap B \bullet C \neq \emptyset$, where $\bullet$ is the shuffle of two strings. Now,

$$\begin{cases} a.ba = aba \in a \bullet ba \\ ab.a = aba \in a \bullet ab \end{cases} \Rightarrow a \bullet ba \cap a \bullet ab \neq \emptyset \tag{9}$$

and

$$\begin{cases} p_1.p_2.u.vu.s_1.s_2 = p_1p_2uvus_1s_2 \in A \bullet D \\ p_1.p_2.uv.u.s_1.s_2 = p_1p_2uvus_1s_2 \in B \bullet C \end{cases} \Rightarrow A \bullet D \cap B \bullet C \neq \emptyset \tag{10}$$

Consequently, our definition of proportional analogy between strings of symbols puts more constraints on parallel infixing thanks to the limitations induced by distances.

[4] This is also trivially implied by the definition mentioned in the above footnote.

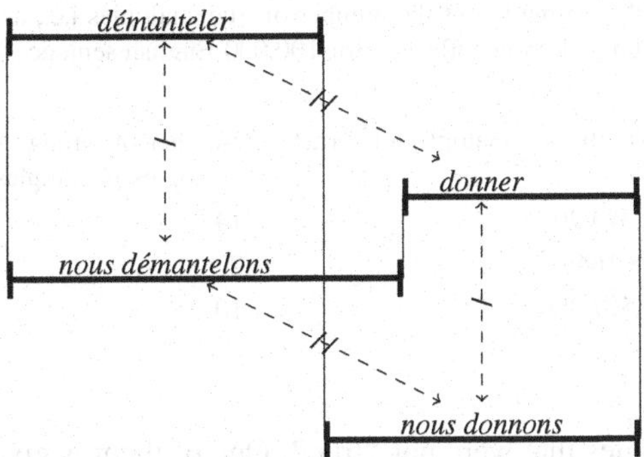

Fig. 3 Visualization of the main results on proportional analogy between strings of symbols

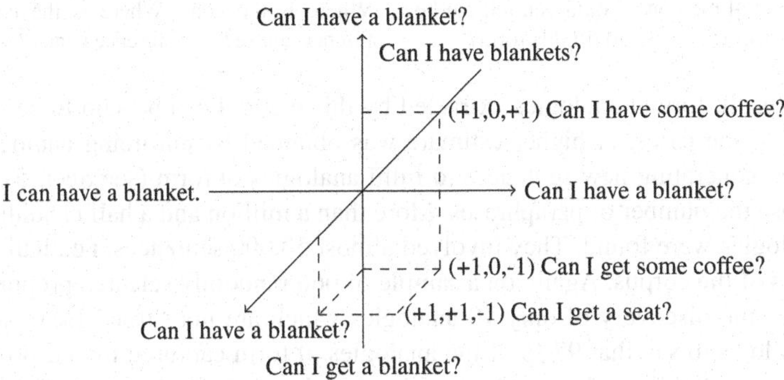

Fig. 4 A three-dimensional vectorial space illustrating three oppositions. Each dimension stands for a cluster of sentences; the two sentences written at both extremities exemplify the ratio. Other sentences can be located in such a space with three possible values on each dimension: −1 or 1 for each side of the opposition, 0 if the opposition is not relevant for the sentence

3 Validity: True Analogies in Corpora

In Lepage (2004), we reported experiments in estimating the number of *true analogies,* i.e., analogies of form *and* meaning, between short sentences contained in an aligned multilingual Chinese-English-Japanese corpus (Takezawa et al. 2002) of almost 100,000 different sentences in each language, making the assumption that translation preserves meaning. We computed a lower and a higher estimates (see Table 6).

We obtained a lower estimate of almost 70,000 true analogies involving almost 14,000 English sentences by intersecting analogies of form between Chinese, English and Japanese extracted using the definition of proportional analogy between strings of symbols presented above. Checking the truth of the proportional analogies extracted, on a sample of 666 randomly selected analogies, allowed to

Table 6 Summary of the estimation of the number of true analogies i.e., analogies of form and meaning, using a multilingual corpus. Results for 100,000 English sentences and test samples of 666 analogies

Sample	Number of analogies of form	Number of wrong analogies in samples	Percentage of true analogies
Raw data	2,384,202	14	96.18 %
Lower estimate	68,164	2	99.04 %
Higher estimate	1,507,380	10	97.05 %

spot only two analogies that were not "true". One of them is given below. Notice the inversion of the 'r' in from/form due to a spelling mistake and in centre/center due to orthographical variation.

Could you tell me how to fill this from? : Could you tell me how to fill this form? :: Where is the conference centre? : Where is the conference center?

As a result, formal analogies extracted by this method can be said to be "true" in 99 % of the cases. A higher estimate was obtained by enforcing analogies of form, i.e., generating new sentences to fulfil analogies of form (see Sect. 5), so as to increase the number of paraphrases. More than a million and a half candidates of true analogies were found. They involved almost 50,000 sentences, i.e., half of the sentences of the corpus. Again, on a sample of 666 randomly selected proportional analogies, the discovery of only 10 analogies which are not "true" (see example below) allows to say that 97 % of the analogies of form captured by our proposed definition are "true" analogies. An analogy which was judged as "false" is given below:

Can I eat? : Can I eat on the train? :: I'm afraid you're wrong. : I'm afraid you're on the wrong train.

In Lepage et al. (2009), we measured in the same way the number of true proportional analogies between chunks in Japanese on a subset of the previous corpus: 20,000 sentences. We tested, with success, a null hypothesis of at least 96 % of true analogies between chunks extracted from these sentences (see Table 7).

This figure of more than 95 % somehow relates to *langage* (as opposed to *parole*), because it establishes the truth of analogies between chunks or sentences attested, at least in a particular corpus. This figure is in blatant contradiction with the generally accepted opinion that analogies of form would almost necessarily lead to nonsense and would have weak connection with meaning. This figure also

Table 7 Statistics for the data and estimation of the number of true analogies, with a 96 % null hypothesis. On average, a chunk is repeated 3.76 times in the corpus

Unit	Data size in			Number of analogies of form	Number of true analogies	
	Total # of units	Words	≠ units		% observed	p-value
Sentences	20,000	173,091	18,454	4,428	100 %	N.r
Chunks	99,719	693,526	27,936	2,131,269	96 %	0.005

shows that analogies can be exploited in natural language processing applications at a higher level than the ordinary level of words it is usually confined to in the general belief. Indeed, different research already exploit analogy on a higher level than words, like Stroppa and Yvon (2005), or (Claveau and L'Homme 2005) with complex terms. In the previous experiment on Japanese (Lepage et al. 2009), it was observed that the number of analogies between chunks is thousand times higher than the number of analogies between the sentences containing these chunks.

Without being concerned with the truth or not of the analogies collected, (Takeya and Lepage 2011, 2013) systematically explored the number of analogies between chunks obtained by marker-based chunking from 2,500 sentences in each of the 11 European different languages of the Europarl corpus (Koehn 2005). Several tens of thousands of analogies between chunks were extracted in each language, again thousand times more than the number of analogies between sentences. This meets the intuition that the number of analogies between smaller units like chunks should be bigger than between larger units like sentences. And this opens the question of determining the linguistic unit which would be the most productive with regard to proportional analogy.

4 Structuring Data by Proportional Analogy

In morphology, proportional analogy is undeniably the force at work that structures conjugation or declension paradigms (Skousen 1989). The notion of paradigm can be extended to sentences by exhibiting series of sentences with commutations. On the left below a series of commutations of the word 'Japanese' with 'Spanish', 'French', etc. is shown. It does not just exchange nationality-related adjectives but crosses the boundaries between (derivational) morphology and syntax as the last two examples clearly show: 'Japanese food' is exchanged with 'seafood' and 'almost all kinds of food'. On the right, commutations around 'Japanese food' happen both at the front and at the end of sentences with a certain degree of freedom.

I like Japanese food.	Japanese food would be fine.
I like Spanish food.	I'd prefer Japanese food.
I like French food.	Japanese food is fine with me.
I like seafood.	I'd like to have Japanese food.
I like almost all kinds of food.	Does Japanese food suit your taste?

Paradigms can be visualized in the form of tables anchored around a sentence placed at the top left corner of a two-dimensional table ('I like Japanese food' in Fig. 5). But a two-dimensional representation is a limitation. The structure induced by proportional analogies is indeed a multi-dimensional space (see Fig. 4) where each dimension is given rise by the existence of a cluster of pairs of sentences that share the same oppositions, like the one below.

I like Japanese food.	I prefer Japanese food.	I'd prefer Japanese food.	I feel like Japanese food.
I enjoyed the food.			*I feel enjoyed the food.
I prefer French food.			*I feel prefer French food.
I like Italian food.	I prefer Italian food.	I'd prefer Italian food.	I feel like Italian food.
I like seafood.	I prefer seafood.	I'd prefer seafood.	I feel like seafood.
I'd like local food.	I'd prefer local food.	*I'd'd prefer local food.	I'd feel like local food.
I like Mexican food.	I prefer Mexican food.	I'd prefer Mexican food.	I feel like Mexican food.
I'd like the local food.	I'd prefer the local food.	*I'd'd prefer the local food.	I'd feel like the local food.
I like Western food.	I prefer Western food.	I'd prefer Western food.	I feel like Western food.
I'd like some Italian food.	I'd prefer some Italian food.	*I'd'd prefer some Italian food.	I'd feel like some Italian food.
I'd like Western food.	I'd prefer Western food.	*I'd'd prefer Western food.	I'd feel like Western food.
I like Chinese food.	I prefer Chinese food.	I'd prefer Chinese food.	I feel like Chinese food.
I like Spanish food.	I prefer Spanish food.	I'd prefer Spanish food.	I feel like Spanish food.
I'd like some famous local food.	I'd prefer some famous local food.	*I'd'd prefer some famous local food.	I'd feel like some famous local food.
Do you like Italian food?	Do you prefer Italian food?	*Do you'd prefer Italian food?	Do you feel like Italian food?

Fig. 5 Filling a paradigm table. The sentences on the first line and the first column are from the corpus. Empty cells have no analogical solution. *Gray* cells were produced by analogy. Cells with a *white* background contain sentences from the corpus. Incorrect sentences are marked with *

Can I have a blanket? : I can have a blanket.
Can I get some small change? : I can get some small change.
Can I board on the next flight? : I can board on the next flight.

Lepage and Denoual (2005) reports experiments in outputting such series of oppositions on roughly 40,000 short sentences again from the BTEC corpus in English and Japanese. The method allowed to extract not only linguistically relevant oppositions between short sentences in English and Japanese, but also constructions (in line with construction grammars, CxG, (Croft 2001). The clusters obtained illustrate a wide range of phenomena of different order, like:

- orthographical variations (e.g.: centre : center);
- fronting of interjections (e.g.: Do…, please. : Please do…);
- exchange of place names, document names, item names etc.;
- positive versus comparative forms of adjectives (e.g.: green : greener);
- structural transformations, like interrogative versus affirmative;
- exchange of predicates in the same grammatical subject and object context (as illustrated by the first cluster in Table 8);
- questions in different levels of politeness (as illustrated by the second cluster in Table 9);
- etc.

Table 8 A cluster of short sentences obtained automatically. It illustrates the exchange of the predicate 'keep this baggage' with 'draw me a map'

Could you keep this baggage?	:	Could you draw me a map?
Keep this baggage, please.	:	Draw me a map, please.
Will you keep this baggage?	:	Will you draw me a map?
Please keep this baggage.	:	Please draw me a map.

Table 9 A cluster of short sentences obtained automatically. It illustrates the structural transformation of 'I'd like to…' into 'Can I… here?'

I'd like to cash this traveler 's check.	:	Can I cash this traveler's check here?
I'd like to make a hotel reservation.	:	Can I make a hotel reservation here?
I'd like to make a reservation.	:	Can I make a reservation here?
I'd like to check my baggage.	:	Can I check my baggage here?
I'd like to leave my baggage.	:	Can I leave my baggage here?
I'd like to leave my luggage.	:	Can I leave my luggage here?
I'd like to reserve a room.	:	Can I reserve a room here?
I'd like to have dinner.	:	Can I have dinner here?
I'd like to check in.	:	Can I check in here?
I'd like to swim.	:	Can I swim here?

5 Generating Data by Proportional Analogy

As said above, in Fig. 5, for reasons of visibility, we use a projection on two dimensions. At the beginning, the first line and the first column of the matrix contain the same sentences in the same order (the matrix is symmetrical). In the inner cells of the matrix, we place sentences in proportional analogy with the top left corner of the matrix, the leftmost sentence on the same line, and the sentence at the top of the same column. A good number of these sentences did not exist in the corpus. Then, by deleting lines or columns which contain too many holes, the proportion of sentences in the matrix raises. It is observed that the number of new correct sentences retained in the tables raises too (see Table 10). In an experiment on 22 matrices and using only 1,500 sentences, up to 70 % (1,201) of the newly created sentences were found to be correct (Lepage and Peralta 2004).

The previous technique can be generalized to massively add new sentences to a corpus. In Lepage and Denoual (2005) the application of the technique was limited to the generation of paraphrases. There, the technique works in two steps. The first step over-generates whilst the second one over-eliminates candidate paraphrases by just filtering out any sentence that contain an unattested *N*-sequence, for some fixed *N*. In the experiment reported in Lepage and Denoual (2005) using 97,769 English sentences it was possible to generate 17, 862 paraphrases so as to increase the size of the original resource by 18.32 %. The quality of the total resource was left untouched at 99 % grammatical correctness. More than 96 % of the candidate paraphrases were judged to be good paraphrases or valid entailments (see Table 10 for examples).

A further generalization of the technique removes the constraint on producing only paraphrases. We currently use this to construct a Chinese-Japanese quasi-parallel corpus from sentences collected from the Web (Yang et al. 2013). We first over-generate new sentences using proportional analogy: from sentences in Chinese and Japanese, we independently construct analogical clusters of the type

Table 10 Paraphrases for 'Can we have a table in the corner?' after filtering by N-sequences (N = 20). These sentences did not exist in the original resource

Number of times the paraphrase was generated	Paraphrase
1678	Could we have a table in the corner?
1658	We would like a table in the corner.
1652	I'd like a table in the corner.
878	Can we have a table in the corner?
50	Can I get a table in the corner?
8	We'd like a table in the corner.
2	I prefer a table in the corner.

shown in Tables 8 and 9 and use these clusters as rewriting models to generate new sentences. Then, to ensure fluency of expression and adequacy of meaning, we filter the newly generated sentences by attested N-sequences and obtain new sentences which are at least 99 % correct on the grammatical level. Finally, relying on the similarity between the clusters across languages and the similarity between the seed sentences, we deduce translation relations between the newly generated sentences and assess their strength to obtain a quasi-parallel Chinese-Japanese bicorpus made of sentence pairs with associated similarity scores. In a preliminary experiment, among 1,837 pairs of Chinese-Japanese sentences obtained from several tens of thousands sentences, 1,124 sentence pairs (61 %) were judged to be exact translations.

The previous technique can be seen as a sketch of a general method to perform translation. Indeed, when applied in parallel to pieces of languages aligned by translation across two languages, the previous technique leads to the principle of translation by proportional analogy. This principle extends the initial proposal of translation by analogy (Nagao 1984). It has been known for long:

$$f(A) : f(B) :: f(C) : D \Leftrightarrow A : B :: C : f^{-1}(D)$$

The first experiments in using this principle were reported in Lepage and Denoual (2005) to translate short sentences as a whole. It has also been thought that the principle can apply to particular pieces of texts, like unknown words (Denoual 2007; Langlais and Patry 2007), terms from a particular domain (Langlais et al. 2008), or transliteration of proper names or cognates (Dandapat et al. 2010; Langlais 2013) Another possible use in the frame of statistical machine translation, is to populate a translation table in advance with phrases obtained by application of the principle. In Luo and Lepage (2013), it is shown that the methods pays off when used with small amounts of data as demonstrated on excerpts of the Europarl coups in 110 language pairs. The technique is not so good on a training set of 350,000 sentence pairs but is worth being applied for a training set of 10,000 sentences pairs. As, in fact, phrases in translation tables are small N-grams, it is certainly worth exploring analogy to separate N-grams that can be reconstructed by proportional analogy from those which cannot. Gosme and Lepage (2011) explores this path and even proposes a smoothing technique for trigram language models. The work relies on the following observation made on the 11 languages of version 3 of the Europarl corpus. Massively, unknown trigrams, which by definition have a frequency of 0 in the training data, can be reconstructed by proportional analogy with hapax trigrams (i.e., trigrams with a frequency of 1 in the training data). In other words, unknown trigrams are massively close, in structure and frequency, to hapax trigrams.

6 Conclusion

This paper summarized some of the results obtained over several years in looking for proportional analogy in written language data. We reported results obtained in the formalization of proportional analogy between strings of symbols and its application to various problems of natural language processing, which extend from structuring Chinese characters to machine translation, through paraphrase generation.

Two important points should be stressed. Firstly from the point of view of *langue*, i.e., when looking at given language data, the number of formal proportional analogies which are true analogies, is found to be surprisingly high, more that 95 %. Secondly, from the point of view of *parole*, i.e., producing new language data, it seems possible to limit the over-generation of proportional analogy in practical systems to drive the systems to output pieces of text that are not worse in quality than those output by some probabilistic systems (we do not think only of machine translation here).

Acknowledgments I would like to mention the contribution of many colleagues, researchers or students in getting many of the experimental results presented here over the years. They are listed in alphabetical order below: Nicolas Auclerc, Etienne Denoual, Chooi Ling Goh, Erwan Guillerm, Juan Luo, Jin Matsuoka, Kota Matsushita, Julien Migeot, Guilhem Peralta, Kota Takeya, Hao Wang, Wei Yang.

References

Anttila, R. (1989). *Historical linguistics and comparative linguistics*. Amsterdam: John Benjamins.

Becker, T. (1990). *Analogie und morphologische Theorie*. München: Whilhelm Fink. Retrieved from http://opus4.kobv.de/opus4-bamberg/files/4324/BeckerThomasDissocrseA2.pdf.

Claveau, V., & L'Homme, M. C. (2005). Terminology by analogy-based machine learning. In: *Proceedings of the 7th International Conference on Terminology and Knowledge Engineering, TKE 2005, Copenhagen (Denmark)*.

Croft, W. (2001). *Radical construction grammar: Syntactic theory in typological perspective*. Oxford: Oxford University Press (Oxford Linguistics). Retrieved from http://books.google.co.jp/books?id=ESa_E-q8hbwC.

Dandapat, S., Morriessy, S., Naskar, S. K., & Somers, H. (2010). Mitigating problems in analogy-based EBMT with SMT and vice versa: A case study with named entity transliteration. In: *Proceedings of the 24th Pacific Asia Conference on Language Information and Computation (PACLIC 2010), Sendai, Japan* (pp. 146–153).

Denoual, E. (2007). Analogical translation of unknown words in a statistical machine translation framework. In: *Proceedings of Machine Translation Summit XI. Copenhagen*.

Gentner, D. (1983). Structure mapping: A theoretical model for analogy. *Cognitive Science, 7*(2), 155–170.

Gil, D. (2002). *From repetition to reduplication in Riau Indonesian*. Paper presented at the Graz Reduplication Conference, p. s: 2. Retrieved from http://www-classic.uni-graz.at/ling2www/veranst/redup2002/abstracts/gil.pdf.

Gosme, J., & Lepage, Y. (2011). Structure des trigrammes inconnus et lissage par analogie. In M. Lafourcade & V. Prince (Eds.), *Actes de TALN-2011* (vol. articles longs, pp. 345–356). ATALA.

Hoffman, R. R. (1995). Monster analogies. *AI Magazine, 11*, 11–35.

Itkonen, E. (2005). Analogy as structure and process: Approaches in linguistics, cognitive psychology and philosophy of science. In M. Dascal, R. W. Gibbs, & J. Nuyts (Eds.), *Human cognitive processing* (Vol. 14, p. 250). Amsterdam: John Benjamins.

Koehn, P. (2005). Europarl: A parallel corpus for statistical machine translation. In *Proceedings of the Tenth Machine Translation Summit (MT Summit X), Phuket, Thailand* (pp. 79–86). Retrieved from http://www.mt-archive.info/MTS-2005-Koehn.pdf.

Langlais, P. (2013). Mapping source to target strings without alignment by analogical learning: A case study with transliteration. In *Proceedings of the 51st Annual Meeting of the Association for Computational Linguistics* (Volume 2: Short Papers, pp. 684–689). *Association for Computational Linguistics, Sofia*, Bulgaria. Retrieved from http://www.aclweb.org/anthology/P13-2120.

Langlais, P., & Patry, A. (2007). Translating unknown words by analogical learning. In *Proceedings of the 2007 Joint Conference on Empirical Methods in Natural Language Processing and Computational Natural Language Learning (EMNLP-CoNLL)* (pp. 877–886). Retrieved from http://www.aclweb.org/anthology/D/D07/D07-1092.

Langlais, P., Yvon, F., & Zweigenbaum, P. (2008). Analogical translation of medical words in different languages. In *Gotal'08*: *Proceedings of the 6th international conference on Advances in Natural Language Processing, Lecture Notes in Artificial Intelligence*, (Vol. 5221, pp. 284–295). Berlin: Springer. doi: 10.1007/978-3-540-85287-2.

Lavie, R. J. (2003). Le locuteur analogique ou la grammaire mise à sa place. Thèse de doctorat, Université de Nanterre—Paris X. Retrieved from http://tel.archives-ouvertes.fr/tel-00285173.

Lehmann, W. P. (1967). *A reader in nineteenth-century historical indo-european linguistics*. Bloomington: Indiana University.

Lepage, Y. (2001). Analogy and formal languages. *Proceedings of FG/MOL 2001, Helsinki* (pp. 1–12).

Lepage, Y. (2003). De l'analogie rendant compte de la commutation en linguistique. Mémoire d'habilitation à diriger les recherches, Université de Grenoble. Retrieved from http://tel.ccsd.cnrs.fr/tel-00004372.

Lepage, Y. (2004). Analogy and formal languages. *Electronic Notes in Theoretical Computer Science, 53*, 180–191. Retrieved from http://www.sciencedirect.com/.

Lepage, Y. (2004). Lower and higher estimates of the number of "true analogies" between sentences contained in a large multilingual corpus. In *Proceedings of COLING-2004, Geneva* (Vol. 1, pp. 736–742). Retrieved from http://aclweb.org/anthology//C/C04/C04-1106.pdf.

Lepage, Y. (2014). *Analogy between binary images: Application to Chinese characters.* In H. Prade & G. Richard (Eds.), *Computational approaches to analogical reasoning*: *Current trends*. (pp. 1–33). Berlin: Springer.

Lepage, Y., & Denoual, E. (2005). Adding paraphrases of the same quality to the C-STAR BTEC. In *11th Conference in Natural Language Processing* (pp. 1141–1144). Yokohama University. Retrieved from http://www.slt.atr.co.jp/~lepage/pdf/nlpj05-1.pdf.gz.

Lepage, Y., & Denoual, E. (2005). BLEU in characters: Towards automatic evaluation in languages without word delimiters. In *Companion Volume to the Proceedings of the 2nd International Joint Conference on Natural Language Processing (IJCNLP-05)* (pp. 81–86). Jeju. Retrieved from http://www.slt.atr.co.jp/~lepage/pdf/ijcnlp05.pdf.gz.

Lepage, Y., & Denoual, E. (2005). Purest ever example-based machine translation: Detailed presentation and assessment. *Machine Translation, 19*, 251–282. Retrieved from http://www.springerlink.com/content/tqj32n0m5v8w3m6u/fulltext.pdf.

Lepage, Y., Migeot, J., & Guillerm, E. (2007). A corpus study on the number of true proportional analogies between chunks in two typologically different languages. In *Proceedings of the seventh international Symposium on Natural Language Processing (SNLP 2007)* (pp. 117–122). Pattaya, Thailand: Kasetsart University (ISBN 978-974-623-062-9).

Lepage, Y., Migeot, J., & Guillerm, E. (2009). A measure of the number of true analogies between chunks in Japanese. *Lecture Notes in Artificial Intelligence, 5603*, 154–164.

Lepage, Y., & Peralta, G. (2004). Using paradigm tables to generate new utterances similar to those existing in linguistic resources. In *Proceedings of the 4th internation conference on Language Resources and Evaluation* (*LREC 2004*) (Vol. 1, pp. 243–246), Lisbon.

Luo, J., & Lepage, Y. (2013). A comparison of association and estimation approaches to alignment in word-to-word translation. In *Proceedings of the tenth international Symposium on Natural Language Processing* (*SNLP 2013*) (pp. 181–186), *Phuket*, Phuket, Thailand.

Nagao, M. (1984). A framework of a mechanical translation between Japanese and English by analogy principle. In A. Elithorn & R. Banerji (Eds.) *Artificial & Human Intelligence* (pp. 173–180). Amsterdam: Elsevier.

Osthoff, H. (1979). Kleine Beiträge zur Declinationslehre. Morphologische Untersuchungen auf dem Gebiete der Indogermanischen Sprachen II.

Paul, H. (1920). *Prinzipien der Sprachgeschichte*. Tübingen: Niemayer.

Richard, G., Prade, H. (2014). A short introduction to computational trends in analogical reasoning. In H. Prade & G. Richard (Eds.) *Computational Approaches to Analogical Reasoning: Current Trends*, (pp. i–xx). Berlin: Springer.

de Saussure, F. (1995). Cours de Linguistique Générale, [1ère éd. 1916] edn. Lausanne et Paris: Payot.

Skousen, R. (1989). *Analogical Modeling of Language*. Dordrecht: Kluwer.

Stankiewicz, E. (1986). *Baudouin de Courtenay I Podstawy Współczesnego Jezykoznawstwa*. Wrocław: Ossolineum.

Stroppa, N. (2005). Définitions et caractérisation de modèles à base d'analogies pour l'apprentissage automatique des langues naturelles. Thèse de doctorat, École nationale supérieure des télécommunications.

Stroppa, N., & Yvon, F. (2004). Analogies dans les séquences: un solveur à états finis. In: *Actes de la 11e Conférence Annuelle sur le Traitement Automatique des Langues Naturelles* (*TALN-2004*), p. [pas de numérotation]. Fès. Retrieved from http://aune.lpl.univ-aix.fr/jep-taln04/proceed/actes/taln2004-Fez/Stroppa-Yvon.pdf.

Stroppa, N., & Yvon, F. (2005) An analogical learner for morphological analysis. In *Proceedings of the 9th Conference on Computational Natural Language Learning* (*CoNLL 2005*), (pp. 120–127). Ann Arbor, MI.

Takeya, K., & Lepage, Y. (2011). A study of the number of proportional analogies between marker-based chunks in 11 European languages. In Z. Vetulani (Ed.) Proceedings of the 5th Language & Technology Conference (LTC'1), (pp. 284–288). Poznań: Fundacja uniwersytetu im. Adama Mickiewicza.

Takeya, K., & Lepage, Y. (2013) Marker-based chunking in eleven European languages for analogy-based translation. Lecture Notes in Artificial Intelligence *8387*, pp. XX–YY.

Takezawa, T., Sumita, E., Sugaya, F., Yamamoto, H., & Yamamoto, S. (2002). Toward a broad coverage bilingual corpus for speech translation of travel conversation in the real world. In *Proceedings of LREC 2002*, (pp. 147–152). Las Palmas.

Tkaczyk, B. (2004). Re 'cloning', i.e. 'reduplicative' process. In KUL (Ed.) 36th Poznań Linguistics meetings.

Turney, P. (2008). A uniform approach to analogies, synonyms, antonyms, and associations. In *Proceedings of the 22nd International Conference on Computational Linguistics* (*Coling 2008*), (pp. 905–912). Manchester, UK: Coling 2008 Organizing Committee. Retrieved from http://aclweb.org/anthology//C/C08/C08-1114.pdf.

Turney, P. D. (2006). Similarity of semantic relations. *Computational Linguistics 32*(2), 379–416. Retrieved from http://aclweb.org/anthology//P/P06/P06-1040.pdf.

Turney, P. D., & Littman, M. L. (2005). Corpus-based learning of analogies and semantic relations. *Machine Learning 60*(1–3), 251–278. Retrieved from http://www.citebase.org/abstract?id=oai:arXiv.org:cs/0508103.

Varro, M. T. (1954). De lingua latina. Coll. Belles-lettres, Paris. Trad. J. Collart.

Veale, T., & Chen, S. (2006). Learning to extract semantic content from the orthographic structure of Chinese words. In *Proceedings of the 17th Irish conference on Artificial Intelligence and Cognitive Science* (*AICS2006*). Retrieved from http://citeseerx.ist.psu.edu/viewdoc/summary?doi=10.1.1.77.6982.

Veale, T., & Li, G. (2014). Analogy as an organizational principle in the construction of large knowledge-bases. In H. Prade & G. Richard (Eds.) *Computational Approaches to Analogical Reasoning: Current Trends, Studies in Computational Intelligence* Vol. 548 (pp. 58–77). Berlin: Springer.

Welcomme, A. (2010). Hermann Paul et le concept d'analogie. *CÍRCULO de Lingüstica Aplicada a la Comunicación* (*clac*) *43*, 49–122. Retrieved from http://pendientedemigracion.ucm.es/info/circulo/no43/welcomme.pdf.

Yang, W., Wang, H., & Lepage, Y. (2013). Using analogical associations to acquire Chinese-Japanese quasi-parallel sentences. In *Proceedings of the tenth symposium on natural language processing* (*SNLP2013*), (pp. 86–93). Phuket, Thailand.

Yvon, F., Stroppa, N., Miclet, L., & Delhay, A. (2004). Solving analogical equations on words. Rapport technique ENST2004D005, ENST.

Multilingual Projections

Pushpak Bhattacharyya

Abstract Languages of the world, though different, share structures and vocabulary. Today's NLP depends crucially on annotation which, however, is costly, needing expertise, money and time. Most languages in the world fall far behind English, when it comes to annotated resources. Since annotation is costly, there has been worldwide effort at leveraging multilinguality in development and use of annotated corpora. The key idea is to project and utilize annotation from one language to another. This means parameters learnt from the annotated corpus of one language is made use of in the NLP of another language. We illustrate multilingual projection through the case study of word sense disambiguation (WSD) whose goal is to obtain the correct meaning of a word in the context. The correct meaning is usually denoted by an appropriate sense id from a sense repository, usually the wordnet. In this paper we show how two languages can help each other in their WSD, even when neither language has any sense marked corpus. The two specific languages chosen are Hindi and Marathi. The sense repository is the IndoWordnet which is a linked structure of wordnets of 19 major Indian languages from Indo-Aryan, Dravidian and Sino-Tibetan families. These wordnets have been created by following the expansion approach from Hindi wordnet. The WSD algorithm is reminiscent of expectation maximization. The sense distribution of either language is estimated through the mediation of the sense distribution of the other language in an iterative fashion. The WSD accuracy arrived at is better than any state of the art accuracy of all words general purpose unsupervised WSD.

Keywords Annotation · Projection · Lexical resource scarcity · WSD · Multilingual computation · Expectation maximization · Indowordnet · Sense marked corpora · Unsupervised WSD

P. Bhattacharyya (✉)
Department of Computer Science and Engineering, IIT Bombay, Bombay, India
e-mail: pb@cse.iitb.ac.inpushpakbh@gmail.com

© Springer International Publishing Switzerland 2015
N. Gala et al. (eds.), *Language Production, Cognition, and the Lexicon*,
Text, Speech and Language Technology 48, DOI 10.1007/978-3-319-08043-7_11

1 Introduction

The world is very multilingual. Ethnologue[1] which is a web based publication containing the most comprehensive and accessible language catalog, mentions 7,105 languages and dialects in its 17th edition, released in 2013. These languages are grouped into 225 language families. The diversity of human languages is tremendous; innovative lexical items and structures get created all the time. For example, the signage "Baby Changing Room" in Amsterdam Airport intrigues the reader with its alternate possibilities of meaning. Similarly the announcement "No smoking areas will allows hookah inside" displayed in Amman airport at Jordan has exactly opposite meanings depending on how much of the text the negation particle "No" qualifies.

Ethnologue also lists 1,300 languages with 100,000 speakers or more, 750 with 300,000 or more, some 400 with a million or more, 200 with at least 3 million, 80 with 10 million, and 40 with 30 million. These language speakers have their needs, hopes and aspirations expressed in diverse ways. As the varied panorama of human activities, so is the number and diversity of language phenomena.

Natural Language Processing (NLP), Computational Linguistics (CL), Text Mining, Text Analytics (TA), Data Analytics (DA)- all these in one way or other involve computer processing of language. Advent of web has created unimaginably huge repositories of text in electronic form. Such textual data contain information and knowledge whose utilization can make a difference to peoples' lives, countries' economies and global relationships.

NLP is really an activity in three dimensions (Bhattacharyya 2012), as shown in Fig. 1. The X-axis is the language axis showing languages like English, Hindi, Marathi, and German and so on. The Y-axis is the problem or tasks axis describing different tasks in language processing, like morphology analysis, parsing and so on. The Z-axis is the algorithms axis mentioning techniques like Hidden Markov Model (HMM), Maximum Entropy Markov Model (MEMM), and Conditional Random Field (CRF). Any NLP system, therefore, is a language-task-technique trinity.

NLP is also a layered activity (Fig. 2; Bhattacharyya 2013). At the lowest layer is the task of morphology processing which takes in a word form and produces the lemma, affix(es) and features. POS tagging is the next layer that produces grammatical categories like noun, verb, adjective, adverb etc. on words. Chunking groups words which are typically non-recursive NPs and Verb groups (main verb + auxiliaries). Parsing produces the parse tree. Discourse and coreference layer processes larger pieces of text consisting of multiple sentences, resolving coreferences and ensuring coherence. Each layer makes use of information supplied by lower layers and cannot typically make assumptions about information from next higher layer.

[1] http://en.wikipedia.org/wiki/Ethnologue.

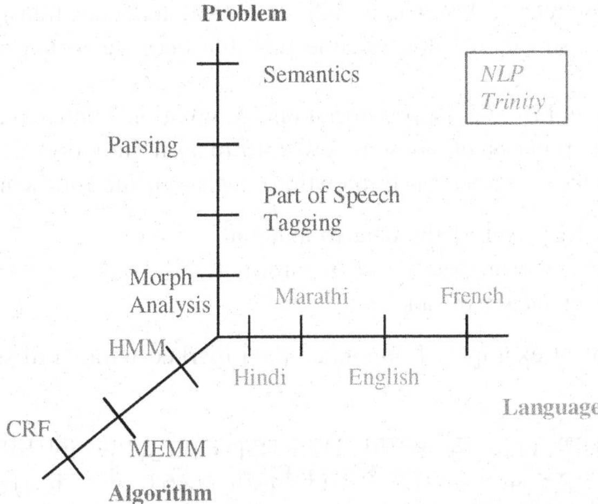

Fig. 1 NLP trinity

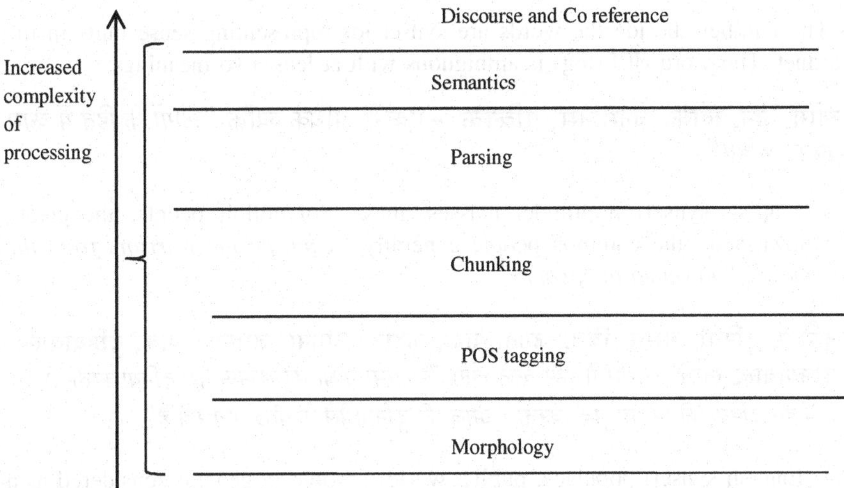

Fig. 2 NLP layers

2 Annotation

At the heart of most NLP tasks is annotation. Since mid 80s, motivated by IBM speech group's research, statistical approaches got introduced in NLP, eventually dominating the field. POS tagging achieved great success through noisy channel modeling (technique borrowed from speech) and HMM (Church 1988 and DeRose 1988). So did shallow parsing (Sha and Perreira 2003), probabilistic parsing

(Manning and Schutze 1999, Chap. 12), statistical machine translation (Brown et al. 1993), and so on. All this became possible because of large quantities of annotated data.

Eduard Hovy in his ACL 2010 tutorial on "Annotation", defines 'annotation' or 'tagging' as the process of adding new information into raw data by human annotators. A typical annotation framework consists of the following:

- Decide which fragment of the data to annotate
- Add to that fragment a specific bit of information
- chosen from a fixed set of options

Here is a typical example of annotated data marked with word sense ids from Hindi wordnet.[2]

एक_4187 नए शोध_1138 के अनुसार_3123 जिन लोगों_1189 का सामाजिक_43540 जीवन_125623 व्यस्त_48029 होता है उनके दिमाग_16168 के एक_4187 हिस्से_120425 में अधिक_42403 जगह_113368 होती है।

(According to a new research, those people who have a busy social life, have larger space in a part of their brain).

The numbers beside the words are synset ids representing sense units in the wordnet. The word लोग (log) is ambiguous with at least two meanings:

- **लोग, जन, लोक, जनमानस, पब्लिक** - एक से अधिक व्यक्ति *"लोगों के हित में काम करना चाहिए"*
  - (English synset) multitude, masses, mass, hoi_polloi, people, the_great_unwashed—the common people generally *"separate the warriors from the mass" "power to the people"*
- **दुनिया, दुनियाँ, संसार, विश्व, जगत, जहाँ, जहान, ज़माना, जमाना, लोक, दुनियावाले, दुनियाँवाले, लोग** - संसार में रहने वाले लोग *"महात्मा गाँधी का सम्मान पूरी दुनिया करती है / मैं इस दुनिया की परवाह नहीं करता / आज की दुनिया पैसे के पीछे भाग रही है"*
  - (English synset) populace, public, world—people in general considered as a whole *"he is a hero in the eyes of the public"*

The two senses of "log" are close to each other. Senses as recorded in sense repositories can be quite fine grained. Therefore creating sense marked data is demanding in terms of linguistic expertise, meaning comprehension, domain knowledge and grip on tags. This combination is not easy of get and costs time and money.

While word based annotations like POS tagging, sense marking, named entity marking etc. target words, "structural annotation" targets phrases and clauses. Here is an example from Stanford parser:

---

[2] http://www.cfilt.iitb.ac.in/wordnet/webhwn.

Sentence: "my dog also likes eating sausages"

```
(ROOT
  (S
    (NP
      (PRP$ My) (NN dog))
    (ADVP (RB also))
    (VP (VBZ likes)
      (S (VP (VBG eating)
        (NP (NN sausage))))) (. .)))
poss(dog-2, My-1)
nsubj(likes-4, dog-2)
advmod(likes-4, also-3)
root(ROOT-0, likes-4)
xcomp(likes-4, eating-5)
dobj(eating-5, sausage-6)
```

The first annotation is the constituent structure of the sentence while the second is the dependency structure. These annotations need understanding of structures besides meaning. A nice example is the Hindi sentence

आओ	मत	जाओ
Come	don't	go

Though not apparent in English, the Hindi sentence has two structures:

Structure-1:
"(come don't) go" meaning "Don't come, go"
Structure-2:
"come (don't go)" meaning "Come, don't go"

Annotation of such sentences need understanding of the larger context.

2.1 Complexities Involved in Annotation

Through the discussions so far, we are driving at the fact that good annotators and good annotation tag designers are rare to find:

- An annotator has to understand BOTH language phenomena and the data
- An annotation designer has to understand BOTH linguistics and statistics

To explain this better we take the example of Penn Treebank Tagset (Marcus et al. 1993). We consider tags for verbs[3]:

A first time computational linguist wonders why there are so many tags for verbs. After all, in elementary grammar she had learnt just 4 main grammatical categories—*Noun, Verb, Adjective* and *Adverb* and a few secondary categories—*preposition, conjunction, interjection*, and so on. Why then so many categories just for verbs?

Answering such questions requires insight into algorithmic, probabilistic and linguistic factors involved in tagging. Remember that POS tagging is just the 2nd layer in the NLP hierarchy with only morphological information available to it (Fig. 2). *No knowledge of syntax or semantics may be assumed.* Thus POS tagging is perforce a limited context task.

The main role of any NLP layer is to *feed useful information to the next higher layers.* The finer the tags at any layer, the better it is for higher layers. However, this begs the question! Fine graining of tags needs processing larger contexts, i.e., processing at higher layers, which in turn needs fine grained tags. This is a chicken and egg problem. NLP in recent times attempts a way out of this quandary by employing deep learning (Bengio 2009) where feedforward neural networks (Rumelhart et. al 1986) of many layers perform computation up and down the layers from input to output, trying to resolve ambiguities on the way.

An example will help illustrate the idea. Consider the classic sentence with structural ambiguity "I saw the boy with a telescope"[4] with additional text as follows:

I saw the boy with a telescope which he dropped accidentally
and
I saw the boy with a telescope which I dropped accidentally

For these sentences, the Stanford parser produces the collapsed typed dependency relations as follows:

"I saw the boy with a telescope which he dropped accidentally"

```
nsubj(saw-2, I-1)
root(ROOT-0, saw-2)
det(boy-4, the-3)
dobj(saw-2, boy-4)
det(telescope-7, a-6)
(*) prep_with(saw-2, telescope-7)
dobj(dropped-10, telescope-7)
nsubj(dropped-10, he-9)
rcmod(telescope-7, dropped-10)
advmod(dropped-10, accidentally-11)
```

[3] https://www.ling.upenn.edu/courses/Fall_2003/ling001/penn_treebank_pos.html.

[4] The PP "with a telescope" can get attached to either "saw" ('I have the telescope') or "the boy" ('the boy has the telescope').

"I saw the boy with a telescope which I dropped accidentally"

```
nsubj(saw-2, I-1)
root(ROOT-0, saw-2)
det(boy-4, the-3)
dobj(saw-2, boy-4)
det(telescope-7, a-6)
prep_with(saw-2, telescope-7)
dobj(dropped-10, telescope-7)
nsubj(dropped-10, I-9)
rcmod(telescope-7, dropped-10)
advmod(dropped-10, accidentally-11)
```

The second dependency graph is correct, while the first is not. For both the sentences the "telescope" is attached with "saw". Since the person dropping the instrument is different in the two cases (*nsubj* of "dropped"), the PP attachment also should be different. In fact, in the first sentence we should have had:

```
prep_with(boy-4, telescope-7)
```

The reason why the parser could not do the attachment correctly in the first sentence is that it could not collate the information of *who dropped the telescope* with *who had the instrument*. A number of higher level NLP tasks like semantic role labeling and co reference resolution need to be performed before doing the attachment correctly. But these tasks need correct parsing! Hence the chicken-and-egg situation.

The deep learning framework would do partial parsing work in syntax layer(s), advance to semantics layer(s) (semantic role) and to the discourse layer(s) (co reference) and come back to the parsing layer to fix attachments. These ideas are still in their nascent stage. But they underline the importance of back and forth movement between NLP layers to solve complex ambiguity problems.

We note that in English almost all nouns can be used as verbs. Take for example the word "tree". Predominantly the word is a noun, but it can be a verb too (*this plot should be treed so that the house will be shaded in summer*). Now "trees" can denote either plural of the noun "tree" or 3rd person, singular number, present tense of the verb "tree". We need context to disambiguate the POS. An auxiliary like "will" denotes verb and a determiner like "The" denotes noun.

We had digressed a bit from our discussion on verb tags in Penn Treebank (Table 1). We were wondering why there are so many tags for verbs. Let us focus our attention to the two verb tags from the set: *VB* and *VBP*. The former is typically used in infinitives, imperatives and subjunctives and the latter in non-3rd person singular present, e.g.,

I want to study_VB here (infinitive)
Please study_VB here (imperative)
I recommend they study_VB here (subjunctive)
versus
I study_VBP here

Table 1 Verb tags in Penn Treebank tagset

Tags	Meaning
VB	Verb, base form
VBD	Verb, past tense
VBG	Verb, gerund or present participle
VBN	Verb, past participle
VBP	Verb, non-3rd person singular present
VBZ	Verb, 3rd person singular present

Now the POS tagger can be easily fooled by the pair of sentences:

I recommend they study here.
I know they study here.

Most POS taggers make the mistake of tagging "study" with VB in both cases. Had the POS tagger had the knowledge of properties of the verbs "recommend" and "know" and their arguments structure and selectional preferences, it would have produced the correct tags of VB and VBP respectively. But these are tasks at higher NLP layers (syntax and semantics). The chicken-and-egg situation of NLP disambiguation is illustrated again.

One might then suggest "why complicate life with two tags VB and VBP, when the verb forms and their nearby contexts do not provide sufficient clues for disambiguation? Let us merge these two tags". We need probabilistic insights to understand why we need to retain both VB and VBP. The argument is frequentist.

VB with "to" infinitive is very frequent (*they like to study*), and so also is non-3rd person, singular number, present tense (*I study*). The preposition "to" is very common and is a strong clue for favouring VB. This clue *should be* used. Similarly should be used the strong clue for VBP, viz., non-3rd person (*I, you*). If the two cases of VB and VBP are not distinguished, it is likely that parsers will not be sufficiently informed to produce correct parses. The situation is made more complicated by the fact that "to" can be a preposition (*went to the market*) and an infinitive (*went to buy from the market*), both of which are very frequent. Additionally, *almost all nouns in English can act as verbs*. Plural noun forms are almost always indistinguishable from 3rd person singular number verb forms.

To summarize the example, in English the preposition "to", the nouns and the verbs forming a complex rubric of grammatical entities whose tag set design and whose annotation need deep linguistic and probabilistic insights and a fine balance between granularity and utility. Too coarse, and the usefulness to higher layers is lost; too fine, and the possibility of tagging using current and lower layer information is lost. To repeat, the complexities are:

(a) "To": very frequent; both preposition and infinitive
(b) Nouns: very frequent; can function as verbs

(c) Verbs: very frequent; can function as nouns
(d) 3rd person, singular number present tense forms of verbs identical to plural forms of nouns; both very frequent

2.2 Annotation Is Costly

The discussion above was meant to show that annotation is a complex and intricate task. This fact is borne out by actual evidences too. The scale of effort involved in practical annotation situations is typically large. Here are some facts and figures:

- Penn Treebank
  - 8 million words (needed *20–25 man years @5 persons for 4-5 years*)
- Ontonotes (very rich resource): Annotated 300 K words per year (*1 person per year*)
  - news, conversational telephone speech, weblogs, usenet newsgroups, broadcast, talk shows,
  - with structural information (syntax and predicate argument structure) and shallow semantics (word sense linked to an ontology and co reference)
  - in English, Chinese, and Arabic
- Prague Discourse Treebank (Czeck): 500,000 words, 20–25 man years (*4–5 persons for 5 years*)
- Sense marked corpora created at IIT Bombay[5]
  - English: Tourism (~170,000), Health (~150,000)
  - Hindi: Tourism (~170,000), Health (~80,000)
  - Marathi: Tourism (~120,000), Health (~50,000)
  - man years for each <L,D> combination (3 persons for 2 years)

3 Leveraging Multilinguality to Solve Annotation Crisis

Annotation is costly, needing expertise, money and time. Most languages in the world fall far behind English, when it comes to annotated resources. Since annotation is costly, there has been worldwide effort at leveraging multilinguality in development and use of annotated corpora. Here is a listing of papers from different areas of NLP involved in such efforts:

[5] http://www.cfilt.iitb.ac.in/wsd/annotated_corpus.

- (Projection in parsing) Greg Durrett, Adam Pauls, and Dan Klein, *Syntactic Transfer Using Bilingual Lexicon*, EMNLP-CoNLL, 2012
- (Projection in POS tagging) Dipanjan Das and Slav Petrov, *Unsupervised Part of Speech Tagging with Bilingual Graph-Based Projections,* ACL, 2011
- (Projection in Grammar and Parsing) Benjamin Snyder, Tahira Naseem, and Regina Barzilay, *Unsupervised multilingual grammar induction*, ACL-IJCNLP, 2009
- (Projection in sentiment analysis) B. Wei and C. Pal, "Cross lingual adaptation: An experiment on sentiment classifications," in ACL, 2010
- (Projection in document classification) X. Ling, G. Xue, W. Dai, Y. Jiang, Q. Yang, and Y. Yu, "Can Chinese web pages be classified with English data source?", WWW, 2008

The key idea is to *project and utilize annotation* from one language to another. This means parameters learnt from the annotated corpus of one language is made use of in the NLP of another language.

4 Cooperative Word Sense Disambiguation

We illustrate multilingual projection through the case study of word sense disambiguation (WSD). WSD is a fundamental tasks in NLP. The goal is to obtain the correct meaning of a word in the context. The correct meaning is usually denoted by an appropriate sense id from a sense repository, usually the wordnet (Fellbaum 1988).

Consider, for example, the word "operation" with the following three senses from Princeton Wordnet (PWN)[6]:

- **Operation**, surgery, surgical operation, surgical procedure, surgical process—(a medical procedure involving an incision with instruments; performed to repair damage or arrest disease in a living body; "they will schedule the operation as soon as an operating room is available"; "he died while undergoing surgery") TOPIC-> (noun) surgery#1
- **Operation**, military operation—(activity by a military or naval force (as a maneuver or campaign); "it was a joint operation of the navy and air force") TOPIC-> (noun) military#1, armed forces#1, armed services#1, military machine#1, war machine#1
- mathematical process, mathematical **operation**, **operation**—((mathematics) calculation by mathematical methods; "the problems at the end of the chapter demonstrated the mathematical processes involved in the derivation"; "they were learning the basic operations of arithmetic") TOPIC-> (noun) mathematics#1, math#1, maths#1

[6] http://wordnet.princeton.edu/.

The 3 senses are from medical, military and scientific domain respectively. In a sentence like "It was a joint operation of the navy and air force", the clues are navy and air force and the sense is the 2nd sense.

In general, it has been the experience of WSD researchers that domain specific WSD achieves high accuracy. This is intuitive, of course; word senses are restricted in specific domains (e.g., "bank" is likely not to have the meaning of river-bank in the finance domain). Also, multilingual WSD is still in its infancy; English is far ahead of any other language in terms of WSD systems that have reasonable accuracy.

WSD approaches are categorized as (Agirre and Edmonds 2006; Navigli 2009):

- Knowledge based
- Machine learning based
  - Supervised
  - Semi-supervised
  - Unsupervised
- Hybrid

Out of these approaches, the most successful ones have been based on machine learning, especially the supervised ones. Sense marked corpora is used to train a classifier like Naïve Bayes, SVM, decision list, feed forward neural network etc. (Yarowsky 1994; Ng and Lee 1996; Escudero et al. 2000; Klein et al. 2002; Lee et al. 2004). The reported accuracy of supervised WSD on various semeval tasks hovers around 60–65 %. Mostly the WSD tasks are for a target set of words. All words, multilingual, general purpose WSD is still a distant dream.

This dream that the field of WSD nurtures is depicted in Table 2:

That is, one would create WSD systems for a specific language domain pair-which is an easier task than general purpose WSD- and apply domain and language adaptation to expand to other cells, thus eventually establishing a *general purpose all words multilingual WSD system.*

In supervised WSD what is learnt from the training corpus is sense distribution, i.e., probability of sense of a word given the word and its context. In this chapter we present the intriguing idea borne out of our research (Bhingardive et al. 2013, Khapra et al. 2009, 2010, 2011a, b) that:

Given **linked wordnets** of two languages L_1 and L_2, it is possible to do WSD for:
(a) L_2 (L_1) even when L_2 (L_1)'s own sense marked corpora is not available; the only requirement is that sense marked comparable corpora of L_1 (L_2) should be available. *Then*, going a step further, it is possible to do WSD for (b) both L_1 and L_2, even when sense marked corpora of neither is available; only, they both should have comparable raw corpora.

Table 2 Domain (D) versus language (L) grid of WSD

D ↓ L →	English	German	Hindi	Marathi	…
Tourism					
Health					
Finance					
Sports					
…					

4.1 Linked Wordnets

A very rich and powerful lexical resource is created by putting in place a collection of linked wordnets. In 2008, the Global Wordnet Association (GWA)[7] launched the idea of completely open worldwide wordnet grid.[8] Inspired by Princeton Wordnet, wordnets in many languages got created across the world, some of them through *merge approach* and some through *expansion* approach. In the former the wordnet of a language is created ab initio, word by word and meaning and by meaning; in the latter, synsets of an existing wordnet is used to create the synsets of another language. For example, Eurowordnet- a linked structure of European language wordnets got set up in 1998 (Vossen 1998) through a mixture of merge and expansion approaches. Indowordnet got created completely through expansion approach with Hindi wordnet as the pivot (Bhattacharyya 2010).

A wordnet is a graph in which nodes are *synsets* and edges are semantic relations. A synset is a set of synonymous words denoting a unique meaning. The instrument of unique meaning denotation is *relational semantics*, where words disambiguate one another by virtue of being present in the same synset and also by virtue of the synsets being linked to one another through lexico-semantic relations (Cruze 1986). For example, *{firm, house, business firm}* is a synset that denotes the business organization sense of the highly polysemous word "house". Figure 3 shows the hypernymy hierarchy of this synset:

Synsets can also be linked to other synsets through *meronymy, pertainymy, troponymy* and such other relations. The first wordnet of the world was the English wordnet created in Princeton University (Fellbaum 1998).

[7] http://globalwordnet.org/.

[8] http://globalwordnet.org/global-wordnet-grid/.

firm, house, business firm-- (the members of a business organization that owns or operates one or more establishments; "he worked for a brokerage house")
=> business, concern, business concern, business organization, business organisation -- (a commercial or industrial enterprise and the people who constitute it; "he bought his brother's business"; "a small mom-and-pop business"; "a racially integrated business concern")
=> enterprise -- (an organization created for business ventures; "a growing enterprise must have a bold leader")
=> organization, organisation -- (a group of people who work together)
=> social group -- (people sharing some social relation)
=> group, grouping -- (any number of entities (members) considered as a unit)
=> abstraction -- (a general concept formed by extracting common features from specific examples)
=> abstract entity -- (an entity that exists only abstractly)
=> entity -- (that which is perceived or known or inferred to have its own distinct existence (living or nonliving))

[7] http://globalwordnet.org/
[8] http://globalwordnet.org/global-wordnet-grid/

Fig. 3 Hypernymy hierarchy of *business organization* sense of "house"

4.2 Indowordnet and Multidict

IndoWordnet[9] is a linked structure of wordnets of 19 major Indian languages from Indo-Aryan, Dravidian and Sino-Tibetan families. These wordnets have been created by following the expansion approach from Hindi wordnet which was made freely available for research in 2006. Since then a number of Indian languages have been creating their wordnets. Figure 4 shows some of the Indian language wordnets.

The synsets of wordnets of different languages are aligned with synsets of Hindi wordnet, that is, they have the same sense ids. Within these linked synsets, words are also cross-linked. This defines a structure that we call MultiDict (Mohanty et al. 2008) and is the foundation of our work on multilingual projection.

Table 3 and Fig. 5 illustrate MultiDict. The concept of *{boy, male child}* with synset id of 04831 in English wordnet 2.1 is linked with identical concepts in Hindi and Marathi. The words inside English, Hindi and Marathi are again interlinked (e.g., "mulgaa" of Marathi linked to "ladkaa" of Hindi which in turn is linked to "boy" of English).

[9] http://www.cfilt.iitb.ac.in/indowordnet/.

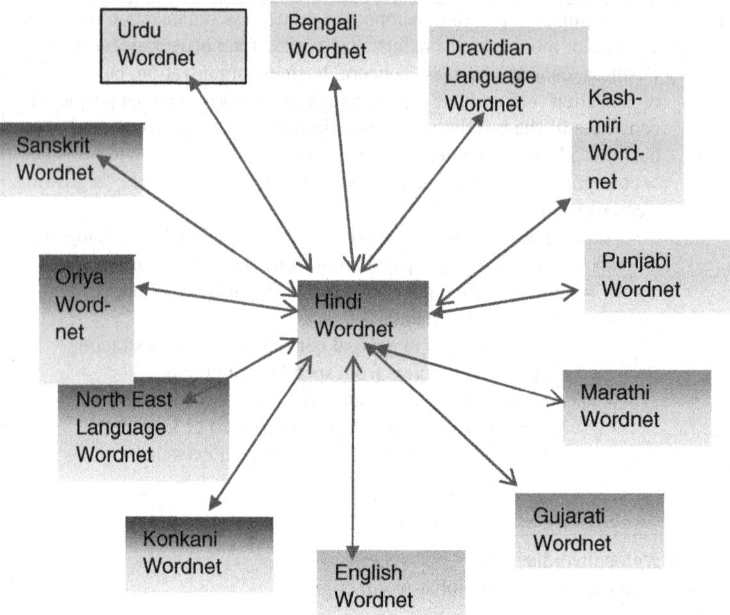

Fig. 4 Indowordnet

Table 3 A row of MultiDict

Concepts	L1 (English)	L2 (Hindi)	L3 (Marati)
04321: a youthful male person	(Malechild, boy)	{लड़का (ladkaa), बालक (baalak), बच्चा (bachchaa)}	{मुलगा (mulgaa), पोरगा (porgaa), पोर (por)}

We close this section with the reminder that WSD is a task that needs two costly resources: (1) wordnets and (2) sense marked corpora. While the first cannot be avoided—since wordnets provide sense ids, the second requirement can be considerably reduced if we employ multilingual projection. This we now proceed to do.

4.3 Parameters for WSD, a Scoring Function and an Iterative WSD Algorithm (Khapra et al. 2010)

Consider the following sentence:

The river flows through this region to meet the sea.

The word *sea* is ambiguous and has three senses as given in the Princeton Wordnet (PWN):

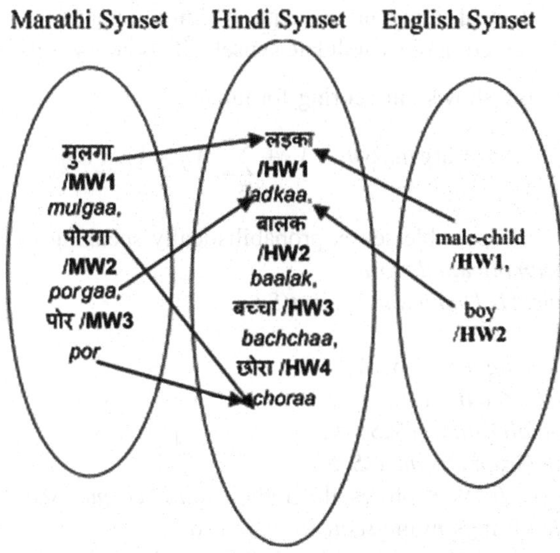

Fig. 5 Word linkages across linked synsets

S1: (n) sea (a division of an ocean or a large body of salt water partially enclosed by land)

S2: (n) ocean, sea (anything apparently limitless in quantity or volume)

S3: (n) sea (turbulent water with swells of considerable size) "heavy seas"

The first parameter for WSD is obtained from *Domain specific sense distributions*. In the above example, the first sense is more frequent in the tourism domain (verified from manually sense marked tourism corpora).

There are other parameters for WSD as follows:

Wordnet-dependent parameters
belongingness-to-dominant-concept
conceptual-distance
semantic-distance
Corpus-dependent parameters
corpus co-occurrences.

However, we find from our study and systematic procedures like ablation test that domain specific sense distribution information is the most important parameter for WSD.

For WSD, we desired a scoring function which:

1. Uses the strong clues for disambiguation provided by the monosemous also the already disambiguated words.
2. Uses sense distributions learnt from a sense tagged corpus.

3. Captures the effect of dominant concepts within a domain.
4. Captures the interaction of a candidate synset with other synsets in the sentence.

Equation 1 below shows our scoring formula:

$$S* = \arg\max_{i}(\theta_i \times V_i + \sum_{j \in J} W_{ij} \times V_i \times U_i) \quad (1)$$

where, $S*$ is the best possible sense, probabilistically speaking.

J = *Set of disambiguated words*
θ_i = *BelonginessToDominantConcept*(S_i)
V_i = *P*($S_i|W$)
Uj = *P(sense assigned to* $W_j|W_j$)
W_{ij} = *CorpusCooccurence*(S_i,S_j) *X*
1/WNConceptualDistance(S_i,S_j) *X*
1/WNSemanticGraphDistance(S_i,S_j)

The component θ_i*V_i captures the rather *static corpus sense*, whereas the second expression brings in the *sentential context.*

We give a greedy iterative algorithm *IWSD* as follows:

1. Tag all monosemous words in the sentence.
2. Iteratively disambiguate the remaining words in the sentence in increasing order of their degree of polysemy.
3. At each stage select that sense for a word which **maximizes the score of a sense as given in Eq.** 1.

For evaluation of the algorithm we used sense marked corpora in the tourism domain. Prior to our work large scale all words domain specific corpora were not available in any language including English. Hence, as part of our earlier work, we set upon the task of collecting data from two domains, viz., *Tourism* and *Health* for *English*. The data for Tourism domain was downloaded from Indian Tourism websites, whereas the data for Health domain was obtained from two doctors. The data was then sense annotated by two lexicographers adept in English. Princeton Wordnet 2.1[10] was used as the sense inventory. Some files were sense marked by both the lexicographers, and the Inter Tagger Agreement (ITA) calculated from these files was around 85 %. This was a first of its kind effort at collecting all-words domain specific sense marked corpora. This data is now available freely for research purposes[11] and should help to advance the research for domain-specific all-words WSD.

IWSD algorithm achieved an accuracy of about 75 % in both tourism and health domains, which is almost same as the most frequent sense baseline (MFS) and is about 10 points more than the standard wordnet first sense (WFS) baseline.

[10] http://wordnetweb.princeton.edu/perl/webwn.

[11] http://www.cfilt.iitb.ac.in/wsd/annotated_corpus.

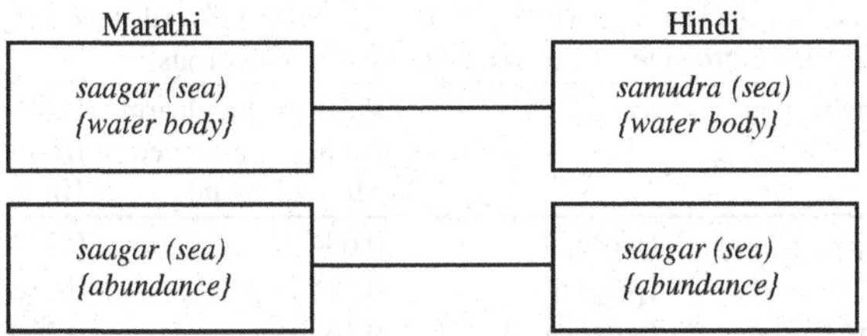

Fig. 6 Two senses of the Marathi word सागर *(saagar)*, viz, {*water body*} and {*abundance*}, and the corresponding cross-linked words in Hindi (One of the senses shows the same word *saagar* for both Marathi and Hindi. This is not uncommon, since Marathi and Hindi are sister languages)

4.4 Parameter Projection

Suppose a word (say, ***W***) in language L_1 (say, Marathi) has *k* senses. For each of these *k* senses we are interested in finding the parameter $P(S_i|W)$- which is the probability of sense S_i given the word *W* expressed as:

$$P(S_i|W) = \frac{\#(S_i, W)}{\sum_j (S_j, W)}$$

where '#' stands for 'count-of'. Consider the example of two senses of the Marathi word सागर *{saagar}*, viz., *sea* and *abundance* and the corresponding cross-linked words in Hindi (Fig. 6):

The probability *P({water body}|saagar)* for Marathi is

$$\frac{\#(\{Water\_body\}, saagar)}{\#(\{Water\_body\}, saagar) + \#(\{abundance\}, saagar)}$$

These counts *could have been* obtained easily if we had sense marked corpora of Marathi. But we assume that is not the case. We propose that this probability of *P({water body}|saagar)* can be approximated by the counts from Hindi sense marked corpora by replacing *saagar* with the cross linked Hindi words *samudra* and *saagar*, as per Fig. 6:

$$\frac{\#(\{Water\_body\}, samudra)}{\#(\{Water\_body\}, samudra) + \#(\{abundance\}, saagar)}$$

Thus, the following formula is used for calculating the **sense distributions of Marathi words using the sense marked Hindi corpus** from the same domain:

$$P(S_i|W) = \frac{\#(S_i, cross\_linked\_hindi\_words)}{\sum_j \#(S_j, cross\_linked\_hindi\_words)}$$

Table 4 Comparison of the sense distributions of some Marathi words learnt from Marathi sense tagged corpus with those projected from Hindi sense tagged corpus

Sr. No	Marathi word	Synset	P(S|word) as learnt from sense tagged Marathi corpus	P(S|word) as projected from sense tagged Hindi corpus
1	किमत (kimat)	{worth }	0.684	0.714
		{price }	0.315	0.285
2	रस्ता (rasta)	{roadway }	0.164	0.209
		{road, route}	0.835	0.770
3	ठिकाण (thikan)	{land site, place}	0.962	0.878
		{home}	0.037	0.12
		{abundance}	0	0

Note that we are not interested in the *exact* sense distribution of the words, but only in their relative values.

To prove that the projected relative distribution is faithful to the actual relative distribution of senses, we obtained the sense distribution statistics of a set of Marathi words from a sense tagged Marathi corpus (we call the sense marked corpora of a language its *self corpora*). These sense distribution statistics were compared with the statistics for these same words obtained by *projecting from* a sense tagged Hindi corpus. The results are summarized in columns 5 and 6 in Table 4. It is seen that relative ranks of sense probabilities for the three words किमत (kimat), रस्ता (rasta) and ठिकाण (thikan) are same whether they are obtained from self corpora or from Hindi's sense marked corpora. The Spearman Correlation coefficient between the two columns is found to be 0.77 and the average KL divergence is 0.29.

The other corpus based parameter *corpus cooccurrence* was similarly projected from Hindi to Marathi and it was found that the two distribution (self and projected) remains well correlated. Table 5 depicts this fact.

After establishing the fact that parameter projection is well grounded (direct evaluation), we proceeded to evaluate performance on actual WSD task (indirect evaluation). IWSD was run on Marathi and Bengali test corpora, after being trained on Hindi training corpora. That is IWSD parameters were learnt from Hindi sense marked corpora and was *used* for Marathi and Bengali.

Table 6 shows the accuracy figures with and without projection. The values lend ample credence to the belief that projection works. The performance when projection is used, is lower by about 10 points than the performance self corpora is used for training. Still the figures are well above the wordnet baseline by about 20 points. The same behavior is seen even when a familialy distant language, viz., Tamil is chosen.

Table 5 Projection of co occurence

Sr. No	Synset	Co-occurring synset	P(co-occurrence) as learnt from sense tagged Marathi corpus	P(co-occurrence) as learnt from sense tagged Hindi corpus
1	{रोप, रोपटे} {small bush}	{झाड, वृक्ष, तरुवर, द्रुम, तरू, पादप} {tree}	0.125	0.125
2	{मेघ, अभ्र} {cloud}	{आकाश, आभाळ, अंबर} {sky}	0.167	0.154
3	{क्षेत्र, इलाक़ा, इलाका, भूखंड} {geographical area}	{यात्रा, सफ़र} {travel}	0.0019	0.0017

Table 6 Precision, recall and F-scores of IWSD, PageRank and Wordnet baseline

Algorithm	Language					
	Marathi			Bengali		
	P %	R %	F %	P %	R %	F %
IWSD (training on self corpora; no parameter projection)	81.29	80.42	80.85	81.62	78.75	79.94
IWSD (training on Hindi and reusing parameters for another language)	**73.45**	**70.33**	**71.86**	**79.83**	**79.65**	**79.79**
PageRank (training on self corpora; no parameter projection)	79.61	79.61	79.61	76.41	76.41	76.41
PageRank (training on Hindi and reusing parameters for another language)	**71.11**	**71.11**	**71.11**	**75.05**	**75.05**	**75.05**
Wordnet Baseline	58.07	58.07	58.07	52.25	52.25	52.25

Values are reported with and without parameter projection

4.5 Two Languages Helping Each Other: Unsupervised WSD

Now we consider a scenario with two languages wherein neither language has any sense marked corpora. However, they have their linked wordnets (linked synsets and within linked synsets, linked words) in place. They also have comparable corpora. We show that by an ingenious use of expectation maximization (EM) like iterative procedure, the words of these languages can be disambiguated.

The above technique rests on a hypothesis:

Universality of sense distributions: Distributions of commonly occurring senses are identical across languages

That is, the proportion of times the *sense* of "sun" (for example) appears through the word "sun" and its synonyms is invariant across languages. The ratio of the times the sense of sun appears in the corpora (written, spoken) to the total number of senses is the same in all languages!

We describe our technique through two Indian languages Hindi and Marathi. The word chosen is Marathi word मान (maan), two of whose synsets are given below:

Synset ID	: 3260 POS : noun
Synonyms	: प्रतिष्ठा, इज्जत, आब, मान, आदर, इभ्रत, दबदबा, पत, अब्रू, लौकिक,
Gloss	: प्रतिष्ठित असण्याचा भाव
Example statement	: "समाजात त्याची प्रतिष्ठा आहे."
Gloss in Hindi	: प्रतिष्ठित होने की अवस्था या भाव
Gloss in English	: a high standing achieved through success or influence or wealth etc.; "he wanted to achieve power and prestige"

Synset ID	: 3627 POS : noun
Synonyms	: मान, ग्रीवा,
Gloss	: डोके व धड यांना जोडणारा शरीराचा भाग
Example statement	: "जिराफची मान खूप लांब असते."
Gloss in Hindi	: शरीर का वह भाग जो सिर को धड़ से जोड़ता है
Gloss in English	: the part of an organism that connects the head to the rest of the body; "he admired her long graceful neck"

Our task is to disambiguate the word "maan" for its two senses of 'respect' and 'neck'. The only resources we have are comparable corpora of Hindi and Marathi and their linked wordnets. The corresponding linked Hindi synsets are also shown below:

Synset ID	3260 POS : noun
Synonyms	प्रतिष्ठा, इज्जत, इज़्ज़त, आदर, सम्मान, मान-सम्मान, पूछ, रुतबा, नाम, नाक, मर्यादा, आनबान, अस्मिता, आबरू, लाज, पत, आन- बान, धाक, साख, इफ़्तख़ार, इफ़्तिख़ार, इफ्तखार, इफ्तिखार, पतपानी,
Gloss	प्रतिष्ठित होने की अवस्था या भाव
Example statement	"उसकी समाज में बड़ी प्रतिष्ठा है / यह चुनाव मुझे हर हालत में जीतना ही है क्योंकि मेरी नाक का सवाल है"
Gloss in Hindi	प्रतिष्ठित होने की अवस्था या भाव
Gloss in English	a high standing achieved through success or influence or wealth etc.; "he wanted to achieve power and prestige"

Synset ID	3627 POS : noun
Synonyms	गर्दन, गरदन, गला, ग्रीवा, हलक, हलक़, कंधर, शिरोधरा, शिरोधि, घेंट,
Gloss	शरीर का वह भाग जो सिर को धड़ से जोड़ता है
Example statement	"जिराफ की गर्दन बहुत लम्बी होती है"
Gloss in Hindi	शरीर का वह भाग जो सिर को धड़ से जोड़ता है
Gloss in English	the part of an organism that connects the head to the rest of the body; "he admired her long graceful neck"

The words in these synsets- Marathi and Hindi- form a bi-partite graph, part of which is shown in Fig. 7. Starting from "maan" which appears in the two senses of "respect" and "neck", we can navigate to the Hindi side, linking with "aadar", "izzat", "gardan", "galaa".

The first two of these Hindi words come from cross linkages in the *respect* sense, and the next two come from cross linkages in the *neck* sense. However, these Hindi words themselves have multiple senses, and *their* cross linkages on the Marathi side produce words "satkaar" *(respect)*, "sanmaan" *(respect)*, "greeva" *(neck)*, "awaaz" *(voice)* and "swar" *(voice)*.

The actual correspondences are depicted in Table 7. We introduce a new notation π called *projection*. $S^{hin} = \pi(S^{mar})$ is the projection of Marathi sense into Hindi.

There is something interesting about this example. The navigation in and out of Marathi side into the Hindi side does not remain confined to the starting two senses, but introduces a third sense, viz., *voice*. This *pulling in* of new senses is crucial to the progress of our algorithm which based on expectation maximization and is iterative in nature.

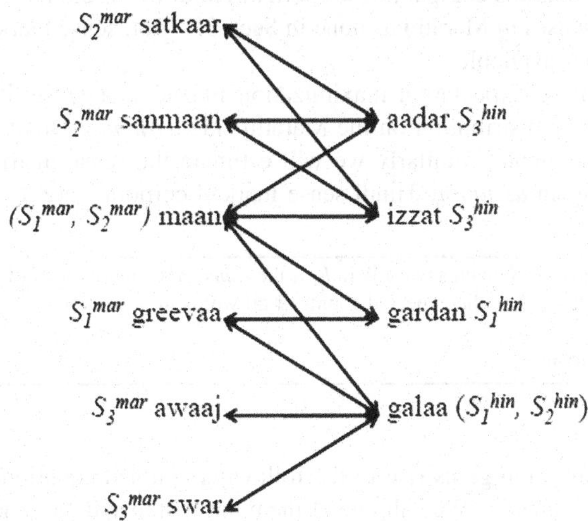

Fig. 7 Bi-partite graph of Marathi and Hindi words linked by identical senses; S_1^{mar}, S_2^{mar} and S_3^{mar} are Marathi senses, while S_1^{hin}, S_2^{hin} and S_3^{hin} are Hindi senses

Table 7 Sense projections along with constituent words

Sense in English	S^{mar} (Marathi sense number)	words^{mar} (partial list)	$S^{hin} = \pi(S^{mar})$ (projected Hindi sense number)	words^{mar} (partial list of words in projected Hindi sense)
Neck	1	maan, greeva	1	gardan, galaa
Respect	2	maan, satkaar, sanmaan	3	izzat, aadar
Voice	3	awaaz, swar	2	galaa

4.5.1 Intuitive Description of the Algorithm

If sense tagged Marathi corpus were available, we could have estimated

$$P(S_1^{mar}|maan) = \frac{\#(S_1^{mar}, maan)}{\#(S_1^{mar}, maan) + \#(S_2^{mar}, maan)}$$

However, such a corpora is not available.

Now, refer Table 7. The cross linked words of "maan" in Hindi in the first sense S_1^{mar} are "galaa" and "gardan" (sense of *neck*). Similarly the cross linked words of "maan" in Hindi in the second sense S_2^{mar} are "izzat" and "aadar" (sense of *respect*). If we had sense marked comparable corpora of Hindi we would have estimated the probability of senses in Marathi as done in Sect. 3.3. But, sense marked corpora of Hindi is also not available.

At this point an expectation maximization like idea suggests itself. We will estimate the sense distribution on the Marathi side *assuming* Hindi sense marked corpora were available. Similarly we will estimate the sense distribution on the Marathi side, again *assuming* Hindi sense marked corpora were available!

The probability of sense S given a word W in L_1 is the *expected* count of all words in the projected sense of S in L_2, divided by the expected counts of all words in projections of all senses of W in L_2.

Similarly for words in L_2.

The above intuition gives rise to the following coupled equations for our running example of "maan". We call one of them the E-step and the other the M-step. We keep Table 7 in mind.

$$P(S_1^{mar}|maan) = \frac{sum\ of\ \exp ected\ counts\ of\ words\ in\ projection\ \pi(S_1^{mar})}{sum\ of\ \exp ected\ counts\ of\ words\ in\ projections\ of\ all\ senses\ of\ maan}$$

"maan" maps to "gardan" and "galaa" in the *neck* sense and izzat and aadar in the respect sense. So,

E-step (1st equation)

$$P(S_1^{mar}|maan) = \frac{P(S_1^{hin}|gardan).\#(gardan) + P(S_1^{hin}|galaa).\#(galaa)}{P(S_1^{hin}|gardan).\#(gardan) + P(S_1^{hin}|galaa).\#(galaa) + P(S_2^{hin}|izzat)..\#(izzat) + P(S_2^{hin}|aadar)..\#(aadar)}$$

The probability values on the right hand side of the equation are obtained as:
M-step equations

$$P(S_1^{hin}|gardan) = \frac{P(S_1^{mar}|maan).\#(maan) + P(S_1^{mar}|greeva).\#(greeva)}{P(S_1^{mar}|maan).\#(maan) + P(S_1^{mar}|greeva).\#(greeva)} = 1$$

and

$$P(S_1^{hin}|galaa) = \frac{P(S_1^{mar}|maan).\#(maan) + P(S_1^{mar}|greeva).\#(greeva)}{P(S_1^{mar}|maan).\#(maan) + P(S_1^{mar}|greeva).\#(greeva)} = \frac{P(S_1^{mar}|maan).\#(maan) + P(S_1^{mar}|greeva).\#(greeva)}{P(S_1^{mar}|maan).\#(maan) + P(S_1^{mar}|greeva).\#(greeva) + P(S_1^{mar}|awaaz).\#(awaaz) + P(S_1^{mar}|swar).\#(swar)}$$

All the probability values on the Marathi side can be similarly estimated. They will form the set of equations on E-step.

4.5.2 EM Based Algorithm

Input: comparable corpora of languages L_1 and L_2

Output: senses of words U in L_1 and V in L_2

1. Initialize randomly sense distributions in one of the languages, say in L_2, the $P(S^{L2}|V)$ values
2. For any word U in L_1

   a. For all senses S^{L1} of U in L_1
   b. For each word V in the projected sense $\pi(S^{L1})$ in L_2 of S

   i. Get $P(S^{L1}|U)$ using Eq. (2); call this equation E-step
   ii. For each probability on the RHS of Eq. 2 get the values symmetrically using Eq. (3); call this equation M-step
   iii. Repeat (i) and (ii) until probabilities settle to some values

3. Do step 2 for all words in L_1; L_2 sense distributions get calculated automatically

Table 8 Comparative performance in 3 settings of training in self-corpora, projection from Hindi, EM with no sense marked corpora in either language

Algorithm	Marathi		
	P %	R %	F %
IWSD (training on self corpora; no parameter projection)	81.29	80.42	80.85
IWSD (training on Hindi and projecting parameters for Marathi)	73.45	70.33	71.86
EM (no sense corpora in either Hindi or Marathi)	68.57	67.93	68.25
Wordnet baseline	58.07	58.07	58.07

$$P(S_i^{L_1}|u) = \frac{\sum\limits_{v \in \pi_{L_2}(S_i^{L_1})} P(\pi_{L_2}(S_i^{L_1})|v).\#(v)}{\sum\limits_{S_j^{L_1}} \sum\limits_{x \in \pi_{L_2}(S_j^{L_1})} P(\pi_{L_2}(S_j^{L_1}|x)).\#(x)} \quad E\text{-}step \tag{2}$$

$$P(S_k^{L_2}|v) = \frac{\sum\limits_{v \in \pi_{L_2}(S_i^{L_1})} P(\pi_{L_1}(S_k^{L_2})|v).\#(v)}{\sum\limits_{S_m^{L_2}} \sum\limits_{y \in \pi_{L_2}(S_m^{L_2})} P(\pi_{L_1}(S_m^{L_2}|y)).\#(y)} \quad M\text{-}step \tag{3}$$

$$where\ S_k^{L_2} = \pi_{L_2}(S_i^{L_1})$$

5 Results

On testing the algorithm on Hindi and Marathi tourism and health corpora the Table 8 shows results for Marathi in tourism domain.

Following are the salient observations:

- Performance of EM is within 10-12 points of Self-Training—remarkable since no additional cost incurred in target language
- EM gives 10 points improvement over Wordnet First Sense Baseline
- *Knowledge based and unsupervised approaches come nowhere close to EM performance* (observed in separate experiments)

Observations of similar kind were obtained in health domain and for Hindi also.

6 Conclusions and Future Work

In this chapter we have argued that annotation marking and annotation set design are complex tasks requiring both linguistic and probabilistic insights. This fact, coupled with NLP systems' requirement of huge amounts of annotated data, makes creation of annotated data very demanding in terms of time, money and manpower. Therefore, it makes sense to explore possibilities of languages *helping* one another in annotation.

After mentioning that such efforts are afoot all over the world, we describe our experience of working with multiple Indian languages for their NLP tasks. A specific case study chosen is in word sense disambiguation (WSD). WSD needs two costly resources: wordnets and sense marked corpora. While the first requirement cannot be by-passed-wordnet senses being ingrained in the definition of WSD-, the requirement of annotated corpora can be greatly reduced. The trick is to use **projection**. Parameters learnt from one language can be used to do WSD in another language.

Perhaps the most innovative and intriguing idea we have presented here is the idea of mutual disambiguation—albeit probabilistic—by two languages of each other's comparable corpora. The key points are (a) assumption that distributions of commonly occurring senses are invariant across languages and (b) an iterative EM like algorithm that goes back and forth between the two languages using their linked wordnets to do disambiguation.

The work can be advanced in several ways. Bhingarvide et al. (2013) have shown how to incorporate context in the EM-WSD framework. Their system performs well for verbs whose disambiguation has traditionally proved to be difficult. WSD of a language with help from multiple languages is another interesting line of investigation.

The fabrique of linked Indian language wordnets is in place as also are resources like Eurowordnet, Babelnet[12] and Asian languages' wordnets. We hope our work will pave ways for building a cooperative world of NLP.

References

Agirre, E., & Edmonds, P. (2006). *Word sense disambiguation*. New York: Springer.

Bengio, Y. (2009). Learning deep architectures for AI. *Foundations & Trends in Machine Learning, 2*(1), 1–127.

Bhattacharyya, P. (2010). IndoWordNet. *Lexical Resources Engineering Conference 2010 (LREC 2010), Malta.*

Bhingardive, S., Shaikh, S., & Bhattacharyya, P. (2013). *Neighbor help: Bilingual unsupervised WSD using context*. Sofia, Bulgaria: ACL.

Bhattacharyya, P. (2012). Natural language processing: A perspective from computation in presence of ambiguity, resource constraint and multilinguality. *CSI Journal of Computing, 1*(2).

Brown P. F., Pietra V. J. D., Pietra S. A. D., & Mercer R. L. (1993). The mathematics of statistical machine translation: parameter estimation. *Computational Linguistics, 19*(2): 263–311.

Church, K. W. (1988). A stochastic parts program and noun phrase parser for unrestricted text. *ANLP*.

Cruze, D. A. (1986). *Lexical semantics*. Cambridge: Cambridge University Press.

[12] http://babelnet.org/.

DeRose, S. J. (1988). Grammatical category disambiguation by statistical optimization. *Computational Linguistics, 14*(1), 31–39.

Escudero, G., Màrquez, L., & Rigau, G. (2000). *Naive bayes and exemplar-based approaches to word sense disambiguation revisited: European Conference on AI* (pp. 421–425).

Fellbaum, C. (Ed.). (1998). *WordNet: An electronic lexical database*. Cambridge: MIT Press.

Khapra, M., Shah, S., Kedia, P., & Bhattacharyya, P. (2009). Projecting parameters for multilingual word sense disambiguation. *EMNLP*.

Khapra, M., Shah, S., Kedia, P., & Bhattacharyya, P. (2010). Domain-specific word sense disambiguation combining corpus based and wordnet based parameters. *5th International Conference on Global Wordnet, Mumbai, India.*

Khapra, M., Joshi, S., & Bhattacharyya, P. (2011a). It takes two to tango: A bilingual unsupervised approach for estimating sense distributions using expectation maximization. *IJCNLP, Chiang Mai, Thailand.*

Khapra, M., Joshi, S., Chatterjee, A., & Bhattacharyya, P. (2011b). *Together we can: Bilingual bootstrapping for WSD*. Oregon, USA: ACL.

Klein, D., Toutanova, K., Ilhan, H. T., Kamvar, S. D., & Manning, C. D. (2002). *Combining heterogeneous classifers for word-sense disambiguation*: Proceedings of the ACL-02 workshop on Word sense disambiguation: recent successes and future directions WSD'02 (Vol. 8, pp 74–80), Stroudsburg, PA: Association for Computational Linguistics.

Lee, K. Y., Ng, H. T., & Chia T. K. (2004). *Supervised word sense disambiguation with support vector machines and multiple knowledge sources: Proceedings of Senseval-3: Third International Workshop on the Evaluation of Systems for the Semantic Analysis of Text* (pp. 137–140).

Manning, C. D., & Schutze, H. (1999). *Foundations of statistical natural language processing*. Cambridge: MIT Press.

Marcus, M., Santorini, B., & Marcinkiewicz, M. A. (1993). Building a large annotated corpus of English: The Penn Treebank. *Computational Linguistics*, *19*(2), 313–330.

Mohanty, R., Bhattacharyya, P., Pande, P., Kalele, S., Khapra, M., & Sharma, A. (2008). Synset based multilingual dictionary: Insights, applications and challenges. *Global Wordnet Conference, Szeged, Hungary.*

Navigli, R. (2009). Word sense disambiguation: A survey. *ACM Computing Surveys*, *41*(2), 1–69.

Ng H. T., & Lee H. B. (1996). *Integrating multiple knowledge sources to disambiguate word sense: an exemplar-based approach: Proceedings of the 34th annual meeting on Association for Computational Linguistics, Morristown, NJ, USA* (pp. 40–47).

Rumelhart, D. E., Hinton, G. E., & Williams, R. J. (1986). *Learning internal representations by error propagation*. In D. E. Rumelhart & J. L. McCleland (Eds.), Vol. 1, Chapter 8, Cambridge, MA: MIT Press.

Sha, F., & Perreira, F. (2003). Shallow parsing with conditional random fields. *HLT, NAACL.*

Vossen, P. (Ed.). (1998). *EuroWordNet: A multilingual database with lexical semantic networks*. Dordrecht, Netherlands: Kluwer.

Yarowsky, D. (1994). *Decision lists for lexical ambiguity resolution: Application to accent restoration in Spanish and French: Proceedings of the 32nd Annual Meeting of the association for Computational Linguistics (ACL)*, (pp. 88–95).

Part III
Semantics

Personal Semantics

Gregory Grefenstette

Abstract Quantified self, life logging, digital eyeglasses, technology is advancing rapidly to a point where people can gather masses of data about their own persons and their own life. Large-scale models of what people are doing are being built by credit companies, advertising agencies, and national security agencies, using digital traces that people leave behind them. How can individuals exploit their own data for their own benefit? With this mass of personal data, we will need to induce personal semantic dimensions to sift data and find what is meaningful to each individual. In this chapter, we present semantic dimensions, made by experts, and by crowds. We show the type of information that individuals will have access to once lifelogging becomes common, and we will sketch what personal semantic dimensions might look like.

Keywords Information extraction · Semantic annotation · Personal data · Lifelogging

1 Introduction

Extracting and finding information in large quantities of unstructured data requires assigning data to semantic classes, so that information can be filtered merged, and labelled. In applied Natural Language Processing, experts produced validated taxonomies and ontologies, such as the Medical Subject Heading (MeSH) and the NASA thesaurus for classifying text. With the expansion of the Internet and Web 2.0, new, crowd-sourced knowledge structures began to appear, for example, the DMOZ hierarchy of the Open Directory Project, and the category hierarchy of Wikipedia. Both formal and crowd-sourced taxonomies allow semantic annotation of information, and are used to accelerate search, allowing the user to choose categories and other metadata before examining results. In a sense, the categories used are an agreed-upon (either by experts or the crowd) way of looking at the

G. Grefenstette (✉)
INRIA, Saclay, France
e-mail: gregory.grefenstette@inria.fr

© Springer International Publishing Switzerland 2015
N. Gala et al. (eds.), *Language Production, Cognition, and the Lexicon*,
Text, Speech and Language Technology 48, DOI 10.1007/978-3-319-08043-7_12

world, and classifying things in it. I believe we will soon need a new third type of semantics, a personal semantics that can be automatically generated but limited to one person's view of the world. This new type of semantics will be needed to organize the digital traces that individuals create. In the near future, due to advances in video and audio processing, in GPS tracking and in memory storage, people will be able to record their lives unobtrusively in video, audio, and position. Buttonhole audio cameras, devices such as Google Glass, will soon be cheaply available to the general public. Each person will be generating personal multimodal Big Data about their lives. In order to process (index and retrieve) this multimodal data, it will have to be semantically annotated in an automatic fashion, since people will not have the time to manually review their own captured date. Contrary to the first two types of shared semantics (expert, crowd-sourced), each person will have personal semantic categories: places, people, events and other categories that meaningful to them alone. This chapter will examine how personal semantics can be generated from the personal data gathered from portable lifelogging devices, mixed with digital traces, and open linked data.

2 Semantic Dimensions

Semantic dimensions help people find things faster. In modern search engines, semantic dimensions are materialised as *facets*. Facets (Tunkelang 2009) are usually presented as a list of expandable categories. For example, if you type "wool" on a popular shopping website, you see the following "Departments" on the left side of the screen: *Arts and Crafts, Clothing and Accessories, Books, Home and Kitchen,…* . Each of these "Departments" is a facet, or semantic dimension, that allows you to divide the universe into two parts: things that belong to that dimension and things that do not belong. Expanding one of the department facets opens up further subdivisions. For example, click on *Clothing and Accessories* and the shopping site displays the narrower facets: *Women, Men, Accessories, Novelty and Special Use, Boys, Girls, Baby, Luggage, Handbags*. When we shop, these subdivisions seem natural, or at least immediately comprehensible, even though, of course, the semantic categories *Boys*, *Girls* and *Baby* are not mutually exclusive.[1] The shopping user is not bothered by the lack of formality, and naturally assumes that the dimension *Boys* covers clothings designed for male children somewhere between roughly the ages of 2 and 17, with *Baby* being the dimension of younger humans and *Men* for older male humans.

Other semantic dimensions that appear under *Clothing and Accessories* > *Baby* on this same web site are *Price* (with intervals such as *\$25 to \$50*), *Brand*, *Size*, *Average Customer Review*.

[1] When you click on *Baby* on this site, you find the following three dimensions: *Baby Boys*, *Baby Girls* and *Unisex*.

Common users who shop online are now experienced in using facets to focus in on the items they are searching for. Naturally and intuitively, they have learned over the past decade to combine the query box method of search as they use on Google, with the use of facets to restrict or refine their search while they shop.

Business users, using modern enterprise search systems also use facets to speed retrieval. An enterprise search will index the documents within an enterprise using keyword indexing, but also using the metadata associated with business documents to create facets. In this case, common facets are type of document (Word, PDF, Powerpoint, email, posting), the date of production of the document, the business department that the document is attached to (Marketing, Communication, Customer Relations, Management, etc.), the creator of the document, the sender and receivers, the language, and the product and the people named in the document. Most of this information is not considered semantic information by the Natural Language Processing community, but users use these facets in exactly the same way as in the case of shopping facets, to reduce the space of search. These facets can be considered semantic dimensions since they associate typed information with the document, information that is not necessarily found in the keyword-indexed text of the document.

In general, where do semantic dimensions come from? In the rest of this chapter, we will examine three different ways of creating semantic dimensions: via experts, via crowd-sourcing, and via induction from data.

3 Expert Semantic Resources

Ever since collections of writings have existed, there has been a need for knowing how to order the collection. In libraries of printed books, this physical need to be in one place and desire to group books about the same subject together gave rise to library classification schemes, such as the Library of Congress Classification (1897), the Dewey Decimal system (1876), etc. (See Fig. 1).

Before computers, search was performed using printed catalogs (Fig. 2). There was a real cost, associated with the paper it was written on, of including a piece of information in the catalog. The constraints of space and cost naturally led to controlling the indexing language, which led to "authority lists" of the categories and subcategories which could be associated with a piece of information.

WordNet is another example of organizing concepts (at least single word concepts) in a semantic hierarchy. To provide a resource for analyzing psychological text, Miller and his team (Miller 1995) collected definitions from a number of dictionaries, and arranged words in a hierarchy of synsets (a synset is a set of synonyms). Dictionary definitions are often of the structure: A is a type of B in which C, where A is the head word, B is a more general class and C are the differentiators that distinguish C from other elements of the class B. B is called the hypernym of A and A is called a hyponym of B. WordNet is a hierarchy of hypernyms and hyponyms over words (including a few proper nouns) of English.

Class 000	Computer science, information & general works
Class 100	Philosophy and psychology
Class 200	Religion
Class 300	Social sciences
Class 400	Language
Class 500	Science
Class 600	Technology
Class 700	Arts & recreation
Class 800	Literature
Class 900	History & geography

Fig. 1 The Dewey Decimal System is a long-used classification system for libraries. It divides subjets into a hierarchy, with the uppermost classes shown here. Still in use, the lower nodes of the hierarchy are modified once a month (http://oclc.org/dewey/updates.en.html)

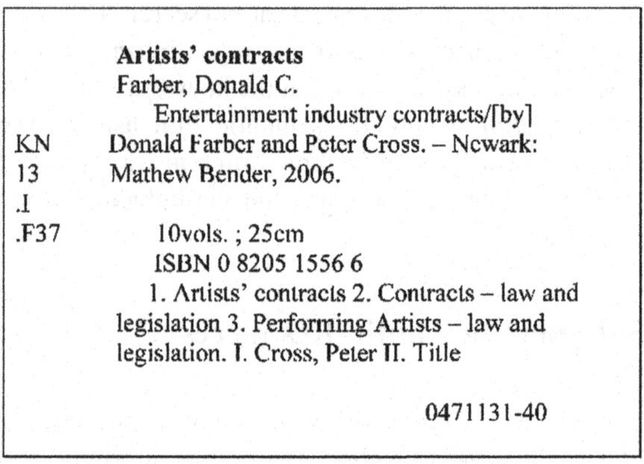
Artists' contracts
Farber, Donald C.
Entertainment industry contracts/[by]
KN Donald Farber and Peter Cross. – Newark:
13 Mathew Bender, 2006.
.I
.F37 10vols. ; 25cm
ISBN 0 8205 1556 6
1. Artists' contracts 2. Contracts – law and legislation 3. Performing Artists – law and legislation. I. Cross, Peter II. Title

0471131-40

Fig. 2 Supplementing the one-book, one-place paradigm, printed card catalogs allowed a book to be indexed under different dimensions (author, title, subjects)

An ambiguous word can be found in many synsets, but each individual meaning is found in only one place in the hierarchy (Fig. 3).

Shiyali Ramamrita Ranganathan, developed the Colon Theory of Classification in the early 1930s (Svenonius 1992). It was widely adopted by libraries afterwords. This colon based notation assigned different semantic classes to each work, separated by colons, whence the name. Each hierarchical class corresponds to a facet in modern information retrieval.

Beyond general classification of human knowledge, domain-specific classifications also began to appear in the 1950s. The National Library of Medicine in the US, first developed a Subject Heading Authority List in 1954, that evolved over time into the Medical Subject Headings (MeSH). MeSH headings are used to index the more than 20 million medical articles appearing in the bibliographic database MedLine.[2] It is updated regularly by a permanent staff of ten doctors, veterinarians, and PhDs at the National Library of Medicine in the US (Fig. 4).

[2] https://www.ncbi.nlm.nih.gov/pubmed.

- S: (n) peritoneum
  - S: (n) serous membrane, serosa
    - S: (n) membrane, tissue layer
      - S: (n) animal tissue
        - S: (n) tissue
          - S: (n) body part
            - S: (n) part, piece
              - S: (n) thing
                - S: (n) physical entity
                  - S: (n) entity

Fig. 3 A slice of the WordNet hierachy, showing the hypernyms (more general classes) for the word *peritoneum* which is a *serous membrane, or serosa* which is a *membrane, or tissue layer* which is an *animal tissue* which is a *tissue body part* which is a *part or piece* which is a *thing* which is a *physical entity* which is a *entity*. These are all nouns (indicated by the *n*). The *S* stands for synset. Wordnet also contains verbs, adjectives and adverbs

Body Regions [A01]
Torso [A01.923]
Abdomen [A01.923.047]
Abdominal Cavity [A01.923.047.025]
Peritoneum [A01.923.047.025.600]
Douglas' Pouch [A01.923.047.025.600.225]
Mesentery [A01.923.047.025.600.451] +
Omentum [A01.923.047.025.600.573]
Peritoneal Cavity [A01.923.047.025.600.678]

Fig. 4 A sample of the MeSH semantic hierarchy. The Abdomen (A01.923.047) is part of the Torso (A01.923) which is a Body Region (A01). The category *A* concerns Anatomy (of humans and animals). Other categories are *B* for Organisms, *C* for Diseases, *D* for Chemicals and Drugs, etc. (See http://www.nlm.nih.gov/mesh)

In the 1960s, the National Aeronautics and Space Administration (NASA) produced its first thesaurus. It is updated monthly by engineers and lexicographers in the NASA Scientific and Technical Information program http://www.sti.nasa.gov/about-us/. The thesaurus contains over 18,000 terms in the fields of aeronautics and engineering. This semantic resource has been used for automatically annotating new documents since at least 1994 (Silvester et al. 1994) (Fig. 5).

The MeSH and NASA thesaurus are examples of expert-directed semantic structuring of a domain. They are expensive to maintain, updated monthly by committee decision, and directed to an audience of specialists.

4 Crowd-Sourced Semantic Hierarchies

In contrast to expert design and maintained semantic structures, we have seen crowd-sourced semantic hierarchies developed over the past 20 years. Crowd-sourcing here means that a large number of "ordinary" people, for example, web users, can contribute and alter entries in the semantic hierarchy.

① **microbursts (meteorology)**
② *(added January 1993)*
③ SN (EXCLUDES IONOSPHERIC RADIATION MICROBURSTS)
④ DEF A strong, localized downdraft that strikes the ground creating an outflow of severe winds near the ground that diverge radially from the impact point.
⑤ UF *bow echo microburst events*
⑥ GS meteorology
. micrometeorology
. . **microbursts (meteorology)**
storms
. storms (meteorology)
. . downbursts
. . . **microbursts (meteorology)**
⑦ RT aviation meteorology
flight hazards
thunderstorms
vertical air currents
wind shear

Key
1. Postable Term
2. Date Added
3. Scope Note
4. Definition
5. Used For Term
6. Generic Structure
7. Related Term

Fig. 5 A typical hierarchical entry in the Nasa thesaurus. *Microbursts* appear under two facets: Meteorology, and Storms. (See http://www.sti.nasa.gov/thesvol1.pdf)

One of the first crowd-sourced efforts to structure the information on the Web was the Open Directory Project (ODP, at dmoz.org), begun in 1998 by two SUN engineers, Rich Skrenta and Bob Truel, beginning with a hand-built hierarchy derived from USENET news groups. The original idea here was to allow anyone on the internet to become a directory editor, after proving their ability to correctly edit a small portion of Web pages (Sherman 2000). This open community-created semantic hierarchy is used by a number of other search engines: Netscape Search, AOL Search, Alexa, and Google (until 2011) (Fig. 6).

Inspired in part by ODP, Wikipedia created an open source encyclopedia, allowing anyone to create and edit pages, depending on the crowd to police edits, and remove errors and spam (certain offending IP addresses can be banned). Wikipedia pages can be categorized. Categories are also crowd-sourced. For example, in the German version of Wikipedia, the article for *Fersental* (in English, the Mocheni Valley) was categorized as in the following categories: *Sprachinsel* (Isolated languages), *Tal im Trentino* (Valleys in Trento), *Deutscher Dialekt* (German dialects). Some categories are listed in Wikipedia as subcategories of other categories. for example, *Valleys in Trento* is a subcategory of *Valleys of Italy*. Gerard de Melo and Gerhard Weikum described how this graph, which extends over language versions of Wikipedia can be structured into a semantic hierarchy (de Melo and Weikum 2010) (Fig. 7).

Fig. 6 The front page of dmoz.org. There are over 5 million web pages hierarchically indexed in over 1 million categories by almost 100,000 editors

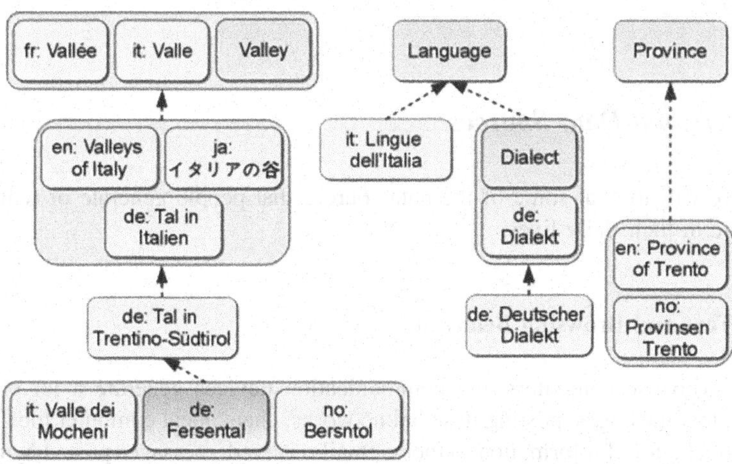

Fig. 7 A multilingual semantic hierarchy induced from the Wikipedia category graph, by Gerard de Melo and Gerhard Weikum into METANET (de Melo and Weikum 2010)

These two semantic hierarchies are controlled by the crowd, which collectively decides what should appear and what should not, the content of the hierarchies resulting from consensus over shared community viewpoints.

5 Personal Hierarchies

The semantic hierarchies presented categorize public information into classes that anyone from the user community can understand. Public information, public semantics. We will soon need more.

Computer technology in wearable and portable computing has reached a point where individuals are able to passively gather large quantities of information about themselves, stored in digital format. As this information grows in size and storage costs continue to drop, it is probable that people will collect their own life logs, with the data that the user generates and interacts with. In this mass of data, individuals will have the same need for classifying information, grouping information into classes, so that search and retrieval can be efficiently performed. The difference with systems developed for public data, is that the semantic classes used need only make sense to the individual. This information is his or her private information, and they may order it in any way they like, without having to explain.

Certainly some dimensions may be comprehensible to others, but this will not be a necessity.

Above all, it will be necessary to automatically create many of these semantic dimensions, and to automatically annotate the data that the user generates. It is enough to live one life, without having spend another life annotating and classifying it.

5.1 Personal Data Sources

Here we will look at some of the data sources that people generate or will soon generate in their daily lives.

5.1.1 Text and Browsing Behavior

People who use computers and communication devices generate a lot of text: emails, text messages, posting in social networks, chats, local computer files. They also attract a lot of information to them: email received, messages posted by others on their personal walls (such as on Facebook or Google+), content of web pages that they browse.

Currently much of this information is exploited by third parties (advertisers, national security agencies) because this text reveals some of the personality of the

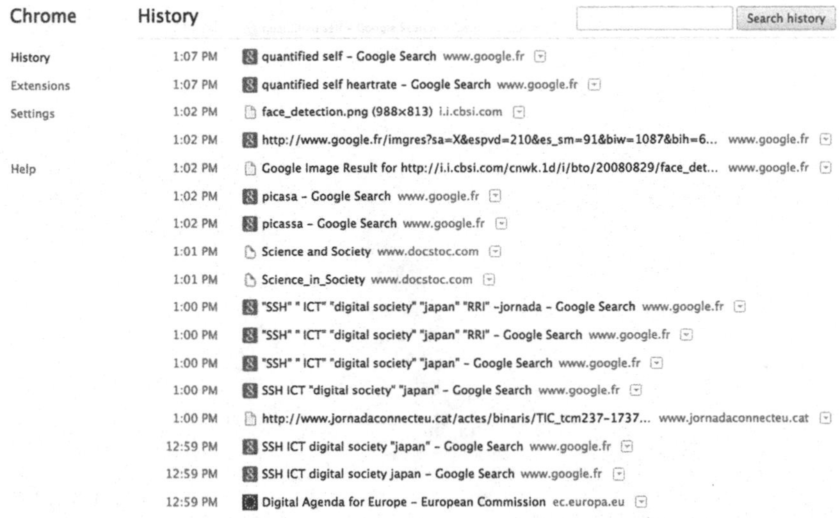

Chrome	History	
		Search history
History	1:07 PM	quantified self - Google Search www.google.fr
Extensions	1:07 PM	quantified self heartrate - Google Search www.google.fr
Settings	1:02 PM	face_detection.png (988×813) i.i.cbsi.com
	1:02 PM	http://www.google.fr/imgres?sa=X&espvd=210&es_sm=91&biw=1087&bih=6... www.google.fr
Help	1:02 PM	Google Image Result for http://i.i.cbsi.com/cnwk.1d/i/bto/20080829/face_det... www.google.fr
	1:02 PM	picasa - Google Search www.google.fr
	1:02 PM	picassa - Google Search www.google.fr
	1:01 PM	Science and Society www.docstoc.com
	1:01 PM	Science_in_Society www.docstoc.com
	1:00 PM	"SSH" " ICT" "digital society" "japan" "RRI" -jornada - Google Search www.google.fr
	1:00 PM	"SSH" " ICT" "digital society" "japan" "RRI" - Google Search www.google.fr
	1:00 PM	"SSH" " ICT" "digital society" "japan" - Google Search www.google.fr
	1:00 PM	SSH ICT "digital society" "japan" - Google Search www.google.fr
	1:00 PM	http://www.jornadaconnecteu.cat/actes/binaris/TIC_tcm237-1737... www.jornadaconnecteu.cat
	12:59 PM	SSH ICT digital society "japan" - Google Search www.google.fr
	12:59 PM	SSH ICT digital society japan - Google Search www.google.fr
	12:59 PM	Digital Agenda for Europe - European Commission ec.europa.eu

Fig. 8 Search engines, such as Google, keep a history of the web sites you visit. They keep an index of the titles of the pages viewed, along with a timestamp. This information can model user interests

user, what interests them, what they might want to do.[3] For example, Google and other companies offer free e-mail services to user. In exchange, Google will analyze the contents of your email, in order to "sell" space on your screen to advertisers in function of that email content. Similarly, many web pages or web servers introduce invisible 1 × 1 pixel images into web pages served to users. When the web page is displayed, a request for the image is sent to the web site that owns the 1 × 1 pixel image, along with the URL of the requesting page and your IP address. When this image is owned by an advertising agent, they learn from analyzing the content of the web page (from its URL address) and from your IP address (associated with your computer), what subjects you are looking at, and from this, these agents can create a model of your interests that can be used to serve ads. This is why, after looking for a vacation hotel on a travel website, you can see ads appearing for other hotels in that locality on completely different websites. Advertisers do a semantic analysis of your behaviour to serve targeted ads. Browser add-ons such as Ghostery can block this traffic.

This information can be used for your own benefit, too, if you capture it and analyze it. In a business setting, browsing behavior of employees can be used to identify expertise within an organization. In US Patent 6,446,035, a system is described that stores and analyzes web pages browsed by workers, browsing in work mode, in an organization. The textual content of the page is reduced to normalized noun phrases, and categorized, and stored along with the bowser's

[3] Christina Tsuei's explanation at http://vimeo.com/12204858.

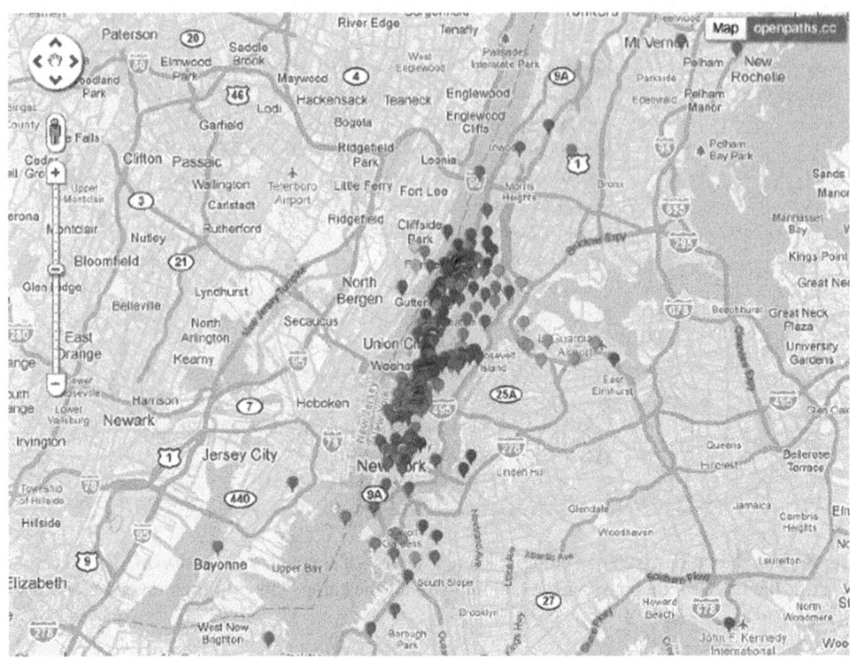

Fig. 9 Passive location tracking applications, such as OpenPath, can capture GPS coordinates from a cell phone, and display personal position during a given time period. Repeated paths and locations can be used to identify common routes taken by the wearer. Information along these routes could be gathered from open business directories to help the user conveniently find items on a shopping list, for example

identity. When someone else is searching for someone knowledgeable about some area within their organisation, they can search this stored information for people who have also browsed that topic.

Currently, people do not use their own browsing behavior to create any stored version of their own interests, relying on actively set bookmarks, or simple search histories (Fig. 8) containing only the title of the pages visited, to keep a record on things that they have browsed. Searching though email, chats and posting is also limited to simple string search.

There have been many research attempts to automatically classify emails, given an existing set of directories, or into two classes of spam or not-spam (Tang et al. 2013), or class it into mail directories using topic-detection techniques (Cselle et al. 2007).

5.1.2 Wearable Computing and Quantified Self

In addition to explicitly written text, soon people will be generating a lot of data from devices that they carry with them. The most ubiquitous example of such

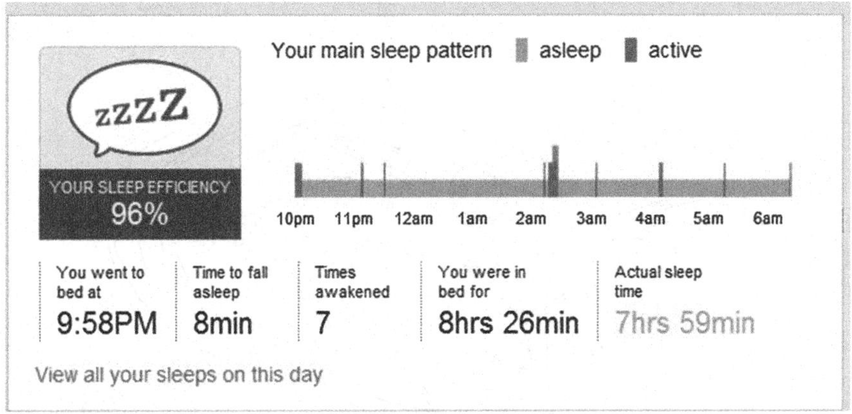

Fig. 10 One output of the wearable quantified self bracelet, FitBit, is an image of how the wearer slept, measuring periods of calm and activity during the night

wearable computing is a person's cell phone, which interacts with communication towers to pinpoint the user's location, in order to receive and send calls. This information is exploited by security agencies for tracking "persons of interest", and can be exploited by a user via a number of tracking apps that they can install on their cell phone. For example, My Running Pal will track a bicycle route, or a run, that can then be sent to another user or social website.

OpenPaths is an application that keeps track of your GPS coordinates, sends them to a central repository where the owner can access them, or allow an approved third-party to download an anonymised version for scientific study.

An application of such tracking for a user's own benefit could be the following scenario. From the timestamped GPS information in OpenPaths, it is possible to detect common routes taken by the wearer. These routes can be crossed with information about stores along these routes, using open source maps such as OpenStreetMap. This crossed information would reveal to a user where they could buy an item that they need, by indicating stores that might carry it along their daily path (Fig. 9).

In addition to tracking GPS information, wearable computing can capture a range of other data: a person's heart rate, the number of steps taken in a certain period, temperature, blood pressure, and other vital signs. A movement called Quantified Self, of people who are tracking this data about themselves, for their own use or to share, has led to great number of commercial products: FitBit (Fig. 10), FuelBand, Jawbone Up, Basis Band, Cardiio, Azumio, Beyobe, … .

These time-stamped personal data can be mapped onto emotional and physical states: calm, happy, agitated, active, sleeping, ill, … , that are specific to a given person, and which that person might use to find and retrieve certain events in their logged lives (Swan 2013).

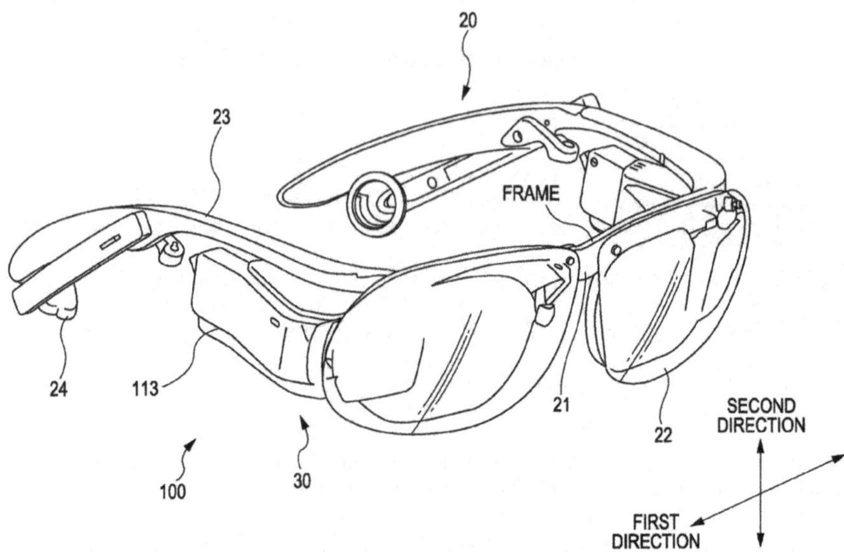

Fig. 11 Google Glass has many competitors appearing. Here is an image from a Sony patent application for a similar wearable digital eyeglass. Sony has also filed a patent, US 20130311132, for a smart-wig that embeds sensors inside a false hairpiece

5.1.3 Digital Eye Glass

In 2012, Google announced Google Glass, a prototype of a wearable video and sound capture device, set to be commercialized in 2014. By 2013, a great number of competitors have appeared (Telepathy One, Sony Smart Glass, Microsoft Augmented Reality, Vusix, ReconJet, MetaSpace Glasses, Oakley, GlassUp, Oculon Electronics, OptiVent, Epiphany Eyewear, castAR, 13th Lab). The inventor Steve Mann has been wearing and developing digital eye glasses since the 1980s. Though currently constrained by battery life, soon these glasses will allow their user to record their entire days, in video, image and sound.

This data can be converted into symbolic, storable data through video and image processing, and through speech-to-text analysis. An example of personal semantics applied to image processing is the family-and-friend recognition that was made available in Picasa (Schwartz 2005) in the early 2010s. In this photo processing system, all your locally stored photos were analyzed to identify faces (essentially ovals with two eyes) and these faces were clustered. Picasa would then present you with an interface in which you could associate a name with tight, precise clusters, removing faces if need be. With this cleaned and labeled information, Picasa would create a model of each named person in your local photos, that would be used to identify less evident faces. Facebook has also adopted a similar software (Figs. 11, 12).

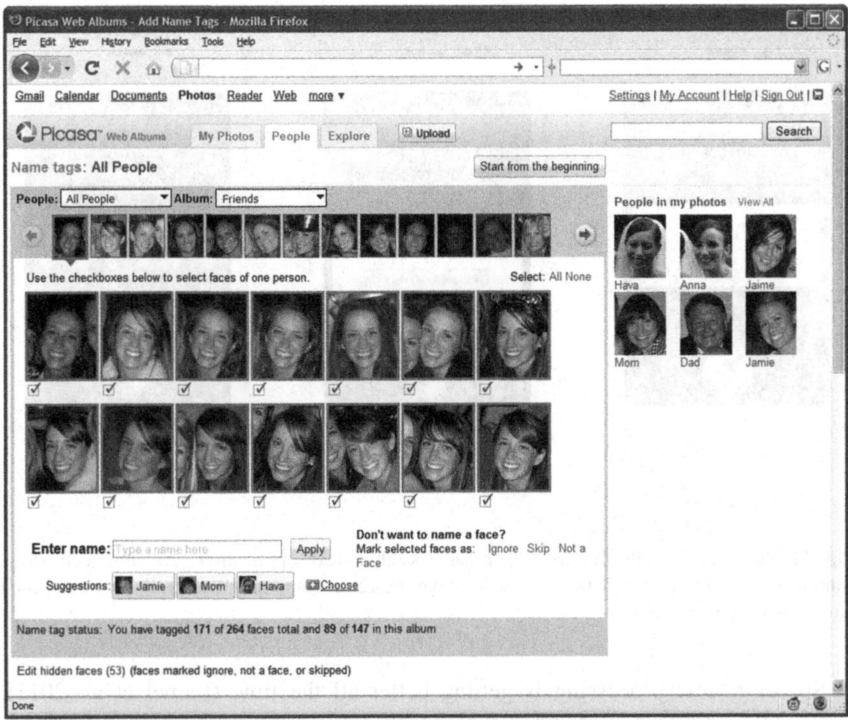

Fig. 12 Picasa, now part of Google Images, introduced a level of personal semantics by creating personal models of faces found in one user's photographs. These faces were clustered and the cluster was presented to the user for editing and for labeling. Newly added labeled images were used to reinforce the model of the labeled face

Fig. 13 Video processing can currently recognize a number of events in video: cars and people moving, fire, crowds, etc. Here in a system produced for the TrecVid by the Informatics and Telematics Institute, Centre for Research and Technology Hellas (CERTH-ITI), *smoke* is automatically detected, even when someone with a white shirt passes in front of it. (Avgerinakis et al. 2013)

Video processing is currently limited to a few large classes: detecting crowds, movement of people, smoke/fire, indoor, outdoor, etc. (Fig. 13). But as the number of classes grow these classes could also be used to annotate personal data. Identifying persons through face identification is well advanced.

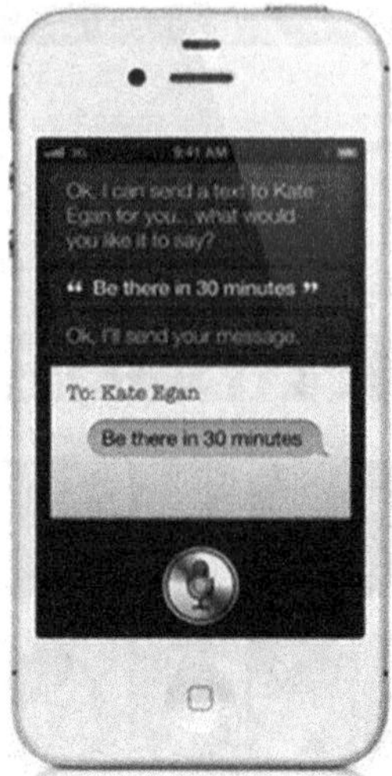

Fig. 14 Siri is currently the most popular speech-to-text application. As this technology continues to improve, it will be possible to have wearable computing passively capture speech throughout the user's day

Speech-to-text processing is getting better all the time (Lamel et al. 2011). Since 2012, Apple has included the speech recognition application SIRI in its iPhone offer (Fig. 14). Spoken questions are transmitted to a distant server for recognition, but the recognition is biased towards items found in the user's local context: contact names, physical location, time of day.

5.2 *Sketch for Personal Semantic Dimensions*

It is easy to project that, in the near future, people will have access to the following information passively collected about their own lives:

- their GPS position at any given moment
- all the things that are around those GPS points
- their vital signs at any given moment
- all the emails they have written
- all the web pages they have browsed
- all the chats, text messages, phone calls they participated in
- all the mails and messages received
- all the things they have seen or read
- all the words that they have said or heard
- all the noises they have heard

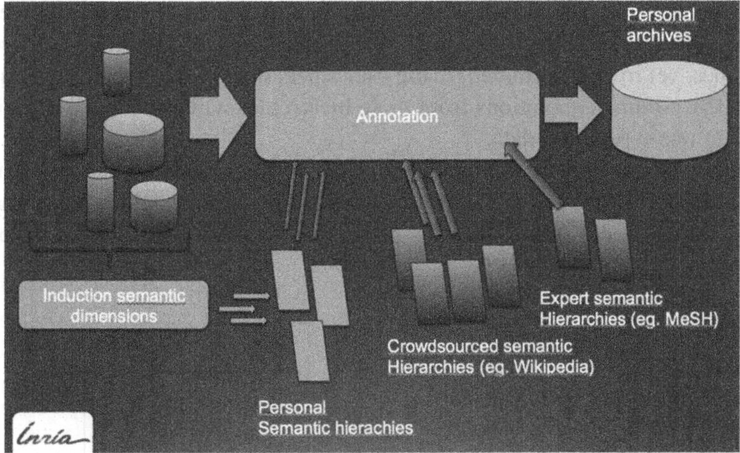

Fig. 15 From many different personal information sources shown on the *left* of this diagram, we will have to use image, speech, video and text processing to extract personal semantic dimensions. These dimensions as well as crowd-sourced semantic hierarchies, and expert defined hierarchies can then be used to annotate a user's personal data

As in a cluttered house, it will be difficult to find things in this data without some type of organisation. To retrieve some piece of information, we can imagine that "the mental dictionary is a huge semantic network composed of words (nodes) and associations (links)'' that can lead us to the information we want (Zock 2002). Some of these links will be socially shared and we can assume that the associations between items are those found in socially shared views of the world, such as are found in the semantic resources prepared by experts (MeSH,[4] WordNet[5]), or those created by crowd-sourcing (DMOZ,[6] Wikipedia categories[7]). But other associations and links will depend on the person's own mental lexicon, on what places and objects mean to the person, on whom the person knows and cares about, and why.

From psychology research on personal semantics, we see that people structure their memories in terms of autobiographical facts (facts about their own lives), episodic memories (repeated or unique events), general knowledge, and autobiographically significant events linking events to general events in the world (Renoult et al. 2012). In addition to this structuring, people can have procedural knowledge, lexical knowledge, and certain brain injuries can affect one of these memories structures and not the others, so one can remember how to use a machine but not remember any of the words for the individual parts of the machine. One can remember personal events and lose track of general knowledge, or the contrary.

4 https://www.nlm.nih.gov/mesh/filelist.html.

5 https://wordnet.princeton.edu/wordnet/download/.

6 http://rdf.dmoz.org/.

7 http://en.wikipedia.org/wiki/Wikipedia:Database_download.

To structure the passively collected information, we will need to apply expert semantic hierarchies, crowd-sourced hierarchies and hierarchies induced by techniques, yet to be determined, to the user's personal passively collected data (as in Fig. 15). Adding annotations from these hierarchies will provide the association links into one's personal data.

A rough example of these hierarchies might be the following. Suppose that one searches in one's personal archives for "wool". This query might produce the following search facets (in addition to presenting snippets and thumbnails of top matches):

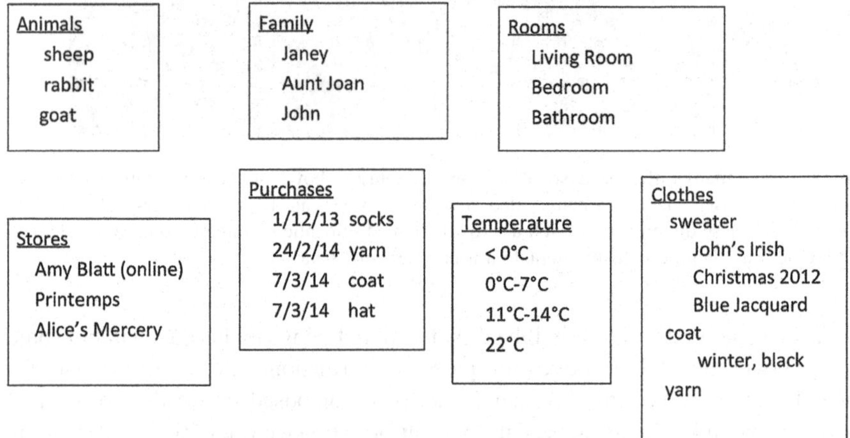

Clicking on a facet here would select items in the personal archive that are annotated with that part of the multiple hierarchies. These items could be images, videos, events, places on a map, records of purchases, documents, or any of the other types of data captured in personal archive.

6 Conclusion

Technology has reached a point where it will soon be feasible to capture, store and process great portions of people's lives, for good or for bad. One may always chose not to record one's life, as one may choose not to use a cell phone, or credit cards today. I believe that the advantages of having traces of our lives will outweigh the drawbacks. Beyond being able to visualise where you parked the car, or left your keys, we will be able recollect important things: what we read, what was said, and recall in detail what happened in a given situation. We will also be able to choose to share parts of lives with given people, a new, vivid type of autobiography. Before this happens, just consider how often you try to recall some fact about your life, and transmit this information to someone else.

I am not sure what exactly the personal semantic dimensions will be. Will they resemble each other from person to person, or be completely incomprehensible to another person? I believe we will soon see, because in the mass of information that we can collect, only categorization will allow rapid search and retrieval. And these categories must make sense to the individual.

References

Avgerinakis, K., Briassouli, A., & Kompatsiaris, I. (2013). Activity detection and recognition of daily living events. In *Proceedings of the 1st ACM international workshop on multimedia indexing and information retrieval for healthcare* (pp. 3–10). ACM.

Cselle, G., Albrecht, K., & Wattenhofer, R. (2007). Buzztrack: topic detection and tracking in email. In *Proceedings of the 12th international conference on intelligent user interfaces* (pp. 190–197). ACM.

de Melo, G., & Weikum, G. (2010). Menta: Inducing multilingual taxonomies from wikipedia. In *Proceedings of the 19th ACM international conference on information and knowledge management* (pp. 1099–1108). ACM.

Lamel, L., Courcinous, S., Despres, J., Gauvain, J. L., Josse, Y., & Kilgour, K., et al. (2011). Speech recognition for machine translation in quaero. In *Proceedings of the international workshop on spoken language translation (IWSLT)*, San Francisco, CA.

Miller, G. A. (1995). Wordnet: A lexical database for english. *Communications of the ACM, 38*(11), 39–41.

Renoult, L., Davidson, P. S., Palombo, D. J., Moscovitch, M., & Levine, B. (2012). Personal semantics: At the crossroads of semantic and episodic memory. *Trends in cognitive sciences, 16*(11), 550–558.

Schwartz, S. (2005). Organizing and editing your photos with picasa: Visual QuickProject guide. Peachpit Press.

Sherman, C. (2000). Humans do it better: Inside the open directory project. *Online, 24*(4), 43–50.

Silvester, J. P., Genuardi, M. T., & Klingbiel, P. H. (1994). Machine-aided indexing at nasa. *Information Processing and Management, 30*(5), 631–645.

Svenonius, E. (1992). Ranganathan and classification science. *Libri, 42*(3), 176–183.

Swan, M. (2013). Next-generation personal genomic studies: extending social intelligence genomics to cognitive performance genomics in quantified creativity and thinking fast and slow. Data driven wellness: From self-tracking to behavior change.

Tang, G., Pei, J., & Luk, W. S. (2013). Email mining: Tasks, common techniques, and tools. *Knowledge and Information Systems* 1–31.

Tunkelang, D. (2009). Faceted search. *Synthesis lectures on information concepts, retrieval, and services, 1*(1), 1–80.

Zock, M. (2002). Sorry, what was your name again, or how to overcome the tip-of-the tongue problem with the help of a computer? In *Proceedings of the 2002 workshop on building and using semantic networks* (Vol. 11, pp. 1–6). Association for Computational Linguistics.

Comparisons of Relatedness Measures Through a Word Sense Disambiguation Task

Didier Schwab, Andon Tchechmedjiev, Jérôme Goulian and Gilles Sérasset

Abstract Michael Zock's work has focussed these last years on finding the appropriate and most adequate word when writing or speaking. The semantic relatedness between words can play an important role in this context. Previous studies have pointed out three kinds of approaches for their evaluation: a theoretical examination of the desirability (or not) of certain mathematical properties, for example in mathematically defined measures: distances, similarities, scores, …; a comparison with human judgement or an evaluation through NLP applications. In this article, we present a novel approach to analyse the semantic relatedness between words that is based on the relevance of semantic relatedness measures on the global level of a word sense disambiguation task. More specifically, for a given selection of senses of a text, a global similarity for the sense selection can be computed, by combining the pairwise similarities through a particular function (sum for example) between all the selected senses. This global similarity value can be matched to other possible values pertaining to the selection, for example the F1 measure resulting from the evaluation with a gold standard reference annotation. We use several classical local semantic similarity measures as well as measures built by our team and study the correlation of the global score compared to the F1 values of a gold standard. Thus, we are able to locate the typical output of an

D. Schwab (✉) · A. Tchechmedjiev · J. Goulian · G. Sérasset
Université de Grenoble Alpes, LIG-GETALP, Grenoble, France
e-mail: Didier.Schwab@imag.fr
URL: http://getalp.imag.fr/WSD/

A. Tchechmedjiev
e-mail: Andon.Tchechmedjiev@imag.fr
URL: http://getalp.imag.fr/WSD/

J. Goulian
e-mail: Jerome.Goulian@imag.fr
URL: http://getalp.imag.fr/WSD/

G. Sérasset
e-mail: Gilles.Serasset@imag.fr
URL: http://getalp.imag.fr/WSD/

© Springer International Publishing Switzerland 2015
N. Gala et al. (eds.), *Language Production, Cognition, and the Lexicon*,
Text, Speech and Language Technology 48, DOI 10.1007/978-3-319-08043-7_13

algorithm compared to an exhaustive evaluation, and thus to optimise the measures and the sense selection process in general.

Keywords Semantic relatedness · Word sense disambiguation · Semantic similarity measures · Evaluation of semantic similarity measures · Best atteignable score · Correlation global score/F1 measure · Lesk measures · Gloss overlap measures · Tversky's similarity measure · Gloss vector measure

1 Introduction

Michael Zock's work has focussed these last years on finding the appropriate and most adequate word when writing or speaking (Zock et al. 2010; Zock and Schwab 2011). The semantic relatedness between words can play an important role in this context. Previous studies have pointed out three kinds of approaches for their evaluation: a theoretical examination of the desirability (or not) of certain mathematical properties, for example in mathematically defined measures: distances, similarities, scores, …; a comparison with human judgement or an evaluation through NLP applications.

In this article, we present a novel approach to analyse the semantic relatedness between words that is based on the relevance of semantic relatedness measures on the global level of a word sense disambiguation task. More specifically, for a given selection of senses of a text, a global similarity for the sense selection can be computed, by combining the pairwise similarities through a particular function (sum for example) between all the selected senses. This global similarity value can be matched to other possible values pertaining to the selection, for example the F1 measure resulting from the evaluation with a gold standard reference annotation.

We use several classical local semantic similarity measures as well as measures built by our team and study the correlation of the global score compared to the F1 values of a gold standard. Thus, we are able to locate the typical output of an algorithm compared to an exhaustive evaluation, and thus to optimise the measures and the sense selection process in general.

In this article, we first present the notion of similarity measures and we give some examples of measures that can be used on words of any part of speech. Secondly, we present the evaluation of similarity measures in the state of the art before introducing our proposition of a new evaluation method. To that end, we first present Word Sense Disambiguation (WSD) and, the ways the task can be evaluated and then we present our own method by introducing two metrics: the best atteignable score and the correlation between the global score and the F1 measure. We test it on five semantic similarity measures: two implementations of the Lesk and extended Lesk measures (one implementation from our team and one implementation from Pedersen's WordNet similarity library) and Pedersen's implementation of the gloss vector measure.

2 Similarity Measures and Their Evaluation

For most natural language processing methods and applications, there is a need to determine lexico-semantic relatedness between word senses, words or text segments. The goal is mainly to determine whether two words or text segments have some closeness in their meanings. We focus in this article on resource-based measures of semantic relatedness that have been proposed for use in natural language applications. In this context, four principal categories of semantic relatedness measures can be distinguished: feature based measures, taxonomic path length measures, information-based measures and hybrid measures. For a complete state of the art, the reader can refer for instance to Budanitsky and Hirst (2006), Cramer et al. (2010), Pedersen et al. (2005) or Navigli (2009). We briefly present the features based measures that we aim at evaluating (Lesk, Extended Lesk and Gloss Vector Measures).

2.1 Features Based Measures

Semantic relatedness measures have first been studied in the context of cognitive psychology and involve the consideration of features that characterize (positively or negatively) the similarity of two objects.

2.1.1 Tversky's Similarity Measure

Tversky (1977) first proposed an approach based on the overlap of features between two objects. The similarity between two objects is expressed as the number of pondered common properties minus the pondered specific properties of each object. The proposed model is therefore non symmetric (Fig. 1).

Formally, reprising the notations of Pirrò and Euzenat (Pirró and Euzenat 2010) where $\Psi(s)$ is the feature's set of a sense s, the Tversky's similarity can be expressed by:

$$sim_{tvr}(s_1, s_2) = \theta F(\Psi(s_1) \cap \Psi(s_2)) - \alpha F(\Psi(s_1) \backslash \Psi(s_2)) - \beta F(\Psi(s_2) \backslash \Psi(s_1))$$

where F is a function that expresses feature relevance, where \ denotes the set difference operator and where θ, α and β respectively denote the relative importance between senses similarity, the dissimilarities between s_1 and s_2, and the dissimilarities between s_2 and s_1.

This measure can be normalized (with $\theta = 1$):

$$sim_{tvtr}(s_1, s_2) = \frac{F(\Psi(s_1) \cap \Psi(s_2))}{F(\Psi(s_1) \cap \Psi(s_2)) + \alpha F(\Psi(s_1) \backslash \Psi(s_2)) + \beta F(\Psi(s_2) \backslash \Psi(s_1))}$$

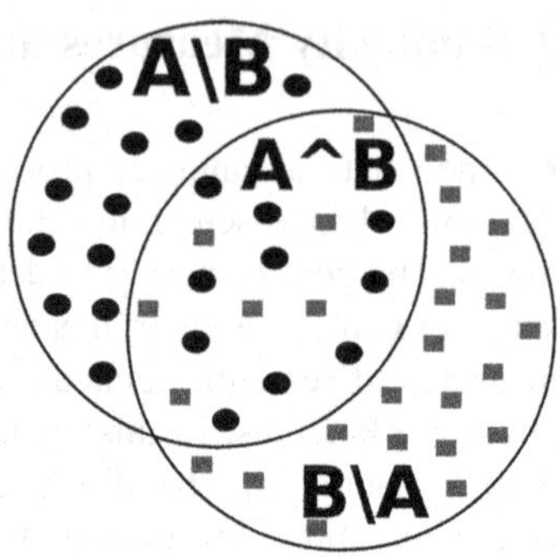

Fig. 1 Contrast between two objects

As mentioned by Pirrò and Euzenat (2010), depending on the values of α and β the Tversky index becomes one of several feature overlap similarity measures. If $\alpha = \beta = 0$, only the common features between the two senses are taken into account. If $\alpha > \beta$ or $\alpha < \beta$ we focus asymmetrically on the similarity of s_1 with s_2 or of s_2 with s_1. If $\alpha = \beta \neq 0$ the mutual similarity between s_1 and s_2 is considered. When $\alpha = \beta = 1$ Tversky's similarity measure is then equal to Tanimoto's index (Rogers and Tanimoto 1960). When $\alpha = \beta = 0.5$ the similarity is equivalent to the Dice coefficient (Dice 1945).

2.1.2 The Lesk Similarity Measure

Lesk proposed more than 25 years ago, a very simple algorithm for lexical disambiguation that evaluates the similarity between two senses as the number of common words (space separated tokens) in the definition of the senses in a dictionary (Lesk 1986) . In the original version, neither word order in the definitions (bag-of-words approach), nor any syntactic or morphological informations are taken into account. In this context, it appears that such a method can be seen as a particular case of Tversky's similarity with $\alpha = \beta = 0$ and where $\Psi(s) = D(s)$ is the set of words in the definition of s. We have:

$$sim_{lesk}(s_1, s_2) = |D(s_1) \cap D(s_2)|$$

This similarity measure is thus very simple to evaluate and only requires a dictionary and no training. The original Lesk algorithm evaluated similarity exhaustively between all senses of all words in the context. According to Navigli (2009), there are variants that select the best sense by computing the relatedness between the definition of the sense and the words in the surrounding context (with a fixed window size), rather than computing the score of all sense combinations. The similarity thus corresponds to the overlap of the sense's definition and a bag of words that contains all the words of the definitions of the context words: $Lesk_{var} = |context(w) \cap D(s_{w_n})|$. As pointed out by Navigli (2009), one important problem of Lesk's similarity is that it is very sensitive to the words that are present in the definition; if important words are missing in the definitions used, the quality of the results will be worse. Moreover, if the definitions are too concise (as it is often the case) it is difficult to obtain fine distinctions between the similarity scores. However, many improved measures, derived from Lesk, have been proposed, as detailed in the next section.

2.1.3 Extended Lesk Measures

Wilks and Stevenson (1998) have proposed to give weights to each word of the definition, depending on the length of the definition, in order to give the same importance to all definitions instead of systematically favoring the longest definitions.

More recently Banerjee and Pedersen (2002) have proposed an extended Lesk measure that considers not only the definition of a sense but also the definitions of related sense through taxinomical links in WordNet. To calculate the overlap between two senses, they propose to consider the overlap between the two definitions of the senses but also between the definitions from different relationships: hyperonymy, hyponymy, meronymy, holonymy and troponymy but also the relations *attribute*, *similar-to*, *also-see*.

To ensure that the measure remains symmetric, the overlap is evaluated on pairs of similar relations in retaining a pair relations (R_1, R_2) only if the reverse pair (R_2, R_1) is present. This produces a set *RELPAIRS*. In addition, the overlap between the two definitions A and B, is calculated as the sum of the squares of the lengths of all substrings of words from A to B, which is expressed with the $\cap$ operator. We have:

$$Lesk_{extended}(s_1, s_2) = \sum_{\forall (R_1, R_2) \in RELPAIRS^2} (|D(R_1(s_1)) \cap D(R_2(s_2))|)$$

2.1.4 Gloss Vector Measure

Similarly, relations in WordNet are used by Patwardhan and Pedersen (2006) to augment glosses for their Gloss Vector measure. This measure combines the structure and content of WordNet with co-occurence information derived from raw text. The idea is based on textual context vectors (second order co-occurrence vectors) and was created by Schutze (1998) for the purpose of Word Sense Discrimination. Word senses are represented by second-order co-occurrence vectors of their WordNet definitions. The relatedness of two senses is then computed as the cosine distance of their representative gloss vectors. This measure allows comparisons between any two concepts without regard to their parts of speech.

2.2 Evaluation of Relatedness Measures

It is commonly accepted that there are three ways to evaluate a semantic similarity measure:

- through a theoretical point of view with its mathematical properties as these scores may be similarities (in the mathematical sense) and therefore have a value between 0 and 1, distances—and therefore satisfy the axioms of reflexivity, symmetry and triangle inequality—and so on;
- through the comparison to human judgement if it is possible to collect a large set of reliable subjects-independent judgments;
- through the performance of the measures in the context of a particular application.

In this article, we will use the third method to compare different measures in the framework of a Word Sense Disambiguation (WSD) task. We focus on three features-based measures that use WordNet: Lesk (Lesk 1986), Extended Lesk (Banerjee 2002), and Gloss Vector measure (Patwardhan and Pedersen 2006) that have been presented Sect. 2.1.

3 Word Sense Disambiguation

Word Sense Disambiguation (WSD) is an essential task in Natural Language Processing applications, as it deals with the resolution of lexico-semantic ambiguities in natural language texts. Let us first make a general introduction of what constitutes a WSD system.

3.1 Generalities

The Word Sense Disambiguation process can be divided in three main steps:

1. build or select raw lexical material(s) (dictionaries, lexical databases, unannotated corpora, sense annotated corpora, …);
2. build an elaborate resource (a computational representation of a inventory of possible word senses);
3. use this resource to lexically disambiguate a text.

Lexical resources thus constitute a crucial element of Word Sense Disambiguation algorithms. The principle behind such algorithms is to exploit one or more resources and extract as many useful and meaningful features as possible, in order to disambiguate a text. Naturally, if no features can be selected and extracted from a given resource, the algorithm will have nothing to work on, thus limiting the usefulness of that particular resource. In this manner, feature selection and extraction are a key process to the success of any WSD algorithm and are strongly dependent on the type and quality of the resources exploited.

3.2 Evaluation of Word Sense Disambiguation

We will first present the principle that governs the evaluation of WSD algorithms, followed by a description of how gold standards are built and what evaluation metrics are customarily used.

3.2.1 Principle

There are two means of evaluating Word Sense Disambiguation algorithms:

- In vivo evaluation, where WSD systems are evaluated through their contributions to the overall performance of a particular NLP application. It is the most natural evaluation method, but also the harder to set up.
- In vitro evaluation where the WSD task is defined independently of any particular application. In this case, systems are evaluated using specifically constructed benchmarks.

In this article, we are more particularly going to focus on the in vitro approach

3.2.2 Gold Standard

In vitro evaluation uses a reference sense-annotated corpus. In WSD, several sense-annotated corpora are commonly used:

- The Defense Science Organization corpus provided by Ng and Lee (1996), is a non-freely available sense-annotated English corpus. 192,800 word occurrences were manually tagged with WordNet synsets. The annotation of this corpus covers 121 nouns (113,000 occurrences) and 70 verbs (79,800 occurrences) that are both the most frequent and the most ambiguous. The authors claim that their coverage corresponds to 20 % of verb and noun occurrences in English texts.
- SemCor (Miller et al. 1993) is a subset of the Brown Corpus (1961). Out of 700,000 words, almost 230,000 words are manually tagged with Wordnet synsets, over a span of 352 texts. In 186 of the texts, 192,639 (all nouns, verbs, adjectives, and adverbs) are annotated, while on the remaining 166, only 41,497 verbs are annotated.
- BabelCor (Navigli 2012) is certainly the most recent annotated corpus as it was released in July 2012. It is a corpus annotated with Babel synsets. It is constituted of two parts. The first is built from SemCor, where each WordNet

synset is simply mapped to the corresponding BabelNet synsets and the other is built from Wikipedia where each hyperlink is similarly mapped to the corresponding Babel synsets.
- Corpora from evaluation campaigns: Since 1998, there have been several campaigns (SemEval–SensEval) to evaluate Word Sense Disambiguation over several languages. Most of them have been English evaluation tasks, but there have also been Japanese, Spanish and Chinese tasks. It is uncommon for WSD evaluation corpora to go beyond 5,000 tagged words.

The three first corpora are commonly used in WSD to build supervised WSD systems (WSD systems based on machine learning principles), the last ones for evaluation. We choose one text of the Semeval 2007 corpus to illustrate the method introduced here.

3.2.3 Metrics

In WSD tasks, four standard metrics are traditionally used to evaluate the quality of the solutions provided (Navigli 2009):

The first metric is Coverage (C) and is defined as the number of answers provided over the number of expected answers, in other words it represents how much of the text has been disambiguated.

The second metric is Precision (P) and is defined as the number of correct answers provided over the total number of answers provided.

The third is Recall (R) and is defined as the number of correct answers provided over the total number of answers expected to be provided.

The last metric is the F1 measure represents the "weighted harmonic mean of Precision and Recall" and combines that P and R in a single measure. It is defined as $F_1 = \frac{2 \cdot P \cdot R}{P+R}$.

3.3 *Similarity-Based Word Sense Disambiguation*

3.3.1 Principle

Similarity-based methods for WSD rest on two algorithms: a local algorithm and a global algorithm. Local algorithms aim at providing a score based on the proximity of the semantic content of two compared linguistic items (usually words or word senses). Similarity measures have been described in Sect. 2. For WSD, these measures are used locally between two senses, and are then applied on the global level. A global algorithm is a method that allows to extend a local algorithm to an entire text in order to infer the appropriate sense for each word. The most direct algorithm is the exhaustive (brute force) method, used for example by Banerjee and Pedersen (2002). The combinations of all the senses of the words in a given context (word window or text) are considered in order to assign a score to each combination and then to choose the combination with the highest score. The main problem with this method is the combinatorial explosion it creates. Hence, the BF method is very difficult to apply in real conditions and moreover, makes the use of a longer analysis context impossible. To circumvent this problem, several approaches are possible. The first, called complete approaches, try to reduce the number of combinations by using pruning techniques and choice heuristics. In the context of WSD, a good example is the approach proposed by Hist and St-Onge (1998) that is based on lexical chains (a taxonomic semantic similarity measure based on the overall relations of WordNet) that combines restrictions during the construction of the global lexical chain with a greedy heuristic. According to Navigli (2009), the major problem of this approach is its lack of precision caused by the greedy strategy used. However, various improvements have been proposed among others by Silbert (2000). Other interesting complete approaches have been applied in the context of word sense disambiguation, in particular by Brody and Lapata (2008). The other approaches are called 'incomplete', as they explore only a part of the search-space using heuristics to guide them to areas that seem more promising. These heuristics are generally based on probabilities: choices are made stochastically.

Two main methods can be distinguished:

- neighborhood approaches (new configurations are created from existing configurations), among which are approaches from artificial intelligence such as genetic algorithms or optimization methods (e.g. simulated annealing);
- constructive approaches (new configurations are generated by iteratively adding solutions to the configurations under construction), among which are for example ant colony algorithms.

The reader may consult (Schwab et al. 2012) for more information.

3.3.2 Problem Configuration

To perform a Word Sense Disambiguation task, is to affect to each word w_i of a text of m words one of the senses of that word $w_{i,j}$. The definition of a sense j of word i is noted $d(w_{i,j})$. The search-space corresponds to all the possible sense combination for the text being processed. Therefore, a configuration C of the problem can be represented as an array of integers such that $j = C[i]$ is the selected sense j of w_i. For example, if we consider the simple text "*The mouse is eating cheese*", it has 3 words to be annotated ('*mouse*'; '*eat*'; '*cheese*'). If we consider the second sense for '*mouse*', the first sense for '*eat*'; and the third for '*cheese*', the configuration is [2;1;3].

4 New Ways to Evaluate Semantic Measures

While standard evaluation methods have been extremely useful for the development and improvement of the field of WSD, we have now reached a plateau in the development of such algorithms. Thus new ways of evaluating are required to go beyond that limit. We first set our working hypothesis and then go on and present the principles that governs our evaluation method.

4.1 Working Hypothesis

Two main working hypotheses have to be set in order to place an appropriate context for our work in this article.

4.1.1 Text as Context

In this article, we choose to consider a text in its entirety as the context window to be disambiguated. This choice is also made by Cowie (1992) for their WSD simulated annealing algorithm, made by Gelbukh et al. (2003) for their WSD genetic algorithm and the idea being taken up more recently by Navigli and Lapata (2010) and in our team Schwab et al. (2011, 2013, 2012). Many approaches, however, use a smaller context, especially for computational reasons, even if it is sometimes not explicitly reported. From our point of view, this leads to two problems. The first is that we have no way to ensure the consistency between the selected senses. Two generally incompatible senses can be chosen by the algorithm, because the context does not include the key word that can make the difference. For example, even with a window of six words before and six words after, the sentence "*The two planes were parallel to each other. The pilot had parked them meticulously*", "pilot" does not help to disambiguate the term "planes". The second problem is that texts usually hold some semantic unity. For example, as noted by Gale et al. (1992) or Hirst and St-Onge (1998), a word used several times in a text has generally the same sense; this information, better known as *one sense per discourse*, cannot be exploited within a windowed disambiguation context.

4.1.2 Uniform Global Score

The algorithms require some *fitness* measure to evaluate how good a configuration is. Even with the text as the context, it is possible to use several methods to compute a global score. For instance, one can weight relatively to the surrounding words proportionally to their distance from that particular word. There are two approaches to a distance-based weighing:

- with respect to the distance in the number of interceding words
- with respect to the distance in a structure: syntactic structure, discourse structure, ...

Such a criterion is important, however it is orthogonal to our object of study. We therefore chose a fixed weight of one for each word as a working hypothesis.

Hence, in this work, the score of the selected sense of a word is expressed as the sum of the local scores between that sense and the selected senses of all the other selected senses for the words of the text: for a full configuration, we simply sum the scores for all selected senses of the words of the text:

$$Score(C) = \sum_{i=1}^{m} \sum_{j=i}^{m} measure\left(w_{i,C[i]}, w_{j,C[j]}\right) \tag{1}$$

4.2 Principle

From a combinatorial optimization point of view, the ideal global score is a fitness value. In other terms, for a given local measure, the global score is an adequate estimator of the F1 score. This implies that the relationship between the global score and the F_1 should ideally be monotonic: the higher the global score, the higher the F1 measure. Various meta-heuristic approaches (simulated annealing, genetic algorithms,...) devise a heuristic global score function that exploits limited knowledge about the problem. The monotonicity prerequisite is often assumed to be true, as it is hoped that the global function will be a good estimator of the maximum a posteriori distribution of the optimal disambiguation. However, in truth, it is extremely difficult to construct a good estimator for the overall disambiguation of natural language texts. Such heuristics lead to biased and often noisy estimators, for which the monotonicity of the relationship between the global score and any form of score based on human judgement (for example F1 measure over a gold standard) can hardly be guaranteed.

Despite the very centrality of this issue, there has been little interest in the community to address such questions.

We study this problem through several measures that we can use to attempt to evaluate the adequacy of a given global score as a good estimator of the disambiguation of a text.

Starting from one or several texts extracted from a sense-annotated gold standard, the idea is to generate a sufficient[1] quantity of uniformly sampled configurations and to compute their F1 measure. Then, starting from this set, we can

[1] Sufficient in the sense of permitting the exhibition of statistical significance, even though in practice we generate several orders of magnitude more samples that the bare minimum necessary to obtain statistically significant differences in the average values.

compute, for each of its members the global score with one or more semantic measures. We can then represent the relationship between a configuration, its global score and F1 measure as a triple:

$$\langle C_i; F_i; S_i^{measure} \rangle \tag{2}$$

where C_i is the ith configuration of the dataset, F_i its corresponding F1 measure and $S_i^{measure}$ the corresponding global score for the measure *measure*.

From these triples, we can compute the measure we need to evaluate the appropriateness of the global score with relation to the F1 measure. We introduce here the notion of best attainable score and the correlation of the global score against the F1 measure.

4.2.1 Best Attainable Score

The best attainable score for a given global score formula, $Score_{best}^{measure}$, is the F1 measure that is obtained with the semantic measure *measure* so that the resulting global score is optimal. We assume the unicity of this value. Even though, in practice we should verify that it is indeed unique.

$$S_{best}^{measure} = \underset{F_i \in \langle C_i; F_i; S_i \rangle}{\text{argmax}} \{score^{measure}(F_i)\} \tag{3}$$

4.2.2 Correlation Global Score/F1 Measure

Principle

As mentioned before, similarity-based WSD rest on the assumption that the global score is an adequate estimator of the F1 measure. The dynamics of such algorithms are based on maximizing the global score. We hence propose to evaluate a semantic measure through the correlation between the global score and the F1 measure. Of course the choice of the correlation measure defines different properties that we are trying to detect. For example a Pearson's correlation tests for can be used linear relationships, while the Spearman rank correlation coefficient imposes the weaker condition of monotonicity. In our case, we are just interested in ensuring monotonicity and thus, we use the Spearman rank correlation coefficient:

$$correlation(F, S) = r = \frac{\Sigma(F_i - \bar{F})(S_i - \bar{S})}{\sqrt{\Sigma(F_i - \bar{F})^2 \Sigma(S_i - \bar{S})^2}} \tag{4}$$

A correlation is a value between -1 and 1 with the following semantics:

- if the correlation is close to 1, the datasets are strongly correlated. In other word, there is a linear relationship between the distributions for the pearson correlation and an exact monotonic relationship in the case of the spearman coefficient. In simple terms when the value of A increases, the value of B as well.
- if the correlation is close to -1, the distributions are strongly inversely correlated and there exists an inverse monotonic or linear relationship between them. As A increases, B decreases, and vice versa.
- if correlation is around 0, there is no linear or monotonic relationship between the distributions.

An ideal measure would give a perfect monotonic relationship between the global score and the F1 measure. In other terms the correlation score would be 1.

How Representative is a Sample?

For our problem, a configuration is a vector of several hundred dimensions in the problem space. A score is assigned to each configuration. An optimal solution to the problem is a configuration with a score of 1. The search space is manifestly too large to explore exhaustively in search of an optimal solution. We, hence, sampled some configurations uniformly as an approximation of the whole search space. Of course we have no way of knowing if the sampling is representative, thus we adopted a technique that attempts to ensure that it is as representative as possible.

In simple terms, we divide the dataset in n different parts (with $n \geq 100$) and compute the correlation on each subset so as to be able to estimate if the variation in correlation is statistically significant over the total F1 measure. This exactly corresponds to a classical randomization test.

5 Construction of the Dataset

5.1 Gold Standard

Our dataset needs to be big enough to permit correlations that are statistically significant and well balanced between configurations with low F1 measure and configurations with high F1 measure to be computed. We choose to build the dataset from the first text of the Semeval 2007 task 7 coarse-grained all words corpus. This text is categorized by the task organiser as a news article, published in the Wall Street Journal.[2]

[2] The article is available here https://wiki.csc.calpoly.edu/CSC-581-S11-06/browser/trunk/treebank_paper/buraw/wsj_0105.ready.buraw.

In this text, there are 368 words to annotate. 66 of them are monosemic. Among the 302 remaining words, there is an average of 6.06 senses per words. We can then approximate the number of combinations as $6.06^{302} = 2 \times 10^{236}$.

The dataset will be accessible through the companion page of this article.[3]

5.2 Random Construction of Configurations

We randomly generated the configurations by starting from one of the configuration that obtained the best score (100 % of precision/recall/F1 measure). The idea of the generation algorithm is to randomly (uniformly) modify one or several senses in the configuration. Of course, it usually leads to new configurations with lower scores. Iterating this process several times permits to obtain configurations in the whole range of possible F1 measure values.

On this text, we obtained 1,910,332 configurations from which 1,184,125 were unique. Yet, the sample represents only 5.84×10^{-229} % of the search space. Figure 2 presents the likelihood density of our dataset, in function of the F1 measure. One can note that we don't have the same number of configurations for each possible F1 measure. It is not a problem, as it doesn't affect our method to have more configurations in one part of the F1 measure range, given that we cut our space in n different parts to compute our correlations. Moreover, it would be difficult and certainly impossible to obtain lot of configurations for the highest and the lowest F1 measure values.

6 First Experiments on Various Semantic Measures

6.1 Similarity Measures Evaluated

In this experiment we endeavour to evaluate and compare the global score function resulting from different similarity measures, and try to find commonalities and differences in terms of which one is the best estimator. In this particular experiment, we have our own implementation of the Lesk and Extended Lesk methods (respectively denoted GETALP-Lesk and GETALP-ExtLesk), and wish to compare them to the same measures as implemented in the `WN::Similarity` Perl package (denoted WNSIM-Lesk and WNSIM ExtLesk).[4] We will similarly consider its vector-based similarity measure (denoted WNSIM-Vectors).

---

[3] http://getalp.imag.fr/static/wsd/Schwab-et-al-SemanticSimilarity2014.html.

[4] http://wn-similarity.sourceforge.net.

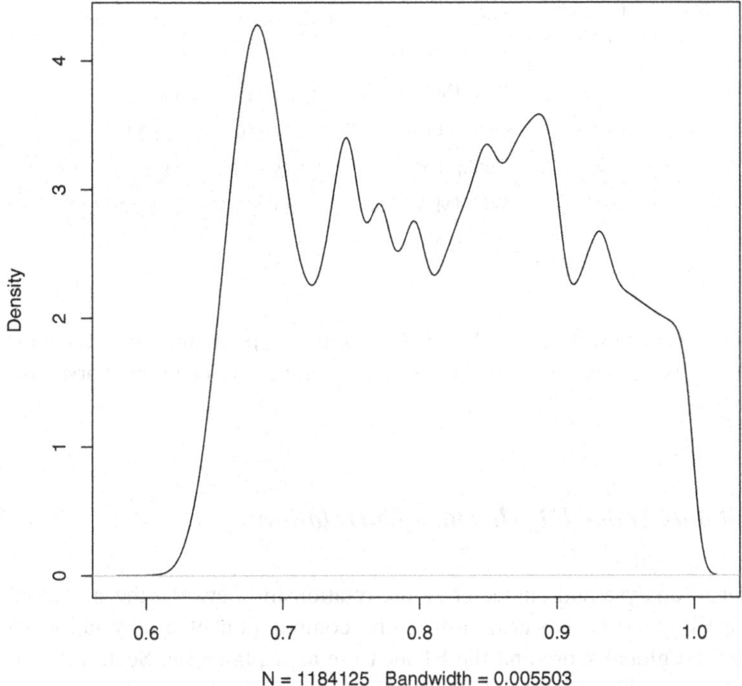

Fig. 2 Density of our dataset in function of the F1 measure

6.2 Best Atteignable Score

For each measure, we computed the best attainable scores on our dataset. Table 1 shows the corresponding F1 measure for each best global score.

First of all, we can note that Lesk obtains better results than Extended Lesk in both implementations. This is a quite surprising result. On previous known results with various gold standards and languages, Lesk always obtains worse results than Extended Lesks. It was the case with our implementation (Schwab et al. 2011), with Pedersen's implementation (Pedersen et al. 2005), with Baldwin et al.'s (2010) and with Miller et al.'s (2012).

It possibly means that global algorithms that use Lesk fall in a local maximum and are not able to find highest global scores. We will try to shed more light on this point.

If we compare the two implementations, Pedersen's appears to be better than our own, especially his WNSIM-Lesk, which obtains a very high F1 measure, 98.37 %, very close of 100 %. This result is certainly caused by squaring the overlap counted for the longest overlapping substring (see Sect. 6.1). We don't use that heuristic here, however, especially as it is computationally very expensive.

Table 1 Best atteignable scores of the measures on our dataset

Measure	Max score	Corresponding F1 measure
WNSIM-Lesk	360,793	0.9837
WNSIM-ExtLesk	2,804,835	0.8533
Getalp-Lesk	311,950	0.8533
Getalp-ExtLesk	3,555,160	0.8505
WNSIM-Vectors	43,795.3	0.8478

As shown in (Schwab et al. 2013), Pedersen's implementation's computational complexity is exactly $O(n \times m)$ while ours's complexity is, in the worst case, $O(n)$ with $n > m$.

6.3 Global Score/F1 Measure Correlation

In order to analyse and characterize the relationship between the global measure and the F1 measure, we now turn to the computation of a correlation measure between the global score and the F1 measure as explained in Sect. 4.2.2. Table 2 show this correlation calculated over the whole sampling of the search space. As we can see, the results vary wildly between the different measures, ranging from −0.2261 with our Extended Lesk, followed closely by Pedersen's Extended Lesk (−0.1755) and the vector similarity measure (−0.1664) all the way up to 0.9137 with Perdersen's Lesk measure. Our own Lesk measure has a correlation of 0.6968. Clearly, we see that some of the correlation are consistent with the F1 measure corresponding to maximal global scores, however, other correlation values are much more surprising. Indeed, if one considers the difference in correlation between ExtLesk and our own implementation of Lesk of $\delta_\rho = 0.4707$ and then the difference in the maximal F1 measure that is of only $\delta_F = 0.028$, the question of what explains such big correlation differences compared to the actual maximal F1 measure arises.

Table 2 Global score/F1 measure correlations on our dataset

Measure	Correlation global score/F1 measure
WNSIM-Lesk	0.9137
WNSIM-ExtLesk	−0.1755
Getalp-Lesk	0.6968
Getalp-ExtLesk	−0.2261
WNSIM-Vectors	−0.1664

Table 3 Correlations global score/F1 measure on our dataset

Measure	Min	1st quartile	Median	Mean	3rd quartile	Max
WNSIM-Lesk	0.9096	0.9124	0.9137	0.9136	0.9146	0.9170
Getalp-Lesk	0.6536	0.6924	0.6968	0.6960	0.7007	0.7135
WNSIM-Vectors	−0.1927	−0.1712	−0.1664	−0.1659	−0.1603	−0.1193
WNSIM-ExtLesk	−0.3898	−0.1815	−0.1755	−0.1776	−0.1697	−0.1462
Getalp-ExtLesk	−0.2493	−0.2326	−0.2261	−0.2270	−0.2233	−0.1370

Could this behaviour be the result of the convergence to a local maximum that is more difficult to escape with one measure over the other? Could it simply be that the correlation measure does not capture the relationship between the global score and the F1 measure? A large quantity of noise in the global score would certainly have a role to play in this discrepancy. If the monotonicity assumption between the scores is violated due to that potentially large presence of noise, can the correlation measures help identify the regions of the search space where the amount of noise is lesser and where the monotonicity assumption holds?

In order to have a better idea about the relationship between the global score and the F1 measure, it may be interesting to look at the distribution of correlation scores more closely, by first breaking down the distributions (Table 3).

Overall, the extrema of the distribution are relatively close to the mean. This seems to indicate a clearly significant difference[5] and thus does not give any further indications to explain what causes such a discrepancy between the maximal F1 measure and the correlation distribution.

Given that the correlation distribution encompasses the entire sampling, regardless of the F1 measure, it is difficult to draw any conclusion, thus we have broken down the correlation distribution depending on the F1 measure and represented it in a separate plot for each measure (Figs. 3, 4, 5, 6 and 7). Depending on the granularity of the increments in the F1 measure we would show more or less of the noise in the relationship. As we are interested in the general behaviour and not on minor artefacts due to noise, we selected a sliding window of 3 % F1 measure around each point of the plot. If the window size is any smaller, the noise makes any interpretation difficult and if the window size is any higher, interesting variations start being “smoothed away”. The five lines on the plot, from top to bottom, respectively represent the maximum value, the 1st quartile, the mean, the 3rd quartile and the minimum value. Thus, we can have a more precise idea of the behaviours and of the distribution of correlation values for particular F1 measure neighbourhoods.

[5] Given that we have over a million configuration and that the correlation is calculated in chunks of 100 scores, each group contains over 10,000 samples, which at a 10^{-4} difference range should guarantee a sufficient statistical power.

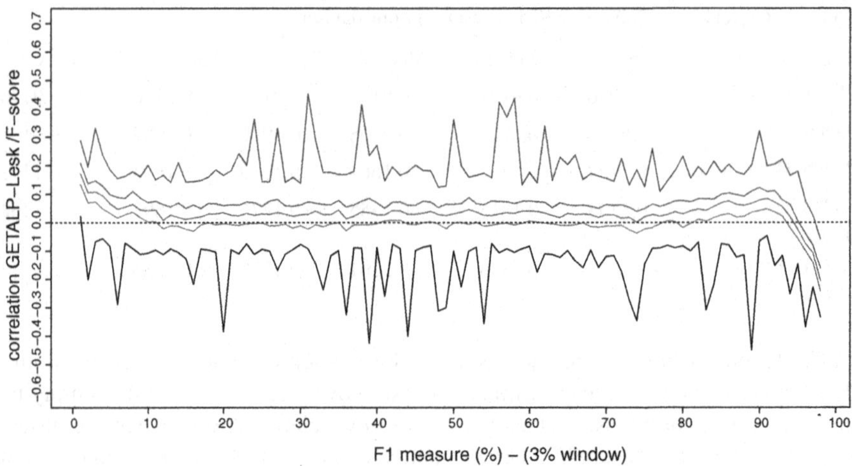

Fig. 3 Correlation of F1 measure and global score for our Lesk measure broken down by F1 measure in a 3 % sliding window

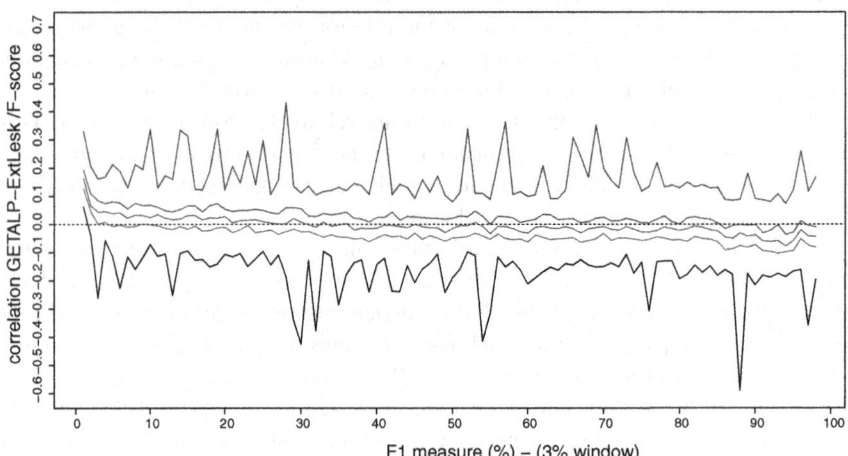

Fig. 4 Correlation of F1 measure and global score for our Extended Lesk measure broken down by F1 measure in a 3 % sliding window

We can immediately see that what explains the huge differences from earlier, is the position of the bulk of the distribution (inter-quartile portion) relative to the zero axis. Our Lesk implementation, for example exhibits consistently positive interquartile range throughout the F1 measure spectrum, while on the other hand, ExtLesk, WNSIM-ExtLesk or WNSIM-Vector the interquartile values are consistently negative.

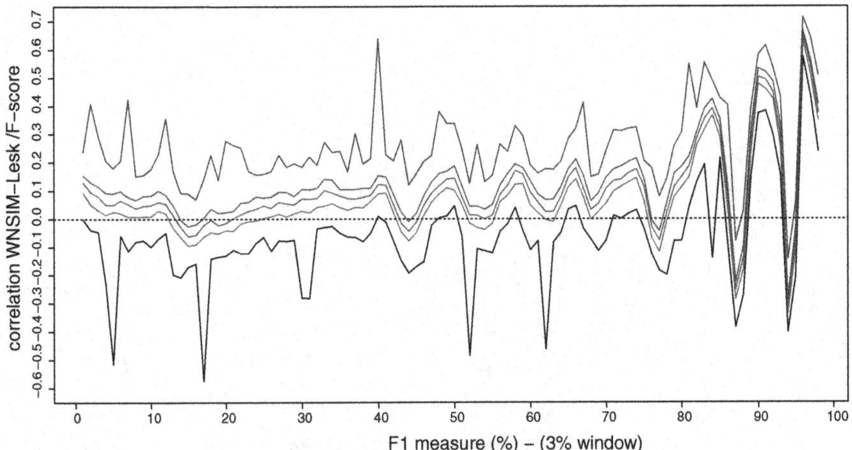

Fig. 5 Correlation of F1 measure and global score for the WNSim Lesk measure broken down by F1 measure in a 3 % sliding window

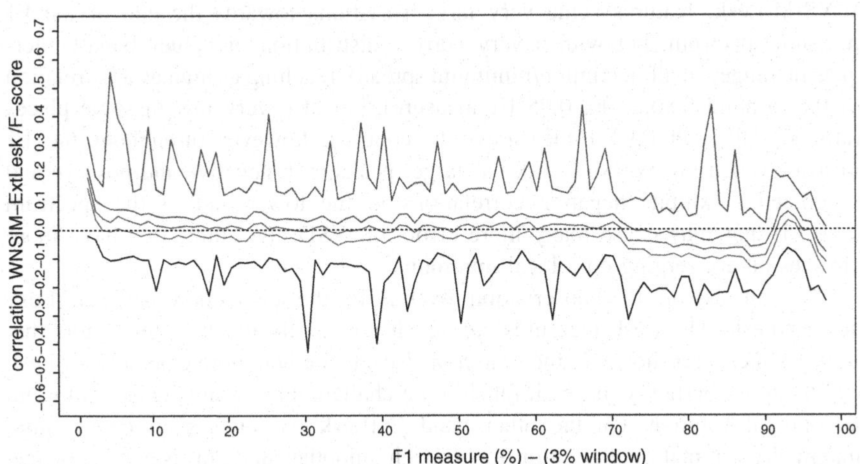

Fig. 6 Correlation of F1 measure and global score for the WNSim Extended Lesk measure broken down by F1 measure in a 3 % sliding window

One commonality between all the distributions is that there is a very wide divide between the maximal and minimal values that is roughly symmetric. In other words, when we have a correlation peak at the top of the distribution, there is often a matching low at the bottom of the distribution. Be it with GETALP-Lesk, GETALP-ExtLesk, WNSim-ExtLesk the maximum peaks tend to reach similar values in many places, this alone explain why we can get a good F1 measure despite a very negative overall correlation. The WNSim-Lesk and WNSim-ExtLesk consistently have a somewhat higher maximum peaks. Furthermore, the

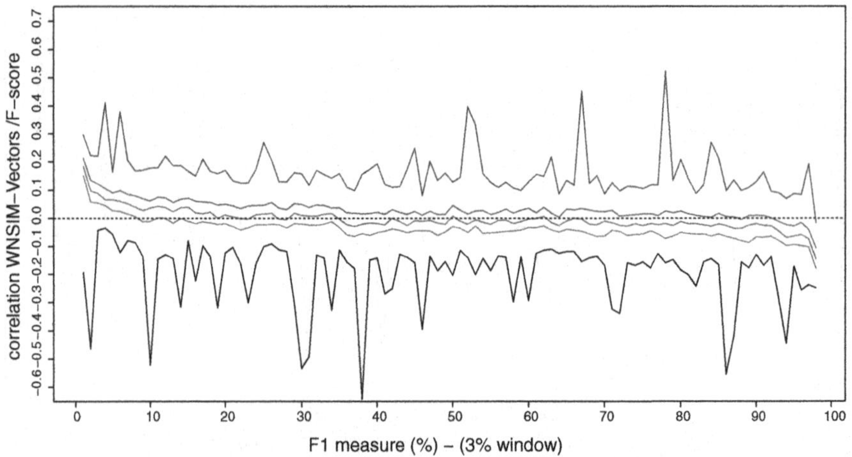

Fig. 7 Correlation of F1 measure and global score for the WNSim Vector similarity measure broken down by F1 measure in a 3 % sliding window

WNSIM-Lesk, features some very large variations towards the end of the F1 measure spectrum, but with a very narrow distribution of values (small inter-quartile range, small maximum/minimum spread), reaching as high as a correlation of 0.6 (around 0.80, 0.90, 0.95 F1 measure), but also very low in some places (around 0.85 and 0.93 F-measures). In contrast, however throughout the F1 measure spectrum, WNSim-Lesk has larger peaks both negative and positive and specifically, exhibits negative correlations in the lower end of the spectrum ($\sim$0.15) that may cause many more errors in WSD algorithms that have more chances on converging on a local minimum.

We can extend this observation overall to the distinction between Lesk and ExtLesk. The Lesk measures can reach potentially much better results that ExtLesk measures, however the search landscape is much more chaotic with Lesk and the noise certainly makes it much more challenging for any algorithm to find an optimal solution. On the other hand ExtLesk measures sacrifice potential maximally optimal configuration for a much smoother and consistent landscape, with much less minima or maxima traps. Thus the Lesk Extensions are merely a compromise to smooth the search space and make its exploration easier in exchange for lower potential scores. In practice, the trade-off is largely worth it as algorithms using extended Lesk yield much better results.

7 Conclusion

In our experiment, we sample the search space of WSD algorithms at the text level through different local similarity metrics summed into a global fitness score for a given configuration in the search space. Then, we move on to attempting to characterize the properties and distribution of the global scores compared to a F1 measure computed with relation to a human annotated gold standard that constitutes a reference disambiguation. Since what interests us is the behaviour of the global function compared to the F1 measure and more specifically a monotonous relationship between the global score and the F1 measure, we compute the Spearman rank correlation coefficient, which quantifies exactly the relative behaviour of the two scores towards one another under an assumption of monotonicity. We then group the samples of our search space by 100 and compute a distribution of correlation values, which gives us an overall idea of the correlation. We then break down the correlation values with relation to the F1 measure in a 3 % sliding window, so as to perform a more fine-grained analysis. The analysis reveals that the main distinction between Lesk and Extended Lesk measures is that the Lesk measures have potentially much higher maximal scores and correlations, at the cost however, of much noisier search landscapes and numerous minima and maxima in the correlation values. Thus there are many variations and local non-monotonic behaviour that in turn makes the job of disambiguation algorithms much more challenging. In contrast, Extended Lesk measures incorporate information from related concepts from the taxonomy of a lexical resource and in a way potentially introduces more *linguistic noise*. On average, this leads to much lower correlations with the F1 measure, at the added benefit of greatly reducing the amount of variation in the correlation values and thus in the presence and density of local non-monotonous behaviour. As a result, WSD algorithms have a much easier time finding solutions and better than they would with the Lesk measure. Overall, the algorithms are very sensitive to local maxima, despite the numerous meta-heuristic countermeasures that they set in place and the landscape with a Lesk score is possibly among the most difficult search spaces for them.

We believe that our own findings give a promising window on what happens in WSD search spaces and open a new avenue of research towards their study and the improvement of search heuristics in the solving of WSD problems. We will continue to explore new ways of efficiently characterizing the search space and new improvements that leverage such findings and insight, in order to get even better disambiguation with knowledge-rich approaches.

References

Baldwin, T., Kim, S., Bond, F., Fujita, S., Martinez, D., & Tanaka, T. (2010). A reexamination of MRD-based word sense disambiguation. *ACM Transactions on Asian Language Information Processing*, *9*(1), 4:1–4:21. doi:10.1145/1731035.1731039, http://doi.acm.org/10.1145/1731035.1731039.

Banerjee, S., & Pedersen, T. (2002). An adapted Lesk algorithm for word sense disambiguation using wordnet. In *CICLing 2002*, Mexico City.

Brody, S., & Lapata, M. (2008). Good neighbors make good senses: Exploiting distributional similarity for unsupervised WSD. In *Proceedings of the 22nd International Conference on Computational Linguistics* (*Coling 2008*), Manchester, UK (pp. 65–72).

Budanitsky, A., & Hirst, G. (2006). Evaluating WordNet-based measures of lexical semantic relatedness. *Computational Linguistics, 32*(1), 13–47.

Cowie, J., Guthrie, J., & Guthrie, L. (1992). Lexical disambiguation using simulated annealing. In *COLING 1992* (Vol. 1, pp. 359–365). Nantes, France.

Cramer, I., Wandmacher, T., & Waltinger, U. (2010). *WordNet: An electronic lexical database, chapter modeling, learning and processing of text technological data structures*. Heidelberg: Springer.

Dice, L. R. (1945). Measures of the amount of ecologic association between species. *Ecology, 26*(3), 297–302.

Gale, W., Church, K., & Yarowsky, D. (1992). One sense per discourse. In *Fifth DARPA Speech and Natural Language Workshop* (pp. 233–237). Harriman, New York: États-Unis.

Gelbukh, A., Sidorov, G., & Han, S. Y. (2003). Evolutionary approach to natural language WSD through global coherence optimization. *WSEAS Transactions on Communications, 2*(1), 11–19.

Hirst, G., & St-Onge, D. D. (1998). Lexical chains as representations of context for the detection and correction of malapropisms. In C. Fellbaum (Ed.) *WordNet: An electronic lexical database* (pp. 305–332). Cambridge, MA: MIT Press.

Lesk, M. (1986). Automatic sense disambiguation using mrd: How to tell a pine cone from an ice cream cone. In *Proceedings of SIGDOC '86* (pp. 24–26). New York, NY, USA: ACM.

Miller, G. A., Leacock, C., Tengi, R., & Bunker, R. T. (1993). A semantic concordance. In *Proceedings of the Workshop on Human Language Technology, HLT '93* (pp. 303–308). Stroudsburg, PA, USA: Association for Computational Linguistics. doi:10.3115/1075671.1075742, http://dx.doi.org/10.3115/1075671.1075742.

Miller, T., Biemann, C., Zesch, T., & Gurevych, I. (2012). Using distributional similarity for lexical expansion in knowledge-based word sense disambiguation. In *Proceedings of COLING 2012* (pp. 1781–1796). Mumbai, India: The COLING 2012 Organizing Committee. Retrieved from http://www.aclweb.org/anthology/C12-1109.

Navigli, R. (2009). WSD: A survey. *ACM Computing Surveys, 41*(2), 1–69.

Navigli, R. (2012). A quick tour of word sense disambiguation, induction and related approaches. In *Proceedings of the 38th Conference on Current Trends in Theory and Practice of Computer Science (SOFSEM)* (pp. 115–129).

Navigli, R., & Lapata, M. (2010). An experimental study of graph connectivity for unsupervised word sense disambiguation. *IEEE Transactions on Pattern Analysis and Machine Intelligence, 32*, 678–692.

Ng, H. T., & Lee, H. B. (1996). Integrating multiple knowledge sources to disambiguate word sense: An exemplar-based approach. In *Proceedings of the 34th annual meeting on Association for Computational Linguistics, ACL '96* (pp. 40–47). Stroudsburg, PA, USA: Association for Computational Linguistics. doi:10.3115/981863.981869, http://dx.doi.org/10.3115/981863.981869.

Patwardhan, S., & Pedersen, T. (2006). Using wordnet based context vectors to estimate the semantic relatedness of concepts. In *EACL 2006 Workshop Making Sense of Sense—Bringing Computational Linguistics and Psycholinguistics Together* (pp. 1–8).

Pedersen, T., Banerjee, S., & Patwardhan, S. (2005). Maximizing semantic relatedness to perform WSD. Research report, University of Minnesota Supercomputing Institute.

Pirró, G., & Euzenat, J. (2010). A feature and information theoretic framework for semantic similarity and relatedness. In P. Patel-Schneider, Y. Pan, P. Hitzler, P. Mika, L. Zhang, J. Pan, I. Horrocks, & B. Glimm (Eds.), *The semantic web—ISWC 2010* (Vol. 6496, pp. 615–630)., Lecture Notes in Computer Science Berlin/Heidelberg: Springer.

Rogers, D., & Tanimoto, T. (1960). A computer program for classifying plants. *Science, 132*(3434), 1115–1118.

Schutze, H. (1998). Automatic word sense discrimination. *Computational Linguistics, 24*(1), 97–123.

Schwab, D., Goulian, J., & Guillaume, N. (2011). Désambigusation lexicale par propagation de mesures sémantiques locales par algorithmes à colonies de fourmis. In *Traitement Automatique des Langues Naturelles* (*TALN*), Montpellier, France.

Schwab, D., Goulian, J., & Tchechmedjiev, A. (2013). Worst-case complexity and empirical evaluation of artificial intelligence methods for unsupervised word sense disambiguation. *International Journal of Web Engineering* and *Technology 8*(2), 124–153. doi:10.1504/IJWET.2013.055713, http://dx.doi.org/10.1504/IJWET.2013.055713.

Schwab, D., Goulian, J., Tchechmedjiev, A., & Blanchon, H. (2012). Ant colony algorithm for the unsupervised word sense disambiguation of texts: Comparison and evaluation. In *Proceedings of the 25th International Conference on Computational Linguistics* (*COLING 2012*), Mumbai (India).

Silber, H. G., McCoy, K. F. (2000). Efficient text summarization using lexical chains. In *Proceedings of the 5th International Conference on Intelligent User Interfaces, IUI '00* (pp. 252–255). New York, NY, USA: ACM.

Tversky, A. (1977). Features of similarity. *Psychological Review, 84*(4), 327–352.

Wilks, Y., & Stevenson, M. (1998). Word sense disambiguation using optimised combinations of knowledge sources. In *COLING '98* (pp. 1398–1402). Stroudsburg, PA, USA: ACL. Retrieved from http://dx.doi.org/10.3115/980432.980797.

Zipf, G. K. (1949). *Human behavior and the principle of least effort*. Reading, MA: Addison-Wesley.

Zock, M., Ferret, O., & Schwab, D. (2010). Deliberate word access: An intuition, a roadmap and some preliminary empirical results. *International Journal of Speech Technology, 13*(4), 107–117. Retrieved from http://hal.archives-ouvertes.fr/hal-00953695.

Zock, M., & Schwab, D. (2011). Storage does not guarantee access: The problem of organizing and accessing words in a speaker's Lexicon. *Journal of Cognitive Science*, *12*, 233–258. Retrieved from http://hal.archives-ouvertes.fr/hal-00953672. (Impact-F 3.52 estim. in 2012).

How Can Metaphors Be Interpreted Cross-Linguistically?

Yorick Wilks

Abstract Research on metaphor as a phenomenon amenable to the techniques of computational linguistics received a substantial boost from a recent US government funding initiative (iARPA, http://www.iarpa.gov/Programs/ia/Metaphor/metaphor.html) that set up a number of teams in major universities to address the issues of metaphor detection and interpretation on a large scale in text. Part of the stated goal of the project was to detect linguistic metaphors (LMs) computationally in texts in four languages and map them all to a single set of conceptual metaphors (CMs). Much of the inspiration for this was the classic work of George Lakoff (Lakoff and Johnson 1980) which posited a set of universal metaphors in use across cultures and languages. I wish to examine the assumptions behind this goal and in particular to address the issue of how and in what representation such CMs can be expressed. I shall argue that a naïve approach to this issue is to make very much the same assumptions as the work of Schank and others in the 1970s: namely that there can be a universal language of "primitives" for the expression of meaning, which in practice always turns out to be a form of simple English. Reviving that assumption for the study of metaphor raises additional issues since, even if the *senses* of the terms in those CM representations could be added to the representations, metaphors often deploy new senses of words which will not be found in existing sense inventories like computational lexicons. The paper is not intended just to present a negative conclusion; I also argue that the representation of metaphors in a range of languages can be brought together within some CM scheme, but that simply reviving the *English-as-interlingua* assumptions of 40 years ago is not a good way to make progress in this most difficult area of meaning computation. In what follows I discuss first the representation of CMs: in what language are they stated? I argue the need for some inclusion of the representation of the senses of their constituent terms within the CM, or at least a default assumption that the major sense (with respect to some lexicon such as WordNet) is the intended one. I then consider the issue of conventional metaphor

Y. Wilks (✉)
Florida Institute of Human and Machine Cognition, Ocala, FL, USA
e-mail: ywilks@ihmc.us

© Springer International Publishing Switzerland 2015
N. Gala et al. (eds.), *Language Production, Cognition, and the Lexicon*,
Text, Speech and Language Technology 48, DOI 10.1007/978-3-319-08043-7_14

and its representation in established lexicons (again such as WordNet) and the effect that can have on detection strategies for metaphor such as selectional preference breaking. I then argue that the mapping of text metaphors to CMs, as well as the empirical, rather than intuitive, construction of CM inventories require further use of preference restrictions in lexicons by means of a much-discussed process of projection or coercion. I conclude that only the use of (computable) procedures such as these for metaphor detection and mapping can lead to a plausible program for the large scale analysis of metaphor in text and that Lakoff's views on metaphor lack these empirical underpinnings.

Keywords Metaphor · Interlingua · Semantics · WordNet · Preference · Word-sense

1 Introduction

Michael Zock's long-term interest in the lexicon, and in particular the mental lexicon (Zock 2006), allow me to presume upon his interest in metaphor in so far as it is undoubtedly a phenomenon both cognitive and tightly tied to the state of a lexicon, one that must for individuals and groups change with time.

Understanding unstructured information such as prose in any natural language rests first on it being in a language one understands, let us say English. But problems in understanding arise even in English and even with translations, human or mechanical, from other languages. One way of capturing the additional understanding needed that goes "beyond having the words" is captured by the term "metaphor". This notion conveniently expresses aspects of culture and figurative expression that go beyond literal or ostensive meaning and are crucial to understanding. These aspects are often opaque even to those who are expert in the language concerned. Metaphor as a notion also has the advantage that it has been an area of research in computer language processing for decades, and one that has yielded real results. That research has been driven in part by the writings of George Lakoff at Berkeley (Lakoff and Johnson 1980) who has developed an approach to metaphor that rests on the following assumptions (in my terms but I think uncontentious):

- There are metaphors found in all cultures that are crucial to understanding language:
- These metaphors can be discovered and listed, even if not exhaustively.
- We can proceed with analysis as if these metaphors can be not only paraphrased but expressed in English.

For example, such a universal metaphor might be expressed (in English) as LIFE IS A JOURNEY and we shall refer to items like this as Conceptual Metaphors (CM). There is then an initial analytic issue of detecting actual surface metaphors in text, possibly related to or "expressing" that CM such as *The pensioner was nearing the end of his road*, and then the task of matching them to such a stored generalized form. We shall refer to linguistic strings like the one quoted as Linguistic Metaphors (LM). There is then the problem, if one believes in the universal nature of CMs, of how to match expressions of "similar" metaphors in, say, Farsi to that CM since the capitalised words in English may have many senses and the question immediately arises as to how an algorithm is to determine which sense is intended by "LIFE" in that CM: that it is not, say, a "a life as in a childrens' game of hide and seek, a score token".

One complexity in metaphor research, at least from a computational or Natural Language Processing (NLP) perspective, is that universal theories like the one above (expressed by the three bullets) have proved resistant to computational implementation, which has not been the case with other, quite different, empirical approaches based on bottom-up detection of LMs in text, rather than starting from a set of a priori CMs (e.g. Fass and Wilks 1983; Shutova et al. 2012). We shall now address serious questions about *the representational language in which CMs are stated* and how they to be intuitively understood, since their terms (e.g. LIFE) do not disambiguate themselves. Let us now turn to the core issue of how CMs are to be represented.

2 The Language of Conceptual Metaphors (CMs)

A crucial aspect of the research problem, which many seem to believe is a solution, is that CMs are classically expressed in English words but without any realization of what that entails. When this is pointed out, a frequent response is that this is an accidental fact of no significance and we can just carry on. I believe this is profoundly inadequate response. It is very close to the early discussion in AI and NLP in the 1960s and 1970s on the role of interlinguas in machine translation and in cognitive representations generally. There was a fashion at that time for limited languages expressed by English primitives terms in systems for the semantic representation of language content (e.g. in the work of Schank 1975; Wilks 1968 and many others). I am not here defending that approach, only pointing out that the extended discussion 40 years ago (e.g. in Wilks 1977/2007) of the adequacy or otherwise of this limited language of (English-like) primitives to carry the general meaning of language expressions has many similarities to what we are discussing now in regard to CMs.

There was no real resolution to that controversy of long ago: key references are Pulman's (1983) attack on the practice from a linguistic perspective, and Lewis (1972) from a philosophical one, in the course of which he invented the term "markerese" for the self-description of language in linguistics by means of word-like *markers* with no illumination or benefit. But the critiques were not heeded and much such representational work continued, simply because researchers in semantics could see no alternative (outside radical connectionism) to continuing to use symbols to represent the meanings of other symbols. Language content had to represented somehow, they reasoned, so why not in this English-like language? Dictionaries, after all, describe word meanings within the very language under description, and so the practice has continued, ignoring the waves of philosophical and linguistic criticism, simply because there seem to be no alternative. What has happened is that the language terms used for representation have been embedded in more logical and formal-seeming structures so as to make them more palatable, but the underlying issue has not gone away. That issue is: How can I describe semantic content with a term such as MAN, HUMAN or ANIMATE and be confident I know what it means, and not just "means in English"? I shall now turn to how CM representation problems can be ameliorated with the aid of a sense-lexicon.

3 Representing CMs Unambiguously with Major Word Senses

If we are to use CMs at all, no matter how derived or expressed, they must be in as word-sense-neutral a form as we can manage. To my knowledge this has never yet been fully considered as problem, perhaps an insurmountable problem, let alone a solved problem. We cannot just ignore this as we do when we say, that [POVERTY IS A GAP] is a CM, and underlies the metaphor "poverty gap", and that we just know what the senses of the words there are present and that they make a CM. Just suppose that we had two CMs in our inventory of universal metaphors that could be written as:

POVERTY IS A GAP

POVERTY IS AN ABYSS

Now suppose we want to locate Russian metaphors and find the text string (LM) containing the keywords : *беДносТь -NA-провал*, which mean roughly "poverty" and "failure". But, and here is the problem "**провал**" can also means "abyss" and "gap" in English; in which case how do we know which of these so-called universal CMs to match the LM to? Or should be seek for or construct a third CM [POVERTY IS FAILURE]? It seems clear to me that either:

(1) The CMs are in some language other than English, in which case how do we know what English word senses the terms above correspond to, since "poverty", "failure" and "abyss" all have multiple senses in, say, WordNet (Vossen 1998). If the terms are not English but some universal language of indeterminate syntax and semantics, how can LMs ever be matched to CMs as *any* theory of metaphor seems to require?
(2) If however, the terms in the two CMs *are* in English, and they certainly appear to be, then we need to know what senses those words have, so as to match any word in an English or Russian LM to them, what senses those words have.

A natural way of carrying out the second possibility is to tag the English words in the CMs (and the words in any putative LMs) with WordNet senses. Since the EuroWordNet project (Vossen 1998) in which the present author participated, we now have a convenient way of setting up such a match since that project took the core Princeton WordNet for English as, essentially, an interlingua, and linked senses in the Wordnets for other languages to those core senses. So, for example (and the correctness of these correspondences does not matter for the argument): there may well be an English WordNet sense of "failure", namely Failure#1 that is deemed by a EuroWordNet mapping to be the same sense as Провал#1 in Russian WordNet. Again, there may be a "Провал#3" that similarly corresponds to "abyss#1".

What do we want to say about universal CMs and their ability to support analysis of metaphor instances in such a case? The first natural thing to say is that the original Russian string "бедность провал"—can express both CMs and we cannot decide which. But that is only true if we cannot decide which sense the last word bears in the Russian LM. If it bears only one of the two noted senses then the Russian LM matches one and only one of the CMs—assuming now the CM terms are tagged with WordNet senses. Russianists should note here that I am ignoring the case issues for the proper expression of that string in Russian and just concentrating on the main forms of the words. Also, I am not suggesting it would be destructive if a LM were to match to two possible CMs, though I do not believe that need be the case here. It could be that other, perhaps pragmatic, factors outside the text would settle the choice. My only pint here is that a systematic empirical account of mapping LMs to CMs should take account of this possibility and standard contemporary theories do not consider the issue.

Now a Russian speaker may take that phrase to have one and only one of those senses in context—assuming the Russian speaker can understand the distinction we are making with the words "failure" and "abyss" in English—let us assume they can. The string certainly seems too short and vague for a wordsense disambiguation program to determine the sense in that LM context.

Or, and this is a quite different possibility, is it the case that, in a metaphorical string such as the LM "Poverty is failure" we cannot rely on the normal psychological or computational methods to resolve a word sense for us? Since the content is, more or less, novel, at least on first encounter, and the standard disambiguation techniques do not work because they are all, to some extent, based on redundancy, which does not apply to novel utterances? So, to use an old and hackneyed example, if someone says *The shepherd swung his crook*, we infer that "crook" is a tool for shepherds not a gangster, simply because of the redundant presence of "shepherd". But in LMs this may not be available, unless the metaphor is dead, or lexicalized or otherwise familiar (in which case wordsense disambiguation hardly applies). What I am suggesting is that perhaps in metaphors, especially novel ones, the words must be taken in the basic senses by default, as it were, *because we lack the familiar context in a metaphor, by definition, to resolve a participating word to any non-basic sense.*

This conclusion is perhaps not very striking but rather obvious: words of a real language, like English, can only function in an interlingua (such as CMs constitute) on condition that they bear their "basic" senses, which will, in WordNet terms, usually mean #1 for any given word. This implies that in the capitalized English CMs above, each term implicitly has whatever its #1 sense is in WordNet.

So to return to the purported sense correspondence in Euroword-net style:

Failure#1 is deemed by a EuroWordNet mapping to be the same sense as Провал#1. Again, there may be a "Провал#3" that similarly corresponds to "abyss#1".

This would imply that we should take the CMs (and LMs, with the caveat below) in their default #1 senses, since we have no information to allow us to do anything else. Hence "Провал" should be taken in the context above to be Провал#1, its first sense, and so as a CM about failure not about an abyss, even thought the latter could conceivably be indicated by another context for the same words. This suggestion that the senses in a CM are major senses of the relevant words also implies that the two CMs are different from each other, which preserves the insight of the tradition that metaphors are strictly speaking lies (attributed variously to Mark Twain, Nietzsche et al.) rather than the less acceptable alternative that CMs are tautologies, where the senses simply recapitulate each other.

This risk of tautology in the expression of CMs is very real even if we are wary and assign (implicitly as main senses) interpretations to the symbols in CMs. If, in the CM [POVERTY IS A GAP], we allow the first WordNet sense interpretation to "gap" we get:

S: (n) **gap**, spread (a conspicuous disparity or difference as between two figures) "gap between income and outgo"; "the spread between lending and borrowing costs"

Thus, and depending on the sense assigned to "poverty", we have a very real risk of tautology since this sense of "gap" is itself abstract (and not, say, a gap between two pieces of wood) and itself very close to any definition of poverty. This unfortunate fact can be dismissed or just accepted as a weakness in WordNet, or as a reason for excluding [POVERTY IS A GAP] as a CM.

One important inference from this discussion, if it has any value, is that we cannot just say, as many researchers in the Berkleyan universal metaphor tradition seem to want to, that some metaphor "in one language" is commoner than in another. As we have seen, it is a very sophisticated matter to establish whether LMs in two languages point to a single CM or not, given the problems of how that CM is to be unambiguously represented and given the need for some lexical resource of at least the size and scope of (Euro)WordNet. In the example above the LM word strings in question in the two languages—Russian and English, in this example—actually point to different CMs in the common interlingua, a conclusion that, we argued, undermines the foundation of the Berkeley approach to understanding metaphor, since the LMs could be interpreted as "meaning the same thing". At this point, we shall step back and review the basic role of "preference" in detecting, then mapping, metaphors.

4 The Role of Preference in Detecting and Matching Metaphors

The exception to the rule of "main senses", as far as LMs are concerned, is the situation we have defined elsewhere as one of "conventional metaphor" (Wilks et al. 2013), where a lexical resource such as WordNet actually encodes a metaphorical sense as a (dead or) conventional metaphor. Our general approach to detecting metaphor has been that an initial sufficient criterion for a surface (LM) metaphor to be present is that a verb or adjective "preference" is broken (Wilks 1968) e.g. in the simplest case the verb does not receive the agent or object it expects (whether that last notion is unpacked linguistically or statistically) in a stereotypical case. Verbs and adjectives will, of course, have multiple senses in the lexicon, each with its own preferences. So to write *fall into poverty* is to break the preference for a space-like object for the basic sense of "fall into". This general criterion reappears frequently in the literature (e.g. the recent work of Shutova et al. 2012); indeed it is not clear there is any alternative as a basic criterion for recognition unless one believes that metaphors are detected by direct matching to stored CMs. As we have seen above this a notion whose sense dissolves somewhat under scrutiny.

If such preferences, and the associated noun-senses for fillers, are thought of as stored in a respository like WordNet or VerbNet, then what counts as a broken preference depends crucially on the state of lexicon, temporally expressed, since sense inventories extend with time and indeed often come to store senses that were in origin metaphorical. Where that is the case, a dead, or as we would prefer to say conventional, metaphor will not result in a broken preference with respect to WordNet because in such a case the metaphorical sense is itelf stored in WordNet and so will fit the demands of the corresponding verb.

So, to take a very simple and uncontentious example:

Public employees' unions have built a fortress around their pension systems

In VerbNet (Windish Brown et al. 2011) we find the following:

[[VerbNet: build

Member of

§build%2:31:03 (member of VN class base-97.1)
§build-26.1-1

- WordNet Sense 1
- Agent [+ animate | +machine]

So "Unions" violates Agent restriction

- WordNet Sense 8
- Agent [+ animate | +organization]

"Unions" satisfies the Agent restriction —as an organization]]

The situation is one where the primary sense of "build" is not satisfied by the first sense of the agent the sentence provides but by a "lower" (in the entry, in this case #8) sense. In (Wilks et al. 2013) I proposed that this could serve as a useful heuristic for detecting conventionalized metaphors of the sort this sentence contains, since such metaphors would be missed by any "preference breaking" heuristic for metaphor detection as there is a (lower) sense of "build" available for which the agent preference here is satisfied. The heuristic was that a main sense fails and a lower sense satisfies; and both parts must be true.

The point here is not to draw attention to this metaphor detection heuristic against a large lexicon for its own sake, but only to show a limitation on the above suggestion that metaphor detection (and as we shall discuss below, metaphor mapping to CMs) must depend on the main senses, as listed in a lexicon. Our claim here is that this heuristic for detecting conventional or lexicalized metaphor does not compromise the general value of that rule. In the case of the above example (of Unions), there are arguably two CM metaphors present: the major one is to do with barriers and the protection of assets, however expressed, and the other is more simply:

ORGANIZATIONS ARE PEOPLE

which is expressed (in major senses of the relevant words) by the process of detection we have described.

The latter move is the basis of how preferences, and their violations in metaphor, are also central to the subsequent process of mapping from a detected metaphor to some stored form, what we are calling CMs. If we were again dealing with "He fell into poverty" we might expect the broken preference for the object of "fall into" to be some coding for hole/abyss/gap/aperture. The inference from that detection to the underlying metaphor in play is generally to assert that the metaphor's subject (poverty in this case) is being asserted to be equivalent to the preferred filler that is made available in the lexical coding (e.g. in VerbNet, see Windisch Brown et al. 2011) but not in the sentence itself. This would lead to some form such as:

POVERTY IS AN ABYSS

As a potential CM, empirically derived from text rather than a linguist's intuition. The interesting difficulty is to determine at exactly what level the last term is to be expressed, since "abyss" is in general a very magnified form of hole. The mapping process from a metaphor instance to a CM, however expressed, will require an ontology of the kind that underlies WordNet to navigate from what appears in a VerbNet coding (perhaps "hole") to an already stored CM (perhaps "abyss"). This method, merely sketched here, can in principle serve to map LMs to CMs, and to create potential CMs from text.

This process using the preferred constituents of lexical codings has been central to a number of systems based on inferences in lexical semantic structures under names such as "projection" and "coercion" in work such as (Wilks 1968; Pustejovsky 1995; Nirenburg and Raskin 2004; Hanks 2013) among many others. It provides at least the beginning of a process of determinate empirical construction of CMs from text cases quite different from the intuitive creation of CMs in the Berkeley tradition. Further possible examples of the method would be with a failed subject preference in *Israel has inflicted this wound on itself*, we can get (from the stored VerbNet subject preference for "inflict" as PERSON) we can link the existing target (Israel) to the preferred subject (as source), namely PERSON, plus the WordNet type of "Israel" as COUNTRY to give as a possible CM: COUNTRY IS PERSON. We could do the same for verb + object failure as in: *The bank hyenas are feeding on money*, assuming we have access to "feed on" as a verb with its own preferences FOOD or EDIBLES. Then, using similar reasoning to that for subjects above, and again using the assigned object and the preferred object, we can derive directly a potential CM MONEY IS FOOD. Again, the preferred class yields the source directly. For adjective preferences, similar routines are possible, as in *Brazil's economic muscle will become increasingly important.* If we have a preference established for the preferred type of the noun associated with the adjective "economic" as COMPLEX-SYSTEM, then from the existing adjective object "muscle" (and taking its semantic type from WordNet as BODY) we then have directly a propositional form linking TARGET IS SOURCE, which is instantiated here as COMPLEX-SYSTEM IS BODY.

Notice that no claims here depend on the actual quality or completeness of resources such asVerbNet or WordNet. These are always variable, depending on the language used, and always contain errors and omissions, as well as being constantly changing with the language itself. The only claim is that some such resource will be needed to carry out the processes described here, even if augmented in practice by statistical corpus computations (some of which augmented these resources in the work described in Wilks et al. 2013).

There has been criticism of processes of this sort applied to mapping to, and empirical construction of, CMs in this manner: during a recent large-scale metaphor detection and interpretation project a project manager wrote:

> *[CMs that were] proposed….. were inconsistent and generally unmotivated. For the most part, the relationship of an LM (for a Target) and a proposed CM was semantically extremely shallow with generally no mapping at all. This process caused a huge proliferation of "lexical" CMs, often dependent on a synset label from WordNet.*

To this one must respond (a) that there is no known correct *level* for the expression of CMs beyond the intuitions of metaphor theorists, so no level is demonstrably "too lexical" and (b) more fundamentally, the CMs are inevitably in some language (usually English) and require sense disambiguation of their terms, as we argued at length above, They are not in a language that is self-disambiguating, since nothing is. Hence the presence of WordNet labels, even if implicit, and indicating main senses as we suggested above, is inevitable. That would be a feature not a bug.

The problems of the appropriate level for the expression of CMs, their distance and separation from LMs and their very origins in intuiion, is not one that preoccupies only NLP researchers, as is clear from:

"…. at some points in the development of [Conceptual Metaphor Theory], there has been a tendency for researchers to propose new conceptual metaphors using limited linguistic evidence. For instance, Gibbs et al. (1997) take the idioms "he really couldn't swallow it" and "[leave] a bad taste in the mouth" as instantiations of a conceptual metaphor termed ACCEPTING SOMETHING IS EATING IT. It is not clear how many other realizations there might be of this conceptual metaphor, and in what way it differs from the more-often cited IDEAS ARE FOOD. Kovecses (2002) lists as a conceptual metaphor CONSIDERING IS CHEWING, which again is difficult to separate from IDEAS ARE FOOD. If this tendency becomes widespread, the notion of a conceptual metaphor loses clarity, along with any predictive power it may have had" (Deignan 2005, p.105).

5 The Lakoff-Berkeley View of Metaphor Revisited

This view, against which I have argued, seems to me to rest on the following, very questionable, assumptions:

1. There is a set of universal CMs, determinable by linguistic intuition and found in all languages.

As I have argued, there is no empirical evidence for their existence or how many of them there are, and intuition as a source of linguistic insight is no longer considered reliable, taken alone. However, there may be a discovery procedure for them from text along the lines suggested here (and in Wilks 1968).

2. These CMs can be expressed in an English-like language, whatever their real underlying representation.

I have argued that they are in fact in English, as they appear to be, and not as an inevitable approximation; this is made clear by the problem of expressing exactly what senses their constituent words are to be taken in. This situation is only tolerable as a heuristic if some form of cross-lingual sense representation is incorporated into the representation as suggested here.

3. Surface metaphors (LMs) in languages can be mapped to these CMs in a determinate way.

I have argued that no procedure is ever given, within this tradition, for performing this crucial step and it can only be attempted at all with the aid of some fairly reliable, cross-sense mapping of the languages concerned, such as (Euro)WordNet.

If LMs can be matched bottom up to CMs in this way—as opposed to being the subject of some imaged direct matching top-down from stored CMs to LMs in text—it should be possible to count how many LMs correspond to a given CM. That would then make it possible to estimate quantitatively the frequency of occurrence of CMs in a reliable manner. That analysis could be extended cross-lingually and cross-culturally if parallel text were available. Suppose we have an

English-Spanish parallel text in which sentences are aligned. We could then ask whether LMs are detected in parallel (synonymous) sentences and, if so, do they map to the same CMs. If they do, that would be independent confirmation of the utility or universality of such a CM. Quantitative and distributional questions about universal metaphor can only be asked, it seems to me, if procedures of the kind I sketch here are developed, and these are not obviously compatible with standard Lakoffian approaches to metaphor.

My main conclusion is that, for these reasons, Berkeley metaphor theory cannot easily be the basis of any empirical exploration of metaphors in texts in multiple languages, and that any research program aimed at the interpretation and translation for metaphor instances so based will have been mistaken.

Acknowledgements The paper is indebted to comments from Patrick Hanks, Robert Hoffman and Sergei Nirenburg, though the errors are all mine as always.

References

Deignan, A. (2005). *Metaphor and corpus linguistics*. Amsterdam: Benjamins.

Fass, D., & Wilks, Y. (1983). Preference semantics, ill-formedness and metaphor. *Journal of Computational Linguistics, 9*, 178–187.

Gibbs, R., Bogdonovich, J., Sykes, J., & Barr, D. (1997). Metaphor in idiom comprehension. *Journal of Memory and Language, 37*, 141–154.

Hanks, P. (2013). *Lexical analysis: Norms and exploitations*. Cambridge, MA: MIT Press.

Kovecses, Z. (2002). *Metaphor: a practical introduction*. Oxford: Oxford University Press.

Lakoff, G., & Johnson, M. (1980). *Metaphors we live by*. Chicago: University of Chicago Press.

Lewis, D. (1972). General Semantics, In: D. Davidson & G. Harman (Eds.), *Semantics of natural language*. Reidel: Dordrecht.

Nirenburg, S., & Raskin, V. (2004). *Ontological semantics*. Cambridge, MA: MIT Press.

Pulman, S. (1983). *Word meaning and belief*. London: Croom Helm.

Pustejovsky, J. (1995). *The generative lexicon*. Cambridge, MA: MIT Press.

Schank, R. (Ed.). (1975). *Conceptual information processing*. Amsterdam: Elsevier.

Shutova, E., Teufel, S., & Korhonen, A. (2012). Statistical metaphor processing. *Computational Linguistics, 39*(2)

Vossen, P. (Ed.). (1998). *EuroWordNet: A multilingual database with lexical semantic networks*. Amsterdam: Kluwer.

Wilks, Y. (1968/2007). Making preferences more active. In K. Ahmad, C. Brewster & M. Stevenson (Eds.), *Word and Intelligence I*. Berlin: Springer (Reprinted).

Wilks, Y. (1977/2007). Good and bad arguments for semantic primitives. In K. Ahmad, C. Brewster & M. Stevenson (Eds.), *Word and Intelligence I*. Berlin: Springer (Reprinted).

Wilks, Y., Dalton, A., Allen, J., & Galescu, L. (2013). Automatic metaphor detection using large-scale lexical resources and conventional metaphor extraction. *Proceedings 1st Workshop on Metaphor in NLP (Meta4NLP 2013)*. Atlanta, GA.

Windisch Brown, S., Dligach, D., & Palmer, M. (2011). VerbNet class assignment as a WSD task. In *IWSC 2011*: *Proceedings of the 9th International Conference on Computational Semantics*, January 12–14, 2011. Oxford, UK.

Zock, M. (2006). Needles in a haystack and how to find them? The case of lexical access. In E. Miyares Bermudez & L. Ruiz Miyares (Eds.), *Linguistics in the twenty first century*. Cambridge: Cambridge Scholars Press.

Recursion and Ambiguity: A Linguistic and Computational Perspective

Rodolfo Delmonte

Abstract In this chapter I will be concerned with what characterizes human language and the parser that computes it in real communicative situations. I will start by discussing and dismissing the Hauser et al. (2002) (HC&F) disputed claim that the "only uniquely human component of the faculty of language" be "recursion". I will substantiate my rejection of HC&F's claims, with the fact that recursion only appears in mature and literate language—an opinion also shared by some papers in a book on recursion by Harry van der Hulst (2010). I will then present in detail Chomsky's proposal—now part of the Minimalist Theory (MT)—of the architecture of the human parser as being based on Phases. I will accept this part of the theory and compare it with the computational architecture contained in a system for deep text understanding called Getaruns (Delmonte 2007, 2009). I will then argue in favour of what I regard the peculiar component of human language faculty that is "the ability to associate meaning to deficient propositions and generic linguistic expressions, which are highly ambiguous in their structure". And this is also due to the presence of recursion (but not only). I will then speak in favour of a parser that takes "context" into account and strives for a "complete" syntactic representation. As to the problem of ambiguity, I will introduce the use of a computational device, a lookahead mechanism, which is presented in association with the need to specify UG parameters characterizing a given language. I will discuss the use of psychologically viable Parsing Strategies implemented in the parser to overcome ambiguity and prevent Garden Path, whenever possible. This will be highlighted by reference to peculiar features associated to different languages, Italian and English. Eventually, I will present a theory that encompasses all my previous proposals and is called LSLT.

R. Delmonte (✉)
Computer Linguistics Laboratory, Venice, Italy
e-mail: delmont@unive.it

© Springer International Publishing Switzerland 2015
N. Gala et al. (eds.), *Language Production, Cognition, and the Lexicon*,
Text, Speech and Language Technology 48, DOI 10.1007/978-3-319-08043-7_15

Keywords Human language faculty · Human language parser · Recursion · Linguistic maturation · Natural language understanding · Parsing arguments and adjuncts · Ambiguity and meaning · Lookahead and parsing strategies · Garden path structures universal grammar parameters · Lexical semantic language theory (LSLT)

1 Introduction

Recursion has received a lot of attention lately, after HC&F's (2002) article which claims that recursion is the "only uniquely human component of the faculty of language", and the book edited by Harry van der Hulst (2010) which collects papers focusing on the same issue from a variety of different perspectives. The book is a mixture of different theories, levels of analysis, perspectives and points of view, none of which addresses the issue in the same manner as will be done here.

I will develop the notion of recursion from a distinct point of view which encompasses both properties of the language faculty and of the parser, this one simulated by a real parser, the central component of the system called GETARUNS. My point of view is partly hinted at in A. Verhagen's chapter (2010), where he points to two important notions: long distance dependencies, and center-embedding, which is phrased as "the specification of certain phrases which requires the application of a rule to its own output". It is just these two elements of a computational architecture of the human/computational parser that make recursion a highly specialized and complex phenomenon. Looked at from inside the parser it is possible to distinguish two basic types of recursion as Pinker and Jackendoff put it, tail recursion and true recursion (2005, p. 211). Tail recursion can be mimicked by iteration (see Karlsson 2010), it is said, but as will be shown below, it requires coping and solving ambiguities and the attachment problem. True recursion on the contrary coincides with clausal recursion and the problem of long-distance dependencies. This latter case requires a computational device with a stack and pointers: but it is much more than that. Sentences are the only structure in a parser that cannot be fed on the output of previous computation. Sentences are semantically closed structures: in our case, extraposition variables for long distance dependencies may be passed on to the next structure in the case of complement clauses, or they may be passed inside a clause in the case of relative clauses. But the essence is that semantically speaking, finite clauses are totally independent of previous computation.

I will use the term "recursion" to refer to a syntactic property of sentence-level constructions focussing only to two types of syntactic constructions: sentential complements and relative clauses. Neither adverbial nor subordinate clauses will be taken into account, because in fact they do not constitute real embedded recursive structures. Adverbial clauses like temporal, concessive, causal and other similar subordinate sentence structures prevent the existence of long distance dependencies between a preceding and a following phrase or sentence. Besides, only sentential level recursion is able to generate semantically plausible—but the higher limit of clause embedding in real performance cases is language dependent and is however equal or below 3 (see Karlsson, 63)—infinite grammatical constructions: in this sense it is only sentence structure that is strictly speaking linked to recursion as a unique element of human language faculty. For instance in

- John said that it will rain yesterday

the adverbial can be bound to the main higher clause. But if we add an adverbial clause then the dependency is no longer possible,

- *John wanted to come because it will rain yesterday

As Verhagen comments in his chapter, recursion is relevant for grammar only for some rather specific phenomena, and it may as well be a product of cultural evolution which involves literacy, rather than be an intrinsic part of genetic evolution as Hauser and Chomsky maintain. We assume it may only come about as a consequence of linguistic maturation and triggered by the need to satisfy communicative goals in highly articulated conversational exchanges—more on this below.

From a linguistic point of view, neither constructions can be regarded a product of lexical selection: relative clauses are totally independent being adjuncts in nature. As to sentential complements, they are selected as such by certain communication verbs, but semantically speaking they are "closed" complements in the sense that they do not share any internal element with a higher governor or controller seen that a sentence or a tensed clause is a semantically independent propositional structures. In this sense, they are syntactic structure which may be motivated by semantic and pragmatic triggers: by the need to identify and describe referents and to report other people's utterances, or as commented again in Verhagen (ibid.:102), "perspective-taking a cognitive capacity—putting oneself in someone else's shoes, thus ascribing to them one's own cognitive capacities, including perspective taking—that implies recursivity". Further on, Verhagen (ibid.:103) links maturational factors with the increase of writing abilities as the main trigger of clause embedding, and frequency criteria that make "type-frequency of complement taking predicates to increase in people's linguistic experience".

Besides, we believe that the most distinctive ability humans show in their use of natural language for communication purposes, is syntactic and semantic disambiguation. This ability is usually ascribed to the existence of a "context" (see Kuhn 2013), a general term that encompasses, amongst other things, elliptical/unexpressed and/or implicit/entailed/implicated linguistic material, presumed intentions and aims of the interlocutor/s, and encyclopaedic knowledge of the world. In the best current systems for natural language, the linguistic components are kept separate from the knowledge representation, and work which could otherwise be done directly by the linguistic analysis is duplicated by the inferential mechanism. The linguistic representation is usually mapped onto a logical representation which is in turn fed onto the knowledge representation of the domain in order to understand and validate a given utterance or query. Thus the domain world model or ontology must be priorly built, usually in view of a given task the system is set out to perform. This modeling is domain and task limited and generality can only be achieved from coherent lexical representations. We assume that access to knowledge should be filtered out by the analysis of surface linguistic forms and their abstract representations of the utterances making up the text. However, we have to admit that world knowledge can be an integral part of the parsing process only in specific domains. No system is yet able to account for all the unexpressed linguistic material that is nonetheless essential for the complete semantic representation of a text or dialogue. We will discuss some of these unexpressed linguistic materials. The appropriate definition of the Context to be used here is the one related to the existence of a rich lexical representation. Consider now some ambiguous examples taken from P. Bosch (246), which cover some types of ambiguity:

1. Five companies sold two hundred installations
2. Fred saw the woman with the binoculars
3. Visiting relatives can be boring
4. Pete went to the bank this morning
5. This paper is ten pages long
6. Faulkner is hard to understand
7. a. The school made a major donation
   b. The school has a flat roof
   c. He enjoys school very much
   d. School is one of the pillars of our civilization

Ambiguity problems to be tackled are not all the same, as can be noticed. In 1. we have a problem of quantifier scope, which we think is only solvable by allowing a Quantifier Raising (hence QR) module produce two different representations for the same f-structure and then letting the semantic/pragmatic component do the rest. In our system, QR would compute as a preferential reading the one in which the subject NP takes scope over the object NP when both are numerals. In case the ambiguity had to be solved in favour of the second reading a distributive floating quantifier (each) should have been added. In 2 and 3 the parser would have come out with the most likely interpretation of the sentence and that might very well happen to be the wrong one: however the feeling one gets when discussing such sentences, is that they are very unlikely to be found in real texts—or at least this is what we assume. If we consider in more detail example 2, we could come up with common sense knowledge that prevents "binoculars" to be computed as an adequate adjunct of the head "woman". To be sure, this is what at present our system does, and assigns it rather as a predicative (Instrumental) complement of the verb SEE. However, there might be special scenarios in which women walk around carrying binoculars around their neck: this does not happen in

Venice(Italy), where everything can be comfortably looked at without binoculars, but could happen in the Grand Canyon where distances require it.

As to 4. we are in presence of a case of ambiguous lexical semantics, and represents a typical case of Word Sense Disambiguation. We should note here that since the semantic role associated to the PP "to the bank" would always be Locative, disregarding its semantic features, the actual meaning or sense associated to the noun "bank" could be easily accommodated by the semantic/pragmatic component, and this would in no way affect syntactic analysis. It is also important to note that the system may have to look for the most adequate referent to the singular definite NP, in the "Discourse Model"—a semantic/pragmatic module of Getaruns (See Delmonte 2007). The same applies to example 5 and 6, provided that a "Discourse Model" is available in the system where previous referents with additional information may be searched for.

Coming now to the last set of examples, where the "school" is assigned different meanings according to context. Here, we may easily assume that the system of linguistic description—WordNet in this case—should cover the whole of them. In a. the school is the SUBJect of the predicate MAKE and this requires an Agent which may be a Social_Institution, but not an object, i.e. a building, as is required by the meaning of the b. example. In this case, the meaning is not conveyed by the verb BE which has non-thematic arguments, but by contents of the predicate NP "the flat roof": this would be classified as [object, part_of], thus implying that the predication requires also an Object as its controller. In c. we have a psych verb "enjoy" which has an EXPERIENCER as SUBJect NP and a CAUSER_EMOT as OBJect NP, in our lexicon—but see also VerbNet and PropNet. The school in this case will be assigned a semantic value by the semantic roles associated to verb predicate, as happened with the a. example. The same applies to the c. example. In other words, it is the linguistic description which enables the semantic interpreter do its job properly by means of the conjoined information made available by semantic roles and semantic features.

The chapter is organized as follows: the second section below presents the parsers and argues for its being compliant with Phases as proposed by Chomsky; in Sect. 3. we present the parser; in Sect. 4. we discuss the psycholinguistic and cognitively founded parsing strategies; in 5 an evaluation and a conclusion.

2 The Parser and Phases

In the last 10 years or so Chomsky has been referring to the human parser as a gauge of the way in which syntactic processes are carried out in the mind of the language user. The parser has also been referred to as a metaphor of grammatical processes underlying sentence comprehension as is being purported within the current Minimalist Theory (hence MT). This interest for performance related notions can be regarded as an attempt on Chomsky's side to support/endow MT with a psychological and computational basis, thus making MT a unified theory for language. However, a parser based on any linguistic theory that aims to realize such a goal, should account also for the determining factor in sentence comprehension, that is ambiguity. This in turn is the cause of Garden Path on the one side, and on the other it motivates the existence of parsing preferences in the human processor. So, in the last resort, a theory that aims at the explanation of performance facts should satisfy three different types of requirements: psycholinguistic plausibility, computational efficiency in implementation, coverage of grammatical principles and constraints. This is also what a parser should satisfy, but see below.

It is plausible to say that for the first time performance facts can be brought to bear on theoretical assumptions based on competence. In fact this is also what HC&F seem to be aiming at.[1] In particular, the notion of Phases will be used in this chapter to test its validity in coping with the effects of ambiguity and Garden-Path related examples. We will try to show that the way in which Phases have been formulated is plausible, even though their final status and their theoretical status are still under debate (see Svenonius 2001, 2004; Legate 2002, 2003; Epstein 2004). But it is both too strong and too weak. Rather than Phases, we will be referring to a related and/or derivable notion, that of Argument and Adjunct as the semantically complete object of any step the parser should pursue in its process of analysis. Sentence level parsing requires in turn a first clause-level preliminary structure (something close to pseudo-syntax, as Townsend and Bever (2001) (hence T&B) call it), which is then submitted to proper interpretation—and possible LF computation, before interacting with higher structures than clause level for complex sentences, which can eventually license the parser output for PF.

To reduce computational complexity Chomsky (1998/2000) introduced the idea of Phases—units of syntactic computation—within MT. The general idea is that of limiting the burden of syntactic operations in order to ease workload or what must be retained in active memory. This seems a counterargument to the fact that human language (actually FLN) exhibits an intrinsic defining property that makes computation hard, that of recursion (HC&F). So it would seem that Chomsky's concern in proposing Phases is double-fold: on the one side it is motivated by performance related issues, on the other hand it is coupled to theory internal motivations. In fact, we will only tackle performance questions and not questions affecting the Minimalist Program. We would like to prove Phases to be a theory-independent principle governing the functioning of the human parser which we will investigate from a psycholinguistic and a computational point of view. The human parser is so efficient that it must obey some principle-based criterion in coping with recursion: Phases are Chomsky's solution.

---

[1] "Recent work on FLN suggests the possibility that at least the narrow-syntactic component satisfies conditions of highly efficient computation to an extent previously unsuspected…. [T]he generative processes of the language system may provide a near-optimal solution that satisfies the interface conditions to FLB. Many of the details of language that are the traditional focus of linguistic study … may represent by-products of this solution, generated automatically by neural/ computational constraints and the structure of FLB—components that lie outside of FLN." (Note that FLN stands for Faculty of Language Narrow, and FNB stands for Faculty of Language Broad).

Constituency-based parsing models are lately starting to be supplanted by word-level parsing models in the vein of Dependency-Based parsing (See Kuhn 2013). These parsers are organized in such a way as to limit the scope of syntactic operations to adjacent head-dependent word pairs. Recursion is thus eliminated from the grammar and computational efficiency is usually guaranteed. The same applies to bottom-up cascaded ATN-like parsers, which decompose the task of syntactic structure building into a sequence of intermediate steps, with the goal of avoiding recursion as much as possible. However, both coverage, precision and recall don't speak in favor of such parsers which working bottom-up adopt parsing policies which are not strictly left-to-right. In this respect, we believe that a parser should embody a psycholinguistically viable model, i.e. it should work strictly left-to-right and be subject to Garden Path effects. We also believe that by eliminating constituents from the parsing process, and introducing the notion of Head-Dependent relations, grammaticality principles may become harder to obey. Parsers today are required to produce a semantically interpretable output for any text: in order to achieve such a goal, Grammatical Relations need to be assigned to words in some kind of hierarchical (constituent-based) representation, before some Logical Form can be built. Word-based head-dependent parsers are not good candidates for the generation of such an output. In fact, no implicit categories are usually computed by such parsers, hampering in this way any semantic mapping from taking place (See Delmonte 2013a, b).

2.1 Phases and Semantic Mapping

Quoting from Chomsky,

> A phase is a unit of syntactic computation that can be sent to the Spell-Out. Syntactic computation proceeds in stages: a chunk of structure (a vP or a CP) is created and then everything but its edge can be sent off to the interfaces.

Phases are semantically complete constituents or "complete propositions", which could be independently given a Logical Form and a Phonetic Form. Carnie and Barss (2006) propose to relativize the definition of phase to that of Argument which we subscribe fully here below: in their words,

"Each phase consists of an argument, the predicative element that introduces the argument (V or vP) and a functional category that represents a temporal operator which locates the predicate in time or space (Asp, T, etc.). Phases consist of:

(a) a predicative element (v or V)
(b) a single argument
(c) a temporal operator that locates the predicate and argument in time and space (Asp or T)"

To this definition we will add the need to regard arguments as semantically complete constituents with their adjuncts and modifiers, something which is asserted by Epstein (2004) and introduced in Chomsky (2004), when they assume that the specification of a phase has "full argument structure". In addition this could be derived where they assume that a partial LF could be produced. It goes without saying that in order to produce a partial or complete LF from syntactic chunks, they need to be semantically interpretable: this includes semantic role assignment, being exempt from quantificational related problems like the presence of unbound variables. The LF we are referring to is a flat version with unscoped quantifiers.

In line with Pinker and Jackendoff's paper (hence P&J 2005) produced as an answer to HC&F, we assume that lexical information is the most important static knowledge source in the processing of natural language. However, we also assume that all semantic information should be made to bear on the processing and this is only partially coincident with lexical information as stored in lexical forms. In particular, subcategorization, semantic roles and all other semantic compatibility evaluative mechanisms should be active while parsing each word of the input string. In addition, Discourse Model and External Knowledge of the World should be tapped when needed to do coreference and anaphora resolution. Antecedents in turn would be chosen on the basis of grammatical information like Grammatical Relations and Semantic Roles, and not independently of it.

In that perspective, we believe that a sound parsing strategy should opt for a parser that strives for an even higher than constituent semantically closer level: i.e. arguments and adjuncts, where mixed/hybrid strategies (bottom-up and top-down) are activated by the use of a strongly language-dependent lookahead mechanism. We would like to speak in favour of such an approach in which locality is sacrificed for a mixed or hybrid model, partially bottom-up, which uses both grammatical function driven information and lexical information from subcategorization frames to direct the choices of the argument vs adjunct building parsing process.

On the one side we endorse a position purported by linguistic theories like MT which require LF licensing of constituency at some level—and clause level Phases are here assumed as the only possible counterpart to LF; on the other side, we speaks against MT as in a sense—at least some MT linguist would accept it—Dependency Parsing implements it because it assumes that parsing cannot just be bottom-up word level parsing, but some top-down guidance is needed. Furthermore, neither MT nor Dependency Parsing would accommodate a strictly semantic and lexicalist notion like "Argument-Adjunct" parsing together with a performance related notion like ambiguity and the accompanying effect of Garden Path, which is familiar in psycholinguistic literature. In addition, language dependent rules would suit best an MT-like approach with parameters driven options or any other linguistic theory which allows rule of Core Grammar to be set apart from rules of the Periphery.

3 GETARUNS: An A-As Hybrid Parser

As commented above, to be Phase-compliant a parser needs to build up each constituent as a fully interpreted chunk with all its internal arguments and adjuncts if any. In this process, we know that there are two boundaries which need to be taken into account: the CP level and the Ibar level, where the finite verb is parsed. From a computational perspective we might paraphrase the concomitant contribution of the two Phases as follows:

v. parse all that comes before the finite verb and then reset your internal indices.

Our parser is not a dependency parser in that it imposes constituent-based global restrictions on the way in which words can be parsed: only legal constituents are licensed by the parser.

We defined our parser "mildly bottom-up" because the structure building process cycles on a call that collects constituents until it decides that what it has parsed might be analysed as Argument or Adjunct. To do that it uses Grammatical Function calls that tell the parser where it is positioned within the current parse. We use Grammatical Functions because in LFG theory they are regarded as linguistic primitives. This proceeds until finite verb is reached and the parse is continued with the additional help of Verb Guidance by subcategorization information. The recursive procedure has access to calls collecting constituents that identify preverbal Arguments and Adjuncts including the Subject if any. When the finite verb is found the parser is hampered from accessing the same preverbal portion of the algorithm and switches to the second half of it where Object NPs, Clauses and other complements and adjuncts may be parsed. Punctuation marks are also collected during the process and are used to organize the list of arguments and adjuncts into tentative clauses.

When the parser reaches the Verbal Phrase the syntactic category associated to the main verb—transitive, unergative, unaccusative, impersonal, atmospheric, raising, psych, copulative—and the lexical form of the predicate, are both used as topdown guidelines for the surface realization of its arguments. Italian is a language which allows for empty or morphologically unexpressed Subjects, so that no restriction may be projected from the lexicon onto c-structure: in case it is empty, a little pro is built in subject position, and features are left as empty variables until the tensed verb is processed.

The clause builder looks for two elements in the input list: the presence of the verb-complex and punctuation marks, starting from the idea that clauses must contain a finite verb complex. Dangling constituents will be adjoined to their left adjacent clause, by the clause interpreter after failure while trying to interpret each clause separately. The clause-level interpretation procedure interprets clauses on the basis of lexical properties of the governing verb: verbless clauses are not dealt with by the bottom-up parser, they are passed down—after failure—to the top-down parser which can license such structures.

The final processor takes as input fully interpreted clauses which may be coordinate, subordinate, main clauses. These are adjoined together according to their respective position. Care is taken to account for Reported Speech complex sentences which require the Parenthetical Clause to become Main governing clause.

We opted to deal with Questions and Imperatives with the top-down parser rather than with the bottom-up one. Also sentences with Reported Direct speech are treated in that way due to the presence of inverted commas that must be interpreted accordingly. Noun-clausal Subject sentences and extraposed That-clause fronted sentences are also computed top-down. The advantage of using fully top-down processing is that the clause-building stage is completely done away with. The parser posits the clause type as a starting point, so that constituents are searched for and collected at the same level in which the parsing has started. However, this is only conceivable in such non-canonical structures as the ones listed here above.

If the parser does not detect any of the previous structures, control is passed to the bottom-up/top-down parser, where the recursive call simulates the subdivision of structural levels in a grammar. All sentential fronted constituents are taken at the CP level and the IP (now TP) level is where the SUBJect NP must be computed. Otherwise SUBJect NP will be either in postverbal position with Locative Inversion structures, or the parser might be trying a subjectless coordinate clause. Then again a number of ADJuncts may be present between SUBJect and verb, such as adverbials and parentheticals. When this level is left, the parser is expecting a verb in the input string. This can be a finite verb complex with a number of internal constituents: but the first item must be definitely a tensed verb. After the (complex) verb has been successfully built, the parser looks for complements: the search is restricted by lexical information. If a copulative verb has been taken, the constituent built will be labelled accordingly as XCOMP where X may be one of the lexical heads, P,N,A,Adv.

The clause-level parser simulates the sentence typology where we may have as SUBJect a verbal clause, Inverted postverbal NPs, fronted that-clauses, and also fully inverted OBJect NPs in preverbal position. We do that because we purport the view that the implementation of sound parsing algorithm must go hand in hand with sound grammar construction. Extragrammaticalities can be better coped with within a solid linguistic framework rather than without it.

The parser has a manually-built grammar and is written in Prolog, a programming language that provides for backtracking freely and has a variable passing mechanism useful to cope with a number of well-known grammatical problems like agreement (local and non-local) as well as Long-Distance Dependencies. The parser is a rule-based deterministic parser in the sense that it uses a lookahead and a Well-Formed Substring Table to reduce backtracking. It also implements Finite State Automata in the task of tag disambiguation, and produces multiwords whenever lexical information allows it. Recovery procedures are also used to cope with elliptical structures and uncommon orthographic and punctuation patterns. In particular, the parser is written in Prolog Horn-clauses and uses Extraposition variables to compute Long-Distance Dependencies.[2]

---

[2] We use XGs (extraposition grammars) introduced by Pereira (1981, 1983). Prolog provides naturally for backtracking when allowed, i.e. no cut is present to prevent it. Furthermore, the instantiation of variables is a simple way for implementing the mechanism for feature percolation and/or for the creation of chains by means of index inheritance between a controller and a controllee, and in more complex cases, for instance in case of constituent ellipsis or deletion. Apart from that, the grammar implemented is a surface grammar of the chosen languages.

Being a DCG (see Pereira and Warren1980), the parser is strictly a top-down, depth-first, one-stage parser with backtracking. Differently from most principle-based parsers presented in Berwick et al. (1991), which are two-stage parsers, our parser computes its representations in one pass. This makes it psychologically more realistic. The final output of the parsing process is an f-structure which serves as input to the binding module and logical form: in other words, it constitutes the input to the semantic component to compute logical relations. In turn the binding module may add information as to pronominal elements present in the structure by assigning a controller/binder in case it is available, or else the pronominal expression will be available for discourse level anaphora resolution.

Grammatical functions are used to build f-structures and the processing of pronominals. They are crucial in defining lexical control: as in Bresnan (1982, 2001), all predicative or open functions are assigned a controller, lexically or structurally. Lexical control is directly encoded in each predicate-argument structure, and it will bind the empty subject of all predicative open functions built in all predicative structures (or small clauses) to the appropriate syntactic controller (or binder).

The parser is made up of separate modules:

1. The Grammar, based on DCGs, incorporates Extraposition to process Long Distance Dependencies, which works on annotated c-structures: these constitute the output to the Interpretation Module;
2. The Interpretation Module checks whether f-structures may be associated to the input partially annotated c-structure by computing Functional Uniqueness, Coherence and Completeness. Semantic roles are associated to the input grammatical function labels at this level, after semantic selectional restrictions are checked for membership;
3. The Mapping scheme, to translate trees into graphs, i.e. to map c-structures onto f-structures. The parser builds annotated c-structure, where the words of the input sentence are assigned syntactic constituency and functional annotations. This is then mapped onto f-structure, i.e. constituent information is dropped and DAGs are built in order to produce f-structure configuration.

3.1 Parsing Ambiguities Coping with Recursion

The lexicon as the source of syntactic variation is widely accepted in various theoretical frameworks. We assume that be it shallow or deep, parsing needs to be internally parameterized in order to account for ambiguities generated both at structural and at semantic level.

As said above, a parser that achieves psychological reality should closely mimic phenomena such as Garden Path effects, or an increase in computational time in presence of semantically versus syntactically biased ambiguous structures. We also assume that a failure should ensue from strong Garden Path effects and that this should be justified at a psycholinguistic interpretation level. In other words, looking at parsing from a performance-based perspective, the parser should anticipate ambiguities that may cause unwanted Garden-Paths and Crashes, in order to refrain from unwanted failures in order to mimic human processing. But how should a "sound" parser be told which ambiguous structures are expected in which language?

In general terms, ambiguity is generated by homophonous words in understanding activities and by homographs in reading activities. In both cases Garden Paths or Crashes may only result in a given language in presence of additional conditions which are strictly dependent on the structure of the lexicon and the grammar (see Hindle and Roth1993). But some UG related parameters, like the "OMISSIBILITY OF THE COMPLEMENTIZER" in English may cause the parser to crash or freeze. Generally speaking, all types of ambiguity affecting parsing at a clause level will cause the parser to go into a Garden Path. Developing this line of thought, we assume that from a psycholinguistic point of view, parsing requires setting up a number of disambiguating strategies, like for instance telling arguments apart from adjuncts and reducing the effects of backtracking. And this is how it has been implemented.

Whenever a given predicate has expectancies for a given argument to be realized either optionally or obligatorily, this information will be passed below to the recursive portion of the parsing process: this operation allows us to implement parsing strategies like Minimal Attachment, Functional Preference and other ones (See Delmonte 2009).

The DCG grammar allows the specification of linguistic rules in a highly declarative mode: it works topdown and by making a heavy use of linguistic knowledge may achieve an almost complete deterministic policy. Parameterized rules are scattered throughout the grammar so that they can be made operative as soon as a given rule is entered by the parser. In particular, a rule may belong either to a set of languages, e.g. Romance or Germanic,[3] or to a subset thereof, like English or Italian, thus becoming a peripheral rule. Rules are activated at startup and whenever a switch is being operated by the user, by means of logical flags appropriately inserted in the right hand side of the rule. No flags are required for rules belonging to the common core grammar.

Some such rules include the following ones: for languages like Italian and Spanish, a Subject NP may be an empty category, either a referential little pro or an expletive pronoun; Subject NPs may be freely inverted in postverbal position, i.e. preverbal NP is an empty category in these cases. For languages like Italian and French, PP or adverbial adjuncts may intervene between Verb and Object NP; adjectival modifiers may be taken to the right of their head Noun. For languages like English and German, tense and mood may be computed in CP internal

[3] As to multilinguality, the basic tenet of the parser is based on a UG-like perspective, i.e. the fact that all languages share a common core grammar and may vary at the periphery: internal differences are predicted by parameters.

position, when taking the auxiliary or the modal verb. English allows an empty Complementizer for finite complement and relative clauses, and negation requires do-support. Italian only allows it for a highly genre marked (literary style) untensed auxiliary in Comp position.

Syntactic and semantic information are accessed and used as soon as possible: in particular, both categorial and subcategorization information attached to predicates in the lexicon is extracted as soon as the main predicate is processed, be it adjective, noun or verb, and is used to subsequently restrict the number of possible structures to be built. Adjuncts are computed by semantic compatibility tests on the basis of selectional restrictions of main predicates and adjuncts heads.

Thus, we build and process syntactic phenomena like wh-movement before building f-structure representations, where quantifier raising and anaphoric binding for pronominals takes place. In particular, all levels of Control mechanisms which allow coindexing at different levels of parsing give us a powerful insight into the way in which the parser should be organized. In addition, we find that topdown parsing policies are better suited to implement parsing strategies that are essential in order to cope with attachment ambiguities. Also functional Control mechanisms—both structural and lexical—have been implemented as close as possible to the original formulation, i.e. by binding an empty operator in the subject position of a propositional like open complement/predicative function, whose predicate is constituted by the lexical head.

3.2 Lookahead and Ambiguity

Lookahead is used in a number of different ways: it may impose a wait-and-see policy on the topdown strategy or it may prevent following a certain rule path in case the stack does not support the first or even second match:

a. to prevent expanding a certain rule
b. to prevent backtracking from taking place by delaying retracting symbols from input stack until there is a high degree of confidence in the analysis of the current input string.

It can be used to gather positive or negative evidence about the presence of a certain symbol ahead: symbols to be tested against the input string may be more than one, and also the input word may be ambiguous among a number of symbols. Since in some cases we extend the lookahead mechanism to include two symbols and in one case even three symbols, possibilities become quite numerous. The following list of 14 preterminal symbols is used (Table 1):

As has been reported in the literature (see Tapanainen and Voutilainen 1994; Brants and Samuelsson 1995), English but also Italian (see Delmonte 1999) is a language with a high level of homography: readings per word are around 2 (i.e. each word can be assigned in average two different tags depending on the tagset).

Table 1 Preterminal symbols used for lookahead

1. v = verb-auxiliary-modal-clitic-cliticized verb
2. n = noun—common, proper;
3. c = complementizer
4. s = subordinator;
5. e = conjunction
6. p = preposition-particle
7. a = adjective;
8. q = participle/gerund
9. i = interjection
10. g = negation
11.d = article-quantifier-number-intensifier-focalizer
12. r = pronoun
13. b = adverb
14. x = punctuation

Lookahead in our system copes with most cases of ambiguity: however, we also use disambiguating before passing the input string to the parser.

Consider now failure and backtracking which ensues from it. Technically speaking, by means of lookahead we prevent local failures in that we do not allow the parser to access the lexicon where the input symbol would be matched against. It is also important to say that almost all our rules satisfy the efficiency requirement to have a preterminal in first position in their right-hand side. Cases like complementizerless sentential complements are allowed to be analysed whenever a certain switch is activated. Suppose we may now delimit failure to the general case that may be described as follows:

- a constituent has been fully built and interpreted but it is not appropriate for that level of attachment: failure would thus be caused only by semantic compatibility tests required for modifiers and adjuncts or lack of satisfaction of argument requirements for a given predicate. Technically speaking we have two main possibilities:

A. the constituent built is displaced on a higher level after closing the one in which it was momentarily embedded. This is the case represented by the adjunct PP "in the night" in example below:

(8) The thieves stole the painting in the night.

The PP is at first analysed while building the NP "the painting in the night" which however is rejected after the PP semantic features are matched against the features of the governing head "painting".

B. the constituent built is needed on a lower level and there is no information on the attachment site. In this case a lot of input string has already been consumed before failure takes place and the parser needs to backtrack a lot before constituents may be safely built and interpreted. This is the case of an NP analysed as OBJect of a higher clause but is needed as SUBJect of a following clause.

To give a simple example, suppose we have taken the PP "in the night" within the NP headed by the noun "painting". At this point, the lookahead stack would be set to the position in the input string that follows the last word "night". As a side-effect of failure in semantic compatibility evaluation within the NP, the PP "in the night" would be deposited in the backtrack WFST storage. The input string would be restored to the word "in", and analysis would be restarted at the VP level. In case no PP rule is met, the parser would continue with the input string trying to terminate its process successfully. However, as soon as a PP constituent is tried, the storage is accessed first, and in case of non emptiness its content recovered. No structure building would take place, and semantic compatibility would take place later on at sentence level. The parser would only execute the following actions:

- match the first input word with the (preposition) head of the stored term;
- accept new input words as long as the length of the stored term allows it by matching its length with the one computed on the basis of the input words.

Differences in reanalysis are determined by structural requirements and by analysis load imposed on the parser by backtracking: in case a sentential adjunct has to be destroyed/broken up and reconstructed it represents a far lighter load than a subordinate/main clause. Let's say, that whenever a clausal structure has to be destroyed/broken up a whole set of semantic decisions have to be dismantled, and structure erased.

4 Linguistically-Plausible Relaxation Techniques

With the grammar above and the parameters we are now in a position to establish a priori positions in the parser where there could be recovery out of recursion with ungrammatical structures with the possibility to indicate which portion of the input sentence is responsible for the failure. At the same time, parsing strategies could be devised in such a way to ensure recovery from local failure. We will start by commenting on Parsing Strategies first and their implementation in our grammar.[4] Differently from what is asserted by global or full paths approaches (see Schubert 1984; Hobbs et al. 1992), we believe that decisions on structural ambiguity should be reached as soon as possible rather than deferred to a later level of representation. In particular, Schubert assumes "…a full paths approach in which not only complete phrases but also all incomplete phrases are fully integrated into (overlaid) parse trees dominating all of the text seen so far. Thus features and partial logical translations can be propagated and checked for consistency as early as possible, and alternatives chosen or discarded on the basis of all of the available information (ibid., 249)." And further on in the same paper, he proposes a system

[4] We also assume that a failure should ensue from strong Garden Path effects and that this should be justified at a psycholinguistic interpretation level (See Pritchett 1992).

of numerical 'potentials' as a way of implementing preference trade-offs. "These potentials (or levels of activation) are assigned to nodes as a function of their syntactic/semantic/pragmatic structure and the preferred structures are those which lead to a globally high potential. Among contemporary syntactic parsing theories, the garden-path theory of sentence comprehension proposed by (Frazier 1987a, b), Clifton and Ferreira (1989) among others, is the one that most closely represents our point of view. It works on the basis of a serial syntactic analyser, which is top-down, depth-first—i.e. it works on a single analysis hypothesis, as opposed to other theories which take all possible syntactic analysis in parallel and feed them to the semantic processor. From our perspective, it would seem that parsing strategies should be differentiated according to whether there are argument requirements or simply semantic compatibility evaluation for adjuncts. As soon as the main predicate or head is parsed, it makes available all lexical information in order to predict the complement structure if possible, or to guide the following analysis accordingly. As an additional remark, note that not all possible syntactic structure can lead to ambiguous interpretations: in other words, we need to consider only cases which are factually relevant also from the point of view of language dependent ambiguities.

The parser has been built to simulate the cognitive processes underlying the grammar of a language in use by a speaker, taking into account the psychological nuances related to the well-known problem of ambiguity, which is a pervading problem in real text/communicative situation, and it is regarded an inseparable benchmark of any serious parser of any language to cope with.

We implemented in our parser a number of strategies that embody current intuitions on the way in which sentence comprehension mechanisms work at a psychological level. The parsing strategies are the following: Minimal Attachment/Late Closure (MA), Argument Preference (AP), Thematic Evaluation (TE), Referential Individuation (RI), Cross Compatibility Check (CCC). From the way in which we experimented them in our implementation it appears that they are strongly interwoven. In particular, MA is dependent upon AP to satisfy subcategorization requirements; with semantically biased sentences, MA and AP, and finally TE should apply in hierarchical order to license the phrase as argument or adjunct. RI seems to be required and activated every time a singular definite NP is computed. However, RI is a strategy that can only become operative whenever a full parse of possible modifiers is available and not before. In addition, subcategorization and thematic requirements have priority over referential identification of a given NP: a violation of the former is much stronger than the latter. Generally speaking, redundancies in referential properties might simply be accommodated by the speaker: but lack of consistency, uniqueness and completeness lead to ungrammaticality.

As discussed above, we follow a mixed topdown depth-first strategy which we believe better accounts for the way in which human psychological processes work. In order to prevent failures and control backtracking, depth-first analysis should be organized as much as possible deterministically. Nondeterminism can be very time consuming and it should be reduced or at least controlled according to the parsing strategy selected.

As Altmann (1989)[5] comments in his introduction (ibid.86), and we also believe, it is an empirical question whether the constraints assumed by the thematic processor (single initial syntactic analysis, semantic evaluation only within the domain of this analysis) are constraints actually observed by the parser, or whether a less-constrained mechanism that makes appeal to context and meaning at the earliest stages of sentence comprehension is a more adequate description of the true state of affairs. It is our opinion that all lower level constraints should work concurrently with higher level ones: in other words, all strategies are nested one inside another, where MA occupies the most deeply nested level. The higher level strategy has control over the lower level one in case some failure is needed. Suppose we have the following examples which can be disambiguated only at the level of pronominal binding.

i. The doctor called in the son of the pretty nurse who hurt herself.
ii. The doctor called in the son of the pretty nurse who hurt himself.

Pronominal binding is a level of computation that takes place after f-structure has been completely checked and built in LFG—the same applies in GB framework, where S-structure gives way to L-structure and this is where binding takes place. In this case however, it would be impossible to address the appropriate level of representation after destroying all previous structures with backtracking. In this case, backtracking by itself would be inefficient and would not assure termination—simply because the same structure could be constructed at sentence level. We assume, instead, that a specific mechanism should be activated before f-structure is licensed in order to check the presence of a reflexive pronoun, i.e. an anaphoric pronoun or short anaphora, that needs the SUBJect to be an appropriate antecedent, agreeing in all features with the anaphora itself (See Delmonte 2002).

The following two examples are also computed without any special provision for the ambiguous structural position of the final temporal adverbial, simply by matching semantic information coming from verb tense and temporal configuration associated to the adverbial in its lexical entries in terms of a precedence relation between td (discourse time), and tr (reference time). Thus, in the case of "tomorrow" the parser will have td < tr and the opposite will apply to "yesterday". In turn, this configuration is matched against tense, "past" or "future" and a failure will result locally, if needed.

iii. Mary will say that it rained yesterday.
iv. Mary said that it will rain yesterday.

[5] Altmann offers a functional argument against a system in which choices are initially made by a syntactic processor, and later corrected by appeal to meaning and context. He says that if referential or discourse information is available, only a strange processor would make decisions without appealing to it. However, syntactic information is always available and always informative.

4.1 Graceful Recovery Actions from Failures

As discussed above, recovery from garden-path requires a trial and error procedure, i.e. the parser at first has to fail in order to simulate the garden-path effect and then the recovery will take place at certain conditions. Now consider the well-known case of Reduced Relatives[6] which have always been treated as a tough case (but see Stevenson and Merlo 1997). From an empirical point of view we should at first distinguish cases of subject attachment reduced relatives from all other cases, because it is only with subject level attachment that a garden-path will actually ensue (see Filip 1998). In fact, this is easily controllable in our parser, given the fact that NPs are computed by means of functional calls. In this way the information as to where the NP is situated in the current sentence analysis is simply a variable that is filled with one of the following labels: subj, obj, obj2, obl, adj, ncomp, where the last label stands for predicative open complements.

From a purely empirical point of view, we searched the WSJ corpus in order to detect cases of subject attachment vs all other cases for reduced relatives and we came up with the following figures: SUBJECT-ATTACHEMENT 530; OTHERS 2982; Total 3512. If we subtract present participle cases of reduced relatives which do not constitute ambiguous words the total number is lowered down to 340. Subject-attachment thus constitute the 9.68 % of all cases, a certainly negligible percentage. In addition, 214 of all subject-attachment are passive participles and lend themselves to easy computation being followed by the preposition "by". So there will reasonably be only 116 possible candidates for ambiguous reduced relatives. The final percentage comes down 3.3 % which is very low in general, and in particular when computed over the whole 1 million occurrences, it comes down to a non classifiable 0.0116 %. The same results can be obtained from an investigation of the Susanne Corpus, where we found 38 overall cases of reduced relatives with ambiguous past participles, 0.031 % which is comparable to the 0.035 % of the WSJ (Table 2).

If we look into matter closely, then we come up with another fairly sensible and easily intuitive notion for reduced relatives disambiguation: and it is the fact that whenever the governing Noun is not an agentive, nor a proto-agent in any sense of the definition (see Stevenson and Merlo), no ambiguity may arise simply because non agentive nominal governors may end up with an ambiguous interpretation only in case the verb is used as ergative. However, not all transitive verbs can be

[6] The typical example quoted in psycholinguistic literature is the reduced relative case, reported here below, determined by the lexical ambiguity of English verbs being at the same time interpretable as Past Participle—Past Tense and shown below in the Reduced Relative Clause well-known example, (9) The horse raced past the barn fell.is one such case. The English speaker will attempt treating the verb "raced" as main tensed verb, but on discovery of sentence final verb "fell" which can only be interpreted as tensed past tense the whole sentential level analysis crashes and a Garden Path ensues causing a complete restart of the mental parser.

Table 2 List of 27 verb-types used in WSJ in subject-attached reduced relatives

Accused	Afforded	Based	Boosted
Bought	Canceled	Caught	Caused
Completed	Contacted	Derived	Designed
Filed	Honed	Involved	Led
Listed	Made	Managed	Owned
Paid	Purchased	Related	Represented
Requested	Sold	Unsettled	

Table 3 List of 36 verb-types used in SUSANNE in subject-attached reduced relatives

Altered	Become	Bent	Burned
Charged	Clouded	Compared	Cooled
Cut	Deserted	Distilled	Dominated
Estimated	Fed	Figured	Filmed
Focused	Frozen	Internalized	Intertwined
Known	Left	Made	Opened
Posted	Proposed	Puckered	Put
Removed	Reported	Seen	Shown
Shut	Soiled	Studied	Torn

made ergatives and in particular none of the verbs used in WSJ in subject-attachment for reduced relatives can be ergativized apart from "sell". We report here above verb-types, i.e. verb wordforms taken only once. As can be easily seen none of the verbs are unergative nor unaccusatives (Table 3).

If we look at the list of verb-types used in Susanne Corpus we come up with a slightly different and much richer picture. The number of ergativizable verbs increases and also the number of verb types which is strangely enough much higher than the one present in WSJ. We also added verbs that can be intransitivized, thus contributing some additional ambiguity. In some cases, the past participle is non ambiguous, though, see "frozen, seen, shown and torn". In some other cases, the verb has different meanings with different subcategorization frames: this is case of "left".

In any case, the parser will procede by activating any possible disambiguation procedure, then it will consider the inherent semantic features associated to the prospective subject: in order to be consistent with a semantic classification as proto-agent, one of the following semantic classes will have to be present: "animate, human, institution, (natural) event, social_role, collective entity".

In the affirmative case, and after having checked for the subject position/ functional assignment, the analysis will proceed at NP internal adjunct modifier position. If this is successful, the adjunct participial clause will be interpreted locally. Then the parser will continue its traversal of the grammar at i_double_bar position, searching for the finite verb.

In case no finite verb is available, there will be an ensuing failure which will recovered gracefully by a recovery call for the same main constituent expected by the grammar in that position. Two actions will take place:

1. the current input word will have to be a nonfinite verb;
2. the already parser portion of the input sentence must contain a possibly ambiguous finite verb;
3. this token word should correspond to the predicate lemma heading the modifier adjunct clause computed inside the NP which is scanned to search for the appropriate structural portion.

The first two actions are carried out on the lookahead stack, while the third action is carried out on the NP structure already parsed and fully interpreted by the parser.

5 LSLT: A Comprehensive Theory

To motivate our criticism and our approach we now introduce the foundations of our theory LSLT—Lexical Semantic Language Theory. LSLT encompasses a *psycholinguistic theory* of the way the language faculty works, a *grammatical theory* of the way in which sentences get analysed and generated—for this we will be using Lexical-Functional Grammar, a *semantic theory* of the way in which meaning gets encoded and expressed in utterances—for this we will be using Situation Semantics, and a *parsing theory* of the way in which components of the theory interact in a common architecture to produce the needed language representation to be eventually spoken aloud or interpreted by the *phonetic/acoustic language interface*.

As a start, we assume that the main task the child is faced with is creating an internal mental LEXICON, where we further assume (with Pinker and Jackendoff 2005) each word should contain two types of information: Grammatical—to feed the Grammatical component of the language faculty—and Semantic—to allow for meaning to be associated to each lexical entry. This activity is guided by two criteria: the Semantic and the Communicative Criteria.

Semantic Criterion

The goal of the language faculty is that of creating meaning relations between words and (mental) reality, that is events, entities and their attributes

Communicative Criterion

The goal of the language faculty is that of allowing communication between humans to take place

We start by addressing the *psycholinguistic theory* in which the basic goal is the creation of meaning relations between linguistic objects—words—and bits of reality—situations for short. To do that we set forth the strong claim that in order to have Analysis and Generation become two facets of the same coin, Semantics needs to be called in and Lexical information be specified in such a way to have the Parser/Generation work properly. However, language generation implies the existence of a planning phase which may be driven by communicative needs. On the contrary, language understanding is substantially conditioned by what is usually referred to by "Shared Knowledge" between two or more interlocutors. Syntax only represents a subcomponent of the Grammatical theory and as such has no relevance in the definition of the primitives of the LSLT.

We will take the stance that the existence of a backbone of rewriting rules with reference to recursion is inherently innate (see HC&F). However, at the same time we agree with Tomasello and others supporting a "usage-based theory of language acquisition", that the major part of linguistic competence "… involves the mastery of all kinds of routine formulas, fixed and semi-fixed expressions, idioms, and frozen collocations. Indeed one of the distinguishing characteristics of native speakers of a language is their control of these semi-fixed expressions as fluent units with somewhat unpredictable meanings"(Tomasello 2006, p. 259). The two hypothesis about language acquisition are not in contrast and coalesce in the need to have a Grammatical Maturation or Development Phase, where children start (over)generalising linguistic knowledge to new combinations. In this case, we can say that both the *Communicative Criterion* together with the *Semantic Criterion* converge on the need to express more and more complex concepts from simple holophrases to event related fully accomplished predicate-argument structures: these alone contain both functions of predicating and referring.[7]

This leads us to the second important goal of a psycholinguistic theory, that is motivating the necessity the child has to communicate with the external world. All complex constructions will appear only in a later phase of linguistic development and, in particular, they include sentential complement and relative clause constructions. As to the role of recursion in language acquisition, we believe it will only take place when the child is aware of the existence of a point of view external from his own. As said above, high level recursion in utterances is represented basically by two types of structures: sentential complements which have a *reportive* semantic content, and relative clauses which have a *supportive* semantic content.

[7] "... from the beginning children are attempting to learn not isolated words, but rather communicatively effective speech act forms corresponding to whole adult constructions…" Tomasello (2006, p. 261). And further on, "… The language learning child is thus faced with a prodigious task: acquiring simultaneously many dozens and dozens (perhaps hundreds) of constructions based on input in which all of the many different construction types are semirandomly strewn. On the other hand, the task is made a bit easier by the fact that many of, indeed the majority of, the utterances children hear are grounded in highly repetitive item-based frames that they experience dozens, in some cases hundreds, of times every day. Indeed, many of the more complex utterances children hear have as a major constituent some well-practiced item-based frame. This means that the more linguistically creative utterances that children hear every day constitute only a small minority of their linguistic experience, and even these quite often rest on the foundation of many highly frequent and relatively simple item-based utterance frames." (ibid., 262).

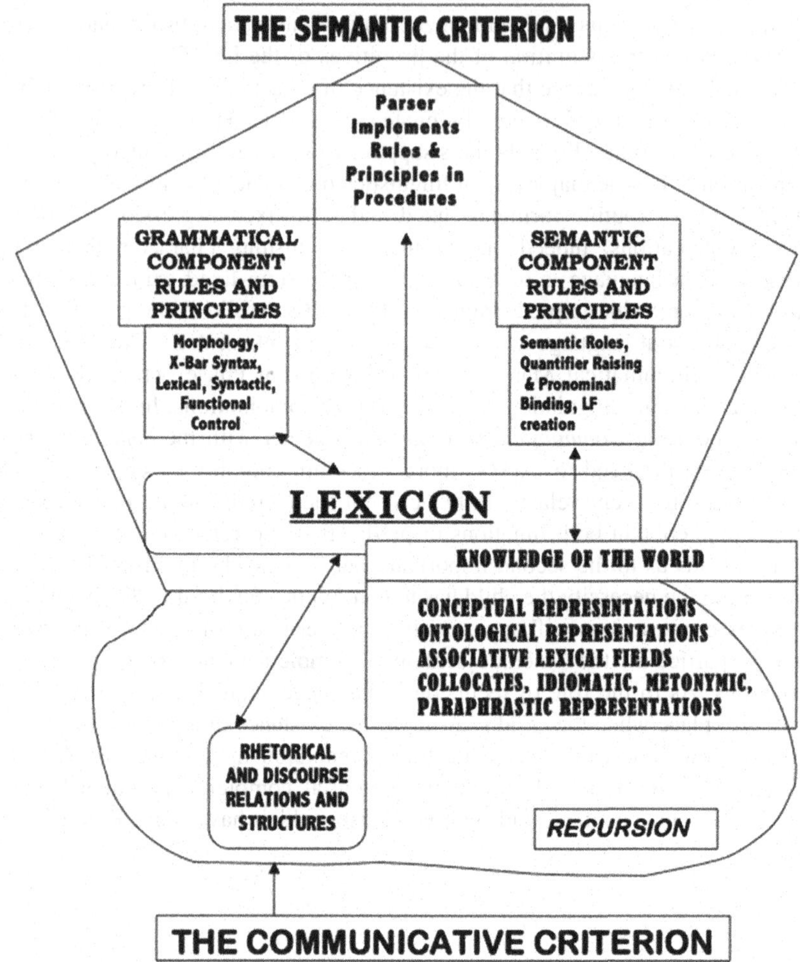

Reportive contents are governed by *communication* predicates, which have the semantic content of introducing two propositions related to two separate situations in spatiotemporal terms. Supportive contents are determined by the need to bring in at the interpretation level a situation which helps better individuate the entity represented by the governing nominal predicate. These two constructions only appear at a later phase of linguistic development, as indicated also in Tomasello (2006, p. 276). And now some details on how LSLT implements its principles.

The *Grammatical Theory* (hence GT) defines the way in which lexical entries need to be organized. However, the Lexicon is informed both by the Grammatical and the Semantic Theory which alone can provide the link to the Ontology or Knowledge of the World Repository. At the analysis/comprehension level, we assume as in LFG, the existence of lexical forms where lexical knowledge is encoded, which is composed of grammatical information—categorial, morphological, syntactic, and selectional restrictions. These are then mapped onto semantic forms, where semantic roles are encoded and aspectual lexical classes are associated. In Analysis, c-structures are mapped onto f-structures and eventually turned into s-structures. Rules associating lexical representations with c-structures are part of the GT. The mapping is effortless being just a bijective process, and is done by means of FSA—finite state automata. C-structure building is done in two phases. After grammatical categories are associated to inflected wordforms, a disambiguation phase takes place on the basis of local and available lexical information. The disambiguated tagged words are organized into local X-bar based head-dependent structures, which are then further developed into a complete clause-level hierarchically based structure, through a cascaded series of FSA which make use of recursion only when there are lexical constraints—both grammatical, semantic and pragmatic—requiring it. C-structure is mapped onto f-structure by interpretation processes based on rules defined in the grammar and translated into parsing procedures. This would be a simplistic view of the parsing process, backed by constructional criteria in which syntactic/semantic constructions are readily available in the lexicon and only need to be positioned in adjacency and then glued together, as maintained by Tomasello and other constructionalists. The question is that whenever a new sentence is started there is no way to know in advance what will be the continuation at the analysis level and telling dependencies between adjacent constituents is not an easy task, as has been shown above.

It is a fact that Grammatical relations are only limited to what are usually referred to as Predicate-Argument relations, which may only encompass obligatory and optional arguments of a predicate. The Semantic Theory will add a number of important items of interpretation to the Grammatical representation, working at propositional level: negation, quantification, modality and pronominal binding. These items will appear in the semantic representation associated to each clause and are activated by means of parsing procedures specialized for those two tasks. Semantic Theory also has the task of taking care of non-grammatical objects usually defined with the two terms, Modifiers and Adjuncts. In order to properly interpret meaning relations for these two optional component of sentential linguistic content, the Semantic theory may access Knowledge of the World as represented by a number of specialized lexical resources, like Ontology, for inferential relations; Associative Lexical Fields for Semantic Similarity relations; Collocates for most frequent modifier and adjunct relations; Idiomatic and Metonymic relations as well as Paraphrases for best stylistic purposes.

In Generation, a plan is created and predicates are inserted in predicate-argument structures (hence PAS) with attributes—i.e. modifiers and adjuncts. Syntax plays only a secondary role in that PAS are hooked to stylistic, rhetorical rules which are in turn genre and domain related. They are also highly idiosyncratic, strongly depending on each individual social background. Surface forms will be produced according to rhetorical and discourse rules, by instantiating features activated by semantic information.

5.1 LSLT and Contextual Reasoning

There are two main additional tenets of the theory: one is that it is possible to reduce access to domain world knowledge by means of contextual reasoning, i.e. reasoning triggered independently by contextual or linguistic features of the text under analysis. In other words, we adopt what could be termed the Shallow Processing Hypothesis: access to world knowledge is reduced and substituted whenever links are missing through inferences on the basis of specifically encoded lexical and grammatical knowledge, and are worked out in a fully general manner. In exploring this possibility we make one fundamental assumption and it is that the psychological processes needed for language analysis and understanding are controlled by a processing device which is completely separated from that of language generation with which it shares a common lexicon though.

In our approach there is no language model for probabilistic processing even though we use statistical processing for strongly sequential tasks like tag disambiguation. Our algorithms are based on symbolic rules and we also use FSA to help tag disambiguation and parsing (but see Carroll2000). The reason for this is twofold: an objective one, machine learning for statistical language models need linguistic resources which in turn are both very time-consuming to produce and highly error-prone activities. On a more general level, one needs consider that highly sophisticated linguistic resources are always language and genre dependent, besides the need to comply with requirements of statistical representativeness. No such limitations can be deemed for symbolic algorithms which on the contrary are more general and easily portable from one language to another. Differences in genre can also be easily accounted for by scaling the rules adequately. Statistics could then fruitfully be used to scale rules in the parser appropriately according to genre adaptation requirements.

It is sensible to assume that when understanding a text a human reader or listener does make use of his encyclopaedia parsimoniously. Contextual reasoning is the only way in which a system for Natural Language Understanding should tap external knowledge of the domain. In other words, a system should be allowed to perform an inference on the basis of domain world knowledge when needed and only then. In this way, the system could simulate the actual human behaviour in that access to extralinguistic knowledge is triggered by contextual factors independently present in the text and detected by the system itself. This would be required only for implicit linguistic relations as can happen with bridging descriptions, to cope with anaphora resolution phenomena, for instance. In other words, we believe that there are principled ways by which linguistic processes interact with knowledge representation or the ontology—or to put it more simply, how syntax interacts with pragmatics.

In fact, no solution for such an interaction has yet been found, nor even tackled by current deep systems (See papers in Bos and Delmonte 2008). In these systems, linguistic components are kept separate from knowledge representation, and work which could otherwise be done directly by the linguistic analysis is duplicated by inferential mechanism. The output of linguistic analysis is usually mapped onto a logical representation which is in turn fed onto the knowledge representation of the domain in order to understand and validate a given utterance or query. Thus the domain world model or ontology must be priorily built, usually in view of a given task the system is set out to perform. This modeling is domain and task limited and generality can only be achieved from coherent lexical representations. In some of these systems, the main issue is how to make the two realms interact as soon as possible in order to take advantage of the inferential mechanism to reduce ambiguities present in the text or to allow for reasoning on linguistic data, which otherwise couldn't be understandable. We assume that an integration between linguistic information and knowledge of the world can be carried out at all levels of linguistic description and that contextual reasoning can be thus performed on the fly rather than sequentially. This implies that access to knowledge must be filtered out by the analysis of the linguistic content of surface linguistic forms and their abstract representations of the utterances making up the text. Thus the two important elements characterizing human language faculty, that is "ambiguity" and "recursion", find a fully justified role in the theory and are also entirely justified by it (see also Kinsella2010).

6 An Evaluation and a Conclusion

The system and the parser have gone through an extended number of evaluations: starting from the latest one, where they been used to produce the output for the Events Workshop (2013); then, Sentiment, Factuality and Subjectivity analysis, (Delmonte and Pallotta 2011); Relational Models of Semantics, (Tonelli and Delmonte 2011); Automatic Identification of Null Instantiations, at SEMEVAL (Delmonte and Tonelli 2010); Semantic Processing for Text Entailment, (Delmonte et al. 2009, 2005, 2006, 2007); Semantic and Pragmatic Computing in STEP (Delmonte 2008); Causality Relations in Unrestricted Text, (Delmonte et al. 2007); Evaluation of Anaphora Resolution, Delmonte and Bianchi (1991) (Delmonte et al. 2006); Comparing Dependency and Constituency Parsing, (Delmonte 2005); Evaluating Grammatical Relations, (Delmonte 2004).

All these evaluations have shown the high resiliency of the system for the different applications with little adjustments. Results are comparable if not better, thus showing that manually organized linguistic grammars and parsers are better suited for semantically related tasks. It is a fact that Machine Learning does not easily adapts to the presence of null elements in the training set and this represents a fatal drawback for any further improvement along the lines indicated in the paper.

References

Altman, G. T. M. (Ed.) (1989). Language and Cognitive Processes. *Special Issue—Parsing and Interpretation, 4*(3/4).

Berwick, R. C., Abney, S., & Tenny, C. (1991). *Principle-based parsing: Computation and psycholinguistics*. New York: Kluwer Academic Publishers.

Bresnan, J. (1982). *The mental representation of grammatical relations*. Cambridge Mass: MIT Press.

Bresnan, J. (2001). *Lexical-functional syntax*. Oxford: Blackwells.

Brants, T., & Samuelsson, C. (1995). Tagging the teleman corpus. *In Proceedings 10th Nordic Conference of Computational Linguistics* (pp. 1–12). Helsinki.

Carnie, Andrew, & Barss, Andrew. (2006). Phases and nominal interpretation. *Research in Language, 4*, 127–132.

Carroll, J. A. (2000). Statistical parsing. In R. Dale, H. Moisl, & H. Somers (Eds.), *Handbook of natural language processing* (pp. 525–543). New York: Marcel Dekker.

Chomsky, N. (1998/2000). Minimalist Inquiries: the framework. In R. Martin, D. Michaels, & J. Uriagereka (Eds.), *Step by Step: Essays on minimalist syntax in honor of Howard Lasnik*. Cambridge, MA: MIT Press.

Chomsky, N. (2004). Beyond explanatory adequacy. In A. Belletti (Ed.), Structures and beyond. The cartography of syntactic structures (Vol. 3, pp. 104–131). Oxford: Oxford University Press.

Clifton, C., & Ferreira, F. (1989). Ambiguity in context. In G. Altman (Ed.), *Language and cognitive processes* (pp. 77–104). op.cit.

Delmonte, R., & Bianchi, D. (1991). Binding pronominals with an LFG parser. *Proceeding of the Second International Workshop on Parsing Technologies, Cancun (Messico)* (pp. 59–72). ACL 1991.

Delmonte, R. (1999). From Shallow Parsing to Functional Structure, in Atti del Workshop AI*IA—"Elaborazione del Linguaggio e Riconoscimento del Parlato", IRST Trento, pp. 8–19.

Delmonte, R. (2013a). Coping with implicit arguments and events coreference in Eduard Hovy, Teruko Mitamura, Martha Palmer. *Proceedings of the Conference The 1st Workshop on EVENTS, HLT-NAACL 2013, Atlanta, Georgia* (pp. 1–10) .

Delmonte, R. (2013b). Predicate argument structures for information extraction from dependency representations: Null elements are missing. In C. Lai, A. Giuliani & G. Semeraro (Eds.), *Studies in Computational Intelligence*, Distributed Systems and Applications of Information Filtering and Retrieval. DART 2012 (pp. 1–25). New York: Springer.

Delmonte, R., & Vincenzo, P. (2011). Opinion mining and sentiment analysis need text understanding. In V. Pallotta, A. Soro & E. Vargiu (Eds.), *Advances in distributed agent-based retrieval tools: Studies in computational intelligence* (Vol. 361, pp. 81–96). New York: Springer.

Delmonte, R., & Tonelli, S. (2010). VENSES ++-UNIVE: Adapting a deep semantic processing system to the identification of null instantiations. *In Proceedings of the 5th International Workshop on Semantic Evaluation* (pp. 296–299). ACL 2010.

Delmonte, R., Tonelli, S., & Tripodi, R. (2009). Semantic processing for text entailment with VENSES. *In Proceedings of Text Analysis Conference (TAC) 2009 Workshop—Notebook Papers and Results* (pp. 453–460). Gaithersburg, MA: NIST.

Delmonte, R. (2009). *Computational linguistic text processing—lexicon, grammar, parsing and anaphora resolution*. New York: Nova Science Publishers.

Delmonte, R. (2008). Semantic and pragmatic computing with GETARUNS. In J. Bos & R. Delmonte (Eds.), *Semantics in text processing (STEP), research in computational semantics* (Vol. 1, pp. 287–298). London: College Publications.

Delmonte, R. (2007). *Computational linguistic text processing—logical form, semantic interpretation, discourse relations and question answering*. New York: Nova Science Publishers.

Delmonte, R., Nicolae, G., Harabagiu, S. (2007). A linguistically-based approach to detect causality relations in unrestricted text. *In Proceedings of MICAI-2007* (pp. 173–185). IEEE Publications.

Delmonte, R., Bristot, A., Piccolino Boniforti, M. A., & Tonelli, S. (2006). Another evaluation of anaphora resolution algorithms and a comparison with GETARUNS' knowledge rich approach. *ROMAND 2006, 11th EACL* (pp. 3–10). Trento: Association for Computational Linguistics.

Delmonte, R., Bristot, A., Piccolino Boniforti, M. A., & Tonelli, S. (2006). Coping with semantic uncertainty with VENSES. In B. Magnini & I. Dagan (Eds.), *Proceedings of the Challenges Workshop—The 2nd PASCAL Recognizing Textual Entailment Challenge* (pp. 86–91).

Delmonte, R., Tonelli, S., Piccolino Boniforti, M. A., Bristot, A., Pianta, E. (2005). VENSES—a linguistically-based system for semantic evaluation. In J. Quiñonero-Candela et al. (Ed.), *Machine learning challenges. Evaluating predictive uncertainty, visual object classification, and recognising textual entailment: First pascal machine learning challenges workshop* (pp. 344–371). Southampton, UK, Revised Selected Papers.

Delmonte, R. (2005). Deep & shallow linguistically based parsing. In A. M. Di Sciullo (Ed.), *UG and external systems* (pp. 335–374). Amsterdam/Philadelphia: John Benjamins.

Delmonte, R. (2004). Evaluating GETARUNS parser with GREVAL test suite. *Proceedings of the ROMAND—20th International Conference on Computational Linguistics—COLING* (pp. 32–41). Geneva.

Delmonte, R. (2002). Relative clause attachment and anaphora: A case for short binding. *Proceedings of TAG + 6* (pp. 84–89). Venice.

Delmonte, R. (2000a). Parsing with GETARUN. *Proceedings of TALN2000, 7° conférence annuel sur le TALN* (pp. 133–146). Lausanne.

Delmonte, R. (2000b). Parsing Preferences and Linguistic Strategies, in LDV-Forum—Zeitschrift fuer Computerlinguistik und Sprachtechnologie—"Communicating Agents", Band 17, 1,2, pp. 56–73.

Epstein, S. D. (2004). *On intermodular, i-functional explanation. Manuscript*. Ann Arbor: University of Michigan.

Filip, H. (1998). Reduced relatives: Lexical constraint-based analysis. *Proceedings of the Twenty-Fourth Meeting of the Berkeley Linguistic Society* (pp. 1–15).

Frazier, L. (1987a). Sentence processing. In M. Coltheart (Ed.), *Attention and performance XII*. Hillsdale, N.J: Lawrence Elbaum.

Frazier, L. (1987b). Theories of sentence processing, In J. Garfield (Ed.), *Modularity in knowledge representation and natural language understanding* (pp. 291–308). Cambridge: MIT Press.

Johan, Bos, & Delmonte, Rodolfo (Eds.). (2008). *Semantics in text processing (STEP), Research in computational semantics* (Vol. 1). London: College Publications.

Hauser, M. D., Chomsky, N., & Tecumesh Fitch, W. (2002). The faculty of language: What it is, who has it, and how did it evolve? *Science, 298*, 1569–1579.

Hobbs, J. R., Appelt, D. E., Bear, J., & Tyson, M. (1992). Robust processing of real-world natural language texts. *Proceedings of the 2nd Conference on NLP*, pp. 186–192.

Hindle, D., & Roth, M. (1993). Structural ambiguity and lexical relations. *Computational Linguistics, 19*(1), 103–120.

Hulst, H.G. van der (Ed.) (2010). *Recursion and Human Language*. Berlin: Mouton de Gruyter.

Karlsson, F. (2010). Syntactic Recursion and Iteration, In: H. van der Hulst (Ed.), *Recursion and human language* (pp. 43–67). Berlin: De Gruyter Mouton.

Kinsella, A. (2010). Was recursion the key step in the evolution of the human language faculty? In: H. van der Hulst (Ed.), *Recursion and human language* (pp. 179–192). Berlin: De Gruyter Mouton.

Kuhn, J. (2013). On the "Spirit of LFG" in current computational linguistics. *In Proceedings of LFG13* (pp. 356–376). CSLI Publications online.

Legate, J. (2002). Some interface properties of the phase. *Linguistic Inquiry 34*, pp. 506–516.

Legate, J. (2003). *Phases in "Beyond Explanatory Adequacy." Manuscript*. Cambridge: Massachusetts Institute of Technology.

Pereira, F. (1983). Logic for Natural Language Analysis, Technical Note 275, Artificial Intelligence Center, SRI International.

Pereira, F. (1981). Extraposition grammars. *American Journal of Computational Linguistics, 7*(4), 243–256.

Pereira, F., & Warren, D. (1980). Definite clause grammar for language analysis—a survey of the formalism and a comparison with ATN. *Artificial Intelligence, 13*, 231–278.

Pinker, S., & Jackendoff, R. (2005). The faculty of language: What's special about it?*. *Cognition, 95*, 201–236.

Pritchett, B. L. (1992). *grammatical competence and parsing performance*. Chicago: The University of Chicago Press.

Schubert, L. K. (1984). On parsing preferences. *Proceedings of COLING* (pp. 247–250). Stanford.

Stevenson, S., & Merlo, P. (1997). Lexical structure and parsing complexity. In M. C. MacDonald (Ed.), *Lexical Representations and Sentence Processing* (pp. 349–399). UK: Psychology Press.

Svenonius, P. (2001). Locality, phases and the cycle, Manuscript, University of Tromsø, Draft 19.07.01.

Svenonius, P. (2004). On the Edge. In D. Adger, C. de Cat, & G. Tsoulas (Eds.), *Peripheries* (pp. 259–287). Dordrecht: Kluwer.

Tapanainen, P., & Voutilainen, A. (1994). Tagging accurately—don't guess if you know. *Proceedings of ANLP '94* (pp. 47–52). Stuttgart, Germany.

Tomasello, M. (2006). Acquiring linguistic constructions. In R. Siegler & D. Kuhn (Eds.), *Handbook of child psychology: Cognitive development* (pp. 255–298). New York: Wiley.

Tonelli, R., & Delmonte, R. (2011). Desperately seeking Implicit arguments in text. In S. N. Kim, Z. Kozareva, P. Nakov, D. Ó Séaghdha, S. Padó, S. Szpakowicz (Eds.), *Proceedings of the ACL 2011 workshop on relational models of semantics (RELMS'2011)* (pp. 54–62). Portland, USA.

Townsend, D. J., & Bever, T. G. (2001). *Sentence comprehension—the integration of habits and rules*. Cambridge: MIT Press.

Verhagen, A. (2010). What do you think is the proper place of recursion? Conceptual and empirical issues. In H. van der Hulst (Ed.), *Recursion and human language* (pp. 93–112). Berlin: De Gruyter Mouton.

Part IV
Language and Speech Analysis and Generation

Consonants as Skeleton of Language: Statistical Evidences Through Text Production

Kumiko Tanaka-Ishii

Abstract In this chapter, the role of consonants is reconsidered through analysis of the statistical structure of text in terms of ambiguity. The discussion proceeds through scientific interpretation of the poet Mallarmé's statement comparing consonants to the skeleton of language. Since the contrast between consonants and vowels is most apparent through text production, as represented in abjad writing systems, different kinds of text production procedures are discussed and analyzed. The statistical nature underlying the consonant/vowel contrast is explained in a manner consistent with the findings reported so far in the domain of cognitive linguistics.

Keywords Entropy · Consonants · Vowels · Bathtub effect · Information bias · Writing systems · Text entry systems · Information theory · Corpus · Cognitive bias

1 Introduction

The French poet Mallarmé mentioned once that "vowels are like flesh whereas consonants are like skeleton"[1] (Mallarmà 1980). If one writes in a language whose writing system is of the abjad type, then this statement would be intuitive, but Mallarmé was a French poet. Still, poets are especially sensitive to language: in making this statement, Mallarmé must have been guided by his heightened

[1] The original quote in French is "À toute la nature apparenté et se rapprochant ainsi de l'organisme dépositaire de la vie, le Mot présente, dans ses voyelles et ses diphtongues, comme une chaire; et, dans ses consonnes, comme une ossature délicate à disséquer."

K. Tanaka-Ishii (✉)
Department of Advanced Information Technology, Graduate School of Information Science and Electrical Engineering, Kyushu University, Fukuoka, Japan
e-mail: kumiko@ait.kyushu-u.ac.jp

© Springer International Publishing Switzerland 2015

N. Gala et al. (eds.), *Language Production, Cognition, and the Lexicon*,
Text, Speech and Language Technology 48, DOI 10.1007/978-3-319-08043-7_16

sensitivity to language. What does Mallarmé mean exactly by the term "skeleton"? Does this universally apply to any language in general?

For this book volume, whose theme involves cognition and language, I would like to discuss this question in part and reconsider how essential consonants are in language. As in the abjad example raised just now, the contrast of consonants and vowels is apparent in text production, in particular. Since text production concerns the cognitive processing of language and produces text, a conjecture on the role of consonants in text production would involve consideration of the two aspects of cognition and the statistical structure of text. Specifically, the former should be reflected by cognitive phenomena and thus be reported in the cognitive science domain, whereas the latter would be reflected by the statistical structures underlying language corpora, with reports appearing in the language processing domain. I thus consider the notion of consonants as the "skeleton" of language in terms of both domains, and I interpret the cognitive phenomena in term of text statistics.

2 Deciphering Through Consonants

The term "skeleton" can be intuitively appreciated through an abjad writing system. Studies on writing systems have sought to plausibly classify the wide variety of existing writing systems; one notable approach (Daniels 1996) classifies all writing systems into six kinds: alphabet, abugida, abjad, featural, syllabary, and logosyllabary. This classification covers the axis of character representation size from phonemes to syllables, and each class is characterized by how it denotes a unit containing consonants and vowels.

An abjad is a consonantal writing system in which texts are represented through consonants only, in an unvocalized form. According to Coulmas (2002), the ancestors of the alphabet system in fact only used consonants in their writing systems: this includes systems for Phoenician, Akkadic and Sumeric. Thus, an entire human language can be expressed only through consonants, and the original linguistic phrases can be deciphered. This is the case not just for one exceptional language but throughout a large family of languages. Although studies of automatic vocalization have shown that it is not obvious how to insert vowels back into an abjad text (Nelken and Shieber 2005), this language family shows that humans can do without vowels, at least in texts, through which the essence of human civilization has been transferred. In contrast, representation of human language through only vowels is very exceptional: It seems that Silbo Gomera, a Spanish whistling language used to communicate over long distances is one such case, but the coverage of its linguistic resources is limited (CNN 2003).

Others who do not write using abjad systems probably don't have much awareness of the fact that we communicate via consonants and vowels when we speak. Yet such orientation towards consonants is not only for abjad-based languages: the contrast of consonants and vowels appear in text production as well. For example, a consonantal text production system for English has been proposed.

In this system, the user enters text with only consonants, and the system predicts entire words (Shieber and Baker 2003). For example, if the user enters "bldg", the system suggests "building". This is a systematic extension of the daily use of abbreviations. There is a universal tendency throughout the world that one strategy for abbreviating words is to drop vowels and retain consonants.

Japanese adopts a writing system consisting of a syllabary, in which the notion of consonants is the least present among writing systems based on phonetic representation. In a syllabary, according to (Daniels 1996), a character represents a syllable, but phonetically similar syllables do not have a similar graphical shape. For example, the sounds of 'ka', 'ki', and 'ku' in Japanese are written as 'か', 'き', and 'く', respectively, and the forms of these characters do not suggest that they include the same consonant. Therefore, in a syllabary, no systematic organization is apparent in terms of consonants and vowels. With the recent popularity of mobile phones, however, consonants in Japanese have increased in importance. Each digit is assigned a consonant, and the phone user enters Japanese with only consonants. For example, to enter "みかえる" ("Michael"), the corresponding numbers are "7721111999", where each digit indicates a different consonant and the number of times a digit repeats represents the subsequent vowel. Since the number of major consonants is 10, Japanese text entry with a 10-digit keypad is well suited to consonant entry.

Since predictive methods have been used for text production of the Japanese logosyllabary, adopted in addition to the syllabary, such ways of entering text have naturally triggered studies on generalized predictive entry systems for Japanese. The prediction procedure is the same as that described previously for abbreviated text entry, and commercially this approach resembles the T9 system (Tegic9 2000). Here, a digit is entered once for any vowel, and the word is predicted by a software application. For example, the entry of "Michael" in Japanese is made by the sequence "7219" only (Tanaka-Ishii et al. 2001).[2] This corresponds to entering a word through consonant sequences only, just like in an abjad. The system would suggest "みかえる" and other words[3] with the same consonant sequence of 'm', 'k', 'ϕ' and 'r', but with different vowel sequences suggested by the system from searching its dictionary. The user then chooses the target term from among these candidates.

The idea of predictive entry so far serves to allow text production in a more efficient way than without such a system. The user needs to push a smaller number of keys than with entering an entire word. Moreover, the system helps the user produce text when the target word has a difficult spelling or character form (MacKenzie and Tanaka-Ishii 2007). In addition to such appreciative advantages, predictive entry opens a new way to reconsider what counts for text production,

---

[2] In Japanese, the name "Michael" is pronounced as "mikaeru", therefore, the entry is made by consonant sequence of "m", "k", "ϕ" (no consonant) and "r", each corresponding to 7,2,1,9, respectively.

[3] Some examples are "迎える" (reads "mukaeru", to welcome), "見返り" (reads "mikaeri", reward) and "報いる" (reads "mukuiru", to compensate).

and more broadly, human language generation. This can be studied through the efficiency of the *code*, the design of the sequence to be predicted: for example, in abbreviated entry, the code corresponds to the abbreviation, while in an abjad system and Japanese mobile phone entry, the code corresponds to the consonant sequence. The efficiency of a code indicates whether its design conforms with human linguistic procedures. We have seen that consonants frequently serve as this type of code across different writing systems, in alphabets, abjads, and even syllabaries.

Then, can a vowel sequence not serve as the code? The investigation involves studies on information amount accommodated by consonants and vowels in words. One of the earliest studies on this probably dates back to (Markov 1913), where Markov reports the stationary probabilities of vowels and consonants in a literary text. Since, the notion of entropy (Shannon 1948) has been invented to quantitatively measure the complexity of a sequence. Without noting, Markov models and Shannon's entropy serve as the most basic tools in natural language processing. Along this line, in order to consider the question of the possibility of vowel to serve as the code, the information amount carried by vowels is measured by calculating the ambiguity of codes underlying predictive entry. The more ambiguous a code, the larger the number of suggested candidates, and the text production load becomes larger since the user must go through the candidates. The ambiguity to guess a word w given a code sequence c can be quantified through the conditional entropy as follows:

$$H(W = w|C = c) = -P(W = w|C = c) log P(W = w|C = c), \qquad (1)$$

where W and C are random variables denoting the sets of words and codes, respectively, and $P(W = w|C = c)$ is the conditional probability of a word for a given sequence c. The total ease of guessing for an encoding method is then measured by averaging the whole product of $H(W = w|C = c)$ and $P(C = c)$:

$$H(W|C) = \sum_{w,c} P(C = c) H(W = w|C = c). \qquad (2)$$

When the estimation of w is more ambiguous, $H(W|C)$ has a larger value.

This value can be calculated for a corpus, and as an example, I used the BNC (574 MB, 353248 different words). Since we are interested in how the ease of deciphering text varies between consonants and vowels, every character must be transformed into a phoneme sequence, with each tagged by a consonant or a vowel. Tagging of alphabet characters as consonants or vowels cannot be automated, since some characters are used as consonants or vowels depending on the context (such as 'r', 'j', and 'y'). Therefore, the words were transliterated into phonemes by using the CELEX database.[4] For example, in CELEX the word

[4] http://www.ru.nl/celex/.

Table 1 English consonants and vowels in IPA, following the classification in The CELEX Manual (1990)

24 vowels	ɪ ɛ æ ʌ ɒ ʊ ə iː ɑː ɔː uː ɜː eɪ aɪ ɔɪ əʊ aʊ ɪə ɛə ʊə æ̃ ɑ̃ː æ̃ː ɒ̃ː
30 consonants	p b t d k g ŋ m n l r f v θ ð s z ʃ ʒ j x h w tʃ dʒ ŋ̩ m̩ n̩ l̩ *
Proportion of consonants in words	63.6 %

"clever" is broken down into syllables and phonemes as [klɛvə*] in IPA (International Phonetic Alphabet) format. Words that are not included in the CELEX database were not considered for measuring the conditional entropy of phonemes. Every CELEX phoneme was tagged as a consonant or vowel, based on (The CELEX Manual 1990, [4–25, Sect. 2.4.1]) as listed in Table 1. The exact numbers of consonants and vowels vary depending on the decomposition strategy, especially for diphthongs. Here, every diphthong appearing in the classification provided by (The CELEX Manual 1990) was counted as one unit.

In English, the conditional entropy with the code consisting of consonants is 0.79, whereas that with the code consisting of vowels is 4.37 (Tanaka-Ishii 2012). This reveals that entry by consonants is far less ambiguous, and the difference represents the relative ease of deciphering text through consonants or vowels. The reader might wonder, however, whether this ambiguity difference is present simply because consonants greatly outnumber vowels in English. As shown in Table 1, the proportion of consonants amounts to 63.6 % in English words when measured according to CELEX. One reason for consonants being more efficient than vowels indeed lies in their frequency difference. In general for a given language, the number of consonants is larger than that of vowels, so it is likely easier to enter text through consonants.

Regarding this difference, in fact, an experiment in Japanese can be designed to compare the ambiguity of consonants and vowels through the same number of code elements. This is so because the number of major consonants is 10, whereas that of vowels is 5. Therefore, comparison can be made by using text entry with a code system having five elements. In a system based on consonants, two consonants are assigned to each code element, whereas in a system based on vowels, one vowel is assigned to each element. Conditional entropy calculation using the Mainichi newspaper from 1994 gives 3.599 for vowels, compared with 3.173 for one possible consonant assignment (Tanaka-Ishii et al. 2003). Note that there is arbitrariness in assigning 10 consonants to 5 elements, and it is possible to assign consonants to give entropy larger than with the vowel assignment. Such an assignment is biased where a code element is assigned two frequent consonants. For a reasonable assignment, however, entry through consonants is less ambiguous than that through vowels.

The amount of ambiguity lies in the statistical nature of texts. As mentioned earlier, a more ambiguous code design will suggest a larger number of candidates, and the user's cognitive load for the task will become larger (Tanaka-Ishii 2006; Tanaka-Ishii et al. 2002). The ambiguity correlates with the number of candidates appearing, and also with the entry speed, when conducting user experiments.

To sum up, the discussion so far indicates that consonants are less ambiguous than vowels, and this could be the reason for the strong preferences towards consonants as code sequences for text production—in abjad systems, abbreviations, and Japanese mobile phone entry. This statistical phenomenon could, in fact, be a chicken and egg problem. It might be the case that humans have preferences in memory towards consonants, so we produce texts in which consonants give less ambiguity.

3 Articulating Through Consonants

Humans are capable of *raeding tihs wtih quit amzaing esae*. This example uses the trick that the order of the original consonants is preserved. From this example as well, Mallarmé's notion of "skeleton" can be intuitively understood, in that when consonants are present as in the original text, we can decipher the correct text.

This capability to correct and recognize jumbled words has raised a controversy over how words are processed (Wheeler 1970). Substantial studies have been conducted on the cognitive processing of words. Within these studies, two common cognitive preferences are frequently addressed with respect to human recognition of words, namely *locational* and *consonantal preferences*. For the locational preference, (Aitchison 1994) indicates that humans remember the beginnings of words better than endings, and endings better than middles; she calls this phenomenon the "bathtub effect". For example, when people try to predict the word "building", they can do so better from "buildi" than from "ilding", and even better than from "uildin". For the consonantal preference, it is known that consonants are more informative than vowels for recalling words (Nespor et al. 2003; Perea and Lupker 2004; Buchwald and Rapp 2006). For example, guessing "building" from the jumble "bld" is easier than from "uii".

The reports referred to here belong to the cognitive science domain, and the findings are based on user experiments, thereby illuminating the human cognitive processing of words. If the chicken and egg problem mentioned previously exists, the statistical properties of text should reflect the consequences of human preference. Using the same prediction framework seen previously, we could measure whether there are statistical structures corresponding to such preferences. We have seen that consonants are less ambiguous than vowels for word prediction. Similarly, regarding the location preference, are both ends of words less ambiguous than the middles of words?

Using the same phonemically transcribed BNC data presented in the previous section, it can be shown that word ends are not necessarily less ambiguous; rather, word ends are *more* ambiguous than the middles, in terms of predicting the whole word given different parts of the same length. In other words, the statistical structure contradicts the locational preference.

This can be shown by measuring the ambiguity of prediction from different subparts of words. Given a part of length n in a fixed location, all words having

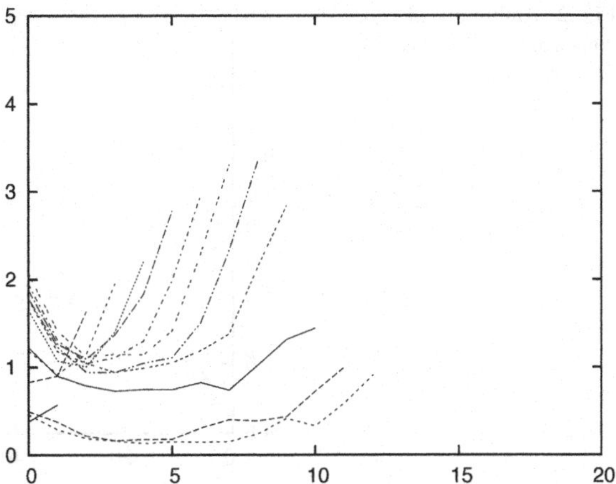

Fig. 1 Locational ambiguity in English words in terms of phonemes (prediction from three phonemes)

that part at that location appear as candidates and the complexity is measured through the conditional entropy. Figure 1 shows the ambiguity of word prediction when $n = 3$. Each line in the graph corresponds to the locational ambiguity for words of a certain length $|w| > n$. The horizontal axis indicates the absolute offset—the location of the part—from the beginning of the word, while the vertical axis indicates the conditional entropy. Therefore, the length of each line is $|w| - n + 1$, which was increased until the total frequency of words of that length was above a threshold.[5] The vertical location of the line thus depends on the overall complexity of words of length $|w|$.

The lines are relatively smooth, and the tendency of high ambiguity at both edges is clear. For relatively short words, in particular, the middle part clearly appears less ambiguous. There is a tendency that words are extended at word edges through inflection: in particular, English is a strongly suffixing language. Thus, regular patterns such as "-ed" and "-ing" do not identify words better than do word cores located in the middle. Such tendency for word middles being less ambiguous was present for different experimental conditions with the value of n ranging from 1 to 5, and also in terms of characters, as well.

How, then, can the location preference be explained? One way to explain it through statistical ambiguity is via consonantal preference. As we have seen previously, a consonant sequence is less ambiguous than a vowel sequence. The ambiguity can be further detailed by location, for both consonants and vowels.

Locational ambiguity data for $n = 1$, similar to that shown in Fig. 1 for $n = 3$, was decomposed into the information carried by consonants and vowels, with the result shown in Fig. 2. This result was obtained by masking words. For example, the English word "clever" was transcribed in CELEX notation as k-l-ɛ-v-ə-* and masked as k-l-?-v-?-* for consonants and as ?-?-ɛ-?-ə-? for vowels. This was done for all words, and the locational ambiguity was calculated. The horizontal axis

[5] The threshold was set to 100.

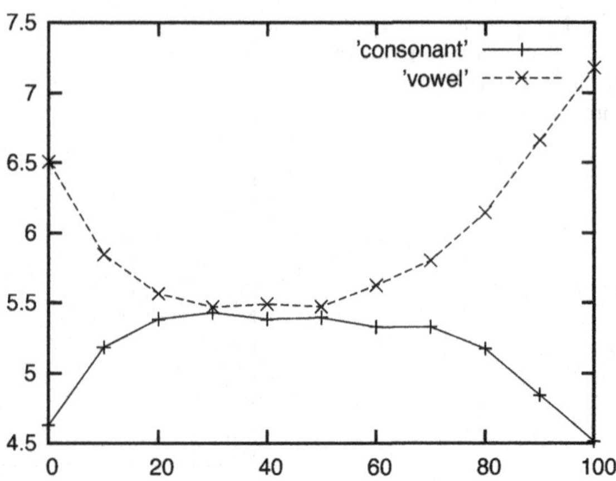

Fig. 2 Ambiguity of consonants and vowels in English words

indicates the *relative* offset within the word by merging words of different length, and the vertical axis indicates the conditional entropy. There are two lines, one for consonants and the other for vowels.

The consonant ambiguity shows a clear hill, with high ambiguity in the middle and low ambiguity at the ends. Thus, guessing words from consonants is much easier if it is done from word edges than from middles. Moreover, the vowel plot forms a vertical mirror of the consonant plot. Thus, consonants and vowels complement each other.

Since the consonant line is located lower than the vowel line, except in the middle, consonants are less ambiguous than vowels almost throughout a word. Consequently, text indeed has a statistical structure that explains the two preferences, and the locational preference might be justified by the evidence that consonants are less ambiguous at word ends than at word middles.

Previous reports on studies of word segmentation in linguistics (Harris 1955) and cognitive linguistics (Saffran et al. 1996), and on methods of unsupervised segmentation in natural language processing (Tanaka-Ishii and Jin 2008; Goldwater et al. 2009; Zhikov et al. 2010), suggest that segmentation is made through information existing outside words. All of these studies captured the variety increase at the border outside a word and defined the atomically conjunct part as a word.

In contrast, the fact that a consonant sequence decreases in ambiguity at the word border suggests that consonants provide word delimitation from *inside* the word. This result suggests that word segmentation could possibly be supported partially by using consonant sequences. Indication of such an intrinsic statistical structure of words enhancing word segmentation is still rare, to the best of my knowledge. Consonants delimit words, with ambiguity smaller than that of vowels when calculated word-wise. At the same time, this delimitation could be further enhanced by exhibiting even less ambiguity at both ends of words, thus indicating word borders.

The verification so far has only been made in English, and it is unknown whether consonant sequences are less ambiguous at the ends of words in other languages in the same way as in English. Especially, whether consonant clusters are allowed or not must be taken into consideration. It is the western languages' characteristic to have consonant clusters, and many languages do not have them. For example in Japanese and Korean, syllables are composed of one single consonant in front of a vowel and a maximum of two consonants which have to belong to certain phonological classes. In these languages, the shape of the ambiguity shift within a word in terms of consonants would probably depend on the phonetic characteristics of a language. In this sense, there might not even be a cognitive phenomenon that corresponds to the "bathtub" effect, as (Aitchison 1994) indicated for other languages besides English. At least, however, the discussion suggests the possibility that semantic delimitation of language sequences, such as in words, would occur not only from the information increase outside a word but also from the information existing within the word, and this could be expressed by the consonant sequence.

4 Statistical Signification of "Skeleton"

Given the discussion so far, what does the term "skeleton" signify? It is known among anthropologists that non-human primates hardly pronounce consonants (Savage-Rumbaugh and Lewin 1996).[6] On a related note, at the beginning of life, human babies mostly utter vowel sounds and learn consonants gradually. It could be said, therefore, that the primate sound inventory includes fewer consonantal sounds from an evolutionary point of view. According to (Deacon 1998), consonants appeared when humans began to walk erect, when the orientation of the head changed and humans became better able to pronounce consonants.

Listening to a newborn baby's cry consisting mainly of vowels, it is hard to delimit inside such an utterance. The utterance forms a unit as a whole, delimited only by the beginning and end of the continuous sound, and nothing corresponding to a segment within is truly distinguishable. The vowels sounds may shift from one vowel to another, but the shift is continuous as the shape of the mouth changes. Therefore, it is difficult to define which part of the utterance was the vowel 'a' and which part was 'e', for example. Clear segments appear only when babies start making consonantal sounds, and they play an important role in delimiting utterances into syllables.

On a related note, a musical conductor writes of the difficulty of detecting the instrument type only from the middle part of a sound (Akutagawa 1971). Instead,

[6] According to a private discussion with an anthropologist, it is not entirely the case that non-human primates do not pronounce consonants. They seem able to make acute consonantal sounds to alert peers. Nevertheless, it appears to remain true that the pronunciation is limited in these utterances. The anthropologist also notes the limited number of complete reports overviewing analysis of non-human primate utterances; the representative study is (Savage-Rumbaugh and Lewin 1996).

information on the instrument type occurs in the characteristic of the sound at the very moment when it begins to be played. As another kind of sound, human utterances might be a similar case: it could be this characteristic of the beginning of every syllable, the consonants, that defines the characteristic of the sound. Consonants thus have the function of delimiting utterances and differentiating sounds. In other words, the functionality of *delimitation* gives a set of sounds through *differentiation*.

Once such a set of basic sounds is given, the possibility for *combination* appears. Linear ordering of combined syllables would generate a combinatorial variety of utterances, which gives the possibility of signifying the complex reality of this world. Within such combination, consonants are organized to serve well for human communication. According to the discussion in the previous two sections, consonants can represent a writer's thoughts without vowels. A consonant sequence allows one to "predict back", or *decipher*, the original utterance. This is partly because a consonant sequence is less ambiguous than a vowel sequence. Moreover, consonants not only allow delimitation of syllables to define different kinds of sounds but also help articulate words, by giving a consonantal pattern of change in ambiguity. To sum up, it is reasonable to suggest that consonants carry the core structure of language, i.e., the skeleton.

5 Concluding Remark

Consonants provide the framework for delimitation of syllables and words. Mallarmé's statement about the "skeleton" of language can be understood as such a linguistic framework of delimitation. In this small chapter, I have reconsidered this simple role of consonants by verifying the statistical structure underlying text, through examination of the amount of information accommodated by consonants.

References

Aitchison, J. (1994). *Words in the mind*. London: Blackwell.

Akutagawa ,Y. (1971). *Basics of music*. Tokyo: Iwanami Shinsho (in Japanese).

Buchwald, A., & Rapp, B. (2006). Consonants and vowels in orthographic representations. *Cognitive Neuropsychology*, *23*(2), 308–337.

CNN. (2003). *Nearly extinct whistling language revived*. Retrieved from http://www.cnn.com/2003/TECH/science/11/18/whistle.language.ap/.

Coulmas, F. (2002). *Writings systems: An introduction to their linguistic analysis*. Cambridge: Cambridge University Press.

Daniels, P. T. (1996). *The world's writing systems*. Oxford: Oxford University Press.

Deacon, T. (1998). *Symbolic species*. New York: W. W. Norton.

Goldwater, S., Griffiths, T. L., & Johnson, M. (2009). A baysian framework for word segmentation: Exploring the effects of context. *Cognition*, *112*(1), 21–54.

Harris, Z. S. (1955). From phoneme to morpheme. *Language*, 31(2), 190–222.

MacKenzie, S., & Tanaka-Ishii, K. (Eds.). (2007). *Text entry systems: Accessibility, mobility, universality*, (co-authored Chaps. 2, 5, 10, 11, 13). San Fransisco: Morgan Kaufmann (Elsevier).
Mallarmé, S. (1980). *Oeuvres complète*. Gallimard.
Markov, A. (1913). Essai d'une recherche statistique sur le texte du roman 'eugene onegin'. Bull de l'Academie Imperiale des Sciences de St Petersboug.
Nelken, R., & Shieber, S. (2005). Arabic diacritization using weighted finite-state transducers. In *Proceedings of the ACL Workshop on Computational Approaches to Semitic Languages*, pp. 79–86.
Nespor, M., Peña, M., & Mehler, J. (2003). On the different roles of vowels and consonants in speech processing and language acquisition. *Lingue e Linguaggio, 2*, 221–247.
Perea, M., & Lupker, S. J. (2004). Can caniso activate casino? Transposed-letter similarity effects with nonadjacent letter positions. *Journal of Memory and Language* (elsevier), *51*(2), 231–246.
Saffran, J. R., Aslin, R., & Newport, E. (1996). Statistical learning by 8-month-old infants. *Science, 274*, 1926–1928.
Savage-Rumbaugh, S., & Lewin, R. (1996). *The ape at the brink of the human mind.* New York: Wiley.
Shannon, C. (1948). A mathematical theory of communication. *Bell System Technical Journal, 27*, 379–423, 623–656.
Shieber, S., & Baker, E. (2003). Abbreviated text input. In *International Conference on Intelligent UserInterfaces*, pp. 293–296.
Tanaka-Ishii, K. (2006). Word-based predictive text entry using adaptive language models. *Journal of Natural Language Engineering, 13*(1), 51–74.
Tanaka-Ishii, K. (2012). Information bias inside English words. *Journal of Quantitative Linguistics, 19*(1), 77–94.
Tanaka-Ishii, K., & Jin, Z. (2008). From phoneme to morpheme—another verification using corpus in English and Chinese. *Studia Linguistica* (Blackwell Publishing), *62*(2), 155–179.
Tanaka-Ishii, K., Inutsuka, Y., & Takeichi, M. (2001). Japanese input system with digits–Can Japanese text be estimated only from consonants? In *Proceedings of Human Language Technology Conference (HLT)*, pp. 211–218.
Tanaka-Ishii, K., Inutsuka, Y., & Takeichi, M. (2002). Entering text with a four-button device. In *Proceedings of the International Conference on Computational Linguistics (COLING)*, pp. 988–994.
Tanaka-Ishii, K., Inutsuka, Y., & Takeichi, M. (2003). Japanese text entry using small number of buttons. *Journal of Information Processing, 44*(2), 433–442. in Japanese.
Tegic9. (2000). Tegic9 home page. Retrieved from http://www.t9.com.
The CELEX Manual. (1990). English linguistic guide by Center for Lexical Information.
Wheeler, D. (1970). Processes in word recognition. *Cognitive Psychology, 1*, 59–85.
Zhikov, V., Takamura, H., & Okumura, M. (2010). An efficient algorithm for unsupervised word segmentation with branching entropy and MDL. In *EMNLP 2010*, pp. 832–842.

MacKenzie, S., & Tanaka-Ishii, K. (Eds.). (2007). *Text entry systems: Accessibility, mobility, [illegible]* [illegible]. Morgan Kaufmann [illegible]
Mallarmé, S. (1998). *Oeuvres complètes*. Gallimard.
Markov, A. (1913). Essai d'une recherche statistique sur le texte du roman [illegible]. Bulletin de l'Académie Impériale des Sciences de St. Pétersbourg.
Nelken, R., & Shieber, S. (2005). Arabic diacritization using weighted finite-state transducers. In *Proceedings of the [illegible] Workshop on Computational Approaches to Semitic Languages* (pp. [illegible]).
[illegible]
[illegible]
[illegible]
[illegible]
[illegible]
[illegible]
[illegible]
[illegible]
[illegible]
[illegible]
[illegible]
[illegible]

How Natural Are Artificial Languages?

Rebecca Smaha and Christiane Fellbaum

Abstract A full account of the structure and rules of natural languages remains an elusive goal for linguists. One way to gain insights into the mechanics of human language is to create an artificial language. Such languages are often constructed by speakers who are motivated by the desire to design a language with a "perfect" structure that lacks the idiosyncrasies of natural languages (e.g. Lojban). Others are invented by people interested in creating a utopia (as in the case of Esperanto) or a dystopia, as portrayed in certain works of science fiction (e.g. *Star Trek* and its Klingon language). In all cases, creators of the artificial languages strove to make them functional languages that would or could be accepted and usable by speakers. It seems therefore reasonable to assume that the inventors of these languages drew on their native linguistic knowledge and intuitions. They deliberately designed a lexicon appropriate to their purposes and probably reflected on the morphological and syntactic properties of their languages. By contrast, the statistical properties of natural languages are opaque to everyday speakers, although they have been shown to play a role in language acquisition (Safran et al. 1996) and linguistic behavior (Fine et al. 2013). Just as phonological and syntactic features of natural languages arguably draw from a universal inventory, statistical properties may set natural languages apart from other forms of superficially similar information-encoding systems. Rao et al. (2009) undertook a statistical analysis of several natural languages and non-linguistic systems including human chromosome sequences and the programming language Fortran. Rao et al. showed that the two kinds of data can be clearly differentiated in particular with respect to entropy, which measures the unpredictability of elements (such as words) in a sequence (such as a phrase or sentence). We extend this approach by comparing the statistical properties, including entropy, of two different artificial languages, Klingon

R. Smaha · C. Fellbaum (✉)
Princeton University, Princeton, NJ, USA
e-mail: fellbaum@princeton.edu

R. Smaha
e-mail: rsmaha@Princeton.EDU

© Springer International Publishing Switzerland 2015
N. Gala et al. (eds.), *Language Production, Cognition, and the Lexicon*,
Text, Speech and Language Technology 48, DOI 10.1007/978-3-319-08043-7_17

and Lojban, to Rao et al.'s data. The results reveal both similarities with, and differences from patterns that characterize natural languages and non-linguistic sequences.

Keywords Natural languages • Artificial languages • Klingon • Lojban • Statistical properties • Word frequencies • Zipf's law • Type-token distribution • Block entropy

1 Introduction

As Herodotus' famous story of the pharaoh Psamtik and his experiment into the origins of language indicates, people have long been fascinated by this unique form of human behavior. One approach to better understand the nature of language is to create a new one from scratch. Artificial languages have been designed by people interested in forming a utopia—or a dystopia, as is the case for some science fiction authors. A strong sense of power and idealism is linked to the culturally embedded idea that the language spoken by a group of people is connected to their worldview and their shared identity. Several movements have, with varying success, relied on newly created languages to transcend national, ethnic, political, and linguistic barriers. Esperanto (Zamenhof 1887) is perhaps the most famous among a long list of man-made languages, some of which are spoken natively. (http://en.wikipedia.org/wiki/List_of_constructed_languages).

Traditional linguistic analyses have examined the phonological, morphological syntactic, lexical and semantic properties of a language. More recently, people have come to view language more abstractly, as data consisting of strings of units (sounds, letters, words) whose sequencing follows statistical patterns. In this paper, we ask whether the statistical patterns that have been observed for natural languages are also found in constructed languages.

2 Statistical Properties of Natural Language

We investigate two artificial languages, Klingon and Lojban, in terms of two statistical measures, type-token ratios and block entropy.

2.1 Zipf's Law

The frequency of words in natural languages, as measured in terms of types (distinct word forms, normalized to their uninflected forms) and tokens (the number of occurrences of such forms) follows a power law, formulated by George Kingsley Zipf in 1935 and known as Zipf's Law. Zipf's Law states that the frequency (the number of tokens) of a word type is inversely proportional to its rank in a frequency table. Thus, tokens of the second most frequent word type (rank 2) should occur ½ times as often as tokens of the highest ranked word; tokens of the third most frequent word type should occur 1/3 times as often as tokens of the first-ranked word type, etc. (Zipf 1935). A general version of this distribution is given in Eq. 1:

$$f(k; s, N) = \frac{1}{k^s H_{N,s}} \tag{1}$$

where k is the rank, s is the exponent (classically, 1), N is the number of elements, and H is the harmonic number. Informally put, few words are used very frequently and many words are rarely used. In fact, an inspection of the Brown Corpus shows that the law does not hold for words at the top of the rank list but does apply if one discounts the most frequent words. Zipf's Law has been argued to apply to other statistics, such as income and population rankings, though it was originally observed specifically for natural languages. We conclude that it is a good initial metric against which to compare artificial languages.

2.2 Entropy

Entropy is a central concept in Information Theory, first described by Claude Shannon (1948), who equated informativeness with unexpectedness. Entropy is a measure of the unexpectedness, or uncertainty, of a random variable and is commonly used to estimate the expected value of a message's information. Intuitively, the entropy of a rare, less probable event is high, making its occurrence "surprising" and informative, whereas the entropy of a frequent and thus unsurprising word is low. Conditional entropy measures the expectedness of a variable given the presence of another, known variable. For example, an occurrence of a vowel following the sequence *spl* in an English word is highly probably and thus carries little information (or low entropy). The reason is, of course, that the phonotactic rules of English constrain the sequences of possible sounds and thus condition the probability of a given sound following a preceding one. Similar rules govern syntax and lexical collocations, which tend to be idiosyncratic (the word *neck* following the verb *crane* carries low information, unlike its near-synonym *turn*, which is found much less often in this semi-fixed expression). As one would expect, natural languages, which must both serve effective communication and convey new information encoded in novel phrases and sentences, show entropy values somewhere between the maximum (totally random) and minimum (fully ordered and predictable).

Our work examines the entropy of sequences of words in Klingon and Lojban, specifically the entropy of blocks of six consecutive words, or hexagrams. The values are compared with the equivalent values for several natural languages as well as those for non-linguistic sequences. Entropy is thus our principal measure for determining whether artificial languages show the same or similar statistical properties as natural languages or whether they pattern like non-linguistic sequences (or neither).

Shannon entropy has been measured to determine whether or not other sequences of symbols could be natural languages; in 2010, the entropy of the undeciphered Pictish symbols was calculated, and it was concluded that they form part of a written system instead of a heraldic or random one (Lee et al. 2010).

3 Related Work

We were inspired by a 2009 article in *Science*, where Rajesh Rao asserts that analyses of the statistical entropy of a corpus can differentiate natural languages from nonlinguistic systems (Rao et al. 2009). In particular, he compares the conditional entropy of some natural languages to that of other systems such as protein sequences and programming languages, finding a clear distinction among them. Our work extends Rao's analyses to data from artificial languages and asks whether they pattern more like natural languages or like the non-linguistic sequences Rao examines.

Rao's paper tries to determine whether the so-called Indus script–some 3,000 short sequences of symbols found in northern India on pottery, seals, and other objects dating from roughly 2,600–1,900 BCE in northern India—likely represents a natural language. To date, no bilingual text or other clues to the decipherment of this script have been found (Yadav et al. 2010). As his critics have pointed out, Rao's corpus—the total number of inscriptions–is quite small, making statistical analyses not fully reliable.

Farmer et al. (2009) dispute the claim that conditional entropy can be used to distinguish types of languages, arguing that Rao's data is misleading by comparing natural languages only to fully ordered or random datasets. Instead, they believe that the Indus Script is nonlinguistic due to the brevity of the known inscriptions and the paucity of symbols. Yet many people, including Rao, claim that the Indus Script text is too complex to be a heraldic or other nonlinguistic symbol system, arguing that the corpus exhibits more similarities to natural languages than one could expect by chance: it has similar entropic structure, follows a Zipfian distribution, has linearity and directionality, and seems to have syntactic structure (Rao et al. 2010).

Given these disagreements about the ability of conditional entropy calculations to differentiate types of languages, this work examines the block entropy of several known artificial languages. Their entropy has not previously been measured or compared to that of natural languages, and it is possible that this measure, along with type-token distribution, will provide insight about the similarities or differences between natural and artificial languages.

4 The Data

Our analyses of two artificial languages, Klingon and Lojban, is based on corpora of written data that we compiled and examined. Like Rao's examination of the Indus script, it falls within the broader enterprise of corpus linguistics. Linguistic analyses based on corpora are necessarily limited to the data included in the corpora, which may not be representative of the language as a whole. It is therefore important to examine a corpus that is neither too small nor biased; as described in Sect. 4.3, we attempted as best as possible to construct representative corpora of the two languages under investigation. On the other hand, the advantages of corpus linguistics are clear: a corpus is stable and can serve as a reference for many kinds of analyses by linguists interested in diverse aspects of a language.

4.1 Klingon

Klingon is the language spoken by a warrior race in the Star Trek science fiction television series and movies. It was first spoken on screen in 1979 and was later developed by Marc Okrand into a full language in the 1985 book *The Klingon Dictionary* (Okrand 1985). Okrand allegedly designed Klingon to be dissimilar to natural languages by endowing it with unusual phonetics, phonology, and word order. Although Klingon's lexicon is necessarily particularly rich in words related to its science fiction setting, well-known texts like the Bible and some of Shakespeare's plays have been translated into Klingon. For the non-Klingon speaker, we cite here the first lines of Hamlet's famous "To be, or not to be" soliloquy as translated by Nicholas and Strader (2000) along with the modern English version:

taH pagh taHbe'. DaH mu'tlheghvam vIqelnIS.
(*To be, or not to be*: *—that is the question: —*)
quv'a', yabDaq San vaQ cha, pu' je SIQDI'?
(*Whether 'tis nobler in the mind to suffer*
The slings and arrows of outrageous fortune,)
pagh, Seng bIQ'a'Hey SuvmeH nuHmey SuqDI',
Or to take arms against a sea of troubles,
'ej, Suvmo', rInmoHDI'?
And by opposing end them?

Klingon today claims to have the largest number of speakers of any artificial language.

4.2 Lojban

Lojban, known as the "logical language," was created in the 1950s in an attempt to construct an unambiguous language. It is based on the rules of predicate logic (Brown 1960) and its lexicon draws inspiration from multiple unrelated natural languages. Lojban features several broad word classes: small function words (cmavo), proper nouns (cmene), and predicate words (brivla). The brivla can be subdivided into five-letter root words (gismu) of which there are about 1,350, borrowed words (fu'ivla), and compound words (lujvo), which are composed of combinations of gismu in a shortened form and/or cmavo.

Here are the first sentences of Lewis Carroll's *Alice in Wonderland* as translated into Lojban (Xorxes), which exemplify its unusual phonemes, syntax and punctuation:

> Ni'o la.alis. co'a tatpi lo nu zutse lo rirxe korbi re'o lo mensi gi'e
> zukte fi no da.i.abu cu so'u roi sutra zgana lo cukta poi my
> tcidu.i ku'i cy vasru no pixra ja nuncasnu.i « lu ji'a ma prali—
> sei la.alis. cu pensi—fi lo cukta poi vasru no pixra ja nuncasnu li'u»
> (*Alice was beginning to get very tired of sitting by her sister on the bank, and of having nothing to do*: *once or twice she had peeped into the book her sister was reading, but it had no pictures or conversations in it, 'and what is the use of a book,' thought Alice 'without pictures or conversation?'*)

Lojban and Klingon appear to be very different languages, both from each other and from natural languages, and thus provide a good basis for statistical comparison.

4.3 The Corpora

We constructed a corpus of Klingon novels, plays, short stories, and poems. Most of these sources were manually translated from English or other natural languages, but they also include works composed originally in Klingon. The corpus consists of 51,125 words: 15,787 distinct tokens—including punctuation—and 3,730 types. The corpus was tokenized using the Natural Language Toolkit software (Bird et al. 2009) and stemmed by removing known prefixes and suffixes iteratively, matching the affixes to a dictionary if the tokens were five characters or longer.

A corpus of Lojban texts—plays, poems, short stories, novels—consisting of 112,122 words was gathered from online sources. It has 4,619 distinct tokens and 2,285 types. The Lojban corpus was tokenized using the NLTK software. Compound words were expanded into their component forms using preexisting software (Curnow 2001).

5 Analyses

We present the different statistical analyses of our data.

5.1 *Word Frequency*

Tables 1 and 2 show the most frequent words in Klingon and Lojban, respectively, and the comparison with the corresponding rank list for English words from the one million word Brown Corpus (Francis and Kučera 1982).

Despite the relatively small corpora, both Klingon and Lojban show great similarity to English. The existence of Klingon words that differ significantly from English (e.g. *lord, honor*, and *situation*) are due to the corpus's domain specificity and small size. The unusual nature of Lojban and its dependence on small function words is clearly shown in its most common words, but in fact they serve to a large degree the same purpose as function words in natural languages like English.

5.2 *Type-Token Ratio*

We calculated the type-token ratios for Klingon and Lojban in order to see whether they follow a Zipfian distribution, similar to natural languages (Zipf 1935). The number of instances of each type and token could be counted and graphed as shown below.

Figure 1 shows the type-token distributions for both Klingon and Lojban for the 300 most common types. The graphs show a pseudo-Zipfian distribution, similar to natural languages, with a long tail of infrequently occurring types. Klingon (left panel) follows this trend relatively smoothly, meaning that the instances of each type (the number of tokens corresponding to it) decrease rapidly.

As shown in the right panel of Fig. 1, the type-token relation is pseudo-Zipfian for Lojban, like natural languages and Klingon, but the drop-off of the trend is much steeper than the usual Zipfian inverse relationship. The frequencies of the most common words decrease precipitously, which is likely due to the small corpus size.

There are more words in Lojban that are among the most frequent (upper left corner of the graph), and the words in the tail are still more frequent than those in the Klingon tail. This may be due (in part) to a very careful construction of the Lojban lexicon.

Table 1 Comparison of the 20 most frequent words in English (Brown Corpus, Francis and Kučera 1982) and Klingon

Rank	Most common English words	Type	Brown corpus frequency	Most common Klingon Words	Frequency in this corpus	Rough translation	Rank in brown corpus (Eng. word at that rank)
1	the	article	69,975	‘ej	1,392	and (for sentences)	4 (and)
2	be	verb	39,175	ghaH	1,068	3rd sing, pronoun	7 [he), 19 [she)
3	of	prep.	36,432	je	1,021	and (for nouns)	4 (and)
4	and	co. conj	28,872	‘e’	878	that (rel. pronoun)	17 (that)
5	a	article	23,073	vaj	731	so. then, thus	88 [so)
6	in	prep.	20,870	jatlh	631	say, speak (verb)	33 [say)
7	he	pron.	19,427	neH	493	desire, only	66 (only), 134 (want.)
8	to	infin.	15,025	Hoch	475	all. every, everyone	34 (all)
9	have	verb	12,458	chaH	441	3rd pl. pronoun	14 (they)
10	to	prep.	11,165	“ach	380	but even	28 (but)
11	it	pron.	10,942	joH	346	lord. lady, king (noun)	1,475 (lord)
12	for	prep.	8,996	ja’	318	tell, report (verb)	103 (tell)
13	I	pron.	8,387	quv	305	honor (noun)	2,228 (honor)
14	they	pron.	8,284	‘oH	292	it (pronoun)	11 (it)
15	with	prep.	7,286	ghaj	272	have, own (verb)	9 (have)
16	not	neg adj	6,976	DaH	260	now	69 (now)
17	that	sub conj	6,468	ta’	249	do (verb)	27 (do)
18	on	prep.	6,188	legh	240	look, see (verb)	61 (see)
19	she	pron.	6,039	pagh	236	none, nothing	223 (nothing)

(continued)

Table 1 (continued)

Rank	Most common English words	Type	Brown corpus frequency	Most common Klingon Words	Frequency in this corpus	Rough translation	Rank in brown corpus (Eng. word at that rank)
20	as	sub conj	6,029	ghu'	235	situation (noun)	418 (situation)

The Klingon corpus was stemmed using a regular expression stemmer to remove affixes on words of length 5 or higher

5.3 Block Entropy

In order to compare the results with those of Rao et al. the block entropy (Eq. 2) for n-grams with $1 \leq n \leq 6$ was calculated for the Klingon and Lojban corpora, using the formula given in Eq. 2:

$$H_N = -\sum_i p_i^{(N)} \log p_i^{(N)} \tag{2}$$

In this equation, p(i) is the frequency of n-gram i divided by all possible n-grams in the corpus (corpus length − (n + 1)). The block entropies were normalized by taking the base of the logarithm as the alphabet size (number of distinct tokens), following Rao (2010). The results were graphed as a function of n and can be compared to those provided by Rao for natural languages, the Indus script, and some nonlinguistic systems. Rao (Rao 2010) calculated the block entropy of English with two types of tokens: words and characters (the tokens of the other systems were their symbols or, in the case of Fortran, a combination of words, punctuation, and variables). This study calculates the block entropy of Klingon and Lojban for words only. Thus a valid comparison can only be drawn between Rao's English words data and our data.

Block entropy of n-grams was calculated for the Klingon and Lojban corpora and normalized by the number of distinct tokens for each, as shown in Fig. 2. The left panel contains the results for Klingon and Lojban; the right panel shows Rao's results for comparison to the Indus script, English words, English characters, Sumer, Tagalog, Sanskrit, Tamil, DNA, a protein sequence, music, Fortran, and minimum and maximum entropy (Rao 2010). The calculated block entropy values for Klingon and Lojban are shown in Fig. 2 as a function of n; note that the $n = 6$ value for Klingon is in fact smaller than the $n = 5$ value. Table 3 gives the normalized values for n grams with $1 \leq n \leq 6$ for Klingon and Lojban.

Table 2 Comparison of the 20 most frequent words in English (Brown Corpus, Francis and Kučera 1982) and in Lojban

Rank	Most common English words	Type	Brown corpus frequency	Most common Lojban words	Frequency in this corpus	Type	Rough translation
1	the	article	69,975	lo	13,481	cmavo	the really is (descriptor)
2	be	verb	39,175	.i	5,534	cmavo	links sentences
3	of	prep.	36,432	nu	4,119	cmavo	abstractor: general event
4	and	co. conj	28,872	cu	4,079	cmavo	separates selbri
5	a	article	23,073	se	2,620	cmavo	places
6	in	prep.	20,870	mi	1,909	cmavo	me/we
7	he	pron.	19,427	la	1,858	cmavo	that named (descriptor)
8	to	infin.	15,025	le	1,529	cmavo	the described (descriptor)
9	have	verb	12,458	ni'o	1,408	cmavo	new topic
10	to	prep.	11,165	lu	1,347	cmavo	start quote
11	it	pron.	10,942	gi'e	1,344	cmavo	and (for sentences)
12	for	prep.	8,996	li'u	1,311	cmavo	end quote
13	I	pron.	8,387	be	1,238	cmavo	links sumti
14	they	pron.	8,284	na	1,113	cmavo	negator (for sentences)
15	with	prep.	7,286	cusku	948	gismu	say. express
16	not	neg adj	6,976	ca	918	cmavo	during
17	that	sub conj	6,468	do	858	cmavo	you
18	on	prep.	6,183	ka	708	cmavo	abstractor: property/ quality
19	she	pron.	6,039	noi	694	cmavo	non-restrictive rel. clause
20	as	sub conj	6,029	da	687	cmavo	something

The Lojban corpus was parsed so that its compound words were separated into their components, which were then counted as separate words

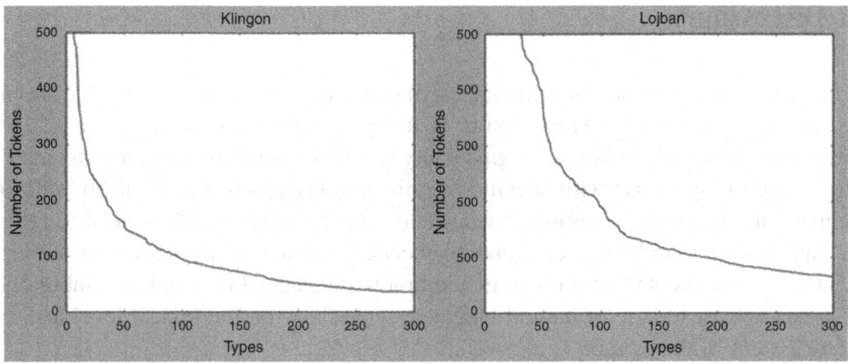

Fig. 1 Magnified type-token distributions for Klingon and Lojban

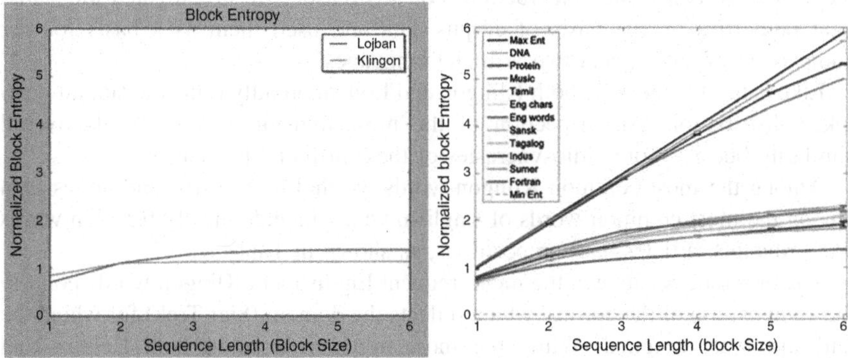

Fig. 2 *Left* Normalized block entropy for n grams with $1 \leq n \leq 6$ for the Lojban and Klingon corpora plotted together. *Right* Block entropy of several natural languages and nonlinguistic systems taken from Rao (2010), graphed on the same scale for ease of comparison. The order of languages in each legend matches the order of data on the *right* y-axis of each graph

Table 3 Values of the normalized block entropy for n grams with $1 \leq n \leq 6$ for the Lojban and Klingon corpora

n-gram	Klingon	Lojban
1	0.832699	0.686294
2	1.092725	1.097504
3	1.119228	1.280360
4	1.122231	1.345388
5	1.122825	1.366140
6	1.122823	1.366142

6 Discussion

The statistical properties of artificial languages have not, to our knowledge, been previously investigated. Their design is likely to be influenced by some of the properties that their creators, linguistically astute speakers of natural languages, are aware of and chose with specific intentions: a lexicon that lends itself well to convey the meanings of entities, events and properties that speakers need to refer to; appropriate morphology or syntax to encode the structural dependencies among sentence constituents, etc. Lojban in addition was designed to avoid the ambiguity that is so characteristic of natural languages especially on the lexical level and to some extent in the syntax.

Phonological, morphological, syntactic and lexical aspects of Klingon and Lojban are man-made and truly "artificial." But the statistical properties of these languages are less likely to be open to introspection and do not easily lend themselves to deliberate construction. For this reason, we investigated the statistical properties on the basis of corpus data and used them as a basis for our comparison of natural and two artificial languages.

Like natural languages, both Klingon and Lojban broadly follow a Zipfian type-token distribution. An inspection of the most frequent words reveals overall similarity but also some idiosyncrasies of these artificial languages.

Among the most common Klingon words we find more verbs and nouns than among the most common words of English, which include mostly function words like pronouns, articles, and prepositions, as shown in Table 1.

The differences between the most frequent English and Klingon words point to the composition of the corpus, which reflects the domain (Star Trek) for which the language was designed. While the most frequent verbs in both English and Klingon are "light" verbs (*do, be, have*) the Klingon corpus includes highly frequent speech verbs (*say, tell/report*). Among the nouns, *joH* (*lord, lady*, or *king*) occurs far more frequently in Klingon than in English—this is likely due to Klingon's norms of politeness (e.g. *Mister*, a possible analog to *joH*, is ranked number 96 in the Brown Corpus). Overall, the frequency distribution demonstrates that Klingon shares many similarities with natural languages.

Lojban's type-token relationship is similarly pseudo-Zipfian, but the curve is bumpier and shows a much steeper drop-off than Klingon. This may be due to bias in the contents of both corpora and their small sizes; the slope of the type-token curves may reflect the artificial nature of the language. In addition, the twenty most common words in Lojban—shown in Table 2—are almost exclusively *cmavo*, or small function words rather than content words. While function words are also among the most frequent tokens in English and other natural languages, Lojban has more function words, a fact resulting most likely from its design based on predicate logic. Besides their greater number, Lojban function words do not map easily onto English, making appropriate English translations and hence rankings difficult, unlike in the case of Klingon. For instance, *lu* (ranked 10) and *li'u* (ranked 12), signify the beginning and end of a grammatical quote, respectively.

Not surprisingly then, the Lojban frequency rank list contains more function words than the corresponding English list; we find only one verb and two pronouns, whereas the corresponding ranks for English include several (modal and auxiliary) verbs. While both English and Lojban exhibit a similar type-token distribution, a closer analysis of the most common words reveals large systematic differences in the nature and use of these words. But despite the lexical differences, the type-token graphs of Klingon and Lojban roughly follow Zipf's law: the frequencies of their words is inversely proportional to the rank of the words' frequencies, with function words ranking the highest. The fact that these corpora are much smaller than those that serve as the basis for studies of the properties of natural languages can likely explain the bumpiness of the trends, which are shown magnified in Fig. 1. Notwithstanding the paucity of data, the pseudo-Zipfian distributions indicate structural similarity between natural languages and these two artificial languages.

The second statistical analysis, block entropy, has been used by Rao to argue for the Indus script's status as a natural language, as distinct from non-linguistic sequences. Our block entropy calculations for the two artificial languages show that Klingon and Lojban cluster with the natural languages examined by Rao and, interestingly, the programming language Fortran (Fig. 2, Table 3). A more fine-grained look reveals that the Lojban and Klingon trends fall between the minimum entropy and Fortran (as calculated by Rao). Even though the values for $n = 1$ are nearly the same for the natural languages, the artificial languages and Fortran, the slope at $n > 1$ is slightly larger for natural languages. Comparing the left and right panels of Fig. 2 suggests that Klingon and Lojban bear a greater resemblance to Fortran—which could be considered a very specialized artificial language—than English or any other natural language. This is not surprising given that the methodologically valid comparison between the block entropies of the artificial languages and English words reveals wide differences, which supports Rao's claim that the Indus script is most likely linguistic as its behavior falls within the natural language cluster. Future studies with larger and possibly more balanced Lojban and Klingon corpora might reveal the robustness of our findings (but note that Rao's Indus script data were much more sparse).

The results for the type-token distribution reflects the robustness of Zipf's law and its application to many other, non-linguistic systems. The entropy calculations, while more specific and thus possibly a better measure for distinguishing natural languages from non-linguistic systems, may be more sensitive to the size of the corpus. Further work needs to be done to confirm the contribution of this statistical measure to the characterization of natural and artificial languages.

7 Conclusion

An initial statistical study of the properties of Klingon and Lojban reveals both similarities and differences with natural languages. The type-token ratio—a small number of words with high frequency and long tail of many infrequent words—is the same for both types of language, extending this apparently universal feature to artificial languages. The entropy calculations, while broadly clustering Klingon and Lojban with natural languages, reveal a closer similarity with Fortran than with English and Tagalog. Our investigation indicates that future work with additional constructed languages and larger datasets might well provide promising insights into the statistical properties of natural and constructed languages.

Acknowledgments Funding for this work, which was performed as part of R. S.'s graduation requirement, was generously provided by the Princeton University Program in Linguistics. R. S. is grateful to Constantine Nakos and Vyas Ramasubramani for technical help.

References

Bird, S., Loper, E., & Klein, E. (2009). *Natural language processing with Python*. Sebastopol: O'Reilly Media Inc.

Brown, J. C. (1960). Loglan. *Scientific American, 202*, 43–63.

Curnow, R. (2001). Jbofihe. Retrieved from http://www.rc0.org.uk/jbofihe/ and http://www.rpcurnow.force9.co.uk/jbofihe/.

Farmer, S., Sproat, R., & Witzel, M. (2009). A refutation of the claimed refutation of the nonlinguistic nature of Indus symbols. Retrieved from http://www.safarmer.com/Refutation3.pdf.

Fine, A. B., Jaeger, T. F., Farmer, T. A., & Qian, T. (2013). Rapid expectation adaptation during syntactic comprehension. *PLoS ONE, 8*(10), e77661.

Francis, W. N., & Kučera, H. (1982). *Frequency analysis of English usage: Lexicon and grammar*. Boston: Houghton Mifflin.

Lee, R., Jonathan, P., & Ziman, P. (2010). Pictish symbols revealed as a written language through application of Shannon entropy. *Proceedings of the Royal Society A, 466*, 2545–2560.

Lujvo expander version 0.2. (2001). Retrieved from the Lojban electronic mailing list http://tech.groups.yahoo.com/group/lojban/message/11387.

Nicholas, N., & Strader, A. (2000). *Hamlet Prince of Denmark: The restored Klingon version*. New York: Pocket Books.

Okrand, M. (1985). *The Klingon dictionary*. New York: Pocket Books.

Rao, R., Yadav, N., Vahia, M. N., Joglekar, H., Adhikari, R., & Mahadevan, I. (2009). Entropic evidence for linguistic structure in the Indus script. *Science, 324*, 1165. doi:10.1126/science.1170391.

Rao, R., Yadav, N., Vahia, M. N., Joglekar, H., Adhikari, R., & Mahadevan, I. (2010). Entropy, the Indus script, and language: A reply to R. Sproat. *Computational Linguistics, 36*(4), 795–805.

Rao, R. (2010). Probabilistic analysis of an ancient undeciphered script. *IEEE Computer, 43*(4), 76–80.

Safran, E., Aslin, R., & Newport, E. (1996). Statistical learning by 8-months old infants. *Science, 274*(5294), 1926–1928.

Shannon, C. E. (1948). A Mathematical theory of communication. *Bell System Technical Journal, 27*(3), 379–423.

Yadav, N., Joglekar, H., Rao, R., Vahia, M. N., Adhikari, R., & Mahadevan, I. (2010). Statistical analysis of the Indus script using n-grams. *PLoS ONE, 5*(3), e9506. doi:10.1371/journal.pone.0009506.

Zamenhof, L. L. (1887). *Unua Libro*. Warsaw.

Zipf, G. K. (1935). *The psychobiology of language*. Boston: Houghton-Mifflin.

Handling Defaults and Their Exceptions in Controlled Natural Language

Rolf Schwitter

Abstract Defaults are statements in natural language that generalise over a particular kind of objects or over what a particular kind of objects does. Defaults are very useful in human communication since we often do not have complete information about the world, but we must be able to draw conclusions about what is normally the case. However, these conclusions are only tentative and sometimes we have to withdraw them and revise our theory if new information becomes available. In this paper, we propose the use of a controlled natural language as a high-level specification language for modelling commonsense reasoning problems. We investigate how defaults and exceptions can be incorporated into an existing controlled natural language and what kind of formal machinery is required to represent and reason with them in a non-monotonic way. Our controlled natural language looks completely natural at first glance since it consists of a well-defined subset of English but it is in fact a formal language that is computer-processable and can be translated unambiguously via discourse representation structures into an executable answer set program. Answer set programming is a relatively new logic-based knowledge representation formalism and is well-suited to solve commonsense reasoning problems.

Keywords Controlled natural language · Automated reasoning

1 Introduction

Most of what we learn and know about the world can be expressed in terms of defaults. Defaults are statements that often contain words such as *normally*, *generally* or *typically* and are used in commonsense reasoning to express general laws and

---

R. Schwitter (✉)
Department of Computing, Macquarie University, Sydney, NSW 2109, Australia
e-mail: Rolf.Schwitter@mq.edu.au

© Springer International Publishing Switzerland 2015
N. Gala et al. (eds.), *Language Production, Cognition, and the Lexicon*,
Text, Speech and Language Technology 48, DOI 10.1007/978-3-319-08043-7_18

regularities (Pelletier and Asher 1997). Defaults allow us to make non-monotonic inferences based on what we currently know in the absence of complete information. The resulting conclusions have always a tentative character and sometimes we have to withdraw these conclusions and revise our theory later in the light of new information. The most interesting feature of defaults is that they allow for exceptions that can refute a default's conclusion or render the default inapplicable.

In this paper, we discuss how defaults and their exceptions can be incorporated into a controlled natural language and how this controlled natural language can be translated automatically into a non-monotonic formalism for automated reasoning. In our context, a controlled natural language is a well-defined subset of a natural language that allows for formal knowledge representation and automated reasoning from seemingly informal textual specifications (Schwitter 2010). These specifications are parsed and translated into a target knowledge representation formalism. There exist a number of non-monotonic formalisms for representing defaults and exceptions in a mathematically precise manner (Brewka et al. 2007; Gebser et al. 2012; Gelfond and Kahl 2014; McCarthy 1980; McDermott and Doyle 1982; Moore 1985), but these formalisms have not been used so far in a systematic way as target languages for controlled language processing. We want to change this and propose the use of Answer Set Programming (ASP) (Gebser et al. 2012) as knowledge representation formalism for controlled natural language processing because of its support for non-monotonic reasoning and its high degree of elaboration tolerance, i.e., ASP programs are relatively easy to modify.

The rest of this paper is structured as follows: In Sect. 2, we give a brief introduction to ASP and present the most important language constructs that are required for representing and reasoning with commonsense knowledge. In Sect. 3, we introduce the controlled natural language PENG^{ASP} that is used to write specifications that are translated via discourse representation structures into executable ASP programs. In Sect. 4, we discuss how defaults and exceptions can be expressed in PENG^{ASP} and how these statements are further processed and translated into an ASP program. In Sect. 5, we show how we can refer from exceptions written in PENG^{ASP} to conflicting defaults and how we can establish preferences among these defaults. Finally, in Sect. 6, we conclude.

2 Answer Set Programming

ASP is a relatively novel logic-based knowledge representation formalism that has its roots in logic programming with negation, deductive databases, non-monotonic reasoning and constraint solving (Brewka et al. 2011; Gebser et al. 2012). ASP combines a rich modeling language for knowledge-intensive applications with high-performance solving capabilities. In contrast to Prolog where a solution for a problem representation is computed by a derivation for a query, in ASP an answer set solver is used to perform search and search problems are reduced to computing one or more stable models (= answer sets) (Eiter et al. 2009; Gelfond and Lifschitz 1988;

Lifschitz 2008). An ASP program consists of a set of rules that have the following form:

$$L_0 \ or \ \cdots \ or \ L_k \leftarrow L_{k+1}, \ldots, L_m, \ not \ L_{m+1}, \ldots, not \ L_n. \quad (1)$$

where all L_i's are literals. A literal is an atom or its negation. A positive atom has the form $p(t_1, \ldots, t_n)$ where p is a predicate symbol of arity n and $t_1, \ldots, t_n$ are object constants or variables. A negative atom has the form $\neg\, p(t_1, \ldots, t_n)$ where the symbol $\neg$ denotes strong negation. The symbol $\leftarrow$ stands for an implication. The expression on the left-hand side of the implication is called the *head* of the rule and the expression on the right-hand side is called the *body* of the rule. The head may consist of an epistemic disjunction of literals denoted by the symbol *or*. Literals in the body may be preceded by negation as failure denoted by the symbol *not*. The head or the body of a rule can be empty. A rule with an empty head is called an *integrity constraint* and a rule with an empty body is called a *fact*. Finally, a rule with a single positive atom in the head and without negation as failure in the body is called a *definite rule*. In order to make rules executable, we replace $\neg$ with -, $\leftarrow$ with :-, and *or* with |.

Facts and Definite Rules. The following is a simple ASP program that consists of a number of facts and a definite rule:

```
o(1). o(2). o(3).
p(1). p(2).
q(1).                                   (2)
r(1,2). s(3,2).
t(Y) :- r(X,Y), s(Z,Y).
```

This program has a single answer set:

```
{o(1) o(2) o(3) p(1) p(2) q(1) r(1,2) s(3,2) t(2)}          (3)
```

that consists of all facts of the program plus the literal `t(2)` that has been derived from the definite rule.

Negation as Failure. The addition of the following rule with a negation failure operator (`not`) to the program in (2):

```
-u(X) :- p(X), not q(X).                (4)
```

adds the literal `-u(2)` to the answer set in (3). Note that this rule uses strong negation in the head of the rule and negation as failure (weak negation) in the body. In contrast to strong negation, weak negation does not support the explicit assertion of falsity of an atom; it rather assumes that an atom is false if it is not provable that the atom is true.

Epistemic Disjunction. The addition of the following rule with an epistemic disjunction (|) in its head to the program:

$$\texttt{w(X)} \mid \texttt{v(X)} :- -\texttt{u(X)}. \quad (5)$$

results in two answer sets: one that extends the existing answer set with the literal w(2) and another one that extends it with the literal v(2). Under the interpretation of epistemic disjunction there exists no third answer set that contains both literals because epistemic disjunction subscribes to a minimality criterion where an answer set that is a superset of another answer set is not considered as a solution since it contains redundant information.

Integrity Constraints. The addition of the following integrity constraint to our program:

$$:- \texttt{w(X)}. \quad (6)$$

removes the first answer set that contains w(2) but keeps the second one that contains v(2). Integrity constraints specify conditions that must not become true in any answer set.

Choice Rules. The addition of the following choice rule to our program:

$$1 \{ \texttt{r (X,Y)} : \texttt{o(X)} \} 1 :- \texttt{t(Y)}. \quad (7)$$

makes sure that if t(Y) holds, then all resulting answer sets will contain exactly one literal of the form r(X,Y), under the condition that o(X) holds. This is the case for our existing answer set that contains all the literals in (3) plus the literals -u(2) and v(2). However, as soon as we add a new fact, for example, of the form r(3,2) to our program, then the choice rule is violated and we will end up with an unsatisfiable program.

Aggregates. An aggregate is a function that is applied to a symbolic set and calculates a value. For example, the addition of the following rule to our program:

$$\texttt{a(C)} :- \texttt{\#count}\{\texttt{X} : -\texttt{u(X)}\} = \texttt{C}. \quad (8)$$

with the aggregate function #count in the body applies to the symbolic set {-u/1} and returns the literal a(1) as part of the answer set. In our context, aggregates are helpful to find answers to quantitative questions.

The combination of strong negation (-) and weak negation (not) allows us to express the closed world assumption (Reiter 1978) for a specific literal. For example, the addition of the following rule to our program:

$$-\texttt{t(X)} :- \texttt{o(X)}, \texttt{not t(X)}. \quad (9)$$

adds the two negative literals -t(1) and -t(3) to our answer set and guarantees that the answer set of our program is complete with respect to a given literal. That means the following three literals -t(1), t(2), -t(3) are now part of the answer set. For some literals such as -u/1, the opposite to rule (9) is more appropriate to express the closed world assumption:

$$\texttt{u(Y) :- o(Y), not -u(Y).} \tag{10}$$

This rule adds the two literals `u(1)` and `u(3)` to our answer set that finally looks as follows:

$$\begin{array}{l}\{\ \texttt{o(1) o(2) o(3) p(1) p(2) q(1) r(1,2) s(3,2) t(2)} \\ \quad \texttt{-u(2) -t(1) -t(3) a(1) u(1) u(3) v(2)}\}\end{array} \tag{11}$$

It is important to note that an ASP program with strong and weak negation can include closed world assumption rules for some of its literals and leave the other literals in the scope of the open world assumption (under the open world assumption failure to derive a fact does not imply the opposite).

3 Controlled Natural Language Processing and ASP

The controlled natural language PENG^{ASP} (Schwitter 2013) is similar to PENG Light (White and Schwitter 2009) and Attempto Controlled English (Fuchs et al. 2008), in particular with regard to the use of discourse representation theory (DRT) (van Eijck and Kamp 2011; Kamp and Reyle 1993) as intermediate representation language, but PENG^{ASP} does not rely on full first-order logic (FOL) as target language as the use of DRT would suggest. This is because the language of FOL is in certain aspects more expressive than the language of ASP and allows to express complex (nested) formulas that can result in undecidable theories. Moreover, FOL is not adequate for representing commonsense knowledge because it has difficulties to deal with non-monotonic reasoning. ASP, in contrast, allows us to represent and process commonsense knowledge because of its unique connectives and non-monotonic entailment relation. Beyond that, ASP is still expressive enough to represent function-free FOL formulas of the $\exists^*\forall^*$ prefix class in form of a logic program (Lierler and Lifschitz 2013). Of course, the specific features of the ASP language have an impact on what we can express on the level of the controlled natural language and require a modified version of DRT that links the controlled natural language to the ASP program.

Let us introduce the controlled natural language PENG^{ASP} with the help of a logic puzzle that is known as the *Martian-Venusian Club* (Smullyan 1987). This puzzle is part of the TPTP problem library (PUZ006-1.p) and has been used for testing and evaluating automated theorem proving systems (Sutcliffe 2009). The problem specification of the puzzle is available in English and it is usually the task of the programmer to encode this puzzle in a suitable formal language so that it can be processed by an automated theorem proving system.

Martian–Venusian Club
Here's the situation: human observers in this exclusive club on Ganymede can't distinguish Martians from Venusians, males from females, except for the fact that Venusian women and Martian men always tell the truth and Venusian man and Martian women always lie.
Ork says "Bog is from Venus."
Bog says "Ork is from Mars."
Ork says "Bog is male."
Bog says "Ork is female."
Who's what? (sex & race). (12)

Instead of encoding this puzzle in a formal language, we reconstruct it in PENG^{ASP} and translate the resulting specification automatically via discourse representation structures into an executable ASP program. A possible reconstruction of the puzzle in PENG^{ASP} looks as follows:

Every Martian is from Mars.
Exclude that a Venusian is from Mars.
Every Venusian is from Venus.
Exclude that a Martian is from Venus.
Every person is a Martian or is a Venusian.
Every person is female or is male.
Every person who is a male Martian or who is a female Venusian is truthful.
Every person who is a female Martian or who is a male Venusian lies.
Exclude that a person who lies is truthful.
Ork is a person and Bog is a person. (13)
If Ork is truthful then Bog is from Venus.
Exclude that Bog is from Venus and that Ork lies.
If Bog is truthful then Ork is from Mars.
Exclude that Bog lies and that Ork is from Mars.
If Ork is truthful then Bog is male.
Exclude that Ork lies and that Bog is male.
If Bog is truthful then Ork is female.
Who is a Martian?
Is Ork male?

As this example illustrates, a PENG^{ASP} specification is a sequence of declarative, imperative, and interrogative sentences that are possibly anaphorically connected. It is important to note that the syntactic structure of these sentences is enforced by an authoring tool similar to (Schwitter et al. 2003) that informs the author of a specification during the writing process about the approved constructions of the controlled language. The language processor of PENG^{ASP} consists of a unification-based grammar, a lexicon, and a chart parser. The grammar is crucial since it specifies the admissible linguistic structures of PENG^{ASP} and guarantees for example that a noun phrase that triggers an existential quantifier cannot occur in the scope of a noun phrase that triggers a universal one (this would violate the $\exists^*\forall^*$ prefix class). Parsing of sentences and their translation into a discourse representation structure occurs in parallel. During the incremental translation of a sentence into a discourse representation structure, the language processor generates for each word form look-ahead information that tells the author which linguistic construction can follow the current input. In this way, the author can only write syntactically correct PENG^{ASP} sentences. The interpretation of the input by the machine is additionally made transparent for the author via a paraphrase in PENG^{ASP} that shows – among other things – how anaphoric expressions have been resolved.

After processing the first five sentences of our specification, the discourse representation structure looks as follows:

```
[]
  [A]
  object(A,martian)
  ==>
    [B,C]
    named(B,mars),predicate(C,be,A),property(C,origin,B)
  CSTR
    [D,E,F]
    object(D,venusian),named(E,mars),predicate(F,be,D),
    property(F,origin,E)
  [G]
  object(G,venusian)
  ==>
    [H,I]
    named(H,venus),predicate(I,be,G),property(I,origin,H)
  CSTR
    [J,K,L]
    object(J,martian),named(K,venus),predicate(L,be,J),
    property(L,origin,K)
  [M]
  object(M,person)
  ==>
    []
      [N,O]
      object(N,martian),predicate(O,isa,M,N)
    OR
      [P,Q]
      object(P,venusian),predicate(Q,isa,M,P)
```

(14)

This discourse representation structure uses a reified notation for logical atoms with a small number of predefined predicates. In contrast to classical DRT (van Eijck and Kamp 2011; Kamp and Reyle 1993), we use here an additional non-standard logical operator (CSTR) that denotes constraints. The entire discourse representation structure is then further translated recursively into an ASP program (15). Note that during this translation process to ASP, we unreify our notation: variables for named objects are replaced by their names and variables for relations that link predicates to properties are eliminated. We will see later, in particular when we speak about defaults, why the reified notation for discourse representation structures is helpful. Note also that disjunction that occurs in the consequent of an implication in the discourse representation structure results in a disjunctive ASP rule and that disjunction that occurs in the antecedent of an implication is distributed and results in more than one ASP rule:

```
origin(A, mars) :- martian(A).
:- venusian(B), origin(B, mars).
origin(C, venus) :- venusian(C).
:- martian(D), origin(D, venus).
martian(E) | venusian(E) :- person(E).
female(F) | male(F) :- person(F).
lie(G) :- person(G), female(G), martian(G).
lie(G) :- person(G), male(G), venusian(G).
truthful(H) :- person(H), male(H), martian(H).
truthful(H) :- person(H), female(H), venusian(H).
:- person(I), lie(I), truthful(I).
person(ork).                                              (15)
person(bog).
origin(bog, venus) :- truthful(ork).
:- origin(bog, venus), lie(ork).
origin(ork, mars) :- truthful(bog).
:- lie(bog), origin(ork, mars).
male(bog) :- truthful(ork).
:- lie(ork), male(bog).
female(ork) -truthful(bog).
:- lie(bog), female(ork).
answer(J) :- martian(J).
answer(yes) :- male(ork).
```

This ASP program is further processed by *clingo* (Gebser et al. 2012), a state-of-the-art answer set tool, that generates the subsequent answer set as solution for the puzzle:

$$\{\, \texttt{person(ork)}\ \texttt{person(bog)}\ \texttt{origin(bog, mars)}\ \texttt{martian(bog)}\ \texttt{venusian(ork)}\ \texttt{female(bog)}\ \texttt{male(ork)}\ \texttt{origin(ork, venus)}\ \texttt{lie(ork)}\ \texttt{lie(bog)}\ \texttt{answer(bog)}\ \texttt{answer(yes)} \,\} \tag{16}$$

Note that the first four sentences of our PENG^{ASP} specification in (13) are not strictly required to find the correct solution, but they help us to use a terminology that is close to the original problem specification in (12). If we replace the two prepositional phrases *from Mars* and *from Venus* by the indefinite noun phrases *a Martian* and *a Venusian* in the specification, then the two literals `origin(bog,mars)` and `origin(ork,venus)` are not generated but the relevant information about sex and race of the participating persons is still available in the resulting answer set.

4 Defaults and Exceptions

Classical logic is monotonic in the sense that adding new information to a knowledge base never invalidates any previous conclusions. Commonsense reasoning is non-monotonic in the sense that additional information may invalidate previous conclusions and then require a revision of the theory. Most rules that we use in commonsense reasoning are defaults that state what is normally the case and allow us to draw conclusions in the absence of complete knowledge. These defaults do not necessarily hold without exceptions.

4.1 Defaults and Exceptions in ASP

Most defaults can have two forms of exceptions: weak and strong exceptions (Gelfond and Kahl 2014). Weak exceptions render a default inapplicable and strong exceptions defeat a default's conclusion. In order to represent defaults and to reason with them in ASP, we need a mechanism that checks if exceptions exist that interfere with a default. Technically, this can be achieved with the help of an abnormality predicate (`ab(.)`) and the combination of strong (`-`) and weak negation (`not`). The idea behind the abnormality predicate is that individuals should not be considered to be abnormal unless there is positive information in the knowledge base to that effect. Formally, a default of the form:

$$\textit{Elements of class}\ \texttt{C}\ \textit{normally have property}\ \texttt{P}. \tag{17}$$

can be represented by the following ASP rule:

$$\texttt{p(X)} :- \ \texttt{c(X)}, \texttt{not ab(d, X)}, \texttt{not} -\texttt{p(X)}. \tag{18}$$

This rule states that `p(X)` holds if `c(X)` holds and it is `not` provable that `X` is abnormal (`ab`) with respect to the default d and that it is `not` provable that `-p(X)` holds. Note that `X` might be abnormal and that `-p(X)` might hold, but we currently cannot find any evidence in the knowledge base that this is the case.

A weak exception `e(X)` to a default `d` can be represented by a so-called cancellation axiom that contains the abnormality predicate (`ab(.)`) in the head of the rule:

```
ab(d,X) :- c(X), not -e(X).
```
(19)

This rule states that `X` is abnormal with respect to the default `d`, if `c(X)` holds and it is not provable that `-e(X)` holds. Note that if our knowledge base contains information about `-e(X)`, then (19) fails and `not ab(d,X)` in (18) succeeds, since it is `not` provable that `X` is abnormal with respect to `d`. However, if our knowledge base is incomplete and does neither contain information for `e(X)` nor for `-e(X)`, then (19) succeeds, but `not ab(d,X)` in (18) fails and the default will not be applicable. Note also a technical detail here: the literal `c(X)` in the body of (19) is used to guarantee rule safety; that means all variables that appear in an ASP rule have to appear for efficiency reasons in a positive literal in the body of the rule.

If `e(X)` is a strong exception, then an additional rule is required:

```
-p(X) :- e(X).
```
(20)

This rule states that `-p(X)` holds if the strong exception `e(X)` holds. Note that if `e(X)` holds, then (20) succeeds and defeats the default (18) since `not -p(X)` fails. If no information for `e(X)` is available in the knowledge base, then the default is not applicable as we have seen above.

4.2 Defaults and Exceptions in PENG^ASP

In this section, we discuss how defaults and exceptions can be expressed on the level of the controlled natural language PENG^ASP and show how the resulting specification can be translated via discourse representation structures into an ASP program. We do this with the help of a concrete example (21) taken from Gelfond and Kahl (2014) but show only those discourse representation structures that contain a new aspect that is relevant for the translation into an ASP program.

Cowardly Students
Normally, students are afraid of math.
Mary is not. (21)
Students in the math department are not.
Those in CS may or may not be afraid.

The first sentence of this text corresponds to a default. The next two sentences are strong exceptions to this default and the last sentence is a weak exception to the default. In order to get a working example in ASP that uses the default in (21) together with the corresponding exceptions, we specify first a simple knowledge base with the help of PENG^{ASP}:

Dave, Mary, Bob and Pat are students.
Dave is located in the Department of English.
Mary is located in the Department of Computer Science.
Bob is located in the Department of Computer Science.
Pat is located in the Department of Mathematics.
Every student is located in exactly one department.
Every Department of X is a department.
If a student is not provably located in a department then the student is not located in that department.

(22)

This specification classifies a number of named objects as students; specifies in which department individual students are located; relates each student to exactly one department, provides terminological information for a relational noun and specifies the closed world assumption for a particular predicate (*located*). This specification can be translated into the following ASP program:

```
student(dave; mary; bob; pat).
located(dave, sk1). department(sk1, english).
located(mary, sk2). department(sk2, computer_science).
located(bob, sk2).
located(dave, sk3). department(sk3, mathematics).                (23)
1 { located(E, F) : department(F) } 1 :- student(E).
department(G) :- department(G, H).
-located(I, J) :- student(I), department(J),
  not located(I, J).
```

As (23) shows, the translation of the first sentence in (22) results in ASP in a single atom with pooled arguments. The translation of the subsequent four sentences leads to a number of facts that contain Skolem constants. The sixth sentence with a cardinality constraint leads to a choice rule and the next sentence that specifies a terminological relationship results in a definite rule. Finally, the last sentence that specifies the closed world assumption for the predicate `located/2` translates into an ASP rule with strong negation (`-`) in its head and weak negation (`not`) in its body.

Now, let's have a look at the default in (21). Defaults require the introduction of a new linguistic structure in PENG^{ASP} that relies on a specific keyword (*normally*). We represent this default exclusively in the following form in PENG^{ASP}:

Students normally are afraid of math. (24)

The noun (*students*) in subject position is a bare plural (without an overt quantifier) followed by the adverb *normally* and a characterising property (*are afraid of math*). Note again that the linguistic structure of this default is enforced by the authoring tool. The default is then translated into the following discourse representation structure that uses a new non-standard operator (~~>) to mark the default:

```
[]
  [A]
  object(A, student)
  ~~>
    [B, C]
    named(B, math), predicate(C, be, A), property(C, afraid, B)
```
(25)

This discourse representation structure is then further translated into the ASP rule in (26). The translation is determined by the default operator (~~>) that triggers the construction of the two extended literals `not ab(d_afraid, A)` and `not -afraid(A, math)` in the context of the information available in (25). Note that the constant `d_afraid` serves as a name for the default. The reified notation for discourse representation structures is particularly helpful for the translation of defaults since we can exploit the information of the predefined predicates (e.g., `property/3`) for the construction of the ASP rule:

```
afraid(A, math) :-
  student(A),
  not ab(d_afraid, A),
  not -afraid(A, math).
```
(26)

The two strong exceptions in (21) do not require the introduction of a new construction in PENG^{ASP}, but in contrast to (21) where these exceptions are expressed in a very compact way with the help of elliptical structures (and rely on the linguistic knowledge of a human reader), we have to make the relevant information explicit on the level of the controlled natural language:

Mary is not afraid of math.
If a student is located in a Department of Mathematics then the student is not afraid of math.

(27)

Both sentences in (27) use strong negation. The subsequent translation of the first sentence results in a negative literal and the translation of the second sentence in a rule with a negative literal in its head:

```
-afraid(mary, math).
-afraid(B, math) :-
  student(B),                                   (28)
  department(C, mathematics),
  located(B, C).
```

The representation of the weak exception in (21) in PENG^{ASP} is more complex than the strong exceptions, since we need to be able to specify a cancellation axiom on the level of the controlled natural language. This requires a linguistic construction that allows us to express weak and strong negation in a compact (positive) manner:

If a student is provably located in a Department of Computer Science then the student abnormally is afraid of math.

(29)

The reserved keyword *provably* provides exactly this functionality in PENG^{ASP} and triggers the required combination of weak negation (NAF) and strong negation (NEG) in the discourse representation structure. Note that the NAF operator for negation as failure is a non-standard operator and is not used in classical DRT (van Eijck and Kamp 2011; Kamp and Reyle 1993):

```
[U, V, W]
student(U),
department(V, W),
named(W, computer_science)
  NAF
    []
      NEG
        [X]                                     (30)
        predicate(X, be, V),
        property(X, located, V)
[Y, Z]
modifier(Y, abnormally),
predicate(Y, afraid, U, Z),
named(Z, math)
```

The interpretation of the keyword *provably* is reflected in the paraphrase that the language processor generates for the author of the specification:

If a student is <ins> not </ins> provably <ins> not </ins> located in a Department of Computer Science then <ana> the student </ana> abnormally is afraid of math. (31)

The translation of the discourse representation structure in (30) results in an ASP rule that uses a combination of weak and strong negation in the body of the rule and an abnormality predicate in its head:

```
ab(d_afraid, U) :-
   student(U),
   department(V, computer_science),
   not -located(U, V).
```
(32)

Our theory is now complete and we can feed it to an ASP tool such as *clingo* (Gebser et al. 2012). The ASP tool creates one answer set for the theory that contains – among other literals – the following positive and negative literals that are of interest here:

```
{ -afraid(mary, math) -afraid(pat, math) afraid(dave, math) }
```
(33)

Our approach to handle defaults and their exceptions works fine as long as we do not have more than one default with the same name (in our case `d_afraid`). This name has been derived from the linguistic structure of the characterising property that occurs in the default. In the next section, we discuss how we can fix this problem and generalise our approach.

5 Referring to Defaults and Establishing Preferences

We show now how we can refer to conflicting defaults in PENG^{ASP} and establish a preference relation between these defaults. Let us assume for this purpose the following simple specification written in PENG^{ASP} that consists of terminological information and specifies the closed world assumption for a number of classes:

Tweety is a penguin and Sam is an eagle.
Every eagle is a bird.
Every penguin is a bird.
Every bird is an animal. (34)
Every animal that is not provably an eagle is not an eagle.
Every animal that is not provably a penguin is not a penguin.
Every animal that is not provably a bird is not a bird.

The translation of this specification via discourse representation structures generates the following ASP program:

```
penguin(tweety).
eagle(sam).
bird(A) :- eagle(A).
bird(B) :- penguin(B).
animal(C) :- bird(C).
-penguin(D) :- animal(D),  not penguin(D).
-eagle(E) :- animal(E),  not eagle(E).
-bird(F) :- animal(F),  not bird(F).
```
(35)

For illustrative purposes, we add now a number of default properties in PENG^{ASP} to (34) that characterise our domain:

Animals normally do not fly.
Birds normally fly. (36)
Penguins normally do not fly.

These defaults are automatically translated into the following default rules in ASP:

```
-fly(G) :-
  animal(G),
  not ab(d1, G),
  not fly(G).
fly(H) :-
  bird(H),
  not ab(d2, H),
  not -fly(H).
-fly(I) :-
  penguin(I),
  not ab(d3, I),
  not -fly(I).
```
(37)

It is important to note that each of these default rules has now a unique name (`d1, d2, d3`). These names are made transparent for the author in the paraphrase by the language processor:

*d*1 : *Animals normally do not fly.*
*d*2 : *Birds normally fly.* (38)
*d*3 : *Penguins normally do not fly.*

If we run the ASP program in (35) together with the default rules in (37), then the following four answer sets are generated:

```
Answer: 1
{ -fly(sam) -fly(tweety) }
Answer: 2
{ -fly(sam) fly(tweety) }
Answer: 3
{ fly(sam) fly(tweety) }
Answer: 4
{ fly(sam) -fly(tweety) }
```
(39)

The first three answer sets are clearly wrong and we have to exclude them with the help of exceptions in the form of cancellation axioms. The following two weak exceptions allow us now to refer in an explicit way to a specific default in (38) and finally to exclude the irrelevant answer sets in (39):

If an animal is provably a bird then the animal is abnormal with respect to d1.
If an animal is provably a penguin then the animal is abnormal with respect to d2.
(40)

These weak exceptions are translated into the following ASP rules that have an abnormality predicate in their heads:

```
ab(d1, J) :- animal(J), not -bird(J).
ab(d2, K) :- animal(K), not -penguin(K).
```
(41)

The first exception in (41) alone excludes the first and the second answer set in (39) and the second exception in (41) alone excludes the second and the third answer set in (39). Used together, they leave behind the correct answer set:

```
{ fly(sam) -fly(tweety) }
```
(42)

Note that the first rule in (40) prohibits the application of default `d1` and expresses preference of default `d2` over default `d1`. The second rule in (40) does the same for default `d3` and default `d2`, and the result `-fly(tweety)` is actually derived by default `d3` since this default is more specific than default `d1`. This nicely corresponds to the commonsense specificity principle (Gelfond and Kahl 2014; Touretzky 1986) that states that more specific defaults should be preferred over less specific ones.

6 Conclusion

In everyday life, we often have to draw plausible conclusions in situations in which we only have incomplete information. We then simply assume that the world in which we live in and reason about is normal as expected and revise our theory if a situation turns out to be abnormal in some respect. Most rules that we use in commonsense reasoning are defaults that describe what is normally the case, but these rules do not necessarily hold without exceptions. In this paper, we proposed the use of a controlled natural language as a high-level specification language for modelling commonsense reasoning problems that involve the processing of defaults and exceptions.

We showed how defaults and exceptions can be expressed in PENG^{ASP}, a controlled natural language that can be translated automatically via discourse representation structures into an executable ASP program. Defaults and exceptions in PENG^{ASP} have a specific linguistic structure that is restricted by the rules of the underlying grammar and enforced by an authoring tool. PENG^{ASP} specifications are incrementally translated during the parsing process into discourse representation structures that are based on a modified version of discourse representation theory. These discourse representation structures use a reified notation for logical atoms together with a number of predefined predicates and a number of non-standard operators for constraints, negation as failure and defaults. The resulting discourse representation structure of a PENG^{ASP} specification is translated recursively into an ASP program. ASP is an interesting formalism for non-monotonic reasoning because of its unique connectives (strong and weak negation) and entailment relation where the addition of new information to a program may invalidate previous conclusions.

References

Brewka, G., Niemelä, I., & Truszczyński, M. (2007). Nonmonotonic reasoning. In V. Lifschitz, B. Porter, & F. van Harmelen (Eds.), *Handbook of knowledge representation* (pp. 239–284). San Diego: Elsevier.

Brewka, G., Eiter, T., & Truszczyński, M. (2011, December). Answer set programming at a glance. In *Communications of the ACM* (Vol. 54, No. 12).

van Eijck, J., & Kamp, H. (2011). Discourse representation in context. In J. van Benthem & A. ter Meulen (Eds.), *Handbook of logic and language* (2nd ed., pp. 181–252). New York: Elsevier.

Eiter, T., Ianni, G., & Krennwallner, T. (2009). Answer set programming: A primer. In *Reasoning Web Semantic Technologies for Information Systems*, LNCS (Vol. 5689, pp. 40–110).

Fuchs, N.E., Kaljurand, K., & Kuhn, T. (2008). Attempto controlled english for knowledge representation. In C. Baroglio, P.A. Bonatti, J. Maluszynski, M. Marchiori, A. Polleres, & S. Schaffert (Eds.), *Reasoning Web Fourth International Summer School 2008* (pp. 104–124). LNCS 5224.

Gebser, M., Kaminski, R., Kaufmann, B., & Schaub, T. (2012). Answer set solving in practice. In *Synthesis Lectures on Artificial Intelligence and Machine Learning* (Vol. 6, No. 3, pp. 1–238).

Gelfond, M., & Lifschitz, V. (1988). The stable model semantics for logic programming. In R. Kowalski & K. Bowen (Eds.), *Proceedings of International Logic Programming Conference and Symposium* (pp. 1070–1080).

Gelfond, M., & Kahl, Y. (2014). *Knowledge representation, reasoning, and the design of intelligent agents: The answer-set programming approach*, Cambridge University Press: Cambridge.

Kamp, H., & Reyle, U. (1993). *From discourse to logic*. Dordrecht: Kluwer.

Lierler, Y., & Lifschitz, V. (2013). Logic programs vs. first-order formulas in textual inference. In *Proceedings of the 10th International Conference on Computational Semantics (IWCS 2013)* (pp. 340–346), Potsdam, Germany.

Lifschitz, V. (2008). What is answer set programming? In *Proceedings of AAAI'08* (Vol. 3, pp. 1594–1597).

McCarthy, J. (1980). Circumscription—A form of non-monotonic reasoning. *Artificial Intelligence, 13*(1–2), 27–39.

McDermott, D., & Doyle, J. (1982). Non-monotonic logic I. *Artificial Intelligence, 13*, 41–72.

Moore, R. C. (1985). Semantic considerations on nonmonotonic logic. *Artificial Intelligence, 25*, 75–94.

Pelletier, F.J., & Asher, N. (1997). Generics and defaults. In J. van Benthem & A. ter Meulen (Eds.), *Handbook of logic and language* (Chapter 20, pp. 1125–1177). Elsevier Science, Amsterdam.

Schwitter, R., Ljungberg, A., & Hood, D. (2003, May, 15-17). ECOLE—A Look-ahead editor for a controlled language. In *Proceedings of EAMT-CLAW03* (pp. 141–150). Dublin City University, Ireland.

Schwitter, R. (2010). Controlled natural languages for knowledge representation. In *Proceedings of COLING 2010* (pp. 1113–1121). Beijing, China.

Schwitter, R. (2013). The jobs puzzle: Taking on the challenge via controlled natural language processing. *Journal of Theory and Practice of Logic Programming, 13*(4–5), 487–501.

Smullyan, R. (1987). *Forever Undecided: a Puzzle Guide to Gödel*. New York: Alfred A. Knopf.

Sutcliffe, G. (2009). The TPTP problem library and associated infrastructure: The FOF and CNF Parts, v3.5.0. *Journal of Automated Reasoning, 43*(4), 337–362.

Reiter, R. (1978). On closed world data bases. In H. Gaillaire & J. Minker (Eds.), *Logic and data bases* (pp. 55–76). New York: Plenum Press.

Touretzky, D.S. (1986). *The mathematics of inheritance systems (Research notes in artificial intelligence)*. Los Altos, California: Morgan Kaufmann.

White, C., & Schwitter, R. (2009). An update on PENG light. In L. Pizzato & R. Schwitter (Eds.), *Proceedings of ALTA 2009* (pp. 80–88), Sydney, Australia.

Ontology in Coq for a Guided Message Composition

Line Jakubiec-Jamet

Abstract Natural language generation is based on messages that represent meanings, and goals that are the usual starting points to communicate. How to help people to provide this conceptual input or, in other words, how to communicate thoughts to the computer? In order to express something, one needs to have something to express as an idea, a thought or a concept. The question is how to represent this. In 2009, Michael Zock, Paul Sabatier and Line Jakubiec-Jamet suggested the building of a resource composed of a *linguistically motivated ontology*, a *dictionary* and a *graph generator*. The ontology guides the user to choose among a set of concepts (or words) to build the message from; the dictionary provides knowledge of how to link the chosen elements to yield a message (compositional rules); the graph generator displays the output in visual form (message graph representing the user's input). While the goal of the ontology is to generate (or analyse) sentences and to guide message composition (what to say), the graph's function is to show at an intermediate level the result of the encoding process. The Illico system already proposes a way to help a user in generating (or analyzing) sentences and guiding their composition. Another system, the Drill Tutor, is an exercise generator whose goal is to help people to become fluent in a foreign language. It assists people (users have to make choices from the interface in order to build their messages) to produce a sentence expressing a message from an idea (or a concept) to its linguistic realization (or a correct sentence given in a foreign language). These two systems led us to consider the representation of the conceptual information into a symbolic language; this representation is encoded in a logic system in order to automatically check conceptual well-formedness of messages. This logic system is the Coq system used here only for its high level language. Coq is based on a typed λ-calculus. It is used for analysing conceptual input interpreted as types and also for specifying general definitions representing messages. These definitions are typed and they will be instantiated for type-checking the conceptual well-formedness of messages.

L. Jakubiec-Jamet (✉)
Laboratoire d'Informatique Fondamentale de Marseille, Aix-Marseille Université, CNRS, LIF UMR 7279, 163, Avenue de Luminy - Case 901, 13288 Marseille Cedex 9, France
e-mail: Line.Jakubiec@lif.univ-mrs.fr

© Springer International Publishing Switzerland 2015
N. Gala et al. (eds.), *Language Production, Cognition, and the Lexicon*,
Text, Speech and Language Technology 48, DOI 10.1007/978-3-319-08043-7_19

Keywords Conceptual input · Message composition · Interactive natural language generation · Symbolic representation · Typed logic · Semantic analysis

1 Introduction

Natural language generation is typically based on messages, i.e. meanings, and goals, the usual starting points. We present our views on how to help people to provide this kind of input. Guiding a user to compose sentences can be done in many ways, a lot depending on the user's knowledge state.[1] We will present here *Illico* (Pasero and Sabatier),[2] some of its shortcomings and our solution. Illico can be helpful in many ways. For example, it can analyze and synthesize expressions (words, phrases, clauses, sentences), as well as offer possible continuations for a sentence that has not been completed yet, whatever the reasons may be (lexical, syntactic, semantic, conceptual or contextual). All the suggestions made by the system are possible expressions fitting into this place and being in line with the constraints at hand. To achieve this goal a powerful mechanism is used to process in parallel knowledge of different sorts (lexical, syntactic, semantic, conceptual and even contextual ones).

Written in Prolog, *Illico*'s engine is based on a mechanism of coroutine processing. Both for analysis and synthesis, it checks and executes the different constraints (lexical, syntactic, semantic, conceptual and contextual) as soon as the structures of the different representations on which they apply are built, the process being dynamic and taking place in parallel. Representations are processed non deterministically in a top-down manner. The implemented strategy is powerful enough to allow for analysis and synthesis to be simultaneously performed in a single pass. The same principle is used for guiding composition incrementally, i.e. by means of partial synthesis.

If you want to compose a sentence step-by-step, from left to right, *Illico* automatically and dynamically offers at each step a list of candidates for continuing the

---

[1] The problem we are dealing with here is search. Obviously, knowledge available at the onset (cognitive state) plays also a very important role in this kind of task, regardless of the goal (determine conceptual input, lexical access, etc.). Search strategies and relative ease of finding a given piece of information (concept, word) depend crucially on the nature of the input (knowledge available) and the distance between the latter and a given output (target word). Imagine that your target word were 'guy' while you've started search from any of the following inputs: 'cat' (synonyme), 'person' (more general term), or 'gars' (equivalent word in French). Obviously, the type of search and ease of access would not be the same. The nature and number of items among which to choose would be different in each case. The influence of formally similar, i.e. close words ('libreria' in Spanish vs. 'library' in English) is well known. Cognates tend to prime each other, a fact that depending on the circumstances can be helpful or sheer nuisance.

[2] For more details and references concerning *Illico* and its applications (natural language interfaces to knowledge bases, simultaneous composition of sentences in different languages, linguistic games for language learning, communication aid for disabled people, software for language rehabilitation, etc.) you may want to take a look at http://pageperso.lif.univ-mrs.fr/paul.sabatier/ILLICO/illico.html.

sentence built so far. Figure 1 illustrates this mode. Having reached a certain point in the chain ("The child takes a picture of the...") the user is waiting for suggestions to be made by the system. Offering possible continuations is but one way among others to assist a user in sentence composition. One can imagine richer kind of assistance where the user accesses various kinds of knowledge (linguistic, conceptual, etc.) to select then the one fitting best his communicative goals.

This aspect could concretely help a user in sentence composition to be fluent in a foreign language. Becoming fluent in a language requires not only learning words and methods for accessing them quickly, but also learning how to place them and how to make the necessary morphological adjustments. The Drill Tutor (Zock and Lapalme 2010) aims to help people to produce a sentence expressing some message. In the system, the user chooses the goal of communication (to introduce someone for example). The goals is tree-structured. The user can either drill down to a given goal by clicking on a goal name to expand the sub-goals until a pattern is displayed, or search for them via a term because goals are indexed. The Drill Tutor gets from the starting point, the goal, to its linguistic realization. The system presents sequentially:

1. a model: the user chooses one of the patterns proposed by the system (a pattern is a general sentence needing to be instanciated; for example, to introduce someone, one can use the model: *This is <title><name>* or *That is <title><name> from <origin>*);
2. the stimulus (chosen word): this step allows the instanciation of the chosen pattern. For example, for <title> , the user can use *Mr, Mrs, Dr., Professor*, and for <origin> , he can choose *Japan, Germany, France*;
3. the user's answer and the system's confirmation: the system has now all the information needed to create the sentence (or the exercise) expressing the conceptual input. Finally, a set of possible outputs representing the message is depicted on the screen and the user can express his message.

This approach is much more economical for storing and accessing patterns, than storing a pattern for every morphological variant. This approach also allows faster authoring, i.e., message building, than long-winded navigation through a conceptual ontology (for more details see Zock and Afantenos (2009)).

2 Limitation of Sentence Completion or the Need of Controlling Conceptual Input

The objectives of *sentence completion systems* are different from those of conventional surface generators (Bateman and Zock 2003; Reiter 2000). The latter start from a *goal* and a set of *messages* (input) in order to produce the corresponding surface form (output). Working quietly in the background, *Illico* tries to be pro-active, making reasonable guesses about what the author could say next.

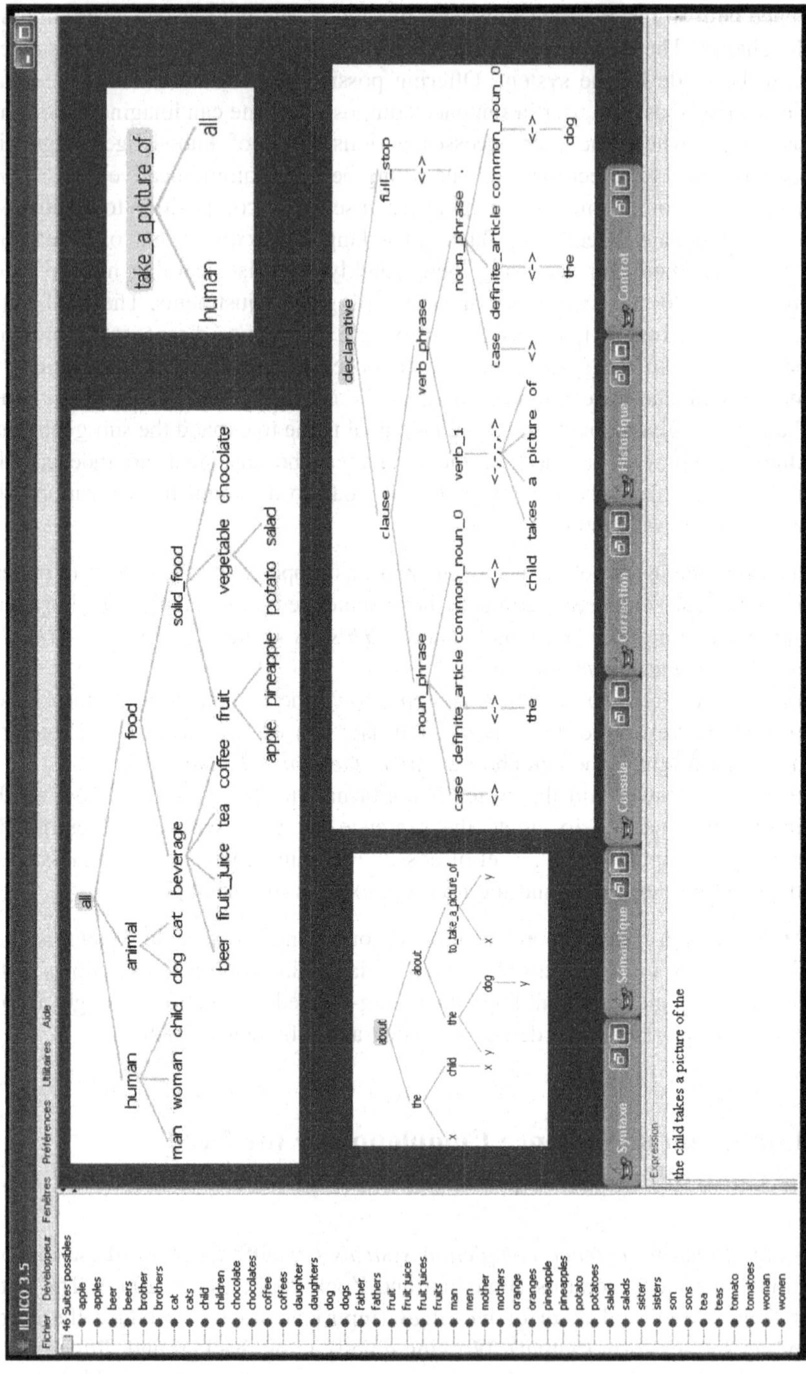

Fig. 1 Illico screen printing

Hence, it supposes somehow that the author knows at least to some extent what he is/was going to say.[3]

Illico performs analysis by synthesis (top-down strategy) and, while it does not need any help from the user for analysis, it does so for synthesis, as, otherwise, it would produce unreasonably large sets of possible continuations, most of which do not even correspond to the users' intention. Figure 1 should give you a rough idea of how *Illico* works. You'll see basically three windows with, at the bottom, the output produced so far (generally an incomplete sentence, here: *the child takes a picture of the*); at the very left, the candidates for the next slot (*apple*, *beer*, *brother*,...) and in the main frame, various kinds of representation, like the system's underlying ontology, pragmatic, semantic and syntactic information concerning the sentence in the making.

Offering rich assistance during sentence composition was not the main goal of the designers of *Illico*. The production of possible continuations is but one functionality among others, though a very useful one[4] and easily implemented due to the power of Prolog's core mechanisms.

A system providing more sofisticated assistance system would look quite a bit differently: (a) the nodes of the tree would be *categories* (types) rather than *instances* (words), the latter being shown only at the leave-level; (b) frequency would be taken into account (the words' likelihood varying with the topic); (c) *governors* (e.g. nouns) would precede their *dependants* (e.g. determiners, adjectives), and (d) *variables* would be used rather than extensive lists of possible morphological *values*, etc.

Another problem linked to set size (i.e. great number of words from which to choose) is the fact that large sets tend to be distracting and to cause forgetting. Indeed, as the number of candidates grows (as is typically the case at the beginning of a clause) the danger to get drowned. Likewise, with the distance between the governor and its dependant increasing, grows the danger to end up producing something that, while in line with the language, does not correspond anymore to what one had in mind. Memory and divided attention have taken their toll. In order to avoid this, we suggest to determine the governing elements first and to keep the set of data from which to choose small. In other words, filtering and navigation become a critical issue and there are at least two ways to deal with them.

In order to reduce the number of candidates from which to choose, one can filter out linguistically and conceptually irrelevant material. This strategy is generally used both by the speaker and the listener as long as optimal transmission of information, i.e. reasonable input/output are considered as a major means to achieve a given communication goal (default case). Hearing someone say: "I'd love to smoke a....", our mind or ears will be "tuned" to smokeable items (cigar,

---

[3] Of course, we can also assume that the author does not even know that. But this is a bit of an extreme case.

[4] For example, it allows the testing of well-formedness and linguistic coverage of the application one is about to develop. This being so, we can check now whether all the produced continuations are expected and none is missing.

cigarette, pipe) rather than to any noun, no matter how correct all of them may be from a syntactic point of view. With regard to our problem (sentence completion or message composition) this means that the list to be presented should be small and contain but "reasonable" items.[5] How can this be achieved without sacrificing coverage? Indeed, even a filtered list can still be quite large. Imagine that you were to talk about people, food, or a day of the year, etc. The number of representatives of each category is far too big to allow for fast identification, if the candidates are presented extensively in an unstructured or only alphabetically structured list. This can be avoided and navigation can considerably be eased by categorizing items, presenting them as a conceptually structured tree (type hierarchy) rather than as a flat list. Instead of operating at the concrete level of instances (all days of the year) the user will now operate (navigate or choose) at a much higher level, using more abstract words (generic concepts, type names, hyperonymes) like month, week-days, hour, etc. Of course, ultimately he will have to choose one of the concrete instances, but having eliminated rapidly, i.e. via categories, most of the irrelevant data, he will now choose from a much smaller list. The gain is obvious in terms of storage (at the interface level) and speed of navigation.

3 Incremental Building and Refining a Message Graph

To show what we have in mind, take a look at Fig. 2. It is reminiscient of SWIM, an ontology-driven interactive sentence generator (Zock 1991). Let's see how this is meant to work. Suppose you were to produce the underlying message of the following sentence "Zidane hammered the ball straight into the net". This would require several walks through the conceptual network, one for each major category (Zidane, hammer, ball, straight, net).[6] The path for "Zidane" would be "scene/idea/objects/entity/person", while the one for the shooting-act would be "scene/idea/relation/action/verb". Concerning this yet-to-be-built resource, various questions arise concerning the components (nature), their building and usage. The three problems are somehow related.

What are the components? In order to allow for the interactive building of the message graph we will need three components: a *linguistically motivated ontology*, a *dictionary* and a *graph generator*. The *ontology* is needed for guiding the user to make his choices concerning the elements to build the message from concepts/words. The fact that the user has chosen a set of building blocks (concepts, i.e. class names, or words) does not mean that we have a message. At this point we

---

[5] This idea is somehow contained in Tesnière's notion of *valency* (Tesnière 1959), in Schank's *conceptual dependancy* (Schank 1975) and McCoy and Cheng's *discourse focus trees* (McCoy and Cheng 1991).

[6] The upper part shows the conceptual building blocks structured as a tree and the lower part contains the result of the choices made so far, that is, the message built up to this point. To simplify matters we have ignored the attitude or speech-act node in the lower part of our figure.

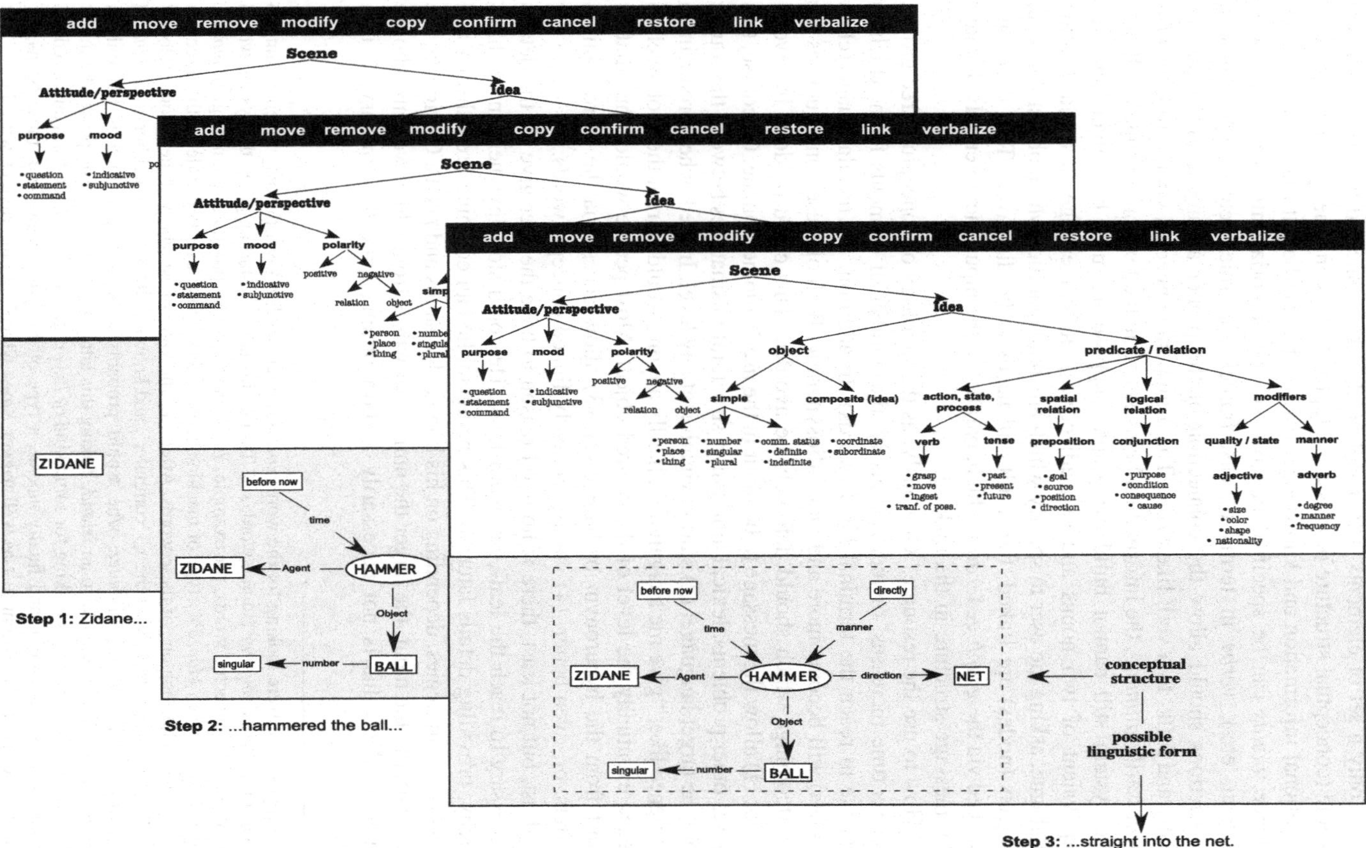

Fig. 2 An interactive graph editor for incremental message composition

have only a set of elements which still need to be connected to form a coherent whole (conceptual structure or message graph). To this end the system might need additional information and knowledge. Part of this can be put into the *dictionary*. Hence, *nouns* can be specified in terms of subcategorial information (animate, human, etc.), *verbs* in terms of case-frames and roles, etc. These kinds of restrictions should allow the connection of the proper arguments, for example, baby and milk, to a verb like *drink*. The argument connected via the link *agent* is necessarily *animate*, the information being stated in the lexicon. In spite of all this, the system still cannot build the graph (suppose the user had given only the equivalent of two nouns and two adjectives), it will engage in a clarification dialogue, asking the user to specify which attribute qualifies which object. Once all objects (nodes) are linked, the result still needs to be displayed. This is accomplished via the *graph generator* which, parallel to the input, incrementally displays the message structure in the making.

How to use the resource? Obviously, as the ontology or conceptual tree grows, access time increases, or more precisely, the number of elements from which to choose to reach the terminal level (words). In addition, the metalanguage (class names) will become more and more idiosyncratic. Both of these consequences are shortcomings which should definitely be avoided. This could be done in several ways: (1) allow the message to be input in the user's mother tongue. Of course, this poses other problems: lexical ambiguity, structural mismatches between the source and the target language; (2) start navigation at any level. Indeed, when producing a sentence like, "give me a cigarette", hardly anyone would start at the root level, to reach eventually the level of the desired object. Most people would immediately start from the hyperonym or base level; (3) allow access via the words' initial letters, or, even better, (4) via associatively linked concepts/words..[7]

Last, but not least, there is no good reason to have the user give all the details necessary to reach the leaf-, i.e. word-level. He could stop anywhere in the hierarchy, providing details later on. This being so, he can combine breadth-first and depth-first strategies, depending on his knowledge states and needs. Obviously, the less specific the input, the larger the number of words from which we must choose later on. Yet, this is not necessarily a shortcoming, quite the contrary. It is a

---

[7] Suppose you were looking for the word *mocha* (target word: t_w), yet the only token coming to your mind were *computer* (source word: s_w). Taking this latter as starting point, the system would show all the connected words, for example, *Java, Perl, Prolog* (programing languages), *mouse, printer* (hardware), *Mac, PC* (type of machines), etc. querying the user to decide on the direction of search by choosing one of these words. After all, s/he knows best which of them comes closest to the t_w. Having started from the s_w 'computer', and knowing that the t_w is neither some *kind of software* nor a *type of computer*, s/he would probably choose *Java*, which is not only a *programming language* but also an *island*. Taking this latter as the new starting point s/he might choose *coffee* (since s/he is looking for some kind of *beverage*, possibly made from an ingredient produced in Java, coffee), and finally *mocha*, a type of *beverage* made from these beans. Of course, the word *Java* might just as well trigger *Kawa* which not only rhymes with the s_w , but also evokes *Kawa Igen*, a javanese volcano, or familiar word of *coffee* in French. For more details, see Zock and Schwab (2008).

quality, since users can now decide whether they want to concentrate first on the big picture (general structure or frame of the idea) or rather on the low level details (which specific words to use). Full lexical specification is probably not even wanted, as it is not only tiresome as soon as the ontology grows (imagine the time it might take just to produce the conceptual equivalent to a message like 'a beer, please!'), but also it may pose problems later on (surface generation), as the words occurring in the message graph might not be syntactically compatible with each other. Hence, we will be blocked, facing a problem of expressibility (Marie 1992).

4 Conceptual, Computational and Psychological Issues

Building the kind of editor we have in mind is not a trivial issue and various problems need be addressed and solved:

- **coverage**: obviously, the bigger the coverage, the more complex the task. For practical reasons we shall start with a small domain (soccer), as we can rely already on a good set of resources both in terms of the ontology and the corresponding dictionary (Sabatier 1997). Kicktionary, developped by Thomas Schmidt (http://www.kicktionary.de/Introduction.html), is a domain-specific trilingual (English, German, and French) lexical resource of the language of soccer. It is based on Fillmore's Frame Semantics (Baker et al. 1998) and uses WordNet style semantic relations (Fellbaum 1998) as an additional layer to structure the conceptual level.
- **language specificity**: there are good reasons to believe that the conceptual tree will be language dependant. Think of Spanish or Russian where verb-form depends on *aspect*, that is, on the speaker's choice of considering an action as completed, i.e. perfective, or not, yielding two, morphologically speaking, entirely different lemmas (ser/estar, meaning *to be* in Spanish, or "uchodits" vs "uitsi" *to walk* in Russian).
- **ergonomic aspects (readability)**: the graph's readability will become an issue as soon as messages grow big. Imagine the underlying graph of a multiple embedded relative-clause. Also, rather than frightening the user by showing him the entire tree of Fig. 2, we intend to show only the useful (don't drown the user), for example, the children nodes for a given choice.
- **the limits of symbolic representation**: as shown elsewhere for *time* (Ligozat and Zock 1992) and *space* (Briffault and Zock 1994), symbolic representations can be quite cumbersome. Just think of gradient phenomena like colors or sounds, which are much easier represented analogically (for example, in terms of a color-wheel) than categorially.
- **the problem of metalanguage**: we will discourage the user if learning the target language is only possible by learning yet another (meta) language.
- **the conceptual tree**: there are basically two issues at stake: which categories to put into the tree and where to place them. Indeed, there are various problematic

points in Fig. 2. Where shall we put negation? Shall we factor it out, or put it at every node where it is needed?

There are several other issues that we have hardly touched upon, yet they are all relevant for natural language generation, in particular for interactive language generation which is our case:

1. in what terms to encode the message (concepts vs. words),
2. at what level of abstraction (general vs. specific);
3. size of the planning unit (concepts vs. messages);
4. processing strategy: is planning done as a one-shot process or is it performed in various steps, i.e. incrementally?;
5. direction: is planning done left to right or top to bottom?
6. processing order. Do thoughts precede language, and if so, is this always the case?

We will touch upon these points here only very briefly (for more details see Zock (1996)). Let's suppose you wanted to produce the following sentence: *When the old man saw the little boy drowning in the river, he went to his canoe in order to rescue him.* Obviously, before producing such a sentence its content must be planned and represented somehow, but how is this done? There are several good reasons to believe that this sentence has not been planned entirely in advance, neither from left to right, nor in a single pass.

Psychological reasons: The sentence is simply too long for a speaker to hold all its information in short-term-memory. It is highly unlikely that the speaker has all this information available at the onset of verbalization. The need of planning, that is, the need to look ahead and to plan in general terms, increases with sentence length and with the number and type of embeddings (for example, center embedded sentences). There is also good evidence in the speech error literature for the claim that people plan in abstract terms. False starts or repairs, like "I've turned on the *stove* switch, I mean the *heater* switch" suggest that the *temperature increasing device* has been present in the speakers mind, yet at an abstract level (Fromkin 1993; Levelt 1989).

Linguistic reasons: as is well known, the order of words does not necessarily parallel the order of thought. For example, the generation of the first word of the sentence here above, the temporal adverbial "when", requires knowledge of the fact that there is another event taking place. Yet, this information appears fairly late in the sentence.

5 Checking Conceptual Well-Formedness

Obviously, messages must be complete and well-formed, and this is something which needs to be checked. The problem of well-formedness is important, not only in systems where a message is built from scratch or from incomplete sentence fragments (ILLICO), but also in message-specification systems.[8] Suppose you were to make a comparison, then you must (at least at the beginning) mention the two items to be compared (completeness), and the items must be comparable (well-formedness). In other words, having chosen some predicate, a certain number of specific variables or arguments are activated, waiting for instantiation. Arguments are, however, not only of a specific kind, playing a given role, they also have specific constraints which need to be satisfied. While checking well-formedness for single words does not make sense (apart from spell checking, which is not our concern here), it does make sense to check the compatibility and well-formedness of the combination of concepts or words, to see whether they produce an acceptable conceptual structure.

To illustrate this further, lets take up again the sentence illustrated in Fig. 2, Zidane hammered the ball straight into the net. This means that, having received as input something like to shoot (or, to hammer), we know that there is someone, performing this action, with a specific target in mind (the goal), and that the action can only be performed in so many ways (manner). While not all of this information is mandatory, some of it is (agent, object, target), and there are definitely certain constraints on the various arguments (the agent must be animate, the object some kind of sphere, typically used in soccer games, etc.). Being formalized and stored in a conceptual dictionary, this information can now be used by our system to check the well formedness of a given structure and its compatibility with the users'input.

The idea according to which types allow well-formedness checking of mathematical objects is well-known. We use them them for a different domain (messages and sentences), because they allow the checking of the adequacy of the elements used to build or complete a message. Having a rigorous representation, we can reason about objects not only to check the well-formedness of the users'input, but also its soundness.

To test this hypothesis we rely on the Coq proof assistant (Coq Development Team 2008) as it allows us to:

- take advantage of its type system and its powerful representation mechanisms: polymorphism, dependent types, higher-order logic…;
- propose natural and general specification;
- check automatically the well-formedness of the users'input.

The Coq system provides a formal language to specify mathematical definitions and prove them. The Coq language implements a higher-order typed λ-calculus, the calculus of constructions. Its logic is constructive and relies on the Curry-Howard isomorphism. Each Coq proposition is of type *Prop* and describes a predicate. There are also objects of type *Set*, but they are not used in the context of this work.

[8] Of course, conceptual well-formedness, i.e. meaningfulness, does not guarantee communicative adequacy. In other words, it does not assure that the message makes sense in the context of a conversion. To achieve this goal additional mechanisms are needed.

Coq allows an hierarchical organization of types via the coercion mechanism. In other words, it contains a mechanism to represent conceptual information in the form of a tree of concept types. We use coercions here to inject terms implicitly from one type into another, which can be viewed as a subtyping mechanism. Given this facility a user may apply an object (which is not a function, but can be coerced to a function) to the coercion, and more generally, consider that a term of type A is of type B, provided that there is a declared coercion between the two.

For example, in Fig. 2 we see that a *Scene* contains both an *Attitude_Perspective* (speech-act, if you prefer) and an Idea (core part of the message). This is expressed in Coq as follows:

```
Coercion Attitude_Perspective_is_Scene :
     Attitude_Perspective >->Scene.
Coercion Idea_is_Scene : Idea >-> Scene.
```

where *Attitude_Perspective*, Idea and Scene are declared as parameters of type Prop. These coercions declare the construction of the conceptual type *Scene* that can be seen as the composition of an *Idea* and an *Attitude_Perspective*.

The coercions used for this study are described by an inheritance graph in Coq. Moreover, Coq detects ambiguous paths during the creation of the tree, and it checks the uniform inheritance condition according to which at most one path must be declared between two nodes. The relevant part of the inheritance graph for our example is:

```
Parameter hammer : Agent ->Object -> Target -> Prop.
Parameter Zidane : human.
Parameter ball : soccer_instrument.
Parameter net : soccer_equipment.
```

These four parameters describe the variables used in our example of Fig. 2. *Prop* stands in Coq for the type of proposition. Roles (*Agent*, *Object*, *Target*) and features (*human*, *soccer_instrument*, *soccer_equipment*) are generic types. To express conceptual constraints such as Agents must be animate, Coq uses the subtype principle in order to check that all constraints are satisfied, defining *human*, *soccer_instrument* and *soccer_equipment* respectively as subtypes of *Agent*, *Object* and *Target*.

When all constraints are satisfied, the semantics of a sentence can be represented, which yields in our case "there is an agent who did something in a specific way, by using some instrument". In other words: "there is a person p, an object o and a target t that are linked via an action performed in a specific way". The user message can be defined generically and typed as follows:

```
Parameter is_someone : Agent -> Prop.
Parameter is_something : Object -> Prop.
Parameter is_manner : Target -> Prop.
Parameter relation : Agent -> Object -> Target -> Prop.
```

```
Definition message : = exists p, exists o, exists t,
           is_someone p/\is_something o/\
           is_manner t/\relation p o t.
```

This definition is a λ-expression taking as parameters the following variables (type names are referred to via their initial capital):

$$(\lambda s : A \rightarrow P)(\lambda o : O \rightarrow P)(\lambda t : T \rightarrow P)(\lambda r : A \rightarrow O \rightarrow T \rightarrow P)$$

Hence, to produce the global message Zidane hammered the ball straight into the net, we must instantiate the composite propositions respectively by *is_Zidane* (of type *human* → *Prop*), *is_ball* (of type *soccer_instrument* → *Prop*), *is_net* (of type *soccer_equipment* → *Prop*). *Hammer* is already declared. Once this is done, the parameters *Zidane*, *ball* and *net* can be applied to produce the desired result, the system type-checking the compatibility of the involved parameters.

More generally speaking, checking the conceptual well-formedness and consistency of the messages amounts basically to type-checking the composite elements of the message.

Another approach implemented in Coq allows the formalization of general patterns used for representing sentences. Then, these patterns are instanciated and a semantic analysis of simple sentences can been performed. This analysis relies on a hierarchy of types for type-checking the conceptual well-formedness of sentences in the same spirit of this paper.[9] The motivation for using Coq is to define general representations in order to have a more economical way for storing and analysing sentences that are built according patterns (for more details see Jakubiec-Jamet (2012)).

6 Conclusion and Perspectives

The goal of this paper has been to deal with a problem hardly ever addressed in the literature on natural language generation, conceptual input. In order to express something, one needs to have something to express (idea, thought, concept) to begin with (input, meaning). The question is how to represent this something. What are the building blocks and how shall we organize and index them to allow for quick and intuitive access later on?

Dealing with interactive sentence generation, we have suggested the building of a *linguistically motivated ontology* combined with a dictionary and graph generator. While the goal of the ontology is to generate (or analyse) sentences and to guide message composition (what to say), the graph's function is to show at an intermediate level the result of the encoding process. This reduces memory load,

---

9 Actually I gratefully acknowledge Michael from many fruitful discussions about this approach. He always has been very attentive to others'works and our collaboration is due to him.

allowing at the same time the checking of well formedness. Does the message-graph really encode the author's intention?

Of course, there are many ontologies. Unfortunately, we cannot draw on any of them directly, as they have not been built for message composition. As we have seen, different applications may require different strategies for providing input. In Illico it was driven via an ontology, taking place fairly late. Part of the message was known and expressed, thus, constraining further inputs.

Michael Zock also worked on another message-specification system (the SPB system), a multi-lingual phrasebook designed to convert meanings into speech. In SPB, conceptual input consisted mainly in searching (for existing sentences or patterns) and performing local changes. Rather than starting from scratch, data are accommodated. Given the fact that we have a translation memory, input can be given in any language (mother tongue) we are comfortable with, provided that it is part of the translation memory. If there is a translation between two sentences, any element is likely to evoke its equivalent and the sentence in which it occurs in the target language. Obviously, this is a nice feature, as it allows not only for natural input, but also to speed up the authoring process.[10]

In the case of Drill Tutor, conceptual input is distributed over time, specification taking place in three steps: first via the choice of a goal, yielding an abstract, global structure or sentence pattern (steps 1), then via the variables'concrete lexical- and morphological values (steps 2 and 3). In the case of Drill Tutor, input is clearly underspecified at the earliest stage. Messages are gradually refined: starting from a fairly general idea, i.e., sentence pattern, one proceeds gradually to the specifics: lexical and morphological values. This seems a nice feature with respect to managing memory constraints. Many ideas presented here are somehow half-baked, needing maturation, but, as mentioned earlier, conceptual input is an area in Natural Language Generation where more work is badly needed.

References

Baker, C. F., Fillmore, C. J., & Lowe, J. B. (1998). The Berkeley Framenet project. In *COLING/ACL-98* (pp. 86–90). Montreal.

Bateman, J., & Zock, M. (2003). Natural language generation. In R. Mitkov (Ed.), *Oxford handbook of computational linguistics*, Chap. 15 (pp. 284–304). Oxford: Oxford University Press.

Boitet, C., Bhattacharyya, P., Blanc, E., Meena, S., Boudhh, S., Fafiotte, G., Falaise, A., & Vacchani, V. (2007). Building Hindi-French-English-UNL resources for SurviTra-CIFLI, a linguistic survival system under construction. In *Seventh international symposium on natural language processing*.

Briffault, X., & Zock, M. (1994). What do we mean when we say to the left or to the right? How to learn about space by building and exploring a microworld? In *6th International Conference on ARTIFICIAL INTELLIGENCE: Methodology, Systems, Applications* (pp. 363–371). Sofia.

[10] For a similar goal, but with a quite different method, see Boitet et al. (2007).

Fellbaum, C. (Ed.). (1998). *WordNet: An electronic lexical database and some of its applications*. Cambridge: MIT Press.

Fromkin, V. (1993). Speech production. In J. Berko-Gleason & N. Bernstein Ratner (Eds.), *Psycholinguistics*. Austin, TX: Harcourt, Brace and Jovanovich.

Jakubiec-Jamet, L. (2012). A case-study for the semantic analysis of sentences in Coq. Research report, LIF.

Levelt, W. (1989). *Speaking : From intention to articulation*. Cambridge, MA: MIT Press.

Ligozat, G., & Zock, M. (1992). How to visualize time, tense and aspect. In *Proceedings of COLING '92* (pp. 475–482). Nantes.

McCoy, K., & Cheng, J. (1991). Focus of attention: Constraining what can be said next. In C. Paris, W. Swartout & W. Mann (Eds.), *Natural language generation in artificial intelligence and computational linguistics* (pp. 103–124). Boston: Kluwer Academic Publisher.

Meteer, M. W. (1992). *Expressibility and the problem of efficient text planning*. London: Pinter.

Reiter, E., & Dale, R. (2000) *Building natural language generation systems*. Cambridge: Cambridge University Press.

Sabatier, P. (1997). Un lexique-grammaire du football. *Lingvistic Investigationes, XXI*(1):163–197.

Schank, R. (1975). Conceptual dependency theory. In R. C. Schank (Ed.), *Conceptual information processing* (pp. 22–82). Amsterdam and New York: North-Holland and Elsevier.

Tesnière, L. (1959). *Éléments de syntaxe structurale*. Paris: Klincksieck.

Zock, M. (1991). Swim or sink: The problem of communicating thought. In M. Swartz & M. Yazdani (Eds.), *Intelligent tutoring systems for foreign language learning* (pp. 235–247). New York: Springer.

Zock, M. (1996). The power of words in message planning. In *International Conference on Computational Linguistics, Copenhagen.*

Zock, M., & Afantenos, S. (2009). Using e-learning to achieve fluency in foreign languages. In N. Tsapatsoulis & A. Tzanavari (Eds.), *Affective, interactive and cognitive methods for e-learning design: Creating an optimal education experience*. Hershey: IGI Global.

Zock, M., & Lapalme, G. (2010). A generic tool for creating and using multilingual phrasebooks. In *Natural Language Processing and Cognitive Science, Funchal.*

Zock, M. & Schwab, D. (2008). Lexical access based on underspecified input. In *Proceedings of the Workshop on Cognitive Aspects of the Lexicon (COGALEX 2008)* (pp. 9–17). Manchester, UK, August 2008 (Coling 2008).

Bridging Gaps Between Planning and Open-Domain Spoken Dialogues

Kristiina Jokinen

Abstract In social media, Wikipedia is the outstanding example of a collaborative wiki. After reviewing progress in open-domain question answering systems, the paper discusses a recent system, WikiTalk, that supports open-domain dialogues by using Wikipedia as a knowledge source. With the collaboratively-written sentences and paragraphs from Wikipedia, the WikiTalk system apparently succeeds in enabling "open-domain talking". In view of recent advances in web-based language processing, the paper proposes steps towards open-domain "listening" that combine anticipated progress in open vocabulary speech recognition with recent developments in named entity recognition, where Wikipedia is now used as a dynamically updated knowledge source instead of fixed gazetteer lists. The paper proposes that Wikipedia-based open-domain talking and open-domain listening will be combined in a new generation of web-based open-domain spoken dialogue systems. Technological and social development affects our interaction with the environment: interactive systems are embedded in our environment, information flow increases, and interaction becomes more complex. In order to address challenges of the complex environment, to respond to needs of various users, and to provide possibilities to test innovative interactive systems, it is important to investigate processes that underlie human-computer interaction, to provide models and concepts that enable us to experiment with various types of complex systems, and to design and build tools and prototypes that demonstrate the ideas and techniques in a working system. In this article, I will discuss the "gap" between dialogue management and response planning and focus on the communicatively adequate contributions that are produced in the context of a situated robot agent. The WikiTalk system supports open-domain conversations by using Wikipedia as the knowledge source, and a version of it is implemented on the Nao-robot.

K. Jokinen (✉)
University of Helsinki, Helsinki, Finland
e-mail: kristiina.jokinen@helsinki.fi

© Springer International Publishing Switzerland 2015

N. Gala et al. (eds.), *Language Production, Cognition, and the Lexicon*,
Text, Speech and Language Technology 48, DOI 10.1007/978-3-319-08043-7_20

Keywords Wikitalk interaction · Open-domain dialogues · Newinfo · Topic trees · Planning · Generation

1 Prologue

In the mid-1990's I organised an ECAI workshop *GAPS AND BRIDGES: New Directions in Planning and Natural Language Generation*, together with Michael Zock and Mark Maybury. It was my first international workshop, and I was excited at the possibility to collaborate with two famous senior researchers of the field.

The workshop focussed on the planning of communicatively adequate contributions, and especially on the gap which at that time was recognized between natural language generation and AI-based planning for autonomous cooperative systems. In NLG, a focus shift directed research from grammatical well-formedness conditions towards exploration of the communicative adequacy of linguistic forms, while dialogue system research investigated how natural and rational communication could be equipped with NLG techniques so as to be able present the message to the user in a flexible way.

The gap has since been bridged, or at least it seems less deep, thanks to research and development on interactive systems and response planning. Generation challenges, e.g. Challenge on Generating Instructions in Virtual Environments (GIVE), have brought the NLG tasks closer to the planning of communicative contributions, while spoken dialogue systems need a module which effectively corresponds to a NLG component to be able to produce system output (see e.g. Jokinen and Wilcock 2003, or Jokinen and McTear 2009 for an overview). A recent indication of the mutual interests is a shared session which has been planned to take place in the SIGDial (Special Interest Group in Disourse and Dialogue) and the INLG (International Conference on Natural Language Generation) conferences organised by the respective communities in the summer 2014, in order to "highlight the areas of research were the interests of the two communities intersect and to foster interaction in these area".

The workshop topics seem timely and relevant even today, after 20 years of the original workshop, although they need to be formulated in a slightly different way. In fact, it is possible to argue that new bridges are needed to overpass the gaps between intelligent agents and open-domain generation tasks. On one hand, research in speech-based dialogue systems has extended communicative adequacy to cover not only grammatical forms of written language, but also meaningful exchanges of "ungrammatical" spoken utterances. An established view in dialogue research is that speaking is a means for achieving communicative goals, and dialogues are jointly constructed by the partners through communicatively appropriate utterances which can overlap with each other time-wise, and consist of elliptical structures as well as of discourse particles and backchannelling elements. Thus interactive agents, ranging from speech-enabled applications to situated conversational robot companions, need to reason on the communicative context, including previous dialogue, physical situation, and the partner's knowledge and interest, in order to interpret the utterances and to engage the partner in the conversation. In generation research, on the other hand, information retrieval and summarization techniques have allowed NLG to extend research toward question-answering systems and thus the context also plays an important role in the planning and realization of responses: it has impact on the interpretation of the question and the information relevant to the answer, as well as on the user's knowledge, preferences, and interest regarding the topic of the question.

In this article, I will discuss the "gap" between dialogue management and response planning and focus on the communicatively adequate contributions that are produced in the context of a situated robot agent. The WikiTalk system supports open-domain conversations by using Wikipedia as the knowledge source (Wilcock and Jokinen 2012, 2013; Jokinen and Wilcock 2013), and a version of it is implemented on the Nao-robot (Csapo et al. 2012). The article is structured as follows. Section 2 reviews recent progress in open-domain interactive systems. Section 3 presents the WikiTalk application and discusses our approach to an open-domain dialogue system which can talk about any topics found in Wikipedia. Section 4 addresses the dichotomy of topic and New information, and Sect. 5 addresses the issues concerning Topic trees. Some notes on generation are presented in Sect. 6, and conclusions and future prospects are discussed in Sect. 7.

2 Open-Domain Interactive Systems

Open domain spoken dialogue systems that aim at serving as conversational companions must be capable of talking about any topic that the user introduces. The WikiTalk system (Wilcock 2012; Jokinen and Wilcock 2012) proposes to meet this requirement by using Wikipedia as a knowledge source. Wikipedia is a collaboratively produced encyclopaedia and it is constantly updated, so the range of topics that the WikiTalk system can talk about is unrestricted, and continuously growing. Contrary to traditional dialogue systems, dialogue management in WikiTalk is not based on a task but on the user's interest in the dialogue topics and on the system's ability to engage the user in an interesting conversation. The interaction management thus resembles the Question-under-Discussion approach (Ginzburg 1996), implemented as the Information State Update model in TrindiKit (Traum and Larsson 2003): the structure of the dialogues is determined by the information flow, and the dialogue is managed by updating the system's information state according to the user's questions and introduction of relevant pieces of information in the dialogue context. An important difference, however, is the availability of the topics in WikiTalk. In TrindiKit, the QUDs are limited to relevant information in a particular task, while in WikiTalk, topics are open to any information for which an article can be found in Wikipedia.

The most famous open-domain dialogue system was, and still is, ELIZA (Weizenbaum 1966). ELIZA could maintain an on-going dialogue, with no restriction on the topics that the user might care to mention. However, this was possible precisely because ELIZA did not use any domain knowledge about anything. Moreover, the user soon noticed that the dialogues lacked a goal and coherence: the system could maintain the dialogue for only a few turns and there was no global coherence or structure in the replies.

Modern versions of Eliza use chatbot technology based on the Artificial Intelligence Markup Language (AIML) standard. Such applications are designed specifically for web-based interaction on mobile devices such as handsets and tablets. For instance, Alice (http://www.alicebot.org/) provides a chatbot personality with a human-like face and interactive features, and it can be used on website or mobile app to chat with the user. However, the limit of the Alice framework is that it requires a hand-tailored database on the basis of which interaction takes place. Although the chatbot applications may sound fairly free and natural, they still require manually built domain models and question-answer pairs for smooth operation.

On the other hand, research with Embodied Conversational Agents (ECAs) has especially brought forward multimodal interaction, focussing on the different types of multimodal signalling that are important in human-human natural conversations, and which are also necessary when supplying natural intuitive communication models for interactions between humans and ECAs (André and Pelachaud 2010; Misu et al. 2011).

Recently, a new type of question-answering (QA) systems have appeared (Greenwood 2006) that are open-domain in the sense that the user can ask a question about any topic. One of the most famous ones of the new QA systems is IBM's Watson (Ferrucci 2012), whereas Apple's SIRI exhibits personal assistant and knowledge navigator with a capability to answer questions which are not directly related to its knowledge-base. Open-domain QA systems use sophisticated machine-learning techniques, question classifiers, search engines, ontologies, summarization, and answer extraction techniques to enable efficient and accurate response. Moriceau et al. (2009) give an overview of the information retrieval and automatics summarization systems, and Franz and Milch (2002) discuss various issues related to voice enabled search. Evaluation of such complex systems is also complicated, and e.g. El Ayari and Grau (2009) provide a glass-box evaluation framework for QA systems.

Different approaches to Interactive Question Answering are reviewed by Kirschner (2007). Although these more interactive developments have brought QA systems closer to dialogue systems, the aim of a QA system is still to find the correct answer to the question, not to hold a conversation about the topic as such. For example, an interaction may consist of a question "What is the second largest city in France?" and of the answer "Marseille." Efforts have also been made to build more interactive QA systems by combining them with aspects of a spoken dialogue system. For example, in the RITEL system (Rosset et al. 2006) the QA component has a capability to ask clarification questions about the user's question.

The combination of RITEL with another QA-system, QAVAL, extends the system with different answer extraction strategies which are then merged at different levels to the final answer (Grappy et al. 2012). However, QA systems are still primarily intended to function as interactive interfaces to information retrieval tasks, rather than as conversational companions.

In this context, a notable exception is the WikiTalk system that can be described from two points of view: it is a QA system in that it operates as an "open-domain knowledge access system" (Wilcock 2012), and it is a conversational dialogue system in that it allows "talking about interesting topics" (Jokinen and Wilcock 2012, 2013; Wilcock 2012). WikiTalk uses Wikipedia as its knowledge source, and by dynamically accessing the web, WikiTalk differs from traditional QA systems in that it is able to maintain a conversation about the topic introduced by the user. Wikipedia has been used by question-answering systems, as described for example by Buscaldi and Rosso (2006). However, their main aim is to use Wikipedia for validation of answers, not as a knowledge source for conversations: Wikipedia "category" entries are used as a kind of ontology which the QA's question type taxonomy can base its answers. The application domain envisaged in WikiTalk is not a fancy chatbot that provides clever answers on a predefined domain, but rather an interactive "agent" which has its cognitive capability extended by internet knowledge.

3 The WikiTalk Application

The WikiTalk (Jokinen and Wilcock 2012, 2013; Wilcock 2012) is an interactive application that allows the user to query and navigate among Wikipedia articles. By using Wikipedia as its knowledge source, WikiTalk is an open-domain spoken dialogue system as compared with traditional task-based dialogue systems, which operate on a closed-domain, finite application database.

The WikiTalk system works as a web application with a screen interface, but the implementation on the Nao humanoid robot greatly extends its natural dialogue capability. As described in Csapo et al. (2012), the robot implementation includes multimodal communication features, especially face tracking and gesturing. Face-tracking provides information about the user's interest in the current topic, while suitable gesturing enables the robot to emphasise and visualise its own information presentation. The human's proximity to the robot and their focus of visual attention are used to estimate whether the user follows the robot's presentation, whereas head nodding, hand gestures, and body posture are combined with the robot's own speech turns to make its presentations more natural and engaging. Figure 1 shows some users interacting with the Nao WikiTalk system during the ENTERFACE summer school 2011, and an annotated video of a Wikipedia-based open-domain human-robot dialogue can be seen at: http://vimeo.com/62148073.

The theoretical foundation of WikiTalk is Constructive Dialogue Modelling (CDM, Jokinen 2009), which integrates topic management, information flow, and

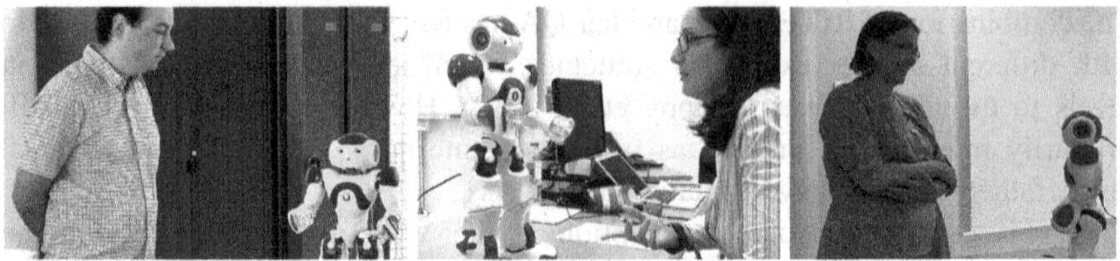

Fig. 1 Users interacting with the Nao WikiTalk

the construction of shared knowledge in the conversation by communicative agents. According to CDM, interlocutors are rational agents who coordinate and control their interaction in cooperation. Moreover, the agents monitor their partner's behaviour and give feedback to each other concerning the basic enablements of communication: Contact, Perception, Understanding, and Reaction (cf. Allwood 1976). Contact and Perception are understood as modelling the agent's awareness of the communication, while Understanding and Reaction concern the agent's intentional and cooperative behaviour: producing a semantic interpretation of the partner's utterance and to the planning and generation of one's own behaviour as a reaction to it, respectively. Signalling whether the basic enablements are fulfilled (the person hears what is said, understands the meaning of the partner's message, or is willing to be involved in the interaction) is often done via non-verbal and multimodal means, i.e. not explicitly by words but by head movements, facial expressions, gesturing, and body posture.

According to the CDM, dialogue management should support interaction that *affords* natural information flow (Jokinen 2009). In the context of WikiTalk, the main challenge is to present Wikipedia information in a way that makes the structure of the articles clear. The users should easily navigate among the topics that interest them, be able to pick up links for new information, and select new topics. WikiTalk keeps track of what is currently salient in the interaction (a model of the interlocutor's attention), and anticipates what is the likely next topic (a model of the interlocutor's communicative intentions). An interactive WikiTalk also distinguishes between two conditions: the user shows interest and allows the system to continue on the current topic, or the user is not interested in the topic and the system should stop or find some other topic to talk about. The interaction model thus includes a user model and a representation for the partner's mental states, to keep track of the topics being talked about and the user's interest and attitude towards the presented information.

The conversational strategy of the WikiTalk agent is designed to be verbose, with a goal of initiating topics which are likely to engage the user in the conversation. The dialogue control model in WikiTalk uses a finite-state approach, and Fig. 2 (next page) shows a pertinent state transition diagram (this diagram also shows speech recognition states, cf. Wilcock 2012). The diagram differs from traditional finite state models in that dialogue states are related to the information flow ("select New Topic", "continue Topic", etc.), not to specific domain-related

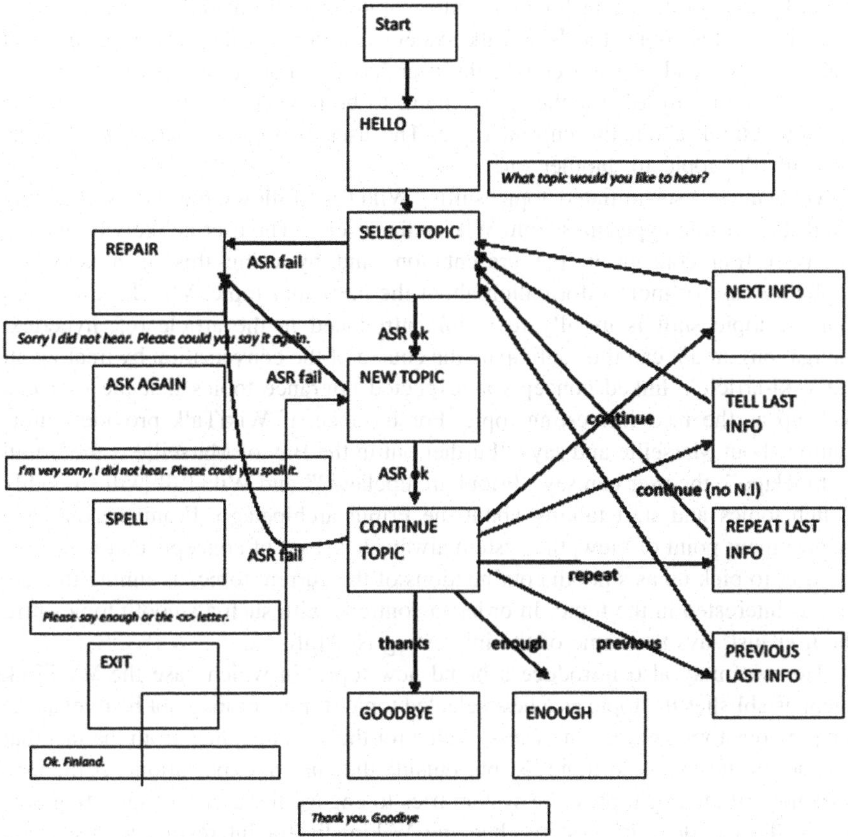

Fig. 2 A state transition diagram for WikiTalk

knowledge states (such as "know departure day" or "know destination city"). The state transitions concern the exchange of information with the user, and they are managed with the help of techniques related to topic-tracking and topic shifting. The dialogue actions are thus reduced to very general actions, namely presenting information and listening to the partner's response, rather than being related to particular task-domain actions. This approach makes it possible for a finite number of states to manage dialogues with an infinite number of topics.

When a new topic is selected, the WikiTalk system gets the text for the topic from Wikipedia and divides it into chunks (paragraphs and sentences) suitable for spoken dialogue contributions. The system then manages the presentation of the chunks according to the user's reaction. The user can respond verbally or non-verbally, and WikiTalk thus needs to be able to "listen" and "see", i.e. it needs to understand the user's verbally expressed commands (such as "continue"), and also interpret the user's multimodal behaviour (such as looking away to signal one is not interested). If the user shows interest in the topic, by explicitly asking for more information or multimodally signalling their curiosity on the topic, the WikiTalk system continues with presenting the next chunk. At the end of each chunk, the user has an opportunity to continue with the next chunk, to ask for the same chunk to be repeated, or to go back to the previous chunk about the current topic. The user also can initiate a new topic, i.e. shift the topic to another one.

To manage user-initiated topic shifts, WikiTalk follows the user's changing interests by using hyperlinks from Wikipedia articles. The user is likely to pick up an interesting concept in the presentation, and by using this as a keyword, explicitly ask for more information about the particular topic. WikiTalk assumes that the topic shift is usually to a link introduced in the article (cf. hypertext navigation), and it can thus anticipate the course of the conversation by treating all the wiki-article's linked concepts as expected utterance topics that the user can pick up as the next interesting topic. For instance, if WikiTalk provides information about Marseille and says "Further out in the Bay of Marseille is the Frioul archipelago", the user can say "Frioul archipelago?" and WikiTalk will smoothly switch topics and start talking about the Frioul archipelago. From the dialogue management point of view, the system always has a set of concepts that it expects the user to pick up as smooth continuations of the current topic, assuming that the user is interested in the topic. In order to continue with such a smooth topic-shift, the user just says the name of the interesting NewInfo.

The user may also introduce a brand new topic, in which case the WikiTalk agent establishes the topic as a new selected topic. It may or may not be relevant to the previous topic, but its "newness" value for the system comes from the fact that it is not in the expected topic list but outside the current expectations. If the user does not initiate any topics, the system tries to engage the user by suggesting new topics. This is done by system checking Wikipedia for interesting topics in the daily "Did you know?" or "On this day" sections, and suggesting randomly some of these topics for the user. Again, if the user is interested in hearing more from the particular topic, the user is likely to indicate their interest by explicitly requesting "tell me more", or implicitly inviting WikiTalk to talk more about the issue with the help of multimodal signalling, e.g. raising eyebrows or uttering "really" with a raising intonation. At the moment, WikiTalk understands user utterances consisting of short commands or simple keywords, but we are experimenting with complex natural language utterances. Depending on the speech recognition engine, this works fairly well for English. The same applies for different speakers and accents: the ASR expects the user to speak fairly standard form of language.

It is also possible that the user wants to interrupt the current chunk without listening to it all, and ask to skip forward to the next chunk on the same topic. If WikiTalk is interrupted, it stops talking and explicitly acknowledges the interruption. It then waits for the user's input, which can range from telling the systems to continue, to go back to an earlier chunk, to skip forward to the next chunk, or to switch to a new topic.

4 NewInfos and Topics in WikiTalk

CDM follows the common grounding models of dialogue information (Clark and Brennan 1991; Traum 1994) in that the status of information available in a particular dialogue situation depends on its integration in the shared context. New information needs to be grounded, i.e. established as part of the common ground by the partner's acknowledgement, whereas old information is already grounded, or part of the general world knowledge. Normally the knowledge of a dialogue system is included in the system's task model that contains concepts for the entities, events and relations relevant for the task in hand, and the concepts are instantiated and grounded in the course of the dialogue.

In WikiTalk, however, the system's knowledge consists of the whole Wikipedia. Wikipedia articles are regarded as possible *Topics* that the robot can talk about, i.e. elements of its knowledge. Each link in the article is treated as a potential *NewInfo* to which the user can shift their attention by asking for more information about it. If the user follows a link in the article, the linked article thus becomes a new Topic and the links in it will be potential NewInfos. The conceptual space in WikiTalk is thus quite unlike that in a closed-domain task models: it consists of a dynamically changing set of Wikipedia articles and is structured into Topic and NewInfos according to the article titles and the hyperlinks in the articles.

The paragraphs and sentences in the article are considered propositional chunks, or pieces of information that form the minimal units for presentation. To distinguish the information status of these units of presentation, we use the term *focus text*: this is the paragraph that WikiTalk is currently reading or presenting to the user and which is thus at its focus of attention. We could, of course, apply the division of Topic and NewInfo also to paragraphs if we consider the Wikipedia articles only in terms of being presented to the user. However, we wanted to have an analogous structure for the Wikipedia article reading as we already had used for sentential information, where the concepts of Topic and NewInfo are instantiated as concepts that can be talked about and which form a concept space for the surface generator. In WikiTalk, Topic and NewInfo refer to the particular issues that the speakers can talk about or decide to talk about next (Wikipedia articles and the hyperlinks therein which form a conceptual network to navigate in), while the parts of the message (paragraphs) that are new in the context of the current Topic, are called focus texts. The focus texts provide new information about the current Topic (the title of the Wiki-article), but they cannot be selected by the user directly as something the user wants to talk about (e.g. it is not possible to issue a command in WikiTalk to read the third paragraph of the article Marseille). The focus text paragraphs are only accessible by the system when it reads the topical article. Unlike articles and hyperlinks, the focus texts are not independent "concepts" or referents in the conceptual space that can be referred to, but more like closely and coherently related pieces of information associated with a specific topic (wiki-article).

It must be emphasized that dialogue coherence is considered straightforward in WikiTalk; discourse relations between consecutive utterances rely on the structure of Wikipedia. Since the articles have already been written as coherent texts and the links between the articles have been inserted so that they make the articles into coherent hypertexts, we can assume that by following the topics and the NewInfo links in Wiki-articles the listener is able to infer what the connection between the topics is. We make a strong assumption in that the user selects links to continue dialogue, rather than any other words in the Wiki-article. The users can, of course, select any article as their next topic, and this is often the case if the user explores the Wikipedia randomly. On the other hand, most users are already used to navigating through Wikipedia and using the hyperlinks to select the next topic, so in WikiTalk, they simply follow the same principle. However, one of the relevant questions in WikiTalk is how to point to the users which of the words are linked and which are not—in speech this is not as easy as in visual texts. In the robot implementation, Nao WikiTalk can use the whole repertoire of communicative means, i.e. it uses rhythmic gesturing to mark the linked words.

Situated dialogue systems impose requirements on the generation of multimodal responses, e.g. to build models that determine appropriate prosody and the appropriate type of hand gesturing to accompany a spoken utterance. We will not go into details of these, but refer to André and Pelachaud (2010) for multimodal aspects, and to the seminal work by Theune (2000) on marking of pitch accents and phrasal melodies for the realizer to synthesize the correct surface form, or to introductory textbook like Holmes and Holmes (2002).

5 Topic Trees and Smooth Topic Shifts

In dialogue management, topics are usually managed by a stack, which conveniently handles topics that have been recently talked about. However, stacks are a rather rigid means to describe the information flow in cases where the dialogues are more conversational and do not follow any particular task structure. We prefer topic trees, which enable more flexible management of the topics. The trees can be traversed in whatever order, while the distance of the jumps determines the manner of presentation of the information.

Originally "focus trees" were proposed by McCoy and Cheng (1991) to trace foci in NL generation systems. The branches of the tree describe what sort of shifts are cognitively easy to process and can be expected to occur in dialogues: random jumps from one branch to another are not very likely to occur, and if they do, they should be appropriately marked. The focus tree is a subgraph of the world knowledge, built in the course of the discourse on the basis of the utterances that have occurred. The tree both constrains and enables prediction of likely next topics, and provides a top-down approach to dialogue coherence.

The notion of a topic (focus) has been a means to describe thematically coherent discourse structure, and its use has been mainly supported by arguments regarding anaphora resolution and processing effort. WikiTalk uses topic information in selecting likely content of the next utterance (the links contained in the article), and thus the topic tree consists of Wiki-article titles that describe the information conveyed by the utterance (the article that is being read). We can say that the topic type or theme is more important than the actual topic entities. The WikiTalk system will not do full syntactic parsing, but will identify chunk boundaries (paragraph and sentence endings), so instead of tracing salient discourse entities and providing heuristics for different shifts of attention with respect to these entities, WikiTalk seeks for a formalisation of the information structure in terms of Topic and NewInfo that deal with the article titles and links.

In previous research, the world knowledge underlying topic trees was hand-coded, and this of course was time-consuming and subjective. In WikiTalk, it is the Wikipedia which is the "world knowledge" of the system, and our topic trees are a way to organise domain knowledge in terms of topic types found in the web. The hypertext structure is analogous to the linking of world knowledge concepts (although not a graph but a network), and through the interaction with the user, the system selects topics and builds a topic tree. The topic shifts which occur following the information structure in the Wikipedia will be *smooth* topic shifts, while the shifts which the user introduces and which are not part of the immediate information structure are called *awkward*. Consequently, smooth topic shifts are straightforward continuations of the interaction, but awkward shifts require that WikiTalk marks the shift verbally. This maintains the interaction coherence and clear.

6 Notes on Generation

In the standard model of text generation systems (Reiter and Dale 2000), information structure is recognised as a major factor. This model usually has a pipeline architecture, in which one stage explicitly deals with discourse planning and another stage deals with referring expressions, ensuring that topic shifts and old and new information status are properly handled. As already mentioned, spoken dialogue systems impose further requirements on generation, such as how to handle prosody, but there are some fundamental issues involved too, stemming from the facts that in spoken interaction, the listener also immediately reacts to the information presented, and the speaker can modify the presentation online based on the listener's feedback. This kind of anticipation of the partner's reaction and immediate revision of one's own behaviour brings us to the old NLG question of *Where does generation start from?* Previously it has been argued that attempts to answer this question push the researchers on sliding down a slippery slope (McDonald 1993) in that the starting point seems to evade any definition. However, considering generation in interactive systems, we can argue that it starts simultaneously with interpretation, in the perception and understanding phase of the presented information. In other words, generation starts already when one is listening to the partner, as a reaction to the presented information. Although the actual realisation of the thoughts as spoken language appears later on (and is regulated by turn-taking conventions), the listeners can also produce immediate feedback in the form of backchannelling and various non-verbal signals.

The model of generation in WikiTalk loosely follows that introduced by Jokinen et al. (1998). In this model, response planning starts from the information focus, *NewInfo*, which can be thought as the content of the speaker's intention. The generator's task is to convey this message to the partner, so it decides how to present NewInfo to the user: whether to realise just the "naked" NewInfo by itself, or whether to add appropriate hedging information that would help the partner to understand how the NewInfo is related to the joint goals of the dialogue. For this, the manager creates an *Agenda*, a set of specifically marked domain concepts which have been designated as relevant in the dialogue. The Agenda is available for the generator, which can freely use the concepts in the agenda in order to realise the system's intention, but is not forced to include all the concepts in its response.

The prototype response generator described by Jokinen and Wilcock (2001) and Jokinen and Wilcock (2003) has a simple pipeline including an aggregation stage, a combined lexicalization and referring expressions stage, and a surface realization stage. In WikiTalk, the generation does not deal with the sentence realisation, since the Wikipedia articles are read aloud as such (using a TTS-system), while the system utterances are simple questions and canned phrases. However, the notions of Agenda and NewInfo are used when the system deals with the "information chunks", i.e. with the paragraphs and sentences of the articles. Following the NewInfo-based model, the WikiTalk Agenda is used to keep track of the "concepts", i.e. the focus texts that belong to the current topical article, and the generator can then select from Agenda those texts that will be realised and read to the user. All focus text paragraphs are marked as NewInfo, i.e. as potential information to be conveyed to the user, and the system realises them by selecting one at the time to be read aloud to the user. As mentioned earlier, the NewInfo presentation continues depending on the user's reaction: the next focus text will be presented to the user if the user seems interested or explicitly requests "continue".

7 Conclusion

A communicatively competent interactive system should provide communicatively adequate responses. In the Gaps and Bridges workshop, this was addressed by inviting submissions e.g. on *interactions between situational, motivational (speaker and addressee goals), cognitive and linguistic constraints*; as well as on *the effect of the various constraints on the generation process as a whole (resource-bounded agency and planning constraints; open-world assumption; time and space constraints)*. In this article I have returned back to the pertinent issues presented in the workshop, and considered issues related to the two above mentioned workshop themes. In particular, I have discussed a situational robot application WikiTalk and its dialogue management model that supports open-domain interactions. It is noticed that in spoken interactive systems, the generation of responses can be seen as starting already when the system is listening to the partner, or in other words, besides open-domain talking, it is necessary to have "open-domain listening". As is clear, there is much still to be done in order to bridge the gap and address the workshop themes, but much active research is being conducted, and rapid progress can be expected.

References

Allwood, J. (1976). *Linguistic communication as action and cooperation*. Gothenburg Monographs in Linguistics 2. University of Gothenburg.

André, E., & Pelachaud, C. (2010). Interacting with embodied conversational agents. In F. Cheng, & K. Jokinen (Eds.), *Speech technology: Theory and applications* (pp. 123–150). Berlin: Springer.

Buscaldi, D., & Rosso, P. (2006). Mining knowledge from Wikipedia for the question answering task. In *Proceedings of 5th Language Resources and Evaluation Conference* (LREC 2006), Genoa.

Clark, H. H., & Brennan, S. E. (1991). Grounding in communication. In L. B. Resnick, J. M. Levine, & S. D. Teasley (Eds.), *Perspectives on socially shared cognition* (pp. 127–149). Washington: APA Books.

Csapo, A., Gilmartin, E., Grizou, J., Han, J. G., Meena, R., & Anastasiou, D., et al. (2012). Multimodal conversational interaction with a humanoid robot. In *Proceedings of 3rd IEEE International Conference on Cognitive Infocommunications* (CogInfoCom 2012), Kosice.

El Ayari, S, & Grau, B. (2009). A framework of evaluation for question-answering systems. *ECIR, Lecture notes in computer science* (vol. 5478, pp. 744–748). Berlin: Springer.

Franz, A., & Milch, B. (2002). Searching the web by voice. In *Proceedings of 19th International Conference on Computational Linguistics* (COLING 2002) (pp. 1213–1217). Taipei.

Ferrucci, D. A. (2012). Introduction to this is watson. *IBM Journal of Research and Development, 56*(3.4), 1:1–1:15.

Ginzburg, J. (1996). Interrogatives: Questions, facts and dialogue. In S. Lappin (Ed.), *The handbook of contemporary semantic theory* (pp. 385–422). Blackwell: Blackwell Textbooks in Linguistics.

Grappy, A., Grau, B., & Rosset, S. (2012). Methods combination and ML-based re-ranking of multiple hypothesis for question-answering systems. In *Proceedings of the Workshop on Innovative Hybrid Approaches to the Processing of Textual Data* (pp. 87–96). Avignon, France, April 2012.

Greenwood, M. A. (2006). Open-domain question answering. PhD Thesis,Department of Computer Science, The University of Sheffield.

Holmes, J. N., & Holmes, W. J. (2002). *Speech synthesis and recognition*. UK: Taylor Francis Ltd.

Jokinen, K. (2009). *Constructive dialogue modelling: Speech interaction and rational agents*. New York: Wiley.

Jokinen, K., & McTear, M. (2009). *Spoken dialogue systems.Synthesis lectures on human language technologies*. San Rafael, CA: Morgan and Claypool.doi:10.2200/S00204ED1V01Y200910HLT005.

Jokinen, K., Tanaka, H., & Yokoo, A. (1998). Planning dialogue contributions with new information. *Proceedings of the ninth international workshop on natural language generation* (pp. 158–167). Ontario: Niagara-on-the-Lake.

Jokinen, K., & Wilcock, G. (2003). Adaptivity and response generation in a spoken dialogue system. In J. van Kuppevelt, & R. W. Smith (Eds.), *Current and new directions in discourse and dialogue*. (pp. 213–234). UK: Kluwer Academic Publishers.

Jokinen, K., & Wilcock, G. (2012). Constructive interaction for talking about interesting topics. In *Proceedings of Eighth International Conference on Language Resources and Evaluation (LREC 2012)*, Istanbul.

Jokinen, K., & Wilcock, G. (2013). Multimodal open-domain conversations with the nao robot. In J. Mariani, L. Devillers, M. Garnier-Rizet, & S. Rosset (Eds.), *Natural interaction with robots, knowbots and smartphones—putting spoken dialog systems into practice*. Berlin: Springer.

Kirschner, M. (2007). Applying a focus tree model of dialogue context to interactive question answering. In *Proceedings of ESSLLI'07 Student Session*, Dublin, Ireland.

McCoy K. F., & Cheng, J. (1991). Focus of attention: Constraining what can be said next. In C. Paris, W. Swartout, & W. Mann (Eds.), *Natural language generation in artificial intelligence and computational linguistics*, (pp. 103–124). UK: Kluwer Academic Publishers.

Misu, T., Mizumaki, E., Shiga, Y., Kawamoto, S., Kawai, H., & Nakamura, S. (2011). Analysis on effects of text-to speech and avatar agent on evoking users' spontaneous listener's reactions. In *Proceedings of the Paralinguistic Information and its Integration in Spoken Dialogue Systems Workshop* (pp. 77–89), Granada.

Moriceau, V., SanJuan, E., Tannier, X., & Bellot, P. (2009). Overview of the 2009 QA track: Towards a common task for QA, focused IR and automatic summarization systems. In *Focused Retrieval and Evaluation, 8th International Workshop of the Initiative for the Evaluation of XML Retrieval, INEX 2009*. Brisbane, Australia, (pp. 355–365). Springer Verlag. Lecture Notes in Computer Science (LNCS 6203).

McDonald, D. (1993). Does natural language generation start from a specification?.In: H. Horacek & M. Zock (Eds.), New concepts in natural language generation(pp. 275–297). London: Pinter Publishers.

Rosset, S., Galibert, O., Illouz, G., & Max, A. (2006). Integrating spoken dialogue and question answering: The RITEL project. In *Proceedings of InterSpeech 06*, Pittsburgh.

Reiter, E., & Dale, R. (2000). *Building natural language generation systems*.Cambridge: Cambridge University Press. Reissued in paperback in 2006.

Theune, M. (2000). From data to speech: language generation in context. Ph.D. thesis, Eindhoven University of Technology.

Traum, D. R. (1994) A computational theory of grounding in natural language conversation, TR 545 and Ph.D. Thesis, Computer Science Dept., U. Rochester, December 1994.

Traum, D., & Larsson, S. (2003). The information state approach to dialogue management. In J. van Kuppevelt and R. Smith (Eds.), *Current and new directions in discourse and dialogue* (pp. 325–353). South Holland: Kluwer.

Weizenbaum, J. (1966). Eliza—a computer program for the study of natural language communication between man and machine. *Communications of the ACM, 9*(1), 36–45.

Jokinen, K., & Wilcock, G. (2001). Pipelines, templates and transformations: XML for natural language generation. In *Proceedings of the 1st NLP and XML Workshop* (pp. 1–8). Tokyo.

Wilcock, G. (2012). WikiTalk: A spoken Wikipedia-based open-domain knowledge access system. In *Proceedings of the COLING 2012 Workshop on Question Answering for Complex Domains* (pp. 57–69). Mumbai, India.

Wilcock, G. & Jokinen, K. (2013). Towards cloud-based speech interfaces for open-domain coginfocom systems. In *Proceedings of the 4th IEEE International Conference on Cognitive Infocommunications (CogInfoCom) 2013*, Budapest, Hungary.

Wilcock, G., & Jokinen, K. (2011). Adding speech to a robotics simulator. In R. Lopez Delgado, et al. (Eds.) *Proceedings of the Third International Conference on Spoken Dialogue Systems: Ambient Intelligence*. (pp. 375–380). Granada, Spain: Springer Publishers.

JSREAL: A Text Realizer for Web Programming

Nicolas Daoust and Guy Lapalme

Abstract The web is constantly growing and its documents, getting progressively more dynamic, are well-suited to presentation automation by a text realizer. Current browser-based information display systems have mostly focused on the display and layout of textual data, restricting the generation of nonnumerical informations to canned text or formatted strings. We describe JSREAL, a French text realizer implemented in Javascript. It allows its user to build a variety of French expressions and sentences, combined with HTML tags to easily integrate them into web pages to produce dynamic output depending on the content of the page.

Keywords French text realizer · Web browser · Text generation · HTML · Javascript · Dynamic web pages

1 Context

Natural language generation (NLG) is often used to textually describe massive datasets, making the most of computers' ability for rapid analysis. Even in the cases where experts could interpret the data by themselves, it can be useful to present summaries of other pertinent aspects of the data to non-experts.

Beyond rapid analysis, another advantage of computers over humans is their tireless efficiency at carrying out routine tasks. Many people, in the course of everyday work, have to repeatedly express information of which only certain details change from one instance to another, for example in customer support.

N. Daoust · G. Lapalme (✉)
RALI-DIRO, Université de Montréal, C.P. 6128, Succ Centre-Ville, Montreal, QC H3C 3J7, Canada
e-mail: lapalme@iro.umontreal.ca

N. Daoust
e-mail: n@daou.st

© Springer International Publishing Switzerland 2015
N. Gala et al. (eds.), *Language Production, Cognition, and the Lexicon*, Text, Speech and Language Technology 48, DOI 10.1007/978-3-319-08043-7_21

NLG can automate a significant part of that type of textual production, only requiring a human to supply some important aspects and thus saving considerable time and producing consistent grammatically correct output.

Following the classical architecture of Reiter and Dale (2000), NLG involves three stages: macro-planning (content choice and organization), micro-planning (abstract specification of linguistic form by means of finding appropriate referring expressions, doing some aggregation and choosing the words and grammatical forms) and realization (conversion into concrete spoken or written form). In this paper, we focus on this last step, which is further subdivided into surface realization (the sequence of words and sentences) and physical presentation (HTML presentation).

2 Realization

All programming languages can produce textual output with so-called *print* statements and most of them allow some flexibility with *formatting* schemes, some of them being quite sophisticated, but no programming language provides a complete text realizer. So when more fluent text must be generated (especially in morphologically rich languages such as German or French), this requires a dedicated specialized realizer. Such realizers feature patterns for phrases, sentences and documents, but only a few of their aspects (e.g. numeric values or number of different values) are modifiable and they would thus require a thorough overhaul to be adapted for another project. Whereas a complete realizer encodes a large diversity of words, phrases and grammatical rules, a specific realizer only covers whatever few words and structures it needs to, processing them quite naïvely.

Some realizers, such as KPML (2013), SURGE (Elhadad 2013) and RealPro (Lavoie and Rambow 1997; RealPro 2013), are based on complex syntactic theories, taking into account many details in the construction of sentences, which allows powerful realizations. However, that complexity hinders their ease of use: writing specifications for them requires an intimate knowledge of the underlying theory, which is not the case of most programmers.

In fact, most existing realizers are considered so convoluted that SimpleNLG (Gatt and Reiter 2009; SimpleNLG 2013), as its name implies, defines itself by its ease of learning and of use (Downloadable NLG systems 2013). Words, phrases and other structures being Java objects, they can be created and manipulated intuitively by a programmer and they are easily integrated into a Java project. While its fundamentals do not allow for realizations as powerful as some other realizers, they largely suffice for most use. SimpleNLG has been used in a variety of text generation projects such as described by Portet et al. (2009).

Some of the existing realizers, like KPML and RealPro, are technically capable of producing web output, such as HTML; KPML even allows the addition of rudimentary HTML tags to words or phrases. However, no realizer is written in a web programming language, such as JavaScript or PHP, and integrating another language on a web page, while feasible, is only practical in select cases. In any case, this means that web-based text generation projects are currently better-served by their own custom realizers.

3 JSREAL

JSREAL (JavaScript REALizer) is a French text realizer that generates well-formed expressions and sentences and can format them in HTML to be displayed in a browser. It can be used standalone for linguistic demonstrations or be integrated into complex text generation projects. But first and foremost, JSREAL is aimed at web developers, from taking care of morphology, subject-verb agreement and conjugation to creating entire HTML documents.

As its name indicates, JSREAL is written in JavaScript, a programming language that, when used in a web page, runs in the client browser. A web programmer that wishes to use JSREAL to produce flexible French textual output only needs to add two lines in the header of the page (one for loading the French lexicon and one for program), similarly as what is done for other browser frameworks such as JQUERY.

The specifications of JSREAL are similar to those of SIMPLENLG: they are programming language instructions that create data structures corresponding to the constituents of the sentence to be produced. Once the data structure (a tree) is built in memory, it is traversed (a phase called *realization*) to produce the list of tokens that will form the sentence. This data structure is built by function calls whose names are the same as the symbols that are usually used for classical syntax trees: for example, `N` to create a *noun* structure, `NP` for a *Noun Phrase*, `V` for a *Verb*, and so on.

So instead of creating specifically formatted strings, the programmer uses usual JavaScript instructions that can be freely manipulated and that are particularly concise, resembling the syntactic trees of the phrases they represent (see Fig. 1).

Words in upper-case are function calls that create a data structure from the values returned by their parameters. As all these values are objects whose features can be modified by function calls that are specified using the *dot-notation* such as .n('p') in the second line of the left of Fig. 1. In this case, this means that the number of the noun phrase should be plural.

```
S(NP(D('le'),
     N('chat')).n('p'),
  VP(V('manger'),
     NP(D('un'),
        N('souris'))))
```

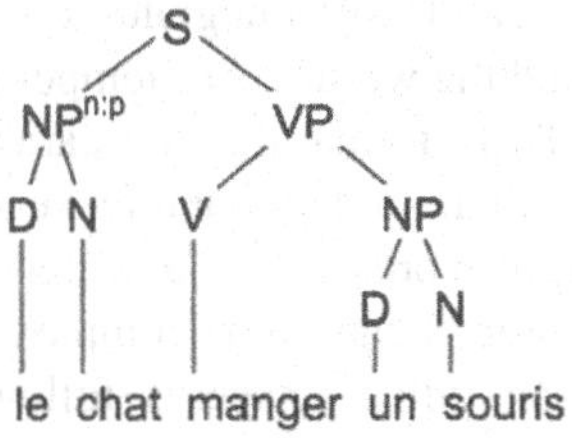

Fig. 1 A sample JSreal expression and the corresponding tree for the sentence `Les chats mangent une souris` (*The cats eat a mouse*)

```
Div(H2(N('propos de ').p('à'),
     Img().class('inline').src('MZ.png')),
    P(CP(S(N('nom').d('p3'),
           VP(V('être'),
              N('Michael Zock').tag('b'))),
         S(Pro('il'),
           VP(V('être'),
              NP(N('pionnier').d('i'),
                 PP(P('de'),
                    N('génération').d('d').add(
                      A('automatique').pos('post'),
                      N('texte').p('de'))
                        .href('http://www.nlg-wiki.org/systems/')))))
            .a2(''),
         Br(),
         S(Pro('vous'),
           VP(V('pouvoir'),
              VP(V('contacter'),
                 Pro('lui'),
                 Email('michael.zock@lif.univ-mrs.fr')
                         .p('à')))))))
```

À propos de 

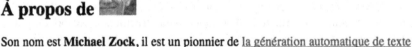

Son nom est **Michael Zock**, il est un pionnier de la génération automatique de texte et vous pouvez le contacter à michael.zock@lif.univ-mrs.fr.

Fig. 2 A more complex specification to produce HTML output

JSREAL 's capabilities are similar to other realizers':

- its lexicon defines word categories, genders, numbers, irregularities and other features;
- its knowledge of French morphologic rules allows it to use the appropriate word forms, such as plurals and conjugations;
- its knowledge of French syntactic rules allows it to properly order words in a sentence, transmit agreement (this is why the verb `manger` (*eat*) is plural in Fig. 1) and carry out other interactions.

JSREAL seamlessly integrates other useful tools, such as the spelling out of numbers and the wordings of temporal expressions. Since it produces web content, it uses HTML formatting for paragraphs, lists and similar structures and can manipulate them in detail and make sure that they do not interfere with the proper processing of words within a sentence.

Specifications can be as complex as needed, as shown in Fig. 2, where a title including an inline image is followed by a paragraph formed by a sentence coordinating three phrases (each of them being full sentences). Links, commas and the conjunction `et` (*and*) are appropriately inserted.

4 The Design of JSReal

The design of JSReal was influenced by the style of programming usually used in JavaScript and web development: that means that the specifications are relatively terse and rely on run-time checking rather than a compile-time type checking of the program used in SimpleNLG.

Previous realizers such as KPML and RealPro take as input files written in a special formalism. Although these realizers can be run from other programs, they mostly behave as black boxes. JSReal 's specifications are inspired by a very simple syntactic tree notation already used in some phrase structure grammar formalisms as shown in Fig. 1; however, to avoid the black box problem, JSReal specifications are made up of JavaScript object-creating functions, similar to SimpleNLG Java objects.

JavaScript objects are simply a set of properties and methods. In JSReal, words, phrases and formatting elements are called `units`, and they all have the same object as prototype, thus sharing methods and possible properties.

The basic units are the *word* categories: noun (`N`), verb (`V`), determiner (`D`), adjective (`A`), pronoun (`Pro`), adverb (`Adv`), preposition (`P` which depending on the context is also used for paragraphs) and conjunction (`C`). Each of the corresponding functions (such as N and V) takes a single lemma as only argument and return a JavaScript object with the appropriate properties and methods. These words can be used standalone or in phrases.

Phrases are higher-level units and are created with functions such as `NP` (noun phrase) and `VP` (verb phrase). They take other units as arguments, incorporating them as constituents, but can also receive constituents by the `add` method. An empty phrase (one that has no constituent) is skipped during realization. *Sentences* and clauses are created with `S`, and if not subordinated, are automatically added a capital and punctuation.

JSReal 's French lexicon is a direct adaptation of that of SimpleNLG-EnFr (Vaudry 2013; Vaudry and Lapalme 2013), a bilingual French and English version of SimpleNLG. That lexicon is in XML and consists of slightly less than 4,000 entries, including most function words and a selection of the most common content words according to the Dubois-Buyse orthographic scale (Echelle orthographique Dubois-Buyse 2013), which studies children's learning as they progress through school. Tools allow the user to add words to the lexicon and edit existing entries.

SimpleNLG-EnFr 's lexicon occupies 673 KB, which is relatively large by web standards. For a given number of entries, JSReal 's lexicon must be as light as possible, so we wrote a Python script to produce a JSON version of the dictionary. This amount to creating an object where each lemma is a key. Figure 3 shows the resulting entry for `son` (*his as adjective, sound as a noun*). This reduced the lexicon to 197 KB. Since JSON is native to JavaScript, it is used directly and combined with the dictionary structure, access speed is highly optimized.

```
"son":[{c:"D",fs:"sa",p:"ses",l:"son",po:1},
       {c:"N",g:"m",p:"sons"}]
```

Fig. 3 JSON entry for the French word son with two uses: a determiner (*his* or *her)*, the singular feminine and plural forms are given; a noun (*sound*), its gender and plural forms are given

4.1 Features

Every unit has multiple properties, such as a category, a lemma (in the case of a word) or constituents (in the case of a phrase). Other properties, called *features*, can be found in the lexicon or specified by the user or the context. There are about 70 features in total and each is represented in JSREAL by a concise set of characters as shown in Table 1:

The user can access features by calling the relevant method of a unit, which is the same string that identifies that feature everywhere else, as shown in earlier examples such as Fig. 1. Usually, the user will input the desired value as an argument or null to remove a previously set feature; in those cases, the method also returns the unit it is called on, allowing a sequence of features to be set. Omitting the argument makes the method return the current value of the feature.

One of the most complex parts of JSREAL is its ability to compute the value of a feature. In general, JSREAL first checks if the user has defined the feature, then if the context imposes a value, then if a value is found in the lexicon, and finally outputs `undefined`, letting the default processing be applied.

Many features follow detailed grammatical rules, in particular number and person, as shown in the two examples of Fig. 4. Some phrases redefine the retrieval of some features. Noun, adjective and verb phrases, as well as clauses and coordinations, can extract features from their constituents. Formatting tags, to be discussed in Sect. 4.2, always defer to their constituents for grammatical features, having none themselves.

Some JSREAL units can accept a JavaScript number instead of a lemma. A number can be used as a noun with no special results; as a determiner, it correctly propagates its number to its associated noun; as an adjective, it becomes an ordinal if associated to a name. With the num feature or by changing a general setting, the user can ask JSREAL to spell out a number or format it in another way. The first four lines of Table 2 show a few examples.

With the `DT` function, JSREAL can automate the writing of dates and times, considering days of the week and redundancies and using expressions such as *yesterday* and *noon*. The date and time can be specified either by a JavaScript Date object (passed as argument), by specific date strings or by methods such as `y`, `d` and `min`. The `DTR` function can make a range from two temporal expressions, removing redundancies. Both `DT` and `DTR` can be used as constituents in other units. The last two lines of Table 2 shows the creation of temporal expressions with their output.

Table 1 Sample values allowed for the main features

Feature	Meaning	Some allowed values
`g`	Gender	`m, f`
`n`	Number	`s, p`
`f`	Verb tense, aspect and mood	`p, i, pc`
`pe`	Person (4–6 are converted to 1–3, but plural)	`1, 5`
`pos`	Position in a phrase	`beg, pre, mid`
`fct`	Function in a phrase	`head, comp, sub`
`d`	Determiner (and makes the unit a noun phrase)	`d, i, dem`
`sub`	Complementize (and makes the clause subordinate)	A word such as `que`
`cap`	Capitalization	`1`
`a`	What comes after (generally punctuation)	`.`
`co`	Comparative form	A word such as `mieux`
`ns`	No space after	`1`
`ell`	Ellipsis of this unit	`1`

All features and their possible values are detailed in the online documentation of JSREAL (Daoust 2013a)

```
S(CP(C('ou'),
     Pro('moi'),
     Pro('toi'),
     Pro('elle')),
  V('manger'))

S(CP(C('et'),
     Pro('moi'),
     Pro('toi'),
     Pro('elle')),
  V('manger'))
```

Fig. 4 The first expression generates `Moi, toi ou elle mange.` (*I, you or she eats.*) in which the verb manger (*eat*) stays singular because of the disjunction `ou` (*or*). The second example generates `Moi, toi et elle mangeons.` (*I, you or she eat.*) with the plural verb because of the conjunction `et` (*and*). In both cases, the verb is conjugated at the first person because French grammar rules that the verb agrees with the *lowest* person

4.2 Formatting

Being web-based, JSREAL uses HTML for its formatting; the most basic is the use of the `P` function to join sentences in a paragraph. Many other HTML tags, like `H4, A` and `B`, also have their own functions, and `DOM` allows the creation of custom tags. Tags can also be added to units with the `tag` method. Figure 1 shows a paragraph preceded by a title and image. In most cases, tags are transparent to grammatical features, so a word can be bolded in the middle of a sentence with no adverse effect.

Table 2 Examples of number and date JSreal expressions and the corresponding output (and English translation)

JSREAL expression	Text output
`S(V('appeler').f('ip').pe(5) .add(N(18005556426).num('t')))`	`Appelez 1-800-555-6426.` (*Call 1-800-555-6426*)
`N(123456).num(''l'')`	`Cent vingt-trois mille quatre cent cinquante-six` (*one hundred twenty-three thousand four hundred fifty-six*)
`N('enfant').d(3).num(''l'')`	`Trois enfants` (*three children*)
`S(A(1).num('o').d('d'), V('gagner'))`	`Le premier gagne` (*The first wins*)
`DT().y(2014).m(7).d(14) .h(16).min(29)`	`Le lundi 14 juillet 2014 à 16 h 29` (*Monday July 14th at 16:29*)
`S(Pro('je'), VP(V('être').f(''f''), Adv('à')), DTR(DT().y(2014) .m(10).d(14), DT().y(2014) .m(10).d(17)).noDay(true) .pos('end'))`	`Je serai là du 14 au 17 octobre 2014.` (*I will be there from October 2014 14 to 17*)

Another important part of HTML formatting are tag *attributes*. As with grammatical features, many attributes, such as `class`, `href` and `src`, have their own methods. Custom attributes can be assigned with the `attr` method.

Some formatting elements do further processing:

- `H1` to `H6` properly capitalize their content;
- `UL` and `OL` add `li` tags to their constituents;
- adding a `href` attribute also adds the `a` tag to the unit;
- `HL` and `Email` automate link input, adding the appropriate href attribute.

4.3 Realization

The final realization of a unit can be obtained in several ways:

- using a unit where JavaScript expects a string realizes that unit as a string;
- the `node` method makes an HTML element from the realization;
- the `toID` and `addToID` place the realization in the web page, at the selected ID.

Once the user asks for the realization of a unit, a syntactic tree is built recursively, down to individual words (and independent HTML tags). In each phrase, constituents are ordered according to their function and features and then by their order of input. Phrases then compute their relevant features (as discussed in

```
var evList = [
 {date:'2013-09-25', ville:'Laval',cat:'at', h:'19:00',
  attr:'nouveau', tit:'Exercices de réalisation', part:'a',
  res:'a'},
 {date:'2013-09-27', ville:'Montréal',cat:'cs',
  attr:'de une demi-heure', part:'r', res:'r'} ,
 {date:'2013-09-30', ville:'Granby', adr:'au 901 rue Principale',
  cat:'cs', attr:'privé', res:'r'} ,
 {date:'2013-09-30', ville:'Granby',cat:'at', h:'13:00',
  attr:'classique', tit:'Principes de réalisation', part:'a'},
 {date:'2013-10-02', ville:'Granby',cat:'at', h:'13:00',
  attr:'nouveau', tit:'Exercices de réalisation', part:'r'},
 {date:'2013-10-02', ville:'Longueuil',cat:'cf', h:'19:00',
  attr:'nouveau', tit:'Pourquoi la réalisation?', part:'n',
  res:'n'},
 {date:'2013-10-03', ville:'Longueuil',cat:'at', h:'13:00',
  tit:'Planification et réalisation', part:'n'}
]
```

Fig. 5 Event list input in JSON format. Each event is a Javascript object with the following fields: `date` the date of the event; `ville` the town in which the event will be held; `cat` the category of the event (`at` atelier (*workshop*); `cs` consultation, `cf` conference); `h` time of the event; `attr` attribute of the event, `tit` title of the event; `part` initial of the participant; `res` initial of the contact person for reservation

Sect. 4.1) and pass them on to their constituents according to their function; for example, a noun phrase can get its number from its determiner and transmit it to its noun, like in the `trois enfants` (*three children*) example of Table 2.

With the syntactic tree complete and all features determined, units are realized from the bottom up. Words return their final form, which can depend on their features and, in cases such as contracting at the request of the neighbouring words (e.g. le `homme` (*the man*) will be transformed to `l'homme`). Phrases then join their constituents with spaces and surround them with punctuation and HTML tags.

5 Use Case

As a use case of JSReal, we want to maintain a web page listing upcoming events that Alice, Robert and I offer the public. Since the information always uses similar syntactical structures, we want to generate it automatically.

We have at our disposal a dataset, shown in Fig. 5, that collects relevant information about the events, namely their date and time, place, category, participants and who to contact for reservations. The data can be assumed to be made available to the web application, it could be the result of parsing a calendar or querying a database. A sample of the desired output is shown in Fig. 6.

Atelier à Laval

Le mercredi 25 septembre 2013 à 9 h, Alice sera à Laval pour le nouvel atelier *Exercices de réalisation*.

Pour réserver, contactez-la au 555-2543.

Consultations à Montréal

Le vendredi 27 septembre 2013, Robert sera à Montréal pour des consultations d'une demi-heure.

Pour réserver, contactez-le au rob@JSreal.js.

Séjour à Granby

Du lundi 30 septembre au mercredi 2 octobre 2013, Alice et Robert seront à Granby, à l'hôtel Castel, au 901 rue Principale, pour des consultations privées et deux ateliers.

- 30 septembre à 9 h: atelier classique « Principes de réalisation » avec Alice
- 2 octobre à 9 h: nouvel atelier « Exercices de réalisation » avec Robert

Pour réserver, contactez Robert au rob@JSreal.js.

Séjour à Longueuil

Les mercredi 2 et jeudi 3 octobre 2013, je serai à Longueuil pour plusieurs événements.

- 2 octobre à 15 h: nouvelle conférence « Pourquoi la réalisation? »
- 3 octobre à 9 h: atelier « Planification et réalisation »

Pour réserver, contactez-moi au 555-6426 ou au nic@JSreal.js.

Fig. 6 Output of a list of events. For the full code, see (Daoust 2013b)

Since our data is already collected, there is no content determination step in this text generation project; we can thus start directly with the microplanning phase.

1. We notice that `Alice` and `Robert` are not in the lexicon, so we add them, specifying their gender.
2. We prepare additional information, such as the contact details for each participant.
3. We go through the data event by event, accumulating for each group the title, date, participants, place, events and reservation details.
4. We integrate the result into the web page (see Fig. 6).

JSReal simplified many aspects of text generation in this project. It:

- added capitals, spaces and punctuation where appropriate;
- took care of verb agreement according to the number and person of the participants;
- created and used clauses, coordinations and lists regardless of if they had any constituents, skipping them seamlessly if they were empty;
- expressed dates and times naturally, looking up the days of the week by itself;
- took care of all the HTML formatting.

The example in this demonstration is fictitious, but it is inspired by a real text generation project (Daoust 2014). The original project, yet less complex, numbered more than 600 lines of Javascript code, whereas the program written for this demonstration has under 200 lines (not counting the 2,000 lines of JSREAL of course).

Starting from concise data instead of manually typing the results has other advantages: it would be easy to use the data to make a summarized table of events in addition to the verbose list (in fact, the original project had such a table). Also, in a future version of JSREAL, bilingual realization could be possible, allowing us to present events to both French and English clients with little more hassle.

6 Other Examples

We have also developed other web based applications whose output is briefly illustrated here. These applications can all be tried online on the RALI website[1]:

- The main advantage of using a text realizer is the fact that the same pattern of code can be reused provided it is appropriately parameterized. Figure 7 shows how a conjugation table for a French verb can be created with the corresponding display in the browser.
- A demo page (Fig. 8) that can be used to build a sentence with a simple syntactic structure and modify some of its components to see how it is realized in French and the corresponding JSreal expression. It was useful to quickly test some features during its development, but it could also be helpful to learn how to write simple French sentences or to learn how to JSreal code.
- We have also developed a JSreal development environment (Fig. 9) integrating the ACE javascript editor[2] in which a JSreal expression can be entered on the left and that shows the corresponding syntactic tree on the right. The realization of the expression is shown at the top of the tree, but it is also possible to get intermediate realization by clicking on any node of the tree.
- Dynamic realization is illustrated with a variant on the Exercices de style of Raymond Queneau which are a classical word play in French. The original book (published initially in 1947) showed 99 stylistic variations on a text describing a situation in which the narrator gets on the *S* bus, witnesses a dispute between a man and another passenger, and then sees the same person 2 h later at the Gare St-Lazare getting advice on adding a button to his overcoat. It has since then been adapted in various languages and in multiple styles. The text at the top of Fig. 10 was produced with JSreal, but by selecting from the menu, we can get a variant in which all the nouns representing persons have

[1] http://rali.iro.umontreal.ca/rali/?q=fr/jsreal-realisateur-de-texte.

[2] http://ace.c9.io.

```
function addTable(verbe,temps){
    // temps is an array of two element arrays each giving
    // the name of a tense and the JSreal code for feature f
    var tableau=$("tableau");     // find the table element
    var row=TR();                 // create a new row
    for (var t=0;t<temps.length;t++) // fill the title of the table
        row.add(TH(N(temps[t][0])))
    tableau.appendChild(row.node()); // add it to the table
    // generate a row for the 6 persons (3 singular and 3 plural)
    for(var p=1;p<=6;p++){
        row=TR();
        for(var t=0;t<temps.length;t++){ // a row at 3 tenses
            var v=S(Pro().pe(p),V(verbe).pe(p).f(temps[t][1]));
            row.add(TD(v.a("")));
        }
        tableau.appendChild(row.node());
    }
}

function conjuguer(verbe){
  H2(V(verbe)).toID("verbe");
  addTable(verbe,[["Présent","p"],
                  ["Imparfait","i"],
                  ["Futur simple","f"]]);
}
```

Tableau de conjugaison

Échanger

Présent	Imparfait	Futur simple
J'échange	J'échangeais	J'échangerai
Tu échanges	Tu échangeais	Tu échangeras
Il échange	Il échangeait	Il échangera
Nous échangeons	Nous échangions	Nous échangerons
Vous échangez	Vous échangiez	Vous échangerez
Ils échangent	Ils échangeaient	Ils échangeront

Fig. 7 JSReal code for producing a conjugation table and its display when called on the verb `èchanger` (*exchange*)

been made plural. The nouns that have been changed are underlined in the resulting text shown at the bottom of Fig. 10; the verbs that have these nouns as subjects have also been changed, but are not underlined.

Démonstrateur de JSreal

Sujet

Déterminant: démonstratif
Nom: chat
Adjectif *antéposé*: gris
Pluriel ☑ Pronominalisé ☐
Pronom

Verbe

Verbe: manger
Mode: indicatif
Temps: présent

Objet direct

Déterminant: indéfini
Nom: souris
Adjectif *antéposé*: petit
Pluriel ☑ Pronominalisé ☐

Objet indirect

Préposition: avec
Déterminant: indéfini
Nom: couteau
Adjectif *antéposé*: bleu
Pluriel ☑ Pronominalisé ☐

Réalisation: `Ces chats gris mangent des petites souris avec des couteaux` [Réaliser]

Code JSreal: [Évaluer]

```
S(NP(N('chat'),A('gris')).d('dem').n('p'),
   VP(V('manger').f('p'),
      NP(N('souris'),A('petit')).d('i').n('p'),
         PP(P('avec'),NP(N('couteau'),A('bleu')).d('i').n('p'))))
```

Cet exemple est adapté de la démonstration de SimpleNLG-ENfr réalisée par Pierre-Luc Vaudry

Fig. 8 Demo page to build a sentence with a subject (*top left*), a verb (*top right*), a direct object (*bottom left*) and indirect object (*bottom right*). For the subject, direct object and indirect object, a determiner, a noun and an adjective can be specified either with a text field or chosen from the menu. Once the fields are filled, clicking on the `Réaliser` button will fill the `Réalisation` text field with the French sentence and the other text field with the corresponding JSREAL code

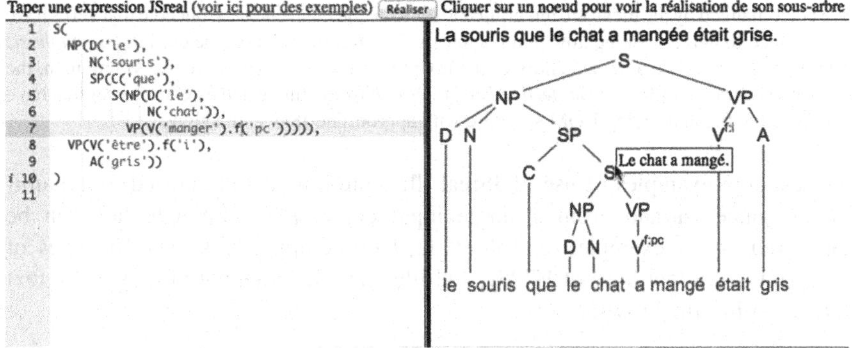
Environnement de programmation JSreal
Taper une expression JSreal (voir ici pour des exemples)
Réaliser
Cliquer sur un noeud pour voir la réalisation de son sous-arbre
S(
NP(D('le'),
N('souris'),
SP(C('que'),
S(NP(D('le'),
N('chat')),
VP(V('manger').f('pc')))),
VP(V('être').f('i'),
A('gris'))
)
La souris que le chat a mangée était grise.
S
NP
VP
D N
SP
V
A
C
S
Le chat a mangé.
NP
VP
D N
V
le souris que le chat a mangé était gris

Fig. 9 JSREAL interactive development environment. The user enters a Javascript expression on the left; this expression is checked for some errors (e.g. mismatched parentheses or brackets) by the underlying ACE javascript editor. By clicking on the `Réaliser` button, the user can see on the right the realization of the expression and the corresponding syntactic tree. Clicking on an internal node of the tree, a tool tip presents the realization of the subtree of this node. In this example, the full sentence reads as The mouse that the cat ate was *grey* in which the proper agreement is made between mouse, which is feminine in French, was made with the adjective *grey* and the past participle in the subordinate sentence; it is feminine because the direct object, `que` standing for the `souris`, appeared before in the sentence. Clicking on the internal `S` node, we get the realization of that sentence only in which the past participle is not changed because it has no direct object

Un *exercice de style* à la Queneau

Choisir le temps, le genre et le nombre du récit ainsi que les éléments à mettre en évidence

présent | masculin | singulier |

Le narrateur rencontre dans un bus bondé de la ligne S un jeune homme au long cou, coiffé d'un chapeau mou. Ce jeune homme échange quelques mots assez vifs avec un autre voyageur, puis va s'asseoir à une place libre. Deux heures plus tard, le narrateur revoit ce jeune homme devant la gare Saint-Lazare. Il est alors en train de discuter avec un ami. Celui-ci lui conseille de faire remonter le bouton supérieur de son pardessus.

Un *exercice de style* à la Queneau

Choisir le temps, le genre et le nombre du récit ainsi que les éléments à mettre en évidence

présent | masculin | pluriel | narrateur

Les *narrateurs* rencontrent dans des bus bondés de la ligne S des jeunes hommes au long cou, coiffés de chapeaux mous. Ces jeunes hommes échangent quelques mots assez vifs avec d'autres voyageurs, puis vont s'asseoir à des places libres. Deux heures plus tard, les *narrateurs* revoient ces jeunes hommes devant la gare Saint-Lazare. Ils sont alors en train de discuter avec des amis. Ceux-ci leur conseillent de faire remonter le bouton supérieur de leurs pardessus.

Fig. 10 A classical French word play in action in the browser. Given a single JSREAL input specification, in which some words have been assigned classes (in the Javascript sense), it is possible to get many variants of a single text: with the menus the user can select the tense of the verbs (one out of four), the gender and the number of the nouns designating persons. The *top figure* shows the initial display and the bottom shows a display in which all nouns have been made plural. The nouns that have been changed by the menu are underlined to indicate the main changes, but note that verbs have also changed to agree with the now plural subjects. The fourth menu can be used to put *emphasis* (here done in *italics*) on a named entity of the text: the narrator shown above, the young man, the friend and the traveler. Both the *underlined* and the *emphasis* are indicated by CSS classes that have be assigned to the underlying DOM structure with appropriate JSREAL functions

These few examples of use of JSreal illustrate how it can be used to dynamically produce variants from a single input expression. Although they can be considered as toy examples, and they are, they comprise less than 100 lines of Javascript and a few lines of HTML and illustrate the potential of a dynamic text realizer within the browser.

7 Current Limitations

Although JSreal is already capable of complex and varied output, its grammatical coverage is relatively limited. In particular, it is missing some irregular verb forms and, because of time limits of the implementer, it does not yet support the specification of interrogative or negative clauses in a declarative way as it is possible in SIMPLENLG-ENFR.

The current lexicon is another weakness, being adapted instead of made from the ground up. Some features are redundant with JSREAL 's grammatical rules and while a limited base vocabulary is understandable considering the size limitations, the words could be selected according to their prevalence on the web.

Finally, JSREAL is currently French-only, a choice dictated by the linguistic expertise of the implementers. An English version would be much more useful, considering there are ten times as many English internet users as there are French (Internet World Users by Language 2014); a multilingual version would even be more useful.

8 Conclusion

We have described the design of JSREAL, a text realizer written in Javascript that can produce flexible French text output and we have given a few illustrative applications. JSREAL reaches its stated objectives: it can easily be integrated to a web page, as much as a tool to more easily obtain some expressions than as the backbone of complex, automatically generated documents from data extracted from databases or through AJAX calls to an information server. We now intend to experiment with JSREAL in the context of data-driven applications in a domain where data is constantly changing such as weather information and combine it with dynamic visualization. It could also be applied to other types of applications such as the verbalization of a personal agenda or to describe personal relations dynamically extracted from a network.

Compared to other realizers, JSREAL integrates little syntactic theory, rather making the user build individual units in a manner similar to a syntactic tree. We prefer to look at this apparent weakness as a strength: as long as the user knows how to group words in phrases and use JavaScript, he can have JSREAL output complex documents. In that respect, JSREAL is very similar to SIMPLENLG, whose specification are also built in its native programming language.

JSREAL being quite flexible, it could be used for teaching French in the context of an interactive language learning environment such as the DRILLTUTOR (Zock and Lapalme 2010) in which the designer of the drill specifies the goals of the sentences to teach. Currently the sentences are simple templates which limits the range of sentences that can be presented to the learner. JSreal would allow a greater flexibility in the design of language drill sentences by enabling the designer of the drills to focus on the high level goals of the interactive generation process. This would create a more interesting and varied type of output for the user of the language tutor.

References

Daoust, N. (2013a). *JSreal*. Retrieved September 10, 2013, from http://daou.st/JSreal.

Daoust, N. (2013b). *Démonstration. JSreal*. Retrieved September 10, 2013, from http://daou.st/JSreal/Demo.

Daoust, N. (2014). *Événements. Luc Lightbringer*. Retrieved January 10, 2014, from http://daou.st/lightbringer/index.php?ong=4.

Downloadable NLG systems. (2013). Association for Computational Linguistics Wiki. Retrieved September 9, 2013, from http://aclweb.org/aclwiki/index.php?title=Downloadable_NLG_systems.

Echelle orthographique Dubois-Buyse. (2013). *Ressources francophones de l'Education*. Retrieved September 9, 2013, from http://o.bacquet.free.fr/db2.htm.

Elhadad, M. (2013). SURGE: A syntactic realization grammar for text generation. Computer Science—Ben Gurion University of the Negev. Retrieved September 9, 2013, from http://www.cs.bgu.ac.il/surge.

Gatt, A., & Reiter, E. (2009). SimpleNLG: A realisation engine for practical applications. In *Proceedings of the 12th European Workshop on Natural Language Generation* (pp. 90–93).

Internet World Users by Language. (2014). Internet World Stats. Retrieved January 16, 2014, from http://www.internetworldstats.com/stats7.htm.

KPML One-Point Access Page. (2013). Universitat Bremen. Retrieved September 9, 2013, from http://www.fb10.uni-bremen.de/anglistik/langpro/kpml/README.html.

Lavoie, B., & Rambow, O. (1997). A fast and portable realizer for text generation systems. In *Proceedings of the Fifth Conference on Applied Natural Language Processing* (pp. 265–268).

Portet, F., Reiter, E., Gatt, A., Hunter, J., Sripada, S., Freer, Y., et al. (2009). Automatic generation of textual summaries from neonatal intensive care data. *Artificial Intelligence, 173*(7–8),789–816.

RealPro. CoGenTex, Inc. (2013). Retrieved September 10, 2013, from http://www.cogentex.com/technology/realpro/index.shtml.

Reiter, E., & Dale, R. (2000). *Building natural language generation systems*. Cambridge: Cambridge University Press.

SimpleNLG. (2013). Retrieved September 9, 2013, from http://code.google.com/p/simplenlg.

Vaudry, P.-L. (2013). *SimpleNLG-EnFr*. Département d'informatique et de recherche opérationnelle de l'Université de Montréal. Retrieved September 10, 2013, from http://www-etud.iro.umontreal.ca/%7Evaudrypl/snlgbil/snlgEnFr_english.html.

Vaudry, P.-L., & Lapalme, G. (2013). Adapting SimpleNLG for bilingual English–French realisation. In *Proceedings of the 14th European Workshop on Natural Language Generation* (pp. 183–187).

Zock, M., & Lapalme, G. (2010). *A generic tool for creating and using multilingual phrasebooks*. In *NLPCS 2010 (Natural Language Processing and Cognitive Science)*, Funchal, Madeira, portugal.

Part V
Reading and Writing Technologies

Simple or Not Simple? A Readability Question

Sanja Štajner, Ruslan Mitkov and Gloria Corpas Pastor

Abstract Text Simplification (TS) has taken off as an important Natural Language Processing (NLP) application which promises to offer a significant societal impact in that it can be employed to the benefit of users with limited language comprehension skills such as children, foreigners who do not have a good command of a language, and readers struggling with a language disability. With the recent emergence of various TS systems, the question we are faced with is how to automatically evaluate their performance given that access to target users might be difficult. This chapter addresses one aspect of this issue by exploring whether existing readability formulae could be applied to assess the level of simplification offered by a TS system. It focuses on three readability indices for Spanish. The indices are first adapted in a way that allows them to be computed automatically and then applied to two corpora of original and manually simplified texts. The first corpus has been compiled as part of the Simplext project targeting people with Down syndrom, and the second corpus as part of the FIRST project, where the users are people with autism spectrum disorder. The experiments show that there is a significant correlation between each of the readability indices and eighteen linguistically motivated features which might be seen as reading obstacles for various target populations, thus indicating the possibility of using those indices as a measure of the degree of simplification achieved by TS systems. Various ways they can be used in TS are further illustrated by comparing their values when applied to four different corpora.

S. Štajner (✉) · R. Mitkov · G. Corpas Pastor
Research Group in Computational Linguistics, University of Wolverhampton, Wolverhampton, UK
e-mail: sanjastajner@wlv.ac.uk

R. Mitkov
e-mail: r.mitkov@wlv.ac.uk

G. Corpas Pastor
e-mail: gcorpas@uma.es

G. Corpas Pastor
Research Group in Lexicography and Translation, University of Malaga, Malaga, Spain

© Springer International Publishing Switzerland 2015
N. Gala et al. (eds.), *Language Production, Cognition, and the Lexicon*,
Text, Speech and Language Technology 48, DOI 10.1007/978-3-319-08043-7_22

Keywords Text simplification · Readability · Automatic evaluation · Readers with Down syndrom and autism spectrum disorder

1 Introduction

Access to written information for people with intellectual disability and people with various reading and comprehension difficulties is a fundamental human right (UN 2006). However, many texts, including newswire texts and healthcare leaflets, are often too complex to understand for many people (Štajner et al. 2012). Although necessary for their better inclusion into society, such lexically and syntactically complex texts can be very difficult to comprehend for non-native speakers (Aluísio et al. 2008; Petersen and Ostendorf 2007), people with intellectual disability (Feng 2009), or language-impaired people such as autistic (Martos et al. 2012; Štajner et al. 2012), aphasic (Carroll et al. 1998; Devlin 1999), dyslexic (Rello 2012) or congenitally deaf people (Inui et al. 2003). For example, the use of infrequent words makes the text difficult to comprehend for people with aphasia[1] (Devlin 1999), autism spectrum disorders (ASD)[2] (Martos et al. 2012; Norbury 2005), and intellectual disability (Feng 2009), and the use of more frequent words reduces the reading time in people with dyslexia (Rello et al. 2013a). Long sentences, noun compounds and long sequences of adjectives (e.g. "twenty-five-year-old blond-haired mother-of-two Jane Smith" (Carroll et al. 1998)), which are typical of the genre of newswire texts, can impose additional problems to people diagnosed with aphasia (Carroll et al. 1998), ASD (Martos et al. 2012), and intellectual disability (Feng 2009).

Since the late nineties, there have been several initiatives to propose guidelines for producing plain, easy-to-read documents, which would be accessible to wider population. The Plain Language Action and Information Network (PLAIN)[3] developed the first version of the "Federal Plain Language Guidelines" (PlainLanguage 2011) in the mid-90s which has been revised every few years since then. The original idea was to help writers of governmental documents (primarily regulations) write in a clear and simple manner so that the users can "find what they need, understand what they find; and use what they find to meet their needs"

[1] Aphasia is a language disorder usually caused by a stroke or a head injury. The impairments in language processing experienced by people with aphasia are quite diverse, but many aphasic people are very likely to encounter problems in understanding written text at some point (Carroll et al. 1998).

[2] Autism spectrum disorder (ASD) is a neurodevelopmental disorder characterised by qualitative impairment in communication and stereotyped repetitive behaviour (American Psychiatric Association 2013). People with ASD have deficits in the comprehension of speech and writing (Štajner et al. 2012).

[3] http://www.plainlanguage.gov/.

(PlainLanguage 2011). The European Guidelines for the Production of Easy-to-Read Information for people with Learning Disability, "Make it Simple" (Freyhoff et al. 1998) were produced by Inclusion Europe[4] in order to assist writers in developing texts, publications and videos that are more accessible to people with learning disability and other people who cannot read complex texts, and thus remove any risk of discrimination or social injustice.

However, manual creation of easy-to-read texts is still very limited, and the manual simplification of existing texts cannot match the speed of new texts being generated. This is particularly important in the domain of news texts which should provide up-to-date information. Therefore, many attempts have been made to completely or at least partially automate this process by means of Text Simplification (TS). The goal of TS is to transform complex texts into their simpler variant which is accessible to a wider audience, while preserving the original meaning. So far, TS systems have been developed for English (Coster and Kauchak 2011; Glavaš and Štajner 2013; Siddharthan 2006; Woodsend and Lapata 2011; Wubben et al. 2012; Zhu et al. 2010), Spanish (Drndarević et al. 2013; Saggion et al. 2011), and Portuguese (Aluísio et al. 2008), with recent attempts at Basque (Aranzabe et al. 2012), Swedish (Rybing et al. 2010), Dutch (Ruiter et al. 2010), and Italian (Barlacchi and Tonelli 2013). These (semi-)automatic TS systems have either been evaluated for the quality of generated output (measured in terms of its simplicity, grammaticality, and meaning preservation, as for example in Drndarević et al. (2013), Glavaš and Štajner (2013) and Woodsend and Lapata (2011)) or for their usefulness measured by reading speed and comprehension achieved by the target population (as for example in (Rello et al. 2013b)).

This chapter addresses the problem of assessment of the level of simplicity of texts, exploring the possibility to employ some of the already existing readability indices for this purpose. If this is possible, the benefits would be two-fold. First, it would enable an easier comparison of the level of simplification achieved by different TS systems, and pinpoint the differences in the simplification strategies used for different target populations. Second, it would enable an easy comparison of the TS output with some gold standard (manually simplified texts or manually produced easy-to-read texts).

2 Related Work

During their long history (since the 1950s), readability formulae have always been regarded as controversial, triggering endless debates about whether they should be used or not. Their initial purpose was to assess the grade level of textbooks. Later, they were adapted to different domains and purposes (e.g. to measure readability of technical manuals (Smith 1967), or healthcare documents intended for the general

[4] http://inclusion-europe.org/.

public (McLaughlin 1969)), resulting in a total of over 200 different readability formulae (for English) and over 1,000 studies of their application (DuBay 2004). The earliest readability formulae were computed only on the basis of average sentence and word length. Due to their simplicity and good correlation with the reading tests, some of them, such as the Flesch-Kincaid Grade Level index (Kincaid et al. 1975) or Flesch readability score (Flesch 1948), are still widely in use. Another type of frequently used readability formulae are those which are a function of the average sentence length and the percentage of the words which cannot be found on a list of "easiest" words, like for example, the Dale-Chall formula (Dale and Chall 1948).

The first readability formulae were developed for English. With the fast spread of their usage, they were soon adapted to other languages by changing the coefficient before the factors. For example, the Flesch-Douma (Douma 1960) and Leesindex Brouwer (Brouwer 1963) formulae for Dutch represent adaptations of the Flesch Reading Ease score, while the Spaulding's Spanish readability formula (Spaulding 1956) could be seen as an adaptation of the Dale-Chall formula (Dale and Chall 1948). Štajner et al. (2012) showed that the four English readability formulae which are solely based on superficial text characteristics (the Flesch readability score (Flesch 1948), the Flesch-Kincaid readability formula (Kincaid et al. 1975), the Fog index (Gunning 1952), and the SMOG grading (McLaughlin 1969)) appear to be strongly correlated with each other (with the Pearson's correlation coefficient between 0.951 and 0.987 depending on the pair), while Oosten et al. (2010) showed that this is the case even across different languages (English, Dutch, and Swedish).

With the recent advances of natural language processing (NLP) tools and techniques, new approaches to readability assessment have emerged. Schwarm and Ostendorf (2005), and Petersen and Ostendorf (2009) showed that more complex features (e.g. average height of the parse tree, average number of noun and verb phrases, etc.) give better readability prediction than the traditional Flesch-Kincaid readability formula. Their studies were based on the texts from Weekly Reader,[5] and two smaller corpora: Encyclopedia Britannica and Britannica Elementary (Barzilay and Elhadad 2003), and CNN news stories and their abridged versions.[6] Feng et al. (2009) went one step further adding a corpus of local news articles which were simplified by human editors in order to make them more accessible for people with mild intellectual disability (MID). Rating of those texts for readability by actual target users (people with MID) indicated that some cognitively motivated features (such as entity mentions, lexical chains, etc.) are better correlated with the user-study comprehension than the Flesch-Kincaid Grade Level index.

In spite of those findings, most of the existing TS systems have still been evaluated by using various readability formulae in combination with human

[5] http://www.weeklyreader.com/.

[6] http://literacynet.org/cnnsf/.

judgments of grammaticality and preservation of meaning. Woodsend and Lapata (2011) evaluated complexity reduction achieved by the proposed TS system using the Flesch-Kincaid (Kincaid et al. 1975) and the Coleman-Liau (Coleman and Liau 1975) readability indices. Zhu et al. (2010) applied the Flesch readability score in combination with n-gram language model perplexity for the evaluation of their system, while Glavaš and Štajner (2013) applied the Flesch-Kincaid Grade Level index and the SMOG index, in combination with the human judgments of simplicity, grammaticality and preservation of meaning. Drndarevic et al. (2013) used three different readability formulae for Spanish to assess the level of simplification achieved by the TS system aimed at people with Down syndrome. The reason for applying readability formulae instead of various aforementioned cognitively motivated features proposed in Feng et al. (2009), Petersen and Ostendorf (2009), and Schwarm and Ostendorf (2005) probably lies in the fact that all those readability formulae are solely based on superficial text characteristics (such as average sentence length and word length), and thus can be computed easily and with high precision.

The goal of evaluation of TS systems using readability formulae should not be to determine the exact reading level (complexity) of the simplified texts and thus replace the user-focused evaluation on the actual target population. It should rather enable an easy comparison of:

- Original and simplified texts in order to assess either the necessary complexity reduction (if comparing original texts with the manually simplified ones); or the achieved complexity reduction (if comparing original texts with the automatically simplified ones);
- Different text simplification systems (i.e. the level of simplification achieved by different TS systems);
- Automatically simplified texts with the manually simplified ones (in order to assess whether the automatic simplification achieves the same level of simplification as the manual one);
- Manually simplified texts with a 'gold standard' (easy-to-read texts which were originally written with the target population in mind) with the aim of assessing whether the manually simplified texts reach the simplicity of the 'gold standard', and thus comply with the easy-to-read standards.

With that goal in mind, it is not necessary that readability formulae give better readability prediction than cognitively motivated features. It would be enough that they correlate well with them. The work of Štajner et al. (2012) showed that many of the linguistically motivated features which can be perceived as an indication of reading obstacles for people with ASD, are significantly correlated with the Flesch Reading Ease score (Flesch readability score). Following this idea, Štajner and Saggion (2013a) explored whether there is a correlation between similar features and three different readability formulae for Spanish, based on the corpora of original and manually simplified news text for people with Down syndrome. The experiments described in this chapter can be seen as an extension of those presented in (Štajner and Saggion 2013a), adding aspects of generalisation and portability, and highlighting the use of readability indices. The validity of the correlations is confirmed on the basis of two corpora which consist of texts belonging to different domains and are aimed at two different target populations. The potential uses of readability indices in text simplification are illustrated by the results of the last two sets of experiments.

3 Methodology

The corpora, readability indices, linguistically motivated complexity features, and experimental settings are presented in the next three subsections.

3.1 Corpora

The following four corpora were used for the experiments presented in this chapter:

1. **FIRST**—The FIRST corpus consists of 25 original texts and their corresponding manually simplified versions,[7] compiled under the FIRST project[8] (Orasan et al. 2013). The texts belong to the news, health, and general culture/literature. A more detailed description of the corpus can be found in Štajner and Saggion (2013b).
2. **Simplext**—The Simplext corpus comprises 200 original news articles (provided by the Spanish news agency Servimedia[9]) and their corresponding manually simplified versions, compiled under the Simplext project[10] (Saggion et al. 2011). A more detailed description of the corpora can be found in (Štajner et al. 2013), and (Štajner and Saggion 2013b).
3. **Automatic**—The *Automatic* Simplext corpus of 100 original news texts (*original*) and three versions of their corresponding automatically simplified texts, using three different simplification strategies: lexical rule-based transformations (*rules*); a rule-based system for syntactic simplification (*syntactic*); and the combination of both (*both*). Details of those simplification strategies and the corpora can be found in (Drndarević et al. 2013). The original articles were obtained from the same source as in the case of the Simplext corpus in order to be comparable.

[7] Available at: http://www.first-asd.eu/?q=system/files/FIRST_D7.2_20130228_annex.pdf.

[8] http://www.first-asd.eu/.

[9] www.servimedia.es.

[10] www.simplext.es.

Table 1 Size of the corpora

Corpus	Texts	Sentences	Words
FIRST (original)	25	325	7,021
FIRST (simplified)	25	387	6,936
Simplext (original)	200	1,150	36,545
Simplext (simplified)	200	1,804	24,154
Automatic (original)	100	557	18,119
Automatic (rules)	100	558	18,171
Automatic (syntax)	100	656	17,884
Automatic (both)	100	657	17,938
Noticias Fácil	200	1,431	12,874

4. **Noticias Fácil**—The corpus of 200 news articles from the Noticias Fácil website[11] written for people with intellectual disability, was compiled with the aim of having the 'gold standard' for comparison with the manually simplified texts in Simplext. Both corpora share the same domains of the articles.

The size of each corpus (and its subcorpora) is detailed in Table 1.

3.2 Readability Indices

This study focuses on three readability formulae for Spanish: two concerned with the lexical complexity—LC (Anula 2007) and SSR (Spaulding 1956); and the third one concerned with the syntactic complexity—SCI (Anula 2007) of the given text.

The Spaulding's Spanish Readability index (SSR) has already been used for assessing the reading difficulty of fundamental education materials for Latin American adults of limited reading ability and for the evaluation of text passages of the foreign language tests (Spaulding 1956). Therefore, it is reasonable to expect that this formula could be used for estimating the level of simplification performed by text simplification systems aimed at making texts more accessible for the same target population (adults of limited reading ability). The index predicts the relative difficulty of reading material based on the vocabulary and sentence structure, using the following formula:

$$SSR = 1.609 \times \frac{|w|}{|s|} + 331.8 \times \frac{|rw|}{|w|} + 22.0 \tag{1}$$

[11] www.noticiasfacil.es.

Here, $|w|$ and $|s|$ denote the number of words and sentences in the text, while $|rw|$ denotes the number of rare words in the text. In his original formula (Spaulding 1956), Spaulding considers as *rare words* those words which cannot be found on the list of 1,500 most common Spanish words (provided in (Spaulding 1956)) plus some special cases of numbers, names of months and days, proper and geographic names, initials, diminutives and augmentatives, etc. The SSR index used in this chapter, can be seen as a simplified (slightly modified) version of the original Spaulding's index. The rules (a)–(g) specified in (Spaulding 1956) were not applied in order to enable a precise and consistent automatic computation.

The Lexical Complexity index (LC) was suggested by Anula (2007) as a measure of lexical complexity of literary texts aimed at the second language learners. It is calculated using the following formula:

$$LC = \frac{LDI + ILFW}{2} \tag{2}$$

where *LDI* and *ILFW* represent the *Lexical Density Index* and *Index of Low-Frequency Words*, respectively:

$$LDI = \frac{|dcw|}{|s|}, \tag{3}$$

$$ILFW = \frac{|lfw|}{|cw|} \times 100 \tag{4}$$

Here, $|dcw|$, $|s|$, $|lfw|$, and $|cw|$ denote the number of distinct content words, sentences, low-frequency words, and content words (nouns, adjectives, verbs, and adverbs), respectively. According to Anula (2007) the *low frequency words* are those words whose frequency rank in the Reference Corpus of Contemporary Spanish (CREA)[12] is lower than 1,000.[13]

The Sentence Complexity Index (SCI) was proposed by Anula (2007) as a measure of sentence complexity in a literary text aimed at second language learners. It is calculated by the following formula:

$$SCI = \frac{ASL + ICS}{2} \tag{5}$$

---

[12] http://corpus.rae.es/lfrecuencias.html.

[13] In this study, both lists (from the Reference Corpus of Contemporary Spanish (CREA) and the Spaulding's list of 1500 most common Spanish words) were lemmatised using Connexor's parser in order to retrieve the frequency of the lemma and not a word form (action carried out manually in the two cited works), and to enable a fully automatic computation of both indices.

where *ASL* denotes the average sentence length, and *ICS* denotes the index of complex sentences. They are calculated as follows:

$$ASL = \frac{|w|}{|s|}, \tag{6}$$

$$ICS = \frac{|cs|}{|s|} \times 100 \tag{7}$$

Here, $|w|$, $|s|$, and $|cs|$ denote the number of words, sentences and complex sentences in the text, respectively. With the aim of computing the SCI index completely automatically, in this study, any sentence which contains multiple finite predicates according to the output of Connexor's Machinese parser was considered as complex. The original definition of a complex sentence used in Anula (2007) (relying on a manual detection of complex sentences), cannot be used for a precise fully automatic computation of the index.

3.3 Linguistically Motivated Features

The syntactic concept of the projection principle (Chomsky 1986) that "lexical structure must be represented categorically at every syntactic level" implies "that the number of noun phrases in a sentence is proportional to the number of nouns in that sentence, the number of verbs in a sentence is related to the number of clauses and verb phrases, etc." (Štajner et al. 2012). Motivated by this principle, Štajner et al. (2012) investigated ten features which can be seen as indicators of structural complexity. Following the same principle and easy-to-read guidelines for writing for people with intellectual disability (Freyhoff et al. 1998), eighteen linguistically motivated complexity features were selected for the present study (Table 2). Features 1–11 are indicators of structural complexity. The average sentence length (ASL) and the average word length (AWL) were added as common features of syntactic and lexical complexity. Features 14–18 are indicators of semantic ambiguity.

The corpora were parsed with the Connexor's Machinese parser.[14] All features were automatically extracted: features 1–14 using the parser's output, and features 15–18 using two additional lexical resources. Extraction of features 15–16 was based on the use of Spanish EuroWordNet (Vossen 1998), which contains 50,526 word meanings and 23,370 synsets. Features 17–18 were extracted using the Spanish Open Thesaurus (version 2),[15] which contains 21,831 target words (lemmas) and provides a list of word senses for each word. Each word sense is, in

[14] www.connexor.eu.

[15] http://openthes-es.berlios.de.

Table 2 Linguistically motivated complexity features

#	Code	Feature
1	Verb	Average number of verbs per sentence
2	Adj	Average number of adjectives per sentence
3	Adv	Average number of adverbs per sentence
4	Det	Average number of determiners per sentence
5	Noun	Average number of nouns per sentence
6	Prep	Average number of prepositions per sentence
7	CC	Average number of coordinating conjunctions per sentence
8	CS	Average number of subordinating conjunctions per sentence
9	Main	Average number of main verbs (verb chains) per sentence
10	Premod	Average number of pre-modifiers per sentence
11	Postmod	Average number of post-modifiers per sentence
12	ASL	Average sentence length (measured in words)
13	AWL	Average word length (measured in characters)
14	Pron	Average number of pronouns per sentence
15	SenseWN	Average number of senses per word (using EuroWordNet)
16	AmbWN	Percentage of ambiguous words in the text (using EuroWordNet)
17	SenseOT	Average number of senses per word (using Open Thesaurus)
18	AmbOT	Percentage of ambiguous words in the text (using Open Thesaurus)

turn, a list of substitute words (total number of word senses is 44,353). For computation of features 15–18, only the lemmas present in the lexical resources used were considered. All occurrences of such lemmas were considered, including repeated lemmas.

3.4 Experiments

After the readability indices and linguistically motivated complexity features were extracted for each text, four sets of experiments were conducted (Table 3).

The first set of experiments was conducted in order to select the features (out of the initial 18 features) which could potentially be correlated with the readability indices. Given that all 18 features reported significantly different values on original and the corresponding simplified texts, they were all used in the next set of experiments. After the second set of experiments indicated many significant correlations between the 18 complexity features and the readability indices, the next two sets of experiments had the aim of presenting the various possibilities of using those readability indices in text simplification. The third set of experiments illustrated the possibility of assessing: the necessary complexity reduction (by comparing the original texts with the manually simplified ones in the Simplext and FIRST corpora); the complexity reduction achieved (by comparing the original texts with the automatically simplified ones in the Automatic corpora); and the

Table 3 Experiments

Set	Experiments	Corpora used in the experiments
I	Comparison of the 18 complexity features and the three readability indices between the original and simplified texts	Simplext, FIRST
II	Correlation between the 18 complexity features and the three readability indices	Simplext, FIRST
III	Comparison of the average sentence length and the readability indices	FIRST, Simplext, Automatic, Noticias Fácil
IV	Comparison of paired relative differences in the three readability indices	FIRST, Simplext, Automatic

success of the manual simplification in reaching the 'gold standard' (by comparing the manually simplified texts in Simplext with the texts in Noticias Fácil). The fourth set of experiments explored the possibility of using the paired relative differences in readability indices for the comparing/ranking of different text simplification systems.

4 Results and Discussion

The results of the first two sets of experiments are presented and discussed in the next two subsections (Sects. 4.1 and 4.2), while the results of the third and forth sets of experiments are presented and discussed in Sect. 4.3.

4.1 Differences Between Original and Simplified Texts

The results of the first set of experiments, comparing the 18 linguistically motivated features and three readability indices between original and simplified texts in two corpora (Simplext and FIRST), are presented in Table 4.

The results (Table 4) indicate that the main simplification strategies in the Simplext corpus were sentence splitting – reflected in a decrease in coordinate conjunctions (*CC*) – and the elimination of adjectives. In the FIRST corpus, however, the main simplification operations were removal of prepositional phrases (*Prep*), adjectives (*Adj*), and post-modifiers (*Postmod*). Although a decrease in prepositions (*Prep*), adjectives (*Adj*), post-modifiers (*Postmod*), average sentence length (*ASL*), and two lexical complexity indices (*LC* and *SSR*) was present in both corpora, the decrease was more pronounced in the Simplext corpus. These observations draw on some important differences in simplification performed when having in mind the people with Down syndrome (Simplext project), and when having in mind the people with ASD (FIRST project). It appears that the first target population needs a higher level of text simplification, including more sentence

Table 4 Differences between original and simplified texts

Feature	Simp (O)	Simp (S)	P.R.Diff.(%)	Sign.	FIRST (O)	FIRST (S)	P.R.Diff.(%)	Sign.
Verb	3.46	1.97	**−39.88**	0.000	3.08	2.92	+0.83	0.397
Adj	2.41	0.67	**−70.96**	0.000	1.65	1.32	**−15.13**	0.003
Adv	0.75	0.46	**−21.11**	0.000	0.97	0.84	−7.86	0.157
Det	4.97	2.35	**−50.19**	0.000	3.19	2.83	−8.77	0.058
Noun	10.99	4.53	**−57.49**	0.000	7.07	6.21	**−8.43**	0.022
Prep	6.61	2.35	**−62.79**	0.000	3.97	3.08	**−20.28**	0.000
CC	1.00	0.22	**−74.85**	0.000	0.90	0.74	−3.33	0.067
CS	0.63	0.35	**−27.97**	0.000	0.51	0.50	+4.18	0.826
Main	3.12	1.86	**−37.21**	0.000	2.78	2.66	+1.20	0.456
Premod	7.07	3.09	**−54.77**	0.000	4.69	4.19	−7.79	0.057
Postmod	5.12	1.70	**−64.91**	0.000	2.83	2.27	**−12.70**	0.004
ASL	32.87	13.54	**−57.63**	0.000	23.00	19.90	**−10.52**	0.012
AWL	5.06	4.81	**−4.79**	0.000	4.92	4.90	−0.25	0.596
Pron	1.81	0.73	**−53.71**	0.000	1.77	1.56	−8.41	0.108
SenseWN	3.78	4.01	**+6.99**	0.000	3.98	4.11	+3.68	0.069
AmbWN	66.02	72.19	**+9.62**	0.000	66.50	68.95	**+3.79**	0.000
SenseOT	3.52	3.65	**+4.47**	0.000	3.37	3.47	**+3.10**	0.006
AmbOT	78.89	82.71	**+5.13**	0.000	77.86	80.90	**+3.93**	0.000
SCI	54.73	35.95	**−34.42**	0.000	46.53	45.69	+1.01	0.699
LC	21.05	12.76	**−39.06**	0.000	18.53	16.17	**−12.88**	0.000
SSR	184.20	123.82	**−32.60**	0.000	149.74	139.61	**−6.69**	0.002

Columns *Simp(O)*, *Simp(S)*, *FIRST(O)*, and *FIRST(S)*, contain the mean value of the corresponding feature on each subcorpus, where *(O)* denotes the original texts, *(S)* the simplified texts, and *Simp* Simplext corpus. Columns *P.R.Diff.* and *Sign.* present the mean value of the paired relative differences for the two subcorpora from the antecedent two columns, and the two-tailed statistical significance of the differences measured by the paired t-test and rounded at three decimals. Differences which are statistically significant at a 0.05 level of significance are shown in bold

splitting (reflected in a decrease in coordinate constructions and verbs) and more elimination of adjective and prepositional phrases (reflected in a greater decrease in adjectives, post-modifiers and prepositions than in the FIRST corpus).

It is interesting to note that while the average number of pronouns (*Pron*), which is an indicator of ambiguity in meaning, is lower in simplified than in original texts, the other four features which indicate ambiguity in meaning (*SenseWN*, *AmbWN*, *SenseOT*, *AmbOT*) show the opposite trend. This is somewhat surprising as we would expect to find a lower number of ambiguous words in simplified texts than in their corresponding originals, if we assume that ambiguous words present obstacles for the target population. However, it is a common lexical simplification strategy to replace infrequent words with their more frequent synonyms, and long words with their shorter synonyms. Given that the shorter words are usually more frequent (Balota et al. 2004), and that the frequent words tend to be more ambiguous than the infrequent ones (Glanzer and Bowles 1976), this lexical simplification strategy would result in having a greater number of ambiguous words and more senses on average per word in the simplified texts than in their corresponding originals. The justification for those substitution decisions might lie in the previous findings of the cognitive psychology that the words with the highest number of possible meanings are actually understood faster, due to their high frequency (Cuetos et al. 1997; Jastrzembski 1981).

Furthermore, the results presented in Table 4 indicate a possibility of finding some correlation between the three readability indices (SCI, LC, and SSR) and the linguistically motivated features. First, all indices show significant differences between original and simplified texts. The only exception to that is the case of the SCI index on the FIRST corpora. However, this is not surprising because the SCI measures syntactic complexity, and there is no significant difference between the linguistic features which would indicate a possible syntactic simplification (*Main*, *Verb*, *CC*) in the original and simplified texts of the FIRST corpora. Therefore, the similarity of the SCI values in the original and simplified texts of the FIRST corpora should not be taken as a sign of SCI not being adequate for estimating the level of syntactic simplification in general, but rather as a specificity of the FIRST corpora, simplified for people with ASD. Second, the relative differences of SCI, LC, and SSR between original and simplified texts are higher for the Simplext than for the FIRST corpora. This corresponds to the higher relative differences of linguistically motivated features in the Simplext than in the FIRST corpora, thus indicating a possible correlation between the readability indices and those linguistically motivated features.

4.2 Correlation Between Readability Indices and Linguistically Motivated Features

The results of the second set of experiments investigating the correlation between the three readability indices (SCI, LC, and SSR) and the 18 linguistically motivated features is presented in Table 5.

From the results presented in Table 5, it can be noted that the readability indices show a significant correlation with many of the linguistically motivated features in both corpora (Simplext and FIRST). As expected, the readability index which measures syntactic complexity of a text correlates best with the average number of verbs (*Verb*) and main verbs (*Main*) on both corpora. Out of the two readability indices which assess lexical complexity of a text, the SSR correlates better than LC with most of the features (on both corpora), the only exceptions being the average number of subordinate conjunctions (*CS*) in the FIRST corpus, and the average number of word senses (*SenseWN*) and the percentage of ambiguous words in the text (*AmbWN*) in the Simplext corpus, computed using the Spanish EuroWordNet.

Table 5 Spearman's correlation between readability indices and linguistically motivated features

Features	Simplext			FIRST		
	SCI	LC	SSR	SCI	LC	SSR
Verb	**0.867**	**0.503**	**0.571**	**0.774**	0.009	−0.001
Adj	**0.550**	**0.540**	**0.732**	0.143	*0.336	**0.584**
Adv	**0.429**	**0.215**	**0.259**	**0.478**	0.061	−0.146
Det	**0.662**	**0.620**	**0.621**	**0.412**	**0.434**	**0.476**
Noun	**0.585**	**0.723**	**0.810**	**0.338**	**0.678**	**0.833**
Prep	**0.658**	**0.704**	**0.759**	**0.398**	**0.592**	**0.782**
CC	**0.543**	**0.621**	**0.703**	**0.411**	**0.365**	0.237
CS	**0.604**	**0.163**	**0.158**	**0.576**	−0.088	−0.148
Main	**0.892**	**0.457**	**0.510**	**0.758**	−0.076	−0.086
Premod	**0.628**	**0.670**	**0.706**	**0.445**	**0.666**	**0.668**
Postmod	**0.546**	**0.621**	**0.750**	0.157	**0.495**	**0.760**
ASL	**0.751**	**0.678**	**0.756**	**0.593**	**0.591**	**0.675**
AWL	**0.169**	**0.326**	**0.517**	−0.177	−0.125	**−0.413**
Pron	**0.644**	**0.567**	**0.577**	**0.418**	0.213	0.035
SenseWN	0.031	**−0.267**	**−0.246**	0.202	**−0.386**	**−0.504**
AmbWN	**−0.196**	**−0.426**	**−0.379**	0.088	*−0.312	**−0.533**
SenseOT	−0.017	*−0.099	*−0.128	0.134	−0.166	−0.049
AmbOT	*−0.118	**−0.195**	**−0.206**	0.010	−0.180	−0.199

The first three columns present the results obtained on the Simplext corpus, and the last three the results obtained on the FIRST corpus. Statistically significant correlations (at a 0.001 level of significance) are presented in bold, while those not significant at a 0.001 level but significant at a 0.05 level is presented with an '*'

It is worth noting that the four features indicating semantic ambiguity (*SenseWN*, *AmbWN*, *SenseOT*, *AmbOT*) are negatively correlated with the two lexical complexity indices (*LC* and *SSR*), i.e. the higher number of senses per word on average and the higher percentage of ambiguous words in a text, the less lexically complex is the text. This brings us back to the previous discussion (Sect. 4.1) about more frequent words (which lead to text being perceived as lexically less complex in terms of LC and SSR) being more ambiguous than their less frequent synonyms, but still easier to disambiguate and understand.

4.3 Use of Readability Indices in Text Simplification

Finally, the possible use of the readability indices in text simplification was investigated by comparing their values on four different corpora:

Table 6 Comparison of readability indices across the corpora

Corpus	ASL	SCI	LC	SSR
FIRST (original)	23.00 ± 5.47	46.53 ± 9.29	18.53 ± 3.18	149.74 ± 25.63
FIRST (simplified)	19.90 ± 5.46	45.69 ± 9.97	16.17 ± 4.09	139.61 ± 27.01
Simplext (original)	32.87 ± 6.34	54.73 ± 10.16	21.05 ± 3.58	184.20 ± 19.10
Simplext (simplified)	13.54 ± 1.97	35.95 ± 12.40	12.76 ± 4.46	123.82 ± 24.13
Automatic (original)	33.43 ± 5.58	56.42 ± 9.37	21.57 ± 3.90	182.21 ± 21.65
Automatic (rules)	33.41 ± 5.61	56.48 ± 9.17	21.28 ± 3.86	174.85 ± 20.97
Automatic (syntactic)	28.10 ± 5.28	49.63 ± 10.19	20.21 ± 3.85	174.40 ± 21.44
Automatic (both)	28.16 ± 5.54	50.01 ± 10.23	19.99 ± 3.66	167.21 ± 20.51
Noticias Fácil	9.26 ± 2.13	30.22 ± 10.88	12.23 ± 4.87	104.50 ± 30.02

1. The *FIRST* corpus of original and manually simplified texts for people with ASD;
2. The *Simplext* corpus of original and manually simplified texts for people with Down syndrome;
3. The *Automatic* Simplext corpus of original texts and three groups of corresponding automatically simplified texts: those which were simplified only by using the lexical rule-based transformations (*rules*); those which were simplified using the rule-based system for syntactic simplification (*syntactic*); and those which were simplified using the combination of both (*both*);
4. The *Noticias Fácil* corpus of news written especially for people with intellectual disability.

The results of the third set of experiments, comparing the average sentence length (ASL), and the three readability indices (SCI, LC, and SSR) are presented in Table 6, showing the mean value with standard deviation of each readability index on each of the four corpora and their sub-corpora.

Comparison of those values across the corpora can provide various interesting insights. For example, the comparison of the results obtained for *Simplext (original)* and *Automatic (original)* show that the starting point (original texts) in both cases had similar values of *ASL*, *SCI*, *LC*, and *SSR* (i.e. texts were of similar complexity). Therefore, the ideal automatic simplification should result in texts with a similar value of those four features as the texts in *Simplext (simplified)* subcorpus. Comparison of the results obtained for *Automatic (both)* with those for *Simplext (simplified)* on all four features indicates how far from ideal (achieved by manual simplification) is the performance of the automatic simplification. Furthermore, the comparison of the manually simplified texts in *Simplext (simplified)* with those in *Noticias Fácil* (which can be considered as a 'gold standard' of texts aimed at people with intellectual disability) could serve as an additional checkpoint as to whether the performed manual simplification complies with the standards for easy-to-read texts.

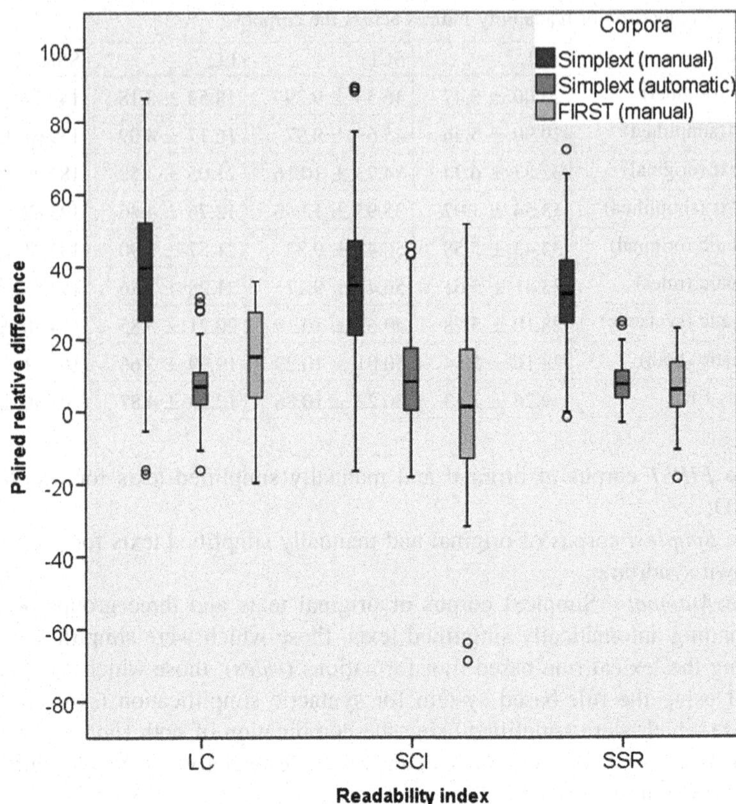

Fig. 1 Paired relative differences of LC, SCI, and SSR across the three corpora

The proposed readability indices could also be used for the comparing or ranking of different simplification systems by the level of simplification achieved, as demonstrated in Fig. 1 (the higher the value of the paired relative differences, the higher the level of simplification). For example, it can be noted that the level of simplification (measured by paired relative differences of SCI, LC, and SSR) achieved by automatic simplification system *Simplext (automatic)* is much lower than the desired one achieved by *Simplext (manual)*. At the same time, the level of simplification achieved in *Simplext (automatic)* is very close to, and in terms of syntactic simplification measured by SCI even better than, the one achieved by manual simplification in *FIRST* (Fig. 1). This could indicate a possibility that some components of the automatic simplification system in Simplext (e.g. the syntactic simplification module) could be used for the syntactic simplification of texts for people with ASD. However, this possibility would need to be carefully investigated especially because the texts in *FIRST* and those in *Simplext (original)* are not from the same domain and do not seem to have the same complexity (Table 6).

5 Conclusions

Text simplification aims to convert written material into a lexically and syntactically simpler variant. It has a significant societal impact, enabling users with limited language comprehension to have better inclusion into society. With the recent emergence of various TS systems, the question we are faced with is how to automatically evaluate their performance given that access to target users might be difficult. This chapter addressed one aspect of this issue by exploring whether existing readability formulae could be applied to assess the level of simplification performed by TS systems.

The results of the first set of experiments showed that there are significant differences between original and manually simplified texts in terms of 18 linguistically motivated complexity features. This supported the idea that those features can be seen as possible reading obstacles for two target populations: people with ASD, and people with Down syndrome. The results of the second set of experiments indicated that the three readability indices (SSR, LC, and SCI) are significantly correlated with many of those features, and that those correlations stand irrespective of the text genre and the target population. The third and fourth sets of experiments illustrated various possible uses of those three readability indices in text simplification: assessing the necessary complexity reduction (by comparing the original texts with the manually simplified ones); the complexity reduction achieved (by comparing the original texts with the automatically simplified ones); the success of the manual simplification in reaching the 'gold standard' (by comparing the manually simplified texts with the 'gold standard'); and the possibility of comparing and ranking different TS systems.

The results presented in this study also complied the well known hypotheses in cognitive psychology: (1) that the shorter and more frequent words are more ambiguous than their longer and less frequent synonyms; (2) that the more frequent words (although having more possible senses on average per word) can be easier understood than their less frequent (and less ambiguous) synonyms, and thus raise fewer problems in text comprehension than their less frequent variants. A more detailed examination of these findings would provide valuable insights into better understanding of the user needs in text simplification, and new ideas as to how to use existing NLP tools for building better TS systems.

Acknowledgements This work has been partially supported by TRADICOR (Ref: PIE 13-054), EXPERT (Ref: 317471-FP7-PEOPLE-2012-ITN), LATEST (Ref: 327197-FP7-PEOPLE-2012-IEF) and FIRST (Ref: 287607-FP7-ICT-2011-7). The authors would also like to express their gratitude to Horacio Saggion for his very helpful comments and input.

References

Alúısio, S. M., Specia, L., Pardo, T. A. S., Maziero, E. G., Caseli, H. M., & Fortes, R. P. M. (2008). A corpus analysis of simple account texts and the proposal of simplification strategies: first steps towards text simplification systems. In *Proceedings of the 26th annual ACM international conference on Design of communication*, SIGDOC '08, (pp. 15–22). New York, NY, USA: ACM.

Anula, A. (2007). Tipos de textos, complejidad lingüística y facilicitacíon lectora. In *Actas del Sexto Congreso de Hispanistas de Asia*, (pp. 45–61).

Aranzabe, M. J., Dı́az De Ilarraza, A., & Gonźalez, I. (2012). First approach to automatic text simplification in basque. In *Proceedings of the first Natural Language Processing for Improving Textual Accessibility Workshop* (NLP4ITA).

American Psychiatric Association. (2013). *Diagnostic and Statistical Manual of Mental Disorders* (5th ed.). Arlington, VA: American Psychiatric Publishing.

Balota, D., Cortese, M. J., Sergent-Marshall, S. D., Spieler, D. H., & Yap, M. J. (2004). Visual word recognition of single-syllabe words. *Journal of Experimental Psychology: General, 133*, 283–316.

Barlacchi, G., & Tonelli, S. (2013). ERNESTA: A sentence simplification tool for childrens stories in italian. In *Computational Linguistics and Intelligent Text Processing.*

Barzilay, R., & Elhadad, N. (2003). Sentence alignment for monolingual comparable corpora. In *Proceedings of the 2003 conference on Empirical methods in natural language processing, EMNLP '03* (pp. 25–32). Stroudsburg, PA, USA: Association for Computational Linguistics.

Brouwer, R. H. M. (1963). Onderzoek naar de leesmoeilijkheden van nederlands proza. *Pedagogische studiën, 40*, 454–464.

Carroll, J., Minnen, G., Canning, Y., Devlin, S., & Tait, J. (1998). Practical simplification of english newspaper text to assist aphasic readers. In *Proceedings of AAAI-98 Workshop on Integrating Artificial Intelligence and Assistive Technology* (pp. 7–10).

Chomsky, N. (1986). *Knowledge of language: Its nature, origin, and use.* Santa Barbara, CA: Greenwood Publishing Group.

Coleman, M., & Liau, T. L. (1975). A computer readability formula designed for machine scoring. *Journal of Applied Psychology, 60*(2), 283–284.

Coster, W., & Kauchak, D. (2011). Learning to simplify sentences using Wikipedia. In *Proceedings of the 49th Annual Meeting of the Association for Computational Linguistics* (pp. 1–9).

Cuetos, F., Domı́nguez, A., & de Vega, M. (1997). El efecto de la polisemia: ahora lo ves otra vez. *Cognitiva, 9*(2), 175–194.

Dale, E., & Chall, J. S. (1948). A formula for predicting readability. *Educational research bulletin, 27*, 11–20.

Devlin, S. (1999). Simplifying natural language text for aphasic readers. Ph.D. thesis, University of Sunderland, UK.

Douma, W. H. (1960). De leesbaarheid van landbouwbladen: een onderzoek naar en een toepassing van leesbaarheidsformules. Landbouwhogeschool Wageningen, Afdeling Sociologie en Sociografie, *Bulletin nr.* 17.

Drndarević, B., Štajner, S., Bott, S., Bautista, S. & Saggion, H. (2013). Automatic text simplication in spanish: A comparative evaluation of complementing components. In *Proceedings of the 12th International Conference on Intelligent Text Processing and Computational Linguistics. Lecture Notes in Computer Science. Samos, Greece, 24–30 March*, (pp. 488–500).

DuBay, W. H. (2004). *The principles of readability.* California: Impact Information.

Feng, L. (2009). Automatic readability assessment for people with intellectual disabilities. In *SIGACCESS Accessibility and Computers.* number 93, (pp. 84–91). New York, NY, USA: ACM.

Feng, L., Elhadad, N., & Huenerfauth, M. (2009). Cognitively motivated features for readability assessment. In *Proceedings of the 12th Conference of the European Chapter of the Association for Computational Linguistics, EACL '09,* (pp. 229–237), Stroudsburg, PA, USA: Association for Computational Linguistics.

Flesch, R. (1948). A new readability yardstick. *The journal of applied psychology, 32*(3), 221–233.

Freyhoff, G., Hess, G., Kerr, L., Tronbacke, B., & Van Der Veken, K. (1998). *Make it simple, European guidelines for the production of easy-to read information for people with learning disability.* Brussels: ILSMH European Association.

Glanzer, M., & Bowles, N. (1976). Analysis of the word frequency effect in recognition memory. *Journal of Experimental Psychology: Human Learning and Memory, 2*, 21–31.

Glavaš, G., & Štajner, S. (2013). Event-centered simplication of news stories. In *Proceedings of the Student Workshop held in conjunction with RANLP 2013, Hissar, Bulgaria* (pp. 71–78).

Gunning, R. (1952). *The technique of clear writing.* New York: McGraw-Hill.

Inui, K., Fujita, A., Takahashi, T., Iida, R., & Iwakura, T. (2003). Text simplification for reading assistance: a project note. In *Proceedings of the second international workshop on Paraphrasing—Volume* 16, *PARAPHRASE '03,* (pp. 9–16), Stroudsburg, PA, USA: Association for Computational Linguistics.

Jastrzembski, J. (1981). Multiple meaning, number or related meanings, frequency of occurrence and the lexicon. *Cognitive Psychology, 13*, 278–305.

Kincaid, J. P., Fishburne, R. P., Rogers, R. L., & Chissom, B. S. (1975). Derivation of new readability formulas for navy enlisted personnel. *Research Branch Report* 8–75.

Martos, J., Freire, S., González, A., Gil, D., & Sebastian, M. (2012). D2.1: Functional requirements specifications and user preference survey. Technical report, FIRST technical report.

McLaughlin, G. H. (1969). SMOG grading—a new readability formula. *Journal of Reading, 22*, 639–646.

Norbury, C. F. (2005). Barking up the wrong tree? lexical ambiguity resolution in children with language impairments and autistic spectrum disorders. *Journal of Experimental Child Psychology, 90*, 142–171.

Orasan, C., Evans, R., & Dornescu, I. (2013). *Towards multilingual Europe 2020: A romanian perspective, chapter text simplification for people with autistic spectrum disorders* (pp. 287–312). Bucharest: Romanian Academy Publishing House.

Petersen, S., & Ostendorf, M. (2009). A machine learning approach to reading level assessment. *Computer Speech and Language, 23*(1), 89–106.

Petersen, S. E., & Ostendorf, M. (2007). Text simplification for language learners: A corpus analysis. In *Proceedings of Workshop on Speech and Language Technology for Education(SLaTE),* 69–72.

PlainLanguage. (2011). Federal plain language guidelines.

Rello, L. (2012). Dyswebxia: a model to improve accessibility of the textual web for dyslexic users. In SIGACCESS *Accessibility and Computers*, number 102, (pp. 41–44) New York, NY, USA: ACM.

Rello, L., Baeza-Yates, R., Bott, S., & Saggion, H. (2013b). Simplify or help? Text simplification strategies for people with dyslexia. In *Proceedings of W4A conference*, Article no. 15

Rello, L., Baeza-Yates, R., Dempere, L., & Saggion, H. (2013a). Frequent words improve readability and short words improve understandability for people with dyslexia. In *Proceedings of the INTERACT 2013: 14th IFIP TC13 Conference on Human-Computer Interaction. Cape Town, South Africa*, pp. 203–219.

Ruiter, M. B., Rietveld, T. C. M., Cucchiarini C., Krahmer E. J., & Strik, H. (2010). Human language technology and communicative disabilities: requirements and possibilities for the future. In *Proceedings of the the seventh international conference on Language Resources and Evaluation (LREC).*

Rybing, J., Smithr, C., & Silvervarg, A. (2010). Towards a rule based system for automatic simplification of texts. In *The Third Swedish Language Technology Conference.*

Saggion, H., Gómez Martínez, E., Etayo, E., Anula, A., & Bourg, L. (2011). Text simplification in simplext: Making text more accessible. *Revista de la Sociedad Española para el Procesamiento del Lenguaje Natural.*

Schwarm, S. E, & Ostendorf, M. (2005). Reading level assessment using support vector machines and statistical language models. In *Proceedings of the 43rd annual meeting of the Association of Computational Linguistics (ACL)*, pp. 523–530.

Siddharthan, A. (2006). Syntactic simplification and text cohesion. *Research on Language and Computation, 4*(1), 77–109.

Smith, E. A., & Senter R. J. (1967) Automated readability index. Technical report, Aerospace Medical Research Laboratories, Wright-Patterson Air Force Base, Ohio.

Spaulding, S. (1956). A Spanish readability formula. *Modern Language Journal 40*, 433–441.

UN. (2006) Convention on the rigths of persons with disabilities.

van Oosten, P., Tanghe, D., & Hoste, V. (2010). Towards an improved methodology for automated readability prediction. In *Proceedings of the seventh international conference on language resources and evaluation (LREC10). Valletta, Malta: European Language Resources Association (ELRA)*, pp. 775–782.

Vossen, P. (Ed.). (1998) *EuroWordNet: A multilingual database with lexical semantic networks.* Dordrecht: Kluwer Academic Publishers.

Štajner, S., Drndarević, B., & Saggion, H. (2013). Corpus-based sentence deletion and split decisions for spanish text simplification. *Computación y Systemas, 17*(2), 251–262.

Štajner, S., Evans, R., Orasan, C., & Mitkov, R. (2012). What can readability measures really tell us about text complexity? In *Proceedings of the LREC'12 Workshop: Natural Language Processing for Improving Textual Accessibility (NLP4ITA)*, Istanbul, Turkey.

Štajner, S., & Saggion, H. (2013b). Adapting text simplification decisions to different text genres and target users. *Procesamiento del Lenguaje Natural, 51*, 135–142.

Štajner, S., & Saggion, H. (2013a). Readability indices for automatic evaluation of text simplification systems: A feasability study for spanish. In *Proceedings of the 6th International Joint Conference on Natural Language Processing (IJCNLP 2013), Nagoya, Japan,* October 14–18, 2013. pp. 374–382.

Woodsend, K., & Lapata, M. (2011). Learning to simplify sentences with Quasi-synchronous grammar and integer programming. In *Proceedings of the 2011 Conference on Empirical Methods in Natural Language Processing (EMNLP).*

Woodsend, K. & Lapata, M. (2011). WikiSimple: automatic simplification of Wikipedia articles. In *Proceedings of the 25th AAI Coference on Artificial Intelligence*, pp. 374–382.

Wubben, S., van den Bosch, A., & Krahmer, E. (2012). Sentence simplification by monolingual machine translation. In *Proceedings of the 50th Annual Meeting of the Association for Computational Linguistics: Long Papers—Volume 1*, ACL '12, (pp. 1015–1024) Stroudsburg, PA, USA: Association for Computational Linguistics.

Zhu, Z., Berndard, D., & Gurevych, I. (2010). A monolingual tree-based translation model for sentence simplification. In *Proceedings of the 23rd International Conference on Computational Linguistics (Coling 2010)*, (pp. 1353–1361).

An Approach to Improve the Language Quality of Requirements

Juyeon Kang and Patrick Saint-Dizier

Abstract In this article, requirement authoring methods are investigated together with the way they impact the tasks carried out by technical writers. A method is proposed, based on natural language processing technology, to improve requirement production and writing. This method is based on the notion of correction memory and correction patterns derived from the observation of the corrections made by technical writers. This work remains preliminary and exploratory. We address in this article the case of fuzzy expressions and of complex sentences, which are major errors found in technical documentation.

Keywords Requirement writing · Correction memory · Correction patterns · Technical documents · Memory-based techniques

1 Introduction

Technical documents form a linguistic genre with very specific linguistic constraints in terms of lexical realizations, including business or domain dependent aspects, grammar and style. Typography and overall document organization are also specific to this genre. Technical documents cover a large variety of types of documents: procedures (also called instructional texts), which are probably the most frequently encountered in this genre, equipment and product manuals, various notices such as security notices, regulations of various types (security, management), requirements (e.g. concerning the design properties of a certain

J. Kang (✉)
IRIT–CNRS, Toulouse, France
e-mail: j.kang@prometil.com

J. Kang · P. Saint-Dizier
IRIT–CNRS, Toulouse, France
e-mail: stdizier@irit.fr

© Springer International Publishing Switzerland 2015

N. Gala et al. (eds.), *Language Production, Cognition, and the Lexicon*,
Text, Speech and Language Technology 48, DOI 10.1007/978-3-319-08043-7_23

product) and product or process specifications. These documents are designed to be easy to read and as efficient and unambiguous as possible for their users and readers. For that purpose, they tend to follow relatively strict authoring principles concerning both their form and contents. However, depending in particular on the industrial domain, the traditions of the company, the required security level, and the target user, major differences in the writing and overall organization quality can be observed (Porter et al. 1995).

Regulations and requirements form a specific subgenre in technical documents: they do not describe how to realize a task but the constraints that hold on certain types of tasks or products, the way they must be manufactured, used, stored and maintained. Requirements can also be process or product specifications describing the properties and the expectations related to a product or a process. These specifications may be used as a contractual basis in the realization of the product at stake. Business rules (as e.g. developed in SBVR) are quite close to requirements. They however contain additional considerations such as means or ways of realizing a task which do not have the injunctive character that requirements have.

Technical documents and, in particular, requirements are seldom written from scratch: they are often the revision, the adaptation, or the compilation of previously written documents. Requirements for a given task or product are often very large, even a small product may require more than ten thousands requirements. Therefore requirements associated with a product result from the collaboration of several technical writers, technicians and validators. Their production may take several months, with several cycles of revisions and validations. Requirement revision and update is a major and complex activity, which requires very accurate authoring principles and text analysis to avoid any form of 'textual chaos'.

Design and software requirements must be unambiguous, short, relevant and easy to understand by professionals. They must form a homogeneous and coherent set of specifications. Safety requirements are often very large documents, they must be carefully checked since they may be as complex as procedures. Requirements must leave as little space as possible for personal interpretations, similarly to procedures (Van der Linden 1993). The functions and the types of requirements are presented in depth in e.g. Hull et al. (2011), Sage et al. (2009), Grady (2006), Pohl (2010), Nuseibeh et al. (2000). A lot of work is devoted to requirement engineering (traceability, organization), via systems such as e.g. Doors and its extensions (e.g. Reqtify, QuaARS). However, very little work has been carried out in the area of natural language processing besides (Gnesi et al. 2005; Yang et al. 2010) and the proceedings of the CNL (Controlled Natural Language) workshops which contain useful observations and projects.

Requirement documents are in general not a mere list of organized requirements. They often start with general considerations such as purpose, scope, or context. Then follow definitions, examples, scenarios or schemas. Then come a series of sections that address, via sets of requirements, the different facets of the problem at stake. Each section may include for its own purpose general elements followed by the relevant requirements. Each requirement can be associated with e.g. conditions or warnings and forms of explanation such as justifications, reformulations or illustrations.

In this paper, we first introduce the notion of requirement and the motivations for improving requirement writing overall quality. Then, we develop two main approaches to writing requirements and propose a method based on the natural language processing to improve requirement authoring based on our LELIE system. Next, a method is proposed, based on natural language processing technology, to improve requirement production and writing. This method is based on the notion of *correction memory and correction patterns* defined from the observation of the corrections made by technical writers. This work remains preliminary and exploratory. We address in this article the case of fuzzy expressions and of complex sentences, which are major errors found in technical documentation.

This notion of error correction memory originates form the notion of translation memory, it is however substantially different in its principles and implementation. An in-depth analysis of memory-based language processing is developed (Daelemans et al. 2005) and implemented in the TiMBL software. This work develops several forms of statistical means to produce generalizations in syntax, semantics and morphology. It also warns against excessive forms of generalizations. Buchholz (2002) develops an insightful memory-based analysis on how grammatical constructions can be induced from samples. Memory-based systems are also used to resolve ambiguities, using notions such as analogies (Schriever et al. 1989). Finally, memory-based techniques are used in programming languages support systems to help programmers to resolve frequent errors.

2 Some Motivations for Improving the Quality of Requirements

Poor requirements often lead to accidents, with major health and ecological consequences. They also lead to social and psycho-social problems (e.g. due to poor management requirements) and, obviously, negative financial situations. Impact studies show the negative consequences of bad or poor requirement, for example, Wiegers (2001) says that *Industry data shows that approximately* 50 % *of product defects originate from incorrect or unreadable requirements. Perhaps* 80 % *of the rework effort on a development project can be traced to requirements defects.* Because these defects are the cause of over 40 % of accidents in safety-critical systems (Chaos reports 2012–2014), poor requirements have even been the ultimate cause of both death and destruction.

Several analysis show that the three major factors of success for a project are user involvement, executive management support and a clear expression of requirements. Each of these features have about the same weight. The factors that cause projects to fail or to be challenged are lack of user input, incomplete requirements and specifications, and changing requirements and specifications. Each of these also have about the same weight.

The two examples below are real-life requirements. They illustrate the necessity of controlling writing quality:

(1) Poor word, choice and syntactic construction: *the fire alarm shall sound when smoke is detected, unless the alarm is being tested and the engineer has suppressed the alarm.*
(2) Undefined word, unclear antecedents and long sentence: *provided that the designated data from the specified columns are received in the correct order so that the application is able to differentiate among the data, the resulting summary data shall comply with the required format in* Sect. 2.

3 Main Functions of Requirements

For a given product or activity, requirements are produced by different participants, often with different profiles. For example, stakeholders are at the initiative of requirements that describe the product they expect. Then, engineers, safety staff, regulation experts and technicians may produce more specialized requirements, for example: quality, tracing, modeling or testing requirements (Hull et al. 2011).

These documents may then undergo several levels of validation and update. Certification is often required for 'strategical' activities (e.g. chemistry, transportation, energy). This requires an accurate compliance of these documents w.r.t. to various norms and regulations which may evolve quite rapidly over time and circumstances.

Requirement production is now becoming a major activity in the industry. The goal is to specify a number of activities in a more rigorous, modular, structured and manageable way. Requirements may be *proper* to a company, an activity or a country. In this latter case, it may be a regulation. We now observe requirements in areas as diverse as product or software design, finance, communication, staff management and security and safety.

Here are a few short illustrations, which have been slightly changed to preserve their anonymous character, that illustrate the above considerations. The first two examples are typical of product requirements. The second example is typical of cases where enumerations specify several components. If enumerations are easy to read and process by engineers, they contribute to making sentences really long.

R1. *For each of the network elements included in our solution, the tenderer shall describe which hardware components* i.e. *racks, chassis, servers, blades, processing units, I/O cards, mother cards, daughter cards* etc. *of its overall platform are redundant.*

R2. *The tenderer shall detail if the following mechanisms are supported:*

- *Protection against DDuS attacks.*
- *Anti-spoofing mechanisms.*

- *Access control list (ACL).*
- *Intrusion prevention and detection mechanisms.*
- *Filtering tools.*

The next example shows a frequent situation where either acronyms (standingfor a number of additional requirements which are not given) or a large numberof references to other documents or norms make the requirement quite difficultto understand:

R3. *When considering the use of surface water drainage channels and or kerbing, the Design Organisation must evaluate the safety aspect in relation to the position of any safety barriers and the relevant set-backs (see HA* 37 [*DMRB* 4.2], *HA 83* [*DMRB* 4.2.4] *and HA* 119 [*DMRB* 4.2.9] *and MCHW-3 Series B and F*).

The last example is a short security notice. Its structure is close to a procedure: motivation or goal followed by a list of instructions to follow. In this example, a somewhat verbose context is specified together with general purpose recommendations before going into the instructions to follow:

R4. *BOMB THREAT. This is a major problem that has to be faced more and more frequently. It is important to remain calm and to contact authorities as early as possible. These will decide on evacuation conditions if appropriate. In this notice different scenarios are given which must be adapted to the context. The following cases are not independent, so it is crucial to read all of them. In case of a bomb threat:*

(a) *Any person receiving a telephone threat should try to keep the caller on the line and if possible transfer the Area Manager. Remain calm, notify your supervisor and await instructions.*
(b) *If you are unable to transfer the call, obtain as much relevant information as possible and notify the Area Manager by messenger. Try to question the caller so you can fill out the 'Bomb Threat Report Form'. After the caller hangs up, notify the Division Manager, then contact* 911 *and ask for instructions. Then contact Maintenance and the Governor's office.*
(c) *The Division Manager will call the police* (911) *for instructions.*

    c1. *If the Division Manager is not available call* 911 *and wait for instructions.*
    c2. *Pull emergency evacuation alarm. Follow evacuation procedures.*

(d) *The person who received the bomb threat will report directly to the police station.*

The reader can note the complexity of this text in terms of language and situation analysis; he may ask himself whether he would read it carefully if such an event occurs. Complexity involves stress and a heavy conceptual load which are not really appropriate in these situations.

4 Requirement Writing and Control

To ensure high quality in requirements, these must follow various authoring principles and recommendations (Weiss 2000; Rushby 2001; Turk 2006; Firesmith 2007). These principles are in general quite close to procedural texts, with some variants since e.g. the use of modals (*shall, must*) is typical of requirements and must not be used in procedure instructions.

A few norms have been produced and international standards have emerged for the production of technical documents, including the principles of simplified language writing. We have implemented some of these in our LELIE project (Barcellini et al. 2012; Saint-Dizier 2014). Concerning requirements, let us note in particular: (1) IEEE (IEEE 1998) Standard 830—Requirement Specification: 'Content and qualities of a good software requirement specification' and (2) IEEE Standard 1233, 'Guide for developing System Requirements Specifications'. Let us now review two of the main approaches to requirement authoring: boilerplates and a posteriori control, which is the strategy adopted in our LELIE project.

Producing requirements, similarly to most authoring activity, requires both global and low level care. The global level requires that requirements are correct, unambiguous, complete, consistent, verifiable, modifiable, and traceable:

- CORRECT: correctly reflects the actual needs;
- UNAMBIGUOUS: should have only one interpretation;
- COMPLETE: a set of requirements must include all significant situations;
- CONSISTENT: should avoid potential conflicts, e.g.: (1) logical and temporal conflicts between two requirements, (2) or two or more requirements describing the same real world object with different properties;
- VERIFIABLE: it is crucial to use concrete words and measurable quantities and to avoid non-verifiable words such as *works well* or *shall usually happen*;
- MODIFIABLE: to implement this property, requirements should not be mixed or redundant;
- TRACEABLE: the main features of the requirement must be accessible in order to facilitate the referencing of each requirement and its components for future developments.

These factors are obviously very difficult to implement in a machine because they require complex language technology coupled with accurate knowledge and inferences. In this document, we present the treatment of errors of a lower level, but which may impact those main characteristics.

4.1 Boilerplates: A Template-Based Approach

The boilerplate approach is essentially used for writing requirements in software and product design. These requirements are often very short sentences which follow strict and very regular formats. The RAT-RQA approach developed by the

Reuse-company is a typical and simple example. Boilerplates are a technique that uses predefined simple language templates based on concepts and relations to guide requirements elicitation. These templates may be combined to form larger structures. Requirement authors must strictly follow these templates. Boilerplates thus define a priori the language of requirements. Defining such a language is not so straightforward for complex requirements such as safety, financial or management requirements. Compliance with boilerplates format is checked e.g. by the *Rubric* system from univerity of Luxemburg. It also checks simple lexical forms which could raise problems in requirements.

The language introduced in boilerplates allows authors to produce general structures such as propositions as well as more specialized components which are treated as adjuncts, such as capability of a system, capacity (maximize, exceed), rapidity, mode, sustainability, timelines, operational constraints and exceptions. Repositories of boilerplates have been defined by companies or research groups, these may be generic or activity dependent.

An average size repository has about 60 boilerplates. Larger repositories are more difficult to manage. These are not in general publicly available. The examples below illustrate the constructions proposed by boilerplates. Terms between < > are concepts which must receive a language expression possibly subject to certain restrictions:

General purpose boilerplates:

- The <system> shall be able to <capability>.
- *The washing machine shall be able to wash the dirty clothes.*
- The <system> shall be able to <action> <entity>.
- *The ACC system shall be able to determine the speed of the eco-vehicle.*

In these examples, the concept action is realized as a verb, the concept entity as a direct object and the concept capability as a verb phrase. The syntactic structures associated with each of these concepts are relatively well identified; their syntax may also be partly controlled. The different words which are used such as e.g. entities can be checked by reference to the domain ontology and terminology.

To develop more complex statements, boilerplates can be defined in terms of a combination of *specialized boilerplates* inserted into general purpose ones. The latter characterize various levels of granularity of the statements which can be built. In these examples, modals, prepositions and quantifiers are imposed. The priority of a requirement can sometimes be evaluated w.r.t. the modal verb that is used (e.g. shall, must, should, may, etc.).

Here are a few templates used to elaborate substructures within the general purpose ones:

- The <system> shall <function> <object> every <performance> <units>.
- *The coffee machine shall produce a hot drink every* 10 s.
- The <system> shall <function> not less than <quantity> <object> while <operational conditions>.

- *The communications system shall sustain telephone contact with not less than 10 callers while in the absence of external power.*
- The <system> shall display status messages in <circumstance>.
- *The Background Task Manager shall display status messages in a designated area of the user interface at intervals of* 60 *plus or minus* 10 s.
- The <system> shall be able to <function> <object> composed of not less than <performance> <units> with <external entity>.
- The <system> shall be able to <function> <object> of type <qualification> within <performance> <units>.
- While <operational condition> the <stakeholder> shall <capability>.
- *While activated the driver shall be able to override engine power control of the ACC-system.*
- The <stakeholder> shall not be placed in breach of <applicable law>.
- *The ambulance driver shall not be placed in breach of national road regulations.*

As the reader may note it, the user of such a system needs some familiarity with the boilerplates concepts to be able to use boilerplates correctly. Some types are relatively vague while others are very constrained. The latter require some training and documentation for the novice technical writer. Boilerplates have some advantages when producing large sets of short requirements in the sense that predefined templates guide the author, limiting the revisions needed at the form level. Revisions are still required at the contents level because a number of types remain general (performance, operational conditions, capability, etc.). It is however an attempt to standardize the requirement sublanguage, at least from a lexical and syntactic point of view. Using predefined attributes makes it to easier to write requirements, in particular for authors with limited experience. Authors can select the most appropriate templates and instantiate concepts such as capability, condition. However, this language may not evolve too much, otherwise large revisions of already produced requirements will need to be done. New templates can be added, but it is not possible to remove existing ones or to transform their structure.

Authors which do not have a good command of the concepts and of what they cover will have a lot of difficulties to use boilerplates; this is obviously the case of stakeholders. Therefore, boilerplates may be used essentially for technical and low level requirements. Our experience is that in a number of companies where boilerplates are used, technical writers try to follow to some degree the boilerplate patterns, but also allow themselves quite a lot of freedom because boilerplates seem to be too rigid for what they must express.

4.2 An a Posteriori Control of the Language Quality of Requirements

A different approach consists in letting requirement writers produce their documents rather freely and to offer them a tool to control their production a posteriori or upon demand. This is obviously a much less constraining view that leaves more freedom and flexibility to the author. This is well-adapted for domains or areas where requirements are complex, for example security requirements or regulations which may be several pages long. In that case, boilerplates are not appropriate.

This approach allows for high-level (writing methodology and guidelines) as well as low-level (lexical items, business terms, grammar) controls. Buddenberg (2011) develops general purpose recommendations and advice to write requirements with this approach. The LELIE system (Saint-Dizier 2014) is based on this approach; it is more closely linked to the production process in which technical writers work, exchange, and revise their documents. Requirement validation can use the same approach, possibly with different types of controls or alerts.

5 Controlling the Writing Quality of Requirements

Let us now develop in more detail the features adopted in the LELIE project. An important element of our approach is that the severity level of an error strongly depends on the domain, the sentence in which it occurs and the familiarity of the reader with the expression and its contents. This is why the term *alert* is preferred to avoid any negative connotation.

In this section, we first show a straightforward implementation of some principles of technical writing applied to requirements. The results are in general good from a language processing point of view. However, requirement authors feel that quite a large proportion of the alerts are not real errors in their context. About 30 % of the alerts are indeed not relevant and do not deserve any attention. This is a very high proportion. Our approach is then to work on a kind of contextual *correction memory* that keeps track, for each alert, of the attitude of authors of a given company working on a specific domain. The goal is (1) to memorize precise situations where alerts do not trigger any correction in the application or business context, so that they are no longer displayed as alerts in the future and (2) to memorize corrections carried out so that they can be proposed in a later stage to authors, after validation, in order to make corrections stable and more homogeneous over large texts. These corrections will also be used in an homogeneous way by a whole population of technical writers. Some light generalizations can be realized so that closely related situations are also taken into account. This approach is essential for requirement authors so that they do not waste time on (1) alerts which are not relevant or (2) working on corrections which have already been elaborated. This is also a way to keep track of the authoring traditions of the company.

The development of this solution is ongoing. It requires a lot of experimentations with technical writers and the treatment of a large number of alerts before the system is really operational.

To illustrate our approach, we develop in this article a few typical situations of technical writing: alerts about fuzzy lexical items and expressions, sentences which are too complex or too long and the use of double negation. We show (1) how a cooperative approach can and must be develop so that only real errors are detected and (2) how a correction memory, similar in its principles to a translation memory, can be implemented. In such an approach, it is necessary to reach a consensus, via discussion and possibly mediation, so that the whole team of writers adopts exactly the same strategy for each alert. For that purpose, and for other reasons developed below, we have introduced an administrator level in our system.

Let us first present in this section the corpus we have considered to carry out our investigations. Let us then focus on the three prototypical alerts advocated above and show how they are managed in LELIE and what the implications are in term of work, management and system flexibility.

5.1 The Development Corpus

Our investigation focuses only on requirements, even if they are included into larger documents. In Kang and Saint-Dizier (2013) we show how requirements can be extracted from such texts based on a few rules typical of requirement structures.

Our analysis of requirement structures is based on a corpus of requirements coming from seven companies, kept anonymous at their request. Documents are in French or in English. Our corpus contains about 500 pages extracted from 27 documents, with about 4,000 requirements, out of which 1,450 requirements have been extracted for our experiments. These 27 documents are composed of 15 French and 12 English documents. The main features considered to validate our corpus are the following:

- Requirement with various structures and language aspects,
- Requirements corresponding to various professional activities: product design, management, finance, and safety,
- Requirements corresponding to different conceptual levels: functional, realization, management, etc.
- Requirements following various kinds of business style and format guidelines imposed by companies,
- Requirements coming from various industrial areas: finance, telecommunications, transportation, energy, computer science, and chemistry.

This corpus allows us to analyze different types of errors in terms of frequency and context. Due to time constraints, the way they are corrected has only been realized on requirements related to the domains of energy and transportation (aeronautics). These two industrial sectors produce long and complex requirement documents which are of much interest for our experiments. Furthermore, technical writers from these areas behave very cooperatively in our experiments.

Our corpus has some very complex situations: abbreviations, technical terms, logical and mathematical formulas, several types of enumerations and possibly examples. They also often refer to standards or to different chapters of the documents which contain additional but essential information. As a consequence, most sentences contain more than 60 words for a single requirement, they often include conditional statements, purposes, circumstances propositions. Finally, in about 20 % of the requirements, several requirements are included into a single statement.

5.2 The Investigated Errors

Let us focus in this article on three types of errors that illustrate our work. These are relatively simple from a language processing point of view. Here are their main characteristics.

The case of fuzzy lexical items is particularly significant of the way lexical errors can be detected and handled. It is important to note that (1) that it is difficult to precisely identify what a fuzzy lexical item is (this is developed in Sect. 5.6) and (2) that there are several categories of fuzzy lexical items. These categories include adverbs (manner, temporal, location, and modal adverbs), adjectives (*adapted, appropriate*) and determiners (*some, a few*), prepositions (*near, around*), a few verbs (*control, increase*) and nouns. These categories are not homogeneous in terms of fuzziness: determiners and prepositions are fuzzier than adjectives in general. The degree of fuzziness is also quite different from one term to another in a category. The context in which a fuzzy lexical item is uttered may also have an influence on its severity level. For example 'progressively' used in a short action (*progressively close the water pipe*) or used in an action that has a substantial length (*progressively heat the probe till* 300 °C *are reached*) may entail different severity levels because the application of 'progressively' may be more difficult to realize in the second case.

The use of negation is often prohibited in requirements, however, in a number of situations it is difficult to go around it, e.g. in *X must not be thrown in the sewer*, it may be difficult to specify all the possible allowed places which may depend on the place where the action is carried out. This is an injunction which cannot easily be replaced by any positive counterpart. We focus here on the use of double negation, which is less frequent but must absolutely be avoided.

Finally, requirements, which are in general expressed by means of a single sentence (possibly with enumerations) are frequently felt to be difficult to understand because they seem to be too long. Requirements with more than 40 words are frequent. In a first stage, in our system, any requirement that is longer than 40 words generates an alert. This is obviously a very rough way of detecting sentence complexity. Indeed, some sentences which are even longer than 40 words may be easier to understand than shorter ones if their structure are simple and the words they contain are common. Instead of just length, as described in authoring guidelines, we switch to complexity. Therefore, in conjunction with technical writers, we developed features that define a metrics that takes into account the various lexical (including acronyms) and syntactic aspects that introduce complexity so that a slightly more acceptable way of detecting long sentences can be implemented (Sect. 5.5).

Table 1 Direct evaluation

Alert	Manually identified	Noise	System precision (%)
Fuzzy lexical item	423	11 %	88
Double negation	12	1 occurence	87
Sentence too long	690	1 %	98

5.3 Initial Error Analysis and Evaluation

Based on the LELIE system presented in Barcellini et al. (2012), where errors are detected on a purely linguistic basis (i.e. the occurrence of an incorrect word or construction triggers an alert, independently of any contextual consideration), we have the following results on our corpus for the three types of alerts developed in this article (Table 1). Before analyzing a set of requirements of a company, it must be noted that the lexical resources which are proper to a domain must be included in the lexicons of LELIE. Although our lexicons are quite large for verbs, adverbs, adjectives, etc. some additional resources need to be included to get an optimal response from the system. So far, this is realized partly manually and therefore largely prone to errors.

The manual analysis in Table 1 indicates that about a third of the 1,450 requirements we have considered contain at least one fuzzy lexical item while about 40 % are too long and therefore difficult to read and to understand. The noise in the automatic recognition of fuzzy lexical items comes from the fact that some items are polysemous and that in those precise cases, the sense considered is not fuzzy, but it has been identified as fuzzy.

5.4 Technical Writers Reactions

Given these first results, which are quite basic, let us now consider the reactions of technical writers. The experiment is conducted as follows. Two technical writers, which are not the authors of the requirements (it is frequent that some writers proof-read the work made by their colleagues) were given a subset of requirements from our corpus with the alert messages. In a first step they read requirements one after the other, alerts are given as MS Word comments. They can then consider the alerts and work on them in the order they want. There is a priori no time limit. Each experiment lasted three hours, after presentation of the task. A discussion always followed the experiments.

The situations which are observed are the following:

(A) the alerts they find relevant or not, with the reasons,
(B) among those which are judged to be relevant, how many they indeed want or can correct. For those not corrected or more difficult to correct, technical

Table 2 Levels of correction

Alert	Number of errors considered in experiment	Errors not relevant	Errors relevant	Errors corrected
Fuzzy lexical item	60	18	42	31
Double negation	6	0	6	5
Sentence too long	51	9	42	25

writers suggest to think about them later or to ask to a more experienced colleague,

(C) they make a correction that entails another alert.

The results obtained are given in Table 2, they are the synthesis of reactions of the two writers who had short discussions between them

The result in Table 2 show that about 25 % of the fuzzy lexical items detected by the system are not really errors and must be left as such in the text. Among the 75 % which have been judged as really inducing fuzziness, about half of them have been corrected relatively easily. The others required a fair amount of revisions. For example how much time (probably a time interval) it takes to heat a probe instead of 'progressively heat the probe' cannot be corrected easily unless the performances of that probe are well known to the technical writer.

Double negation is rather straightforwardly corrected by either improving the syntactic structure of the sentence (most cases) or by using lexical variants such as antonyms. Finally, 9 sentences longer than 40 words have not been judged to be really 'long'. For the 'long' ones, only about half have been corrected, which shows the difficulty of the task and the subjectivity of the measure. After the experiment, we had a discussion with the two technical writers to evaluate what they feel is complex in a 'long' sentence. This discussion enabled us to define features of a preliminary metrics that can be used to characterize complex, instead of just 'long' sentences.

5.5 Investigating the Language Complexity of Requirements

Investigating the reasons why a sentence is complex in general requires the elaboration of an analysis protocol that refers to cognition, psycholinguistics and didactics. Such a protocol needs a lot of investigations and testing to develop something adequate within the domain of technical writing, which is different from classical experiments in reading and understanding texts.

Since, in a first stage, we want to have a coarse-grain solution to test with writers, we developed a rather simple evaluation based on the main linguistic characteristics of requirements felt by writers and readers to introduce forms of complexity. The main linguistic features are the following. Since they have various severity levels which depend on their utterance context and on the reader, they are given as a mere list with comments. Associating precise weights with each of them is beyond the scope of this article:

- At the lexical level, complexity is mainly induced from: acronyms and technical terms (for products, tools, etc.) which are not frequently used (this is a rather fuzzy criterion),
- At the syntactic level, complexity originates from: sequences of coordinated structures (in general NPs, figures with units or acronyms), complex NPs formed from sequences of nouns, passive forms, verbs with more than three complements or adjuncts, expression of numerical intervals of any type, and reference to another requirement,
- At the discourse level, complexity is induced by the presence of more than one construction such as a condition, a purpose clause, a circumstance described by a subordinate clause and illustrations. There are very few reformulations and elaborations. Furthermore, the order in which such structures are observed when there are several in a requirement can also be a complexity factor. The most frequent order is purpose followed by circumstance followed by condition.
- A rather external factor, but that is crucial is the lack of syntactic and style cohesion among groups of requirements. Readers do expect some forms of regularity in order to limit the cognitive load required to process long sentences.

If we consider requirements which are longer than 40 words, the criteria presented above are distributed as follows. The experiment is conducted on 350 requirements (rates are rounded up), results are given in Table 3.

A total of 1,614 reasons of complexity have been observed over the set of 350 requirements, therefore, a factor of 4.6 in average per requirement. A maximum of 7 of these factors has been observed in 5 requirements of about 50 words long. It is however difficult to establish a threshold that would tell when a requirement is difficult to understand, since this depends on the weights associated with each factor and the context in which these factors occur.

The next steps of our investigations are:

1. Develop alerts with a priori graded severity levels: a requirement will be judged too complex from the occurrence of three of the above factors. Graded messages are produced depending on the number of these factors found in a requirement: 3: possibly complex, 4 and 5: complex, probably needs some partial reformulation, 6 and beyond: really too complex, must be completely reformulated.
2. Develop a kind of memory of the changes that have been carried out, if any, so that, statistically, a more relevant evaluation of the severity of these factors, in isolation or in conjunction, can be realized and implemented.
3. Estimate how much of the requirement (in terms of number of words or structures) has been changed. Word positions and more complex factors could also be considered in a later stage. Those changes contribute to evaluating the complexity of the correction to be carried out.

This experiment should give more details about how complexity is analyzed by technical writers and how they really behave. Then, the severity levels can be

Table 3 Complexity factors

Type of alert	Number of requirements in which the alert occurs	Average rate per requirement	Maximum observed
Technical term not frequent	218	2	4
Acronym	287	4	7
Coordinated structures	216	2 nps	6 terms
Complex nps	201	1	3
Passive forms	43	1	1
Verbs with more than	144	1	1
3 complements of adjuncts			
Numerical structures	128	2	3
Conditionals	39	2	3
Purpose clauses	129	1	3
Circumstance	157	1	3
Sequence of 2 or more such clauses	52	2	3

much more fine-grained and relevant for the writers and advice, from corrections observed could be given. Complex requirements being between 35 and 60 words long, the length would be redundant and is not considered at the moment, but the presence of the above factors.

5.6 Developing a Correction Memory for Fuzzy Lexical Items Management

Technical writers have in general a rather rough idea of what a fuzzy lexical item is. They tend to consider that everything that is vague or underspecified is fuzzy. For each of these cases, the corrections to realize are of a different nature. In technical documents, terms such as *high, about* are clearly fuzzy, a term such as *damaged* in *the mother card risks to be damaged* is just vague because the importance and the nature of the damage is unknown, finally, in *heat the probe to reach* 500° is underspecified because the means to heat the probe are not given: an adjunct is missing in the instruction.

Fuzzy lexical items often require a large reformulation of the requirement. Vague terms require in general additional information that make the vague term more precise, e.g. for the above example: *the connectors may be broken*, where there is a kind of entailment between the two propositions. Finally, an underspecified expression often requires a complement or an adjunct to be added, e.g.: *using a constant voltage*. This latter situation is highly dependent on the domain and on the user knowledge.

In the Lelie system, a lexicon has been implemented that contains the most commonly found fuzzy lexical items in our corpus. As indicated above, fuzzy lexical items include adverbs, determiners, adjectives, prepositions, and some nouns and verbs. This lexicon is not very large and contains the terms which are almost always interpreted as fuzzy. Since some terms are a priori more fuzzy than others, a mark, between 1 and 3 (3 being the worse case) has been assigned a priori. This mark is however not fixed, it may evolve depending on technical writers behavior.

For illustrative purposes, Table 4 shows some types of entries our lexicon contains for English.

About 350 terms are included in this lexicon, this is not very large: this reflects the fact that technical writing in general prefers standard terms. Having such a lexicon is necessary so that the fuzzy lexical item identification process can start.

In our experimentation, the following questions are considered:

- Given the above lexicon, for each category, what is the behavior of the technical writers for each of the alerts, what do they think of the errors? how do they feel about making a correction?
- This lexicon is composed of isolated terms, but requirements also contain expressions which are fuzzy because they include a fuzzy lexical item. Such expressions are difficult to characterize and delimit on a syntactic basis. For example, in *progressively close the hot water pipe*, 'progressively' is the fuzzy lexical item, while 'close' is a verb that denotes a punctual action. This verb gets a durative interpretation because of its combination with 'progressively'. Therefore the whole VP is fuzzy. Then what level of analysis do technical writers have of these constructions and how much help do they need?
- The next question is therefore what portion of the requirement was judged fuzzy by the writer and therefore modified even if the alert is given on a single term? Finally, how much of the requirement is modified, besides the fuzzy lexical item? Does the modification affect what the requirement was supposed to state? How difficult is a modification and what resources does this requires (e.g. external documentation, asking someone else)?
- How many corrections have effectively been made? How many are left pending?

Table 4 Main fuzzy lexical item classes

Category	Number of entries	A priori severity level
Manner adverbs	112	2–3
Temporal and location adverbs	87	In general 2
Determiners	26	3
Prepositions	31	2–3
Verbs and modals	43	1–2
Adjectives	57	In general 1

- Finally, how to enrich the lexicon with new fuzzy lexical items from the writers activity? How to capture the experience of technical writers and engineers? The approach considered at the moment is that when an alert is produced for a fuzzy lexical item, relatively frequently, technical writers note that they have used close expressions elsewhere which they think should also be fuzzy.

Answering the fourth question above, namely how to add new fuzzy lexical items to the lexicon, requires an important cooperation from writers. The simplest approach we foresee is to ask them to artificially tag any change they make in this context with the tags used for our alerts. This is feasible since, quite frequently, technical writers are used to document (e.g. as MS Word comments) any change they make on a requirement. The only constraint we impose is to include in the comment the exact name of the alert.

Concerning the three first questions above, in order to be able to have a global view of how fuzzy lexical items are corrected, and in order to be able to provide help to writers, we are developing the following experiment. The tests we make do not include any temporal consideration (how much time it takes to make a correction, or how they organize the corrections) and any consideration concerning the means used by writers. At this stage, we simply examine the results, which are stored in a database. The protocol is the following:

- For each different fuzzy lexical item that originates an alert, create a new entry in the database, include its category and a priori severity level,
- When texts are processed, for each alert concerning this term, include in its database entry the whole requirement before and after the correction made by the technical writer. Indicate who made the correction (several writers often work on similar texts). Tag the term on which the alert is in the input text and tag the text portion that has been changed in the resulting requirement. Changes are basically characterized by the use of new words or a different word order. Indicate in the database if the initial requirement has not been corrected (then no corrected requirement is included).

The database is implemented in Prolog. Its global form is the following: *term, category* (*nous, adverb,...*), *severity level* a priori (*from 1 to 3*), *list of: [error found, tagged correction, author of correction].*

In the database:

```
fuzzyterm([term], [category], [severity],
[[requirement1 before error, resulting requirement with tags,
    name of writer], ....] ).
```

For example:

```
fuzzyterm([progressively], [adverb], [3],
[[[progressively, heat, the, probe],
   [[heat, the, probe, <revised>, progressively,
            in, 5, seconds, </revised>]],  [John] ]]
```

Requirements are stored as lists of words, this enables an easy processing by our TextCoop platform (Saint-Dizier 2012), implemented in Prolog, on which Lelie runs (Saint-Dizier 2014).

With these observations, for each fuzzy lexical item defined in the lexicon, we plan to:

1. Evaluate how many occurrences have been corrected w.r.t. the total number of alerts for this term,
2. Evaluate the complexity of the update, i.e. how and how much of the original requirement has been changed. This requires the development of a metrics that considers the type of the words, since it is not necessarily very useful to just count how many words have been changed before and or after the fuzzy lexical item.
3. Elaborate a strategy so that changes can be somewhat generalized (e.g. using the domain terminology).
4. Since the goal is to be able to provide writers with a simple list of the corrections previously carried out, have each of the corrections validated or rejected by an expert (administrator) or a group of writers so that only the best ones are kept. Each correction will then be accessed by its original context (the words around it in the original requirement).

One of the main advantages of this approach is that technical writers can access, via keywords, the corrections that have been previously realized and validated, so that corrections are more homogeneous. In a second step, we plan to develop *correction patterns* that really reflect the principle of a correction memory. The goal is to be able, in relatively large contexts to abstract over corrections and to propose generic correction patterns. For example, from examples such as:

Close the pipe progressively → *close the pipe progressively in* 30 s.
Progressively heat the probe → *heat the probe in a* 4–5 min *period.*
The power must be reduced progressively to 65 % *to reach 180* knots→ *reduce the power to* 65 % *with a reduction of* 10 % *every* 30 s *to reach* 180 knots.

A correction pattern could be the association of progressively (to keep the manner and its continuous character) with a time interval, possibly complex as in the third example:
progressively → *progressively [temporal indication].*

Obviously, this pattern is just a guide or a correction recommendation which requires the expertise of the technical writer.

This kind of pattern has been tested e.g. in the case of negation with some success. For example, in:

Never leave the doors open but do not forbid the access,
the application of a pattern such as:
negation, verb → *antonym(verb).*
can be applied to produce:

leave the doors closed but allow the access.
However, the injunctive character of the negation has been lost and this correction is much more neutral in terms of persuasion.

6 Perspectives

In this article, we have outlined the difficulty of writing requirements and the reasons why they should be proofread and revised till they become easy to read and unambiguous. Technical document production requires specific authoring guidelines and a specific error analysis, since in general erroneous formulations in technical documents are perfectly acceptable in ordinary language. We have shown that the boilerplate technology, by the constraints it imposes on requirement structures, can partly help to resolve some of these errors, but only for simple forms of requirements, since boilerplates are not used for complex forms.

Based on the LELIE system and technology, we have explored in this article an approach to accurately detect errors, expressed as alerts, in a close cooperation with writers since the severity level of these errors and therefore the necessity to correct them and the way they could be corrected heavily depends on the context, the users and the company's traditions. For that purpose, we have sketched out a few experimental protocols leading to simple solutions which should be helpful. These obviously need further developments, improvements and testing.

In technical document production, there is quite a large literature on how to write technical documents and most technical writers are now aware of what they should avoid (pronouns, modals, fuzzy lexical items, buzz words, future tenses, etc.). If some errors can easily be avoided, such as pronouns, others remain difficult to correct, such as fuzzy lexical items and complex sentences, which have been investigated here. Besides these errors which remain relatively local to a requirement, there are other types of errors which are not so well identified, for which corrections are difficult. Among these types of errors we can note the problem of references (to other requirements and documents that may or may not exist, to equipment, etc.), the problem of the ambiguity of general purpose lexical items (strict terminologies and limited vocabularies are often recommended to overcome this problem but is not sufficient), the problem of text cohesion (regularity of expressions with some necessary flexibility that is acceptable by readers), and the problem of coherence, overlaps, etc. which are rather AI than language problems.

Acknowledgments This project was supported by the French ANR, TextCoop and Lelie projects. We also thank the companies that let us discuss and experiment with their technical writers and for the time they kindly devoted to us. We also thank a number of colleagues who gave us constant advice and hints so that this work can be useful to them.

References

Barcellini, F. et al. (2012). *Risk analysis and prevention: LELIE, a tool dedicated to procedure and requirement authoring: LREC*, Istanbul.

Buddenberg, A. (2011). *Guidelines for writing requirements*, weekly seminars, september-december, IRIT-CNRS.

Buchholz, S. (2002). Memory-based grammatical relation finding (Ph.D, Tilburg).

Daelemans, W., van Der Bosch, A. (2005). *Memory-based language processing*. Cambridge: Cambridge University Press.

Firesmith, D. (2007). Common requirements problems, their negative consequences, and the industry best practices to help solve them. *Journal of Object Technology*, *6*(1), 17–33.

Gnesi, S. et al. (2005). An automatic tool for the analysis of natural language requirements. *International Journal of Computer Systems Science and Engineering special issue*, *20*(1), 1–13.

Grady, J. O. (2006). *System requirements analysis*. USA: Academic Press.

Hull, E., Jackson, K., & Dick, J. (2011). *Requirements engineering*. London: Springer.

Kang, J., & Saint-Dizier, P. (2013) Discourse structure analysis for requirement mining. *International Journal of Knowledge Content Development and Technology, 3*(2), 67–91.

Nuseibeh, B., & Easterbrook, S. (2000). Requirements engineering: A roadmap. In *Proceedings of the 22nd International Conference on Software Engineering, ICSE'00* (pp. 37–46).

Pohl, K. (2010). *Requirements engineering: Fundamentals, principles, and techniques*. Berlin: Springer.

Porter, A., Votta, L. G., & Basili, V. R. (1995). Comparing detection methods for software requirements inspections: A replicated experiment. *IEEE Transactions on Software Engineering, 21*(6), 563–574.

Rushby, J. (2001). Security requirements specifications: How and what? In *Invited paper from Symposium on Requirements Engineering for Information Security (SREIS)*, Indianapolis.

Sage, P. A., & Rouse, W. B. (2009). *Handbook of systems engineering and management*. USA: Wiley.

Saint-Dizier, P. (2012). Processing natural language arguments with the <TextCoop> platform. *Journal of Argumentation and Computation*, *3*(2), 8.

Saint-Dizier, P. (2014). *Challenges of discourse processing: the case of technical documents*. UK: Cambridge Scholars.

Schriver, K. A. (1989). Evaluating text quality: The continuum from text-focused to reader-focused methods. *IEEE Transactions on Professional Communication, 32*, 238–255.

Turk, W. (2006). Writing requirements for engineers. *IET Engineering Management*, *16*(3), 20–23.

Weiss, E. H. (2000). *Writing remedies. practical exercises for technical writing*. Phoenix: Oryx Press.

Wiegers Karl, E. (2001). Inspecting requirements. StickyMinds.com Weekly Column.

Van der Linden, K. (1993). Speaking of actions: Choosing rhetorical status and grammatical form in instructional text generation (Doctoral dissertation, University of Colorado, USA).

Yang, H. et al. (2010). A methodology for automatic identification of nocuous ambiguity. In *Proceedings of the 23rd International Conference on Computational Linguistics (Coling 2010)*, Beijing.

IEEE recommended practice for software requirements specifications IEEE computer society sponsored by the software engineering standards committee 20 Oct 1998.

Learning from Errors: Systematic Analysis of Complex Writing Errors for Improving Writing Technology

Cerstin Mahlow

Abstract In this paper, we describe ongoing research on writing errors with the ultimate goal to develop error-preventing editing functions in word-processors. Drawing from the state-of-the-art research in errors carried out in various fields, we propose the application of a general concept for action slips as introduced by Norman (1981). We demonstrate the feasibility of this approach by using a large corpus of writing errors in published texts. The concept of slips considers both the process and the product: some failure in a procedure results in an error in the product, i.e., is visible in the written text. In order to develop preventing functions, we need to determine causes of such visible errors.

Keywords Writing technology · Error analysis · Writing process · Slips · Writing research · Writing errors · Error classification

1 Introduction

Published texts by native-language, expert writers—or more generally: finished texts, i.e., when the author has no intention to carry out further revisions, but submits the text to the reader or publisher, even if carefully proofread by the author—still contain numerous errors. Examples are sentences without finite verbs (*Dabei es vielfältige Arbeitsbereiche.* [missing *gibt* as second word], *Sie sich viel Zeit für den Bettenkauf.* [missing *Nehmen* as first word]), duplicate words (*Wir fliegen wie geplant am 30. Oktober nach Kairo fliegen* [last *fliegen* should be removed], *This was former camel trading venue was home to the 1982 stock market crash in Kuwait, which wiped out many billions in regional wealth at the time.* [first *was* should be removed]), superfluous words (*like when you're sitting at*

C. Mahlow (✉)
University of Stuttgart Germany, Stuttgart, Germany
e-mail: cerstin.mahlow@ims.uni-stuttgart.de

© Springer International Publishing Switzerland 2015

N. Gala et al. (eds.), *Language Production, Cognition, and the Lexicon*,
Text, Speech and Language Technology 48, DOI 10.1007/978-3-319-08043-7_24

a someone else's computer), or agreement errors (*Von der grauhaarigen Frau sieht Christin nur zuckenden den Rücken.* [should be *den zuckenden Rücken*]).

In a US-wide study on error types in native-language college-student writing using final drafts of essays, Lunsford and Lunsford in (2008) found similar errors as Connors and Lunsford (1988) had identified in a comparable study 20 years before. In the late 1980s, students wrote the essays by hand (or with a type-writer), and thus could not use any automatic checkers. Twenty years later, students used word processors with spelling and grammar checkers. The number of spelling errors had thus decreased dramatically—from over 30 to only 6.5 % of all errors. However, apart from punctuation issues, Lunsford and Lunsford (2008) still found a similar amount of "wrong words," "vague pronoun references," "subject-verb agreement errors," "missing words," "unnecessary shifts in verb tense," "fused sentences," or "sentence fragments" (Lunsford and Lunsford 2008), a clear indication that these errors cannot be detected and corrected by automatic checkers. Additionally, the error rate in 2008 with 2.29 errors per 100 words is very similar to the error rate in 1988 with 2.26 errors per 100 words.

Table 1 gives a comparison of the 20 top-most identified error types and percentages of total errors. As spelling errors had been identified the most common error by far in the 1988-essays, they had been excluded in this listing, however, in 2008, they made rank 5 with only 6.5 % of all errors. This change is a clear indicator that using spell checkers helped students correct most of the spelling errors. However, almost two third of the errors identified as frequent in 1988 still are in the list of frequent errors in 2008—marked bold in Table 1. The order changed, but "wrong words," "no comma after introductory element," and "vague pronoun reference" are the most common errors, summing up to ca. 30 % of all errors. Here, grammar checkers obviously didn't help students.

When produced by skilled writers, these errors can be considered performance errors rather than competence errors. The fact that they appear in published texts—see the collection in appendix A of Mahlow (2011)—indicates that these errors cannot be automatically detected and corrected by state-of-the-art grammar checkers, as Gubelmann (2010) confirmed in a small-scale study for German errors. In the last decade, various studies (Kramer 2004; Rimrott and Heift 2008; Vernon 2000) pointed out general deficits of checkers for English and German in larger studies.

In language-learning scenarios, the focus should be clearly on competence errors and how to advise students. For experienced writers, performance errors are more common, so a different approach is needed for detecting errors and providing appropriate feedback. It would be even better to provide editing functions helping writers to *prevent* performance errors. As shown by Mahlow (2011), a large variety of editing functions based on NLP sources could be developed. The results clearly depend on the quality of the underlying resources. However, from a writing research perspective, the question remains which of these functions are really useful, which kind of errors could be prevented indeed, and how to distinguish performance errors from competence errors.

Table 1 Error types as reported by Connors and Lunsford (1988) and Lunsford and Lunsford (2008), error types found in both studies are marked in bold

	Connors and Lunsford (1988)		Lunsford and Lunsford (2008)	
Rank	Error type	(%)	Error type	(%)
1	**No comma after introductory element**	11.5	**Wrong word**	13.7
2	**Vague pronoun reference**	9.8	**Missing comma after an introductory element**	9.6
3	**No comma in compound sentence**	8.6	Incomplete or missing documentation	7.1
4	**Wrong word**	7.8	**Vague pronoun reference**	6.7
5	**No comma in non-restrictive element**	6.5	Spelling error (including homonyms)	6.5
6	Wrong/missing inflected endings	5.9	Mechanical error with quotation	6.4
7	Wrong or missing preposition	5.5	**Unnecessary comma**	5.2
8	**Comma splice**	5.5	Unnecessary/missing capitalization	5.2
9	**Possessive apostrophe error**	5.1	Missing word	4.6
10	**Tense shift**	5.1	Faulty sentence structure	4.4
11	Unnecessary shift in person	4.7	**Missing comma in a non-restrictive element**	3.8
12	**Sentence fragment**	4.2	**Unnecessary shift in verb tense**	3.8
13	Wrong tense or verb form	3.3	**Missing comma in a compound sentence**	0.6
14	Subject-verb agreement	3.2	**Unnecessary/missing apostrophe including *its/it's***	3.1
15	Lack of comma in serie	2.7	**Fused (run-on) sentence**	3.0
16	**Pronoun agreement error**	2.6	**Comma splice**	2.9
17	**Unnecessary comma with restrictive element**	2.4	**Lack of pronoun-antecedent agreement**	2.7
18	**Run-on or fused sentence**	2.4	Poorly integrated quotation	2.7
19	Dangling or misplaced modifier	2.0	Unnecessary or missing hyphen	2.5
20	***Its/it's* error**	1.0	**Sentence fragment**	2.4

In this paper, we propose the use of a well-defined error typology. We first discuss the state-of-the-art in error research in several fields in Sect. 2, and illustrate relevant methods in writing research, NLP, and writing technology in Sect. 3. In Sect. 4 we then present the application of the general-purpose concept of *slips* proposed by Norman (1981) to writing and in Sect. 5 we illustrate some examples. Using Norman's typology, we can distinguish competence errors from performance errors, and we can determine the best starting point for the design of preventive editing functions.

2 Research on Errors

Errors in writing are investigated in various research fields. In the field of *writing research*, there is only little published research on errors in the last decades (except for learning to write in a second language), for example by Connors and Lunsford (1988), Lunsford and Lunsford (2008), Sloan (1990). However, all studies try to systematize the errors found in writing samples; they take the written evidence as starting point and develop coding schemes. These studies aim to compare writing abilities of students and to design pedagogically motivated writing strategies to help students become better writers. They do not investigate how these errors have been produced nor how to prevent these errors by means of improved writing technology. A common research question in writing research is to explore how writers react to given or produced errors—thus a behavioral focus is chosen.

Mostly, each study comes up with an ad hoc coding scheme, making it difficult to compare findings across studies. As an illustration consider Table 1: Although one of the authors (Andrea Lunsford) was involved in both studies and the study from 2008 clearly was intended to provide a follow-up, the authors used different namings for (probably) identical error classes—e.g., "no comma after introductory element" versus "missing comma after an introductory element."

In *applied linguistics* and *second language acquisition*, research on errors started with the collection of learner data in the late 1980s. The aim was to advance the understanding of language acquisition to develop better pedagogical approaches tailored to language learners' needs. However, even recent studies concerned with cognitive aspects of errors do not focus on the process, but on the produced language units (see for example Gries and Stefanowitsch 2007; Reznicek et al. 2013).

In the context of the online available Falko corpus,[1] Lüdeling et al. (2005) argue for annotation on various levels, to be able to distinguish competence errors and performance errors. They also aim to come up with an explanation for an observed error, but restrict this to meta-explanations referring to the learners language biography like "transfer problems" (Lüdeling et al. 2005), which clearly refer to competence errors only. This is in line with earlier research, restricting possible explanations to psycholinguistic, sociolinguistic, epistemic, or discourse structure sources.

In error annotation in learner corpora, we find various coding schemes, which raises problems for systematic analysis and the application of NLP methods. As Meurers puts it:

> There is so far no consensus, though, on the external and internal criteria, that is, which error distinctions are needed for which purpose and which distinctions can reliably be annotated based on the evidence in the corpus and any meta-information available about the learner and the activity which the language was produced for [Meurers et al. 2013, p. 6].

[1] https://www.linguistik.hu-berlin.de/institut/professuren/korpuslinguistik/forschung/falko.

In the field of *computational linguistics*, most of the research on errors is concerned with students (i.e., writing novices) writing in their first or second language (for an overview, see Leacock et al. (2010))—a similarity to error analysis in writing research and language acquisition. However, the goals are different: Researchers code errors in learner corpora to improve checkers (Gamon 2010), to develop applications for computer-assisted language learning (Meurers et al. 2010), or to make syntax parsers more robust (Foster and Vogel 2004). Coding schemes are generally developed from scratch (for an overview, see Daz-Negrillo and Fernández-Dominguez (2006)) without reference to the coding schemes developed in writing research.

However, an agreed-upon standard on error annotation would be a prerequisite for the development of any writing support in learning scenarios or in tutoring systems (Meurers et al. 2013). Also in computational linguistics, error analyses for experienced writers—i.e., skilled authors writing in L1 and familiar with the topic, genre, and tools involved—are rare. One of the few examples are Napolitano and Stent (2009), who work on a personalizable writing assistance program for advanced learners of English. The target group are thus L2 writers, but familiar with topic, genre, and tools.

Neither writing research, applied linguistics, nor computational linguistics draw on more general research on errors, which is an important topic in *psychology*. With respect to performance errors, in the early 1980s, Norman (1981, 1983) proposed a very strong theoretical framework for the classification of *action slips*:

> Call the highest level specification of a desired action an **intention** […]. An error in the intention is called a **mistake**. An error in carrying out the intention is called a **slip** (Norman 1983, p. 254).[2]

The concept of slips combines the process and the product: some failure in a procedure results in an error in the product. Currently error analyses in writing research, applied linguistics, and computational linguistics focus exclusively on the product: the text produced is explored manually or automatically to find and code errors to deduce error correction and to propose better language-learning approaches. The same strategy is used by checkers: they process written text to detect errors and suggest corrections. How this error might have been produced is not considered.

According to Norman, slips are frequently caused by the design of the tools used: when the user has to carry out a complex sequence of operations to achieve a goal, this will often result in cognitive overload (Norman 1983). Many slips can thus be prevented by better designed tools, which offer functions operating in line with the users' cognitive model and thus reduce cognitive load. To develop such tools to support writing, a detailed and systematic analysis of writing errors and their causes is needed, but has not been carried out so far.

[2] Emphasis in the original.

Although the different nature or competence errors and performance errors is addressed in earlier studies in applied linguistics and second language acquisition, e.g., by Corder (1967) and Ellis (1994), research in this area focuses on competence errors. Surprisingly, we find a divergent terminology. Competence errors ("mistakes" according to Norman) are called "errors"—and are in the focus of research—while performance errors ("slips" according to Norman) are called "mistakes"—and as Corder puts it: "Mistakes are of no significance to the process of language learning" (Corder 1967, p. 167). Additionally, those "mistakes" are not easily distinguishable from "errors" (Ellis 1994, pp. 50–54). With our approach to not only look at the failure in the product, but to consider also the failure in the procedure as inherent in the concept of "slips," we can address this issue. For our purposes, we stick with the terminology proposed by Norman, i.e., mistakes versus slips.

3 Relevant Areas

3.1 Research on Writing Processes

When writers use electronic writing tools, writing process data can be collected using keystroke-logging tools. Van Waes et al. (2006) and Sullivan and Lindgren (2006) provide a good overview of keystroke-logging technology. Originally, logging tools were developed to allow for better analysis of revising operations carried out by writers. The first large-scale study was performed by Flinn (1987), who logged writers using the Milliken Word Processor (Smithson 1986) with the logging program COMPTRACE over the period of a year.

Today's keystroke-logging tools, such as Inputlog[3] (Leijten and Van Waes 2006), can record all user actions in an unobtrusive way. This has lead to an increase in writing studies investigating writing in the workplace or in other natural writing situations (see for example Leijten et al. 2010; Perrin 2006a, b; Van Waes et al. 2009).

However, manual inspection and interpretation of logging data is a demanding task. In the 1990s, S-notation was developed as a standard notation for encoding the evolvement of text—i.e., insertions, deletions, cursor movements, and pauses (Kollberg 1998; Severinson Eklundh 1994). Data from keystroke-logging tools can be transformed into S-notation data automatically. Based on this encoding, it is possible to understand which operations have been carried out by the writer. S-notation may also serve as input for tools that play back the writing session.

In S-notation, the writer's revisions are coded directly in the text. For each insertion or deletion, a break ("|") marks the last position before the action; insertions are enclosed by curly braces, deletions are enclosed by square braces. An index for each of break, insertion, and deletion, indicates the order of those

[3] http://www.inputlog.net.

S-Notation:
Th[r$|_{1}$]^{1}e q{u}^{2}ick$|_{2}$ brown [dog]^{5}{f}^{5}$|_{6}${[i]^{7}$|_{8}${o}^{8}$|_{9}$x}^{6}$|_{7}$ jumps over
the [{old }^{4}$|_{5}$]lazy [d$|_{3}$]^{3}[fox]^{9}|{dog}^{10}$|_{11}$.$|_{4}$ The end[. $|_{12}$]^{12}!

Produced text:
The quick brown fox jumps over the lazy dog. The end!

Fig. 1 Example writing process data presented in S-notation

Doch: {Fast}^{148}$|_{149}$[J]^{149}$|_{150}${j}^{150}$|_{151}$edes dritte
[Medikament]^{199}$|_{200}${[Präparat]^{627}$|_{628}^{200}|_{201}${Medikament}^{628}$|_{629}$, das
{de^{192} [s]^{192} $|_{193}${r }^{193}$|_{194}$Basler Pharmamulti[s $|_{192}$]^{194}$|_{195}$}^{191},
[Novartis]^{195}$|_{196}$ auf den Markt wirft, [ist gar $|_{39}$]^{39}stammt gar
nicht aus der eig[he$|_{40}$]^{40}enen Forschung, sondern wurde [zu einem
bestimmten Zeitpunkt^{41}[von $|_{41}$]^{41}]^{174} $|_{175}${[eingekauft$|_{176}$]^{176},
[eingekauft$|_{177}$]^{177}, [zu einem bestimmten Zeitpunkt]^{641}$|_{642}$
{während der Entwicklungsphase}^{642} $|_{643}$ eingekauft -}^{175}$|_{178}$
von [Uni[versitäten]^{201}$|_{202}$]^{204}$|_{205}$ [{[f]^{205}$|_{206}${F}^{206}$|_{207}$
[a$|_{203}$]^{203}orschern}^{202}$|_{204}$ {der Unis}^{207}$|_{208}$]^{208}$|_{209}$ {Uni-Labors }^{209}$|_{210}$
[doer$|_{42}$]^{42}oder [anderen [P$|_{43}$]^{43}Firmen]^{80}$|_{81}$ {kleine[re]^{179}$|_{180}$n
[Pharma- oder]^{180}$|_{181}$ Biotechfirmen}^{81}$|_{82}$ [eingekauft]^{178}$|_{179}$.

Fig. 2 S-notation example (from writing session `sf zvz 070118 2150 keller novartis snt 1`)

actions. For logging data as presented in the example in Fig. 1, manual inspection of the S-notation data is possible. However, for real-world data as shown in Fig. 2, manual inspection is not feasible.

The extract in Fig. 2 shows the creation of one sentence by a journalist encoded in S-notation. The data has been collected between September 2006 and March 2007 as part of 120 writing sessions from 15 journalists from two Swiss broadcasters (SRF and RTS). The finished texts comprise TV news items ranging from 30 to 270 s (Perrin 2011) The final product produced here is the rather short sentence:

> *Doch: Fast jedes dritte Medikament, das der Basler Pharmamulti auf den Markt wirft, stammt gar nicht aus der eigenen Forschung, sondern wurde während der Entwicklungsphase eingekauft—von Uni-Labors oder kleineren Biotechfirmen.*

Writing processes can also be visualized by progression analysis as a path through the evolving text, as developed by Perrin (2002, 2006a, b), and used in various studies (see for example Ehrensberger-Dow and Perrin 2009; Perrin and Wildi 2009). This representation is also used to collaboratively develop writing strategies together with writers. However, on a more technical level, there is a lack of appropriate analysis and visualization algorithms to be able to investigate writing processes on various levels with different granularity for large amounts of keystroke-logging data.

While S-notation is designed for representing natural language text, it only encodes insertion and deletion of *strings of characters*; it does not take into account *linguistic units*. Leijten et al. (2012) were the first—and up to now the only—researchers who applied natural language processing (NLP) tools to S-notation data for texts in Dutch and English, enriching them with basic linguistic information in order to facilitate higher-level analyses of the data.

3.2 Research on Writing Technology

Research on tools and automated support for *programmers* is an ongoing topic (e.g., Candillon 2013; Ko et al. 2005; Omar et al. 2012). However, as shown in a research survey in Mahlow (2011, pp. 57–63), research on tools for *writers* of natural language text and their influence on the writing process stopped in the 1980s; projects like RUSKIN (Williams et al. 1989) or the Editor's Assistant (Dale et al. 1990) did not result in actual products, systems like AUGMENT (Engelbart 1962)—which was in some respects more advanced than today's word processors—disappeared.

Automated linguistic support for writers available in today's mainstream word processors (e.g., Microsoft Word), is restricted to grammar and spell checking; while technically more advanced (see Heidorn 2000), conceptually it does not go much beyond what tools like the UNIX Writer's Work Bench (Macdonald et al. 1982) offered in the 1970s.

As can be seen at conferences like "Computers and Writing" or in journals like "Kairos",[4] writing research for the most part treats writing technology as a given that cannot be changed; the focus is thus on creative uses of its affordances in order to discover or develop new kinds of writing beyond the production of alphabetical text.

3.3 Incremental Parsing

Applying NLP to writing poses two main challenges: first, the text is growing during writing, so that newly written parts have to be added to the parse tree, and revised parts have to be updated. Second, the text is still unfinished. Parsing has to be robust, so that it can handle ill-formedness, incompleteness, and inconsistency (the "I3", as Van De Vanter (1995) calls them). These two challenges are mostly investigated separately in computational linguistics.

For parsing text as it is created, *incremental parsers* are used. Incremental parsers in the field of computational linguistics analyze their input word by word

[4] http://kairos.technorhetoric.net/.

and start to construct a parse tree immediately. Incremental parsing is typically (though not exclusively) used in the context of acoustic speech recognition; approaches for incremental parsing therefore usually assume a linear evolvement of text. However, writing is not incremental in the sense that speech is incremental; in contrast to speakers, writers *can* actually go back and alter the text produced so far. This means that written text does not evolve linearly, and reparsing is needed if earlier text is changed. In order to avoid costly reparsing, it would be preferable to modify the parse tree built-up so far. This extended understanding of incrementality is well known in computer science, in particular in the context of interactive programming environments, e.g., Cook and Welsh (2001). It is only rarely addressed in NLP, though; one such example is Wirén (1989). In general, incremental parsers for natural languages focus on handling linearly expanding text (e.g., Costa et al. 2003; Huang and Sagae 2010; Nivre 2008; Roark 2001).

Research on *robust parsing*, i.e., on parsers that are able to handle ungrammatical input gracefully, is often done in the context of applications such as processing of learner language or user-generated content (Foster 2010; Leacock et al. 2010), and, of course, grammar checking (Clément et al. 2009; Heidorn 2000; Jensen et al. 1983). The combination of robust and incremental parsing is mainly researched in the context of speech recognition (Foth et al. 2000, 2005); Schulze (2004) shows the implementation of a robust parser applying an incremental grammar formalism (Left-Associative Grammar (Hausser 2001)) outside the domain of speech processing.

4 Approach

4.1 Research Goals

The spelling and grammar checkers in today's word processors are useful tools, since authors tend to overlook errors in their own writing; instead, they read what *should* be there (Perrin 2006b). However, even state-of-the-art checkers are not capable of detecting and correcting *all* errors. Preliminary research indicates that many of the remaining errors can be explained as action slips. Norman (1983) has demonstrated that the occurrence of slips can be minimized by improving the design of systems. The question posed here is thus: How can such non-detectable errors in writing be *prevented* by more ergonomic writing tools, which use online analysis of the writing process?

Our research aims to develop language-aware editing functions integrated into word processors that help to prevent errors. Such functions will be based on a systematic analysis of complex writing errors and interactive incremental NLP resources. We follow a holistic approach, combining methods and resources from writing research, computational linguistics, document engineering, software engineering, and XML technology, thus making this research entirely interdisciplinary. To avoid costly re-implementation of core functionality writers expect (e.g., copy-paste, general navigation, undo function), we rather integrate new functions into existing word processors, but do not build new ones from scratch.

In general, the development of writing technology should (a) be based on insights from writing research—projects like RUSKIN failed, because they did not take into account actual user needs—, (b) make use of NLP methods and tools—since the 1980s, a lot of effort went into the development of NLP resources and tools, so the overall situation today is much better than several decades ago[5]—, and (c) benefit from development in hardware—programs like Epistle from IBM (Jensen et al. 1983) were not commercially successful, because they were computationally too expensive at that time. Here, we address all three obstacles for earlier projects: actual writing process data is used as basis for the implementation, NLP resources today are of a reasonable quality and can be executed fast enough to be integrated into real-world applications running on laptops.

We focus on experienced L1 authors writing in German, where most of the errors could be classified as performance errors—authors would detect the errors themselves when reading the respective text some time later or after a media break (e.g., reading on paper instead of reading on screen or using a different layout or font). Mechanical errors that can be reliably detected and corrected by standard grammar and spell checkers, e.g., sentence-initial capitalization, are not in the scope here.

For errors that can reliably be detected and corrected by state-of-the-art checkers, there is no specific need to prevent them. For errors that are caused by poorly designed tools resulting in cognitive overload of the writer, we should distinguish errors that would be preventable by improving writing tools and errors writers could easily take care of themselves with some support from the word processor. This will allow the development of language-aware functions for writing support, with an emphasis on interaction with the writer and avoiding patronizing.

4.2 Slips in Writing

We start with a detailed analysis of errors, from which we can create a fine-grained taxonomy of writing errors, applying the concept of slips. The scientific value with respect to errors is two-fold: (a) It is the first extensive systematic application of the Norman (1981) classification of slips to writing, and (b) it is the first error analysis to take into account the *process* of writing by exploring keystroke-logging data.

---

[5] As an example, in the project *Integrated language tools for writing and document handling* at KTH Stockholm (http://www.nada.kth.se/iplab/langtools/), the development of linguistic search and editing functions was planned but had to be postponed first and was skipped in the end, because the required NLP resources would have to be developed in the first place.

We use the error corpus collected in the LingURed project[6] as starting point and systematically apply the categorization of slips. The corpus consists of over 200 errors from German texts published in printed or electronic newspapers, books, and advertisements, which contain typical errors not detectable by checkers (the examples used here are from this collection). The corpus data is annotated manually on various levels, e.g., error classes as described by Lunsford and Lunsford (2008); correct and incorrect sub-parse trees; erroneous syntactical elements like agreement error wrt. adjectives in noun phrases as instance of the class "agreement error," missing finite verbs as instance of "missing units," and stranded verb particles as instance of "extraneous units." Based on this annotation, we can develop heuristics for identifying errors. For example, to identify duplicate verbs, as in the example *Wir fliegen wie geplant am 30. Oktober nach Kairo fliegen*, a useful heuristic is the presence of multiple occurrences of the same word form in a sentence.

Additionally, the general design principles for avoiding slips proposed by Norman (1983) can be transferred to editing functions. Some of the classes Norman (1981) proposes can easily be applied to writing errors.

In the rest of this section, we present an overview of applicable classes of slips. The original names and explanations by Norman (1981) are in italic. For each class we give a general example from everyday live Norman used in his proposal and we then give examples from writing taken from our error corpus with an explanation on how this slip had been produced. All examples are German, glosses are given where necessary.

Unintentional activation: when schemas not part of a current action sequence become activated for extraneous reasons, then become triggered and lead to slips

- *Data-driven activation: external events cause activation of schemas*
  - The most common one is the Stroop phenomenon, where names of colors are presented in a color that differs from the name, so participants have difficulties saying the color the word is printed in Norman (1981, p. 9).
- *Capture error* (*When a sequence being performed is similar to another more frequent or better learned sequence, the latter may capture control*)
  - When counting something, you fall into a common counting schema, i.e., instead of counting page numbers, it goes like counting cards (1, 2, 3, 4, 5, 6, 7, 8, 9, 10, Jack, Queen, King) (Norman 1981, p. 8)
  - An example in writing is the mixture of the processes of copy-and-paste and cut-and-paste. Both are very similar and a common failure is to copy something to a different point in text when it should have been cut-and-pasted. So the text appears both at the new place and the original one.

[6] http://lingured.info.

Example from the newspaper "Uckermark Kurier", October 1, 2010, page 21:

Noch gibt es keinerlei Vermutungen, wer in den neu entdeckten Gräbern bestattet wurde. In zwei Wochen werden die archäologischen Arbeiten an den Gräbern gestoppt. Dann werden Umbauarbeiten beginnen. In zwei Wochen werden die archäologischen Arbeiten an den Gräbern gestoppt. Dann werden umfassende Umbauarbeiten beginnen. Die Bischofskirche wird bis 2014 für rund 30 Millionen Euro saniert.

The sentence *In zwei Wochen werden die archäologischen Arbeiten an den Gräbern gestoppt.* appears twice. The following sentence *Dann werden umfassende Umbauarbeiten beginnen.* does not have the adjective *umfassende* in the first place, so here some additional revising took place.

Another example from the newspaper "The New York Times", Article selected for Süddeutsche Zeitung, July 19, 2010:

The great hope for robots, said Patricia Kuhl, co-director of the Institute for Learning and Brain Sciences at the University of Washington, great hope for robots, said Patricia Kuhl, co-director of the Institute for Learning and Brain Sciences at the University of Washington, is that with the right kind of technology at a critical period in a child's development, they could supplement learning in the classroom

Loss of activation: when schemas that have been activated lose activation, thereby losing effectiveness to control behavior

- *Forgetting an intention (but continuing with the action sequence)*
  - You start going to some place but once there, you forgot what you wanted to do there and try to come up with an arbitrary justification (Norman 1981, p. 9).
  - Due to misdesign of word processors, it is often hard to find a certain point in the text. A common situation is to plan a revision at a certain point—the author has a clear idea about what to inspect or change there, but he only vaguely remembers the point in the text. He has to find an action sequence to find this point (by scrolling or invoking a search function). After navigating to a certain point in the text, the author forgot what to change here and most probably does not carry out the intended revision. Here a better navigation in the written text and probably a different kind of displaying or presenting already written text is needed. Severinson-Eklundh (1992) started to address such issues.
- *Misordering the components of an action sequence (including skipping steps and repeating steps)*
  - Starting the engine of a car although you already drive or forgetting to put water in the coffee machine (Norman 1981, p. 10).
  - Following an example from my own writing:

Die Entwickler von von RUSKIN stellten erst beim Ende des Projektes feststellten, dass die Autoren ganz andere Funktionen gewünscht und gebraucht hätten.
('The developers of of RUSKIN discovered at the end of the project discovered, that the authors would have needed totally different functions.')

to discover in German is expressed with a verb with a separable particle (*feststellen*). The finite verb of the main clause occurs twice, although once in an incomplete form (the particle is missing for *stellten*). The complete form *feststellten* is in the last position of the first part, indicating that this would not be a main clause (which would be possible with *stellten... fest*). So if *stellten*—because of he missing particle—would be removed, it would result in an ungrammatical sentence. Removing the finite verb in the wrong position (*feststellten*) would result in an incomplete main clause. This sentence had been produced by splitting a longer version into two parts and then revising it—trying to correct the verb position. Here, help with splitting sentences would be necessary. Additionally, we have a duplicate *von* ('of'), also caused by a revision action.

False triggering: A properly activated schema is triggered at an inappropriate time

- *Falls triggering of acts among the things currently active in mind*
  - Trying to put down your glasses although not wearing them (Norman 1981, p. 7).
  - In writing, a common slip is to paste something from the clipboard without having copied it to the clipboard in the first place. In the best case scenario, the clipboard had been empty before, so the writer sees that nothing has been pasted and will go back to actually copy (or cut) the desired text part. In the worst case, the clipboard contains some text from an earlier action which will be pasted. The writer will not actually read the pasted part as he already knows what should be there, so this slip will go unnoticed.
- *Spoonerism (Reversal of event components)*
  - Reversal of words or parts of
    "You have tasted the whole worm" instead of "You have wasted the whole term" (Norman 1981, p. 10)
  - The example is from the book "*Nur Engel fliegen höher*" by Wim Westfield, published in 2008, page 13:

Von der grauhaarigen Frau sieht Christin nur zuckenden den Rücken.
('From the gray-haired woman, Christin only sees tremoring the back.')

The noun phrase *zuckenden den Rücken* is in wrong order, it should be *den zuckenden Rücken.* Here, the adjective *zuckenden* had been added later and had been positioned at the wrong place.

- *Blends* (*Combinations of components from two competing schemas*)
  - Merging *close* and *shut* into *clut* (Norman 1981 p. 10).
  - From the newspaper "*Süddeutsche Zeitung*", July 16, 2010, page 16:

George Washington heißt bei den Haudenosaunee seitdem Hanadahguyus, Stadzerstörerenn sie einen Brief an den Präsidenten schreiben, dann lautet die Anrede stets: Dear Hanadahguyus!

Here, the form *Stadtzerstörerenn* is a blend from *Stadtzerstörer. Wenn.*

- *Triggering of schemas meant only to be thought, not to govern action*
  - Say something you intend to mention later (Norman 1981, p. 10).
  - In writing, this results in writing the next word in the sentence before the currently needed one, resulting in missing words like in this sentence from the newspaper "*Uckermark Kurier*", March 22, 2010, page 5:

Die Terrorismus und Spionage zuständige Ermittlungsbehörde prüft, ob der Anfangsverdacht einer geheimdienstlichen Straftat vorliegt
('The investigative authority terrorism and spying checks, whether there is a initial suspicion with respect to intelligence crime.')

Here the preposition *für* is missing after the determiner *Die*. This kind of slips occurs when writers "think faster than they can type."

Failure in triggering: When an active schema never gets invoked

- Wondering why person A didn't make coffee—you forgot to ask (Norman 1981 p. 11).
- When writers pause during sentence production they may reread already written text to check for proper use of anaphora. As they have read the pronoun already, they skip writing it down, resulting in a missing word (the pronoun) in the final sentence. Another example are non-finished revisions like replacing one word by another without deleting the first one as in this example from my own writing:

In Abschnitt 2.1.2.1 sind wir auf Taxonomien von Redigieroperationen eingegangen, die mehrheitlich aus der Beobachtung von Änderungen in Texten entwickelt wurden, jedoch nicht die ursprüngliche Redigierabsicht Absicht der Autoren berücksichtigen.

Here two versions of *purpose*, i.e., *Absicht* and *Redigierabsicht*, occur directly one after the other. I don't remember which one I liked most in the end, but I played around with both versions to see which one would read better in the final sentence. And then I forgot to delete one of them.

As we can see from these examples, writing errors that can be categorized as "missing words" or "duplicate" words on the surface level may have various causes. For proper handling—in the best case: preventing these slips—we need to know the actions carried out before the slip. We might not be able to always detect the intention of the writer, however, after having identified certain action patterns, it will be possible to set up experiments triggering those slips where we know the writers' intention beforehand.

Additionally, it will be necessary to investigate keystroke-logging data with respect to pausing information to distinguish performance errors due to revision from misspellings. The latter are often corrected immediately by the writer and can thus be identified by using typing speed. Considering the length of inter-key intervals also helps determining boundaries of linguistic units. From a cognitive point of view it is important to closely relate pausing and revision behavior when analyzing non-linearity. This allows for the isolation of motoric actions.

5 Examples

The following examples illustrate the research process starting with the error analysis.

5.1 Example 1

Let us consider the following example from the corpus:

Alle Studierenden dokumentieren und reflektieren die vorgegebene Kompetenzen
('All students document and reflect on the given [singular] competencies [plural]')

The phrase *die vorgegebene Kompetenzen* is ungrammatical as there is no agreement between determiner, adjective, and noun. If it reads *die vorgegebene Kompetenz* (singular) or *die vorgegebenen Kompetenzen* (plural), the noun phrase would be correct. As the surface of the determiner is ambiguous with respect to number, no change is needed for the determiner. Although it looks like a typo—assuming that the *n* as last letter of the adjective was forgotten—an inspection of the keystroke-logging data (in S-notation) shown below reveals that it is actually a revision error:

Alle Studierenden dokumentieren {und reflektieren}^{1}[fünf$|_{3}$]^{2} {die}^{3} vorgegebene$|_{1}$ Kompetenzen. Dabei$|_{2}$

The author writes *Alle Studierenden dokumentieren fünf vorgegebene* then stops and adds *und reflektieren.* Then she finishes the first sentence with *Kompetenzen.* and begins the next one with *Dabei.* There she stops again and deletes *fünf* after which she adds *die* (probably she wasn't sure about the exact number but still wanted to express that there would be several competencies).

The agreement error could have been prevented if the writer would have been made aware that changing *fünf* into *die* affects a complex noun phrase; this could be done by highlighting the syntactical structure she is editing, helping to focus on side-effects of the revision. The system could also suggest the writer to automatically apply the needed changes, possibly allowing selection from a list of changes, as in this case the intended number may be either singular or plural.

5.2 Example 2

Another error-prone operation is replacing one term in a text by another term. One strategy is deleting the term to be replaced and then typing the new term. However, some writers prefer to make use of letters already typed. Thus, when replacing

Prüfung 'examination' by *Überprüfung* 'test' they delete the capital p, and then type *Überp*. In S-notation this may be coded this way:

```
[P|₂]¹{Überp}²rüfung
```

This is a very complicated approach, as a result we encounter errors like a forgotten *p* as in *Überrüfung* or—having forgotten to delete the *P*—in *ÜberPrüfung*, or a duplicated *p* as in *ÜberpPrüfung*. Again, these errors could be explained as typing errors—especially *Überrüfung*—, we can be sure about the reasons only by looking at the keystroke-logging data.

To prevent these kind of replacement errors, an appropriate query-and-replace function should be used. Today's word processors offer search-and-replace functions, but these functions operate on character sequences only and do not take into account that natural language text consists of word forms. For inflectional languages like German, replacing a word by another involves searching for all word forms of the query word and then replacing it by the corresponding word form of the replace word, i.e., both forms have to have the same morphosyntactic features.

6 Conclusion

The main goal is to support efficient writing by developing appropriate writing technology based on a strong theoretical basis developed in this project: a systematic classification of complex writing errors. For the first time, an error analysis considers both *the product*, i.e., the text where the error is visible for a reader, *and the process*, i.e., the editing operations causing this error. This analysis will lead to a deeper understanding of the relation between cognitive aspects of the writing process and the affordances of the tools used. We develop functions to improve word processors by preventing complex writing errors. These language-aware functions for writing support will be implemented with an emphasis on interaction with the writer and avoiding patronizing. For errors that can reliably be detected and corrected by state-of-the-art checkers, there is no specific need to prevent them.

The scientific impact is on the theoretical level (1 and 2) and on a more practical level (3 and 4):

1. This research opens a new field in error research in writing by a systematic and empirically sound analysis of product and process as two aspects of errors which are intrinsically tied together.
2. We propose a methodological framework for the classification of complex writing errors to be used as starting point for improvement of writing technology.
3. We develop methods and tools for analyzing and visualizing large-scale keystroke-logging data based on XML technology.

4. We implement language-aware editing functions based on incremental interactive NLP resources, to be integrated into word processors that help to prevent errors by offering appropriate support to write efficiently.

References

Candillon, W. (2013). XQuery development in the Cloud(9). XQuery code anywhere, anytime. In: XML Prague 2013, pp. 221–236. Prague: University of Economics, Czech Republic.

Clément, L., Gerdes, K., & Marlet, R. (2011). A grammar correction algorithm: Deep Parsing and minimal corrections for a grammar checker. In P. Groote, M. Egg & L. Kallmeyer (Eds.), *Formal Grammar. 14th International Conference, FG 2009, Bordeaux, France, July 25-26, 2009, Revised Selected Papers, Lecture Notes in Computer Science* (Vol. 5591, chap. 4, pp. 47–63). Berlin/Heidelberg: Springer. doi:10.1007/978-3-642-20169-1_4.

Connors, R. J., & Lunsford, A. A. (1988). Frequency of formal errors in current college writing, or Ma and Pa Kettle do research. *College Composition and Communication, 39*(4), 395–409.

Cook, P., & Welsh, J. (2001). Incremental parsing in language-based editors: User needs and how to meet them. *Software: Practice and Experience 31*(15), 1461–1486. doi:10.1002/spe.422.

Corder, S. P. (1967). The significance of learner's errors. *Produktinformation International Review of Applied Linguistics in Language Teaching, 5*(4), 161–170. doi:10.1515/iral.1967.5.1-4.161.

Costa, F., Frasconi, P., Lombardo, V., & Soda, G. (2003). Towards incremental parsing of natural language using recursive neural networks. *Applied Intelligence, 19*(1–2), 9–25. doi:10.1023/a:1023860521975.

Dale, R. (1990). Automating editorial assistance. In *IEEE Colloquium on Hypertext*, pp. 3/1–3/3.

Daz-Negrillo, A., & Fernández-Dominguez, J. (2006). Error tagging systems for learner corpora. *Revista Española de Lingüística Aplicada, 19*, 83–102.

Ehrensberger-Dow, M., & Perrin, D. (2009). Capturing translation processes to access metalinguistic awareness. *Across Languages and Cultures, 10*(2), 275–288. doi:10.1556/acr.10.2009.2.6.

Ellis, R. (1994). *The study of second language acquisition. Oxford Applied Linguistics*. Oxford: Oxford University Press.

Engelbart, D. C. (1962). Augmenting human intellect: A conceptual framework. Menlo Park: Tech. Rep., Stanford Research Institute.

Flinn, J. Z. (1987). Case studies of revision aided by keystroke recording and replaying software. *Computers and Composition, 5*(1), 31–44. doi:10.1016/s8755-4615(87)80013-0.

Foster, J. (2010). "cba to check the spelling": Investigating parser performance on discussion forum posts. In *Human Language Technologies: The 2010 Annual Conference of the North American Chapter of the Association for Computational Linguistics* (pp. 381–384). Stroudsburg, PA, USA: Association for Computational Linguistics.

Foster, J., & Vogel, C. (2004). Parsing Ill-formed text using an error grammar. *Artificial Intelligence Review, 21*(3–4), 269–291. doi:10.1023/b:aire.0000036259.68818.1e.

Foth, K., Menzel, W., Pop, H.F., & Schröder, I. (2000). An experiment on incremental analysis using robust parsing techniques. In *Proceedings of the 18th conference on Computational Linguistics* (*COLING '00*) (pp. 1026–1030). Stroudsburg, PA, USA: Association for Computational Linguistics. doi:10.3115/992730.992798.

Foth, K., Menzel, W., & Schröder, I. (2005). Robust parsing with weighted constraints. *Natural Language Engineering, 11*(1), 1–25. doi:10.1017/s1351324903003267.

Gamon, M. (2010). Using mostly native data to correct errors in learners' writing. In *Human Language Technologies: The 2010 Annual Conference of the North American Chapter of the*

Association for Computational Linguistics (pp. 163–171). Stroudsburg, PA, USA: Association for Computational Linguistics.

Gries, S. T., & Stefanowitsch, A. (Eds.). (2007). *Corpora in cognitive linguistics: corpus-based approaches to syntax and lexis*. Berlin, New York: De Gruyter Mouton.

Gubelmann, R. (2010). Systematischer Überblick über die Fundstücke im Fehlerforum zu "Making word processors process words". Master's thesis. Zürich, Schweiz: Universität Zürich, Insitut für Computerlinguistik.

Hausser, R. (2001). Foundations of computational linguistics: Human-computer communication in natural language, 2nd rev. and ext. edn. Berlin, Heidelberg: Springer, New York (2001).

Heidorn, G. E. (2000). Intelligent writing assistance: Techniques and applications for the processing of language as text. In R. Dale, H. Moisl, & H. Somers (Eds.), *Handbook of natural language processing* (pp. 181–207). New York, NY, USA: Marcel Dekker.

Huang, L., & Sagae, K. (2010). Dynamic programming for linear-time incremental parsing. In *Proceedings of the 48th Annual Meeting of the Association for Computational Linguistics, ACL '10* (pp. 1077–1086). Stroudsburg, PA, USA: Association for Computational Linguistics.

Jensen, K., Heidorn, G. E., Miller, L. A., & Ravin, Y. (1983). Parse fitting and prose fixing: getting a hold on ill-formedness. *Computational Linguistics, 9*(3–4), 147–160.

Ko, A. J., Aung, H. H., & Myers, B. A. (2005). Design requirements for more flexible structured editors from a study of programmers' text editing. In CHI '05: CHI '05 extended abstracts on human factors in computing systems, pp. 1557–1560. New York, NY, USA: ACM. doi:10.1145/1056808.1056965.

Kollberg, P. (1998). S-notation: A Computer based method for studying and representing text composition. Master's thesis. Kungliga Tekniska Högskolan Stockholm.

Kramer, A. (2004). Rechtschreibkorrektursysteme im Vergleich. DITECT versus Microsoft Word. URL http://www.mediensprache.net/de/networx/docs/networx-35.aspx.

Leacock, C., Chodorow, M., Gamon, M., & Tetreault, J. (2010). Automated grammatical error detection for language learners. *Synthesis Lectures on Human Language Technologies* (Vol. 9). San Rafael, CA, USA: Morgan & Claypool. doi:10.2200/s00275ed1v01y201006hlt009.

Leijten, M., Janssen, D., & Van Waes, L. (2010). Error correction strategies of professional speech recognition users: Three profiles. *Computers in Human Behavior, 26*(5), 964–975. doi:10.1016/j.chb.2010.02.010.

Leijten, M., Macken, L., Hoste, V., Van Horenbeeck, E., & Van Waes, L. (2012). From character to word level: Enabling the linguistic analyses of inputlog process data. In M. Piotrowski, C. Mahlow & R. Dale (Eds.). *Proceedings of the Second Workshop on Computational Linguistics and Writing (CL&W 2012): Linguistic and Cognitive Aspects of Document Creation and Document Engineering* (pp. 1–8). Stroudsburg, PA, USA: Association for Computational Linguistics.

Leijten, M., & Van Waes, L. (2006). Inputlog: New perspectives on the logging of on-line writing. In: K. P. H. Sullivan, E. Lindgren (Eds.), *Computer keystroke logging and writing: Methods and applications, studies in writing* (Vol. 18, chap. 9, pp. 73–94). Amsterdam: Elsevier Science.

Lüdeling, A., Walter, M., Kroymann, E., & Adolphs, P. (2005). Multi-level error annotation in learner corpora. In *Proceedings of Corpus Linguistics 2005*.

Lunsford, A. A., & Lunsford, K. J. (2008). Mistakes Are a fact of life: A national comparative study. *College Composition and Communication, 59*(4), 781–806 (2008).

Macdonald, N. H., Frase, L. T., Gingrich, P. S., & Keenan, S. A. (1982). The writer's workbench: Computer aids for text analysis. *IEEE Transactions on Communication, 30*(1), 105–110.

Mahlow, C. (2011). Linguistisch unterstütztes redigieren: Konzept und exemplarische Umsetzung basierend auf interaktiven computerlinguistischen Ressourcen. Ph.D. thesis, University of Zurich.

Meurers, D. (2013). Natural language processing and language learning. In C. A. Chapelle (Ed.) *Encyclopedia of applied linguistics* (pp. 1–13). Oxford: Blackwell.

Meurers, D., Ziai, R., Amaral, L., Boyd, A., Dimitrov, A., Metcalf, V., & Ott, N. (2010). Enhancing authentic web pages for language learners. In *Proceedings of the NAACL HLT*

2010 Fifth Workshop on Innovative Use of NLP for Building Educational Applications (pp. 10–18). Stroudsburg, PA, USA: Association for Computational Linguistics.

Napolitano, D. M., & Stent, A. (2009). TechWriter: An evolving system for writing assistance for advanced learners of English. *CALICO Journal, 26*(3), 611–625.

Nivre, J. (2008). Algorithms for deterministic incremental dependency parsing. *Computational Linguistics, 34*(4), 513–553. doi:10.1162/coli.07-056-r1-07-027.

Norman, D. A. (1981). Categorization of action slips. *Psychological Review, 88*, 1–15.

Norman, D. A. (1983). Design rules based on analyses of human error. *Communications of the ACM, 26*(4), 254–258. doi:10.1145/2163.358092.

Omar, C., Yoon, Y., LaToza, T. D., & Myers, B. A. (2012). Active code completion. In *Proceedings of the 2012 International Conference on Software Engineering, ICSE 2012* (pp. 859–869). Piscataway, NJ, USA: IEEE Press.

Perrin, D. (2002). Progression analysis (PA): Investigating writing strategies in the workplace. In T. Olive & C. M. Levy (Eds.) Contemporary Tools and techniques for studying writing, *studies in writing* (Vol. 10, pp. 105–117). Boston, Dordrecht, London: Kluwer.

Perrin, D. (2006a). Progression analysis: An ethnographic computer-based multi-method approach for investigate natural writing processes. In L. Van Waes, M. Leijten & C. M. Neuwirth (Eds.), *Writing and digital media, studies in writing* (Vol. 17, pp. 173–179). Amsterdam: Elsevier Science.

Perrin, D. (2006b). Schreibforschung im Kursalltag: Was die Progressionsanalyse praktisch nützt. In O. Kruse, K. Berger & M. Ulmi (Eds.), Prozessorientierte Schreibdidaktik: Schreibtraining für Schule, Studium und Beruf (pp. 279–294). Bern, Stuttgart, Wie: Haupt.

Perrin, D. (2011). Language policy, tacit knowledge, and institutional learning: The case of the Swiss public service broadcaster SRG SSR. *Current Issues in Language Planning, 12*(3), 331–348. doi:10.1080/14664208.2011.604953.

Perrin, D., & Wildi, M. (2009). Statistical modeling of writing processes. In C. Bazerman, R. Krut, K. Lunsford, S. McLeod, S. Null, P. Rogers, & A. Stansell (Eds.), *Traditions of writing research* (pp. 378–393). New York: Routledge.

Reznicek, M., Lüdeling, A., & Hirschmann, H. (2013). Competing target hypotheses in the Falko Corpus. A flexible multi-layer corpus architecture. In: A. Daz-Negrillo (Ed.) *Automatic treatment and analysis of learner corpus data.* Amsterdam: John Benjamins (forthcoming).

Rimrott, A., & Heift, T. (2008). Evaluating automatic detection of misspellings in German. *Language Learning & Technology, 12*(3), 73–92.

Roark, B. (2001). Probabilistic top-down parsing and language modeling. *Computational Linguistics, 27*(2), 249–276. doi:10.1162/089120101750300526.

Schulze, M. (2004). Ein sprachunabhängiger Ansatz zur Entwicklung deklarativer, robuster LA-Grammatiken mit einer exemplarischen Anwendung auf das Deutsche und das Englische. Ph.D. thesis, Friedrich-Alexander-Universität Erlangen-Nürnberg.

Severinson Eklundh, K. (1992). Problems in achieving a global perspective of the text in computer-based writing. In M. Sharples (Ed.) *Computers and writing: issues and implementation* (pp. 73–84). Boston, Dordrecht, London: Kluwer.

Severinson Eklundh, K. (1994). Linear and nonlinear strategies in computer-based writing. *Computers and Composition 11*(3), 203–216. doi: 10.1016/8755-4615(94)90013-2.

Sloan, G. (1990). Frequency of errors in essays by college freshmen and by professional writers. *College Composition and Communication, 41*(3), 199–308.

Smithson, I. (1986). The writing workshop. *Computers and Composition, 4*(1), 78–94. doi:10.1016/s8755-4615(86)80009-3.

Sullivan, K. P. H., & Lindgren, E. (2006). Computer key-stroke logging and writing: Methods and applications. K. P. H. & E. Lindgren (Eds.) *Studies in writing* (Vol. 18). Amsterdam: Elsevier Science.

Van De Vanter, M. L. (1995). Practical language-based editing for software engineers. In *Software Engineering and Human-Computer Interaction, Lecture Notes in Computer Science* (Vol. 896, pp. 251–267). Berlin, Heidelberg, New York: Springer. doi: 10.1007/bfb0035821.

Van Waes, L., Leijten, M., & Neuwirth, C. M. (Eds.). (2006). Writing and digital media, studies in writing (Vol. 17). Amsterdam: Elsevier Science.

Van Waes, L., Leijten, M., & Van Weijen, D. (2009). Keystroke logging in writing research: Observing writing processes with Inputlog. GFL—German as a Foreign Language, *2*(3), 41–64.

Vernon, A. (2000). Computerized grammar checkers 2000: Capabilities, limitations, and pedagogical possibilities. *Computers and Composition, 17*(3), 329–349. doi:10.1016/s8755-4615(00)00038-4.

Williams, N. (1989). Computer assisted writing software: RUSKIN. In: N. Williams & P. O. Holt (Eds.) *Computers and writing: Models and tools* (chap. 1, pp. 1–16). Oxford: Intellect.

Wirén, M. (1989). Interactive incremental chart parsing. In *Proceedings of the Fourth Conference of the European Chapter of the Association for Computational Linguistics* (pp. 241–248). Morristown, NJ, USA: Association for Computational Linguistics. doi:10.3115/976815.976848.

Part VI
Language Resources and Language Engineering

Language Matrices and a Language Resource Impact Factor

Joseph Mariani and Gil Francopoulo

Abstract We feel it is important to have a clear picture of what exists in terms of *Language Resources and Evaluation* (LRE) in order to be able to carry on research investigations in computational linguistics and develop language processing systems. The language coverage is especially important in order to provide technologies that can help multilingualism and protect endangered languages. It implies that one knows what is necessary and exists for some languages, detects the gaps for other languages, and finds a way to address them. In order to have access to that information, we based our study on the *LRE Map*, which was produced within the FLaReNet EC project. The *LRE Map* is built on data gathered at conferences directly from the authors, and therefore provides actual data obtained from the source, not an estimate of such data. At the time of this study, it covered 10 conferences from 2010 to 2012. We consider here *Language Resources* (LR) in the broad sense, including Data, Tools, Evaluation and Meta-Resources (standards, metadata, guidelines, etc.). We took into consideration the names, types, modalities and languages attached to each entry in the *LRE Map*. A huge amount of manual cleaning was necessary before being able to use the data. In order to check the availability of Language Resources for the various languages, we designed a software tool called "*LRE Matrix*" that automatically produces Language Matrices presenting the number of resources of various types that exist for various modalities for each language. We slightly modified the software code in order to also compute the number of times a Language Resource is mentioned, what we may call a "*Language Resource Impact Factor*" (LRIF). Given their quantitative, objective nature, our results are precious for comparing the situation

J. Mariani (✉)
LIMSI-CNRS, Orsay, France
e-mail: Joseph.Mariani@limsi.fr

J. Mariani · G. Francopoulo
IMMI-CNRS, Orsay, France
e-mail: gil.francopoulo@wanadoo.fr

G. Francopoulo
Tagmatica, Paris, France

© Springer International Publishing Switzerland 2015
N. Gala et al. (eds.), *Language Production, Cognition, and the Lexicon*,
Text, Speech and Language Technology 48, DOI 10.1007/978-3-319-08043-7_25

of the various national and regional languages in Europe regarding the availability of Language Resources in a survey conducted within the META-NET network. We faced in our studies the need for a tedious normalization and cleaning process that showed the necessity to assign a Unique and Persistent Identifier to each Language Resource in order to identify it more easily and follow its use and changes over time, a process that requires an international coordination.

Keywords Language resources · Language map · Multilingualism · Standards

1 Introduction

Even if it is not his main research focus, multilingualism always interested M. Zock, should it be for Lexicology (Zock and Quint 2004), Language Production (Zock et al. 1989; Zock 2010), Machine Translation (Zock et al. 1988; Rapp and Zock 2010), or Foreign Language Learning (Zock and Lapalme 2010).

In order to allow for full multilingualism, it is mandatory to possess technologies that are able to process all languages and to benefit from the availability of Language Resources in all those languages.

To this regard, we wish to present here a study that was conducted within the T4ME (*Technologies for a Multilingual Europe*) project supported by the European Commission (EC) from 2011 to 2013, using data produced in the framework of the FLaReNet project (*Fostering Language Resources Network*) supported by the EC from 2008 to 2011.

The objective was to provide a clear picture on what exists in terms of Language Resources (LR), in the broad sense (Data, Tools, Evaluation and Meta-resources (standards, metadata, guidelines, etc.)) for the various languages, and to stress the languages that are missing such Language Resources. The goal would then be to ensure the production of the corresponding resources to fill the gaps for those languages.

Drawing inspiration and experience from the EuroMatrix[1] survey and the structure of the BLARK[2] (Krauwer 1998) matrix, we produced Languages Matrices that aim at drawing a chart of Language Resources (Data, Tools, Evaluation and Meta-Resources (Standards, metadata, guidelines)) for the various languages. The data model of the underlying database goes together with the design of the metadata scheme adopted in the META-SHARE LR sharing infrastructure developed within T4ME.

We present here the results of two successive studies:

In a first study, we built those matrices from the *LREC Map* that has been produced within the EC FLaReNet project from the information provided by the

[1] http://www.euromatrixplus.net/matrix/.

[2] http://www.blark.org/.

authors of the papers submitted at the LREC'2010 conference, which gathers the international community working in the field of Language Resources and Evaluation. It is therefore a unique opportunity to get the freshest information from the community itself. Each author was requested to provide a set of information on the Language Resources that are mentioned in their paper, through an online questionnaire. It resulted in a table of close to 2,000 entries. This information was then made available to the scientific community, through the same interface than the one that was used for the information acquisition.

The first set of Language Matrices was built from this data. It consists in "verticalizing" the information through the pivot of languages, in order to analyze the language coverage of the Language Resources. This operation necessitated the design of a specific piece of software, as it would have been impossible to do it manually.

In a second study, the data was enriched over time through 9 more international conferences. It changed its name accordingly from the *LREC Map* to the *LRE Map* (*Language Resources and Evaluation Map*). The acquisition and consultation software packages have been improved based on the experience gained in the acquisition, consultation and analysis of the initial *LREC Map*. Cleaning the initial *LREC Map* was a very tedious task, and one of the main objectives in this second study was to facilitate this cleaning and normalization process through the use of auto-completion during the insertion of the information by the paper's authors.

The first version of the *LRE Matrix* software package has also been modified in order to improve the visual analysis of the matrices and to extend the analysis to the computation of a *Language Resource Impact Factor* (LRIF) comparable to what is being experimented in the biological area (BRIF: *Bioresource Research Impact Factor*[3]).

2 First Study

2.1 The LREC Map

The *LREC Map*[4] is an initiative proposed by N. Calzolari at the Institute for Computational Linguistics A. Zampolli (ILC) of the CNR in Pisa, in relation with her presidency of the Language Resources and Evaluation Conference (LREC) and her coordination of the FLaReNet (Fostering Language Resource Network) Thematic Network.

She proposed to ask each author submitting a paper at the LREC'2010 conference, held in Malta in May 2010, to fill in a questionnaire related to the Language Resources which were produced or used in the submitted paper. It resulted

[3] http://www.gen2phen.org/groups/brif-bio-resource-impact-factor.

[4] http://en.wikipedia.org/wiki/LRE_Map.

in a database called the *LREC Map*. It is a very appropriate initiative as this conference is specifically devoted to Language Resources and Evaluation, and as it gathers 1,200 specialists working in that field worldwide. Each author submitting a paper had to respond to a questionnaire in order to have his submitted paper be taken into account in the evaluation process. While this input was mandatory, the authors could simply respond that it is not applicable to their paper.

The content of the questionnaire was carefully designed by some members of the conference Program Committee, who happened to be also FLaReNet and META-NET partners (K. Choukri (ELDA), J. Mariani (LIMSI-CNRS) and S. Piperidis (ILSP)), and ILC researchers, under the chairwomanship of N. Calzolari (ILC-CNR). It included the selection of the list of questions, and for some questions, the list of suggested answers, giving the possibility to also provide an answer that was not suggested ("Other").

The questions regarding the LR were the following:

- Resource Type (with 24 suggestions depending on the Resource category):
  - Data (5)

    Corpus, Lexicon, Terminology, Ontology, Grammar/Language Model
  - Tool (11)

    Annotation Tool, Tokenizer, Tagger/Parser, Named Entity Recognizer, Word Sense Disambiguator, Language Identifier, Prosodic Analyzer, Speaker Recognizer, Signal Processing/Feature Extraction, Transcriber, Image Analyzer
  - Guidelines (3)

    Representation-Annotation Formalism/Guidelines, Representation-Annotation Standards/Best Practices, Metadata
  - Evaluation (5)

    Evaluation Data, Evaluation Tool, Evaluation Package, Evaluation Methodology/Formalism/Guidelines, Evaluation Standards/Best Practices
  - Other (1)
- Resource Name (Open)
- Resource Size (Open)
- Resource Production status (with 4 suggestions):
- Newly created-finished, Newly created-in progress, Existing-used, Existing-updated) + Other
- Resource Language(s) (Open)
- Resource Modality (with 4 suggestions):
  - Written, Spoken, Multimodal/Multimedia, Sign Language) + Other

- Use of the resource (with 26 suggestions)
- Resource Availability (with 4 suggestions):
  - Freely available, From Data Center(s), From owner, Not available + Other
- License (Open)
- Resource URL (if available) (Open)
- Documentation (Open)
- Resource Description (Open).

The acquisition software was designed by ILC. It was put online[5] together with explanations[6] in connection with the START software, which is used for submitting papers at LREC. The feedback from the users was very positive and there was no complaint about the extra work it induces for submitting a paper. There were only warnings within the community about the fact that submitting a paper at LREC involved more time than in the past.

The result of this survey was presented at the LREC 2010 conference (Calzolari et al. 2010). Each submitted paper mentioned about 1.5 Language Resources on average. The *LREC Map* contained 1,995 entries, corresponding to 1,576 different language resources. Those numbers show that the redundancy is low, and that the diversity of the LR used is relatively large. In order to transform the *LREC Map* into *Language Matrices*, if was necessary to clean up the data. This was a very tedious activity done by a single person (J. Mariani) after a 2-day meeting on the topic of the *LREC Map* that was held in Pisa in July 2010.

2.2 The LRE Matrix *Software*

The *LRE Matrix* software has been designed and written by G. Francopoulo. It transforms the *LREC Map* into Language Matrices depicting the existence, or absence, of LR for each language.

Its interface is enough intuitive to be used by people not familiar with computer programming (Fig. 1). The goal was to have the selected languages in the columns and the LR information to be analyzed in the rows, and to place in each cell of the matrix the number of existing Language Resources, with the possibility to have access to the corresponding Language Resources and to the attached details of those Language Resources through hyperlinking.

This piece of software includes many parameters and is actually not specific to language analysis. It can also use any other pivot, allowing the study of other aspects, such as the Types of LR which are necessary for different Uses, for example.

---

[5] http://www.resourcebook.eu/LrecMapGUI/faces/views/lrecMapUI.xhtml.

[6] http://www.lrec-conf.org/lrec2010/?LREC2010-Map-of-Language-Resources.

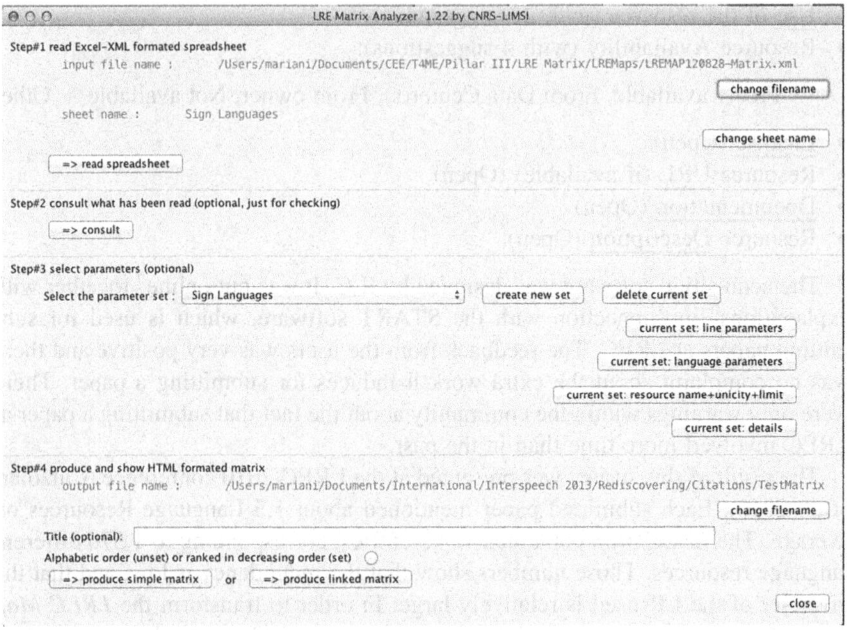

Fig. 1 Screenshot of the interface of the LRE matrix analyzer software

2.3 Analysis

In the first study, the European languages, and especially the 23 EU languages existing at that time,[7] have been especially considered, but the goal was to easily extend it to any set of languages. This matrix representation of the inventory database is well suited for a quick comparison across languages, with a column for every language and the rows corresponding to the relevant Types of resources needed for technology progress. A cell then describes the existing Language Resources in terms of resource Type for a specific language. In the top-level view this state represents a global measure of the resources available for a language, which is most often correlated to the availability of Language Technologies for that language, and to the maturity of research in the countries where this language is spoken, or to the popularity (not to say "the weight") of that language worldwide. By a simple click on any cell, one can find the inventory of the corresponding resources with their descriptions.

In order to keep the Language Matrices manageable for both providers and readers, the data was partitioned into several matrices corresponding to several modalities (Written, Spoken and Multimodal/Multimedia) and categories of resource types (Data or Tools). In addition, Evaluation and Meta-resources were

[7] As of 2014, there are now 24 EU official languages, with the accession of Croatia in July 2013.

depicted by two matrices, which include all the components related to those two kinds of resources. Those matrices could be completed with the EuroMatrix, which provides a special view of translingual resources, in which both rows and columns correspond to languages and each cell represents the number of resources corresponding to each language pair, or the performance of Machine Translation systems for that language pair.

2.4 Conclusions of the First Study

The first Language Matrices based on the LREC 2010 Map provided very interesting results on the comparative status of European languages regarding the availability of Language Resources. It was thus decided in a second study to extend the analysis with more data being harvested at upcoming conferences on speech and natural language processing such as COLING, ACL, EMNLP or Interspeech, and to produce an update of the matrices based on this enriched data.

The analysis of the initial *LREC Map* showed that the authors were using many other LR Types than the ones suggested by the *LREC Map* designers. It was therefore thought necessary to extend the list of those Types, based on the analysis of the data entered by the authors at LREC 2010.

Another major issue that was identified is the naming of the LR. Each author may name the same LR, and the various versions of a LR, with different wordings. It is therefore very difficult to count the LR existing for the various languages. In order to solve this problem, it would be necessary to assign a persistent and unique identifier to each individual LR. This process would necessitate an international coordination in order to avoid the duplication of identifiers. The same problem exists for biological resources.

The information provided by the authors on the languages covered by a LR also lacked homogeneity. It was therefore decided to provide a list of languages to the authors to facilitate their task and improve consistency. It was also wished to extend the initial analysis, which mainly addressed the 23 EU official languages, to more languages, and to also consider Sign Languages.

Finally, the importance of recognizing the contribution of LR producers in the scientific and technological progress within Language Technologies was acknowledged. In order to express this contribution, it was proposed to compute a *Language Resource Impact Factor* (LRIF), just as Citation Indexes exist for papers.

Based on those conclusions, we proposed in a second study to:

- increase the number of the identified LR trough more conferences,
- use the results of the metadata guidelines produced in T4ME META-SHARE,
- improve the coherence of the inputs in a loop where the taxonomy and the metadata are refined through the analysis of the matrices and the work on metadata, and reflected in the suggested terms of the questionnaire,

- improve accordingly the suggested terms in the questionnaire,
- extend the range of languages being considered, including regional and non-European languages,
- include the analysis of the Sign Languages,
- define and compute a *Language Resource Impact Factor* (LRIF),
- discuss at international fora with the main stakeholders and with the scientific community the way to assign a Persistent and Unique Identifier to all LR.

3 The Second Study

3.1 Improved LRE Map

3.1.1 New *LRE Map* Acquisition

Based on the experience gained in the acquisition and cleaning process, and on the analysis of the corresponding data, it was decided to improve the acquisition software by extending the list of suggested Types and Modalities, by harmonizing the LR Names and the languages. A meeting took place in Pisa on July 18, 2011, involving N. Calzolari and colleagues (CNR-ILC (Istituto di Linguistica Computazionale)), G. Francopoulo and J. Mariani.

The analysis of the data showed that most of the 24 suggested Types have been used by the authors, and cover 85 % of the entries. However, the remaining 15 % represents a long tail of 222 "Other" Types, including a small set (13) of resources belonging to several Types (1 %), 100 "Other" Types mentioned several times by authors (7 %) and 99 Types mentioned only once (7 %). As an alternative to a too large extension of the number of LR Types, which may be confusing for the authors, it was proposed to use an auto-completion process which provides to the authors suggestions of Types based on the first characters that he/she types.

After an extensive discussion, the new set of suggestions for LR Types included 29 items (5 more than in the first study):

- Data (5: same)
  - Corpus, Lexicon, Terminology, Ontology, Grammar/Language Model
- Tool (16: 5 new Types and one new wording marked in italics)
  - Annotation Tool, Tokenizer, Tagger/Parser, Named Entity Recognizer, Word Sense Disambiguator, Language Identifier, Prosodic Analyzer, Speaker Recognizer, Signal Processing/Feature Extraction, Image Analyzer, *Corpus Tool, Machine Translation Tool, Language Modeling Tool, Spoken Dialog Tool, Text-to-Speech Synthesizer, Speech Recognizer/Transcriber.*

- Guidelines (4: 1 new Type marked in italics)
  - Representation-Annotation Formalism/Guidelines, Representation-Annotation Standards/Best Practices, Metadata, *Language Resources/Technologies Infrastructure*.
- Evaluation (4: 2 Types merged in a single one with a new wording marked in italics)
  - Evaluation Data, Evaluation Tool, Evaluation Package, *Evaluation Methodology/Standards/Guidelines*.
- Other (1)

Auto-completion was also introduced for entering the name of a LR, with a suggestion to even pre-fill all the slots corresponding to that LR which was finally not implemented in order to avoid wrong inputs induced by the easiness of relying on existing information. The new acquisition software also provides a list of languages encoded according to the ISO 639-3 codes based on the *Ethnologue*[8] survey of existing languages (Lewis 2009), which facilitates and normalizes the input of the 5 first languages corresponding to a LR. In case an LR addresses more languages, the others are entered in a free format. Finally, the suggestions for LR Modalities were extended with "Speech/Written", given the large number of LR belonging to both modalities.

3.1.2 Extended *LRE Map*

The *LREC Map* has been enriched by new data coming from 9 conferences which were organized since the LREC 2010 conference and which agreed to use the software developed for LREC. Those are COLING 2010, EMNL 2010, LTC 2011, ACL-HLT 2011, RANLP 2011, Oriental-Cocosda 2011, Interspeech 2011, IJCNLP 2011 and LREC 2012. It resulted in a new database called the *LRE Map*, containing 4,395 entries, corresponding to 3,121 different Language Resources.

Agreements have been discussed with the conference organizers and the supporting organizations (ACL, ISCA, AFNLP). Some conference organizers expressed the wish to modify the content of the questionnaire. Defining its content in a coordinated way within the (spoken, written and multimodal) language processing communities appears as a major challenge.

In the future, other sources of information may also be considered, such as the *Language Resources and Evaluation* (LRE) journal, or the LR repositories catalogues (LDC, ELRA, META-SHARE, CLARIN, OLAC, etc.).

8 http://www.ethnologue.com/.

3.1.3 *LRE Map* Consultation

The *LRE Map* resulting from the survey conducted at LREC'2010 and at upcoming conferences is made publicly available online by ILC.[9] The design of the consultation software has also been improved, on the same basis as the *LRE Map* acquisition improvements. It is presently possible when consulting the *LRE Map* online to consider one or the full set of the 10 conferences that provided the data.

The data that is put online is the raw data obtained from the authors. It therefore contains duplication of LR, and the spelling errors and input errors coming from the authors themselves. It provides access to this data to the whole community with a nice GUI and received a very positive feedback.

3.1.4 *LRE Map* Cleaning

Just as for the initial *LREC Map* in 2010, it was also necessary to clean up and normalize the new data gathered from the 9 conferences in order to transform the *LRE Map* into Language Matrices. Part of the data has already been cleaned at ILC, but more cleaning was necessary and still resulted in a very tedious activity (Mariani et al. 2014).

The data is kept as entered by the authors, including all the errors they may have introduced, and the cleaned version of the information is added in parallel. The cleaned information is used for all analyses, but the raw data is provided to the users who wish to consult the database, leaving the full responsibility of the information to the authors.

Modifying the data as a collaborative activity is very difficult, as some decisions are specific to the data cleaners. The modifications are related to various issues (cases, spelling errors, introduction of a new term while the concept was already covered by or within a suggested term, etc.), but also raise in some cases more fundamental and theoretical questions, which should be discussed within the scientific community.

The data that was corrected is the following (human interventions are marked in grey):

Resource Type

The errors here concern for example new Types that were introduced by the authors in addition to the suggested ones. It may be possible that the correct Type already existed, but that the author didn't realize. It may also happen that different authors use different terms for the same new Type, that should therefore be harmonized, or that the Type is too specific and that it can be merged in a larger Type (already suggested or new) (Fig. 2).

[9] http://www.resourcebook.eu/.

Not Assigned	Database	Data	B3DB
Database	Database	Data	B3DB
Corpus	Corpus	Data	BABEL Hungarian Speech Databases
Corpus Tool	Corpus Tool	Tool	Babouk
Corpus	Corpus	Data	BabyExp
Evaluation Data	Evaluation Data	Evaluation	BAF corpus
Lexicon	Lexicon	Data	Bagla SyllableNet
Corpus	Corpus	Data	Baidu Zhidao Corpus
Corpus	Corpus	Data	Balanced Corpus of Contemporary Written Japanese (BCCWJ)
Corpus	Corpus	Data	Balanced Corpus of Contemporary Written Japanese (BCCWJ)
Lexicon	Lexicon	Data	BalkaNet
Corpus	Corpus	Data	Baltic Language Named Entity Recognition (NER) corpus
Corpus	Corpus	Data	Bank of Russian Constructions and Valencies
Named Entity Recogniser	Named Entity Recognizer	Tool	BANNER NER system
Resource-Tool: Coreference Resolution	Coreference Resolution Tool	Tool	BART Anaphora Resolution Toolkit
Annotation Tool	Coreference Resolution Tool	Tool	BART Anaphora Resolution Toolkit
Lexicon	Lexicon	Data	Base Concepts
Corpus	Corpus	Data	Base de datos de verbos, alternancias de diátesis y esquemas sintácticos del español (ADESSE)
Language database	Database	Data	Base de datos sintácticos

Fig. 2 Examples of cleaning the inputs of the LR Types (*first column*): spelling normalization ("recognizer"), Harmonization (BART as a "Coreference Resolution Tool"), "Language Database" as "Database" (*second column*) and categorization into "Data", "Tool", "Evaluation" or "Meta-Resources" gross categories (*third column*). The entered LR names appear in the fourth column

The study of the new LR Types provided by the authors also reflects Types that were not thought of by the *LREC Map* designers, due to the difficulty of embracing the whole field. It also allows for identifying new kinds of research conducted somewhere in the world on a given language, and act as a "weak signal" that may indicate new emerging research areas in the field of Language science and technology.

The introduction of the auto-completion process in LREC 2012 greatly improved the homogeneity of the data and reduced the size of the new Types introduced by the author. On the complete table, only 149 Types are not among the suggested ones, the most frequent being Machine Learning Tool (mentioned 21 times), Database (16), Terminology Tool (10) and Search Engine (9).

In addition, information on the "Type Category" (Data, Tool, Evaluation, Guidelines) has been added to each entry in agreement with the need to produce the various matrices.

Resource Name

This information is provided by the authors in an open format. Therefore different authors may use different wordings for the same LR, and those names should be harmonized. The problem of versioning is a more difficult problem to handle:

ACE	ACE	Automatic Content Extraction (ACE)
ACE	ACE	Automatic Content Extraction (ACE)
ACE 2003	ACE 2003	Automatic Content Extraction (ACE)
ACE 2003, 2004, 2005	ACE 2003, 2004, 2005	Automatic Content Extraction (ACE)
ACE 2004 Multilingual Training Corpus	ACE 2004	Automatic Content Extraction (ACE)
ACE 2004 training data	ACE 2004	Automatic Content Extraction (ACE)
ACE 2005	ACE 2005	Automatic Content Extraction (ACE)
ACE 2005	ACE 2005	Automatic Content Extraction (ACE)
ACE 2005	ACE 2005	Automatic Content Extraction (ACE)
ACE 2005	ACE 2005	Automatic Content Extraction (ACE)
ACE 2005	ACE 2005	Automatic Content Extraction (ACE)
ACE 2005	ACE 2005	Automatic Content Extraction (ACE)
ACE 2005 Arabic	ACE 2005 Arabic	Automatic Content Extraction (ACE)
ACE 2005 Handwritten Arabic	ACE 2005 Arabic	Automatic Content Extraction (ACE)
ACE 2007	ACE 2007	Automatic Content Extraction (ACE)
ACE 2007	ACE 2007	Automatic Content Extraction (ACE)
ACE 2007	ACE 2007	Automatic Content Extraction (ACE)
ACE-2 data set	ACE-2	Automatic Content Extraction (ACE)
ACE-2 Version 1.0	ACE-2	Automatic Content Extraction (ACE)
Automatic Content Extraction	ACE	Automatic Content Extraction (ACE)
Automatic Content Extraction	ACE	Automatic Content Extraction (ACE)

Fig. 3 Examples of cleaning the inputs of the LR Names (*first column*): harmonization of various ways of mentioning the "Automatic Content Extraction (ACE)" resource (*second column*), and gathering into the same family resource name (*third column*)

should the different versions of a LR over time be considered as the same LR or as different ones? For the time being, we kept them as different items. Also a LR may have the same name but be constituted by several parts (corresponding to different Types: a dictionary and a corpus, for example) or have varieties in different languages (Wordnets for example). In some cases, we kept them separate (Fig. 3).

The introduction of auto-completion in the questionnaire at LREC 2012 facilitated the naming of resources and only 8 % of the names had to be corrected compared with 45 % at LREC 2010. However, it appeared that 64 entries didn't get any name.

Above this naming issue, the more general question is to identify the same LR, and to merge the corresponding entries in order to avoid counting twice the same LR. Regarding LREC 2010, after doing this merging, the number of entries only decreased from 1,995 to 1,576 different LR (about 20 %), which shows that the diversity of the LR used was large in this first study. For the entire *LRE Map*, it decreased from 4,395 to 3,121 (about 30 %), as the production of new LR may not vary as fast as their use.

This demonstrates the importance of attributing a Persistent and Unique Identifier (LRID) to a LR, just like a book is identified by an ISBN number. The same should be done for LR, in a coordinated way, through a single entity attributing such numbers. This appears as a big challenge if we consider its international dimension, and discussions are presently on going at the international level in order to define the way to perform that task. This would also allow to keep track of the use of the corresponding LR in research through publications, and more generally to trace the use, enrichment, or modification of such LR by all Language Technology stakeholders (Choukri et al. 2012).

Interestingly, the Biology community conducts presently the same reflection on Biological Resources (Cambon-Thomsen et al. 2011).

Resource Languages

Here also, the input format was initially open. It was therefore necessary to clean up the data in order to harmonize the various spellings. Some authors provided the ISO code for languages, instead of the complete name. Some decisions were harder: we chose for example to consider British English, American English and English as a single (EU) language (Fig. 4).

The new acquisition software provides a list of languages encoded according to the ISO 339-3 code also used in the *Ethnologue* survey of existing languages, which facilitates and normalizes the input of the 5 first languages corresponding to a LR. If it is needed to enter more than 5 languages, the next ones are entered in a free format.

In the first study of the Language Matrices, the focus was put on EU languages. We therefore only considered the 23 official EU languages at that time; we merged all the regional EU languages (such as Basque, Catalan, Galician, Sami, Luxemburgish) in a single category ("European Regional languages") and the non-EU European languages (such as Moldavian, Turkish, Norwegian) also in a single category ("Other European languages"). We completed by the "Multilingual", "Language Independent" and "Non Applicable" categories.

Penn Arabic Treebank	Arabic	Arabic
Penn Arabic Treebank	Arabic	Arabic
Penn Arabic Treebank	Arabic	Arabic
Penn Arabic Treebank	Ll,,,,,	Arabic
Penn Chinese Treebank		Chinese
Penn Chinese Treebank	Chinese	Chinese
Penn Chinese Treebank 5		Chinese
Penn Chinese Treebank 5.1	Chinese	Chinese
Penn Chinese Treebank 6.0	Chinese	Chinese
The Penn Chinese Treebank 6.0		Chinese
Penn Chinese Treebank	Chinese	Chinese
Penn Chinese Treebank		Chinese
Penn Chinese Treebank 5.1	Chinese	Chinese

Fig. 4 Examples of cleaning the inputs of the language(s) addressed by a LR (entered input in *first column*): harmonization of the "Penn Arabic Treebank" to cover the Arabic language, and of the "Penn Chinese Treebank" to address Chinese (*third column*)

In the second study, we still considered the 23 official EU languages individually, but also a set of 4 Spanish regional languages (Catalan, Basque, Galician and Asturian). We gathered all the other European languages in a single "Other European Languages" category (comprising 51 national and regional European languages). We considered individually major international languages (Arabic, Hindi, Chinese Mandarin, Japanese and Korean), and gathered all the other ones in a single "Other Languages" category (comprising 133 languages). This represents a total of 216 languages mentioned in the *LRE Map* entries.

We also decided that LRs which concern several languages should be counted for each of those languages in the analysis of the language coverage, while they should be counted only once in the LRIF computation.

Resource Modality(ies)

Here also, a limited set of suggestions is made to the authors. However, some LR may be related to a couple of modalities (such as spoken and written). In this case, we decided to mark them as such in a coherent way and we considered them for both modalities. Some authors introduced modalities that we considered as already covered (such as "Text" instead of "Written", or "Any modality" instead of "Multimodal/Multimedia"), and we therefore had to correct it in a few cases (Fig. 5).

3.1.5 Summary of the Cleaning Process

Table 1 gives some insight on the number of cleaning operations that were made for each conference in the series.

A final cleaning had to be made on the full *LRE Map* after merging the 10 conferences, in order to ensure the overall homogeneity of Names and Types across conferences. 218 Types and 231 Names (about 5 % of the entries) and 6 Modalities were still corrected in this final process.

National Corpus of Polish	Written and Speech	Speech/Written
National Corpus of Polish	Written and Speech	Speech/Written
National Corpus of Polish	Written	Speech/Written
National Corpus of Polish	Written	Speech/Written
National Corpus of Polish	written and spoken	Speech/Written
National Corpus of Polish	Written	Speech/Written

Fig. 5 Examples of cleaning the modality of a LR (*second column*): harmonization of "National Corpus of Polish" to address both spoken and written language (*third column*)

Table 1 Table presenting the number of corrections on Types, Names, Languages and Modalities for the conferences which provided the data contained in the *LRE Map*

Conference	Date, place	Entries	Existing Types	Corrected existing Types	New Types	Corrected new Types	Corrected Names	Corrected Languages	Corrected Modalities	# corrections	(%) corrected cells
Lrec 2010	May 17–23 2010, Valetta, Malta	1,995	1,720	156	104	15	889	179	122	1,361	17 %
COLING 2010	August 23–27 2010, Beijing, China	735	654	52	28	1	126	39	202	420	14 %
EMNLP 2010	October 9–11 2010, Boston, USA	100	94	0	5	1	13	11	4	29	7 %
ACL-HLT 2011	June 19–24 2011, Portland, USA	93	87	4	2	0	5	10	6	25	7 %
Interspeech 2011	August 27–31, 2011, Firenze, Italy	66	61	2	2	1	6	5	6	20	8 %
RANLP 2011	September 12–14 2011, Hissar, Bulgaria	101	93	4	4	0	2	5	0	11	3 %
Oriental-Cocosda 2011	October 26–28 2011, Hsinchu, Taiwan	8	8	0	0	0	0	0	0	0	0 %
IJCNLP 2011	November 8–13 2011,	122	115	6	1	0	7	33	6	52	11 %

(continued)

Table 1 (continued)

Conference	Date, place	Entries	Existing Types	Corrected existing Types	New Types	Corrected new Types	Corrected Names	Corrected Languages	Corrected Modalities	# corrections	(%) corrected cells
	Chiang Mai, Thailand										
LTC 2011	November 25–27 2011, Poznan, Poland	45	38	4	3	0	6	12	8	30	17 %
LREC 2012	May 21–27 2012, Istanbul, Turkey	1,130	1,012	55	43	20	95	13	83	266	6 %
Total	10 conferences	4,395	3,882 (89 %)	283 (6 %)	192	38	1,149 (26 %)	307 (7 %)	437 (10 %)	2,214	13 %

We see in Table 1 that about 2,000 cells had to be modified overall. The number of corrections has been drastically reduced thanks to the new acquisition software regarding the Names (from 45 % at LREC 2010 to 8 % at LREC 2012) and the Languages (from 9 % to 1 %) while it has remained stable for the Types and the Modalities.

3.2 Language Resource Impact Factor (LRIF)

The idea here is to recognize the merits of the producers of Language Resources, just as papers are cited and contribute to the recognition of researchers.

In order to do so, a *Language Resource Impact Factor* (LRIF) is computed, which provides the number of times a LR is mentioned in the papers which served to constitute the *LRE Map*. In this case, we only considered the accepted papers, while in the case of the analysis of language coverage, we considered all the papers submitted for the LREC conferences and only the accepted papers for the other conferences. The LRIF has been computed independently for the 4 kinds of Language Resources: Data, Tools, Evaluation and Meta-Resources.

3.3 Modified LRE MATRIX *Software*

The software has been slightly modified in order to avoid long tails of sparse information and facilitate the reading and the analysis. It is now possible to select the information which needs a close analysis in individual rows, while gathering all the other information (*sparse data*) in a single row, and choosing to display that information or not.

The other main modification of the software is the possibility to compute the *Language Resource Impact Factor* (LRIF) for the various categories of LR (Data, Tools, Evaluation, Meta-Resources). The user may choose to display information with various occurrence thresholds (more than 1, 5 or 10 citations, or unlimited).

4 Language Matrices Analysis

4.1 Analysis of Language Coverage

As in the first study, 8 new Language Matrices have been produced (Written Language Data and Tools, Spoken Language Data and Tools, Multimodal/Multimedia Data and Tools, Evaluation and Meta-Resources). We took into consideration the design of similar matrices that have been built for the 11 national South

African languages in the NHN (*National Human Language Network*) program in South Africa (Grover et al. 2010).[10] As already mentioned, a LR is counted as many times as the number of languages it concerns, but is only considered once, whatever the number of citations. We also checked the progression from 2010 to 2012 (Table 2).

The full matrix, including all modalities and all Type categories shows the global preeminence of the English Language. On the 5,218 entries, it contains 1,364 LR related to English (close to 26 %, compared to 29 % in 2011), followed by French (286), German (265), Spanish (222), Italian (158) and Dutch (110). While still very few exist for Slovak (9), Irish Gaelic (5) or Maltese (4), we note a big increase for the Estonian language (from 7 to 23), for Regional languages (67 to 103) and for non-EU European languages (63 to 293) (Fig. 6).

Other major languages are also well represented (Chinese Mandarin (190), Arabic (157), Japanese (135), Hindi (50) and Korean (17), while the other 133 languages represent only 414 entries.

The largest types of resources are Corpus (2365), Lexicons (682), Taggers/Parsers (315), Annotation Tools (251), Evaluation Data (249), Ontology (172), Grammar/Language Models (100), Terminology (84), Representation-Annotation Standards/Best Practices (83), *Corpus Tools* (78), Named Entity Recognizers (77), *Language Resources/Technologies Infrastructures (62), Machine Translation Tools (61)* and Evaluation Tools (59), which were all suggested by the *LRE Map* designers (the new Types are in italics).

As already mentioned, the Language Matrices can also serve to identify the trends in terms of new tools or data for addressing emerging technologies and innovative applications. In this case, the authors introduced a Type which was not provided by the *LRE Map* designers and the corresponding LR may appear for a single language, or for a limited set of languages. It is therefore up to the person conducting the analysis to decide whether it was a category which already existed in the suggested list with a different wording, a category which can be merged in a larger one, a category which was forgotten and should be added, or a new Type of LR appearing for one language, which may quickly adapt to others.

4.1.1 Multimodal/Multimedia Resources

The suggested Types are marked in bold characters, and the new ones in bold italics (Figs. 7, 8).

- The activity on Multimedia/Multimodal (MM) Resources is continuously increasing.

[10] http://www.meraka.org.za/nhn.

Table 2 Examples of largest and smallest presence of EU languages, and increase from 2010 to 2012

Year	Total	English	French	German	Spanish	Italian	Dutch	Estonian	Irish	Slovak	Maltese	EU Regional	Other Europe
2010	1,889	559 (29 %)	143 (7.5 %)	132 (7 %)	111 (6 %)	90 (5 %)	54 (3 %)	7 (0.4 %)	3 (0.3 %)	3 (0.2 %)	2 (0.1 %)	67 (3.5 %)	63 (3.4 %)
2012	5,218	1,364 (26 %)	286 (5.5 %)	265 (5 %)	222 (4.3 %)	158 (3 %)	110 (2 %)	23 (0.4 %)	5 (0.1 %)	9 (0.2 %)	4 (0.1 %)	103 (1.9 %)	293 (5.6 %)

	Bulgarian	Czech	Danish	Dutch	English	Estonian	Finnish	French	German	Greek	Hungarian	Irish	Italian	Latvian	Lithuanian	Maltese	Polish	Portuguese	Romanian	Slovak	Slovene	Spanish	Swedish	Other Europe	Asturian	Basque	Catalan	Galician	Arabic	Hindi	Japanese	Korean	Mandarin	Other	Multilingual	L.I.	N.A.	Total
Corpus	22	33	32	56	702	13	15	135	133	30	26	1	74	12	10	2	25	48	23	5	15	104	44	157	1	16	18	7	84	32	65	10	94	216	21	37	47	2365
Lexicon	12	12	4	15	162	3	3	46	30	5	7	0	28	1	1	0	13	11	12	2	5	27	11	50	0	9	8	3	22	8	26	2	27	93	5	9	10	682
Tagger/Parser	1	3	0	2	68	1	0	24	14	5	3	1	11	0	1	0	6	5	2	0	0	12	4	17	1	4	2	1	11	1	7	0	15	18	4	51	20	315
Annotation Tool	2	2	1	4	44	1	1	9	5	1	1	0	5	1	1	1	1	2	2	1	2	7	1	4	0	1	2	0	10	0	2	0	5	13	3	93	23	251
Evaluation Data	2	5	2	5	101	0	1	13	14	1	1	1	5	0	0	0	0	4	3	0	1	15	2	11	0	2	1	1	8	4	9	0	14	9	2	4	8	249
Ontology	1	2	0	7	44	0	1	9	6	3	0	0	6	0	2	0	1	3	3	0	0	9	0	7	0	0	0	0	2	0	7	1	7	6	4	32	9	172
Grammar / Language Model	3	1	2	2	20	0	2	8	8	0	1	0	2	1	0	1	3	1	1	1	1	7	3	5	0	0	1	0	1	1	0	0	2	9	0	7	6	100
Terminology	1	1	0	3	22	2	0	11	7	2	1	0	5	1	1	0	1	0	0	0	0	8	0	5	0	2	2	0	0	0	2	0	1	0	1	3	2	84
Representation-Annotation Standards/Best Practices	1	2	0	4	22	1	0	3	3	0	1	0	1	0	0	0	1	0	1	0	0	2	1	4	0	0	0	0	2	0	1	0	4	3	1	20	5	83
Corpus Tool	0	0	0	3	13	1	0	1	1	0	0	0	1	0	0	0	1	2	0	0	1	3	1	5	0	1	1	0	3	0	0	0	1	0	0	36	3	78
Named Entity Recognizer	0	1	0	2	23	0	0	4	4	1	0	0	2	0	0	0	0	2	0	0	0	2	0	3	0	1	0	0	4	0	4	1	3	7	5	6	2	77
Language Resources/ Technologies Infrastructure	1	2	1	2	7	0	0	1	3	1	1	0	4	0	0	0	1	1	0	0	1	3	3	2	0	2	1	0	1	0	2	2	3	1	2	13	1	62
Machine Translation Tool	1	1	2	0	6	1	0	1	3	1	0	0	0	1	1	0	0	0	1	0	1	2	0	4	0	1	1	0	1	1	1	1	1	6	1	17	4	61
Evaluation Tool	0	0	0	1	13	0	0	0	1	0	0	0	0	0	0	0	0	0	0	0	0	1	0	1	0	0	0	0	0	0	0	0	0	0	1	30	11	59
Total	48	68	46	110	1364	23	24	286	265	56	44	5	158	18	18	4	55	87	51	9	28	222	73	293	2	48	41	12	157	50	135	17	190	414	58	532	207	5218

Fig. 6 Complete matrix with all LR types (Ranked order. Only the ones with more than 50 citations appear)

- The MM Data is essentially constituted of Corpus (85 %),[11] Terminology and Ontology.
- The best-covered languages are English (30 % of the LR) and German (8 %).[12]
- Several MM tools are developed, including of course Annotation tools that are especially crucial for producing MM Resources. Those tools are mostly Language Independent.
- Beside Annotation tools, which are especially crucial for producing Multimedia/Multimodal Resources, new kinds of MM tools appear, such as Cross-lingual Information Retrieval ones, which go with the increasing activity on Voice-based Video Search, and tools for Language Learning applications.

[11] This percentage is related to the total number of resources of all types in all languages for that Modality and Type category.

[12] Similarly, this percentage is related to the total number of languages mentioned for that Modality and Type category, etc.

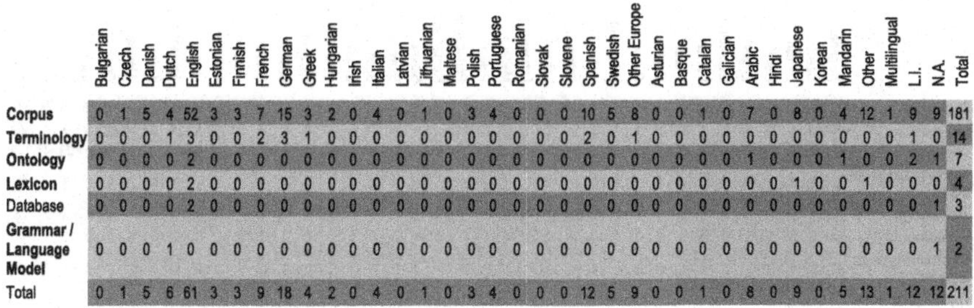

	Bulgarian	Czech	Danish	Dutch	English	Estonian	Finnish	French	German	Greek	Hungarian	Irish	Italian	Latvian	Lithuanian	Maltese	Polish	Portuguese	Romanian	Slovak	Slovene	Spanish	Swedish	Other Europe	Asturian	Basque	Catalan	Galician	Arabic	Hindi	Japanese	Korean	Mandarin	Other	Multilingual	L.I.	N.A.	Total
Corpus	0	1	5	4	52	3	3	7	15	3	2	0	4	0	1	0	3	4	0	0	0	10	5	8	0	0	1	0	7	0	8	0	4	12	1	9	9	181
Terminology	0	0	0	1	3	0	0	2	3	1	0	0	0	0	0	0	0	0	0	0	0	2	0	1	0	0	0	0	0	0	0	0	0	0	0	1	0	14
Ontology	0	0	0	0	2	0	0	0	0	0	0	0	0	0	0	0	0	0	0	0	0	0	0	0	0	0	0	0	1	0	0	0	1	0	0	2	1	7
Lexicon	0	0	0	0	2	0	0	0	0	0	0	0	0	0	0	0	0	0	0	0	0	0	0	0	0	0	0	0	0	0	1	0	0	1	0	0	0	4
Database	0	0	0	0	2	0	0	0	0	0	0	0	0	0	0	0	0	0	0	0	0	0	0	0	0	0	0	0	0	0	0	0	0	0	0	0	1	3
Grammar / Language Model	0	0	0	1	0	0	0	0	0	0	0	0	0	0	0	0	0	0	0	0	0	0	0	0	0	0	0	0	0	0	0	0	0	0	0	0	1	2
Total	0	1	5	6	61	3	3	9	18	4	2	0	4	0	1	0	3	4	0	0	0	12	5	9	0	0	1	0	8	0	9	0	5	13	1	12	12	211

Fig. 7 Multimodal/Multimedia Data (Ranked order)

	Bulgarian	Czech	Danish	Dutch	English	Estonian	Finnish	French	German	Greek	Hungarian	Irish	Italian	Latvian	Lithuanian	Maltese	Polish	Portuguese	Romanian	Slovak	Slovene	Spanish	Swedish	Other Europe	Asturian	Basque	Catalan	Galician	Arabic	Hindi	Japanese	Korean	Mandarin	Other	Multilingual	L.I.	N.A.	Total
Annotation Tool	0	0	0	0	4	0	0	1	1	0	0	0	1	0	0	0	0	0	0	0	0	1	0	0	0	0	0	0	0	0	0	0	2	0	0	18	6	34
Information Retrieval Tool	0	1	0	1	1	0	0	1	1	1	0	0	1	0	1	0	0	0	0	0	0	1	0	0	0	0	0	0	0	0	0	0	0	0	0	0	0	9
Multimedia language learning applications	0	1	0	0	1	0	1	1	1	0	1	0	0	0	0	0	1	1	1	0	0	0	0	0	0	0	0	0	0	0	0	0	0	0	0	0	0	9
Corpus Tool	0	0	0	0	1	0	0	0	0	0	0	0	0	0	0	0	0	0	0	0	0	0	0	1	0	0	0	0	0	0	0	0	0	0	0	4	1	7
Signal Processing/Feature Extraction	0	0	0	0	1	0	0	0	0	0	0	0	0	0	0	0	0	0	0	0	0	0	0	0	0	0	0	0	0	0	0	0	0	0	1	2	1	5
Tagger/Parser	0	0	0	0	1	0	0	1	1	0	0	0	1	0	0	0	0	0	0	0	0	1	0	0	0	0	0	0	0	0	0	0	0	0	0	0	0	5
Image Analyzer	0	0	0	0	0	0	0	0	0	0	0	0	0	0	0	0	0	0	0	0	0	0	0	0	0	0	0	0	0	0	0	0	0	0	0	0	2	2
Proficiency testing tool	0	0	0	0	1	0	0	0	0	0	0	0	0	0	0	0	0	0	0	0	0	0	0	0	0	0	0	0	0	0	1	0	0	0	0	0	0	2
Total	0	2	0	1	10	0	1	4	4	1	1	0	3	0	1	0	1	2	1	0	0	3	0	1	0	1	0	0	0	0	1	0	2	0	1	30	11	82

Fig. 8 Multimodal/Multimedia Tools (Ranked order. Only the ones with more than 1 citation appear)

4.1.2 Written Language Resources

- Written Language Resources constitute the largest part of the mentioned resources (Fig. 9).
- The Types of Written Language Data are mostly Corpus (65 %), Lexicon (22 %), Ontology, Grammar/Language Models and Terminology (more than 95 % all together), which were the Types suggested to the authors.
- The coverage varies greatly among languages. The most resourced languages are English (28 %!), French and German (about 6 % each), then Spanish, Italian, Dutch, Portuguese, Swedish, Bulgarian, Polish and Romanian. Among the less resourced ones (less than 1 %) are Estonian, Finnish, Latvian, Lithuanian, Slovak, Slovene, Maltese and Irish. Other European languages are mentioned and it is interesting to notice that Catalan and Basque are also now well resourced.
- Many Written Language tools are listed. The most common ones (Tagger/ Parser, Annotation Tools, Named Entity Recognizers, Corpus Tools, Machine Translation Tools, Tokenizers, Language Modeling Tools, Language Identifier), which were suggested in the questionnaire (the new ones are in bold italics), constitute 75 % of those tools.

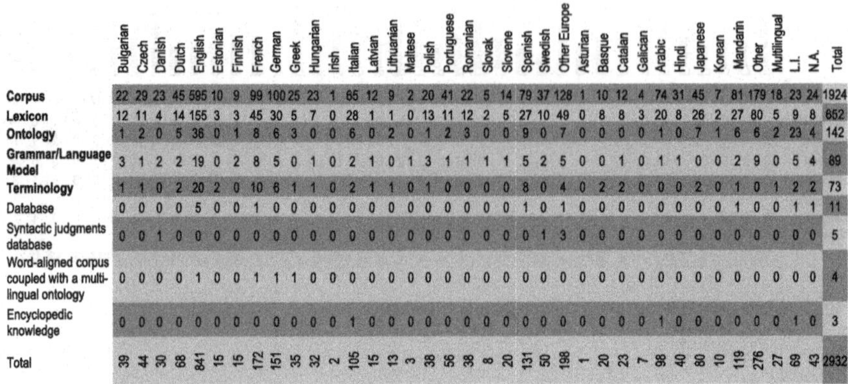

	Bulgarian	Czech	Danish	Dutch	English	Estonian	Finnish	French	German	Greek	Hungarian	Irish	Italian	Latvian	Lithuanian	Maltese	Polish	Portuguese	Romanian
Corpus	22	29	23	45	595	10	9	99	100	25	23	1	65	12	9	2	20	41	22
Lexicon	12	11	4	14	155	3	3	45	30	5	7	0	28	1	1	0	13	11	12
Ontology	1	2	0	5	36	0	1	8	6	3	0	0	6	0	2	0	1	2	3
Grammar/Language Model	3	1	2	2	19	0	2	8	5	0	1	0	2	1	0	1	3	1	1
Terminology	1	1	0	2	20	2	0	10	6	1	1	0	2	1	1	0	1	0	0
Database	0	0	0	0	5	0	0	1	0	0	0	0	0	0	0	0	0	0	0
Syntactic judgments database	0	0	1	0	0	0	0	0	0	0	0	0	0	0	0	0	0	0	0
Word-aligned corpus coupled with a multi-lingual ontology	0	0	0	0	1	0	0	1	1	1	0	0	0	0	0	0	0	0	0
Encyclopedic knowledge	0	0	0	0	0	0	0	0	0	0	0	0	1	0	0	0	0	0	0
Total	39	44	30	68	841	15	15	172	151	35	32	2	105	15	13	3	38	56	38

	Slovak	Slovene	Spanish	Swedish	Other Europe	Asturian	Basque	Catalan	Galician	Arabic	Hindi	Japanese	Korean	Mandarin	Other	Multilingual	L.I.	N.A.	Total
Corpus	5	14	79	37	128	1	10	12	4	74	31	45	7	81	179	18	23	24	1924
Lexicon	2	5	27	10	49	0	8	8	3	20	8	26	2	27	80	5	9	8	652
Ontology	0	0	9	0	7	0	0	0	0	1	0	7	1	6	6	2	23	4	142
Grammar/Language Model	1	1	5	2	5	0	0	1	0	1	1	0	0	2	9	0	5	4	89
Terminology	0	0	8	0	4	0	2	2	0	0	0	2	0	1	0	1	2	2	73
Database	0	0	1	0	1	0	0	0	0	0	0	0	0	1	0	0	1	1	11
Syntactic judgments database	0	0	0	1	3	0	0	0	0	0	0	0	0	0	0	0	0	0	5
Word-aligned corpus coupled with a multi-lingual ontology	0	0	0	0	0	0	0	0	0	0	0	0	0	0	0	0	0	0	4
Encyclopedic knowledge	0	0	0	0	0	0	0	0	0	1	0	0	0	0	0	0	1	0	3
Total	8	20	131	50	198	1	20	23	7	98	40	80	10	119	276	27	69	43	2932

Fig. 9 Written Language Data (Ranked order. Only the ones with more than 2 citations appear)

- Apart from those most common Written Language tools, there exists a long tail of tools for various purposes, some corresponding to new trends in research and applications (Reasoner, Knowledge representation tool, Frequent itemset mining, Text simplification tool, etc.).
- The most covered languages are English (20 % (it was 25 % in 2010)), French German, Spanish and Italian. Many are poorly resourced, although many tools are Language Independent (Fig. 10).

4.1.3 Spoken Language Resources

- The Spoken Language Data that are listed are less numerous than for Written Language. They are also mostly constituted by the types of data that were suggested (corpus (90 %), Lexicon and Grammar/Language Models). The best-covered languages are English (24 %), French, Spanish, German and Dutch (Figs. 11, 12).
- The Spoken Language tools are also less numerous than for Written Language, with a pre-eminence of Corpus Tools, Speech Recognizer/Transcriber, Annotation tools, Text-to-speech Synthesizer, Signal processing/Feature extraction, Tagger/Parser that were suggested (the new ones are in bold italics). Most of those tools are language-independent.
- Tools for Computer Aided Language Learning (CALL) are a new trend within Spoken Language tools.

4.1.4 Evaluation Resources

Evaluation resources (Data, Tools, Methodologies and Packages) exist for some languages, but by far, not for all. English is especially well served (n.b. We didn't make any distinction between British English and American English) (40 %), then

	Bulgarian	Czech	Danish	Dutch	English	Estonian	Finnish	French	German	Greek	Hungarian	Irish	Italian	Latvian	Lithuanian	Maltese	Polish	Portuguese	Romanian	Slovak	Slovene	Spanish	Swedish	Other Europe	Asturian	Basque	Catalan	Galician	Arabic	Hindi	Japanese	Korean	Mandarin	Other	Multilingual	L.I.	N.A.	Total
Tagger/Parser	1	3	0	3	64	1	0	23	10	5	3	1	10	0	1	0	5	5	2	0	0	11	4	17	1	4	2	1	10	1	8	0	13	18	4	49	17	297
Annotation Tool	2	2	1	4	37	1	1	8	4	1	1	0	4	1	1	1	1	2	2	1	2	6	1	3	0	1	2	0	9	0	1	0	3	13	3	60	11	190
Named Entity Recognizer	0	1	0	2	23	0	0	4	4	1	0	0	2	0	0	0	0	2	0	0	0	2	0	3	0	1	0	0	4	0	4	1	3	7	5	6	1	76
Corpus Tool	0	0	0	3	11	1	0	1	1	0	0	0	1	0	0	0	1	2	0	0	1	3	1	3	0	1	1	0	4	0	0	0	0	0	0	29	1	65
Machine Translation Tool	1	1	2	0	8	1	0	2	4	1	0	0	0	1	1	0	0	0	1	0	1	2	0	4	0	1	1	0	1	1	1	1	1	6	1	18	3	65
Tokenizer	0	0	0	0	2	0	0	0	0	0	0	1	1	0	0	0	0	0	0	0	0	2	0	0	0	0	2	0	0	0	0	0	4	3	0	4	3	22
Language Modeling Tool	1	0	0	1	2	0	0	0	1	0	0	0	0	0	0	0	0	0	0	0	0	0	0	1	0	0	0	0	0	0	0	0	1	0	0	10	2	19
Language Identifier	0	0	0	0	0	0	0	0	0	0	0	0	0	0	0	0	0	0	0	0	0	0	0	2	0	1	0	0	1	0	0	0	0	7	1	2	0	14
Coreference Resolution Tool	0	0	0	0	5	0	0	0	2	0	0	0	3	0	0	0	0	0	0	0	0	1	0	0	0	0	1	0	0	0	0	0	0	0	0	0	1	13
Terminology Tool	0	0	0	0	2	0	0	2	1	1	0	0	0	1	0	0	0	0	0	0	1	1	0	1	0	0	0	0	0	0	0	0	1	0	0	2	0	13
Lexicon Tool	0	0	0	0	2	0	0	0	0	0	0	0	0	0	0	0	0	0	0	0	0	0	0	0	0	0	0	0	0	1	2	0	0	1	0	4	0	10
Word Sense Disambiguator	0	0	0	0	5	0	0	0	1	0	0	0	0	0	0	0	0	0	0	0	0	0	0	0	0	1	0	0	0	0	0	0	0	0	0	2	1	10
Information Retrieval Tool	0	0	0	0	2	0	0	0	0	0	0	0	0	0	0	0	0	0	0	0	0	1	0	0	0	1	0	0	0	0	0	0	0	0	0	4	1	9
Morphological Analyzer/Generator	0	0	0	0	0	0	0	0	5	0	0	0	0	0	0	0	0	0	0	0	0	0	0	2	0	0	0	0	1	0	0	0	0	0	0	1	0	9
NLP Development Tool	0	0	0	0	2	0	0	0	1	1	0	0	2	0	0	0	0	0	0	0	0	0	0	1	0	0	0	0	0	0	1	0	0	0	0	0	0	8
Search Engine	0	0	0	0	1	0	0	0	0	0	0	0	1	0	0	0	0	0	0	0	0	0	0	0	0	0	0	0	0	0	3	0	0	0	0	2	0	7
Summarization Tool	0	0	0	0	1	0	0	0	0	0	0	0	0	0	0	0	0	0	0	0	0	1	0	0	0	0	1	0	0	0	1	0	0	0	0	1	2	7
Ontology Tool	0	0	0	0	1	0	0	0	0	0	0	0	0	0	0	0	0	0	0	0	0	1	0	0	0	0	0	0	0	0	0	0	0	0	1	2	0	5
Sentiment Analysis Tool	0	0	0	0	1	0	0	1	1	0	0	0	0	0	0	0	0	0	0	0	0	0	0	0	0	0	0	0	0	0	0	0	0	0	0	1	1	5
Signal Processing/Feature Extraction	0	0	0	0	0	0	0	0	0	0	0	0	0	0	0	0	0	0	0	0	0	0	0	0	0	0	0	0	0	0	0	0	0	0	0	5	0	5
Transliterator	0	0	0	0	0	0	0	0	0	0	0	0	0	0	0	0	0	0	0	0	0	0	0	0	0	0	0	0	0	0	0	0	0	4	0	1	0	5
Wikipedia Tool	0	0	0	0	1	0	0	0	1	0	0	0	0	0	0	0	0	0	0	0	0	0	0	0	0	0	0	0	0	0	0	0	0	0	0	2	1	5
Chunker	0	0	0	0	1	0	0	1	0	0	0	0	0	0	0	0	0	0	1	0	0	0	0	0	0	0	0	0	0	0	0	0	0	0	0	0	1	4
Machine Learning Tool	0	0	0	0	1	0	0	0	0	0	0	0	0	0	0	0	0	0	0	0	0	0	0	0	0	0	0	0	0	0	0	0	0	0	0	2	1	4
Speech Recognizer/Transcriber	0	0	0	0	0	0	0	0	1	0	0	0	0	0	0	0	0	0	0	0	0	0	0	0	0	0	0	0	0	0	0	0	0	1	0	2	0	4
Stemmer	0	0	0	0	0	0	0	1	1	0	0	0	1	0	0	0	0	0	0	0	0	0	0	0	0	0	0	0	0	0	0	0	0	1	0	0	0	4
Concordancer	0	0	0	0	1	0	0	1	0	0	0	0	0	0	0	0	0	0	0	0	0	0	0	0	0	0	0	0	0	0	0	0	0	0	0	1	0	3
Converter	0	0	0	0	0	0	0	0	1	0	0	0	0	0	0	0	0	0	0	0	0	0	0	0	0	0	0	0	0	0	0	0	0	0	0	1	1	3
Open-word-;-concept dependency reprezentations and selectional preferences	0	0	0	0	2	0	0	0	0	0	0	0	0	0	0	0	0	0	0	0	0	0	0	0	0	0	0	0	0	0	0	0	0	0	0	1	0	3
Web Service	0	0	0	0	0	0	0	0	0	0	0	0	0	0	0	0	0	0	0	0	0	0	0	0	0	0	0	0	0	0	0	0	0	0	0	3	0	3
Total	5	7	3	14	192	4	1	45	42	13	4	2	26	3	3	1	7	13	8	1	5	33	6	38	1	13	10	1	31	5	22	2	27	65	16	260	58	985

Fig. 10 Written Language Tools (Ranked order. Only the ones with more than 2 citations appear)

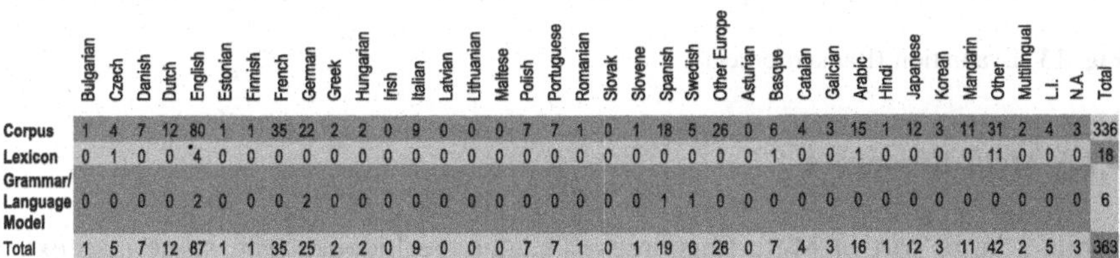

	Bulgarian	Czech	Danish	Dutch	English	Estonian	Finnish	French	German	Greek	Hungarian	Irish	Italian	Latvian	Lithuanian	Maltese	Polish	Portuguese	Romanian	Slovak	Slovene	Spanish	Swedish	Other Europe	Asturian	Basque	Catalan	Galician	Arabic	Hindi	Japanese	Korean	Mandarin	Other	Multilingual	L.I.	N.A.	Total
Corpus	1	4	7	12	80	1	1	35	22	2	2	0	9	0	0	0	7	7	1	0	1	18	5	26	0	6	4	3	15	1	12	3	11	31	2	4	3	336
Lexicon	0	1	0	0	4	0	0	0	0	0	0	0	0	0	0	0	0	0	0	0	0	0	0	0	0	1	0	0	1	0	0	0	0	11	0	0	0	18
Grammar/ Language Model	0	0	0	0	2	0	0	0	2	0	0	0	0	0	0	0	0	0	0	0	0	1	1	0	0	0	0	0	0	0	0	0	0	0	0	0	0	6
Total	1	5	7	12	87	1	1	35	25	2	2	0	9	0	0	0	7	7	1	0	1	19	6	26	0	7	4	3	16	1	12	3	11	42	2	5	3	363

Fig. 11 Spoken Language Data (Ranked order. Only the ones with more than 1 citation appear)

Spanish, French, German, Portuguese, Italian and Dutch, all countries which have or had Language Technologies evaluation activities and programs. But many of such LR are Language Independent. Almost all the LRs fall in a suggested Type, except the one on Synthetic Sign Language performance (Fig. 13).

	Bulgarian	Czech	Danish	Dutch	English	Estonian	Finnish	French	German	Greek	Hungarian	Irish	Italian	Latvian	Lithuanian	Maltese	Polish	Portuguese	Romanian	Slovak	Slovene	Spanish	Swedish	Other Europe	Asturian	Basque	Catalan	Galician	Arabic	Hindi	Japanese	Korean	Chinese Mandarin	Other	Multilingual	L.I.	N.A.	Total
Corpus Tool	0	0	1	0	3	0	0	0	0	0	0	0	0	0	0	0	0	0	0	0	0	0	1	4	0	0	0	0	2	0	0	0	0	0	0	4	0	15
Speech Recognizer / Transcriber	0	0	0	0	3	0	0	0	2	0	1	0	0	0	0	0	0	1	0	0	0	1	0	0	0	1	0	0	0	0	0	0	0	0	0	6	0	15
Annotation Tool	0	0	0	1	1	0	0	0	0	0	0	0	0	0	0	0	0	0	0	0	0	0	0	1	0	0	0	0	0	0	1	0	0	0	0	8	2	14
Text-to-Speech Synthesizer	0	0	0	0	4	0	0	0	2	0	0	0	0	0	0	0	0	0	0	0	0	0	0	3	0	1	0	0	0	0	0	0	0	3	0	0	0	13
Signal Processing/Feature Extraction	0	1	0	0	0	0	0	0	0	0	0	0	0	0	0	0	0	0	1	0	0	0	0	0	0	0	0	0	0	0	0	0	0	0	0	3	2	7
CALL System	0	0	0	1	1	0	0	1	1	0	0	0	0	0	0	0	0	0	0	0	0	0	1	0	0	0	0	0	0	0	1	0	0	0	0	0	0	6
Tagger / Parser	0	0	0	0	1	0	0	1	1	0	0	0	0	0	0	0	0	0	0	0	0	1	0	0	0	0	0	0	0	0	0	0	0	0	0	0	0	4
Prosodic Analyzer	0	0	0	0	0	0	0	0	0	0	0	0	0	0	0	0	0	0	0	0	0	0	0	0	0	0	0	0	0	0	0	0	0	0	0	3	0	3
Language Modeling Tool	0	0	0	0	0	0	0	0	0	0	0	0	0	0	0	0	0	0	0	0	0	0	0	0	0	0	0	0	0	0	0	0	0	0	0	2	0	2
Speaker Recognizer	0	0	0	0	0	0	0	0	0	0	0	0	0	0	0	0	0	0	0	0	0	0	0	0	0	0	0	0	0	0	0	0	0	0	0	2	0	2
Spoken Dialogue Tool	0	0	0	0	0	0	0	0	1	0	0	0	0	0	0	0	0	0	0	0	0	0	0	0	0	0	0	0	0	0	0	0	0	0	0	1	0	2
Tokenizer	0	0	0	0	1	0	0	0	0	0	0	0	0	0	0	0	0	0	0	0	0	0	0	0	0	0	0	0	0	0	0	0	0	0	0	1	0	2
Total	0	1	1	2	15	0	0	2	7	0	1	0	0	0	0	0	0	1	1	0	0	2	2	8	0	3	0	0	2	0	2	0	0	3	0	33	4	90

Fig. 12 Spoken Language Tools (Ranked order. Only the ones with more than 1 citation appear)

	Bulgarian	Czech	Danish	Dutch	English	Estonian	Finnish	French	German	Greek	Hungarian	Irish	Italian	Latvian	Lithuanian	Maltese	Polish	Portuguese	Romanian	Slovak	Slovene	Spanish	Swedish	Other Europe	Asturian	Basque	Catalan	Galician	Arabic	Hindi	Japanese	Korean	Mandarin	Other	Multilingual	L.I.	N.A.	Total
Evaluation Data	2	5	2	5	109	0	1	14	16	1	1	1	6	0	0	0	0	5	3	0	1	16	2	11	0	3	2	2	8	4	9	0	14	9	2	4	8	266
Evaluation Tool	0	0	0	1	13	0	0	0	1	0	0	0	0	0	0	0	0	0	0	0	0	1	0	1	0	0	0	0	0	0	0	0	0	0	1	31	11	60
Evaluation Package	0	0	1	0	14	0	0	2	0	0	0	0	0	0	0	0	0	2	0	0	0	1	0	0	0	0	0	0	2	0	0	0	2	0	0	4	1	29
Evaluation Methodology / Standards / Guidelines	0	0	0	0	7	0	0	1	0	0	0	0	0	0	0	0	0	0	0	0	0	0	1	0	0	0	0	0	1	0	0	0	0	0	0	7	1	18
Synthetic Sign Language performance	0	0	0	0	0	0	0	0	0	0	0	0	0	0	0	0	0	0	0	0	0	0	0	0	0	0	0	0	0	0	0	0	0	0	0	0	1	1
Total	2	5	3	6	143	0	1	17	17	1	1	1	6	0	0	0	0	7	3	0	1	18	3	12	0	3	2	2	11	4	9	0	16	9	3	46	22	374

Fig. 13 Evaluation (Ranked order)

4.1.5 Meta-Resources

While a large part of Meta-Resources is Language Independent, some also exist, and especially Standards and Metadata, which are specific for a given language, and, here also, mostly for English (18 %). The strong presence of the new Type "Language Resources/Technologies Infrastructure" expresses a large activity in this area (Fig. 14).

	Bulgarian	Czech	Danish	Dutch	English	Estonian	Finnish	French	German	Greek	Hungarian	Irish	Italian	Latvian	Lithuanian	Maltese	Polish	Portuguese	Romanian	Slovak	Slovene	Spanish	Swedish	Other Europe	Asturian	Basque	Catalan	Galician	Arabic	Hindi	Japanese	Korean	Mandarin	Other	Multilingual	L.I.	N.A.	Total
Representation-Annotation Standards/Best Practices	1	2	0	4	22	1	0	3	3	0	1	0	1	0	0	0	2	0	1	0	0	2	1	4	0	0	0	0	2	0	1	0	4	3	1	20	5	84
Language Resources /Technologies Infrastructure	1	2	1	2	7	0	0	1	3	1	1	0	4	0	0	0	1	1	0	0	1	3	3	2	0	2	1	0	1	0	2	2	3	1	2	14	1	63
Representation-Annotation Formalism /Guidelines	0	0	0	0	2	0	0	2	0	0	0	0	0	0	0	0	0	0	0	0	0	0	0	1	0	0	0	0	0	0	0	0	1	7	0	4	0	17
Metadata	0	0	0	0	1	0	0	1	0	0	0	0	0	0	0	0	0	0	0	0	0	1	0	0	0	0	0	0	0	0	0	0	0	0	2	5	2	12
Course material	0	0	0	0	1	0	0	1	0	0	0	0	0	0	0	0	1	0	0	0	0	1	0	0	0	0	0	0	0	0	0	0	0	0	0	1	0	5
Format description	0	0	0	0	0	0	0	0	0	0	0	0	0	0	0	0	0	0	0	0	0	0	0	0	0	0	0	0	0	0	0	0	0	0	0	2	0	2
Repository of NLG task materials	0	0	0	0	2	0	0	0	0	0	0	0	0	0	0	0	0	0	0	0	0	0	0	0	0	0	0	0	0	0	0	0	0	0	0	0	0	2
Total	2	4	1	6	35	1	0	8	7	1	2	0	5	0	0	0	4	1	1	0	1	7	4	7	0	2	1	0	3	0	3	2	8	11	5	50	10	192

Fig. 14 Meta-resources (Ranked order. Only the ones with more than 1 citation appear)

4.1.6 Sign Languages

This constitutes a new analysis of the *LRE Map* for Sign Languages. 21 different Sign Languages are mentioned in the *LRE Map*. The data is mostly constituted by Corpus (50 %), while Annotation Tools are the most numerous (12 %). The American Sign Language is the most studied Sign Language (20 %), followed by the French Sign Language (17 %) (Fig. 15).

4.2 Analysis of a Language Resource Impact Factor (LRIF)

While it was mandatory to count only once a LR in order to determine the language coverage, it is necessary here to count the number of time a LR is cited, but only once independently of the number of languages it covers. The analysis provides an interesting panorama of the most popular LR. However, it appears that the way we consider a LR, either globally as a family or making a distinction across the various versions (over time, or as subparts), may greatly modify this Hit Parade.

Here also, the existence and use of a Persistent and Unique Identifier (LRID) would greatly help.

4.2.1 Data

The most cited Data is Wordnet, followed by Europarl, Wikipedia, Penn Treebank, Arabic Treebank (ATB) and the British National Corpus (BNC) (Fig. 16).

	Al-Sayyid Bedouin Sign Language	American Sign Language	Arabic Sign Language	Australian Sign Language	British Sign Language	Catalan Sign Language	Chinese Sign Language	Czech Sign Language	Dutch Sign Language	Finnish Sign Language	French Sign Language	German Sign Language	Greek Sign Language	Irish Sign Language	Italian Sign Language	Japanese Sign Language	Russian Sign Language	South African Sign Language	Spanish Sign Language	Swedish Sign Language	Swiss German Sign Language	Sign Languages in General	Not Applicable	Total
3D toolkit	0	0	0	0	0	0	0	0	0	0	0	0	0	0	0	0	0	0	0	0	0	0	1	1
Annotation Tool	1	1	2	0	1	0	0	0	0	0	0	1	0	1	0	0	0	0	1	0	0	3	0	11
Corpus	0	10	0	1	2	2	1	0	1	3	10	7	1	2	2	0	0	0	3	0	0	0	1	46
Corpus Tool	0	1	0	0	0	0	0	0	0	0	1	0	0	0	1	0	0	0	0	0	0	1	0	4
E-Learning	0	0	0	0	0	0	0	0	0	0	0	0	0	0	0	1	0	0	0	0	0	0	0	1
Evaluation Data	0	0	0	0	1	0	0	0	0	0	0	0	0	0	0	0	0	0	0	0	0	0	0	1
Language Identifier	0	0	0	0	0	0	0	0	0	0	0	0	0	0	0	0	0	0	0	0	0	1	0	1
Lexicon	0	2	0	0	1	0	0	1	0	0	0	0	0	0	0	0	2	0	0	2	1	0	0	9
Ontology	0	0	0	0	0	0	0	0	0	0	2	0	0	0	0	0	0	0	0	0	0	2	0	4
Representation-Annotation Standards / Best Practices	0	2	0	0	1	0	0	0	0	0	0	0	0	0	0	0	0	0	0	0	0	0	0	3
Signal Processing / Feature Extraction	0	1	0	0	2	0	0	0	0	0	2	0	0	0	0	0	0	0	0	0	0	0	0	5
Synthetic Sign Language performance	0	0	0	0	0	0	0	0	0	0	0	0	0	0	0	0	0	0	0	0	0	0	1	1
Tagger/Parser	0	0	0	0	0	0	1	0	0	0	0	0	0	0	0	0	0	1	0	0	0	0	0	2
Total	1	17	2	1	8	2	2	1	1	3	15	8	1	3	3	1	2	1	4	2	1	7	3	89

Fig. 15 Language Resources for Sign Languages (Alphabetical order)

	Bulgarian	Czech	Danish	Dutch	English	Estonian	Finnish	French	German	Greek	Hungarian	Irish	Italian	Latvian	Lithuanian	Maltese	Polish	Portuguese	Romanian	Slovak	Slovene	Spanish	Swedish	Other Europe	Asturian	Basque	Catalan	Galician	Arabic	Hindi	Japanese	Korean	Mandarin	Other	Multilingual	L.I.	N.A.	LRIF*
WordNet	0	0	0	0	46	0	0	0	0	0	0	0	0	0	0	0	0	0	0	0	0	0	0	0	0	0	0	0	0	0	0	0	0	0	0	0	0	47
Europarl	1	0	13	16	38	0	12	26	21	11	0	0	12	0	0	0	0	13	0	0	0	20	20	0	0	0	0	0	0	0	0	0	0	0	1	0	0	44
Wikipedia	0	0	0	1	13	0	0	5	3	0	0	0	1	0	0	0	0	0	0	0	0	2	0	1	0	0	0	0	0	0	0	0	0	0	1	3	3	22
Penn Treebank	0	0	0	0	15	0	0	0	0	0	0	0	0	0	0	0	0	0	0	0	0	0	0	0	0	0	0	0	1	0	0	0	1	0	0	0	0	15
Arabic Treebank (ATB)	0	0	0	0	0	0	0	0	0	0	0	0	0	0	0	0	0	0	0	0	0	0	0	0	0	0	0	0	12	0	0	0	0	0	0	0	1	13
British National Corpus (BNC)	0	0	0	0	13	0	0	0	0	0	0	0	0	0	0	0	0	0	0	0	0	0	0	0	0	0	0	0	0	0	0	0	0	0	0	0	0	13
Penn Discourse Treebank	0	0	0	0	10	0	0	0	0	0	0	0	0	0	0	0	0	0	0	0	0	0	0	0	0	0	0	0	0	0	0	0	0	0	0	0	0	10
Sparse data	30	45	37	77	942	18	20	182	174	29	34	2	107	9	12	3	36	46	32	8	19	138	55	210	1	26	21	8	103	40	120	13	131	343	31	87	74	2038

Fig. 16 LRIF for Data (Ranked order. Only the ones with more than 5 citations appear)

4.2.2 Tools

The most cited Tools are the Stanford Parser, followed by Moses, the Tree Tagger, GIZA++, MaltParser, the ELAN Annotation Tool and the SRI Language Modeling Toolkit (SRILM) (Fig. 17).

4.2.3 Evaluation

The BLEU and ROUGE measures, Aurora and the Document Understanding Conference (DUC) are the most cited Evaluation resources (n.b.: DUC is cited both as such and as its 2002 version. Adding them would put DUC at the first rank) (Fig. 18).

	Bulgarian	Czech	Danish	Dutch	English	Estonian	Finnish	French	German	Greek	Hungarian	Irish	Italian	Latvian	Lithuanian	Maltese	Polish	Portuguese	Romanian	Slovak	Slovene	Spanish	Swedish	Other Europe	Asturian	Basque	Catalan	Galician	Arabic	Hindi	Japanese	Korean	Mandarin	Other	Multilingual	L.I.	N.A.	LRIF*
Stanford Parser	0	0	0	0	20	0	0	0	1	0	0	0	0	0	0	0	0	0	0	0	0	0	0	0	0	0	0	0	1	0	0	0	3	0	0	2	1	24
Moses	0	0	0	0	0	0	0	0	0	0	0	0	0	0	0	0	0	0	0	0	0	0	0	0	0	0	0	0	0	0	0	0	0	0	0	21	2	23
TreeTagger	1	0	0	2	15	0	0	8	5	0	0	0	3	0	0	0	0	1	0	0	0	3	0	1	0	0	0	0	0	0	0	0	1	0	0	5	0	22
GIZA++	0	0	0	0	0	0	0	0	0	0	0	0	0	0	0	0	0	0	0	0	0	0	0	0	0	0	0	0	0	0	0	0	0	0	0	16	0	16
MaltParser	0	0	0	0	3	0	0	1	1	0	0	0	0	0	0	0	0	0	0	0	0	0	2	0	0	0	0	0	0	0	0	0	2	0	0	9	1	14
ELAN annotation tool	0	0	0	0	2	0	0	0	2	0	0	0	0	0	0	0	0	0	0	0	0	0	0	0	0	0	0	0	1	0	0	0	0	0	0	4	1	13
SRI Language Modeling Toolkit (SRILM)	0	0	0	0	0	0	0	0	0	0	0	0	0	0	0	0	0	0	0	0	0	0	0	0	0	0	0	0	0	0	0	0	0	0	0	9	3	12
Sparse data	4	7	3	16	179	3	2	34	34	4	6	2	23	2	3	1	8	10	6	1	5	23	6	37	0	15	5	0	28	5	21	2	23	60	13	312	97	793

Fig. 17 LRIF for Tools (Ranked order. Only the ones with more than 10 citations appear)

	Bulgarian	Czech	Danish	Dutch	English	Estonian	Finnish	French	German	Greek	Hungarian	Irish	Italian	Latvian	Lithuanian	Maltese	Polish	Portuguese	Romanian	Slovak	Slovene	Spanish	Swedish	Other Europe	Asturian	Basque	Catalan	Galician	Arabic	Hindi	Japanese	Korean	Mandarin	Other	Multilingual	L.I.	N.A.	LRIF*
BLEU	0	0	0	0	0	0	0	0	0	0	0	0	0	0	0	0	0	0	0	0	0	0	0	0	0	0	0	0	0	0	0	0	0	0	0	5	1	6
ROUGE	0	0	0	0	0	0	0	0	0	0	0	0	0	0	0	0	0	0	0	0	0	0	0	0	0	0	0	0	0	0	0	0	0	0	0	5	1	6
Document Understanding Conference (DUC)	0	0	0	0	5	0	0	0	0	0	0	0	0	0	0	0	0	0	0	0	0	0	0	0	0	0	0	0	0	0	0	0	0	0	0	0	0	5
AURORA Project Database 2.0 - Evaluation Package	0	0	0	0	3	0	0	0	0	0	0	0	0	0	0	0	0	0	0	0	0	0	0	0	0	0	0	0	0	0	0	0	0	0	0	0	0	3
DUC 2002	0	0	0	0	3	0	0	0	0	0	0	0	0	0	0	0	0	0	0	0	0	0	0	0	0	0	0	0	0	0	0	0	0	0	0	0	0	3
20 Newsgroups	0	0	0	0	2	0	0	0	0	0	0	0	0	0	0	0	0	0	0	0	0	0	0	0	0	0	0	0	0	0	0	0	0	0	0	0	0	2
Emo	0	0	0	0	0	0	0	0	0	0	0	0	0	0	0	0	0	0	0	0	0	2	0	0	0	0	0	0	0	0	0	0	0	0	0	0	0	2
Evaluation des Systèmes de Transcription enrichie d'Émissions Radiophoniques - ESTER	0	0	0	0	0	0	0	2	0	0	0	0	0	0	0	0	0	0	0	0	0	0	0	0	0	0	0	0	0	0	0	0	0	0	0	0	0	2
GALE Phase 4 Chinese Parallel Word Alignment and Tagging Part 1	0	0	0	0	2	0	0	0	0	0	0	0	0	0	0	0	0	0	0	0	0	0	0	0	0	0	0	0	0	0	0	0	2	0	0	0	0	2
KALAKA-2	0	0	0	0	2	0	0	0	0	0	0	0	0	0	0	0	0	2	0	0	0	2	0	0	0	2	2	2	0	0	0	0	0	0	0	0	0	2
Reuters-21578	0	0	0	0	2	0	0	0	0	0	0	0	0	0	0	0	0	0	0	0	0	0	0	0	0	0	0	0	0	0	0	0	0	0	0	0	0	2
SIGA	0	0	0	0	0	0	0	0	0	0	0	0	0	0	0	0	0	0	0	0	0	0	0	0	0	0	0	0	0	0	0	0	0	0	0	0	2	2
TER	0	0	0	0	0	0	0	0	0	0	0	0	0	0	0	0	0	0	0	0	0	0	0	0	0	0	0	0	0	0	0	0	0	0	0	2	0	2
TREC_eval	0	0	0	0	0	0	0	0	0	0	0	0	0	0	0	0	0	0	0	0	0	0	0	0	0	0	0	0	0	0	0	0	0	0	0	2	0	2
Sparse data	2	4	2	5	117	0	1	14	15	1	1	1	5	0	0	0	0	5	3	0	1	12	2	10	0	1	0	0	10	4	9	0	13	7	2	35	17	211

Fig. 18 LRIF for Evaluation (Ranked order. Only the ones with more than 1 citation appear)

4.2.4 Meta-Resources

The ISOcat Data Category Registry (DCR), TectoMT, the Controlled Language in Crisis Management (CLCM) and the Text encoding Initiative (TEI) appear for Meta-Resources (Fig. 19).

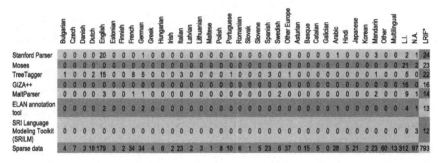

	Bulgarian	Czech	Danish	Dutch	English	Estonian	Finnish	French	German	Greek	Hungarian	Irish	Italian	Latvian	Lithuanian	Maltese	Polish	Portuguese	Romanian	Slovak	Slovene	Spanish	Swedish	Other Europe	Asturian	Basque	Catalan	Galician	Arabic	Hindi	Japanese	Korean	Mandarin	Other	Multilingual	L.I.	N.A.	LRIF*
ISOcat Data Category Registry (DCR)	0	0	0	0	0	0	0	0	0	0	0	0	0	0	0	0	0	0	0	0	0	0	0	0	0	0	0	0	0	0	0	0	0	0	1	2	1	4
TectoMT	0	1	0	0	1	0	0	0	1	0	0	0	0	0	0	0	0	0	0	0	0	0	0	0	0	0	0	0	0	0	0	0	0	0	0	2	0	3
Controlled Language in Crisis Management (CLCM)	0	0	0	0	2	0	0	0	0	0	0	0	0	0	0	0	0	0	0	0	0	0	0	0	0	0	0	0	0	0	0	0	0	0	0	0	0	2
TEI (Text Encoding Initiative)	0	0	0	0	0	0	0	0	0	0	0	0	0	0	0	0	0	0	0	0	0	0	0	0	0	0	0	0	0	0	0	0	0	0	0	2	0	2
Sparse data	2	3	1	6	31	1	0	8	6	1	2	0	4	0	0	0	4	1	1	0	1	7	4	7	0	2	1	0	3	0	3	2	8	11	4	38	6	100

Fig. 19 LRIF for Meta-resources (Ranked. Only the ones with more than 1 citation appear)

	Aragonese	Asturian	Basque	Breton	Catalan	Corsican	Dreents	Faroese	Frisian	Galician	Limburgan	Lombard	Low German	Lule Saami	Luxembourgish	North Saami	Norwegian Bokmal	Norwegian Ny-	Occitan	Romansh	Scottish Gaelic	Scots	Sicilian	South Saami	Swiss German	Venetian	Welsh	Total
Tool																												
AWAdb	0	0	1	0	0	0	0	0	0	0	0	0	0	0	0	0	0	0	0	0	0	0	0	0	0	0	0	1
AhoTTS	0	0	1	0	0	0	0	0	0	0	0	0	0	0	0	0	0	0	0	0	0	0	0	0	0	0	0	1
Eihera	0	0	1	0	0	0	0	0	0	0	0	0	0	0	0	0	0	0	0	0	0	0	0	0	0	0	0	1
Fonema TTS front end	0	0	0	0	0	0	0	0	0	0	0	0	0	0	0	0	1	0	0	0	0	0	0	0	0	0	0	1
FreeLing	0	1	0	0	0	0	0	0	0	1	0	0	0	0	0	0	0	0	0	0	0	0	0	0	0	0	1	3
Giellatekno parser	0	0	0	0	0	0	0	1	0	0	0	0	0	1	0	1	0	0	0	0	0	0	0	1	0	0	0	4
Google AJAX Language API	0	0	1	0	0	0	0	0	0	0	0	0	0	0	0	0	0	0	0	0	0	0	0	0	0	0	0	1
Google Translate	0	0	0	0	0	0	0	0	0	0	0	0	0	0	0	0	0	0	0	0	0	0	0	0	0	0	1	1
Heart of Gold	0	0	0	0	0	0	0	0	0	0	0	0	0	0	0	0	1	0	0	0	0	0	0	0	0	0	0	1
Ihardetsi	0	0	1	0	0	0	0	0	0	0	0	0	0	0	0	0	0	0	0	0	0	0	0	0	0	0	0	1
Matxin	0	0	1	0	0	0	0	0	0	0	0	0	0	0	0	0	0	0	0	0	0	0	0	0	0	0	0	1
Morfeus	0	0	1	0	0	0	0	0	0	0	0	0	0	0	0	0	0	0	0	0	0	0	0	0	0	0	0	1
RelaxCor	0	0	0	0	1	0	0	0	0	0	0	0	0	0	0	0	0	0	0	0	0	0	0	0	0	0	0	1
VenPro	0	0	0	0	0	0	0	0	0	0	0	0	0	0	0	0	0	0	0	0	0	0	0	0	0	1	0	1
Vocon3200 Basque	0	0	1	0	0	0	0	0	0	0	0	0	0	0	0	0	0	0	0	0	0	0	0	0	0	0	0	1
WSD-IXA	0	0	1	0	0	0	0	0	0	0	0	0	0	0	0	0	0	0	0	0	0	0	0	0	0	0	0	1
apertium-es-an	1	0	0	0	0	0	0	0	0	0	0	0	0	0	0	0	0	0	0	0	0	0	0	0	0	0	0	1
iula2standoff	0	0	0	0	1	0	0	0	0	0	0	0	0	0	0	0	0	0	0	0	0	0	0	0	0	0	0	1
Total	3	2	47	3	10	1	2	5	2	12	1	1	1	1	2	1	21	2	1	3	1	1	1	1	1	3	4	133

Fig. 20 Extract from the language matrix giving the existing Language Resources for European Regional and Minority languages: some of the tools and the total of the existing LRs in the *LRE Map*

4.3 *Use of the Language Matrices to Study Less-Resourced Languages*

Language Matrices were also used to study the situation of Less-Resourced Languages, including Regional, Minority and Endangered languages (Soria and Mariani 2013; del Gratta et al. 2014). In that case, the goal was to directly identify the list of resources existing for a selection of languages, and the Language Matrix software has been adapted in order to serve the needs of this new task (Fig. 20).

Table 3 Status of the 30 languages studied in the white papers in terms of Language Resources, and comparison with the actual number of Language Resources existing in the *LRE Map*

Excellent support	Good support	Moderate support	Fragmentary support	Weak/no support
	English (1364)	*Czech (68)* Dutch (110) French (286) German (265) *Hungarian (44)* Italian (158) *Polish (55)* Spanish (222) *Swedish (73)*	Basque (48) Bulgarian (48) Catalan (41) Croatian (NA) Danish (46) Estonian (23) Finnish (26) *Galician (12)* Greek (56) Norwegian (NA) Portuguese (87) Romanian (51) Serbian (NA) *Slovak (9)* Slovene (28)	Irish (5) Icelandic (NA) ***Latvian (18)*** ***Lithuanian (18)*** Maltese (4) Welsh (NA)

(N.B. The languages that haven't been analyzed yet are marked NA. The languages that seem to be overestimated are marked in italics and the languages that seem to be comparatively underestimated are marked in bold italics)

5 Use of the Language Matrices for the Language White Papers

The *Language White Papers* have been produced within the T4ME project.[13] They consist in a set of 30 volumes describing the status of 30 European languages in terms of use and of the availability of Language Technologies (Spoken Language Processing, Natural Language Processing and Machine Translation) and of Language Resources. A qualitative comparison of the status of those languages was then conducted in order to place them in 5 categories (Excellent support, Good support, Moderate support, Fragmentary support, Weak/No support). It resulted in the finding that no language is placed in the first category, that only English may be considered as benefiting from a "Good support", and that the 21 languages placed in the two last categories were in danger of "digital extinction" (Table 3).

The Language Matrices complemented the White Paper for the classification of Language Resources, as an objective and quantitative information. They showed that some languages were underestimated and others were overestimated (Table 3). This advocates for adding a sixth category for the categorization of the languages in terms of LR availability (Table 4).

[13] http://www.meta-net.eu/whitepapers/overview.

Table 4 Proposal for modifying the language table into 5 categories instead of 4

Excellent support	Good support (More than 500)	Relatively good support (From 100 to 500)	Moderate support (From 50 to 100)	Fragmentary support (From 20 to 50)	Weak support (Less than 20)	NA
	English (1364)	French (286) German (265) Spanish (222) Italian (158) Dutch (110)	*Portuguese (87)* *Swedish (73)* *Czech (68)* *Greek (56)* *Polish (55)* *Romanian (51)* *Hungarian (44)*	Basque (48) Bulgarian (48) Danish (46) Catalan (41) Slovene (28) Finnish (26) Estonian (23)	***Latvian (18)*** ***Lithuanian (18)*** *Galician (12)* *Slovak (9)* Irish (5) Maltese (4)	Croatian Norwegian Serbian Icelandic Welsh

6 Conclusions and Perspectives

The availability of data and tools such as the *LRE Map* and the Language Matrices help getting a clear picture of the Language Resource landscape and its changes.

Since the *LREC Map* produced at the LREC'2010 conference, more data have been harvested at upcoming conferences and have in turn fed the Language Matrices. It appears that English is still very present, but new languages are deploying, and the share of the English language is even slightly decreasing. Future developments will allow to increase the number of the identified LR trough more conferences, journals and catalogues, and to extend the range of languages being considered. It will help setting targets that all languages should reach in order to benefit from reliable Language Technologies.

The big challenge for the next steps will be the assignment of an international Persistent and Unique Identifier (LRID or ISLRN) for all LR, which will facilitate the naming process, and will allow for tracking the use of LR in papers and their enrichment or modification, and for the computation of a *Language Resource Impact Factor* (LRIF), which could assess the popularity and usefulness of Language Resources over time, and would recognize the merits of their producers. This process will need an international action, which includes technical, organizational and political dimensions.

Acknowledgments This paper results from the studies conducted within the EC projects FLaReNet (Grant Agreement ECP-2007-LANG-617001) and T4ME (Grant Agreement no. 249119).

References

Calzolari, N., Soria, C., Del Gratta, R., Goggi, S., Quochi, V., & Russo, I., et al. (2010). *The LREC 2010 Resource Map*. LREC'2010, Malta, May 19–21, 2010.

Cambon-Thomsen, A., Thorisson, G. A., & Mabile, L. (2011). The role of a bioresource research impact factor as an incentive to share human bioresources. *Nature Genetics*, *43*, 503–504.

Choukri, K., Arranz, V., Hamon, O., & Park, J. (2012). *Using the international standard language resource number: Practical and technical aspects*. LREC'2012, Istanbul, May 23–25, 2012.

Del Gratta, R., Frontini, F., Fahad Khan, A., Mariani, J., & Soria, C. (2014). *The LREMap for under-resourced languages*. Workshop Collaboration and Computing for Under-Resourced Languages in the Linked Open Data Era, Satellite Workshop of LREC 2014, Reykjavik, May 26, 2014.

Grover, A., van H., Gerhard B., & Pretorius, M. W. (2010). *The South African human language technologies audit*. LREC'2010, Malta, May 19–21, 2010.

Krauwer, S. (1998). ELSNET and ELRA: Common past, common future. *ELRA Newsletter*, *3* (2), May 1998.

Lewis, P. (Ed). (2009). *Ethnologue: Languages of the world* (16th ed., p. 1248). SIL International, ISBN 978-1-55671-216-6.

Mariani, J., Cieri, C., Francopoulo, G., Paroubek, P., & Delaborde, M. (2014). *Facing the identification problem in language-related scientific data analysis*. LREC'2014, Reykjavik, May 28–30, 2014.

Rapp, R. & Zock, M. (2010). *The noisier the better: Identifying multilingual word translations using a single monolingual corpus*. Fourth International Workshop on CrossLingual Information Access (CLIA), Beijing (pp. 16–25).

Soria, C., & Mariani, J. (2013). Searching LTs for minority languages, Talare 2013 Traitement Automatique des langues régionales de France et d'Europe, Les Sables d'Olonne, 21 juin 2013.

Zock, M., Francopoulo, G., & Laroui, A. (1988). *Language learning as problem solving: Modelling logical aspects of inductive learning to generate sentences in french by man and machine*. Budapest: Coling.

Zock, M., Francopoulo, G., & Laroui, A. (1989). *SWIM: A natural interface for the scientific minded language learner, computers and the humanities* N°23, 4/5 (pp. 411–422). Netherlands: Kluwer Academic Publishers.

Zock, M., & Lapalme, G. (2010). *A generic tool for creating and using multilingual phrasebooks*. 7th International Workshop on Natural Language Processing and Cognitive Science, NLPCS, Funchal (Madeira) (pp. 79–89).

Zock, M. (2010). Language production a demanding but feasable task, provided to find the right strategies and tools. In D. Tufis & C. Forascu (Eds.), *Multilinguality and interoperability in language processing*. Bucuresti: Editura Academiei.

Zock, M., & Quint, J. (2004). *Why have them work for peanuts, when it is so easy to provide reward? Motivations for converting a dictionary into a drill tutor*. Papillon-2004, 5th workshop on Multilingual Lexical Databases Grenoble (p. 6).

References

The Fips Multilingual Parser

Eric Wehrli and Luka Nerima

Abstract This paper reports on the Fips parser, a multilingual constituent parser that has been developed over the last two decades. After a brief historical overview of the numerous modifications and adaptations made to this system over the years, we provide a description of its main characteristics. The linguistic framework that underlies the Fips system has been much influenced by Generative Grammar, but drastically simplified in order to make it easier to implement in an efficient manner. The parsing procedure is a one pass (no preprocessing, no postprocessing) scan of the input text, using rules to build up constituent structures and (syntactic) interpretation procedures to determine the dependency relations between constituents (grammatical functions, etc.), including cases of long-distance dependencies. The final section offers a description of the rich lexical database developed for Fips. The lexical model assumes two distinct levels for lexical units: words, which are inflected forms of lexical units, and lexemes, which are more abstract units, roughly corresponding to a particular reading of a word. Collocations are defined as an association of two lexical units (lexeme or collocation) in a specific grammatical relation such as adjective-noun or verb-object.

Keywords Multilingual parser · Complexity of natural language syntax · Grammatical relations

E. Wehrli (✉) · L. Nerima
Laboratoire d'Analyse et de Technologie du Langage – CUI, University of Geneva, Battelle - 7 Route de Drize, Carouge 1227, Switzerland
e-mail: Eric.Wehrli@unige.ch

L. Nerima
e-mail: Luka.Nerima@unige.ch

© Springer International Publishing Switzerland 2015
N. Gala et al. (eds.), *Language Production, Cognition, and the Lexicon*,
Text, Speech and Language Technology 48, DOI 10.1007/978-3-319-08043-7_26

1 Introduction

The Fips parser has been developed at LATL[1] during the last two decades. Needless to say, this parsing model has undergone multiple changes. As a matter of fact, except for the name and the general goal of the project, there are very few similarities between the first version of Fips, presented at ATALA in 1991 (cf. Laenzlinger and Wehrli 1991) and the current version. Linguistic concepts on which the parser relies, as well as the parsing strategy, the development platform and the programming language have changed several times over this period. Some modifications have been triggered by outside considerations, such as replacement of equipment—the first version of Fips was implemented in Modula-2 on a Digital Equipment Corporation (DEC) minicomputer running the VAX/VMS operating system. About 10 years ago, Fips was completely re-engineered using an object-oriented design to enhance its multilingual potentiality. This forced us to leave the Modula-2 language (by then under Windows), and migrate to the BlackBox programming environment using the Component Pascal language (a refinement of Oberon-2), the latest of Niklaus Wirth's programming languages.[2] Still other modifications were motivated by our own experience, or new challenges, for instance when Fips was extended to cover languages with relatively free word order, such as German and Modern Greek.

Today, Fips—still developed under PC/Windows in the BlackBox environment—is a truly multilingual parser, available for several of the main European languages, i.e. French, English, German, Italian, Spanish, with less-developed versions for Modern Greek and Romanian, and mock-ups for Latin, Hindi, Polish, Romansh, Russian, Portuguese and Japanese.

From the beginning, Fips has been conceived as a general parser, that is, a parser that can be used for any natural language application which requires lexical, morphological or syntactic information. Thus, Fips has been applied to several tasks, such as machine translation (Wehrli et al. 2009), speech analysis (Gaudinat et al. 1999a), speech synthesis (Goldman et al. 2000; Mertens et al. 2001), part-of-speech tagging (Scherrer 2008), terminology extraction (Seretan 2011; Seretan and Wehrli 2013), text summarization (Genest et al. 2008), spelling and grammatical correction (L'haire 2004, 2012), information retrieval (Ruch 2002), word translation in context [a terminology aid for non-native readers] (Wehrli 2004, 2006), speech-to-speech translation (Gaudinat et al. 1999b), and others. Notice that for all

[1] LATL stands for Laboratoire d'analyse et de technologie du langage, a language technology lab which is affiliated to the Linguistic department and to the Centre universitaire d'informatique of the University of Geneva. Fips, was originally spelled FIPS, an acronym for French Interactive Parsing System. The interactive feature was abandoned early and when re-engineered with object-oriented design, the parser has become truly multilingual. However, the name Fips was kept, mostly for sentimental reasons.

[2] The BlackBox environment was developed by Oberon Microsystems—a spin-off company of ETH Zurich —and is now freely available as open source at www.oberon.ch/blackbox.html. For a description of the language Oberon-2 see Mössenböck and Wirth (1991) and Mössenböck (1995).

these applications, only input and output components must be adapted to the specific task. The parser itself, as well as the associated lexical resources, stay unmodified.

This paper describes some of the main characteristics of the Fips parser.[3] The grammar, as well as the linguistic assumptions on which it relies are described in Sect. 2. Section 3 shows how the parser assigns a syntactic representation to a particular sentence. A central element of all symbolic parsers is the lexical database, the repository of all the lexical units the parser "knows". Section 4 describes the structure and the content of the Fips lexical database.

Although, to the best of our knowledge, Michael Zock has not been directly involved in the development of natural language parsers, his keen interest for cognitive science made him appreciate the inherent complexity of natural language syntax, as reflected in a "deep" syntactic parser such as Fips. Furthermore, parts of his research make explicit use of syntactic dependency relations (cf. Zock and Tesfaye 2013), corresponding to what we prefer to call grammatical relations.

2 The Grammar of Fips

The linguistic foundation underpinning the Fips parser is a computational adaptation of the Chomskyan model of generative grammar, inspired by the Government and Binding theory (GB) (cf. Chomsky 1981), with some elements from the Minimalist model (Chomsky 1995, 2004). Our syntactic model has also been influenced by Lexical Functional Grammar (LFG) (Bresnan and Kaplan 1982; Bresnan 2001), and by the Simpler Syntax model (Culicover and Jackendoff 2005; Culicover 2009).

The guiding principles for the development of the grammatical framework have been simplicity and computational efficiency. To give a concrete example, simplicity led us to adopt the simplest possible version of X'(X-bar) theory with just two levels, the lexical category level [X] and the corresponding phrasal level [XP], which is the maximal projection.[4] We return to X' and syntactic structures in the next subsection. As for an example of principled decision dictated by computational efficiency, movement and empty categories have been drastically reduced (compared to Minimalist or cartographic representations). To use the movement metaphor, we can say that with very few exceptions, movements have been restricted to "visible" movements, that is movements that modify the surface word order, such as fronting, extraposition or inversion of lexically realized constituents.

Another characteristic of the Fips grammar is the fact that it is in part declarative (i.e., rule-based, see attachment rules below) and in part procedural. The

[3] A preliminary version of parts of this paper was presented at the workshop IWPT/ATALA in Paris, 2009 (cf. Wehrli and Nerima 2009).

[4] As it turns out, a similar view has been adopted in Simpler Syntax (cf. Culicover 2009).

claim is that several linguistic processes are best described by means of procedures rather than rules. Examples include chain formation—the link between fronted elements and their canonical position—, or operations on argument structures, as in the passive construction or (as argued in Wehrli 2014) in the causative construction.[5] Although such operations could be described by rules (as in HPSG or LFG grammars), they are much easier to describe as procedures, and of course, much more efficiently implemented as such.

Finally, lexical information plays a crucial role, specifying selectional properties of functional elements such as prepositions, auxiliaries, determiners, etc. For instance, French "être" and "avoir" auxiliaries select a past participial verbal element, just like the English "have" auxiliary. German "werden" selects an infinitival verbal element, like English modals, and so on. Predicative heads, whether verbal, adjectival or nominal, can select arguments, whose syntactic properties are also specified in the lexicon. For instance, English "want" can take a sentential complement which cannot be tensed (1), while the French equivalent "vouloir" selects both infinitival (2a) and subjunctive (2b) sentential complements.

(1) a. John wants to sleep.
    b. John wants you to sleep.
    c. *John wants you to sleep.

(2) a. Jean veut dormir.
    b. Jean veut que tu dormes.

Other types of information, including some semantic features, are also specified in the lexical entries, as discussed in Sect. 4.

2.1 Syntactic Structures

All the constituent structures built by the parser follow the pattern given in (3), where **X** is a (possibly empty) lexical head, **XP** the phrasal category projected from the head **X**, while **L** and **R** stand for, respectively, (zero of more) left subconstituents and right subconstituents.

(3) $[_{X}$ L X R]

In this schema, **X** is a variable which takes its value in the set of lexical categories (**N**oun, **V**erb, **A**djective, **Adv**erb, **D**eterminer, **P**reposition, **C**onjunction,

---

[5] In a nutshell, passive triggers the suppression of the subject argument, and the optional insertion of an agent argument (e.g. the "by-phrase" in English). In the French causative construction (e.g. *Paul a fait rire les enfants* "Paul made the children laugh", we assume that the causative verb is a sort of verbal operator triggering a modification of the argument structure of the infinitival verb (the verb *rire* in our example), by the addition of an internal argument to express the logical subject of the infinitival verb, the subject slot being used by the causative subject.

Interjection) to which we add two additional categories, **T**ense and **F**unction. **TP** is the phrasal node that dominates the tense marker (T). In short, it corresponds to the traditional **S** sentential node used in many grammatical formalisms. **FP** constituents are secondary predicative structures of nominal, adjectival or prepositional nature. They correspond to the "small clause" structures of standard generative grammar (cf. Haegeman 1994). As already mentioned, this is a rather minimal variant of the X' theory with just two levels, the head and the maximal projection.

Notice that contrary to standard views in Minimalism, the constituent structures are not binary. Also, rather than **Spec**ifier and **Compl**ement, the more neutral **L**eft and **R**ight are used to refer to subconstituents. This choice was motivated by the observation that across languages, complements can occur as left subconstituents, right subconstituents or both. Similarly non complements, such as adjuncts can also occur either to the left, to the right or both with respect to the head.

3 Fips in Action

Fips is a constituent parser that functions as follows: it scans an input string (say, a sentence or a document[6]) from left to right, without any backtracking. The parsing algorithm, iteratively, performs the following three steps:

- Get the next lexical item and project the relevant phrasal category (X → XP)
- Merge XP with the structure in its left context (the structure already built)
- (syntactically) interpret XP.

These three actions are further discussed in the next subsections. Given the fact that each of those steps is non-deterministic (i.e. is likely to produce more than one result), a filtering mechanism can be activated, which filters out the set of analyses after each iteration, to keep the number of analyses below a selected beam size. We return to this filtering mechanism in Sect. 3.4.

If the parser manages to merge all the constituents into a single constituent, the analysis is said to be *complete*. Otherwise, the analysis is *incomplete* and the parser returns a sequence of constituents (usually no more than three or four), which together span the whole sentence.

Notice that the Fips parser does not resort to any preprocessing or postprocessing. As discussed in Seretan and Wehrli (2013), the detection of collocations,

[6] The segmentation of a document into sentence is made by the parser during the analysis, based on punctuation as well as grammatical considerations.

and more generally multi-word expressions, is performed during the parse, as soon as the relevant material is available.[7] Similarly, anaphora resolution also takes place during parsing.

3.1 Projection

The projection mechanism creates ("projects") a constituent of phrasal category on the basis of a lexical item (unmarked case) or of another phrasal constituent. As soon as a lexical item has been retrieved from the lexicon, it is projected to a phrasal level. For instance, the noun *cat* triggers the projection of a NP constituent, with *cat* as its head. Similarly, the adverb *by and large* and the French conjunction *au fur et à mesure que* ("as") trigger the projection, respectively, of an adverbial phrase AdvP and a Complementizer phrase, as illustrated in (4):

(4) a. $[_{\text{adv}}$ by and large$]$ → $[_{\text{AdvP}}$ $[_{\text{adv}}$ by and large$]]$
b. $[_{\text{conj}}$ au fur et *à* mesure que$]$ → $[_{\text{CP}}$ $[_{\text{conj}}$ au fur et *à* mesure que$]]$

Given the systematic character of the projection of a phrase from a lexical item, we will henceforth abbreviate the notation and skip the lexical category label:

(5) a. $[_{\text{AdvP}}$ by and large$]$
b. $[_{\text{CP}}$ au fur et *à* mesure que$]$

Projection is an operation occurring at the interface between the lexicon and the syntax. The Fips grammar, responsible for merging operations, only considers phrasal constituents and never lexical categories.

3.1.1 Metaprojection

There are other types of projections, more complex than the ones just discussed in the sense that they project richer, more elaborate structures. They are referred to as *metaprojections*. One example of metaprojection concerns tensed (and infinitival) verbs, as in the following sentence:

(6) John slept.

Upon reading the word *slept*, the parser retrieves a verbal element from the lexicon. Given the projection mechanism, we get the constituent $[_{\text{VP}}$ slept$]$. However, since the verb bears a tense marker, it also projects a **TP** (TensedPhrase)

[7] To be detected, a multi-word expression must be listed in the lexicon. MWEs of the "word with space" type are entered in the word and lexeme lexicons as compound words (see Sect. 4). They are retrieved during the lexical analysis performed by the parser. Other types of multi-word expressions, for instance collocations and idioms, are listed in the collocation lexicon and their detection occurs at the syntactic level.

node.[8] These two projection operations are combined into a metaprojection which produces the structure in (7):

(7) $[_{TP}$ $[_{VP}$ slept]]

Another example of metaprojection concerns coordination, for which we assign the structure (8b):

(8) a. cats and dogs
b. $[_{NP}$ $[_{ConjP}$ $[_{NP}$ cats] and $[_{NP}$ dogs]]]

The justification for this analysis of coordination is beyond the scope of this paper. Suffice it to say that it is as compliant with X' theory as possible and assigns to the whole structure the category of its parts (**NP**).

3.2 Merge

The constituent structures assigned to a sentence are created by the application of the projection (and metaprojection) mechanism and the merge operation. Merge takes two adjacent constituents and attempts, well, to merge them into one constituent. Not any two adjacent constituents can merge. The operation is constrained by grammar rules that specify which constituents can merge, and under what conditions. Given two adjacent constituents **A** and **B**, two cases must be considered:

- A can attach as a left subconstituent of B;
- B can attach as a right subconstituent of A, or as a right subconstituent of an active subconstituent of A.

The first case is referred to as *left attachment*, the second case as *right attachment*. Examples of left attachment include the attachment of an adjective to a noun (9a), of an adverbial modifier to another adverb (9b) or to an adjective (9c), attachment of an interrogative phrase to a sentential constituent, etc.

(9) a. $[_{NP}$ $[_{AP}$ happy] days]
b. $[_{Adv}$ $[_{Adv}$ quite] systematically]
c. $[_{AP}$ $[_{Adv}$ highly] unlikely]

Right attachment, by far the most frequent in natural languages, concern (in English or French) the attachment of most complements and adjuncts, among others. We assume that determiners are (syntactic) heads of noun phrases,[9] the structure of a noun phrase takes the form in (10):

[8] For personal and historical reasons, we use the category **TP**(TensedPhrase) instead of the **IP** label commonly used in GB theory, or of the traditional **S**(Sentence) category to represent a sentential constituent.

[9] For arguments supporting the so-called DP-hypothesis, see Abney (1987).

(10) a. the cat

$[_{DP}$ the $[_{NP}$ cat$]]$

b. all the cats

$[_{DP}$ all $[_{DP}$ the $[_{NP}$ cats$]]]$

While left subconstituents are attached to the top level of the adjacent constituent, right subconstituents can attach either to the top level of the adjacent constituent, or to a node that is itself a subconstituent of the adjacent constituent. Given two adjacent constituents **A** and **B**, each of the nodes on the right-hand edge of A could be a possible attachment site for B. As an example, consider sentence (10b). When the parser reads the words *cats*, we have the following configuration:

(11) $[_{DP}$ all $[_{DP}$ the$]]$ $[_{NP}$ cats$]$

The word *cats* being a noun, an NP constituent has been projected. The left context contains the DP constituent *all the*. Right attachment of the NP constituent to the DP at the top level is excluded by the fact that the node is not active (all its lexically specified selectional properties have been satisfied). However, its right subconstituent, the DP *the* is active, and can therefore serve as possible attachment site. The attachment takes place if a rule and its conditions are satisfied, which is the case in this example, producing structure (10b).

3.2.1 Fips Grammar Rules

Attachments, whether to the left or to the right, are constrained by conditions associated to rules written in a (pseudo) formalism, both intuitive enough for linguists and easy to code. The conditions bear on selectional properties of the governor, inherent properties (features) of either constituent, agreement conditions, etc., as illustrated in (12) with an example of left-attachment rule (for French) and in (13) with an example of right-attachment rule (for German).

(12) AP + NP

a. HasFeature(prenominalAdj)
a. AgreeWith(b, {number, gender})

(13) DP + NP

a. Select(Ncomplement)
b. IsType(commonNoun)
a. AgreeWith(b,{number, gender, case})

Both examples are fairly straightforward. On the first line, the two adjacent constituents are indicated by means of their category. Optional additional lines specify the conditions associated with the rule. The conditions are stated as boolean predicates expressed in a notation borrowed from object-oriented formalism. In example (12), the first condition states that the first constituent, referred to as **a** must be a prenominal adjective,[10] which means that it must bear the lexical feature [+ prenominalAdj]. The second condition states that the first constituent (**a**) must agree with the second constituent (**b**) in number and gender.

In the second example (13), the conditions state that the first constituent (**a**), which is a determiner, must select a noun complement, i.e. must bear the lexical selectional feature [+ Ncomplement]. The second condition requires that the second constituent (**b**) be a common noun, while the third condition requires a number, gender and case agreement between the two constituents.

3.3 Syntactic Interpretation

Projection and Merge are the two operations responsible for the production of the constituent structure assigned to an input string. A richer information structure, however, is expected from a syntactic parser, providing information about grammatical functions, sentence types (declarative, imperative, etc.), particular syntactic constructions (active vs. passive, relatives, etc.), and so on. The task of providing such information is assumed by so-called syntactic interpretation procedures.

3.3.1 Grammatical Functions

One of the main tasks of syntactic interpretation is the assignment of grammatical functions to argument-type constituents, that is to constituents of category DP, PP, CP and FP. We consider the following grammatical functions: subject, direct object, indirect object, prepositional complement, sentential complement, predicative complement (small clause), and adjuncts. The assignment is triggered by the attachment of an argument-type constituent to a predicate (a verb, for instance). The procedure then checks whether the newly attached constituent can be interpreted as an argument of the verb, by checking if an adequate slot is available in the argument structure associated with the verb, which is built on the basis of the so-called subcategorization frame specified in the lexical entry of each predicative element, stating the number and type of each possible argument.

It is often the case, though, that the decision whether or not a constituent can be interpreted as an argument must be delayed, for instance because the constituent is not attached to the main verb of the clause. In such cases, the constituent is added to a temporary structure, pending the attachment of the main verb. As an example,

---

[10] In French, some modifier adjectives are prenominal, others are postnominal and some can be both.

consider the German sentence (14), where the main verb *gelesen* ("read") occurs at the end of the sentence. The preceding DPs are properly attached in the structure, but their syntactic interpretation must be delayed until the verb is known:

(14) Das Buch hat das Mädchen gelesen.
the book has the girl read
'the girl has read the book'.

Another example of delayed interpretation is found in the so-called *wh*-constructions, such as relative clauses, *wh*-interrogatives, exclamative sentences, and a few other constructions.[11] Consider for instance *wh*-interrogatives, such as (15), in which the *wh*-phrase and the verb with respect to which it can be interpreted are emphasized:

(15) a. **Who** did John **see**?
b. **Who** did you say that John will **invite** to the party?

In English, French and many other languages, *wh*-phrases occur in proposed positions, attached as left subconstituents of CP, a position in which they cannot be interpreted. Furthermore, contrary to our German example, where the relation between the DPs and the main verb is clause-bound, the relation between a *wh*-phrase and the verb which assigns it an interpretation is unbounded, i.e. the distance between the two elements can be arbitrary long, and can cross several clause boundaries.[12]

In the tradition of generative grammar, we consider that such unbounded dependencies are best described in terms of a chain relating the *wh*-phrase and an empty category in the canonical position of the argument (or adjunct) corresponding to its interpretation. In other words, a *wh*-phrase interpreted as a direct object is linked to an empty DP in the canonical direct object position, as illustrated in (16), where $[_{DP}$ e $]$ stands for the empty direct object, and the chain is identified by the **i** index:

(16) a. What book did John buy?
b. $[_{CP}\ [_{DP}$ what book$]_i$ did $[_{TP}\ [_{DP}$ John$]\ [_{VP}$ buy $[_{DP}$ e$]_i]]]$

The chain formation mechanism, by which a constituent in a position where it could not be interpreted is connected to an argument (or adjunct) position[13] has been implemented in the following (somewhat simplified) fashion: when attached in a non-argument position (A'-position), a *wh*-constituent is also put on a special

[11] See Chomsky (1977) for an in-depth discussion of *wh*-constructions.

[12] This does not mean, though, that any type of structure can occur between the two elements. Ross (1967) showed that *wh*-constructions are constrained by "island" constraints. See Chomsky (1977), Rizzi (1990) for subsequent generalizations of those constraints.

[13] The distinction between argument and non-argument positions is referred to as the A versus A' positions in the GB and minimalist literature.

data structure, technically a stack,[14] which is passed down the right edge of the constituent structure. Each time a predicative element is attached to the structure, the parser checks whether the *wh*-element on top of the stack can be interpreted with respect to this predicate. If so, an empty node co-indexed with the *wh*-element is inserted in the argument position of the predicate, and the *wh*-element is popped off the stack.

3.4 Ranking and Filtering

Ambiguities can be found at all levels of linguistic description, the lexical level, the syntactic level and the interpretation level. A natural language parser must consider several (indeed very many) possible analyses. If unchecked, the number of alternatives (the number of analyses at a given point of the parsing process) grows exponentially with respect to the length of the input sentence, and so does the response time. For a parser to be used in "real-life" applications, such as translation, it is thus mandatory to restrict the number of alternatives, in order to ensure reasonable response times.

Another problem in connection with the proliferation of alternatives is the selection of the preferred analysis. In most applications (for instance translation) only one analysis should be considered. Hence a selection must be made.

Ranking analyses provides a solution to both problems. If a score can be assigned to each analysis, the parser can then output the analysis with the best score and the selection problem is solved. Furthermore, if scores can be assigned at each step of the parse, then the proliferation problem is solved, as the set of alternatives can be filtered after each step. The Fips parser can be set with a particular *beam size*, which is the maximum number of alternatives allowed, say 40. After each step, only the 40 best alternatives are kept and all the others are filtered out. Setting a lower beam size speeds up the parser (by a nearly linear function), though at the risk of some degradation of the quality of the analyses, as "good" candidates might have been filtered out.

The quality of score assignment is thus crucial for the selection mechanism. The current version of Fips uses a mix of psycholinguistic (e.g., local attachments are preferred over non local ones), lexical (e.g. word frequency) and syntactic (e.g. rule frequency) considerations to set scores, but altogether score assignment remains largely ad hoc and constitutes a major topic for further improvement.

[14] The stack data structure is appropriate since *wh*-chains can be embedded in each other, but do not cross each other, corresponding to the last-in, first-out flow of a stack.

4 The Lexical Database

Lexical resources are a key component of NLP projects. Unfortunately, reusable and reliable electronic lexicons constitute a scarce resource[15] and, even when they are available, their structure and content rarely fit the needs of a specific project. For those reasons, and since the Fips parser needs extremely detailed lexical information, we choose to build our own lexicons, implemented as a relational database.

The database structure is based on the following concepts:

- **words** representing all morphological forms (spellings) of the words of a language, grouped into inflectional paradigms;
- **lexemes**, describing more abstract lexical forms which correspond to the syntactic and semantic readings of a word (a lexeme corresponds roughly to a standard dictionary entry);
- **collocations** describe multi-word expressions combining two lexical items;
- **variant spellings**, which list all the alternative written forms for a word, e.g. the written forms of British English vs American English, the spellings introduced by a spelling reform, etc.

Each of these concepts results in a separate lexicon (implemented as a table in the relational database), that is (i) the lexicon of words, (ii) the lexicon of lexemes, (iii) the lexicon of collocations and (iv) the lexicon of variant spellings. Figure 1 gives the structure of the lexical database for a language.[16] To be complete, we must also mention the ability to define specific user-defined "private" lexicons containing words of specialized domains (medicine, biology, chemistry, etc.), named entities, and so on. In order to avoid "polluting" the general lexicon, private lexicons are stored in a separate lexical structure.

4.1 The Word Lexicon

An entry of type *word* describes an inflected form with information such as: spelling, category (noun, adjective, etc.), phonetic representation (including, for French, the possible latent consonant), agreement features (number, gender, case, etc.), and for verbal entries, tense and mood, and so on.

Frequency information computed over large corpora has also been added, and is now used as part of the score computation discussed in Sect. 3.4.

[15] With some notable exceptions, such as Lefff (Sagot 2010).

[16] This database structure must be instantiated for each language.

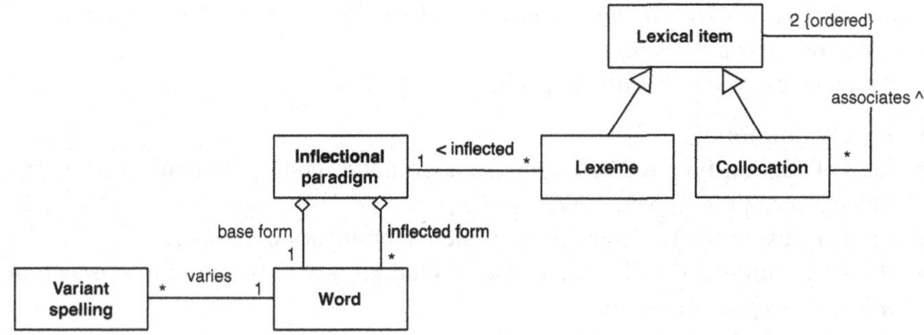

Fig. 1 Lexical database structure (UML class diagram notation)

The insertion of new words in the lexicon is performed manually.[17] The linguist or lexicographer enters the citation form of the word, its category and its morphological class. A morphological engine associated to the user interface generates and enters the whole inflectional paradigm of the word.

4.2 *The Lexeme Lexicon*

An entry of type *lexeme* describes the syntactic and (some) semantic properties of a lexeme (type, subtype, selectional features, argument structure, semantic features, thematic roles, etc.). It is also planned to compute lexeme frequency over large analyzed corpora.

Each lexeme is associated with its inflectional paradigm, stored in the lexicon of words. If several syntactic (or semantic) readings exist for a word, they lead to many entries in the lexeme lexicon. For example, the verb *to play* is represented by at least two entries, one transitive and one intransitive.

4.3 *The Collocation Lexicon*

Collocations are defined as an association of two lexical units (not counting function words) in a specific grammatical relation (for instance verb-object). Since a lexical unit can be a collocation, the definition is recursive (Nerima et al. 2010), allowing for collocations of more than one word, for instance French *tomber en*

[17] When adequate resources are available, word insertion can be made semi-automatically, under supervision of the lexicographer.

panne d'essence (*'to run out of gas'*), or English *guaranteed minimum wage*, *weapons of mass destruction*.

An entry of type *collocation* specifies:

- the citation form;
- the collocation type (adjective-noun, noun-noun, noun-prep-noun, verb-direct object, verb-prep-object, etc.);
- the two lexical units (referred to by their identification number);
- the preposition, for collocation types including a preposition (e.g. *absence* **of** *mind*, *flag* ***of*** *convenience*;
- additional features (e.g., plural collocation, determiner-less complement, bare-noun complement, etc.).

Some examples of entries are given in (17):

(17) *to make an appointment*
type: verb-direct object
lexeme No. 1: *to make*, transitive verb
lexeme No. 2: *appointment*, noun
preposition: Ø
features: { }

(18) *gloomy thoughts*
type: adjective-noun
lexeme No. 1: *gloomy*, adjective
lexeme No. 2: *thought*, noun
preposition: Ø
features: {plural collocation}

(19) *school of fish*
type: noun-prep-noun
lexeme No. 1: *school*, noun
lexeme No. 2: *fish*, noun
preposition: of
features: {determiner-less complement}

To enter a collocation, the lexicographer types its citation form. The lexical user interface then invokes the Fips parser to perform a full parse of the citation form. It returns the lexical units composing the collocation, its type, as well as the features. The lexicographer can then validate or change these settings.

An automatic collocation extraction tool was developed at LATL (Seretan et al. 2004; Seretan 2011). It generates lists of collocations from selected corpora and displays their contexts. With this tool, the lexicographer can browse the list of proposed collocations and quickly validate the relevant ones.

	Lexemes	Words	Collocations
French	41,372	104,486	16,732
English	57,917	241,203	9,415
German	43,552	449,082	3,202
Italian	33,604	277,834	3,101
Spanish	27,838	275,506	3,489

Fig. 2 Number of lexical entries

4.4 The Lexicon of Orthographic Variants

An entry in the lexicon of orthographic variants specifies the variant spelling, its class (for instance GB vs. US, or some spelling reform), and its type (e.g. -ise/-ize), and of course the word it is a variant of (referred to by its identification number). Several variants can be associated to a given word.

4.5 Some Figures

Figure 2 gives the current size of the lexicons (lexemes, words, collocations) for the five best-developed languages of the Fips system.

5 Concluding Remarks

Several aspects of the Fips parser could not be described in this article, such as the object-oriented design, which enables the extension to additional languages without internal modification, recompilation, etc. As for the results, the Fips parser performs well compared to other "deep" linguistic parsers (Delph-in, ParGram, etc.) in terms of speed. Parsing time depends on two main factors: (i) the type and complexity of the corpus, and (ii) the selected beam size, as discussed in Sect. 3.4. By default, Fips runs with a beam size of 40 alternatives, which gives it a speed ranging from 150 to 250 symbols (word, punctuation) per second. At that pace, parsing a one million word corpus takes approximately 2 to 3 h.

As for the quality of the parses, precise evaluations are not available at this time. Evaluations, such as the Passage campaign on French parsers (Paroubek et al. 2010) do not yield reliable results for Fips, largely due to major differences in output formats.

One available large-scale statistical data, though, is the number of complete analyses, along with the number of "unknown" words (i.e. words that are not in the lexical database). While the latter gives a good estimate of the lexical

beam size	words/second	complete analyses
120	59	77.98%
80	93	75.45%
40	198	71.80%
10	579	59.40%
5	793	50.94%

Fig. 3 Number of complete analyses relative to beam size

coverage, the former provides some qualitative indications, under the reasonable assumption that the number of complete analyses correlates with their quality.

Figure 3 below shows results obtained by Fips for a corpus of approximately 75,000 words (approx. 4,000 sentences) from the magazine *The Economist* with various beam sizes. Column 1 indicates the beam size, column 2 gives the parsing speed (words/second), and column 3 the percentage of sentences for which Fips returns a complete analysis.[18]

Finally, besides the never-ending tasks of expansion of the lexical database and of the enhancement of the grammatical coverage, two specific on-going research topics are worth mentioning regarding the Fips project: the first one is the development of an anaphora resolution component, which already shows promising results, in particular with respect to collocation detection—allowing the parser to detect collocations in which a nominal element has been pronominalized (e.g., *to break* **it**, where the pronoun refers to *record*, see Wehrli and Nerima 2013). As for the second on-going research topic, it concerns the use of statistical data that could serve as basis for the score assignment of analyses, as discussed in Sect. 3.4. (see Wehrli and Nerima 2014).

Acknowledgments A significant part of the research reported here has benefited from grants from the Swiss National Science Foundation. Thanks to Yves Scherrer for useful suggestions and observations and to Genoveva Puskas for careful reading.

References

Abney, S. (1987). *The English noun phrase in its sentential aspect.* PhD thesis, MIT. MIT Working Papers in Linguistics.

Bresnan, J. (2001). *Lexical functional syntax.* Oxford: Blackwell.

Bresnan, J., & Kaplan, R. (1982). Introduction: Grammars as mental representations of language. In J. Bresnan (Ed.), *The mental representation of grammatical relations.* Cambridge: The MIT Press.

Chomsky, N. (1977). On wh-movement. In P. Culicover, T. Wasow & A. Akmajian (Eds.), *Formal Syntax.* New York: Academic Press.

Chomsky, N. (1981). *Lectures on Government and Binding.* Dordrecht: Foris.

[18] Recall that a "complete analysis" is a single constituent tree spanning the whole sentence.

Chomsky, N. (1995). *The minimalist program*. Cambridge, Mass: MIT Press.
Chomsky, N. (2004). Beyond explanatory adequacy. In A. Belletti (Ed.), *The cartography of syntactic structures*. Oxford: Oxford University Press.
Culicover, P. (2009). *Natural language syntax*. Oxford: Oxford University Press.
Culicover, P., & Jackendoff, R. (2005). *Simpler syntax*. Oxford: Oxford University Press.
Gaudinat, A., Goldman, J-Ph, & Wehrli, E. (1999a). Syntax-based speech recognition: How a syntactic parser can help a recognition system. *EuroSpeech, 1999*, 1587–1591.
Gaudinat, A., Goldman, J.-P., Kabre, H., & Wehrli, E. (1999b). Syntax-based french-english speech-to-speech translation on restricted domains. *Proceedings of EACL99*.
Genest, P.-E., Lapalme, G., Nerima, L., & Wehrli, E. (2008). Ness: A symbolic summarizer for the update task of TAC 2008. *In Proceedings of TAC 2008, Gaithersburg, MD*.
Goldman, J.-P., Gaudinat, A., & Wehrli, E. (2000). Utilisation de l'analyse syntaxique pour la synthèse de la parole, l'enseignement des langues et l'étiquetage grammatical. *TALN 2000. Lausanne*.
Haegeman, L. (1994). *Introduction to government and binding theory* (2nd ed.). Oxford: Blackwell.
Laenzlinger, C., & Wehrli, E. (1991). FIPS: Un Analyseur interactif pour le français. *TA Informations, 32*(2), 35–49.
L'haire, S. (2004). Vers un feedback plus intelligent. Les enseignements du projet Freetext. *In Proceedings of the workshop "TAL & Apprentissage des langues"*, Journée d'étude de l'ATALA, Grenoble. pp. 1–12.
L'haire, S. (2012). *Traitement automatique et apprentissage des langues par ordinateur: bilan, résultats et perspectives*. Saarbrücken: Presses Académiques Francophones.
Mertens, P., Goldman, J-Ph, Wehrli, E., & Gaudinat, A. (2001). La synthèse de l'intonation à partir de structures syntaxiques riches. *Traitement automatique des langues (TAL), 42*, 145–192.
Mössenböck, H.-P., & Wirth, N. (1991). The programming language Oberon-2. *In Structured Programming 12*, 179–195.
Mössenböck, H.-P. (1995). *Object-oriented programming in Oberon-2*. New York: Springer.
Nerima, L., Wehrli, E., & Seretan, V. (2010). A recursive treatment of collocations. *In Proceedings of the Seventh International Conference on Language Resources and Evaluation (LREC 2010), Valletta, Malta*.
Paroubek, P., Hamon, O., de La Clergerie, E., Grouin, C., & Vilnat, A. (2010). The second evaluation campaign of PASSAGE on parsing of French. *In Proccedings of Seventh International Conference on Language Resources and Evaluation (LREC 2010), Valletta, Malta*.
Rizzi, L. (1990). *Relativized minimality*. Cambridge: MIT Press.
Ruch, P. (2002). *Applying Natural Language Processing to Information Retrieval in Clinical Records and Biomedical Texts*, thèse de doctorat, Université de Genève.
Ross, J. (1967). *Constraints on variables in syntax*. PhD dissertation, MIT.
Sagot, B. (2010). "The Lefff, a freely available and large-coverage morphological and syntactic lexicon for French. *In Proceedings of the Seventh International Conference on Language Resources and Evaluation (LREC 2010), Valletta, Malta*.
Scherrer, Y. (2008). Part-of-speech tagging with a symbolic full parser: Using the TIGER treebank to evaluate Fips. *In Proceedings of the Workshop on Parsing German*. ACL 2008, Columbus, Ohio, USA.
Seretan, V., Nerima, L., & Wehrli, E. (2004). Multi-word collocation extraction by syntactic composition of collocation bigrams. In N. Nicolov, K. Bontcheva, G. Angelova & Ruslan Mitkov (Eds.), *Recent Advances in Natural Language Processing III: Selected Papers from RANLP 2003, Current Issues in Linguistic Theory* (pp. 91–100). Amsterdam/Philadelphia: John Benjamins.
Seretan, V. (2011). *Syntax-based collocation extraction*. New York: Springer.
Seretan, V., & Wehrli, E. (2013). Syntactic concordancing and multi-word expression detection. *In International Journal of Data Mining, Modelling and Management, 5.2*. (pp. 158–181).

Wehrli, E. (2004). Traduction, traduction de mots, traduction de phrases. In B. Bel & I. Marlien (Eds.), *TALN XI*, Fes (pp. 483–491).

Wehrli, E. (2006). "TwicPen: Hand-held scanner and translation software for non-native readers. *In Proceedings of the COLING/ACL 2006 Interactive Presentation Sessions, Sydney, Australia* (pp. 61–64).

Wehrli, E. (2014). Processing pronominal clitics. In J. Blochowiak, C. Grisot & Ch. Laenzlinger (Eds.), *Festschrift for Jacques Moeschler.*

Wehrli, E., & Nerima, L. (2009). L?analyseur syntaxique Fips. *Proceedings of the IWPT/ATALA Workshop "Quels analyseurs syntaxiques pour le français ?"*, Paris, France. [http://alpage.inria.fr/iwpt09/atala/fips.pdf].

Wehrli, E., Nerima, L., & Scherrer, Y. (2009). Deep linguistic multilingual translation and bilingual dictionaries. *In Proceedings of the Fourth Workshop on Statistical Machine Translation, Athens, Greece* (pp. 90–94).

Wehrli, E., & Nerima, L. (2013). Anaphora resolution, collocations and translation. *In Proceedings of the Workshop on Multi-word Units in Machine Translation and Translation Technology, MT Summit XIV* (pp. 12–17). Nice, France.

Wehrli, E., & Nerima, L. (2014). When rules meet bigrams. In A. Gelbukh (Ed.), *Proceedings of Cicling 15.* New York: Springer.

Zock, M., & Tesfaye, D. (2013). Automatic sentence clustering to help authors to structure their thoughts. In B. Sharp & M. Zock (Eds.), *Proceedings of the 10th International Workshop on Natural Language Processing and Cognitive Science* (NLPCS 2013) (pp. 35–48).

The Lexical Ontology for Romanian

Dan Tufiş and Verginica Barbu Mititelu

Abstract Lexical resources have taken different forms throughout time. Nowadays, they occur in forms serving several types of users: the traditional human user, the modern human users and the computer. This last type of user explains the appearance of lexical knowledge representation forms, with semantic networks as one of the most frequently used forms. We present here the semantic network for Romanian. It was created primarily for use in various applications involving natural language: question answering, document and word-alignment, parallel data extraction from comparable documents, machine translation. During its exploitation, several inaccuracies were detected and consistent cleaning steps were necessary due to errors from the initial construction phase (typos in the definitions, alternation of the old and new orthography, duplicate entries, semantic conflicts) or were required by the mapping to the new versions of Princeton WordNet. The first proper content extension was in-line importing of the SUMO/MILO concept labels, via the alignment to the Princeton WordNet. A second extension was the association of each synset with a connotation vector, a representation of the multifactorial meaning variation, according to a generalized Osgoodian methodology. Recently, we started to add a series of new lexical relations (language specific) based on an in-depth analysis of the Romanian derivational morphology. In the end of the paper we present the results of a word sense disambiguation algorithm based on wordnets.

Keywords Wordnet · Romanian · Dictionary · Synset · Semantic relations · Derivation · Differential semantics · Word sense disambiguation · Subjectivity · Connotation

---

D. Tufiş (✉) · V.B. Mititelu
Romanian Academy Research Institute for Artificial Intelligence,
13 Calea 13 Septembrie, Bucharest, Romania
e-mail: tufis@racai.ro

V.B. Mititelu
e-mail: vergi@racai.ro

© Springer International Publishing Switzerland 2015

N. Gala et al. (eds.), *Language Production, Cognition, and the Lexicon*,
Text, Speech and Language Technology 48, DOI 10.1007/978-3-319-08043-7_27

1 Introduction

Language has been a preoccupation of mankind for thousands of years (with the Indian grammarian Panini as one of the first language "researchers", 4th century BC probably). The organization of the lexical material has also been a concern and a practice, even though for didactic purposes at the beginning (Gala 2013). Making a huge leap in time up the second half of the 20th century, facing the steep evolution in computer sciences and in technology, we notice an acute interest in lexical knowledge manifested by linguists, philosophers, psychologists and computer scientists alike. We will focus here on the way lexical knowledge can be stored, with hints to lexical access, both being among Michael Zock's scientific interests (Zock 2010; Zock and Bilac 2004; Zock and Schwab 2013).

Dictionaries have become market products having to answer the needs of their potential users. In the last century we notice the persistence of the learner type user alongside with the emergence of a totally new one (Barbu Mititelu 2013). The former is the human who assumes two roles: a traditional (i.e., using the printed dictionaries) and a technical one (i.e., using a computer). The latter is the computer, which makes use of the knowledge in a dictionary for solving various tasks involving natural language processing. Adopting the perspective of language production, more exactly lexical access, (Zock and Schwab 2013) consider that lexical networks are a good solution for the future dictionaries, meant to simulate the mental lexicon, due to their organization and access facility. The Princeton WordNet (PWN) (Fellbaum 1998) is the most widely known and used lexical network. With its advantages and despite its disadvantages, PWN has been so influencial in the domain of natural language processing that several other projects have been initiated to complement information offered by PWN with various other types of information, useful for a large number of applications. Among the most important such initiatives was the alignment of PWN synsets to the concepts of SUMO/MILO upper and mid-level ontology, which turned the ensemble PWN + SUMO/MILO into a proper lexical ontology. In spite of several other projects aiming at developing alternative lexical ontologies, no one can compete with the extended PWN yet. Another enhancement of PWN was the development of DOMAINS (Bentivogli et al. 2004) hierarchical classification system, which assigns each synset a DOMAINS class.

Among the latest enhancements of the PWN was the development of the SentiWordNet (Baccianella et al. 2010; Esuli and Sebastiani 2006), an explicit annotation of all synsets with subjectivity mark-up. Unlike many other resources used in subjectivity analysis, SentiWordNet rightly considers that word senses may have different subjectivity loads. In SentiWordNet, each synset is associated with a triple $<P:\alpha, N:\beta, O:\gamma>$, where P denotes its Positive subjectivity, N represents the Negative subjectivity and O stands for Objectivity. The values α, β and γ are sub-unitary numbers summing up 1 and represent the degrees of positive, negative and objective prior sentiment annotation of the synset in case.

In this paper we present the Romanian wordnet (RoWN): its content, its development in an international and national context and its use in applications.

2 The Ongoing RoWN Development and Its Current Status

RoWN was started in the BalkaNet (BKN) project (Stamou et al. 2002) and was created in partnership by the Research Institute of Artificial Intelligence of the Romanian Academy and the Faculty of Informatics of the University “Alexandru Ioan Cuza” from Iaşi. By the end of the project 18,000 synsets had been created and aligned to PWN 2.0 and, through it, to the synsets of all BKN wordnets. By exploiting the SUMO/MILO information attached to PWN synsets, the collection of monolingual semantic networks became a multilingual lexical ontology.

After the BKN project ended, the Research Institute for Artificial Intelligence of the Romanian Academy undertook the task of maintaining and further developing the RoWN.

We selected the concepts to be further implemented in our network so that they would serve other tasks that we accomplished throughout time. Thus, we aimed at a complete coverage of the 1984 corpus, of the newspaper articles corpus NAACL2003, of the Acquis Communautaire corpus, of the Eurovoc thesaurus, of VerbNet 3.1, and as much as possible from the Wikipedia lexical stock.

The two basic development principles of the BalkaNet methodology (Tufiş and Cristea 2002; Tufiş et al. 2004), that is the Hierarchy Preservation Principle and the Conceptual Density Principle, were strictly observed. The former served as the assumption for the expand approach we undertook. The compliance with the latter principle ensures that no orphan synsets, i.e. lower-level synsets without direct ancestors, are created. The implementation methodology was decided upon taking into consideration the available language resources. They were: an English-Romanian electronic dictionary (263,283 entries), an electronic synonyms dictionary (SYND), an electronic explanatory dictionary (EXPD) (containing 63,108 entries).

The major tools, designed to help the lexicographers develop the synsets of the RoWN, were WNBuilder and WNCorrect (Tufiş and Barbu 2004). They use the above-mentioned lexical resources.

The structure of the RoWN is inherited from the PWN. Most of the relations it contains are conceptual, so they are transferable from one language to another.

A very important lexical relation is antonymy which may hold between word pairs of any of the four grammar categories. While one could speak about a conceptual opposition between two synsets such as < rise:1 lift:3 arise:4 > and < descent:1 fall:2 go down:2 come down:2 > or < rise:8, come up:10 uprise:2 ascend:3 > and < set:10 go down:1 go under:8 > , the real antonymy relation in the examples above holds only between the members of the pairs rise:1 $\sim$ fall:2 and rise:8 $\sim$ set:10. We decided to mark antonymy at the synset level. Thus, it stands for the conceptual opposition between the members of the two synsets.

RoWN is aligned with EXPD at the sense level. In this dictionary the meanings of a polysemous word are marked differently, depending on their similarity or

Table 1 Statistics about synsets and literals in RoWN

Part of speech	Synsets	Lexical units	Unique literals	NonLexicalized
Nouns	41,063	56,532	52,009	1,839
Verbs	10,397	16,484	14,210	759
Adjectives	4,822	8,203	7,407	79
Adverbs	3,066	4,019	3,248	110
Total	59,348	85,238	76,874	2,787

difference: less related meanings are marked with Roman figures, while closely related ones are marked with Arabic figures. All further refinements (i.e. derived meanings) inside the definition of a meaning are numbered by adding a dot and a further digit (for example, 1.3). We preserved the sense numbers from EXPD whenever possible (the difference in granularity between the dictionary and the wordnet explains the cases when the sense number is not the same; this correlates with the difference in the definitions—see Sect. 5 below). So, unlike PWN, the sense numbers in RoWN do not reflect the frequency of the respective meaning of the word. A detailed presentation of the sense numbering of synsets in RoWN can be found in (Tufiş et al. 2013).

In the tables 1 and 2 we present up to date statistics about our resource.

Table 1 shows that the total number of synsets in RoWN is 59,348. The total number of literals (simple words or multiword expressions) occurring in these synsets is 85,238. As some of them occur several times in the network (as they are polysemous), it is explainable why the number of unique literals is smaller: 76,874. As a consequence of adopting the expand methodology in the wordnet creation, some synsets are empty: the respective concepts are not lexicalized in Romanian. Their total number is 2,787.

Table 2 shows the number of relations in RoWN. By far, the most numerous ones are hyponymy and hyperonymy. This correlates with the fact that nouns are far more numerous than the other parts of speech. Instance relations reflect the number of proper nouns in the network.

Although containing 59,348 synsets, the RoWN3.0 covers most of the DOMAINS-3.2, SUMO/MILO (Niles and Pease 2001) and domain ontologies concepts existing in PWN3.0.

3 Marking Derivational Relations in RoWN

A rather sensitive topic is the derivational relations. Let e_1 and e_2 be two English literals, and r_1 and r_2 their Romanian equivalents; if e_1 is derived from e_2 with a certain affix, it may be the case that r_1 is derived from r_2 with an affix; however, derivational relations marked in PWN at the literal level cannot be transferred into

Table 2 Semantic relations in RoWN

Relation	Number
Hypo/hyperonymy	48,316
Instance_hypo/hyperonymy	3,889
Antonym	4,131
Similar_to	4,838
Verb_group	1,530
Member_holonym	2,047
Part_holonym	5,573
Substance_holonym	410
Also_see	1,333
Attribute	958
Cause	196
Entailment	371

another language. Even in the expand approach it is impossible to tell what correspondence between the literals in aligned synsets is. Nevertheless, as affixes usually carry semantic information, the English derivative relation can be viewed at a conceptual level and can be imported in Romanian not as a derivative one, but as a conceptual reflex of it. This relation is of great help: a base word and all the words derived from it belong to the same semantic field. Nevertheless, for some pairs e_1 and e_2 it may be the case that the equivalent r_1 and r_2 literals are not derivationally related.

This type of relations exists in other wordnets as well: the Turkish WordNet (Bilgin et al. 2004), PWN (Fellbaum et al. 2007), the Czech WordNet (Pala and Hlavackova 2007), the Polish WordNet (Piasecki et al. 2012), the Estonian one (Kahusk et al. 2010), the Bulgarian (Tarpomanova and Rizov 2014), the Croatian wordnet (Sojat and Srebacic 2014). Given the language-specific character of such relations, each team undertook their own strategy for finding the relations in their wordnet.

Derivation presupposes both formal and semantic relatedness between the root and the derived word: the former is ensured by the fact that the root and the derived word contain (almost) the same string of letters that represent the root, while the latter is ensured by the compositionality of meaning of the derived word: its meaning is a sum of the meaning of the root and the meaning of the affix(es). Thus, the Romanian words *alerga* "run" and *alergător* "runner" are derivationally related: the latter is obtained from the former by adding the suffix *-ător* (after removing *-a*, the infinitive suffix) and it means "the one who runs". However, derivational relations cannot be established for all meanings of these words: when considered with their proper meaning, they are related, but when *alerga* is considered with its figurative meaning "to try hard to get something", it does not

Table 3 Semantic labels for prefixed words

Label	Number of occurrences
Together	29
Subsumption	363
Opposition	792
Mero	17
Eliminate	9
Iterative	2
Through	5
Repeat	305
Imply	26
Similitude	61
Instead	6
Aug	5
Before	14
Anti	10
Out	1
Back	2

establish a derivational relation with *alergător*, as it has not developed any related figurative meaning.

In the derivation process only one affix of a type is added. So, a prefix and a suffix can be added to a root in the same derivation step, but never two suffixes or/and two prefixes. If a word contains more than two affixes of the same type, then they were attached in different steps in the derivation. This was the assumption for marking derivational relations in RoWN only between literals directly derived from one another (so without any intermediate step). For a complete description of the methodology we adopted see (Barbu Mititelu 2013). The pairs are labeled with one of the 54 semantic labels we established: 16 for prefixed words (see Table 3) and 38 for suffixed ones (see Table 4). Whenever a type of semantic relation was already labeled in other wordnets, we borrowed the label. For a complete list of labels and examples see (Barbu Mititelu et al. 2014).

These labels hold between concepts, so, in our view, they have cross-lingual validity, although there are cases when there is no derivational relation between the words lexicalizing the respective concepts in other languages.

Marking these derivational relations leads to an increase of the number of links between synsets, especially between synsets of different parts of speech, as presented in (Table 5). Given that the number of relations between synsets and literals of different parts of speech is not so large, adding the derivational relations can ensure a faster access to the target literal, shorter chains between two semantically related words (Barbu Mititelu 2013).

Table 4 Semantic labels for suffixed words

Label	Number of occurrences
Subsumption	42
Member_holo	37
Member_mero	17
Substance_holo	2
Substance_mero	1
Ingredient_holo	1
Holonym	26
Part	12
Agent	394
Result	227
Location	87
Of_origin	29
Job	179
State	284
Period	43
Undergoer	47
Instrument	84
Sound	163
Cause	19
Container	17
Material	4
Destination	5
Gender	13
Dim	50
Aug	1
Object_made_by	50
Subject_to	19
By_means_of	104
Clothes	1
Event	699
Abstract	490
Colour	19
Make_become	89
Make_acquire	110
Manner	436
Similitude	115
Related	1294

Table 5 Distribution of derivational relation on PoS

	Same PoS %	Cross PoS %
Prefixed	97	3
Suffixed	15	85
Total	38	62

4 Differential Semantics Annotation

More and more applications begin to use the prior subjectivity mark-up of PWN senses in order to assess the connotation of a sentence or a paragraph in different contexts. Using SentiWordNet, this assessment is carried out from a single perspective: a negative-positive connotative axe. However, the work of Osgood et al. (Osgood et al. 1957) on the theory of semantic differentiation gives strong evidence that affective meanings can also be outlined and measured on some other connotative axes defined by antonymic pairs of words. They performed intensive experiments on rating the meaning of a word, phrase or text on different scales defined in terms of pairs of bipolar adjectives (good-bad, active-passive, strong-weak, optimistic-pessimistic, beautiful-ugly, etc.). In the semantic differential technique, each such pair of bipolar adjectives is a factor. Osgood and his colleagues found that most of the variance in the text affecting judgment was explained by only three major factors: the evaluative factor (e.g. good-bad), the potency factor (e.g. strong-weak) and the activity factor (e.g. active-passive), out of which the most discriminative is the evaluative one.

Starting with semantic differential techniques, Kamps and Marx (Kamps and Marx 2002) developed algorithmic methods that rely on the structure and content of the WordNet (version 1.7) to assess the subjectivity of all the adjectives contained in PWN. They illustrated their method beginning with the evaluative factor and found 5,410 adjectives related to "good" and "bad". They applied the same method to the next two best discriminative factors identified by Osgood and his colleagues: the potency factor and the activity factor. The set of adjectives related to the bipolar adjectives (the coverage of the factor) from each of the two factors represented the same cluster of 5,410 adjectives.

As many researchers (Andreevskaia and Bergler 2006; Bentivogli et al. 2004; Mihalcea et al. 2007; Valitutti et al. 2004; Wiebe and Mihalcea 2006) agree that the subjectivity load of a given word is dependent on the senses of the respective word, the principal problem of the Kamps and Marx's model is the fact that the sense distinctions are lost, making it impossible to assign different scores to different senses of the word in case. Moreover, while the adjectives make up the evident class of subjectivity words, the other open class categories have an important potential for expressing subjective meanings.

Considering the above facts, we addressed the problem of differential semantics starting along the lines introduced by Kamps and Marx. We have considerably

Table 6 Synsets factors and coverage in PWN2.0 and PWN3.0

POS	PWN2.0 Synset factors	PWN2.0 Synset coverage	PWN3.0 Synset factors	PWN3.0 Synset coverage
Adjectives	332	5,241 synsets	264	4,240 synsets
Nouns	85	10,874 synsets	118	11,704 synsets
Verbs	246	8,516 synsets	246	8,640 synsets
Adverbs	332	1,571 synsets	264	1,284 synsets

amended their approach in order to take into account all open-class grammar categories in PWN and the word senses. We applied our approach on both PWN 2.0 (Tufiş and Ştefănescu 2010) and PWN 3.0 (Tufiş and Ştefănescu 2012).

We called a factor a pair of word-senses which were directly related by antonymy relation and among which there exists a navigation path as defined in (Tufiş and Ştefănescu 2012). The set of synsets that were traversed on a navigation path for a given factor represents the factor's coverage. It may be of interest to say that not all the antonyms make a factor, that is there exist antonymic word senses among which one cannot find (in PWN) a navigation path. Due to the way the adverbial synsets are dealt with in PWN, we considered only those adverbs that were derived from the adjectives and used for them the same factors.

Any synset in the respective part-of-speech coverage receives scores in the interval [−1, 1] for every factor corresponding to its grammatical category. A positive score means that the connotation of the synset is more similar to the right pole of the factor, while a negative one means the synset is more similar to the left pole. Via PWN—RoWN alignments (2.0 and 3.0) we are able to transfer the values determined for the synsets in PWN to synsets in RoWN. The results are in Table 6.

In (Tufiş and Ştefănescu 2011) we presented an application exploiting these scores in evaluating the possibility of connotation shifts when a fragment of text is taken out of the initial context and put into another "well selected" context.

As one can see from Table 6, between PWN2.0 and PWN3.0 there are significant differences in the number of factors and the size of coverage for Nouns and Adjectives (Adverbs). The differences are due to many synset restructuring (merging, deletion, extending) that were considered in version 3.0.

5 The Pre-Processing and Correction of the RoWN Definitions

The most frequent uses of wordnets exploit the relations among the synsets and synsets alignment to an external conceptual structure (a taxonomy such as IRST's DOMAINS or an ontology such as SUMO/MILO). Except a few remarkable works (Moldovan and Novischi 2002) or Princeton's new release PWN3.0, much less used are the synset glosses, in spite of their essential content. In order to develop a lexical chain algorithm similar to (Moldovan and Novischi 2002) we needed to pre-process the glosses of the Romanian synsets. They are, primarily, taken from EXPD. However, given the difference in granularity between a dictionary and wordnet, many of them required refining.

The pre-processing consists in tokenizing, POS-tagging, lemmatizing and dependency linking of each gloss found in the RoWN.

POS-tagging and lemmatizing were performed using TTL (Ion 2007) which outputs a list of tokens of the sentence each with POS tag (morpho-syntactic descriptors) and lemma information. The RoWN glosses contain about 470 K lexical tokens and 60 K punctuation marks.

When performing POS tagging, the tagger identified more than 2,500 unknown words. Most of them proved to be either spelling errors or words written in disagreement with the Romanian Academy regulations (the improper use of the diacritical mark *î* vs. â). We automatically identified all spelling errors with an ad hoc spell checker using Longest Common Sequences between errors and words in our 1.5 million word-form lexicon. After eliminating all spelling errors, we were left with 550 genuine unknown words which we added to our tagging lexicon along with their POS tags and lemmas. Dependency linking was achieved through the use of LexPar (Ion 2007) which generates a planar, undirected and acyclic graph representation of the sentence (called a linkage) that mimics a syntactic dependency-like structure.

6 Word Sense Disambiguation Based on Wordnets

Due to its wealth of encoded information, PWN has become the "de facto" standard for the knowledge-based word sense disambiguation (WSD) algorithms in both the supervised and unsupervised settings. The WSD competition SensEval (http://www.senseval.org/), which now continues as SemEval (http://semeval2.fbk.eu/), has adopted WordNet as the official sense inventory since its second edition (2001).

Due to the alignment between PWN and RoWN two distinct approaches are possible in disambiguating the senses of the words in Romanian texts: monolingual WSD in which RoWN is used alone and a bilingual parallel WSD in which, through word alignment and synset mapping, the common set of meanings of a pair of words which are translation equivalents (TE) is determined (Tufiş et al. 2004a, b). The synsets from an aligned pair have the same identifier. (Ion and Tufiş 2009) showed that multilingual WSD accuracy exceeded the state of the art (with an F-measure of almost 75 %, a fact which still stands) and we presented the entire WSD procedure from word alignment, the identification of common sets of meanings and the clustering of meanings to find word classes which share the same meaning. The identification of the common set of meanings of a pair of translation

Table 7 Results of the RoWN to PWN alignment validation based on the bilingual SemCor

	# of EN-RO TEs	% of EN-RO TEs pairs out of all TEs pairs identified
Synonyms missing from existing RO synsets (incomplete RO synsets)	12,044	13.55 %
Unimplemented senses for Romanian lemmas (missing RO synsets)	11,930	13.42 %
Different POS tags (xpos)	3,694	4.16 %

equivalents was used to pinpoint problems of conceptual alignment between PWN and RoWN. Thus, if for a correct pair of translation equivalents one cannot find at least a common meaning (that is a pair of synsets with the same identifier), then one of the following problems could be identified: the relevant Romanian synset has not been implemented yet, the relevant Romanian synset was wrongly aligned or (most frequently) it did not contain that particular synonym. By doing parallel WSD on George Orwell's 1984 novel (English-Romanian parallel variant), we were able to identify and correct a significant number of such problems with RoWN.

Another corpus that we have worked with and sense-disambiguated with the parallel WSD procedure described above is the English-Romanian SemCor (Ion 2007). We have translated 81 SemCor files into Romanian instructing the translators to translate as literally as possible, avoiding paraphrases or language specific expressions in all cases in which the resulted Romanian translation was fluent. The texts were then word-aligned using YAWA (Tufiş et al. 2006) and the parallel WSD procedure was applied on the parallel English-Romanian SemCor for which we had sense annotations on the English part. On the occasion of this experiment we identified several incomplete RO synsets as well as non-implemented senses of many Romanian words. Based on this evaluation, RoWN has been corrected for the "Incomplete RO synsets" type error and the missing synsets were partially added. The word alignment was performed automatically with a precision of around 80 % (Ion and Tufiş 2009), therefore we estimate that this percent may be taken as a lower bound of the accuracy of the WSD in the Romanian part of the bilingual SemCor. The validation results are summarized in Table 7.

We also performed full parallel WSD (i.e. ignoring the existing sense annotation) on the English-Romanian SemCor with good results: 0.685 F-measure for the English part of the corpus (around 80 K disambiguated occurrences) and 0.515 F-measure for the Romanian part (approx. 50 K disambiguated occurrences). For Romanian, to the best of our knowledge, this is the first, large-scale, WSD disambiguation experiment.

We have developed an English-Romanian MT system for the legalese language of the type contained in JRC-Acquis multilingual parallel corpus (Steinberger et al. 2006), of a cross-lingual question answering system in open domains (Ion et al. 2010) and an opinion mining system (Ştefănescu 2010; Tufiş 2008). For these projects, heavily relying on the aligned Ro-En wordnets, we extracted a series of high frequency Romanian nouns and verbs not present in RoWN but occurring in JRC-Acquis corpus and in the Romanian pages of Wikipedia and proceeded to their incorporation in RoWN.

7 Conclusions

Lexical resources have always been the main repositories of both language and knowledge (Gala and Zock 2013). Nowadays, the electronic format has become indispensable for language study and automatic processing. One of the most valuable lexical resources for processing Romanian is the wordnet, as it contains a large number of literals, both simple and multi-word ones, mainly characterizing the contemporary language. We keep enriching it both quantitatively and qualitatively, thus turning it into a knowledge base to be used effectively in applications. We presented here its actual status and its evolution throughout time. We mentioned all the time the motivation for the decisions we took regarding its further development. And all the time the motivation was practical, explainable by the necessity of using this resource in various projects and applications. In fact, the existence of wordnets is justified mostly by the processing of natural language, and less by the human user interested in clarifying the meaning of a word.

References

Andreevskaia, A., & Bergler, S. (2006). Mining WordNet for a fuzzy sentiment: Sentiment tag extraction from WordNet glosses. In *Proceedings of the 11th Conference of the European Chapter of the Association for Computational Linguistics (EACL-2006)* (pp. 209–216).

Baccianella, S., Esuli, A., & Sebastiani, F. (2010). SENTIWORDNET 3.0: An enhanced lexical resource for sentiment analysis and opinion mining. In *Proceedings of LREC2010* (pp. 2200–2204).

Barbu Mititelu, V. (2013). Sistemul all-inclusive în reprezentarea cunoştinţelor lexicale. In O. Ichim (Ed.), *Tradiţie/inovaţie—identitate/alteritate: paradigme în evoluţia limbii şi culturii române* (pp. 9–18). Iasi: Editura Universitatii Alexandru Ioan Cuza.

Barbu Mititelu, V. (2013). Increasing the effectiveness of the Romanian Wordnet in NLP applications. *CSJM*, *21*(3), 320–331.

Barbu Mititelu, V., Dumitrescu, S. D., & Tufiş, D. (2014). News about the Romanian Wordnet. In *Proceedings of the 7th International Global Wordnet Conference* (pp. 268–275).

Bentivogli, L., Forner, P., Magnini, B., & Pianta, E. (2004). Revising WordNet domains hierarchy: semantics, coverage, and balancing. In *Proceedings of COLING 2004 Workshop on Multilingual Linguistic Resources* (pp. 101–108).

Bilgin, O., Cetinoglu, O., & Oflazer, K. (2004). Morphosemantic relations in and across wordnets: A study based on Turkish. In P. Sojka, K. Pala, P. Smrz, C. Fellbaum & P. Vossen (Eds.), *Proceedings of GWC* (pp. 60–66).

Dimitrova, Ts., Tarpomanova, E., & Rizov, B. (2014). Coping with derivation in the Bulgarian Wordnet. In *Proceedings of the 7th International Global Wordnet Conference* (pp. 109–117).

Esuli, A., & Sebastiani, F. (2006). SENTIWORDNET: A publicly available lexical resource for opinion mining. In *Proceedings of the 5th Conference on Language Resources and Evaluation LREC-06* (pp. 417–422).

Fellbaum, Ch. (1998). *WordNet: an electronic lexical database*. Cambridge: Academic Press.

Fellbaum, C., Osherson, A., & Clark, P. E. (2007). Putting semantics into wordnet's "morphosemantic" links. In *Proceedings of the 3rd Language and Technology Conference* (pp. 350–358).

Gala, N. (2013). Ressources lexicales mono- et multilingues : une évolution historique au fil des pratiques et des usages. In N. Gala, M. Zock (Eds.), *Ressources lexicales: contenu, évaluation, utilisation, évaluation* (pp. 1–42). Amsterdam : John Benjamins Publishing.

Gala, N., & Zock, M. (Eds.). (2013). *Ressources lexicales: contenu, évaluation, utilisation, évaluation*. Amsterdam: John Benjamins Publishing.

Ion, R. (2007). Automatic word sense disambiguation techniques: Applications for romanian and english (in Romanian). *PhD Thesis*. Bucharest: Romanian Academy.

Ion, R., & Tufiş, D. (2009). Multilingual versus monolingual word sense disambiguation. *Int J Speech Technol, 12*(2–3), 113–124.

Ion, R., Ştefănescu, D., Ceausu, A., Tufiş, D., Irimia, E., & Barbu Mititelu, V. A. (2010). Trainable multi-factored QA system. In C. Peters et al. (Eds.), *Multilingual information access evaluation* (pp. 257–264). Heidelberg: Springer.

Kahusk, N., Kerner, K., & Vider, K. (2010). Enriching estonian Wordnet with derivations and semantic relations. In *Proceeding of the 2010 Conference on Human Language Technologies—The Baltic Perspective* (pp. 195–200).

Kamps, J., & Marx, M. (2002). Words with attitude. In *Proceedings of the 1st International Wordnet Conference* (pp. 332–341).

Mihalcea, R., Banea, C., & Wiebe, J. (2007). Learning multilingual subjective language via cross-lingual projections. In *Proceedings of the 45th Annual Meeting of the ACL* (pp. 976–983).

Moldovan, D., & Novischi, A. (2002). Lexical chains for question answering. In *Proceedings of COLING 2002* (pp. 674–680).

Niles, I., Pease, A. (2001). Towards a standard upper ontology. In *Proceedings of the 2nd International Conference on Formal Ontology in Information Systems* (pp. 2–9).

Osgood, E Ch., Suci, G., & Tannenbaum, P. (1957). *The measurement of meaning*. Urbana: University of Illinois Press.

Pala, K., & Hlavackova, D. (2007). Derivational relations in Czech Wordnet. In P*roceedings of the Workshop on Balto-Slavonic Natural Language Processing* (pp.75–81).

Piasecki, M., Ramocki, R., & Maziarz, M. (2012). Recognition of polish derivational relations based on supervised learning scheme. In *Proceedings of LREC 2012* (pp. 916–922).

Stamou, S., Oflazer, K., Pala, K., Christoudoulakis, D., Cristea, D., & Tufiş, D., et al. BALKANET A multilingual semantic network for the balkan languages. In *Proceedings of the International Wordnet Conference* (pp. 12–24).

Steinberger, R., Pouliquen, B., Widiger, A., Ignat, C., Erjavec, T., & Tufiş, D., et al. (2006). The JRC-Acquis: a multilingual aligned parallel corpus with 20 + languages. In *Proceedings of LREC2006* (pp. 2142–2147).

Ştefănescu, D. (2010). Intelligent information mining from multilingual corpora (in Romanian). *PhD Thesis*, Bucharest: Romanian Academy.

Sojat, K., & Srebacic, M. (2014). Morphosemantic relations between verbs in Croatian Wordnet. In *Proceedings of the 7th International Global Wordnet Conference* (pp. 262–267).

Tufiş, D. (2008). Mind your words! You might convey what you wouldn't like to. *IJCCC, 3*, 139–143.

Tufiş, D., & Cristea, D. (2002). Methodological issues in building the Romanian Wordnet and consistency checks in Balkanet. In *Proceedings of LREC2002 Workshop on Wordnet Structures and Standardisation* (pp. 35–41).

Tufiş, D., & Barbu, E. (2004). A methodology and associated tools for building interlingual Wordnets. In *Proceedings of LREC2004* (pp. 1067–1070).

Tufiş, D., Cristea, D., & Stamou, S. (2004). BalkaNet: Aims, methods, results and perspectives. *ROMJIST*, *7*(1–2), 9–43.

Tufiş, D., Ion, R., Barbu, E., & Barbu Mititelu, V. (2004a). Cross-lingual validation of multilingual Wordnets. In P. Sojka, K. Pala, P. Smrz, C. Fellbaum & P.Vossen (Eds.), *Proceedings of the Second International Wordnet Conference*—GWC 2004 (pp. 332–340).

Tufiş, D., Ion, R., & Ide, N. (2004b). Word sense disambiguation as a Wordnets validation method in Balkanet. In *Proceedings of LREC2004* (pp. 741–744).

Tufiş, D., Ion, R., Ceauşu, Al., & Ştefănescu, D. (2006). Improved lexical alignment by combining multiple reified alignments. In *Proceedings of the 11th Conference of the European Chapter of the Association for Computational Linguistics (EACL2006)* (pp. 153–160).

Tufiş, D., & Ştefănescu, D. (2010). A differential semantics approach to the annotation of the Synsets in WordNet. In *Proceedings of LREC 2010* (pp. 3173–3180).

Tufiş, D., & Ştefănescu, D. (2011). An Osgoodian perspective on WordNet. In *Proceedings of Speech Technology and Human-Computer Dialogue (SpeD)* (pp. 1–8).

Tufiş, D., & Ştefănescu, D. (2012). Experiments with a differential semantics annotation for WordNet 3.0. *Decis Support Syst*, *53*(4), 695–703.

Tufiş, D., Barbu Mititelu, V., Ştefănescu, D., & Ion, R. (2013). The Romanian Wordnet in a nutshell. *LRE*, *47*(4), 1305–1314.

Valitutti, A., Strapparava, C., & Stock, O. (2004). Developing affective lexical resources. *Psychol J*, *2*(1), 61–83.

Wiebe, J., & Mihalcea, R. (2006). Word senses and subjectivity. In *Proceedings of the 21st International Conference on Computational Linguistics and 44th Annual Meeting of the ACL* (pp. 1065–1072).

Zock, M. (2010). Language production, a complex, but feasible task, provided to find the right strategy. In D. Tufiş & C. Forascu (Eds.), *Multilinguality and interoperability in language processing with emphasis on Romanian* (pp. 343–359). Bucharest: Romanian Academy Publishing House.

Zock, M., Bilac, S. Word lookup on the basis of associations: from an idea to a roadmap. In *Proceedings of the COLING Workshop on Enhancing and using Electronic Dictionaries* (pp. 89–95).

Zock, M., & Schwab, D. (2013). L'index, une ressource vitale pour guider les auteurs a trouver le mot bloque sur le bout de la langue. In N. Gala, M. Zock (Eds.), *Ressources lexicales: Contenu, évaluation, utilisation, évaluation* (pp. 313–354). Amsterdam : John Benjamins Publishing.

Quo Vadis: A Corpus of Entities and Relations

Dan Cristea, Daniela Gîfu, Mihaela Colhon, Paul Diac, Anca-Diana Bibiri, Cătălina Mărănduc and Liviu-Andrei Scutelnicu

Abstract This chapter describes a collective work aimed to build a corpus including annotations of semantic relations on a text belonging to the belletristic genre. The paper presents conventions of annotations for four categories of semantic relations and the process of building the corpus as a collaborative work. Part of the annotation is done automatically, such as the token/part of speech/lemma layer, and is performed during a preprocessing phase. Then, an entity layer (where entities of type person are marked) and a relation layer (evidencing binary

D. Cristea (✉) · D. Gîfu · P. Diac · L.-A. Scutelnicu
Faculty of Computer Science, "Alexandru Ioan Cuza" University of Iaşi, Iaşi, Romania
e-mail: dcristea@info.uaic.ro

D. Gîfu
e-mail: daniela.gifu@info.uaic.ro

P. Diac
e-mail: paul.diac@info.uaic.ro

L.-A. Scutelnicu
e-mail: liviu.scutelnicu@info.uaic.ro

D. Cristea · L.-A. Scutelnicu
Institute for Computer Science, Romanian Academy - The Iaşi Branch, Iaşi, Romania

M. Colhon
Department of Computer Science, University of Craiova, Craiova, Romania
e-mail: mcolhon@inf.ucv.ro

A.-D. Bibiri
Department of Interdisciplinary Research in Social-Human Sciences, "Alexandru Ioan Cuza" University of Iaşi, Iaşi, Romania
e-mail: anca.bibiri@info.uaic.ro

C. Mărănduc
"Iorgu Iordan-Al. Rosetti" Institute of Linguistics of the Romanian Academy, Bucharest, Romania
e-mail: catalina_maranduc@yahoo.com

© Springer International Publishing Switzerland 2015

N. Gala et al. (eds.), *Language Production, Cognition, and the Lexicon*,
Text, Speech and Language Technology 48, DOI 10.1007/978-3-319-08043-7_28

relations between entities) are added manually by a team of trained annotators, the result being a heavily annotated file. A number of methods to obtain accuracy are detailed. Finally, some statistics over the corpus are drawn. The language under investigation is Romanian, but the proposed annotation conventions and methodological hints are applicable to any language and text genre.

Keywords Semantic relations · Annotated corpus · Anaphora · XML · Annotation conventions

1 Introduction

When we read books we are able to discover in the sequence of words, with apparently zero effort, the mentions of entities, the relationships that connect entities, as well as the events and situations the characters are involved in. Entities, relations, events and situations can be of many types. For instance, entities could be: persons, animals, places, organisations, crafts, objects, ideas, etc. as well as any grouping of the above. Relations linking characters could be anaphoric (when the interpretation of one mention is dependent on the interpretation of a previous one), affectional (when a certain feeling or emotion is expressed in the interaction of characters), kinship (when family relationships are mentioned, sometimes composing very complex genealogical trees), social (when job hierarchies or social mutual ranks are explicitly remarked), etc. Moreover, the text could include mentions about relations holding between characters and other types of entities: persons are in places, persons belong to organisations, mutual positioning of locations in space, etc. Deciphering different types of links is a major step in understanding a book content.

We address in this paper the issue of building a corpus that makes explicit a strictly delimited set of binary relations between entities that belong to the following types: persons, gods, groups of persons and gods, parts of bodies of persons and gods. The relations marked in the corpus belong to four binary types: anaphoric, affectional, kinship and social.

Very often the interpretation of semantic relations is subjective being the result of a personal interpretation of the text, more precisely, of inferences developed by the reader or obtained by putting on stage some extra textual general knowledge. In building this corpus we avoided anything that is not explicitly uttered in the text, trying thus to keep the subjective interpretation to a minimum. Also, we were not interested to decode time moments, nor the different ways in which time could be connected to entities or to the events they participate in.

The motivation for this endeavour is to base on this "gold" corpus the construction of a technology able to recognise these types of entities and these types of semantic relations in free texts. The experience acquired while building such a technology could then be applied in extrapolating it to other types of entities and semantic relations, finally arriving to a technology able to decipher the semantic content of texts. When a human reads a text, she/he first deciphers the semantic links as they are mentioned in the text, and only then these isolated pieces of knowledge are connected by inferences, that often engage particular knowledge of the reader, thus obtaining a coherent, albeit personal, interpretation of the text, as a whole. A novel could be the source of as many interpretations as readers it has. The freedom to build a proper interpretation makes the relish of most readers. The issue of building a machine interpretation of a novel should therefore be considered also from this perspective (which could be a rich source of philosophical questions, too): *how much do we want our technology be able to add above the strict level of information communicated by the text?* We believe that the answer to this question shall be rooted in the actual type of application that is desired, but the primary challenge is this one: *are we capable to interpreted basic assertions expressed in a book?*

We are tempted to conclude this introduction by making a parallel with the way human beings do grow up, the accumulation of their memories and readings assembling in time their personalities, characters, predisposition for certain types of behaviour. Similarly, one may imagine the formation of intelligent behaviours in agents, which could be rooted in the artificial interpretation of books, this way short-circuiting a real life-time formation. Fictional worlds, if proper selected and fed into agents, are extremely rich in life examples, and a plurality of semantic aspects belonging to real or fictional lives could be studied if recognized in other contexts.

The paper is organised as follows. In the following section we give reasons for selecting the text of a novel as the basis for this corpus. Then we make a brief tour in the literature to configure the state-of-the-art in work related to semantic relations. Section 4 presents the annotations conventions for entities and the four categories of relations annotated in the corpus. Then Sect. 5 details the activities for the creation of the corpus. The notations in the corpus allowed to make different counts and comparisons. They are presented in Sect. 6. Finally, Sect. 7 makes concluding remarks and presents ways of exploitations of the corpus.

2 Why a Corpus Displaying Semantic Relations in Free Texts?

To understand a language one needs not only means of expression, but also vehicles of thought, necessary to discover new ideas or clarify existing ones by refining, expanding, illustrating more or less well specified thoughts (Zock 2010). Semantic relations describe interactions, connections. Connections are indispensable for the interpretation of texts. Without them, we would not be able to express any continuous thought, and we could only list a succession of images and ideas isolated from each other. Every non-trivial text describes a group of entities and the ways in which they interact or interrelate. Identifying these entities and the relations between them is a fundamental step in text understanding (Năstase et al. 2013).

Moreover, relations form the basis for lexical organization. In order to create lexical resources, NLP researchers proposed a variety of methods, including lexico-syntactic patterns and knowledge-based methods exploiting complex lexical resources. Somehow similar situations occur when we reverse the task and go from text interpretation to text production. As Michael Zock and collaborators have shown (Zock et al. 2010; Zock and Schwab 2013) lexical resources are only truly useful if the words they contain are easily accessible. To allow for this, association-based indexes can be used to support interactive lexical access for language producers. As such, co-occurrences can encode word associations and, by this, links holding between them.

Developing a lexical-semantic knowledge base to be used in Natural Language Processing (NLP) applications is the main goal of the research described in this chapter. Such resources are not available for many languages, mainly because of the high cost of their construction. The knowledge base is built in such a way as to facilitate the training of programs aiming to automatically recognise in text entities and semantic relations. As we will see in the next sections, it includes annotations for the spans of text that display mentions of entities and relations, for the arguments (poles) of the relations, as well as for the relevant words or expressions that signal relations.

We are not concerned in the research described in this paper neither with the automatic recognition of entities, nor with the recognition of the relationships between entities. Instead we present how a significant corpus marking entities and relations has been built. The recognition problem will be our following objective. Năstase et al. (2013) show many examples of NLP tasks that are based on the ability to identify semantic relations in text, such as: information extraction, information retrieval, text summarization, machine translation, question answering, paraphrasing, recognition of textual entailment, construction of thesauri and of semantic networks, word-sense disambiguation, language modelling. Although the issue of automatic semantic relations recognition has received good attention in the literature, we believe that the problem is far from being exhausted. Moreover, most of the research in this area is focused on corpora composed of press articles or on Wikipedia texts, while the corpus we describe is built on the skeleton of a fictional text.

As a support for our annotations we have chosen a novel, i.e. a species of the epic genre, which is particularly rich in semantic relations. The text used was the Romanian version of the novel "Quo Vadis", authored by the Nobel laureate Henryk Sienkiewicz.[1] In this masterpiece the author narrates an extremely complex society, the pre-Christian Rome from the time of the emperor Nero. The text displays inter-human relations of a considerable extent: love and hate, friendship and enemy, socio-hierarchical relationships involving slaves and their masters, or curtains and the emperor, etc. The story is dynamic, it involves many characters

[1] The version is the one translated by Remus Luca and Elena Linţă and published at Tenzi Publishing House in 1991.

and the relations are either stable (for instance, those describing family links) or change in time (sexual interest, in one case, and disgust, in another, both evolve into love, friendship depreciates in hate, lack of understanding develops into worship). Appreciative affective relations may differ depending on whether they hold between human characters, when it takes the form of love, or between humans and gods, when it shapes as worship. Another aspect of interpretation relates the contrast between the social and affective relationships, dictatorial, based on fear and abeyance, at the court of Nero, and those found in the evolving but poor Christian society, based on solidarity and forgiveness.

Annotating a novel to entities and semantic relations between them represents a significant challenge, given the differences between journalistic and literary style, the first being devoid of figures of speech that create suggestive images and emotional effects into the mind of the reader.

Not the least, the novel "Quo Vadis" is translated in extremely many languages. We have thought at the possibility to exploit the semantic annotations of the Romanian version for other languages, by applying exporting techniques. Rather many results in the last years have shown that, in certain conditions, annotations can be exported on parallel, word-aligned, corpora, and this usually shortens the annotation time and reduces the costs (Postolache et al. 2006; Drabek and Yarowsky 2005).

Of course, the annotation conventions are expressed in English to facilitate their use for similar tasks in other languages. As is usual the case with semantic labels, they are expected to be applicable without adaptation effort to any language. Most of the examples are extracted from the Romanian version of the book and then aligned passages are searched in an English version.[2] The examples are meant to show also the specificities of different language versions: syntactic features, but mainly idiosyncrasies of translation make that in certain cases the notations pertinent to the two versions differ. We make special notes when these cases occur.

3 Similar Work

Murphy (2003) reviews several properties of semantic relations, among them unaccountability, which basically marks relations as an open class. If considered between words and not entities, then relations complement syntactic theories, like functional dependency grammars (Tesnière 1959) or HPSG (Pollard and Sag 1994). Taken to its extreme, we might say that the very meanings of words in contexts is constituted by the contextual relations they are in (Cruse 1986). Lyons (1977), another important schooler of the British structural semantic tradition, considers that (p. 443) "as far as the empirical investigation of the structure of language is concerned, the sense of a lexical item may be defined to be, not only

[2] Translation in English by Jeremiah Curtin, published by Little Brown and Company in 1897.

dependent upon, but identical with, the set of relations which hold between the item in question and the other items in the same lexical system".

In NLP applications, as in this work, the use of semantic relations is, generally, understood in a more narrower sense. We are concerned about relations between concepts or instances of concepts, i.e. conceptualisations, representations on a semantic layer of persons, things, ideas, which should not be confused with relations between terms, i.e. words, expressions or signs, that are used to express these conceptualisations. For instance, novel, as a concept, should be distinguished from *novel*, as an English word, or *roman*, its Romanian equivalent. The concept novel may be expressed by the terms or expressions *novel*, *fiction* or *fantasy writing*. The relation between *novel* and *fiction* is a synonymy relation between two words. These words are synonyms because there exist contexts of use where they mean the same thing. Examples of lexical databases are WordNet (Miller et al. 1990), where lexical items are organized on synonymy sets (synsets), themselves representing concepts placed in a hierarchy, or Polymots (Gala et al. 2010), that reveals and capitalizes on the bidirectional links between the semantic characterization of lexical items and morphological analogies.

We place our work in the semantic register, there where unambiguous meanings about words or expressions in contexts have been formed and what is looked for are the relations that the text expresses between these conceptualisations, or entities. The domain is known as *entity linking*.

One kind of semantic relation is the hyperonym relation, also called *is a* (and usually noted ISA), linking a hyponym to a hyperonym, or an instance to a class, in a hierarchical representation, for instance in a taxonomy or an ontology (*A* is a kind of *B*, *A* is subordinate to *B*, *A* is narrower than *B*, *B* is broader than *A*). Dictionaries usually use the Aristotelian pattern to define a *definiendum* by identifying a *genus proximus* and showing the *diferentiae specificae* with respect to other instances of the same class (Del Gaudio 2014). Long time ago, Quillian (1962) imagined a model of human memory, thus introducing the concept of semantic network, a knowledge graph representation in which meaning is defined by labelled relations (connections) between concepts and their instances. The most common relation in these representations are the ISA relations (for example, "Petronius *is a* proconsul in Bithynia"), but other types include *part of*, *has as part*, etc.

Most of the work in semantic relations and entity linking addresses the recognition problem and, on a secondary scale, the issue of building significant corpora to support this activity. If NLP systems are to reach the goal of producing meaningful representations of text, they must attain the ability to detect entities and extract the relations which hold between them.

The term *entity linking* usually expresses the task of linking mentions of entities that occur in an unstructured text with records of a knowledge base (KB). As such, the most important challenges in entity linking address: name variations (different text strings in the source text refer the same KB entity), ambiguities (there are more than one entity in the KB a string can refer to) and absence where there is no entity description in the KB to which a string in the source text representing an entity could possibly match with (Bunescu and Paşca 2006; Cucerzan 2007). Let's note also that in the interpretation of fictional texts, each time a process starts, the KB is empty and it will be populated synchronously with the unfolding of the text and the encountering of first mentions.

Another point of interest is the detection of relations holding between entities and events. Mulkar-Mehta et al. (2011) for instance, focused on recognising the part-whole relations between entities and events as well as causal relations of coarse and fine granularities. Bejan and Harabagiu (2010) and Chen et al. (2011) showed that coreferences between events can be detected using a combination of lexical, part-of-speech (POS), semantic and syntactic features. Their corpus, the *EventCorefBank*, restricted by the Automatic Content Extraction exercise to the domains of *Life*, *Business*, *Conflict* and *Justice*, contained articles on 43 different topics from the Google News archive. Also, Cybulska and Vossen (2012) annotated the *Intelligence Community Corpus*, at coreference mentions between violent events as bombings, killings, wars, etc.

Corpora detailing semantic relations in fictional texts are rare if not inexistent. Usually supporting the activities of semantic analysis are texts belonging to the print press.

Some have been annotated with predicate-argument structures and anaphoric relations, as the *Kyoto University Text Corpus* (Kawahara et al. 2002) and the *Naist Text Corpus* (Iida et al. 2007). The anaphoric relations are categorized into three types (Masatsugu et al. 2012): coreference, annotated with the "=" tag, bridging reference, that can be expressed in the form *B* of *A*, annotated by "*NO*:*A*" to *B*, and non-coreference anaphoric relations, annotated with "≃". The *Balanced Corpus of Contemporary Written Japanese* (BCCWJ)[3] includes publications (books, magazines) and social media texts (blogs and forums) annotated with predicate-argument structures as defined in FrameNet (Ohara 2011). They do not annotate inter-sentence semantic relations. Although the predicate-argument structures of FrameNet include the existence of zero pronoun, referents are not annotated if not existent in the same sentence. Since anaphoric relations are not annotated, they do not annotate the inter-sentence semantic relations.

Another type of annotation regarding the semantic level, focusses specifically on anaphoric relations, including zero anaphora, as is the *Live Memories Corpus* (Rodríguez et al. 2010), originating in the Italian Wikipedia and blogs. Since in Italian pronoun-dropping only occurs in the subject position (same as in Romanian), they transfer to the corresponding predicates the role of anaphors. To the same category belongs also the *Z-corpus* (Rello and Ilisei 2009), incorporating Spanish law books, textbooks and encyclopedia articles, treating zero anaphora. There too, pronoun-dropping is marked in the subject position.

In all cases, corpora annotated to semantic links are intended to be used to train recognition algorithms. In principle, the annotation layers, the constraints used in the annotation, and the annotation conventions should be related to the set of

[3] http://www.tokuteicorpus.jp/.

features used by the recogniser and not to the learning methods used in training. For that reason, in the following we will revise briefly algorithms and sets of features used in the training of semantic links detection.

As regards the methods used in recognition, some approaches use supervised machine learning to match entity mentions onto their correspondent KB records. Rao et al. (2012) score entities contained in the KB for a possible match to the query entity. Many studies make use of syntactic features extracted by deep or shallow parsing, POS-tagging and named entity annotation (Pantel et al. 2004). The 2012 Text Analysis Conference launched the *Knowledge Base Population Cold Start* task, requiring systems to take a set of documents and produce a comprehensive set of <Subject, Predicate, Object> triples that encode relationships involving named-entities. Starting with (Hearst 1992), many studies have used patterns incorporating information at the lexical and syntactic level for identification of instances of semantic relationships (Banko et al. 2007; Girju et al. 2006; Snow et al. 2006). The system KELVIN, for instance, integrates a pipeline of processing tools, among which a basic tool is the BBN's SERIF (Statistical Entity and Relation Information Finding). SERIF does named-entities identification and classification by type and subtype, intra-document co-reference analysis, including named, nominal and pronominal mentions, sentence parsing, in order to extract intra-sentential relations between entities, and detection of certain types of events (Boschee et al. 2005).

An accurate entity linking technique is dependent on a diversity of NLP mechanisms, which should work well in workflows. Ad hoc linking techniques are on the class of one-document and cross-document anaphora resolution (Bagga and Baldwin 1998; Saggion 2007; Singh et al. 2011). RARE is a system of anaphora resolution relying on a mixed approach that combines symbolic rules with learning techniques (Cristea and Dima 2001; Postolache et al. 2006). A recently improved version of it, developed for the ATLAS project[4] has given good results for a number of European languages (Anechitei et al. 2013).

4 Annotation Conventions

Vivi Năstase, citing Levi (1978) and Séaghdha and Copestake (2008) in her book (Năstase et al. 2013) enumerates a set of principles for relation inventories:

- the inventory of relations should have good coverage;
- relations should be disjunct, and should describe a coherent concept;
- the class distribution should not be overly skewed or sparse;
- the concepts underlying the relations should generalize to other linguistic phenomena;
- the guidelines should make the annotation process as simple as possible;
- the categories should provide useful semantic information.

[4] http://www.atlasproject.eu/.

In this section we present a set of annotation conventions that observe the above principles and were put at the bases of the "Quo Vadis" corpus.

4.1 Layers of Annotation

The Romanian automatic pre-processing chain applied on the raw texts of the book consists of the following tasks, executed in sequence:

- segmentation at sentence level (marks the sentence boundaries in the raw book text);
- tokenization (demarcates words or word compounds, but also numbers, punctuation marks, abbreviations, etc.);
- part-of-speech tagging (identifies POS categories and morpho-syntactic information of tokens);
- lemmatization (determines lemmas of words);
- noun phrase chunking (explores the previous generated data and adds information regarding noun phrase boundaries and their head words) (Simionescu 2012).

Let's note that we have not find a standard for annotating entities and relations. Năstase et al. (2013) says on this issue: "A review of the literature has shown that almost every new attempt to analyze relations between nominals leads to a new list of relations. We observe that a necessary and sufficient list of relations to describe the connections between nominals does not exist". As such, we went on with our own suggestions, knowing well that, at any moment in the future, if a need to adopt a standard will arise, an automatic conversion will be possible.

4.2 Annotating Entities

Let's note that our intention is to put in evidence entities such as are they mentioned in a piece of literature. These are characters or groups that play different roles in the development of the story. A human reader usually builds a mental representation for each of them the very moment those characters (or groups) are mentioned first, and these representations are recalled from memory any time they are evoked subsequently. The mental representation associated with a character may change while the story unfolds, although a certain mapping remains constant. It is just like we associate a box or a container with each character and afterwards we fill it with details (name, sex, kinship connections, composition, beliefs, religion, etc.). Some of these details may change as the story goes on, only the container remains the same. Any mention of that character is a mapping from a text expression to the corresponding container. In text, we annotate mentions, not containers, but recreate them after processing the coreference mappings, as will become clear in the next sections. So, what we call entities are these containers, or empty representation structures, as holders to associate text mentions on. However, as will be shown later in Sect. 4.3, the notation we use for entities' mentions is an XML element also called ENTITY.

We concentrate only on entities of type `PERSON` and `GOD`, but group of persons are also annotated as `PERSON-GROUP`, occupations or typologies—coded as `PERSON-CLASS`, human anatomical parts, coded `PERSON-PART` and names of persons, coded `PERSON-NAME`. Similarly, there will be: `GOD-GROUP`, `GOD-CLASS`, `GOD-PART` and `GOD-NAME`, although very few of these last types, if any, really occurred. It is well known that an isomorphism exists between the world of humans and that of gods. In the Greek and then in the Roman antiquity, co-exist the same types of relations as those holding among humans. The man Christ became a god in the Christian religion. As such, to talk about men and women and to neglect gods was not an option, because would have created an artificial barrier.

Syntactically, the text realisation of entities are nominal phrases (NPs). Using a term common in works dedicated to anaphora, we will also call them referential expressions (REs), because the role of these expressions is to recall from memory (or refer to) the respective containers (where the features add on). We will use the term NP when we discuss syntactic properties of the expression and RE, when we discuss text coverage and semantic properties. It will be normal, therefore, to say that a NP has a syntactic head and a RE mentions (or represents, or refers) an entity. A noun phrase normally has a nominal or pronominal head and can include modifiers: adjectives, numerals, determiners, genitival particles, and even prepositional phrases. Some examples are[5]: [*Ligia*], [*Marcus Vinicius*], [*împăratul*] ([*the emperor*]), [*al lui Petronius*] ([*of Petronius*]), [*el*] ([*he*]), [*imperiul Roman*] ([*the Roman empire*]), [*un grup mare de credincioşi*] ([*a big group of believers*]). There is one exception to this rule: nominal phrases realised by pronominal adjectives, as [*nostru*] (*our*) or [*ale noastre*] (*ours*). We do not include relative clauses (relative pronouns prefixing a verb and, possibly, other syntactic constituents) in the notation of entities. A relative pronoun is marked as an individual entity. Example: [*Petronius*], [*care*] *era*… ([*Petronius*], [*who*] *was*…).

Not marked are also the reflexive pronouns in the reflexive forms of verbs, like in: *ei se spală* (*they* REFL-PRON *wash*); but other reflexive pronouns not appearing in a verbal compound are marked: *sieşi*, *sine* (*herself*, *himself*), etc.

A NP may textually include another NP. We will say they are "imbricated", and, by abuse of language, sometimes we will say the corresponding entities are also "imbricated". It should be noted that imbricated NPs have always separate heads and they represent always distinct entities. NPs heads would be, therefore, sufficient to represent entities. Still, because we want our corpus to be useful inclusively for training NP chunkers, as REs we notate always the whole NP

[5] In all examples of this chapter we will notate occurrences of entities between square brackets, and we will prefix them with numbers to distinguish among them, there where their identities are important.

constructions, not only their heads. When more imbricated NPs have the same head, only the longest is annotated as an entity. Example: [*alte femei din* [*societatea înaltă*]] ([*other women of* [*the high society*]]), and not [*alte* [*femei*] *din* [*societatea înaltă*]] or [*alte* [*femei din* [*societatea înaltă*]], because [*femei*] as well as [*femei din societatea înaltă*] and [*alte femei din societatea înaltă*] all have the same head: "*femei*". Another syntactic constraint imposes that there are not NPs that intersect and are non-imbricated.

We have instructed our annotators to try to distinguish identification descriptions from characterisation descriptions. For instance, in *acest bărbat, stricat până-n măduva oaselor* (*this man, rotted to the core of his bones*), *stricat până-n măduva oaselor* (*rotted to the core of his bones*) is a caracterisation description. It does not help in the identification of a certain men among many and should be neglected in the notation of a RE. Alternatively, in *convoi de fecioare* (*a band of maidens*)—the sequence *de fecioare* (*of maidens*) is an identification description, because it uniquely identifies "the band" among many others and it should be included in the RE aimed to refer that band as an entity group. Only identification descriptions will be marked as REs.

4.3 Annotating Relations

One class of anaphoric relations and three classes of non-anaphoric relations are scrutinised, each with sub-types. We present annotation conventions and methodological prerequisites based on which a corpus that puts in evidence characters and relations mentioned as holding between them has been manually built.

As will be seen in the following sub-sections, each relation holds between two arguments, that we will call *poles*, and, with one exception, is signalled by a word or an expression, that we will call *trigger*. In general, when marking relations we want to evidence the minimal span of text in which a reader deciphers a relation. Excepting for coreferential relations, in which poles can be sometimes quite distant in text and there is nothing to be used as a trigger, usually relations are expressed locally in text, within a sentence, within a clause, or even within a noun phrase. As such, excepting for coreferentiality, each relation span should cover the two poles and the trigger.

Our notations are expressed in XML. Basic layers of annotation include: borders of each sentence (marked as `<S></S>` elements, and identified by unique IDs) and words (marked as `<W></W>` and including unique IDs, lemma and morpho-syntactic information). Above these basic layers the annotators marked three types of XML elements:

- `ENTITY`—delimiting REs, including the attributes: `ID`, `TYPE` and, optionally, `HEAD`; as will be explained below, for included subjects (pronoun-dropping) the verb is annotated instead as an `ENTITY`;

- TRIGGER—marking relations' triggers; it delimits a word (<W>) or an expression (sequence of <W>);
- REFERENTIAL, AFFECT, KINSHIP and SOCIAL—mark relations. With the exception of coreferential relations, these markings delimit the minimal spans of text that put in evidence these types of relations. Their attributes are: a unique ID, the sub-type of the relation (listed below), the two poles and the direction of the relation (the attributes FROM and TO), and the ID of a trigger (the attribute TRIGGER).

The two poles of a relation could be intersectable or not. If they are intersectable, then they are necessarily nested and the direction convention is to consider the FROM entity the larger one and the TO entity the nested one.

1:[*celui de-al doilea* <*soț*> 2:[*al Popeii*]] (1:[*to the second husband* 2:[*of Popeea*]]) $\Longrightarrow$ [1] spouse-of (Bagga and Baldwin 1998)[6]

As already mentioned, the coreferential relation could never be expressed between nested REs. If the RE poles are not nested, we adopted a right-to-left direction in annotating coreferential relations. This decision will be defended in the next sub-section. For the rest of relations the convention is to consider the direction as indicated naturally by reading the trigger and its context. For instance, in the text "X loves Y", the relation love, announced by the trigger *loves*, is naturally read as [X] love [Y], therefore with FROM = X and TO = Y, but in "X is loved by Y", the relation will be [X] loved-by [Y].

It could happen that a pole of a relation is not explicitly mentioned. This happens in cases of included subjects, when the subjects are expressed by null (or dropped) pronouns. In Romanian, the morphological properties of the subject are included in the predicate, such that the missing pole will be identified with the predicate.

Example. *dar* (1:[*îl*]*și* 2:[<*iubeau*>, REALISATION = "INCLUDED"]) *din tot sufletul* (2:[<*loved*> REALISATION = "INCLUDED"] 1:[*him*] *with the whole soul*)) $\Longrightarrow$ [2] loves [1]

It should be noted that a word could be simultaneously marked as a token (<W>), trigger (<TRIGGER>) and entity (<ENTITY>). For instance, *iubeau* (love-PAST-TENSE) in the notation below has all three markings. The value of the FROM attribute of the AFFECT element will filled in by the ID of the verb *iubeau*, marked as an ENTITY, while the value of the TRIGGER attribute in the same relation will be the ID of the TRIGGER element covering the same word.

[6] To save space, in the notations showing relations on our examples, we will mark in labeled square brackets, as before, the entities and in pointed brackets—the triggers; the relations themselves are indicated by their sub-types; sometimes, when there is a need to associate triggers to their corresponding relations, these are also labeled.

```
dar
 <AFFECT ID="..." TYPE="LOVE" FROM="E47" TO="E46" TRIGGER="T17">
   <ENTITY ID="E46">
     <W ID="..." POS="..." LEMMA="el">îl</W>
   </ENTITY>
   şi
   <ENTITY ID="E47" REALISATION="INCLUDED">
     <TRIGGER ID="T17">
        <W ID="W45" POS="..." LEMMA="iubi">iubeau</W>
     </TRIGGER>
   </ENTITY>
</AFFECT>
din tot sufletul
```

When a relation is expressed through the eyes of another character, being perceived particularly as such by this one, or is still uncertain or to be realised in the future we say that the relation is “interpreted”. As such, a relation `R` will be marked as `R-interpret`. All types and sub-types of relations could have `interpret`-ed correspondents.

4.4 Referential Relations

When the understanding of one RE-to-entity mapping depends on the recuperation in memory of a previously mentioned entity (the container together with its accumulated content), we say that a referential relation occurs between this RE (called anaphor) and that entity (called antecedent). In the literature, this definition presents variants, some (as (Mitkov 2003)) insisting on the textual realisation of the relation, the anaphor and the antecedent being both textual mentions, while others (Cristea and Dima 2001) putting in evidence its cognitive or semantic aspects as such, the anaphor being a textual mention and the antecedent—an entity as represented on a cognitive layer, therefore, in our terms—a container plus its content. Supplementary, some authors also make the distinction between anaphora (when a less informative mention of an entity succeeds a more informative one; for instance, a pronoun follows a proper noun) and cataphora (when the other way round is true; for instance, the pronoun mention comes before the proper noun mention). It is to notice however, as (Tanaka 1999) and others have noticed, that cataphora could be *absolute* (when the text includes no more informative reference to the entity before the less informative one) or *relative* (when the inversion takes place at the level of a sentence only, a more informative mention being present in a sentence that precedes the one the pronoun belongs to).

In order to mark the direction of a referential relation, for non-imbricated REs, in connection with text unfolding (a more recent RE mentions an entity introduced or referred by a previously mentioned RE), the annotation of the poles of the coreferential relations are as follows: the source (`FROM`) is the more recent one and the destination (`TO`) is the older one. In Romanian,[7] this direction is from the right of the text to its left. For example, in *pe* 1:[*Ligia*] 2:[*o*] *iubesc* (1:[*Ligia*] *is* 2:[*the one*] *I love*), the relation is marked from (Bagga and Baldwin 1998) to [1]. Although perhaps less intuitive, the direction of cataphoric relations comply with the same right-to-left annotation convention, on the ground that a container (possibly including only scarce details) must have been introduced even by a less informative mention, while the more informative mention, coming after, refers back in memory to this conceptualisation, and injects more information in there (Cristea and Dima 2001). In the text 1:[*îl*] *chemă pe* 2:[*Seneca*] (*he* 1:[*him*_clitic] *summoned* 2:[*Seneca*]) the direction is also from (Bagga and Baldwin 1998) to [1]. Deciphering anaphoric relations in the Romanian language is perhaps more complex than in other languages, mainly due to the duplication of the direct and indirect complements by unaccented forms of pronouns. But we will refrain from making anaphora resolution comments in the present study as this topic is outside our declared intent.

We established nine sub-types of referential relations, listed and exemplified below.

- `coref`: by slightly modifying the definition given above for referentiality, we say that we have a coreferential relation between a RE and an entity E when we understand the RE-to-E identity mapping based on the recuperation in memory of E, a previously mentioned entity. Coref is a symmetric relation, where poles could be of types `PERSON`, `PERSON-GROUP`, `GOD` and `GOD-GROUPS`, but always with both poles of the same category. It is important to notice that a coref relation can never occur between imbricated REs. Examples:

  1:[*Marcus Vicicius*]… 2:[*el*]… (1:[*Marcus Vicicius*]… 2:[*he*]…) ⟹ [2] coref [1];
  1:[*Ligia*]… 2:[*tânara libertă*]… (1:[*Ligia*]… 2:[*the young libert*]…) ⟹ [2] coref [1];
  Nu avea nici cea mai mică îndoială că 1:[*lucrătorul acela*] *e* 2:[*Ursus*]. (*He had not the least doubt that* 1:[*that laborer*] *was* 2:[*Ursus*].)
  ⟹ [2] `coref-interpret` [1];
  L-am prezentat pe 1:[*acest Glaucus*] *ca pe* 2:[*fiul Iudei*] *şi* 3:[*trădător al tuturor creştinilor*]. (*I described* 1:[*Glaucus*] *as* 2:[*a real son of Judas*], *and* 3:[*a traitor to all Christians*].) ⟹ [2] `coref-interpret` [1], [3] `coref-interpret` [1];

- `member-of`(a `PERSON` type RE is a `member-of` a `PERSON-GROUP` entity and, similarly, a `GOD` is a `member-of` a `GOD-GROUP`), a directed relation. Example:

[7] contrary, for instance, to Semitic languages.

1:[*o femeie din* 2:[*societatea înaltă*]] (1:[*a woman of* 2:[*the high society*]]) ⟹ [1] `member-of` [2];

- `has-as-member` (the inverse of `member-of`, from a `PERSON-GROUP` to a `PERSON`, or from a `GOD-GROUP` to a `GOD`), directed:

  1:[*Petronius*]... 2:[*amândurora*] (1:[*Petronius*]... *to* 2:[*both of them*]) ⟹ [2] `has-as-member` [1];
  1:[*Ursus*]... 2:[*Ligia*]... 3:[*voi*] (1:[*Ursus*]... 2:[*Ligia*]... 3: [*you*_PL]) ⟹ [3] `has-as-member` [1]; [3] `has-as-member` [2];

- `isa` (from a `PERSON` type RE to its corresponding `PERSON-CLASS`, or from a `GOD` to its corresponding `GOD-CLASS`), directed;

  1:[*naşă*] *să-mi fie* 2:[Pomponia] (*and I wish* 2:[*Pomponia*] *to be* 1:[*my godmother*]) ⟹ [2] isa [1] only in the Romanian version; in the English version the two REs are inverted, which gives here the inverse relation (*see* next);

- `class-of` (the inverse of isa, from a `PERSON-CLASS` to an instance of it of type `PERSON`, or from a `GOD-CLASS` to a `GOD` type instance), directed:

  Dar nu eşti 1:[*tu*] 2:[*un zeu*]? (*But are* 1:[*thou*] *not* 2:[*a god*]?) ⟹ [2] `class- of-interpret` [1] ([1] is seen as a God by someone);
  daţi-mi-1:[*o*] *de* 2:[*nevastă*] (*Give* 1:[*her*] *to me as* 2:[*wife*]) ⟹ [2] `class-of- interpret` [1][8];
  Se trezise în 1:[*el*] 2:[*artistul*], 3:[*adoratorul frumuseţii*]. (2:[*The artist*] *was roused in* 1:[*him*], *and* 3:[*the worshipper of beauty*]) ⟹ for the Romanian version: [2] `class-of-interpret` [1]; [3] `class-of-interpret` [1]; for the English version, because of the inversion: [1] `isa` [2]; [3] `class-of-interpret` [1];

- `part-of` (a RE of type `PERSON-PART` is a part of the body of an entity of type `PERSON`, or a `GOD-PART` is a part of the body of an entity of type `GOD`), directed:

  1:[*mâna* 2:[*lui*] *dreaptă*] (1:[2:[*his*] *right hand*]) ⟹ [1] `part-of` [2];

- has-as-part (the inverse of `part-of`: a `PERSON` type RE has as a component part a `PERSON-PART` entity, or a `GOD` type RE has as a component part a `GOD-PART` entity), directed;

  chinurile, 1:[*sângele*] *şi moartea* 2:[*Mântuitorului*] (*the torment,* 1:[*the blood*] *and the death* 2:[*of the Saviour*]) ⟹ [2] `has-as-part`[1];

- `subgroup-of` (from a subgroup, i.e. a `PERSON-GROUP` type RE, to a larger group, i.e. also a `PERSON-GROUP` type entity which includes it, and similarly for `GOD-GROUP`'s poles), directed:

---

[8] (Anechitei et al. 2013) could become a wife of the speaker but is actually not.

1:[*a*], 2:[*b*], 3:[*c*] *şi* 4:[*alte femei din* 5:[*societatea înaltă*]] (1:[*a*], 2:[*b*], 3:[*c*] *and* 4:[*other women of* 5:[*the high society*]]) ⟹ [5] has-as-member [1], [5] has-as-member [2], [5] has-as-member [3], [4] subgroup-of [5]; *Christos* 1:[*i*]*-a iertat şi pe* 2:[*evreii*] *care i-au dus la moarte şi pe* 3:[*soldaţii romani*] *care l-au ţintuit pe cruce*. (*Christ forgave* 2:[*the Jews*] *who delivered him to death, and* 3:[*the Roman soldiers*] *who nailed him to the cross*) ⟹ for the Romanian version only: [2] subgroup-of [1]; [3] subgroup-of [1]. The subgroup-of relation holds in the Romanian version because of the existence of the anticipating pronoun 1:[*i*], which signifies both groups. In the English equivalent no such mention appears and a subgroup-of relation cannot be formulated;

- name-of (inverse of has-name, linking a PERSON-NAME RE to a PERSON entity), directed:

  1:[*numele lui* 2:[*Aulus*]] (1:[*the name of* 2:[*Aulus*]]) ⟹ [1] name-of [2]; *Petronius... care simţea ca pe statuia* 1:[*acestei fete*] *s-ar putea scrie*: 2: [*"Primavara"*]. (*Petronius... who felt that beneath a statue of* 1:[*that maiden*] *one might write* 2:[*"Spring."*])⟹ [2] name-of-interpret [1] (-interpret because Petronius is the one that gives this name).

4.5 Kinship Relations

Kinship (or family) relations (marked KINSHIP as XML elements) occur between PERSON, PERSON-GROUP, GOD and GOD-GROUP type of REs and entities. Seven subtypes have been identified, detailed below:

- parent-of (the relation between a parent or both parents and a child or more children; a RE *A* is in a parent-of relation with *B* if *A* is a parent of *B*, i.e. mother, father, both or unspecified), directed:

  1:[*<tatăl>* 2:[*lui Vinicius*]] (1:[2:[*Viniciu's*] *<father>*]) ⟹ [1] parent-of [2];

- child-of (inverse of parent-of; a RE *A* is a child-of *B* if the text presents *A* as a child or as children of *B*), directed:

  1:[*Ligia mea*] *este <fiica>* 2:[*regelui*] (1:[*My Lygia*] *is the <daughter>* 2:[*of that leader*].) ⟹ [1] child-of [2];
  1:[*<copilul> drag al* 2:[*celebrului Aulus*]] (1:[*a dear <child>*] 2:[*of the famous Aulus*]) ⟹ [1] child-of [2];

- sibling-of (between brothers and sisters), symmetric:

  1:[*sora lui* 2:[*Petronius*]] (1:[2:[*Petronius's*] *<sister>*]) ⟹ [1] sibling-of [2];

1:[*nişte* <*fraţi*> *ai* 2:[*tăi*]] (1:[*some of* 2:[*your*] <*brothers*>]) ⟹ [1] `sibling-of` [2];

- `nephew-of` (we have *A* `nephew-of` *B*, if *A* is a nephew/niece of *B*), directed:

  1:[*scumpii* 2:[*săi*] <*nepoţi*>] (1:[2:[*his*] *dear* <*nephews*>]) ⟹ [1] `nephew-of` [2];

- `spouse-of` (symmetric relation between husbands):

  ... *cu* 1:[*care*] *mai târziu* 2:[*Nero*], *pe jumatate nebun, avea să se* <*cun-une*> (... *to* 1:[*whom*] *later* 2:[*the half-insane Nero*] *commanded the flamens to* <*marry*> *him*) ⟹ [2] `spouse-of` [1];
  1:[*Vinicius*] *ar putea să* 2:[*te*] *ia de* <*nevastă*> (1:[*Vinicius*] *might* <*marry*> 2:[*thee*]) ⟹ [2] `spouse-of-interpret` [1];

- `concubine-of` (symmetric relation between concubins)

  1:[<*concubina*> 2:[*ta*]] (1:[2:[*your*] <*concubine*>]) ⟹ [1] `concubine-of` [2];

- `unknown` (a kinship relation of an unspecified type):

  1:[*o* <*rudă*> *de-a* 2:[*lui Petronius*]] (1:[*a* <*relative*> *of* 2:[*Petronius*]]) ⟹ [1] `unknown` [2];
  1:[<*strămoşilor*> 2:[*lui Aulus*]] (1:[2:[*Aulus's*] <*ancestors*>]) ⟹ [1] `unknown` [2]

4.6 Affective Relations

Affective relations (marked as AFFECT elements in our XML notations) are non-anaphoric relations that occur between REs and entities of type `PERSON`, `PERSON-GROUP`, `GOD` and `GOD-GROUP`. There are eleven subtypes, as detailed below:

- `friend-of` (*A* is a `friend-of` *B*, if the text expresses that *A* and *B* are friends), symmetric:

  1:[<*tovarăşii*> 2:[*lui*]] (1:[2:[*his*] <*comrades*>]) ⟹ [1] `friend-of` [2];
  1:[*Vinicius*] *e un nobil puternic, spuse el, şi* <*prieten*> *cu* 2:[*împăratul*]. (1: [*Vinicius*] *is a powerful lord, said he, and a* <*friend*> *of* 2:[*Cæ sar*].) ⟹ [1] `friend-of-interpret` [2];

- `fear-of` (*A* is in a relation `fear-of` with *B* if the text expresses that *A* feels fear of *B*), directional:

  1:[*oamenii*] <*se tem*> *mai mult de* 2:[*Vesta*] (1:[*people*] <*fear*> 2:[*Vesta*] *more*) ⟹ [1] `fear-of` [2];

1:[*Senatorii*] *se duceau la* 2:[*Palatin*], *<tremurând de frică>* (1:[*Senators*], *<trembling in their souls>* , *went to the* 2:[*Palatine*]) ⟹ [1] `fear-of` [2];

- `fear-to` (inverse of `fear-of`: *A* is in a relation `fear-to` *B* if the text expresses that the RE *A* inspires fear to the entity *B*), directional:

  1:[*Nero*] *îi <alarma> chiar şi pe* 2:[*cei mai apropiaţi*] (1:[*Nero*] *did <roused attention>* , *even in* 2:[*those nearest*]) ⟹ [1] `fear-to` [2];

- `love` (*A* is in a relation `love` to *B*, if *A* loves *B*), directional:

  1:[Ligia] simţi că o mare greutate i s-a luat de pe inimă. <Dorul> acela fără margini după 2:[Pomponia] (1:[She][9] felt less alone. That measureless <yearning> for 2:[Pomponia]) ⟹ [1] `love` [2];
  <îndrăgostit> ca 1:[*Troilus*] *de* 2:[*Cresida*] (*<in love>* , *as was* 1:[*Troilus*] *with* 2:[*Cressida*]) ⟹ [1] `love` [2];

- `loved-by`(inverse of love: *A* `loved-by` *B*, if *A* is loved by *B*):

  <iubită> este 1:[*Ligia*] *de* 2:[*familia lui Plautius*] (*<dear>* 1:[*Lygia*] *was to* 2:[*Plautius*]) ⟹ [1] `loved-by` [2];

- `rec-love` (*A* `rec-love` *B* if the text mentions a mutual love between *A* and *B*), symmetric:

  <iubită> 1:[*unul*] *de* 2:[*altul*] (*in <love> with* 1:[*each*] 2:[*other*]) ⟹ [1] `rec-love`[2];

- `hate` (*A* `hate` *B*, if the text mentions that *A* hates *B*), directional:

  Pe 1:[*Vinicus*] *îl cuprinse o <mânie> năprasnică şi împotriva* 2:[*împăratului*] *şi împotriva* 3:[*Acteii*] (1:[*Vinicius*] *was carried away by sudden <anger> at* 2:[*Cæsar*] *and at* 3:[*Acte*].) ⟹ [1] `hate` [2], [1] `hate` [3];

- `hated-by` (*A* `hated-by` *B*, if *A* is hated by *B*), directional:

  <ura> pe care 1:[*i*]*-o purta* 2:[*prefectul pretorienilor*] (*<hatred toward>* 1:[*him*] *of* 2:[*the all-powerful pretorian prefect*]) ⟹ [1] `hated-by` [2]

- `upset-on` (*A* `upset-on` *B*, if the text tells that *A* feels upset, disgust, anger, discontent, etc. on *B*), directional:

  1:[*<Dispreţuia>* `REALISATION` = ”`INCLUDED`”] 2:[*mulţimea*] (1:[*He*] *had a twofold <contempt for>* 2:[*the multitude*]) ⟹ [1] `upset-on`[2];

[9] In the English equivalent, the mention of Ligia is missing.

- `worship` (*A* `worship` *B*, if the text mentions that *A* worships *B*), directional:

  1:[*oamenii aceia*] *nu numai că-şi* <*slăveau*> 2:[*zeul*] (1:[*those people*] *not merely* <*honored*> 2:[*their God*]) ⟹ [1] worship [2];
  1:[*Ligia*] *îngenunche ca să se* <*roage*> 2:[*altcuiva*]. (*But* 1:[*Lygia*] *dropped on her knees to* <*implore*> 2:[*some one else*].) ⟹ [1] `worship` [2];

- `worshiped-by` (*A* `worshiped-by` *B* if the text mentioned that *A* is worshiped by *B*), directional:

  1:[*un zeu cu totul neînsemnat*] *dacă n-are decât* 2:[*două* <*adoratoare*>] (1:[*a very weak god*], *since he has had only* 2:[*two* <*adherents*>]) ⟹ [1] `worshiped-by` [2]

4.7 Social Relations

The group of social relations (marked `SOCIAL` in our XML annotations) are non-anaphoric relations occurring only between `PERSON` or `PERSON-GROUP` REs and entities. They are grouped in six subtypes, as detailed below:

- `superior-of` (*A* `superior-of` *B*, if *A* is hierarchically above *B*), directional:

  <*Eliberând*> -1:[*o*], 2:[*Nero*] (2:[*Nero*], *when he had* <*freed*> 1:[*her*]) ⟹ [2] `superior-of` [1];
  1:[*Nero*] *a ordonat* <*predarea*> 2:[*mea*] (1:[*Nero*] *demanded* 2:[*my*] <*surren*-der>) ⟹ [1] `superior-of` [2];
  1:[*un centurion*] <*în fruntea*> 2:[*soldaţilor*] (1:[*a centurion*] <*at the head*> 2:[*of soldiers*]) ⟹ [1] `superior-of` [2];

- `inferior-of` (inverse of `superior-of`, *A* inferior-of *B* if *A* is hierarchically subordinated to *B*), directional:

  1:[<*consul*> *pe vremea* 2:[*lui Tiberiu*]] (1:[*a man of* <*consular*> *dignity from the time* 2:[*of Tiberius*]) ⟹ [1] `inferior-of` [2];
  1:[*Tânărul*] *luptase* <*sub comanda*> 2:[*lui Corbulon*] (1:[*The young man*] *was serving then* <*under*> 2:[*Corbulo*]) ⟹ [1] `inferior-of` [2];
  1:[<*libertei*> 2:[*lui Nero*]] (1:[2:[*Nero's*] <*freedwoman*>]) ⟹ [1] `inferior-of` [2];

- `colleague-of` (*A* `colleague-of` *B* if the text explicitly places *A* on the same hierarchical level with *B*), symmetrical:

  1:[<*tovarăşii*> 2:[*săi*]] (1:[2:[*his*] <*companions*>]) ⟹ [1] `colleague-of` [2];

- opposite-to (*A* opposite-to *B*, if *A* is presented in a position that makes her/him opposing to *B*), directional:

  Să nici nu-ţi treacă prin gând să 1:[*te*] <*împotriveşti*> 2:[*împăratului*] (*Do not even* 1:[*think*; REALISATION = "INCLUDED"] *of* <*opposing*> 2:[*Cæsar*]) ⟹ [1] opposite-to-interpret [2];
  1:[*Pomponia şi Ligia*] *otrăvesc fântânile,* <*ucid*> 2:[*copiii*] (1:[*Pomponia and Lygia*] *poison wells,* <*murder*> 2:[*children*]) ⟹ [1] opposite-to [2];

- in-cooperation-with (*A* is in-cooperation-with *B* if the text present *A* as performing something together with *B*), directional:

  1:[*Vannius*] *a chemat* T1: <*în ajutor*> *pe* 2:[*iagizi*], *iar* 3:[*scumpii săi nepoţi*] *pe* 4:[*ligieni*] (1:[*Vannius*] *summoned to his* T1: <*aid*> 2:[*the Yazygi*]; 3:[*his dear nephews*] T2: <*called in*> 4:[*the Lygians*]) ⟹ [1] in-cooperation-with [2], trigger: <T1> ; [3] in-cooperation-with [4], trigger: <T2>;

- in-competition-with (*A* is in-competition-with *B*, if *A* is presented as being in a sort of competition with *B*), directional:

  1:[*Petronius*] 2:[*îl*] <*întrecea*> *cu mult prin maniere, inteligenţă* (1:[*Petronius*] <*surpassed*> 2:[*him*] *infinitely in polish, intellect, wit*) ⟹ [1] in-competition-with [2].

4.8 Examples of Combinations of Relations

In the end of this section we will give a few examples showing complex combinations of relations.

1:[*Vinicius*]*... e* 2:[*o* <*rudă*> *de-a* 3:[*lui Petronius*]] (1:[*Vinicius*]*... is* 2:[*a* <*relative*> 3:[*of Petronius*]]) ⟹ [2] coref-of [1], [2] KINSHIP: unknown [3];

Se repezi la 1:[*Petru*] *şi, luându-*2:[*i*] 3:[*mâinile*], *începu să* 4:[*i*] 5:[*le*] *sărute* (*... seized* 3:[*the hand of* 1:[*the old Galilean*]], *and pressed* 5:[*it*] *in gratitude to his lips.*)[10] ⟹ [2] coref [1]; [3] part-of [1] (or [2]); [4] coref [1] (or [2]); [5] coref [3]. It is superfluous to mark [5] as part-of [1] because it results by transitivity from it being coreferential with [3] and [3] being part-of [1].

1:[*Vinicius*] *şi* 2:[<*tovaraşii*> 3:[*săi*]] (1:[*Vinicius*] *and* 2:[3:[*his*] <*comrades*>]) ⟹ [3] coref [1]; [2] SOCIAL:colleague-of [3].

[10] In the English equivalent, two mentions of Peter are missing.

5 Creating the Corpus

The realisation of a manually annotated corpus incorporating semantic relations obliges to a fine-grained interpretation of the text. This triggers the danger of non-homogeneity, due to idiosyncrasies of views, over the linguistic phenomena under investigation, of different annotators working each on different parts of the document. A correlation activity that would nivelate divergent views is compulsory. Let's add to this that many details of the annotation conventions usually settle down in iterative sessions of discussions within the group of annotators, following the rich casuistry picked up along the first phases of the annotation process. As such, the organisation of the work should be done in such a way as to certify that the result of the annotation process contains the least errors possible, and that the conventions are coherently applied over the whole document.

5.1 Organising the Activity

The annotation activity of the "Quo Vadis" corpus was performed over a period of three terms with students in Computational Linguistics.[11] An Annotation Manual, including an initial set of annotation rules, was proposed by the first author to the students at the beginning of the activity and discussed with them. Then, the students went through some practical classes in which they were taught to use an annotation tool. Approximately half of the novel was split in equal slices and distributed to them and they begun to work independently or grouped by two. During the first term, in weekly meetings, annotation details were discussed, difficult cases were presented and, based on them, the Manual was refined. At the end of the first term their activity was individually evaluated and the results showed that only about 15 % of them were trustful enough as to be given a full responsibility.[12] As a by-product, we had, at the time, a consistent set of annotation rules and PALinkA,[13] our annotation tool, could incorporate rather stable preferences settings (describing the XML structural constraints).

---

[11] A master organised at the "Alexandru Ioan Cuza" University of Iași by the Faculty of Computer Science, which accommodates graduate students with either a background in Computer Science or in Humanities.

[12] It was not a surprise that for annotation activities the most dedicated and skillful students were those having a Humanity background.

[13] PALinkA was created by Constantin Orăsan in the Research Group in Computational Linguistics, at the School of Law, Social Sciences and Communications, Wolverhampton. PALinkA was used for annotating corpora in a number of projects, for purposes including: anaphoric and coreferential links in a parallel French-English corpus, summarisation, different versions of the Centering Theory, coreferences in email messages and web pages, or for Romanian name entities.

We continued the activity during the next two terms with only the best ranked members of the former class (among them—a Ph.D. researcher with a Philology background). At the beginning of the next year (September 2013), a few new students with a Philological background went through a rapid training period and joined the team (among them—two Ph.D. researchers in Humanities). The quality improved a lot, but in the detriment of the speed, which continued to be very slow. At that moment it became clear to us that it will be impossible to achieve this ambitious task by going through the text three times or even only twice, as the usual norms for redundant annotation require in order to organise a proper inter-annotator agreement process. As a consequence, we started to think at other methods for obtaining accuracy that would involve only one manual annotation pass. We imagined different methods for clearing up the corpus from errors, which will be detailed in the following sub-sections.

As shown already, the files opened in PALinkA have been previously annotated in XML with markings signalling word (`<W>`) and paragraph (`<P>`) boundaries. Over these initial elements the annotators have marked: entities, coreferential links, triggers of relations, and relation spans, including attributes indicating the poles and the triggers.

In building the manual annotation, there where words are ambiguous, we have instructed our annotators to use their human capacity of interpretation in order to decide the true meaning of words, the types of relations or the entities that are glued by relations.[14] For instance, words and expressions, based on their local sense, could functions as triggers only in some contexts (*father*, for instance should not be taken as signaling a `parent-of` relation if its meaning is that of priest).

5.2 Acquiring Completeness and Correctness

Along the whole process of building the "Quo Vadis" corpus, the two main pre-occupations were: to acquire completeness (therefore to leave behind as few as possible unmarked entities or relations) and to enhance its quality (therefore to clean the corpus of possible errors). As said already, in order to distribute the text to different annotators, we splitted the text of the novel into chunks of relatively equal size (phase 1, in Fig. 1). It resulted a number of 58 chunks, each including on average approximately 123 sentences. The following formula was used to estimate the density of annotations (D) to each chunk:

$$D = (E + 2 \times R + 5 \times (A + K + S))/N$$

[14] Not rare were cases when philologists asked: *And how would the machine recognise this relation when it was difficult even for me to decipher it here?!...*

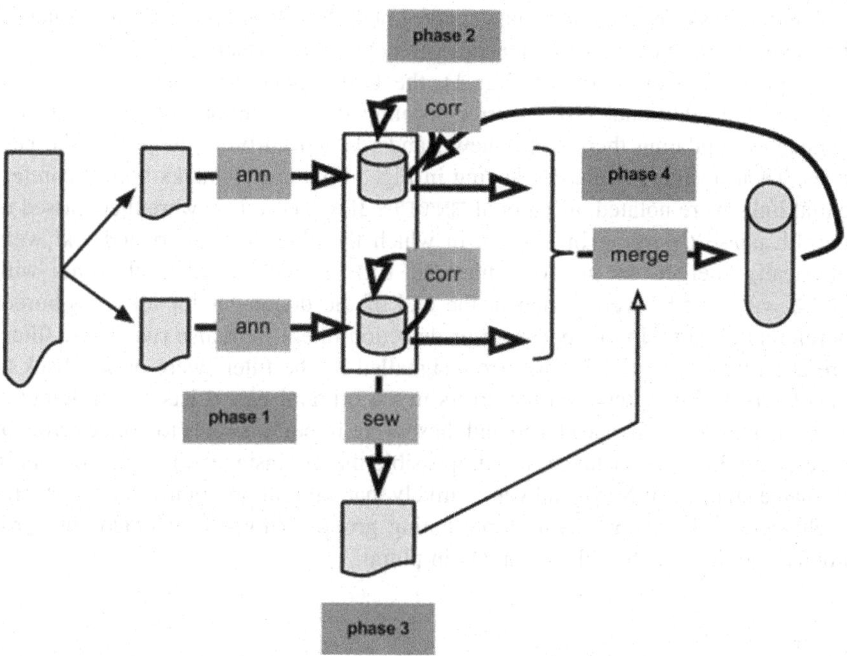

Fig. 1 Annotation-correction-sewing-merging cycles in the building of the "Quo Vadis" corpus

where: E = number of marked entities; R = number of marked REFERENTIAL relations; A, K, S = number of marked AFFECT, KINSHIP and SOCIAL relations, N = number of sentences.

During the annotation process, the density scores per segment varied between 0 to more than 20. Assuming an approximately uniform density all over the novel,[15] these scores allowed us to detect from the blink of an eye those chunks which received too little attention from the part of the annotators and to spot also the most diligent annotators. After the first round, only the best ranked annotators were retained in the team. In the second round, all chunks scored low, therefore contributed by dismissed students, were resubmitted for a second annotation round to the selected members remained in the refreshed team (4). At this moment, all chunks are scored over 5.5, the maximum reaching 20.2 and the whole novel having an average density score of 9.4. But this score does not reflect the correctness.

The final step in the construction of the corpus was dedicated to enhancing the accuracy. As said, because of the very high complexity of the task, which makes it extremely time-consuming, and the scarcity of skilled people able to do an expert

[15] Not necessarily true, because long passages of static descriptions are bare of mentions of entities and, consequently, relations.

annotation task, no inter-annotator agreement has been possible to organise. However, more measures to enhance correctness were assured.

In phase 2 (Correction on Fig. 1), the best trained annotators of the team received the additional task of error-proofing the annotations of their last year colleagues, updating them to the new standards and unifying them with the new ones. Then, in the 3rd phase (Sewing in Fig. 1) the cross-chunks-border coreferential links were notated, as pairs of `ENTITY` IDs. These lists were then passed to the 4th phase (Merging in Fig. 1), in which the chunks of annotated text were physically merged in just one file and `REFERENTIAL XML` elements with `TYPE` = "`coref`" were added at the end of the document for all cross-border coreferential pairs. In this phase, error-detection filters were also run. These filters are described in Sect. 5.3. The errors signalled by the filters were passed back to annotators and they repaired the errors in the original files. Lists of coreferential entity names were also produced and these were important clues to notice errors of coreferentiality. For instance, it is impossible that an instance of Ligia appears in the same chain with Nero, and very unlikely that a plural pronoun would ever refer a character. Moreover, chains representing group characters, if containing pronouns, should include only pronouns in plural.

5.3 Error Correcting Filters

We list in this section a number of filterring procedures that helped to detect annotator errors.

- We call a coreference chain (CC) a list of REs whose occurrences are sequentially ordered in the text and which all represent the same `PERSON/GOD` entity or the same `PERSON-GROUP/GOD-GROUP` entity[16] $\Longrightarrow$ any proper noun that appears in a CC should be a variation of the name of that entity. We have extracted one occurrence for all proper names in CCs and manually verified if they are variations, inflections or nick-names of the name of the same character (Ex. *Marcus*, *Vinicius* and *Marcus Vinicius* for the character [Vinicius], or *Ligia*, *Ligiei*, *Callina*, *Callinei* for the character [Ligia], or *Nero*, *Barbă-Arămie*, *Ahenobarbus*, *Cezar*, *Cezarul*, *Cezarului*, etc. for the character [Nero]);
- All common nouns and pronouns in a CC generally have the same number + gender values[17] $\Longrightarrow$ For each `W` having the category common noun or

[16] Let's note that the `REFERENTIAL:coref` links should separate the whole class of `ENTITY` elements into disjoint trees. Trees and not general graphs, because considering `ENTITY`s as nodes in the graph and `REFERENTIAL:coref` relations as edges, there is just one TO value (parent in the graph) for each `ENTITY` node.

[17] There are exceptions to this rule: a plural may be referred by a singular noun denoting a group, or due to errors of the POS-tagger, etc.

pronoun in a CC we have extracted the pairs number + gender values and reported if they are not identical;

- It is improbable that an entity be referred only by pronouns ⟹ We have listed the CCs that include only pronouns and passed them to the correctors for a second look;
- In most of the cases, gods are referred to by names in capital letters ⟹ We have reported the exceptions;
- There should be a one-to-one mapping between triggers and relations ⟹ Report if a trigger is not referred in any relation or if more relations use the same trigger;
- Triggers could not appear as values of `FROM` and `TO` attributes and no element type other than `TRIGGER` could to a value of a `TRIGGER` argument of a relation ⟹ We performed an argument type checking (see (Năstase et al. 2013)) by citing (Paşca et al. 2006; Rosenfeld and Feldman 2007) for "matching the entity type of a relation's argument with the expected type in order to filter erroneous candidates". Combined (or coupled) constraints, as proposed by (Carlson et al. 2010) in semi-supervised learning of relations in context, were not of primary interest at the moment of building the corpus.
- In the vast majority of cases, the two poles and the trigger belong to the same sentence. For instance, in the example: 1:[*e*; `REALISATION` = "`INCLUDED`"] 2:[-*un patrician*], 3:[*prieten cu* 4:[*împăratul*]] (1:[*he*] *is* 2:[*a patrician*], 3:[*a friend* 4:[*of Caesar*]]), the correct annotation is as follows: [2] `class-of` [1]; [3] `class-of` [1]; [3] `friend-of` [4]. As such, the friend-of relation does not cross the borders of the second sentence. ⟹ We report cross-sentences non-coreferential relation spans and asked the correctors to verify them.

6 Statistics Over the Corpus

In this section we present a number of statistics and comment on the semantic links of the corpus from a global perspective. Table 1 presents the Corpus by numbers.

It can be seen that 20 % of the tokens of the novel are covered by some manual annotation (entity, trigger, relation). The vast majority of relations are those belonging to the `REFERENTIAL` type. A comparison is shown in the diagram of Fig. 2.

If the 17,916 `REFERENTIAL:coref` and `REFERENTIAL:coref-interpret` relations (the most numerous) are left aside, the distribution is depicted in Fig. 3. In Fig. 4, the distributions of different types of `REFERENTIAL` relations (without `REFERENTIAL:coref` and `REFERENTIAL:coref-interpret`) is shown.

Figures 5, 6 and 7 show the distributions of `KINSHIP`, `SOCIAL` and `AFFECT` relations in the corpus.

Table 1 The corpus at a glance

Counted elements	Values
# sentences	7,150
# tokens (W elements, punctuation included)	144,068
# tokens (W elements, excluding punctuation)	123,093
# tokens under at least one annotation (punctuation included)	28,851
# tokens under at least one relation (punctuation included)	7,520
# tokens summed up under all relations (punctuation included)	9,585
# entities	22,310
# REF annotations (all)	21,439
# REF:coref and REF:coref-interpret annotations	17,916
# AKS annotations	1,133
# TRIGGER annotations	1,097
total # annotations (ENTITY + TRIGGER + REF + AKS)	45,979
overall density score	10.21

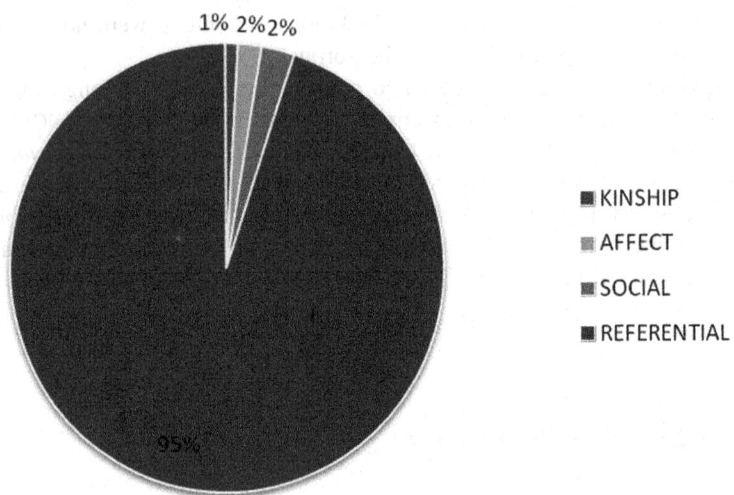

Fig. 2 Comparing families of relations

Long relation spans make the discovery of relations difficult. The graphic in Fig. 8 shows the ranges of lengths of REFERENTIAL relations spans whose lengths can be estimated, thus REFERENTIAL:coref and REFERENTIAL:coref-interpret are not considered.

As can be seen, the average span for this group of relations is placed somewhere around 20 words. In Fig. 9 the same statistics is shown for the other three families of relations. A rapid glance shows that KINSHIP relations are expressed over a shorter context than other types. This is mainly because many KINSHIP relations are contextualised in noun-phrase expressions (*his mother*, *the son of X*, etc.).

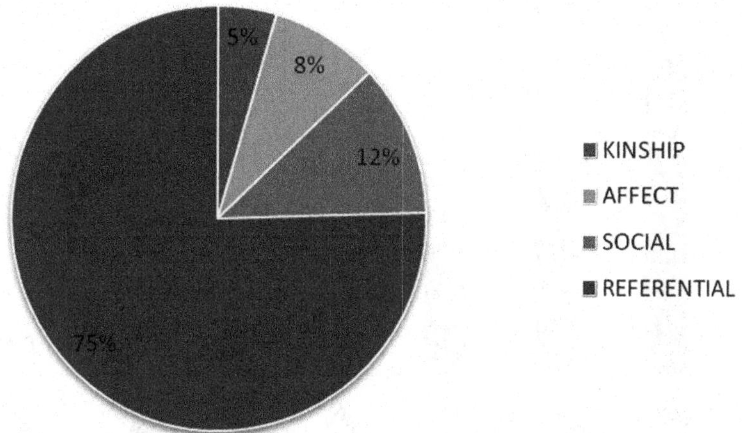

Fig. 3 Comparing families of relations (without REFERENTIAL:coref and REFERENTIAL:coref-interpret)

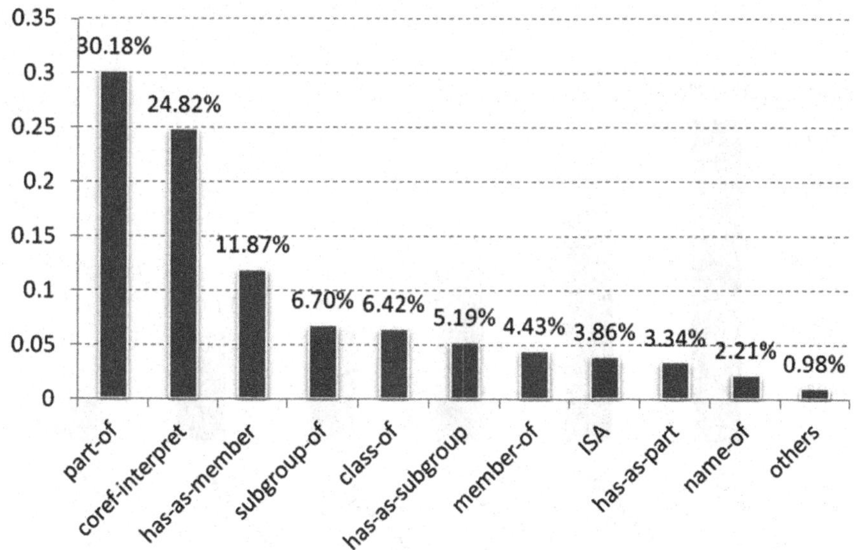

Fig. 4 Distribution of REFERENTIAL relations (without REFERENTIAL:coref and REFERENTIAL:coref-interpret)

To see how often appear in the corpus long spans with respect to short spans, Fig. 10 shows the density of different lengths of relation spans (of course, excluding REFERENTIAL:coref and REFERENTIAL:coref-interpret). Its abrupt descending allure shows that short spans occur much frequently than long spans. There is a nose for length 3, indicating the most frequent span. The longest relation

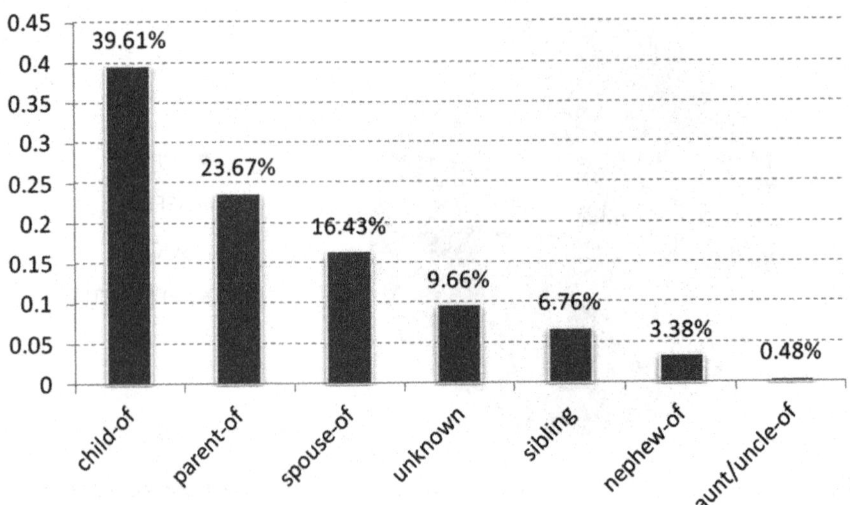

Fig. 5 Distribution of KINSHIP relations

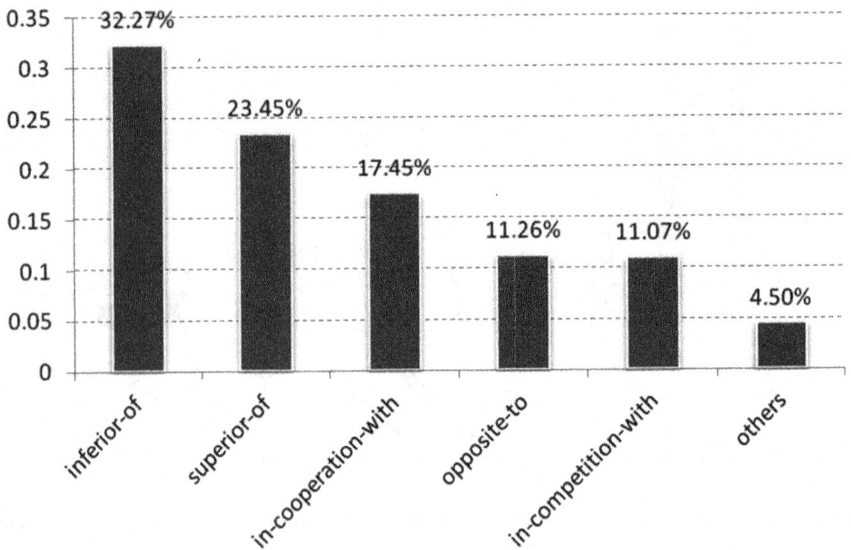

Fig. 6 Distribution of SOCIAL relations

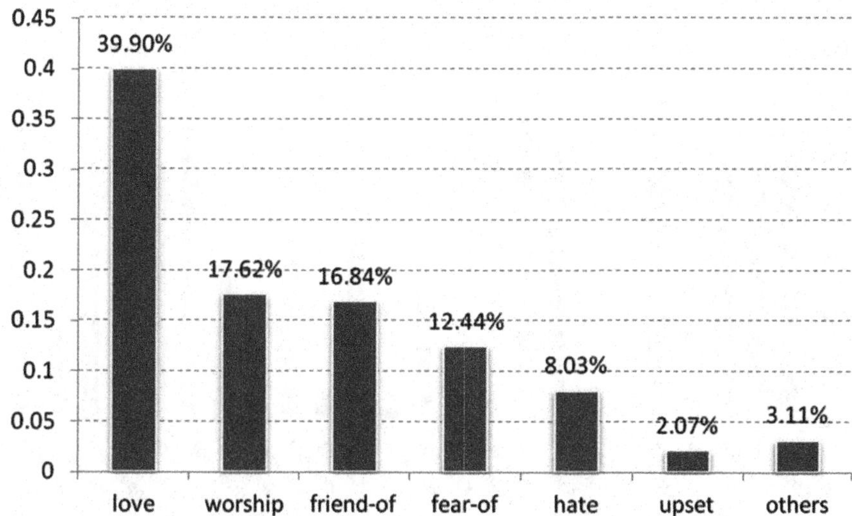

Fig. 7 Occurrences of AFFECT relations

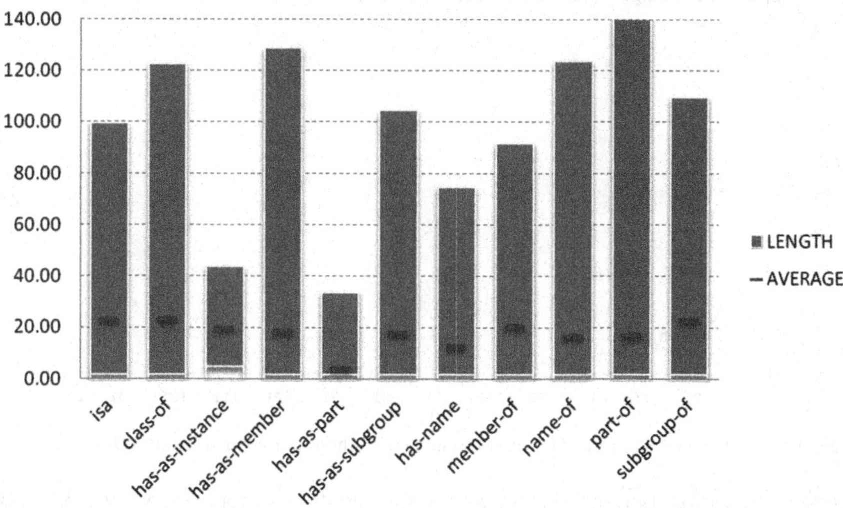

Fig. 8 Span length ranges and averages in number of words for REFERENTIAL relations (excepting REFERENTIAL:coref and REFERENTIAL:coref-interpret)

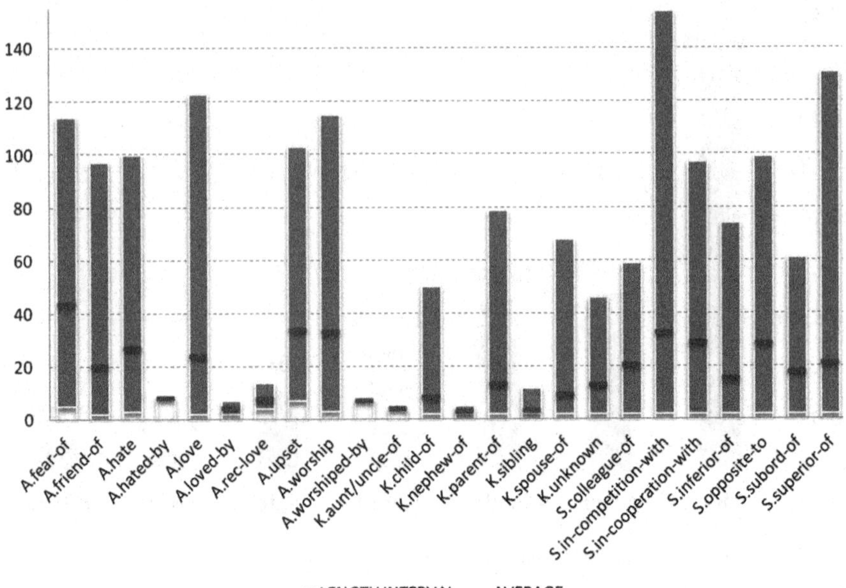

Fig. 9 Span length ranges and averages for AKS relations

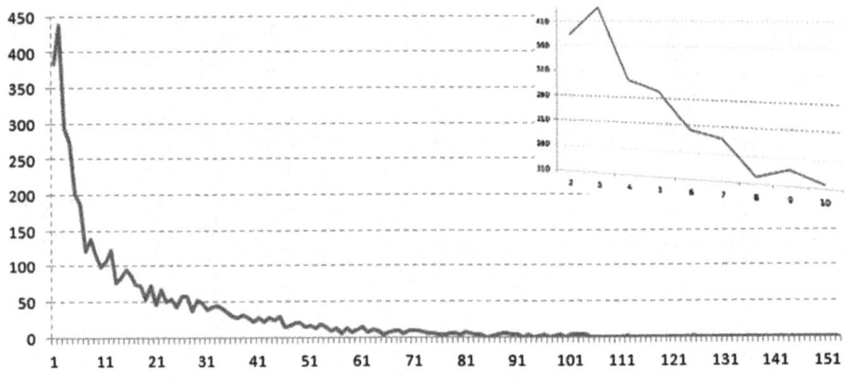

Fig. 10 Relations occurences (Oy) in correlation with the relation span length (Ox)

covers 154 words (but there is only one of this length).[18] Supposing we would mark with $f(x)$ the function in Fig. 10, the total number of words in the spans of the relations would be:

[18] In this version of the corpus we did not make a thorough verification of long relations. We have noticed some errors in the annotation of poles, especially when one of the two poles are null pronouns in the position of subjects and `REALISATION = ''INCLUDED''` has not been marked on the respective verbs. In reality, a long distance coref relation would link the main verb (or its auxiliary) to an named entity, which now stands as one of the poles.

$$\sum_{x=2}^{154} xf(x) = 9{,}585$$

It corresponds with the total count of XML <W>... </W> markings under some relation span different than `REFERENTIAL:coref` and `REFERENTIAL: coref-interpret`. This means approximately 6.66 % of the total area of the book, including punctuation (144,068 tokens).

An analysis of this kind is interesting because it reveals in approximate terms the proportion between positive and negative examples in an attempt to decipher automatically relations and could be of help when designing the sample set in a statistical approach to train from the corpus a recognition program.

Another set of statistics addresses the triggers. We are interested to know to what degree triggers are ambiguous. The sparse matrix in Table 2 allows an analysis of this type. On rows and columns all relations are placed and the number in a cell ($R1$, $R2$) indicates how many triggers, as (sequence of) lemmas, are common between the relations $R1$ and $R2$.

The last set of graphical representations are semantic graphs. Figures 11, 12 and 13 show sets of affection, family and social relations for some of the most representative characters in the novel.

Nodes in these graphs represent entities. Each one of them concentrates all coreferential links of one chain. Nodes names were formed by choosing the largest proper noun in each chain. When a character is mentioned with more different names, a concatenation of them was used (as is the case with *Ligia—Callina*). For the chains (usually small) that do not include proper nouns, one of the common nouns was used. When, doing so, more chains (nodes) got the same name, after verifying that the corresponding chains are indeed distinct, the names have been manually edited by appending digits.

In Fig. 11, for instance, can be read a love relation from Nero towards Acte, his child, his entourage (society) and, accidentally, Ligia. Also, there are reciprocal love relations linking Vinicius and Ligia, while Petronius is loved by Eunice and loves Vinicius.

Figure 12 concentrates both sets of relations `parent-of` and `child-of`, by reversing the sense of relations `child-of`. The family relations (not too many) expressed in the novel are now evident. Ligia-Callina has two fathers, the Phrygian king and Aulus Plautius.

Finally, Fig. 12 reveals the `superior-of–inferior-of` pair of links (also by reversing the sense of relations `inferior-of`). Central in this graph is, as expected, the emperor Nero, socially superior to almost all characters in the novel. There is no edge pointing towards the node representing this character in the graph. Following him come: Vinicius (revealed as being superior to people of Rome, to the two slaves Demas and Croton, as well as to other servants, slaves and liberated slaves) and Petronius (linked to his servants and slaves, to pretorians, but also to his beloved Eunice). As expected, there is no superiority relation between

Table 2 The ambiguity of triggers

Relation	#Triggers	#Common Triggers						
A.fear-of	27	S.in-coop-w:1	S.opp-to: 1					
A.friend-of	37	A.hate: 1	A.love: 2	A.loved-by: 2	A.wship: 1	S.col-of: 2	S.in-coop-w:3	S.inf-of: 1
A.hate	23	A.friend-of: 1	A.hated-by: 1	S.opp-to: 2				
A.hated-by	1	A.hate: 1						
A.love	64	A.friend-of:2	A.loved-by:3	A.rec-love:1	A.wship: 5	A.worsh-by:1	S.inf-of:1	
A.loved-by	3	A.friend-of: 2	A.love: 3	A.rec-love:1	A.wship: 1			
A.rec-love	5	A.love: 1	A.loved-by: 1	A.wship: 2				
A.upset-on	8							
A.wship	53	A.friend-of: 1	A.love: 5	A.loved-by: 1	A.rec-love:2	A.worsh-by: 2	S.inf-of: 3	S.sup-of: 2
A.worsh-by	3	A.love: 1	A.wship: 2					
K.child-of	20	K.parent-of: 7						
K.nephew-of	1							
K.parent-of	16	K.child-of: 7						
K.sibling	3	S.col-of: 1						
K.spouse-of	7							
K.unkn	8	S.col-of: 1						
S.col-of	7	A.friend-of: 2	K.sibling: 1	K.unkn: 1				
S.in-comp-w	50	A.fear-of: 1	S.in-coop-w:1	S.opp-to: 1				
S.in-coop-w	64	A.friend-of: 3	S.sup-of: 1	S.inf-of: 2	S.in-comp-w:1			
S.inf-of	69	A.friend-of: 1	A.love: 1	A.wship: 3	S.in-coop-w:1	S.sup-of: 9		
S.opp-to	41	A.fear-of: 1	A.hate: 2	S.in-comp-w:1				
S.sup-of	52	A.wship: 2	S.in-coop-w:1	S.inf-of: 12				

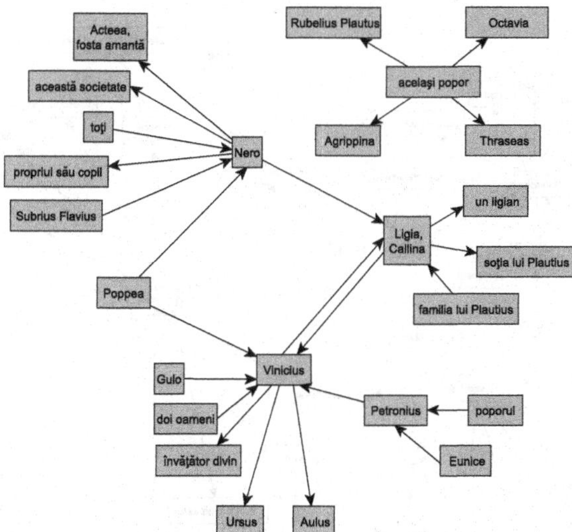

Fig. 11 A network of relations AFFECT:love

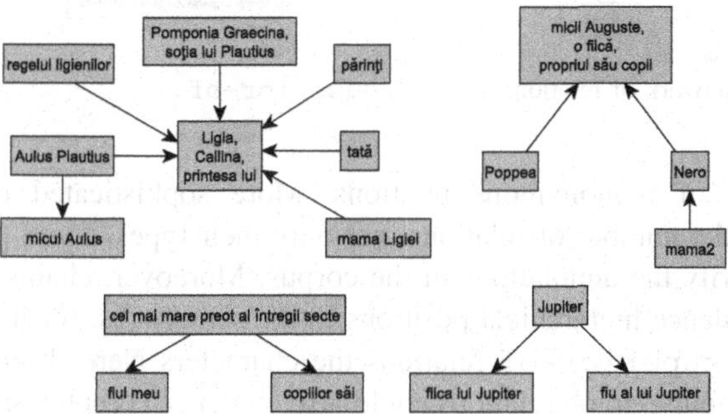

Fig. 12 A network of relations KINSHIP:parent-of

the two close friends Petronius and Vinicius. In weaker relationships with the emperor Nero, Vinicius is not mentioned as his inferior, while Petronius, his cultural counsellor and praise-giver, he is. The only superior Vinicius seems to have over the whole novel is Corbulon, a former military chief.

As remarked in (Năstase et al. 2013), "The importance of an entity in a semantic graph is determined not only by the number of relations the entity has, but also by the importance of the entities with which it is connected. So, for a character to be influential in the novel it is not enough to have many relations, but to be related with influential characters too. The PageRank (Brin and Page 1998) could be applied to measure the centrality/influence of an entity according to its position in the graph". Such estimations are yet to be made in a further research, but even only a simple visual inspection of our graphs puts in evidence the central characters: Vinicius, Petronius, Nero, Ligia. Let's note also that all these graphs display only

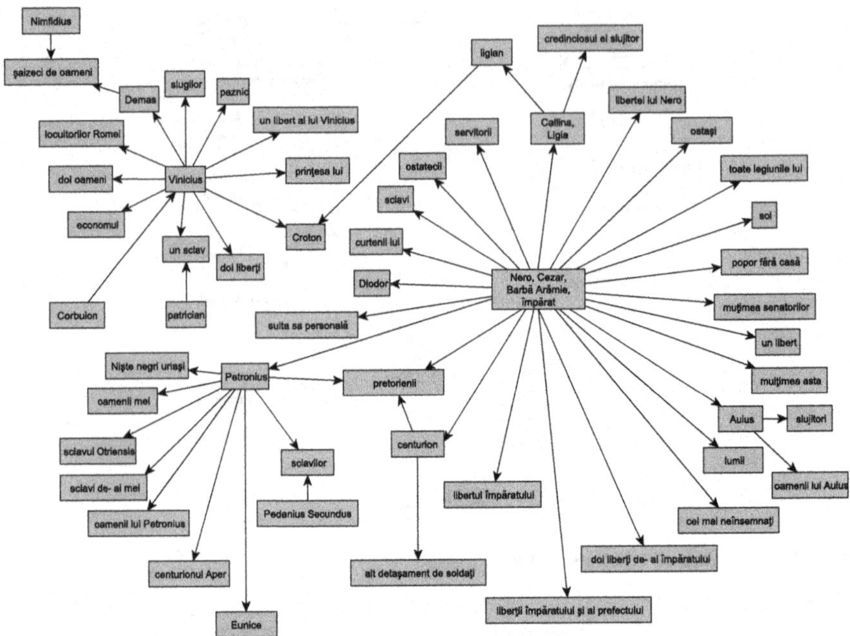

Fig. 13 A sub-network of relations `SOCIAL:superior-of`

once the sets of homonymous relations. More sophisticated representations, showing also the number of relations, not only their types, could put in evidence with more clarity the annotations in the corpus. Moreover, chains of social links could also evidence hierarchical positions in the society (as, for instance, the one connecting in `superior-of` relations the characters Nero, Ligia, a ligian and Croton). Combining graph relations could also evidence complex situations or plot developments, as for instance the distinction between a family type of affection (between Ligia and Plautius's wife, for instance, Plautius's wife being a parent for Ligia) and lovers (the sentiment that Vinicius develops versus Ligia and vice versa, neither of these doubled by any kinship relation).

The examples put forth are bits of complex interpretations. They reveal that the detection of semantic relations could incumber complex reasoning steps, thus including germs for a true understanding of the semantic content of a big coherent text.

7 Conclusions and Further Work

The research aims to formalize relationships between characters of a novel, thus establishing precise criteria that underpin aspects of the interpretation of text. The annotations that we propose can be considered as representation bricks in a project pertaining to the interpretation of free texts. Since the world described in our corpus is a fictional one, free of any constraints, we believe that the representation of entities and their links made explicit in the annotation constitute pieces of knowledge that can be extended to other universes or world structures with minimum adaptations.

The enterprise of building the "Quo Vadis" corpus was an extremely time consuming and difficult one, necessitating iterative refinements of the annotation conventions, followed by multiple corrections, sewing and merging steps. We considered that describing this process could be interesting per se, as a model to apply in building other corpora, when the scarcity of resources do not permit passing the manual work under the critical eyes of more subjects. Instead, an iterative improvement methodology was applied, by designing syntactical and semantic filters, running them and correcting the reported errors.

The corpus is still too fresh to risk a detailed numerical report and interpretation on it. In the next few months it may still undergo further improvements.[19] The graphics and tables we presented should, therefore, be interpreted more qualitatively than quantitatively, e.g. in terms of the rates between different types of relations. They allow to sketch a perception about the density of person and god types of entities and the relations mentioned among them in a literary freestyle text. Of course, from genre to genre, style to style and document to document the densities and rates may vary dramatically, but, we believe, proportions will remain within the same orders of magnitude.

The corpus is intended to be put at the base of a number of investigations in the area of semantic links, mainly oriented towards their automatic identification. For sophisticating the features to be used in the process of training statistical relation recognition programs, other layers of annotation could be useful, the most evident one being the syntactic layer, for instance, dependency links. Then, on top of the annotations already included, other types of entities and relations could be further added. Examples of sophistications include: notation of places and relations between people and places, or between places and places. Such markings could put in evidence descriptions of journeys in travelling guides, or geographical relations in high school manual. Of a different kind, extensively studied (see (Mani et al. 2006) for a survey), are the temporal relations.

Of a certain interest could be the issue of exporting annotations between parallel texts. For instance, from the Romanian version of "Quo Vadis" to its English or Polish version. If this proves possible, then a lot of time and money could be saved.

In the process of deep understanding of texts, on top of discovering inter-human or human-god relationships could be placed superior levels of interpretation, as, for instance, deciphering groups manifesting a distinctive, stable and cohesive social behaviour (as is, in the novel, the group of Romans and that of Christians). If time is added to the interpretation, then developments of stories could be traced

[19] One of the authors is elaborating a personal dissertation thesis (due June 2014) having as theme this corpus, being responsible for its correctness and complete statistics over it.

as well. Sometimes individuals migrate from one group to the other (see Vinicius) and the range of sentiments and social relations might change (Vinicius to Christ: from lack of interest to worship and Vinicius to Nero: from `inferior-of` to insubordination). On another hand, a society, as a whole, can be characterised by the set of inter-individual relationships and interesting contrasts could be determined. The new society of Christians, with their affective relations of love and worship, regenerate the old and decadent society of Romans, especially that cultivated at the court of the emperor. `The inferior-of, fear` and `hate` relations, frequent between slaves and their masters are replaced by `in-cooperation-with, friendship` and love, characteristic to the Christian model.

The corpus includes only explicitly evidenced relations (what the text says), but in many cases a human reader deduces relations on a second or deeper level of inference. Moreover, some relations explicitly stated are false, insincere, as for instance the declared love or worship sentiments of some underdogs with respect to the emperor. To deduce the falsity of relations, it could mean, for instance, to recognise relations of an opposite type, stated in different contexts and towards different listeners by the same characters. All these could be subjects of further investigation, but to do such complicated things one should start by doing simple things first, as is the automatic discovery of clearly stated relations, such as those annotated in the "Quo Vadis" Corpus.

Acknowledgments We are grateful to the master students in Computational Linguistics from the "Alexandru Ioan Cuza" University of Iaşi, Faculty of Computer Science, who, along three consecutive terms, have annotated and then corrected large segments of the "Quo Vadis" corpus. Part of the work in the construction of this corpus was done in relation with COROLA—The Computational Representational Corpus of Contemporary Romanian, a joint project of the Institute for Computer Science in Iaşi and the Research Institute for Artificial Intelligence in Bucharest, under the auspices of the Romanian Academy.<Query ID="Q4" Text=" References 'Hjørland (2007), Malmkjær (1995), Mazlack (2004)' are given in list but not cited in text. Please cite in text or delete from list." –>

References

Anechitei, D., Cristea, D., Dimosthenis, I., Ignat, E., Karagiozov, D., Koeva, S., et al. (2013). Summarizing short texts through a discourse-centered approach in a multilingual context. In A. Neustein & J. A. Markowitz (Eds.), *Where humans meet machines: Innovative solutions to knotty natural language problems*. Heidelberg: Springer.

Bagga, A., & Balwdin, B. (1998). Entity-based cross-document coreferencing using the vector space model. *Proceedings of COLING '98*, 1.

Banko, M., Cafarella, M. J., Soderland, S., Broadhead, M., & Etzioni, O. (2007). Open information extraction from the web. *Proceedings of IJCAI '07.*

Bejan, C. A., & Harabagiu, S. (2010). Unsupervised event coreference resolution with rich linguistic features. *Proceedings of the 48th Annual Meeting of the Association for Computational Linguistics*, Uppsala, Sweden.

Brin, S., & Page, L. (1998). The anatomy of a large-scale hypertextual Web search engine. *Computer Networks and ISDN systems, 30*(1), 107–117.

Boschee, E., Weischedel, R., & Zamanian, A. (2005). Automatic information extraction. *Proceedings of the 2005 International Conference on Intelligence Analysis*, McLean, VA, pp. 2–4.

Bunescu, R. C., & Paşca, M. (2006). Using encyclopedic knowledge for named entity disambiguation. *European Chapter of the Assocation for Computational Linguistics* (EACL 2006).

Carlson, A., Betteridge, J., Wang, R. C., Hruschka Jr., E. R., & Mitchell, T. M. (2010). Coupled semi-supervised learning for information extraction. *Proceedings of the Third ACM International Conference on Web Search and Data Mining* (WSDM 2010).

Chen, B., Su, J., Pan, S. J., & Chew L. T. (2011). A unified event coreference resolution by integrating multiple resolvers. *Proceedings of the 5th International Joint Conference on Natural Language Processing*, pp. 102–110, Chiang Mai, Thailand.

Cristea, D., & Dima, G. E. (2001). An integrating framework for anaphora resolution. *Information Science and Technology, Romanian Academy Publishing House, Bucharest, 4*(3–4), 273–291.

Cruse, D. A. (1986). *Lexical semantics*. Cambridge: Cambridge University Press.

Cucerzan, S. (2007). Large-scale named entity disambiguation based on wikipedia data. *Empirical Methods in Natural Language Processing* (EMNLP).

Cybulska, A., & Vossen, P. (2012). Using semantic relations to solve event coreference in text. *Proceedings of Semantic Relations-II. Enhancing Resources and Applications Workshop*, Istanbul.

Del Gaudio, R. (2014). Automatic extraction of definitions. Ph.D. thesis, University of Lisbon.

Drabek, R., & Yarowsky, D. (2005). Induction of fine-grained part-of-speech taggers via classifier combination and crosslingual projection. *Proceedings of the ACL Workshop on Building And Using Parallel Texts: Data-Driven Machine Translation And Beyond*, June 29–30, 2005, Ann Arbor, Michigan, pp. 49–56.

Gala, N., Rey, V., & Zock, M. (2010). A tool for linking stems and conceptual fragments to enhance word access. *Proceedings of LREC-2010*, Malta.

Girju, R., Badulescu, A., & Moldovan, D. (2006). Automatic discovery of part-whole relations. *Computational Linguistics, 32*(1), 83–135.

Hearst, M. (1992). Automatic acquisition of hyponyms from large text corpora. *Proceedings of COLING '92*.

Iida, R., Komachi, M., Inui, K., & Matsumoto, Y. (2007). Annotating a Japanese text corpus with predicate-argument and coreference relations. *Proceedings of the Linguistic Annotation Workshop*, pp. 132–139.

Kawahara, D., Kurohashi, S., & Hasida, K. (2002). Construction of a Japanese relevance-tagged corpus. *Proceedings of LREC '02*.

Levi, J. N. (1978). *The syntax and semantics of complex nominals*. New York: Academic Press.

Lyons, J. (1977). *Semantics*. Cambridge: Cambridge University Press.

Mani, I., Wellner, B., Verhagen, M., Lee, C. M., & Pustejovsky, J. (2006). Machine learning of temporal relation. *Proceedings of the 44th Annual meeting of the Association for Computational Linguistics*, Australia.

Masatsugu, H., Kawahara, D., & Kurohashi, S.(2012). Building a diverse document leads corpus annotated with semantic relations. *Proceedings of the 26th Pacific Asia Conference on Language, Information and Computation*, pp. 535–544.

Miller G. A., Beckwidth R., Fellbaum C., Gross D., & Miller K. J. (1990). Introduction to WordNet: An on-line lexical database. *International Journal of Lexicography, 3*(4)(winter 1990), 235–244.

Mitkov, R. (2003). Anaphora resolution. In R. Mitkov (Ed.), *The oxford handbook of computational linguistics* (pp. 266–283). Oxford: Oxford University Press.

Mulkar-Mehta, R., Hobbs, J. R., & Hovy, E. (2011). Granularity in natural language discourse. *Proceedings of International Conference on Computational Semantics.*

Murphy, M. L. (2003). *Semantic relations and the lexicon: Antonymy, synonymy, and other paradigms*. Cambridge: Cambridge University Press.

Năstase, V., Nakov, P., Séaghdha, D. Ó., & Szpakowicz, S. (2013). *Semantic relations between nominals*. California: Morgan & Claypool Publishers.

Ohara, K. (2011). Full text annotation with Japanese framenet: Study to annotation semantic frame to bccwj (in japanese). *Proceedings of the 17th Annual Meeting fo the Association for Natural Language Processing*, pp. 703–704.

Pantel, P., Ravichandran, D., & Hovy, E. (2004). Towards terascale knowledge acquisition. *Proceedings of COLING '04.*

Paşca, M., Lin, D., Bigham, J., Lifchits, A., & Jain, A. (2006). Names and similarities on the Web: Fact extraction in the fast lane. *Proceedings of the 21st International Conference on Computational Linguistics and 44th Annual Meeting of the Association for Computational Linguistics*, pp. 809–816, Sydney, Australia.

Postolache, O., Cristea, D., & Orasan, C. (2006). Transferring coreference chains through word alignment. *Proceedings of LREC-2006*, Geneva.

Quillian, M. R. (1962). A revised design for an understanding machine. *Mechanical Translation, 7*, 17–29.

Rao, D., McNamee, P., & Dredze, M. (2012). Entity linking: Finding extracted entities in a knowledge base. In T. Poibeau, H. Saggion, J. Piskorski, & R. Yangarber (Eds.), *Multisource multilingual information extraction and summarization, Springer lecture notes in computer science*. Berlin: Springer.

Rello, L., & Ilisei, I. (2009). A comparative study of Spanish zero pronoun distribution. *Proceedings of the International Symposium on Data and Sense Mining, Machine Translation and Controlled Languages (ISMTCL)*, pp. 209–214.

Rodríguez, K. J., Delogu, F., Versley, Y., Stemle, E. W., & Poesio, M. (2010). Anaphoric annotation of Wikipedia and blogs in the live memories corpus. *Proceedings of the Seventh conference on International Language Resources and Evaluation (LREC '10).*

Rosenfeld, B., & Feldman, R. (2007). Using corpus statistics on entities to improve semisupervised relation extraction from the Web. *Proceedings of the 45th Annual Meeting of the Association for Computational Linguistics*, pp. 600–607, Prague, Czech Republic.

Pollard, C., & Sag, I. A. (1994). *Head-driven phrase structure grammar*. Chicago: University of Chicago Press.

Saggion, H. (2007). SHEF—semantic tagging and summarization techniques applied to cross-document coreference. *Proceedings of SEMEVLA '07.*

Séaghdha, D. Ó., & Copestake, A. (2008). Semantic classification with distributional kernels. *Proceedings of the 22nd International Conference on Computational Linguistics (COLING-08)*, Manchester, UK.

Singh, S., Subramanya, A., Pereira, F., & McCallum, A. (2011). Large-scale cross-document coreference using distributed inference and hierarchical models. *Proceedings of HLT '11*, 1.

Simionescu, R. (2012). Romanian deep noun phrase chunking using graphical grammar studio. In M. A. Moruz, D. Cristea, D. Tufiş, A. Iftene, H. N. Teodorescu (Eds.), *Proceedings of the 8th International Conference "Linguistic Resources and Tools for Processing of the Romanian Language"*, pp. 135–143.

Snow, R., Jurafsky, D., & Ng, A. Y. (2006). Semantic taxonomy induction from heterogeneous evidence. *Proceedings of COLING-ACL '06.*

Tanaka, I. (1999). The value of an annotated corpus in the investigation of anaphoric pronouns, with particular reference to backwards anaphora in English. Ph.d. thesis, University of Lancaster.

Tesnière, L. (1959). *Éléments de syntaxe structurale*. Paris: Klincksieck.

Zock, M. (2010). Wheels for the mind of the language producer: microscopes, macroscopes, semantic maps and a good compass. In V. Barbu Mititelu, V. Pekar, & E. Barbu (Eds.), *Proceedings of the Workshop Semantic Relations*. Theory and Applications.

Zock, M., Ferret, O., & Schwab, D. (2010). Deliberate word access: An intuition, a roadmap and some preliminary empirical results. *International Journal of Speech Technology, 13*, 201–218.

Zock, M., & Schwab, D. (2013). L'index, une ressource vitale pour guider les auteurs a trouver le mot bloque sur le bout de la langue. In N. Gala, & M. Zock (Eds.), *Ressources lexicales: construction et utilisation. Lingvisticae Investigationes*. Amsterdam: John Benjamins.

AusTalk and Alveo: An Australian Corpus and Human Communication Science Collaboration Down Under

Dominique Estival

Abstract Over the past decades, NLP has progressed from hand-crafted rule-based text processing systems to the widely accepted adoption of statistically-based systems. The convergence between techniques inspired by speech processing and detailed analyses embedded in formal linguistic frameworks continues to be negotiated, sometimes painfully, and the divide between empirical resource-intense and formal approaches can still be felt across our field. Michael Zock has always been a pioneer in building bridges across disciplines and he has endeavoured throughout his career to avoid being forced into one or another camp. As a colleague early in my own career, he has inspired and encouraged me in my own efforts at collaborating with related sub-disciplines and at approaching problems from new angles. In this paper, I describe two large-scale Australian projects that both resulted from cross-disciplinary collaboration and are expected to foster further research across a range of speech and language disciplines.

Keywords Audio–visual recordings corpus · Australian English varieties · Visual perception · Human–computer interaction · Cognitive modelling

Over the past decades, NLP has progressed from hand-crafted rule-based text processing systems to the widely accepted adoption of statistically-based systems. The convergence between techniques inspired by speech processing and detailed analyses embedded in formal linguistic frameworks continues to be negotiated, sometimes painfully, and the divide between empirical resource-intense and formal approaches can still be felt across our field. Michael Zock has always been a pioneer in building bridges across disciplines and he has endeavoured throughout his career to avoid being forced into one or another camp on ideological grounds. As a colleague early in my own career, he inspired and encouraged me in my own efforts at collaborating with related sub-disciplines and at approaching problems from new angles. I am fortunate to count Michael as a friend as well as a

D. Estival (✉)
MARCS Institute, University of Western Sydney, Sydney, NSW, Australia
e-mail: D.Estival@uws.edu.au

© Springer International Publishing Switzerland 2015
N. Gala et al. (eds.), *Language Production, Cognition, and the Lexicon*,
Text, Speech and Language Technology 48, DOI 10.1007/978-3-319-08043-7_29

colleague, who demonstrated through his example the value of independence of spirit and non-conformity for multi-disciplinary collaboration.

From the early 1990s, Michael and I crossed paths through various European projects and summer schools, particularly the Summer Schools in Bulgaria,[1] which led to the successful RANLP conference series, and the Summer Schools in Romania.[2] At times, the teaching environment could be challenging: no power on the first morning of classes at the beautiful old building of the Alliance Française in Iasi meant I could not use overheads for my first lecture but had to resort solely to white boards where, due to a mixed audience with different language backgrounds (some students had come by train from Siberia and knew no French, others from Romania did not understand English) I alternated between French and English for 2 h. In the second lecture, Michael had to do the same, and we both enjoyed together a well-deserved lunch break before, to our great relief, the power came back for the rest of the sessions.

Building on the links established during these summer schools, where we usually attended each other's lectures, Michael helped me set up a fruitful collaboration with Dan Tufis.[3] This was one example among many of Michael's generosity, spending time helping others set up projects, as well as helping students and younger researchers. His enthusiasm and willingness to make connections were also evident in his participation in, and support to, the *International Symposium on Social Communication,* Santiago de Cuba, where we met again in 1999 and where he was, as usual, working to help the organisers obtain funding for the following year. Michael also showed his open-mindedness in the breadth of his interests: psycholinguistics, lexicon, language teaching tools, cognitive science, language processing tools. In his teaching, he always seems to be looking for connections and ways to relate advances in one area to further understanding in another.

Continuing in this spirit of European collaborations, whether in academia or industry, after I moved to Australia in 1995, I tried to set up projects with colleagues at other institutions and helped establish organisations such as ALTA[4] and OzCLO[5] (Estival et al. 2013a, b). Following an unsuccessful attempt to set up an Australian Centre of Excellence for language processing, the wider-reaching and more ambitious *Human Communication Science Network* (HCSNet) was finally funded by the Australian Research Council for 5 years (Dale et al. 2004–2010). Summer schools, conferences and workshops gathered researchers across a range

[1] Summer School 'Contemporary Topics in Computational Linguistics' (Tzigov Chark, Bulgaria, 1991, 1992; Vassil Kolarov Lake, Bulgaria, 1993).

[2] Summer School 'EUROLAN'93' and 'EUROLAN'95' (Iasi, Romania).

[3] Research project *Développement d'outils et de données linguistiques pour le traitement du langage naturel*, between ISSCO and the Romanian Academy to develop NLP software, specifically using the ELU platform for the morphological analysis of Romanian (1993–1995), funded by the FNRS-EST (Swiss Government Grant for collaboration with Eastern European countries).

[4] Australasian Language Technology Association: http://www.alta.asn.au/.

[5] Australian Computational and Linguistics Olympiad: http://www.ozclo.org.au/.

of disciplines and resulted in fertile cross-disciplinary collaborations (Dale et al. 2011). *AusTalk* and *Alveo* are two large-scale Australian projects which arose from HCSNet cross-disciplinary connections and which aim at furthering research across a range of speech and language disciplines. As the project manager for both these projects, in this article, I describe the way they were set up, their difficulties and their achievements to date.

1 The Big ASC Project and the AusTalk Corpus

1.1 Background and Aims

The *AusTalk* corpus of audio-visual Australian English was designed and created through the *Big ASC*, a collaborative project funded by the Australian Research Council (ARC) with the two main goals of providing a standardized infrastructure for audio-visual recordings in Australia and producing a large audio-visual corpus of Australian English. Like all spoken dialects, Australian English contains a certain amount of variation, albeit less than UK or US English. The Macquarie Dictionary of Australian English (first ed. 1981) recognised three main varieties of Australian English: broad, general and cultivated. These three varieties were usually taken to be loosely related to social class, while regional variations were not considered sufficiently salient to warrant discussion. Today we can identify a broader range of Australian English varieties (Moore 2008), including ethno-cultural dialects which in more recent years have become increasingly evident and proudly spoken (Cox and Palethorpe 2011). Certain varieties have been investigated to some extent (Clyne et al. 2001) and subtle regional variations are now recognised (Cox and Palethorpe 2007) but much still remains unknown about the extent of variation in Australian English. The only publicly available Australian speech corpus is the *Australian National Database of Spoken Language* (ANDOSL) (Vonwiller et al. 1995). Although still relevant for research, ANDOSL is now outmoded because of, on the one hand its small number of speakers (108) and their non-representative sampling, and on the other hand the limited coverage of Australian English variation and the limited number of tasks performed by the speakers. In addition, the data for each speaker consist in a single recording session which is audio-only and low-fidelity by current standards. A few earlier data sets are now part of the Australian National Corpus (Musgrave and Haugh 2009) but they are even more limited in their coverage.

Thus, the first purpose of the Big ASC project was to establish a much larger and more representative corpus of speakers from all over Australia, using modern technology to obtain higher quality data. The *AusTalk* corpus provides an extensible database for projects charting the extent, degree, and details of social, regional and ethno-cultural variations in Australian English, with up to 1000 geographically and socially diverse speakers recorded in locations across Australia in 2011–2014. The *AusTalk* corpus was also designed to cater for a range of research projects and applications, therefore in order to provide for the needs of different constituencies such as phonetics, forensic studies, language technologies, linguistic analysis, or audio-visual analysis, the project had to strike a balance between high quality studio recording and field data collection. This was achieved through a strict data collection protocol, with high levels of standardisation and automation. Thus the second purpose of the Big ASC project was to establish a common infrastructure with reusable equipment in locations around Australia and to ensure standardisation of the *AusTalk* corpus across all data collection sites (Wagner et al. 2010; Burnham et al. 2011). The infrastructure and the standard data collection protocol also ensure that the *AusTalk* corpus can be extended through further projects in a consistent manner.

1.2 Structure of the Project

Managed by the University of Western Sydney (UWS) as the leading institution, the Big ASC project regrouped thirteen partners and was spread over sixteen recording sites. The equipment was designed by a sub-committee representing the requirements of the various constituencies and the hardware itself was built and tested at UWS. Twelve identical Black Boxes, consisting of a portable demountable DJ case containing the computer and all the audio and video recording equipment, as shown in Fig. 1, were then assembled and distributed to the project partners.

Given the complex data collection protocol, described below, and the precision required in maintaining the recording environment, both for acoustic and light levels, virtual recording with full automation was not an option. Recording Assistants (RAs) were recruited for each site and they all came to a 2 day workshop in Sydney, where they trained together and practiced setting up the equipment and running through the recording sessions with each other. Although

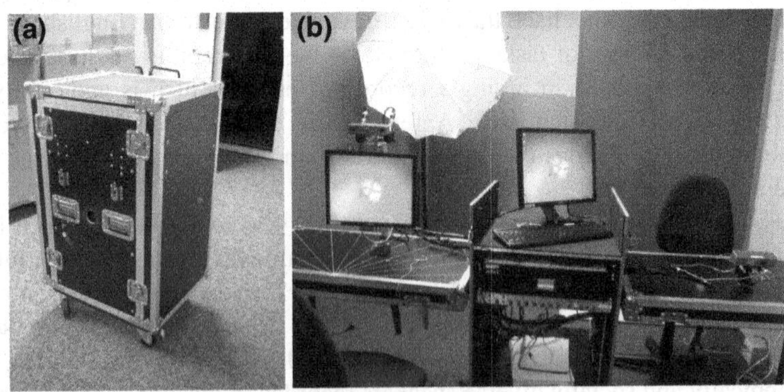

Fig. 1 The big ASC black box **a** closed and **b** deployed

some inevitable delays lessened the impact of this centralised training to some extent and extra training was required when new RAs were recruited, this was an important factor in keeping the data consistent.

1.3 Description of the Corpus

Audio-visual corpora are important for different types of research in linguistics, NLP and Language Technologies, relying of various aspects of variability. In the AusTalk corpus, three 1 h sessions are recorded at intervals of at least 1 week to capture potential *variability over time*, while *geographical variability* is guaranteed by recording at locations covering all the capital cities of Australian states and territories and several regional centres. Wide advertising and high visibility of the project, with a well-publicised launch on Australia Day 2011 and good media coverage, helped recruit speakers from a range of social spheres to ensure *social variability*.[6]

1.4 Collection Protocol

The *AusTalk* corpus contains a variety of speech content from a range of tasks, with four Read Speech and five Spontaneous Speech components, while five microphones and two stereo cameras record audio and video.

Each of the three recording sessions comprises a different sub-set of the Read and Spontaneous speech tasks. In the standard 'Words', 'Digits' and 'Sentences' tasks, the speaker reads aloud a list of prompts from a computer screen, while the 'Story Reading' and 'Story Re-telling' tasks (Session 1) provide material for the study of differences between reading and spontaneous language. The 'Interview', 'Map Task' and 'Conversation' tasks provide material for the analysis of speech acts in dialogues. In the 'Interview' (Session 2), the speakers talk to the RA on a topic which they chose in Session 1. The 'Map Task' (Session 3) is designed along the lines of (Anderson et al. 1991) but adapted for Australian English. In this final session, two speakers are paired for two Map Tasks, so that each participant plays the role of Information Giver and Information Receiver, after which they discuss the experience in the 'Conversation'.[7] At the beginning and end of each session, a set of natural 'Yes/No' questions elicit a range of positive and negative answers. Table 1 shows the distribution of these tasks across the sessions and the average time for each task.

---

[6] Detailed demographic statistics concerning gender, age and education level of the speakers are available at: http://bigasc.edu.au/stats/.

[7] Scheduling three sessions per speaker and coordinating the timing of the sessions were part of the RAs responsibilities, together with strict record-keeping, data management and data upload. The project thus relied heavily on the RAs and the quality of their work.

Table 1 AusTalk corpus components/time per speaker

Components	Session	Time (mins)	Time per speaker
Read speech			53 min
Words (322 × 3)	S1, S2, S3	10	30
Digit strings (12 × 2)	S1, S2	5	10
Sentences (59 × 1)	S2	8	8
Read story	S1	5	5
Spontaneous speech			80 min
Yes/No answers (× 5)	S1, S2, S3	2	10
Re-told story	S1	10	10
Interview	S2	15	15
Map task (× 2)	S3	20	40
Conversation	S3	5	5
Total (average)			133 min

1.5 Quality Control

To guarantee consistency of recordings across locations, the data collection protocol was automated as much as possible via the SSCP software program, designed and developed for the project. The SSCP ensures that all the RAs follow the same scripts and it helps prevents errors in manipulating and saving the data. To ensure data quality as well as consistency across all the sites, we put in place several processes. In addition to the centralised RA training and the automated collection protocol, sample recordings were checked for audio and video quality before the start of data collection at each site. Continuous monitoring of data quality helped provide feedback and advice to the RAs throughout the data collection. A Quality Control RA (QC-RA) was employed at the central receiving site where the data was uploaded, with strict guidelines for both audio and video quality checks.

To help the site RAs and the QC-RA, we also developed the SSCP-QC, a utility to check the number of files along with the quality of parameters such as silence or loudness for audio, and frame skipping or brightness for video. The outcomes of the QC checks are retained and become part of the metadata at the item and component levels. Manual inspection of the data finalises the published QC status, as one of the following:

- A (A-OK)
- B (OK, but imperfect)
- C (bad, not acceptable)
- D (deficient or missing, e.g. “Missing 2nd video camera for Map Task”).

1.6 Data Annotation

Annotation is an important aspect of projects such as the Big ASC for, without annotations, many of the applications and much of the proposed research could not be conducted. Integral to the project is the requirement that new annotations, e.g. detailed phonetic transcriptions or Part-of-Speech tagging, can later be contributed by project partners or other researchers and then integrated into the existing annotation store. From the outset it was decided to automate the annotation process as much as possible, while providing high-quality manual annotation for a subset of the data. In particular, it was expected that forced alignment would be used where appropriate to enhance manual annotation. We thus defined the minimum annotations, with their automation options, as follows:

(a) **Orthographic** level annotation of both Read Speech and Spontaneous Speech. For Read Speech, the prompts provide the basis for an automated orthographic transcription; for Spontaneous Speech, the process might be automated if an automatic speech recognition (ASR) package could be trained on the Read Speech.
(b) **Phonemic** level transcription with segmentation, to be automated as far as possible. For Read Speech, forced alignment can be performed after manual phonemic level transcription of a subset of the data.
(c) **Video**—the automatic alignment of speech with video can be performed from the strobe signal recorded on a separate audio channel (Lichtenauer et al. 2009).

In addition, the following 'wish-list' was to be performed if there were sufficient resources:

(d) **Phonetic** level—manual and labour intensive
(e) **Intonation**—to be explored later
(f) **Part-Of-Speech**—can be automated (see *Alveo* below)
(g) **Morphemic**—to be explored later
(h) **Syntactic**—to be explored later

The Annotation Task itself could only be commenced when sufficient data had been collected and organised, i.e. from April 2012, and is to be continued until mid-2014. As manual annotation is extremely time-consuming and expensive, we decided early on that the project could only afford to annotate around half of the data: only 5 speakers would be fully annotated (at least a, b, c, d, and f above), while the rest of the data would have only the basic levels (a, b, c). Therefore, the manual Annotation Task was limited to (1) word segmentation for the Read Speech and (2) orthographic transcription aligned at the phrase or sentence level for Spontaneous Speech.

A very important aspect of the project has thus been to explore procedures for automated annotation and to work in collaboration with partners who could produce automated alignment for the Read Speech (Schiel 1999) and automated orthographic transcriptions for the Spontaneous Speech Components. As was expected, automating the time alignment of phonemic transcriptions for the Read Speech data and the orthographic transcription of the Spontaneous Speech data proved very challenging, a major obstacle for this part of the project being that people make mistakes when reading material aloud, so scripted data does not always have the integrity required for automatic processing. Another major challenge was the poor quality of the automated transcriptions obtained with ASR systems and this effort was discontinued.

Nevertheless, while the ideal of producing full annotations for 100 % of the *AusTalk* data cannot be realised in this phase of the project, we are providing a full set of manually created phonetic, phonemic and orthographic transcriptions for a selected number of speakers. The *AusTalk* corpus will also contain automatically time-aligned transcriptions for all the Read Speech data and automatically generated orthographic transcriptions for at least a subset of the Spontaneous Speech data. Meanwhile, as described below, the *AusTalk* corpus is now included in the *Alveo* Virtual Laboratory (Burnham et al. 2012), a more recent Australian collaborative project funded under the Australian Government NeCTAR program to build a platform for collaborative research around human communication science data. This will allow the generation of automated Part-of-Speech tagging and syntactic analyses as additional annotations for the corpus.

As the Big ASC project aims both to make *AusTalk* widely available and to allow future contributions, such as further data or additional annotations, audio and video data are stored on a web-accessible server, with corpus metadata and annotations stored in the DADA annotation store (Cassidy and Johnston 2009). The DADA server can support import/export of annotation data in formats used supported by many annotation and analysis tools.

1.7 Challenges

Managing a project of this size and complexity, with partners from different disciplines and therefore different aims (e.g. field work vs phonetic analysis) and different understandings of the requirements, proved quite challenging. The original timeline had to be extended, with the project now in its 4th year (2010–2014).

In addition to the logistics problems posed by coordination between recording sites and working with RAs across a vast continent, the technical issues involved in uploading the enormous amount of recorded data (up to 3,000 h of 2 video channels and 6 audio channels) over the network led to delays while we developed a solution for compressing the stereo video data. Each session requires approximately 30G of space when uncompressed, therefore the original intention of copying data on disks to be mailed turned out not to be feasible. Even with compressed video, each session takes about 2 GB and recording sites sometimes ran out of hard disk space before successfully uploading the data they had recorded. The uploading software had to be redesigned and new processes put in place.

Ensuring there were always two copies of the data in existence was a main concern, especially while the database on the server was redesigned and constantly being populated, and we implemented a system of backup hard disk drives posted to UWS when the Black Box computers were full or when data could not be uploaded.

Nevertheless, one very satisfying aspect of the project was being able to meet so many different Australian English speakers and working with people of such diverse backgrounds.

1.8 Results

The *AusTalk* data collection itself is coming to an end, with less than 200 speakers remaining to be recorded at three sites in order to complete the data set for 1,000 Australian English speakers, each with three 1 h sessions. Follow-on projects have already begun to collect data from different population groups (e.g. particular ethnic backgrounds) in some locations and the analysis of *AusTalk* data is under way at other partner sites, e.g. video analysis for facial gestures (Sui et al. 2012a, b) and close phonetic analysis of the isolated word list data. In another study based on the framework of (Weiss et al. 2013), the Read Sentences provide a set of stimuli to study perceptual dimensions used by listeners to characterise speakers' vocal characteristics and speaking style. Meanwhile annotation and quality assessment continue and more data is made available through a new interface (Estival et al. 2014).

An unforeseen but very exciting addition to *AusTalk* was the inclusion of speakers who originally participated in the ANDOSL project in 1993–1995. Of the eight ANDOSL speakers who were identified and who agreed to participate in AusTalk, four completed the full recording sessions and these constitute invaluable longitudinal data.

2 The Alveo Virtual Lab

2.1 Background and Aims

The Human Communication Science (HCS) field is broadly defined to encompass the study of speech and language from various perspectives but also includes research on music and various other forms of human expression. The Australian HCS community responded very positively to the formation of HCSNet (Dale et al. 2004–2010), a research network funded by the Australian Research Council for 5 years, attending HCSNet workshops and seminars, producing successful grants and publications in the HCS area (Dale et al. 2011), and setting up the Big ASC project. While HCSNet permitted the development of a strong interdisciplinary community, the *Alveo* Virtual Laboratory project (Estival et al. 2013a) is now extending and deepening the links in the HCS community by furthering and strengthening these collaborations.[8]

The primary goal of the *Alveo* project is to foster multi-disciplinarity and to allow the blooming of collaboration in unforeseen ways and directions. HCSNet provided the opportunity for applying novel combinations of old ideas or methods of analysis from different disciplines to new problems. For instance, in the *HCS Compendium*, (Butavicius and Lee 2011) describe a multi-disciplinary approach involving visual perception, human-computer interaction and cognitive modelling to the problem of assisting users to find relevant information in very large data sets. In the same spirit, (Copland et al. 2011) married an existing psycholinguistic semantic priming task with fMRI to address the role of dopamine on neuro-transmitters in semantic processing. However, the HCSNet experience also made it clear that one of the main impediments to such quantum leaps in HCS research was the difficulty for a researcher from one discipline to apply the tools and techniques of another discipline, or to explore data collected under one paradigm via a completely different analytical perspective. Moreover, research conducted in isolation entails inefficient repetition of analysis of local data sets.

Therefore the *Alveo* Virtual Laboratory is designed to provide a platform for easy access to language, speech and other communication-relevant databases and for the integrated use of a range of analysis tools. The hope is that such an environment will not only eliminate the waste of unshared analyses being repeated, but that it will afford the serendipity of new combinations of tools and datasets, facilitating research that will provide new insights into old problems, or the combinations of old ideas to approach new problems. As HCS is such a multi- and cross-disciplinary field, it relies upon various types of data and various tools by which these data can be analysed. *Alveo* will enable easy access to shared tools and data, and overcome the resource and access limitations of individual desktop systems. It will allow a diverse range of researchers to access an amalgamation of existing data collections and corpora and to use analytical tools created by other researchers. Providing access to corpora, tools and the analyses conducted with these, into an easily accessed, shared, and replicable environment will not only promote collaboration between institutions and disciplines, but also dramatically improve scientific replicability. It makes it possible to standardise, define, and capture procedures and data output so that research publications can be supported by re-runnable re-usable data and coded procedure.[9]

A number of projects in the EU and the US aim to develop standard web-service architectures for defining and managing workflows that process audio or textual resources using tools such as parsers, taggers or speech recognisers. One important project with which *Alveo* is associated is the US NSF funded project "The Language Application Grid: A Framework for Rapid Adaptation and Reuse",

---

[8] *Alveo* is funded by NeCTAR, a body set up by the Australian Government as part of the Super Science initiative and financed by the Education Investment Fund.

[9] See, e.g.: http:/www.myexperiment.org.

which aims to make resources available for "intercultural collaboration, using the language resources registered by users around the world".[10] The Language Grid resources are primarily textual and aimed at multilingual applications, particularly Machine Translation while *Alveo* is aimed at researchers and is not limited to textual data. While the EU funded CLARIN project is "aimed at making language resources and technology readily available for the whole European Humanities (and Social Sciences) community",[11] *Alveo* aims to make available to the Australian, and ultimately the international community, more broadly construed HCS resources, i.e. not only text and speech but also video, music and ethnographic data. Another significant EU effort is META-NET (Multilingual Europe Technology Alliance) which aims to establish a platform for resource sharing around Europe and has already made significant contributions relating to meta-data management.[12] The *Alveo* project is working closely with these international partners to ensure that we are building compatible and interoperable toolsets.

2.2 Structure of the Project

Regrouping sixteen partners, including thirteen Australian universities, most of which were Big ASC project partners, the *Alveo* project is managed centrally by UWS as the leading institution (Denis Burnham, project director). It is designed to make use of Australian national infrastructure—including data storage, discovery and research computing services. One of the partners, Intersect, is charged with development under the guidance of the project manager (Dominique Estival, UWS) and the product owner (Steve Cassidy, Macquarie University), while User Acceptance Testing (UAT) is performed by Higher Degree Researchers (HDRs) at the partner institutions across Australia. Scenarios and scripts for testing the environment, access to the corpora and use of the tools are distributed to all the partners and the testing results are collected via a web interface, leading to acceptance reports endorsed by a Steering Committee.

2.3 Technical Description

Alveo incorporates existing tools, some developed by project members, which were adapted to work on the shared infrastructure, together with a web-based data discovery interface for searching and accessing the data sets. The tools are

[10] See: http://langrid.org/file/TheLanguageGrid-en.pdf. One collaborator is the Australian National Corpus, also a member of *Alveo*.

[11] See: http://www.clarin.eu.

[12] See: http://www.meta-net.eu.

Table 2 Alveo corpora

1. PARADISEC (the Pacific and Regional Archive for Digital Sources in Endangered Cultures), including Indigenous languages, music, and speech data (Thieberger et al. 2011)
2. AusTalk, audio-visual speech corpus from the Big ASC project (Burnham et al. 2011)
3. The Australian National Corpus (AusNC) incorporating the Australian Corpus of English (ACE), Australian Radio Talkback (ART), AustLit, Braided Channels, Corpus of Oz Early English (COOEE), Email Australia, Griffith Corpus of Spoken English (GCSAusE), International Corpus of English (Australia contribution is ICE-AUS), the Mitchell and Delbridge corpus, and the Monash Corpus of Spoken English (Musgrave and Haugh 2009)
4. AVOZES, a visual speech corpus (Goecke and Millar 2004)
5. Australian Music Centre archive (collection of sound and text: over 30,000 items by 530 artists)[a]
6. Colloquial Jakartan Indonesian corpus, audio and text (recorded in Jakarta in the early 1990s by Fay Wouk)
7. The ClueWeb dataset (http://lemurproject.org/clueweb12/)

[a] Obtaining access to the AMC proved quite challenging because of technical and copyright issues, so it was decided to replace it with three datasets: (1) a collection of music excerpts from films: samples of Pixar movie theme music expressing different emotions (Emery Schubert, UNSW); (2) a collection of room impulse responses which, through convolution with speech or music, can create the effect of that speech or music in the acoustic environment they represent (Densil Cabrera, Sydney University); (3) a battery of emotional prosody: samples of sung sentences using different prosodic patterns (Bill Thompson, Macquarie University)

orchestrated by a workflow engine with both web and command line interfaces to allow use by technical and non-technical researchers. The corpora and tools that were originally scheduled to be included in the first phase of the project are listed in Tables 2 and 3.

Table 3 Alveo tools

1. EOPAS (PARADISEC tool) for text interlinear text and media analysis
2. NLTK (Natural Language Toolkit) for text analytics with linguistic data (Bird et al. 2009)
3. EMU for search, speech analysis, and interactive labelling of spectrograms and waveforms
4. AusNC Tools: KWIC, Concordance, Word Count, statistical summary and statistical analysis on a user-defined subset of content
5. Johnson-Charniak parser, to generate full parse trees for text sentences (Charniak and Johnson 2005)
6. ParseEval, tool to evaluate the syllabic parse of consonant clusters (Shaw and Gafos 2010)
7. HTK—modifications, a patch to HTK (Hidden Markov Model Toolkit, http://htk.eng.cam.ac.uk/) to enable missing data recognition
8. DeMoLib software for video analysis (http://staff.estem-uc.edu.au/roland/research/demolib-home/)
9. PsySound3 (physical and psycho-acoustical algorithms) of complex visual and auditory scenes (Cabrera et al. 2007)
10. ParGram (grammar for Indonesian) (Arka 2012)
11. The INDRI tool for information retrieval with large data sets (http://www.lemurproject.org/indri/)

The *Alveo* Workflow Engine is built around the Galaxy open source workflow management system (Goecks et al. 2010). An instance of the Workflow engine is run on a virtual machine in the NeCTAR Cloud, with web-based browse/search of corpora using Blacklight. An API is provided to mediate access to data, ensuring that permissions are respected, and providing a way to access individual items, and 'mount' datasets for fast access (Cassidy et al. 2014).

Behind the scenes, *Alveo* uses a Fedora based repository to manage corpus data, Hydra (Awre et al. 2009) tools to help build the interface to the data, and Solr to index meta-data and text. We re-use the AusNC pre-processing module to convert PDF, Word and other formats to plain text, extract metadata and annotations, and standardise formats (RDF).

2.4 Challenges

As the *Alveo* project follows from the *Big ASC*, previous resolution of management issues led to a smoother continent-wide organisation. Having a dedicated team of professional software engineers for design and implementation, rather than relying on graduate students at partner institutions, ensured timely deliveries, thorough regression testing and bug-fixing, under the Agile development process. Nevertheless, the size and complexity of the project and the distributed testing across sixteen sites, with HDRs from varied disciplines and backgrounds, some expert programmers, others pure linguists, resulted in some challenges. The main difficulty was the creation of appropriate testing scenarios for each component, suitable for a range of diverse HDRs.

2.5 Status of the Project

Alveo 2.0 was delivered at the end of 2013, with *Alveo 3.0* scheduled for June 2014, the end of Phase I. Of the corpora listed in Table 2, all are now part of *Alveo* (but see note for Table 2) to some extent, with the two larger ones being special cases: the metadata for *AusTalk* is still being ingested and, as the data collection is not yet complete, more data will be added in the coming months; for ClueWeb, the data is indexed using INDRI and accessible from the Research Cloud. Of the tools listed in Table 3, all have been integrated in *Alveo*, with the added bonus that the Johnson-Charniak Parser has been added to the NLTK Tools and is thus accessed in the same way as the other text processing tools in that toolkit, and the ParGram grammar for Indonesian is made available through the XLE interface (King et al. 2000), thus providing access to all the other XLE grammars as well.

The project will continue for 2 years of Phase II (until June 2016) during which we will focus on the uptake of *Alveo* in the research community and on adding resources and functionalities to the existing tools and corpora. To achieve the first goal, we will run regular training workshops and an annual conference. New corpora will be added, starting with the Liberated Learning Consortium (LLC) corpus of recorded lectures, some with transcriptions (Bain et al. 2012). Next in the pipeline, a semi-parallel corpus of handwritten handover nursing notes that have been transcribed and verbal nursing handover notes (from UWS), a new music dataset (from RMIT), a forensic database (from UNSW) and a corpus of sign language corpus (from Macquarie University) are under negotiation. We are expanding the set of tools by integrating the MAUS forced alignment tool (Schiel 1999) with HTK and will attempt to provide more than a link to the XLE Grammar Environment. We also foresee the inclusion of a new tool for music analysis (from UWS).

It is hoped that more researchers, both from Australia and internationally, will want to join *Alveo* and contribute new tools and new datasets. As important will be the projects which will take advantage of this new facility and which will contribute new results to our understanding of human communication.

3 Conclusion

The *AusTalk* and *Alveo* projects are examples of collaborative projects building new resources and consolidating partnerships across disciplines. I like to think that, were Michael in Australia, he would have been one of the researchers active in both these projects. We certainly would have benefited from his experience and advice.

References

Anderson, A. H., et al. (1991). The HCRC Map task corpus. *Language and Speech, 34*(4), 351–366.

Arka, I. W. (2012). Developing a deep grammar of indonesian within the pargram framework: Theoretical and implementational challenges. *26th Pacific Asia Conference on Language,Information and Computation* (pp. 19–38).

Awre, C., et al. (2009). Project hydra: Designing & building a reusable framework for multipurpose, multifunction, multi-institutional repository-powered solutions. *4th International Conference on Open Repositories*. Atlanta: Georgia Institute of Technology.

Bain, K., et al. (2012). Transcribe your class: Empowering students, instructors, and institutions: Factors affecting implementation and adoption of a hosted transcription service. *INTED201* (pp. 1446–1454).

Bird, S., et al. (2009). *Natural language processing with python—analyzing text with the natural language toolkit*. Sebastopol: O'Reilly Media.

Burnham, D., et al. (2012). *Above and beyond speech, language and music: A virtual Lab for Human Communication Science (HCS vLab)*. NeCTAR (National eResearch Collaboration Tools & Resources) Virtual Laboratory.

Burnham, D., et al. (2011). Building an audio-visual corpus of Australian English: large corpus collection with an economical portable and replicable Black Box. *Interspeech 2011*. Florence, Italy.

Butavicius, M. A. & Lee, M. D. (2011). An empirical evaluation of four data visualization techniques for displaying short news text similarities. In R. Dale, D. Burnham & C. J. Stevens (Eds.), *Human communication science: A compendium* (pp. 125–148). Sydney, Australia: ARC Research Network in Communication Science.

Cabrera, D., et al. (2007). Psysound3: Software for acoustical and psychoacoustical analysis of sound recordings. *International Community on Auditory Display*. Atlanta: Georgia Institute of Technology.

Cassidy, S., et al. (2014). The alveo virtual laboratory: A web based repository API. *9th Language Resources and Evaluation Conference (LREC 2014)*. Reykjavik, Iceland.

Cassidy, S. & Johnston T (2009). Ingesting the auslan corpus into the DADA annotation store. *Third Linguistic Annotation Workshop (LAW III)*. Singapore.

Charniak, E. & Johnson, M (2005). Coarse-to-fine n-best parsing and MaxEnt discriminative reranking. *43rd Annual Meeting on Association for Computational Linguistics, Association for Computational Linguistics* (pp. 173–180).

Clyne, M., et al. (2001). Ethnic varieties of Australian English. In D. Blair & P. Collins (Eds.), *Varieties of English around the World: English in Australia* (pp. 223–238). Amsterdam: Benjamins.

Copland, D. A., et al. (2011). Dopaminergic neuromodulations of semantic procesing: A 4-T fMRI. In R. Dale, D. Burnham & C. J. Stevens (Eds.) *Human communication science: A compendium*. Sydney, Australia: ARC Research Network in Communication Science.

Cox, F., & Palethorpe, S. (2007). Illustration of the I P A: Australian English. *JIPA, 37*, 341–350.

Cox, F. & Palethorpe, S (2011). Timing differences in the VC rhyme of standard Australian English and Lebanese Australian English (submitted). *ICPhS XVII*. Hong Kong.

Dale, R., et al. (2004–2010). ARC research network for human communication science: HCSNet, ARC RN0460284.

Dale, R., et al. (Eds.). (2011). *Human communication science: a compendium*. Sydney, Australia: ARC Research Network in Communication Science.

Estival, D., et al. (2014). AusTalk: an audio-visual corpus of Australian English. *9th Language Resources and Evaluation Conference (LREC 2014)*. Reykjavik, Iceland.

Estival, D., et al. (2013 a). The human communication science virtual lab. *7th eResearch Australasia Conference*. Brisbane, Australia.

Estival, D., et al. (2013 b). Learning from OzCLO, the Australian computational and linguistics olympiad. *Fourth Workshop on Teaching NLP and CL, 51st Annual Meeting of the Association for Computational Linguistics* (pp. 35–41). Sofia, Bulgaria: ACL.

Goecke, R. & Millar, J. B. (2004). The audio-video Australian English speech data corpus AVOZES. *8th International Conference on Spoken Language Processing (INTERSPEECH 2004—ICSLP)* (vol. 3, pp. 2525–2528). Jeju, Korea.

Goecks, J., et al. (2010). Galaxy: a comprehensive approach for supporting accessible, reproducible, and transparent computational research in the life sciences. *Genome Biology, 11*(8), R86.

King, T. H., et al. (2000). Ambiguity management in grammar writing. *Workshop on Linguistic Theory and Grammar Implementation, ESSLI 2000*. Birmingham, Great Britain.

Lichtenauer, J., et al. (2009). Cost-effective solution to synchronized audio-visual capture using multiple sensors. *Sixth IEEE International Conference on Advanced Video and Signal Based Surveillance (AVSS '09)* (pp. 324–329). Washington, DC, USA: IEEE Computer Society.

Moore, B. (2008). *Speaking our language : the story of Australian English*. South Melbourne, VIC: Oxford University Press.

Musgrave, S. & Haugh, M. (2009). The AusNC project: plans, progress and implications for language technology. *ALTA 2009* (p. 29). Sydney.

Schiel, F. (1999). Automatic phonetic transcription of non-prompted speech. *ICPhS* (pp. 607–610). San Francisco.

Shaw, J. A. & Gafos, A. I. (2010). Quantitative evaluation of competing syllable parses. *11th Meeting of the Association for Computational Linguistics. Special Interest Group on Computational Morphology and Phonology* (pp. 54–62). Uppsala, Sweden.

Sui, C., et al. (2012a). A 3D audio-visual corpus for speech recognition. *SST2012* (pp. 125–128). Sydney, Australia: ASSTA.

Sui, C., et al. (2012b). Discrimination comparison between audio and visual features. *Asilomar 2012* (pp. 1609–1612). Pacific Grove, USA.

Thieberger, N., et al. (Eds.). (2011). Sustainable data from digital research: Humanities perspectives on digital scholarship. *A PARDISEC Conference, Custom Book Centre*. http://ses.library.usyd.edu.au/handle/2123/7890.

Vonwiller, J., et al. (1995). Speaker and material selection for the Australian national database of spoken language. *Journal of Quantitative Linguistics, 3*, 177–211.

Wagner, M., et al. (2010). The big Australian speech corpus (The Big ASC). In: M. Tabain, J. Fletcher, D. Grayden, H. J. & A. Butcher (Eds.), *13th Australasian International Conference on Speech Science and Technology* (pp. 166–170). Melbourne: ASSTA.

Weiss, B., Burkhardt, F., & Geier, M. (2013). Towards perceptual dimensions of speakers' voices: Eliciting individual descriptions. Paper presented at the Workshop on Affective Social Speech Signals, Grenoble, France.

Knowledge Services Innovation: When Language Engineering Marries Knowledge Engineering

Asanee Kawtrakul

Abstract With the development of the World Wide Web and mobile devices, an enormous amount of explicit knowledge resources, distributed over multiple websites, can be accessed anywhere and anytime. However, to access this scattered knowledge, in unstructured text format, consumes a great deal of time and processing power, since the semantic relations among such resources are not directly stated and the content is not yet compiled into a meaningful context for effective action. Accordingly, instead of enhancing knowledge accessibility only, the challenge is how to provide a knowledge service that satisfies individual demands in actions and a timely manner. This paper focuses on developing a framework for handling knowledge extraction and integration across websites, using the agriculture domain as a case study, in order to provide more functional knowledge services to the end-user at the right time and in the right context. By merging two technologies, i.e., Knowledge Engineering and Language Engineering, a knowledge base can be constructed from unstructured text to enable the efficient and effective accessing and exploitation of knowledge. Usually, measurements for the success of knowledge service implementation are correctness of knowledge construction. However, this project aims to provide farmer service innovations with a functional knowledge according to crop calendar. Through the measurement of such operations, the farmer will gain maximum income while maximizing yields and minimizing costs through disease control and tailor-made fertilizing. Thus, the key performance indexes of knowledge service system, then, are benefit realization of the service consumer instead of service system correctness only.

Keywords Knowledge service · Ontology-based knowledge base construction · Name entity extraction · Information extraction · Ontology based knowledge integration

---

A. Kawtrakul (✉)
Department of Computer Engineering, Faculty of Engineering, Kasetsart University, Bangkok, Thailand
e-mail: asanee_naist@yahoo.com

© Springer International Publishing Switzerland 2015
N. Gala et al. (eds.), *Language Production, Cognition, and the Lexicon*,
Text, Speech and Language Technology 48, DOI 10.1007/978-3-319-08043-7_30

1 Introduction: Knowledge Services Innovation

To achieve such ambitious goals, i.e., a knowledge society, information and knowledge are needed for decision making, problem solving, and risk prevention, especially for driving an economic society. With the development of the Internet and the World Wide Web, an enormous amount of explicit knowledge resources, which also include best practices and experiences in many domains, can be found and are distributed over multiple websites, in heterogeneous expressions and in an unstructured format. Consequently, to access this scattered knowledge using traditional search methods consumes a great deal of time and processing power, since the semantic relations among such resources are not directly stated.

In order to move beyond conventional information retrieval and simple database query, it is necessary to build a knowledge base interconnecting several websites, which can then offer valuable information sufficiently relevant to support decision-making at the local level. Also, thanks to the development of devices such as personal digital assistants and mobile phones, the use of this technology has given birth to a new concept: Context-Aware and Location-based Knowledge Services. A context-aware service (Kawtrakul et al. 2013), here, is a type of knowledge service that can be automatically processed according to various situations and information. For example, in the agricultural information domain, factors for activating functional knowledge services, such as how to treat disease, may be a stage of plant's growth, weather changes, and so on.

This paper focuses on developing a framework for handling knowledge extraction from unstructured/semi-structured and integration across websites, in order to provide more functional knowledge services to the end-user at the right time. Figure 1 shows an example of the knowledge needed from several websites for rice cultivation, from preparation stage to cultivation stage.

Preparation Stage Thailand has more than 118 rice varieties that are already certified. Almost all farmers grow rice without any deep knowledge of rice variety. Each variety has different attributes, such as disease resistance, ecosystem for growing, and yields depending on soil properties. These kinds of knowledge could help farmers to reduce the risk factors such as disease problems or production optimization.

During the Cultivation Stage The knowledge and best practices acquired from the expertise for managing fertilizing and pest control, throughout the entire rice crop cycle, are also significant factors in reducing risk, thus enhancing crop productivity and quality.

Contextual factors according to a crop calendar, e.g., stage of crop growth, soil nutrients and weather, represent important service execution information. With a farmer's profile, i.e., farmer's identifier, selected rice variety, rice field location and micro climate information, a personal knowledge service can be provided through mobile devices or knowledge brokers with the right information in the right context at the right time, such as tailor-made fertilizing, disease early warning and disease control.

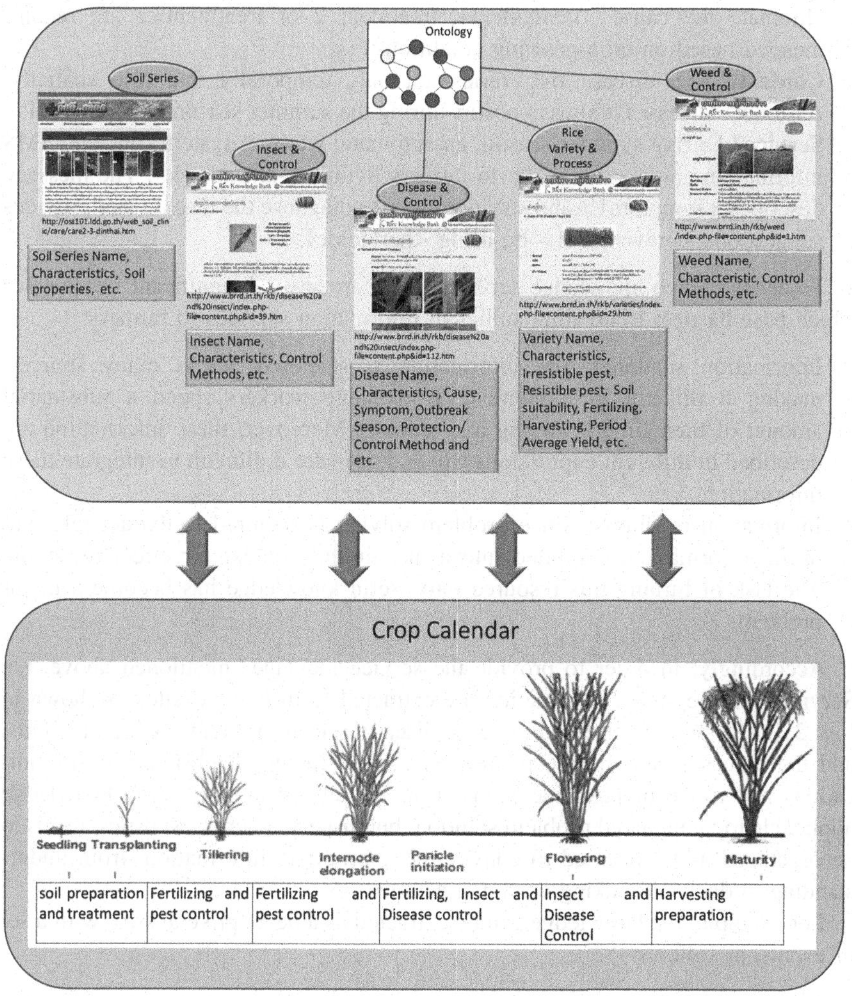

Fig. 1 Different information from several websites needed for providing knowledge services according to each stage of rice growth

To illustrate a context-aware knowledge service, the following two scenarios are given. Context1 activates a service for disease treatment, while context 2 for early warning and disease prevention.

Context1 Assume: <farmers> living in <location1> have some problems in their paddy fields with <disease_symptom1> and <disease_symptom2>; the rice varieties are <variety1, variety2>, the growth stage is <panicle stage>, and the temperature is <high>.

Service1 <symptom1> and <symptom2> are symptoms of <disease1> which are often found in <location1>. Based on disease1, variable treatments to

eliminate the cause <treatement1, treatment 2 or treatment3> are recommended based on crop-growing conditions.
Context2 Rice-disease risk varies not only temporally, but also spatially. Assume: <disease1> always occurs during the summer season at <location1>.
Service2 During summer season, an automatic warning system can send SMS information about <disease1> to farmers living in <location1>. The message describes <symptom1> and <symptom2> to diagnose the disease and provides suggestions <prevention1> by using <herbicide1>.

To develop such knowledge services, there are several significant weaknesses which pose barriers to creating sufficient information services to farmers:

- Information scattered: the information is scattered across many sources, making it difficult to implement. Knowledge workers spend a substantial amount of their time browsing and reading. Moreover, these information are described in different expressions which also make it difficult to integrate these information.
- Information readiness: Since problem solving is required to extract relevant, useful information, compiled into a meaningful context for effective action. The task of turning this resource into useful knowledge has become a major problem.

Accordingly, in order to provide the service messages mentioned above, i.e. Service1 and Service2, information are extracted from two websites as shown in Fig. 2. (Left) shows cause-and-effect of disease, related pesticides without details, and the processes for disease prevention and treatment. (Right) shows the indications and usage of pesticide preparation. As shown in Fig. 2, the knowledge applicable to an intended problem solution, but dispersed across websites, needs to be organized and processed to convey the appropriate information, from understanding to decision making or taking actions.

For example, the knowledge can be extracted as a descriptive answer with a set of events, as follows:

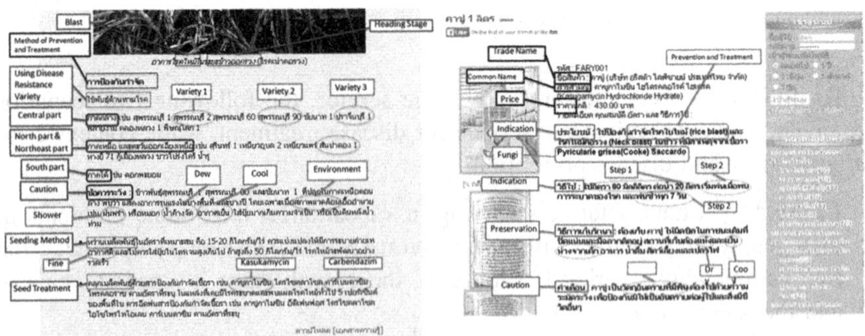

Fig. 2 (*Left*) Disease Knowledge (*Right*) Pesticide Knowledge

A1: To prevent Rice Blast: for those locations where this disease commonly occurs, use a disease-resistant rice variety. Don't sow the rice seed too densely. Don't use too much nitrogen. If a severe outbreak and during the stage of young plants, plow and sow again. If epidemic, use an anti-fungus chemical such as Carbendazim.

A2: Brown spot may be reduced by balanced fertilization, crop rotation, and the use of high quality planting seed. Seed treatment with fungicides reduces the incidence and severity of seedling blight caused by this fungus.

By using knowledge engineering, a knowledge base can be constructed to enable the efficient and effective accessing and exploitation of knowledge, such as knowledge modeling for localized problem solving, knowledge acquisition and structuring of the related information through ontology design. However, without language engineering such as Name Entities (NEs) identification, co-reference resolution and sentence coherence detection, the significant relevant information could not be extracted from unstructured text. Within the MUC framework, NEs were defined as names of persons, organizations, and locations, temporal information (date and time), and numerical expressions (monetary values and percentages). When extending the system to a new domain like agriculture, we need to extend the NE extraction accordingly to fit the new domain such as plant name, animal name, disease name, chemical name, and pathogen name.

Section 2 identifies the challenges and needs of knowledge engineering for developing a knowledge base schema and for providing knowledge services. In Sect. 3, language engineering issues in extracting information and a problem for Thai text processing, especially NE recognition, is explained in detail. Section 4 provides the framework that merges two technologies for extracting related information from unstructured text.

2 Issues in Knowledge Engineering and Related Works

To construct a knowledge base, three main issues need to be discussed: knowledge modeling for supporting functional problem solving, knowledge acquisition, and structuring of the sufficient related information. In this work, ontology is designed to comprehend the basic formal relationships that support these three main issues, and also, the ways in which farmers work in reality.

2.1 Knowledge Modeling and Ontology Design

Many researches influence to this work, such as topical relation (Olivier 2006), mental lexicon (Olivier and Michael 2006), including ontology. Ontology not only acts as a powerful tool for aggregating knowledge based on different expressions, it can also be used for deducing or navigating the concept characteristics or

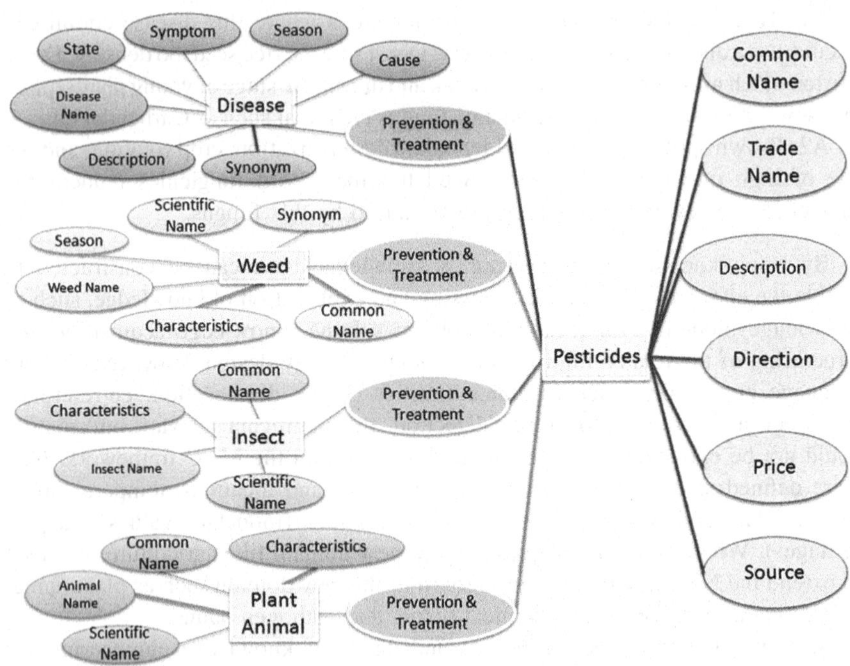

Fig. 3 An ontology design for a pest concept and related pesticide concept

properties that should be extracted. Consequently, ontology can be applied to the reference models for configuring a specific domain knowledge base having the respective details as a template. The most challenging aspect of intelligent use of overloaded information is how to provide knowledge accessibility that enables scattered and heterogeneous knowledge to be exploited fully, and also how to provide knowledge services that serve users with information relevant enough to support making effective decisions in real time. Therefore, domain-specific ontology (Kawtrakul 2012) is designed as a skeleton for constructing and linking information space with the salient information attached (See Fig. 3).

Regarding the given contexts or scenarios in Sect. 1, there are 3 main concepts: Rice Variety, Rice Pests (i.e., pathogens/diseases, weeds, insects), and Pesticide, that need an ontology design for navigating a template to extract the related data or information. For example, the following template for extracting knowledge is derived from the concept of Plant-Disease (see Table 1). In order to develop systems able to extract information or knowledge in an efficient way, it is crucial that the relevant entities be correctly recognized. This is the task of NE recognition and information extraction.

Figure 4 shows the results of extracted information by using ontology as a schema and NE extraction to fill the relevant entities into the templates.

Table 1 A template for plant-disease information extraction

Template: plant-disease
Plant: <Plant name>
Disease: <Plant disease name>
Cause: <Pathogen that causes the disease>
Symptom: <Text that describes symptoms of disease>
Treatment: <Instructions on how to protect this plant from the disease or how to cure this plant from the disease>

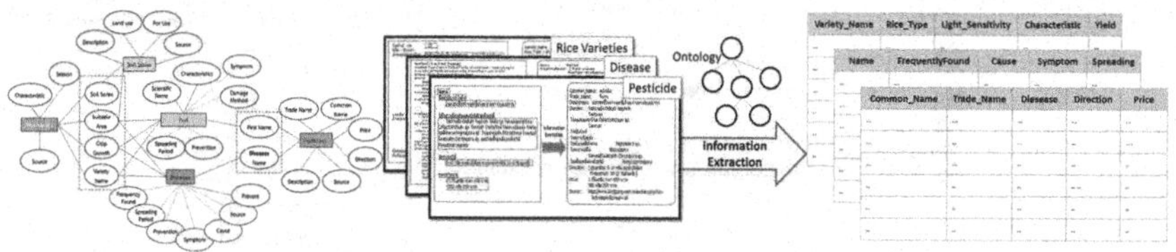

Fig. 4 Ontology designed for constructing a structured knowledge base

2.2 *Cyber-Brain: A Platform for Knowledge Processing and Services*

There are three key issues that we focus on: i.e., how to improve access of unstructured and scattered information for non-specialist users, how to provide adequate information to knowledge workers, and how to provide advice requiring highly focused and related information based on lexical co-occurrence (Michael et al. 2010). To meet these objectives, Cyber–Brain (Kawtrakul et al. 2008), was designed as a platform that combines approaches based on knowledge engineering and language engineering, in order to gather knowledge from various sources and to provide an effective knowledge service. Based on specially designed ontology for practical service scenarios, Cyber–Brain can aggregate knowledge resources from the Internet and expertise in specific domains toward providing constraint-based, location-based and situation-based knowledge services. See Fig. 5.

As shown in Fig. 5, there is a module of information acquisition and extraction as a main part of the platform. By using NE extraction and shallow sentence parsing based on regular expressions, information can be extracted and organized in both a relational database and structured templates. Thereafter, functional knowledge can be activated by the physical conditions of a farm's surrounding environment, e.g. temperature, meteorological conditions and/or images. The system can provide farmers with more specific suggestions for disease control by filtering all of the possible diseases, and provide services to farmers according to a crop calendar through mobile devices, or knowledge brokers, by giving the relevant activity of a specific disease extracted from the web; combined with best practices, the application of fungicides could be prepared and applied appropriately.

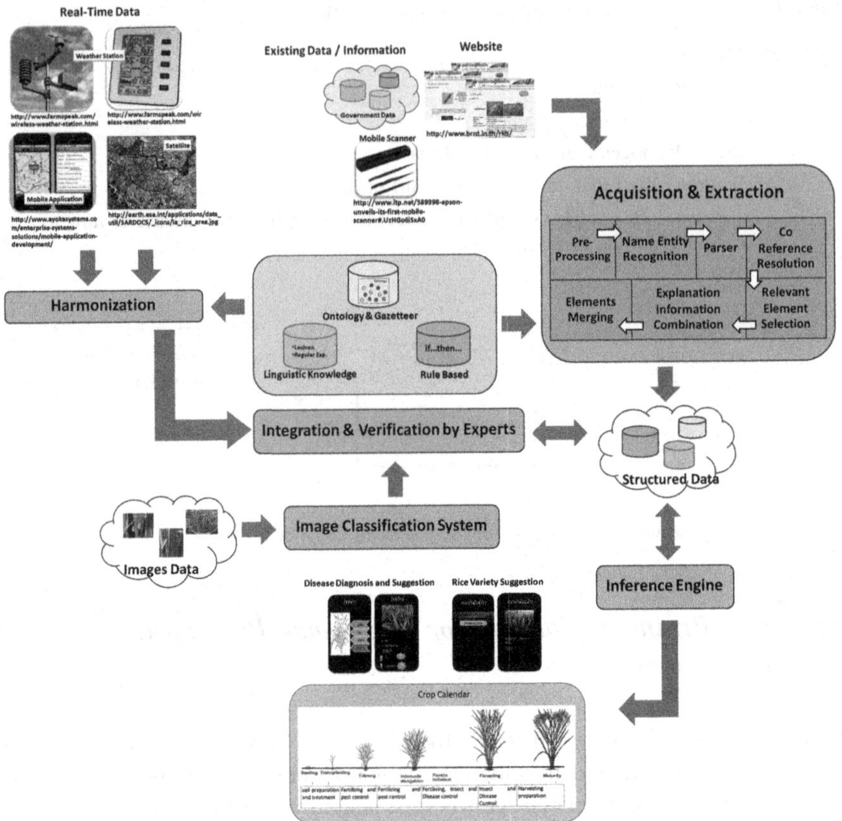

Fig. 5 A platform that merges knowledge engineering and language engineering

3 Language Engineering Issues for Thai Information Extraction

Regarding access to agricultural information, much of the useful information is in an unstructured format and scattered not only across websites, but also organized haphazardly in the document itself; information such as how to analyze symptoms of plant disease and how to protect plants from weeds/insects (see Figs. 1 and 2). Moreover, information is rapidly increasing, causing information to become overwhelming in size, so extraction of only significant and interesting information is necessary. The output of Information Extraction process is represented in the template/frame format (slot and filler as shown in the above table: Plant-Disease).

3.1 Challenges

In order to develop a system capable of extracting information or knowledge in an efficient way, it is crucial that the NEs and relevant information be correctly recognized and extracted respectively. In this work, we suggest enriching the list of traditional NEs with the following terms from the domain of agriculture: plant name, animal name, disease name, chemical name, and pathogen name. While there are many common difficulties between NEs in the domain of agriculture NE (ANE) and the traditional extraction of NE, there are some minor, different, yet difficult problems specific to the task of ANE extraction.

3.2 Named Entities Recognition and Related Works

The work on NE extraction can be divided into 3 main approaches: (1) handcrafted, systems built by human experts, (2) automatic or machine learning approaches, and (3) hybrid approaches (Borthwick 1999a, b).

In the early days, many researches relied on handcrafted systems to extract NEs (Appelt et al. 1993; Gaizauskas et al. 1995; Stevenson and Gaizauskas 2000; Wacholder et al. 1997; Weischedel 1995). The drawback of these systems is that they require a lot of time and effort to build by human experts. In addition, the developers have to rebuild the system every time they want to apply it to a new domain.

This is why many researchers have suggested a new strategy, namely, to use machine learning to extract NEs—the obvious goal being to cut down on the time and effort that the developing process demands. In addition, machine learning could also reduce the time and effort necessary for adapting the system to a new domain, as this can be achieved by training the system with the corpus of a new domain. There have been experiments with many models or learning techniques such as the *maximum entropy model* (Borthwick 1998; Chieu and Ng 2002), the *Hidden Markov Model* (Bikel et al. 1997; Collier et al. 2000; Zhou and Su 2002), *Support Vector Machine* (Isozaki and Kazawa 2002; Takeuchi and Collier 2002), *decision trees* (Buchholz and van den Bosch 2000; Sekine 1998), etc.

Despite the mentioned drawbacks of the handcrafted approach, it does have at least one advantage: hand-coded systems are usually very precise. This is why some researchers (Sassano and Utsuro 2000) have proposed to combine hand-coded, rule-based and statistical approaches (i.e. machine learning) to exploit their respective advantages.

While NE extraction has been recognized as an important component for many NLP applications such as Information Extraction, the number of NE types has remained very low (Sekine et al. 2002). Hence we are faced with a problem of coverage. Different kinds of named entities are needed in different domains and applications. Sekine et al. (2002) proposed a Named Entity hierarchy containing about 150 NE types to extend the coverage of the named entity types.

3.2.1 NE in Asian Languages

One major difficulty that Asian languages (e.g., Thai, Chinese, Japanese) typically encounter when extracting NEs is the identification of word boundaries (Chanlekha and Kawtrakul 2003).

This problem is especially pronounced for Japanese. The character types of this writing system (Kanji, Katakana, etc.) can be used for information extraction or for extracting NEs. Several approaches have been used, such as decision trees (Sekine et al. 1998), decision lists (Sassano and Utsuro 2000; Utsuro and Sassano 2000) Support Vector Machines (Isozaki and Kazawa 2002), Maximum Entropy (Borthwick 1999a, b), etc. Chinese also has the same kind of problem because of its absence of word boundaries. Although there is no character type to distinguish between NEs and other types of words, one can use the information from certain character components to extract NEs. For example, one can rely on the list of characters used in the transliterated version of a person's name to identify a word as the name of the person (Sun et al. 2002; Wu et al. 2003). This can be observed in many researches working in Chinese. Researchers noted that different NE types tend to exhibit different structures; hence, they proposed various approaches based on this observation. Some works (Ye et al. 2002) have used grammatical restrictions to build NEs of different types, so a rational model was proposed for computing the probability of NEs on the basis of structural and contextual information. Other scholars working in Chinese have used different models for recognizing NEs belonging to different categories (Chen et al. 1998; Sun et al. 2002; Wu et al. 2003; Zhang and Zhou 2002).

In Thai, little attention has been paid to the task of NE extraction. While Charoenpornsawat et al. (1998) used Winnow's algorithm (Chanlekha and Kawtrakul 2003; Chanlekha and Kawtrakul 2004) tried Maximum Entropy.

3.2.2 Characteristics of Named Entities in Thai

Unlike English and other European languages, Thai orthography does not encode much linguistic knowledge. For example, Thai orthography cannot signal word classes as in the use of uppercase characters to set off nouns from other classes in German, or the more general use of uppercase characters to set off proper nouns from other nouns. NEs in Thai are formed by the combination of known words and unknown strings. The characteristics of Thai NEs are:

- The Thai language does not have precise orthographical information to identify NEs, such as uppercase letters (like in many western languages), but some orthographical information is still useful when combined with other features.
- Foreign NEs will be transliterated without using any special characters, such as Katakana in Japanese, to signal the transliterated NE. Furthermore, there are no restrictions in transliteration; hence the form of a given foreign NE can be quite

different. For example, "New York" could be transliterated into "นิวยอร์ก", "นิวยอร์ค", or in other ways as well.
- There are no specific construction rules for NEs in Thai; i.e. Thai NEs do not have a specific structure, and NEs can be built from any kind of word.

The characteristics of Thai ANEs are basically the same as traditional ones. Hence, no orthographic information is used to signal NE; there are no rules to build ANEs. Foreign ANEs will be transliterated without the use of any special characters. As such, there are some additional features making ANE extraction difficult:

- ANEs for plants and animals usually occur without any explicit clue word, which is different from NEs where markers do occur occasionally. The information to indicate ANEs usually has to be derived by its head word, or by information contained at the discourse level.
- ANEs, especially plants, animals and diseases, are usually named according to their appearance, behavior, or intrinsic characteristics. For example, "*non jo fakkhaophot*/ caterpillars bore into corn ears" (Corn Ear worm) is named after the perforation behavior of the worm. As a result, many ANEs of this type have the same structure as noun phrases or sentences, which causes a lot of difficulties for their extraction. We will focus here on the development of a model to extract ANEs in an efficient way.

3.3 Problems Concerning the Identification of Thai Agricultural Named Entities

In order to extract Thai ANEs, two major problems must first be solved: identification of ANEs, and their categorization. The problems in Thai ANE identification are as follows:

3.3.1 Ambiguity Between Single-Word ANEs and Common Words

The lack of orthographical information to signal the locus of ANEs in Thai makes their extraction problematic, especially when a given single-word ANE has the same surface form as a common word, for example:

Ex. 1 *khwam phen phit khong* [**lamphong**]*: tuk suan luan mi kunnasombut pen phit* / Toxicity of the **thorn apple**: Every part has a toxic property.

In Thai, the word "lamphong" could be a plant name ("thorn apple") or a common word ("loud speaker"). This being so, we will rely on contextual information to extract the ANE.

3.3.2 Ambiguity Between Multi-Word ANEs and Common Noun Phrases

ANE extraction and the extraction of multi-word ANEs are not trivial problems in Thai because of the already mentioned absence of orthographic information. The problem becomes even worse in the case of multi-word ANEs, where the ANE is composed of known words, which in addition, exhibit basically the same structure as a noun phrase or a sentence. For example:

Ex. 2 *panha thi hob khue rueang pluak thamlai rak lae* [*non jo lamton*]$_{NP}$
The problems are: termites destroy roots, and [caterpillars bore into stems]$_{NP}$.
Ex. 3 [*non jo lamton*]$_{ANIMAL}$ *ja thamlai mali doi karn jo lamton*
[Stem borer]$_{ANIMAL}$ will destroy jasmines by boring into the stems.

In Example 2, "non-cho-lam-ton" is a common noun phrase, meaning "caterpillars bore into stems". However, by looking at Example 3, we notice that the same phrase acts as an animal name, meaning "stem borer". This problem cannot be solved by using simple heuristics. Clearly, more information than POS or syntactic information is needed. Below is another example of ambiguity between a plant name and a compound word.

Ex. 4 [*nommaeo*]$_{PLANT}$ *mak thuk nam sakat namman hom rahoei phuea taeng klin ahan*
[Nommaeo]$_{PLANT}$ is usually distilled for its aromatic essential oil used for food odor. The meaning of "*nommaeo*" could be plant name (Nommaeo) or compound word (cat milk).

From observations based on a corpus, we have found that the proportion of multi-word ANEs composed of known words versus multi-word ANEs are as follows: 53.68 % (plant name), 84.71 % (animal name), 94.65 % (disease name), 28.49 % (pathogen name), 10.55 % (chemical name). The statistics of multi-word ANEs that can be considered as a meaningful common noun phrase or sentence, as well as other kinds of common phrases, such as, "khwan khon/girdle the bole of a tree" (verb phrase) or "nao le/soft rot" (adjective phrase), are shown in Table 2.

3.3.3 Ambiguity in Multi-Word ANE Boundary Identification

The lack of orthographical information causes not only an ambiguity between an ANE and a common word or noun phrase, it also causes a problem of ANE

Table 2 Statistics concerning the structure of multi-word ANEs

NE structure	Plant	Animal	Disease	Pathogen	Chemical
NP/sentence	30.41	41.62	86.53	28.49	10.15
VP/ADJP/…	1.42	0.52	6.46	0	0.39
Not meaningful phrase	68.17	57.86	7.01	71.51	89.46

boundary identification; especially when ANEs are formed by the combination of known words. From the following example, we can see that a Thai ANE does not have any information like characters (uppercase/lowercase) to help boundary identification.

Ex. 5 *ja phob* [**duang nguang kat bai mamuang**]$_{\text{ANIMAL}}$ *chamnuan mak*
(1) *ja phob* [*duang nguang*]$_{\text{ANIMAL}}$ *kat bai mamuang chamnuan mak*
We will find that Pin-Hole Borers cut a lot of mango leaves.
(2) *ja phob* [*duang nguang kat bai mamuang*]$_{\text{ANIMAL}}$ *chamnuan mak*
We will find a lot of mango leaf cutting weevils.

In the above examples, both sentences (1) and (2) are grammatically correct if one considers only the local context. However, if we take the global context into account, i.e. other occurrences of the same name, we see that only (2) is correct.

3.3.4 Problems in Categorization of ANEs in Thai

Contextual Ambiguity

Problems in ANE categorization arise when the immediate contexts of a given ANE do not provide a strong clue, or when the relevant context cannot be captured by the extraction model. The example below shows that ANEs of different types can appear in similar context.

phan [*mamuang*]$_{\text{PLANT}}$ *ti rujak kan tua pai* VS. *phan* [*sunak*]$_{\text{ANIMAL}}$ *ti rujak kan tua pai*
The well known species of [**mango**] are… The well known species of [**dog**] are…

To make things worse, the closest contextual clues sometimes suggest the wrong ANE category. For example:

sankhemipongkanlaekamchartchuea-ra[*mancozeb*]$_{\text{chemical}}$
Chemical substances prevent and destroy fungus Mancozeb
Meaning: Chemical substance for preventing and destroying the fungus: Mancozeb.

In the example above, the closest contextual clue of the CHEMICAL ANEs is "chuea-ra" (fungus). Yet, "chuea-ra" is the typical clue word indicating the PATHOGEN category. This might result in an incorrect categorization of the ANE.

Category ambiguity
ANEs belonging to different categories can have the same surface form, for example:

Ex. 6: [*fakthong*]$_{\text{PLANT}}$ *phan* [*dam*]$_{\text{PLANT}}$ *muea kae plueak cha krukra pen pum pom khlai phio* [*khankhok*]$_{\text{ANIMAL}}$ *bang thi ko riak phan* [*khankhok*]$_{\text{PLANT}}$
Meaning: [**Dum**]$_{\text{PLANT}}$, one of [**pumpkin**]$_{\text{PLANT}}$ varieties, when the fruit ripens, the skin will be rugged, which looks like a [**toad**]$_{\text{ANIMAL}}$'s skin, sometimes call [**toad**]$_{\text{PLANT}}$ variety.

In Example 6, "khangkhok/toad" could be either the name of a plant or an animal. It all depends on the context. Furthermore, the starting word of an ANE, which in Thai is usually considered as a head word, can yield an incorrect ANE category. For example "saiduean-foi-rak-pom/Root-knot Nematode" could be the name of a disease. However, "saiduean-foi/Nematode" here is the name of an animal.

To solve such problems, we have been developing a system (see Fig. 6) that uses the technique of Conditional Random Fields. In addition, we take local and global information into account, together with external knowledge resources such as dictionaries, to extract ANEs in Thai.

3.3.5 NE Extraction Module

The process of NE extraction (Shown in Fig. 6) is composed of 2 steps:

1. Pre-processing, which includes word segmentation and document's section tagging.
2. NE extraction, which includes feature extraction and ANE extraction with the help of the Conditional Random Fields technique.

In this work, an approach to extracting ANEs is proposed by using conditional random fields (CRFs) plus knowledge from dictionaries and the ANEs' surrounding context. To enhance the performance of our NE extraction system, not

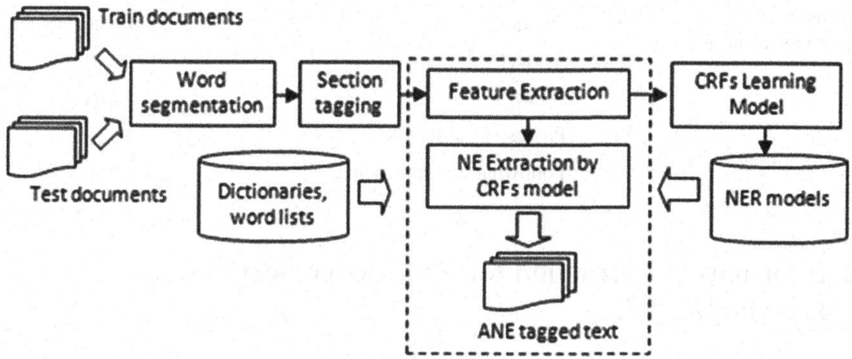

Fig. 6 Process of named entity extraction named entity extraction

only are the features of the local context used, but also those from a more global level, such as other occurrences of ANEs and the document structure: e.g. sections, paragraphs, etc. It has also been found that some ANE categories have special characteristics concerning compound words. For example, many plant names contain information concerning the word's specific color, the plant's original location, etc. Obviously, we will draw on this kind of information by incorporating these characteristics of ANE into our model. The experiment on various feature types to see their impact on the performance of the extraction system is ongoing.

3.4 Zero Anaphora Analysis

Next, we indicate the main problems that influence not only IE, but other applications such as MT and IR systems, i.e. zero anaphora. To provide cohesion in the discourse, the anaphora is used as a reference to "point back" to some entities, called referent or antecedent, given in the preceding discourse. From observing the corpus in news, magazines and agricultural text, there are 4 types of anaphora. Ellipsis or zero anaphora was found most frequently in Thai documents, and other anaphora occurred as follows:

Type of anaphora	Magazines (%)	News (%)	Agricultural (%)
Zero anaphora	49.88	52.38	50.04
Repetition	32.04	27.78	34.49
Personal reference	12.18	12.70	1.87
Nominal substitution	5.90	6.08	6.08

Zero anaphora is the use of a gap in a phrase or clause that has an anaphoric function similar to a pro-form. It is often described as "referring back" to an expression that supplies the information necessary for interpreting the gap.

Table 3 also shows the occurrence of zero anaphora in various parts of a sentence.

Table 3 Position of reference in sentences

Position	Frequency (%)
Subject	49.88
Object	32.04
Possessive pronoun	12.18
Following a preposition	5.90

4 Information Extraction for Knowledge Services: LE Marries KE

In this work, we extract information and knowledge from several websites to support farmers from preparation stage to cultivation stage of rice, that enable farmers to achieve greater efficiency and effectiveness in field-level crop management, such as rice variety knowledge for reducing the risk factors, e.g., disease problems or production optimization, seedling techniques for preventing disease, amount of fertilizer and other crop inputs used to boost yields and reduce cost, and pest control/prevention for reducing risk and getting higher productivity. Therefore, relying on both the agricultural environment, such as growing stage, climate data, and practical knowledge, farmers will be enabled to achieve greater efficiency and effectiveness in field-level crop management. As mentioned in Sect. 2, specific-tasked ontology is designed as a knowledge model to capture highly focused and related information, as example in Fig. 3. This selected ontology was used for templates construction (see Table 1). The template contains slots named, for example, Plant, Disease, Cause/Pathogen, Symptoms and Treatment; these slots have to be filled in with the plant name, plant disease name, pathogen that causes the disease, symptoms of disease, and instructions on how to treat this plant from the disease, respectively. Each template will be activated by a type/category of NE. We define two types of information that we want to extract.

Entity Information is the relevant name entity elements which are extracted by the NE extraction process. It includes names of Plant, Disease, Pathogen, Date, Yield, and etc.

Explanation Information is information that cannot be explained by name entity only, so we have to extract a set of sentences that explains the topic or subtopics and uses shallow discourse analysis technique to combine them together into one unit. It consists of: Symptoms and Treatment.

In the current system, we only focus on NE extraction and co-reference resolution which are the major modules. Extracted NE is a filler of slot that matches the type of NE. Since the proportion of zero anaphora in Agricultural domain is 50.04 % (see Sect. 3.4) and the occurrence of zero anaphora which are in subject and object parts of a sentence are about 82 %, the co-reference resolution is analyzed according to Aroonmanakum (2000) who proposed the combination of

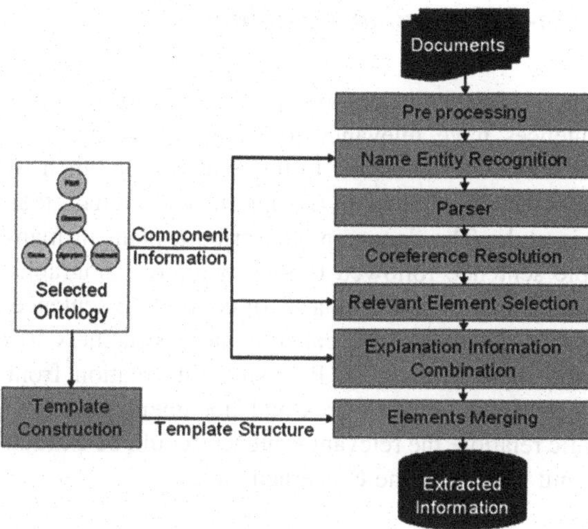

Fig. 7 Process of extracting salient information

centering theory and discourse structure. However, it is hard to implement in systematic works, so this problem is still an area of interest for further research. In this work, we also find the co-relation information, i.e., explanation information such as disease-symptoms, disease-treatment, that appears in discourse units. Figure 7 summarizes the steps of extracting information from unstructured text.

The result of the extraction process is a series of templates that have been filled in with the relevant information. Each template contains information about one disease or one rice variety, which references back to the source document. As such, it contains information that has been extracted from one document, but one document can be extracted to be more than one template, as shown below.

TEMPLATE_ID:	T00001
TEMPLATE_NAME:	Plant-Disease
Plant Name:	กะหล่ำปลี
Disease:	Template_ID:=T00002

TEMPLATE_ID:	T00002
TEMPLATE_NAME:	Disease
Disease Name:	โรคเน่าดำ
Cause:	เชื้อบักเตรี
Symptom:	ใบจะแห้งจากด้านขอบใบเข้าไปเป็นรูปสามเหลี่ยมที่มีปลายแหลมชี้ไปที่เส้นกลางใบ บนเนื้อเยื่อที่แห้งจะมีเส้นใบสีดำเห็นชัดเจน อาการใบแห้งจะลุกลามไปจนถึงเส้นกลางใบและลุกลามลงไปถึงก้านใบทำให้เกิดอาการใบเหลืองเหี่ยวและแห้งตาย กะหล่ำปลีจะชะงักการเจริญเติบโตและอาจตายได้ โดยเชื้อบักเตรีที่เป็นสาเหตุของโรคนี้จะอาศัยอยู่ในดิน เมื่อฝนตกจะระบาดไปทั่ว นอกจากนี้ยังสามารถติดไปกับเมล็ดผักได้อีกด้วย
Treatment:	1. ก่อนนำเมล็ดพันธุ์ผักไปปลูกควรแช่เมล็ดพันธุ์ผักในน้ำอุ่นที่อุณหภูมิประมาณ 50-55 องศาเซลเซียส เป็นเวลา 20-30 นาที เพื่อฆ่าเชื้อโรคที่ติดอยู่ในเมล็ด 2. ไม่ปลูกพืชตระกูลกะหล่ำติดต่อกันเกิน 3 ปี เพราะจะทำให้เป็นแหล่งสะสมโรค

4.1 Explanation–Information Combination

After solving the co-reference resolution/co-relation information problem, we can mark which sentences have relevance to the topic of interest. If a paragraph contains relevant sentences of interest to the related topic, then it is considered a relevant paragraph. The documents in the agricultural domain that we studied are semi-structured in style. The documents describe a plant in many aspects. Each aspect has a topic sentence followed by one or more paragraphs describing the details of that topic. Paragraphs can be a set of continuous sentences, or bulleted or numbered sentences. Therefore, we can use these structures to obtain relevant paragraphs for the topic of interest. By using information from the document context, i.e., concept and family words and document structure, such as topic/sub-topic, thematic relation, the relevant sentences could be extracted and combine them to be one unit for filling the concerned slot.

5 Conclusions and Future Work

This paper proposes a framework for handling knowledge extraction and integration across websites and demonstrates how language processing could add value to such knowledge construction. However, access to knowledge is a critical issue for non-specialist users such as farmers, i.e., it is not always easy for farmers to access such huge amounts of knowledge across several websites in unstructured text. This work therefore aims to develop functional knowledge service and merge two technologies, Language Engineering and Knowledge Engineering, to construct a more easily accessible knowledge base. Based on our ontology design, NE recognition and information extraction system, three key issues are resolved: improving the accessibility of unstructured and scattered information for non-specialist users, providing adequate information to knowledge workers, and providing highly focused and related information. In the future, we plan to validate this work in a real environment, which constitutes a significant step toward formally building context-aware knowledge services in the agriculture domain. In parallel, the ANE recognition module is still experimental and in an early stage of development.

Moreover, in this work, we aim at studying and merging language engineering and knowledge engineering to provide a framework for context-aware knowledge services in order to enable farmers to achieve greater efficiency and effectiveness in field-level crop management. Accordingly, instead of mainly measuring the correctness of NE recognition and information extraction system, we measure whether valuable information sufficiently relevant enough to support decision-making at the local level or not. We use two performance indicators to evaluate the framework—cost and yields. To achieve these two goals, we expect to significantly increase the average income of farmers. Through interviews conducted in

2013, the typical yield per hectare (ha) for Thai farmers, who participate our project, is approximately 700 kg/rai (4,375 kg/ha). We do hope that farmers could increase their productivity to 1,000 kg/rai, or 6,250 kg/ha (compared with the best case gathered from the most successful farmers), if they apply knowledge-based precision farming at each stage of rice cultivation. Moreover, we expected that such knowledge significantly can reduce the cost of production by enhancing a farmer's ability to apply actions effectively according to the crop calendar; i.e. the optimal use of pesticides and nutrients in heterogeneous field situations that affect crop quality and reduce risk.

References

Appelt, D., Hobbs, J., Israel, D., & Tyson, M. (1993). FASTUS: A finite-state processor for information extraction from real-world text. In *Proceedings of the 13th IJCAI-93*, France.

Aroonmanakun, W. (2000). Zero pronoun resolution in Thai: A centering approach. In D. Burnham et al. (Eds.), *Interdisciplinary approaches to language processing: The international conference on human and machine processing of language and speech*. Bangkok: NECTEC, pp. 127–147.

Bikel, D. M., Miller, S., Schwartz, R., & Weischedel, R. (1997). Nymble: a high-performance learning name-finder. In *Proceedings of 5th conference on applied natural language processing*. Washington, DC, pp. 194–201.

Borthwick, A. (1999a) A maximum entropy Approach to named entity recognition. Ph.D. Dissertation, New York University.

Borthwick, A. (1999b). A Japanese named entity recognizer constructed by a non-speaker of Japanese. In *Proceedings of information retrieval and extraction exercise workshop*, Tokyo, Japan.

Borthwick, A., Sterling, J., Agichtein, E., & Grishman, R. (1998). NYU: description of the MENE named entity system as used in MUC-7. In *Proceedings of 7th message understanding conference (MUC-7)*, Fairfax, Virginia.

Buchholz, S., & van den Bosch, A. (2000). Integrating seed names and n-grams for a named entity list and classifier. In *Proceedings of the second international conference on language resources and evaluation* (*LREC 2000*), Greece, pp. 1215–1221.

Charoenpornsawat, P., Kijsirikul, B., & Meknavin, S. (1998). Feature-based proper name identification in Thai. In *Proceedings of national computer science and engineering conference'98* (*NCSEC'98*), Bangkok, Thailand.

Chanlekha, H., & Kawtrakul, A. (2003). Thai name entity extraction by using maximum entropy model knowledge base. In *Proceedings of national computer science and engineering conference'2003* (*NCSEC'2003*), Chonburi, Thailand.

Chanlekha, H., & Kawtrakul, A. (2004). Thai named entity extraction by incorporating maximum entropy model with simple heuristic information. In *Proceedings of IJCNLP*' 2004. HAINAN Island, China.

Chen, H. H., Ding, Y. W., Tsai, S. C., & Bian, G. W. (1998). Description of the NTU system used for MET-2. In *Proceedings of the seventh message understanding conference* (*MUC-7*). Washington DC.

Chieu, H. L., & Ng, H. T. (2002). Named entity recognition: a maximum entropy approach using global information. In *Proceedings of the 19th international conference on computational linguistics* (*COLING 2002*). Taipei, Taiwan. pp. 190–196.

Collier, N., Nobata, C., & Tsujii, J. (2000). Extracting the names of genes and gene products with a hidden markov model. In *Proceedings of international conference on computational linguistics* (*COLING'2000*). Saarbrucken, Germany. pp. 201–207.

Gaizauskas, G., Wakao, T., Huimphreys, K., Cunninghan, H., & Wilks, Y. (1995). University of sheffield. Description of the LaSIE system as used for MUC-6. In *Proceedings of the sixth message understanding conference* (*MUC-6*). Columbia, MD: NIST, Morgan-Kaufmann Publishers.

Isozaki, H., & Kazawa, H. (2002). Efficient support vector classifiers for named entity recognition. In *Proceedings of COLING-2002.* Taipei, Taiwan.

Kawtrakul, A., Sriswasdi, W., Wuttilerdcharoenwong, S., Khunthong, V., Andres, F., Laovay-anon, S., et al. (2008). *"CyberBrain: Towards the next generation social intelligence".* Tokyo: IAALD AFITA WCCA 2008.

Kawtrakul, A. (2012). "Ontology engineering and knowledge services for agriculture domain". *Journal of Integrative Agriculture, 11*(5), pp. 741–751.

Kawtrakul A., Pusittigul A., Ujjin S., Lertsuchatavanich U., & Andres, F. (2013) "Driving connected government implementation with marketing strategies and context-aware service design". In *Proceedings of the European conference on e-government.* Como, Italy, p. 265.

Michael, Z., Olivier, F., & Didier, S. (2010). Deliberate word access: an intuition, a roadmap and some preliminary empirical results. *International Journal of Speech Technology, 13*, 201–218.

Olivier, F. (2006). Building a network of topical relations from a corpus. In *LREC 2006.*

Olivier, F., & Michael, Z. (2006). Enhancing electronic dictionaries with an index based on association. In *Proceedings of the 21st international conference on computational linguistics and 44th annual meeting of the ACL.* Sydney, pp. 281–288.

Sassano, M., & Utsuro, T. (2000). Named entity chunking techniques in supervised learning for Japanese named entity recognition. In *Proceedings of COLING 2000*, pp. 705–711.

Stevenson, M., & Gaizauskas, R. (2000). Using corpus-derived name lists for named entity recognition. In *Proceedings of ANLP-NAACL-2000*, WA.

Sekine, S. (1998). NYU: description of the Japanese NE system used for MET-2. In *Proceedings of 7th message understanding conference* (*MUC-7*). Virginia, USA.

Sekine, S., Grishman, R., & Shinnou, H. (1998). "A decision tree method for finding and classifying names in Japanese texts". In *Proceedings of the 6th workshop on very large corpora.* Montreal, Canada.

Sekine, S., Sudo, K., & Nobata, C. (2002). Extended named entity hierarchy. In *Proceedings of third international conference on language resources and evaluation* (*LREC 2002*). Las Palmas, Spain.

Sun, J., Gao, J., Zhang, L., Zhou, M., & Huang, C. (2002). Chinese named entity identification using class-based language model. In *Proceedings of COLING 2002.* Taipei, Taiwan.

Takeuchi, K., & Collier, N. (2002). Use of support vector machines in extended named entity recognition. In *Proceedings of the sixth conference on natural language learning* (*CoNLL-2002*). Taipei, Taiwan.

Utsuro, T., & Sassano, M. (2000). Minimally supervised Japanese named entity recognition: resources and evaluation. In *Proceedings of LREC2000*, pp. 1229–1236.

Wacholder, N., Ravin, Y., & Choi, M. (1997). Disambiguation of proper names in text. In *Proceedings of the 5th applied natural language processing conference.* Washington, DC, pp. 202–208.

Weischedel, R. (1995). BBN: description of the PLUM system as used for MUC-6. In *Proceedings of the sixth message understanding conference* (*MUC-6*). Columbia, MD: NIST, Morgan-Kaufmann Publishers.

Wu, Y., Zhao, J., & Xu, B. (2003). Chinese named entity recognition combining statistical model and human knowledge. In *Proceedings of he workshop on multilingual and mixed-language named entity recognition.* Sapporo, Japan.

Ye, S., Chua, T., & Liu, J. (2002). An agent-based approach to Chinese named-entity recognition. In *Proceedings of COLING2002*. Taipei, Taiwan.

Zhang, Y., & Zhou, J. F. (2000). A trainable method for extracting Chinese entity names and their relations. In *Proceedings of the 2nd Chinese language processing workshop.* Hong Kong, pp. 66–72.

Zhou, G. D., & Su, J. (2002). Named entity recognition using an HMM-based chunk tagger. In *Proceedings of ACL2002*.

Index

© Springer International Publishing Switzerland 2015

N. Gala et al. (eds.), *Language Production, Cognition, and the Lexicon*,
Text, Speech and Language Technology 48, DOI 10.1007/978-3-319-08043-7

U

V

W

X

Z